W9-AZQ-345

THE SIXTH
Garfield
Fat Cat 3-Pack

BY: JIM DAVIS

The Random House Publishing Group • **New York**

A Ballantine Book
Published by The Random House Publishing Group

GARFIELD ROUNDS OUT copyright © 1988 by Paws, Incorporated. All Rights Reserved.
GARFIELD CHEWS THE FAT copyright © 1989 by Paws, Incorporated. All Rights Reserved.
GARFIELD GOES TO WAIST copyright © 1990 by Paws, Incorporated. All Rights Reserved.
GARFIELD Comic Strips copyright 1987, 1988, 1989 by Paws, Incorporated. All Rights Reserved.

Ballantine and colophon are registered trademarks of Random House, Inc.

"GARFIELD" and the GARFIELD characters are registered and unregistered trademarks of PAWS, Inc.

All rights reserved under International and Pan-American Copyright
Conventions. Published in the United States by The Random House
Publishing Group, a division of Random House, Inc., New York, and
simultaneously in Canada by Random House of Canada Limited, Toronto.

ISBN: 0-345-40884-5

www.ballantinebooks.com

Manufactured in the United States of America

First Edition: September 1996

20 19 18 17 16 15 14 13 12 11

Garfield rounds out

BY: JIM DAVIS

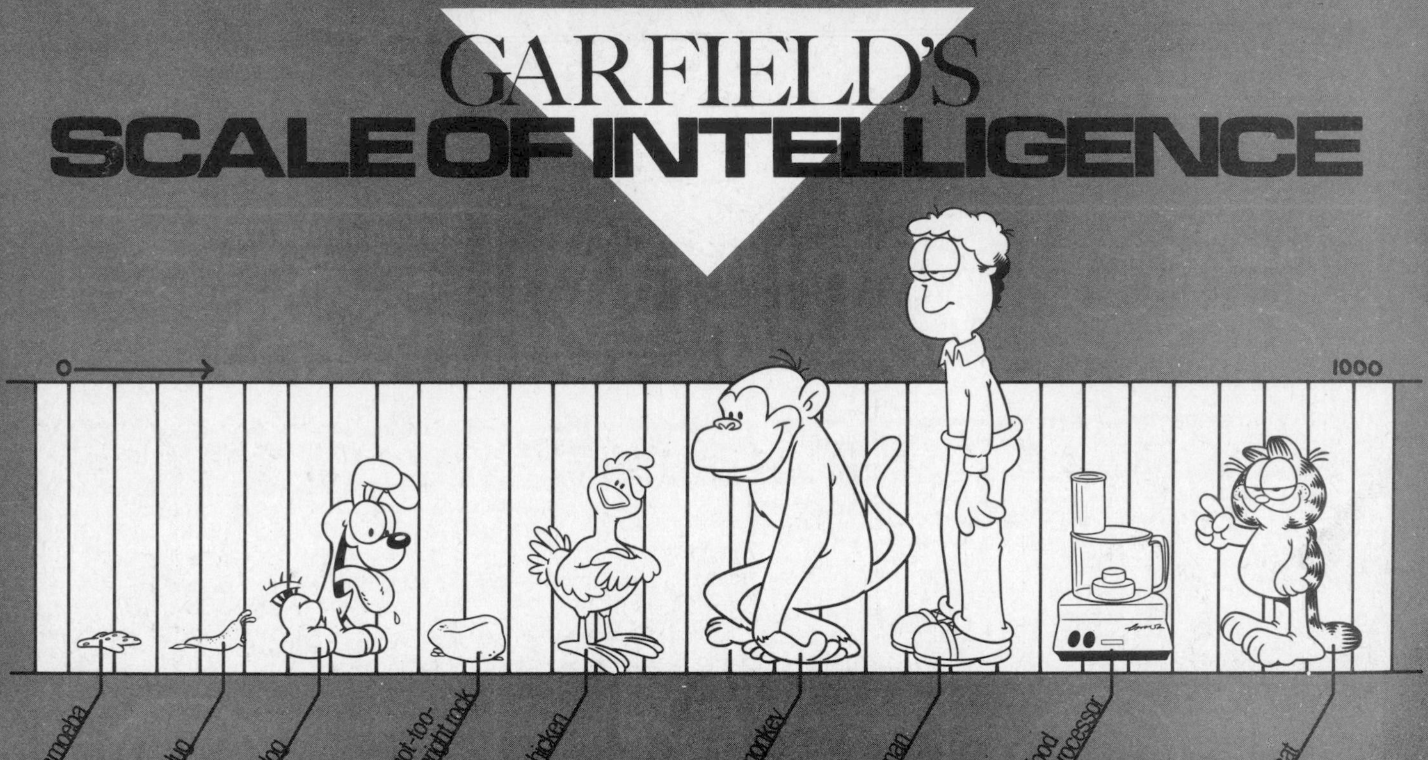
GARFIELD'S
SCALE OF INTELLIGENCE
0
1000
amoeba
slug
dog
not-too-bright rock
chicken
monkey
man
food processor
cat

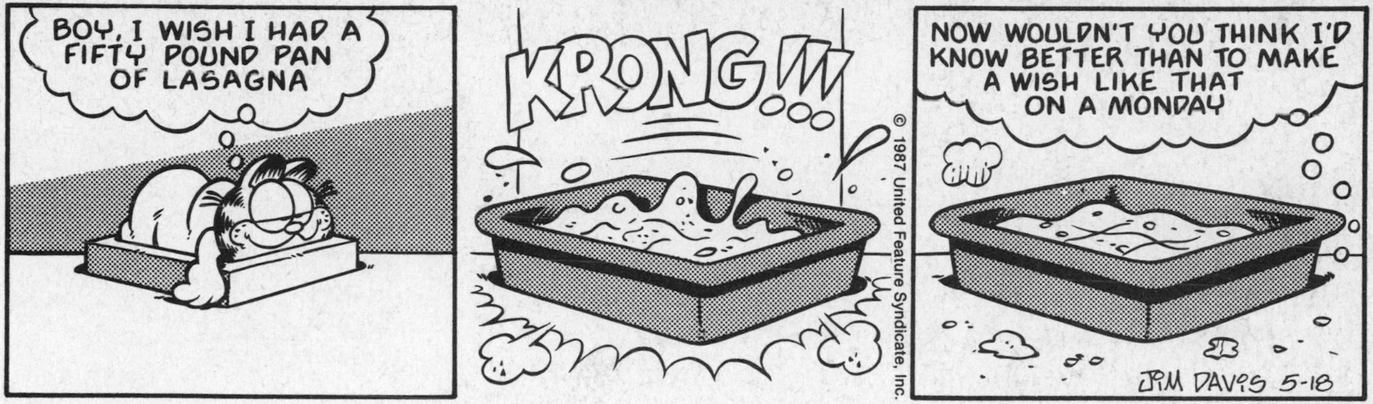
BOY, I WISH I HAD A FIFTY POUND PAN OF LASAGNA
KRONG!!!
NOW WOULDN'T YOU THINK I'D KNOW BETTER THAN TO MAKE A WISH LIKE THAT ON A MONDAY
© 1987 United Feature Syndicate, Inc.
JIM DAVIS 5-18

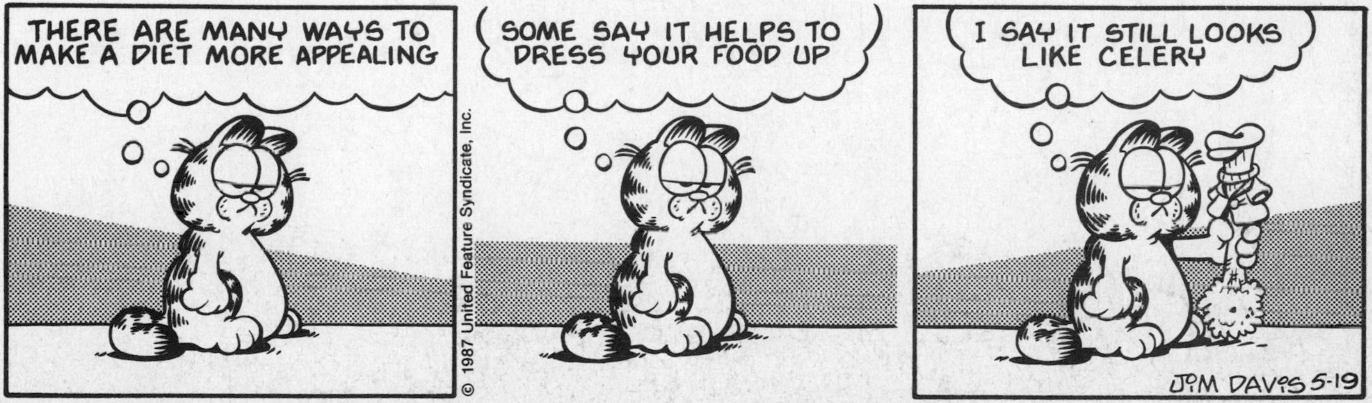
THERE ARE MANY WAYS TO MAKE A DIET MORE APPEALING
© 1987 United Feature Syndicate, Inc.
SOME SAY IT HELPS TO DRESS YOUR FOOD UP
I SAY IT STILL LOOKS LIKE CELERY
JIM DAVIS 5-19

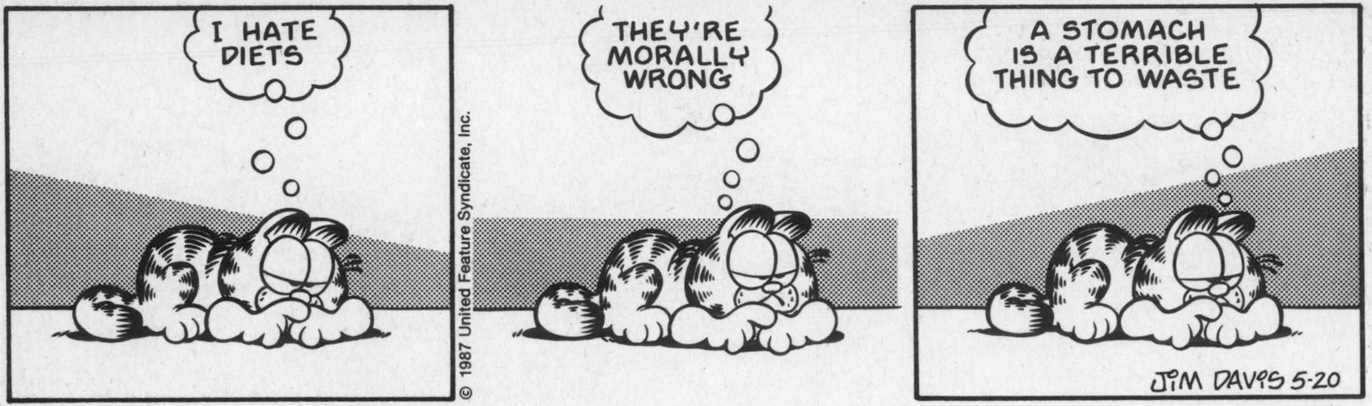
I HATE DIETS
THEY'RE MORALLY WRONG
A STOMACH IS A TERRIBLE THING TO WASTE
© 1987 United Feature Syndicate, Inc.
JIM DAVIS 5-20

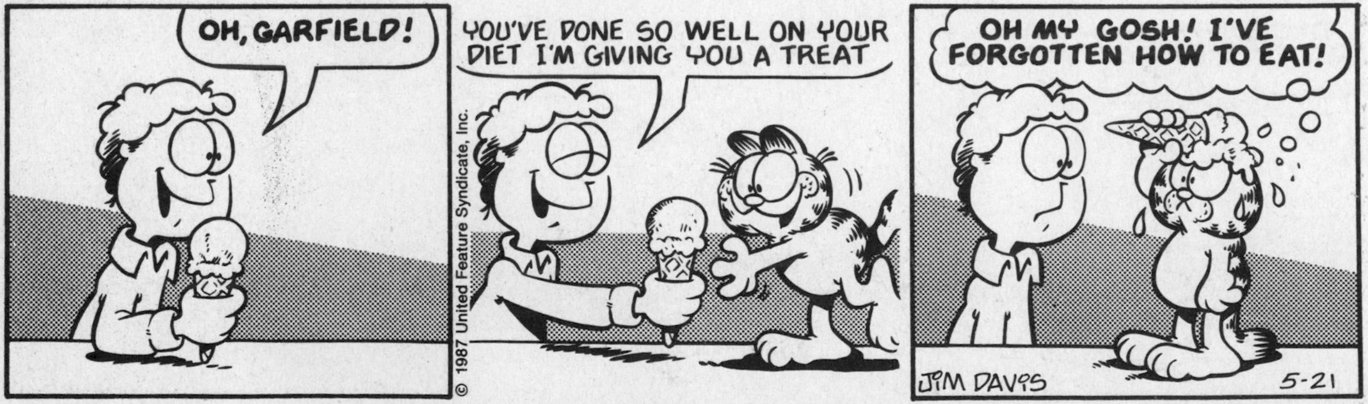
OH, GARFIELD!
YOU'VE DONE SO WELL ON YOUR DIET I'M GIVING YOU A TREAT
OH MY GOSH! I'VE FORGOTTEN HOW TO EAT!
© 1987 United Feature Syndicate, Inc.
JIM DAVIS
5-21

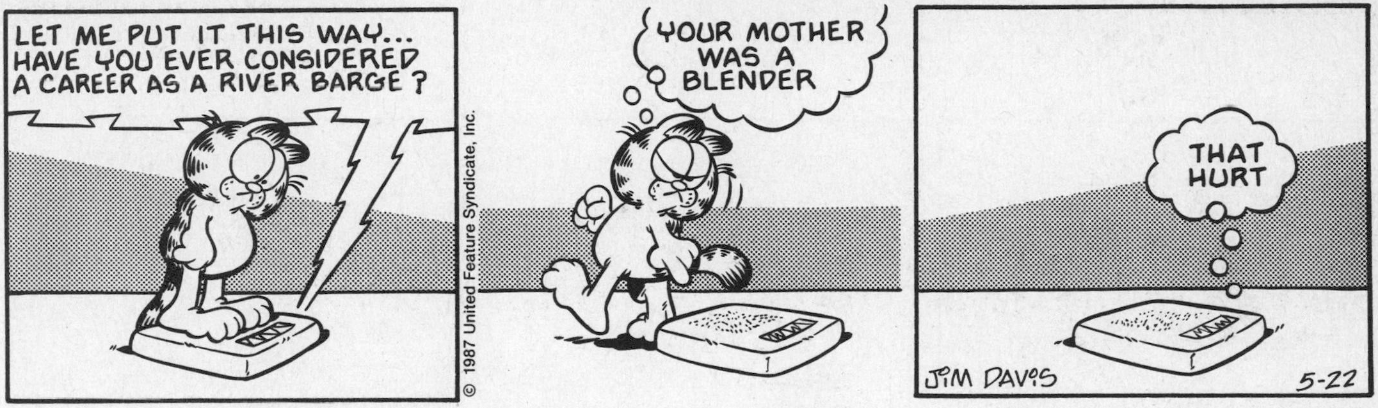
LET ME PUT IT THIS WAY... HAVE YOU EVER CONSIDERED A CAREER AS A RIVER BARGE?
YOUR MOTHER WAS A BLENDER
THAT HURT
JIM DAVIS
5-22
© 1987 United Feature Syndicate, Inc.

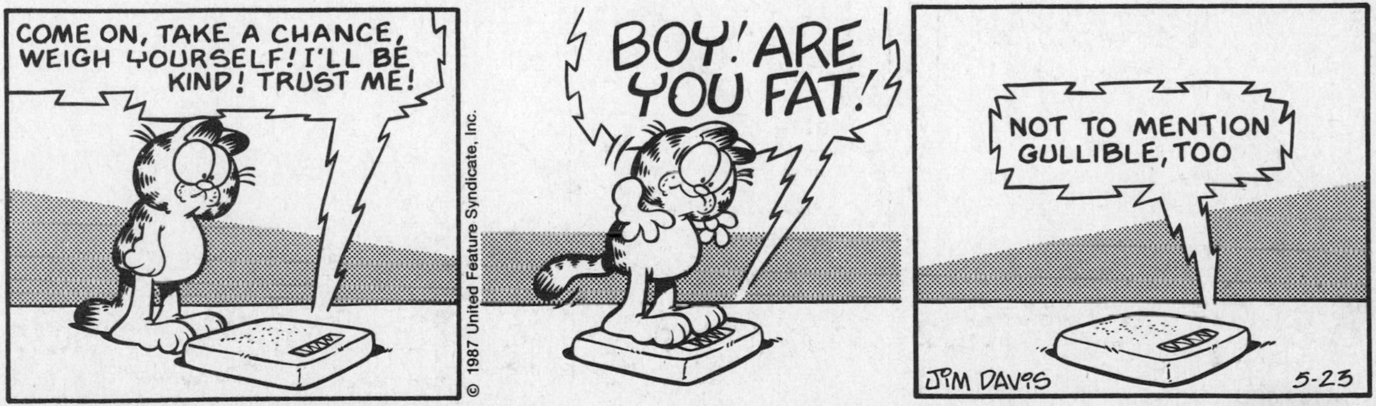
COME ON, TAKE A CHANCE, WEIGH YOURSELF! I'LL BE KIND! TRUST ME!
BOY! ARE YOU FAT!
NOT TO MENTION GULLIBLE, TOO
JIM DAVIS
5-23
© 1987 United Feature Syndicate, Inc.

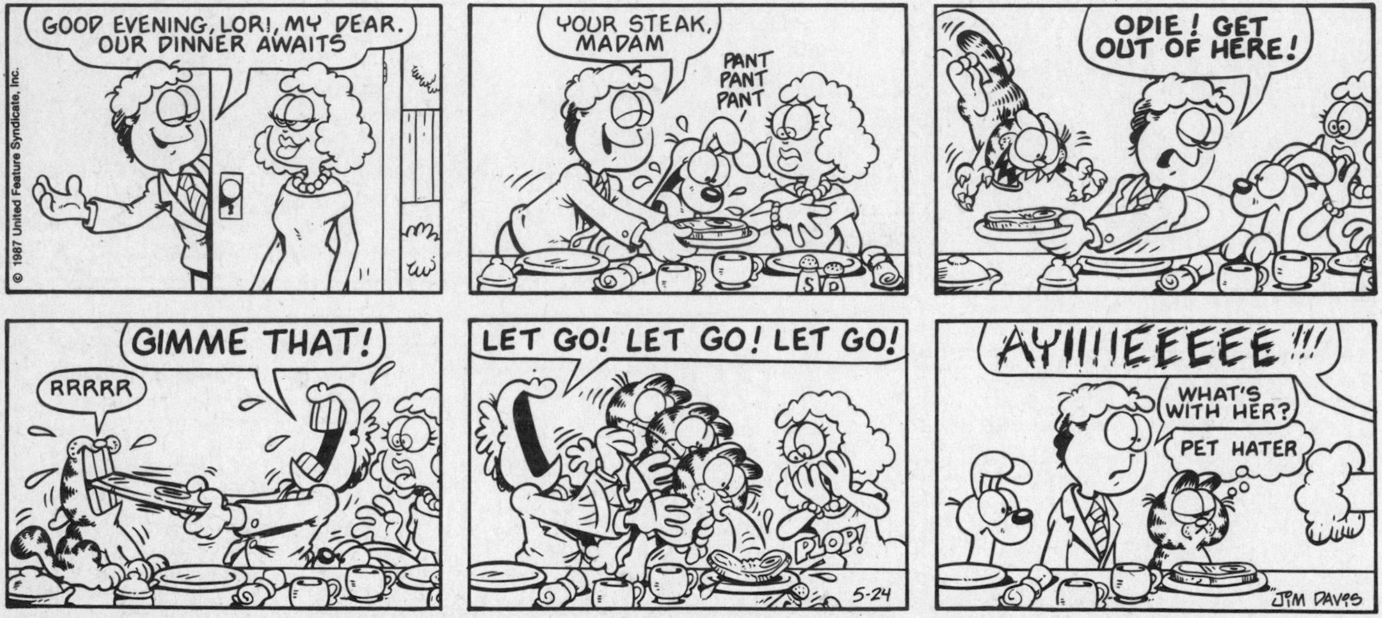
© 1987 United Feature Syndicate, Inc.
GOOD EVENING, LORI, MY DEAR. OUR DINNER AWAITS
YOUR STEAK, MADAM
PANT PANT PANT
ODIE! GET OUT OF HERE!
GIMME THAT!
RRRRR
LET GO! LET GO! LET GO!
PLOP!
5-24
AYIIIIEEEEE!!!
WHAT'S WITH HER?
PET HATER
JIM DAVIS

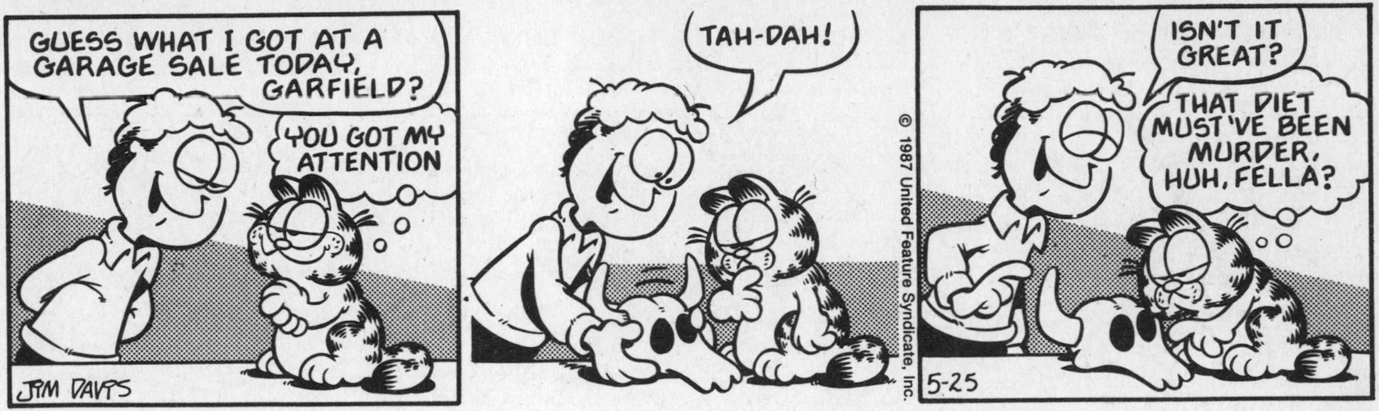
GUESS WHAT I GOT AT A GARAGE SALE TODAY, GARFIELD?
YOU GOT MY ATTENTION
JIM DAVIS
TAH-DAH!
© 1987 United Feature Syndicate, Inc.
ISN'T IT GREAT?
THAT DIET MUST'VE BEEN MURDER, HUH, FELLA?
5-25

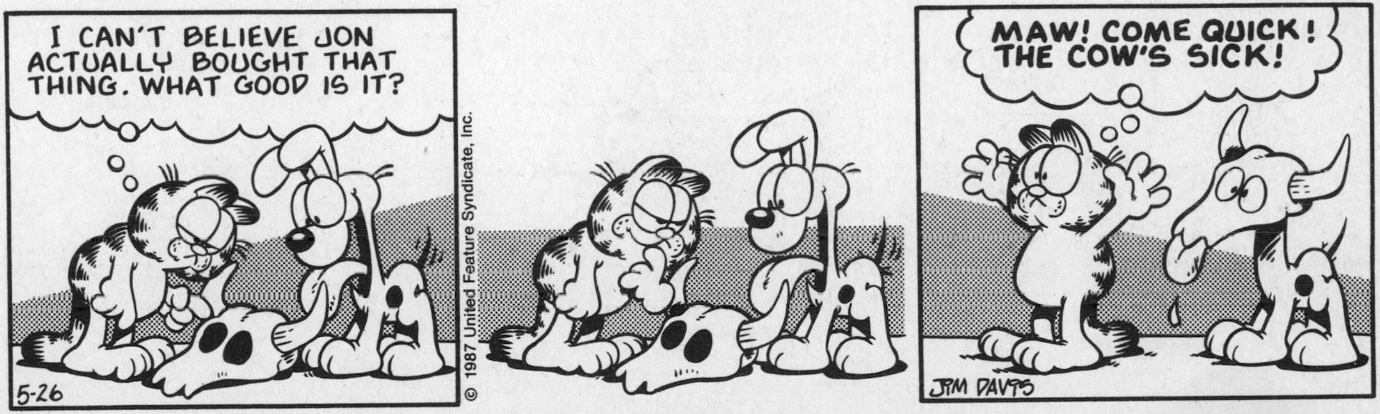
I CAN'T BELIEVE JON ACTUALLY BOUGHT THAT THING. WHAT GOOD IS IT?
5-26
© 1987 United Feature Syndicate, Inc.
MAW! COME QUICK! THE COW'S SICK!
JIM DAVIS

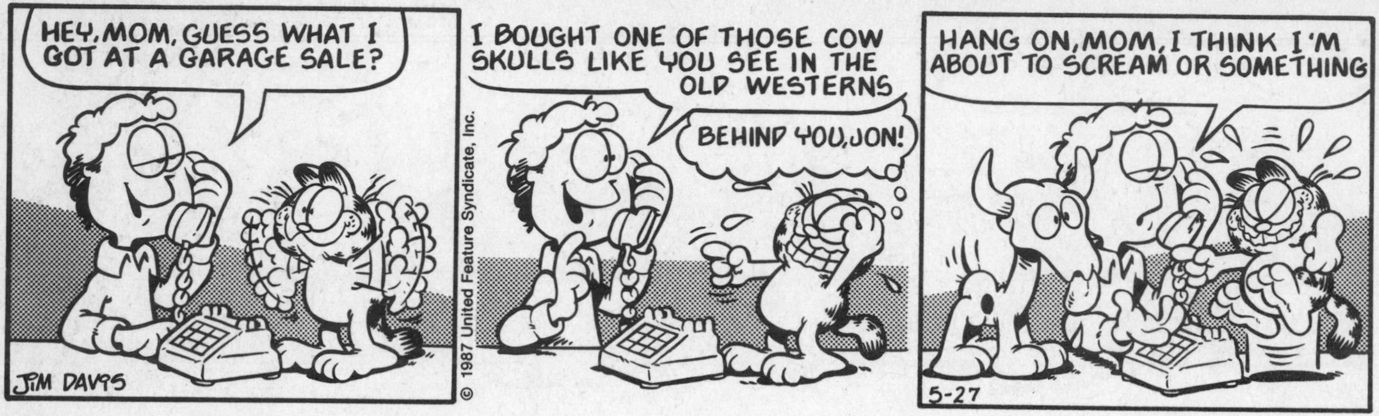
HEY, MOM, GUESS WHAT I GOT AT A GARAGE SALE?
JIM DAVIS
© 1987 United Feature Syndicate, Inc.
I BOUGHT ONE OF THOSE COW SKULLS LIKE YOU SEE IN THE OLD WESTERNS
BEHIND YOU, JON!
HANG ON, MOM, I THINK I'M ABOUT TO SCREAM OR SOMETHING
5-27

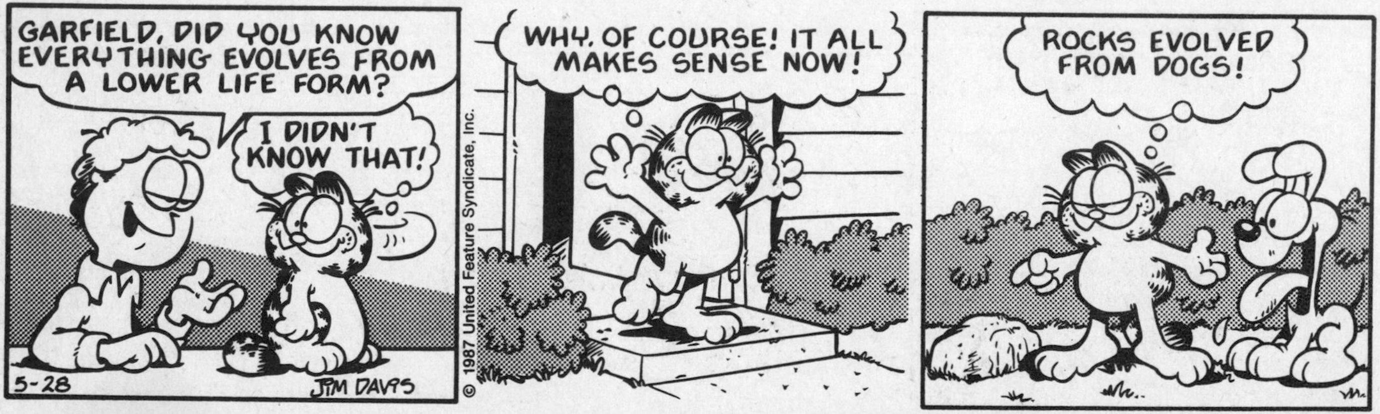
GARFIELD, DID YOU KNOW EVERYTHING EVOLVES FROM A LOWER LIFE FORM?
I DIDN'T KNOW THAT!
5-28
JIM DAVIS
© 1987 United Feature Syndicate, Inc.
WHY, OF COURSE! IT ALL MAKES SENSE NOW!
ROCKS EVOLVED FROM DOGS!

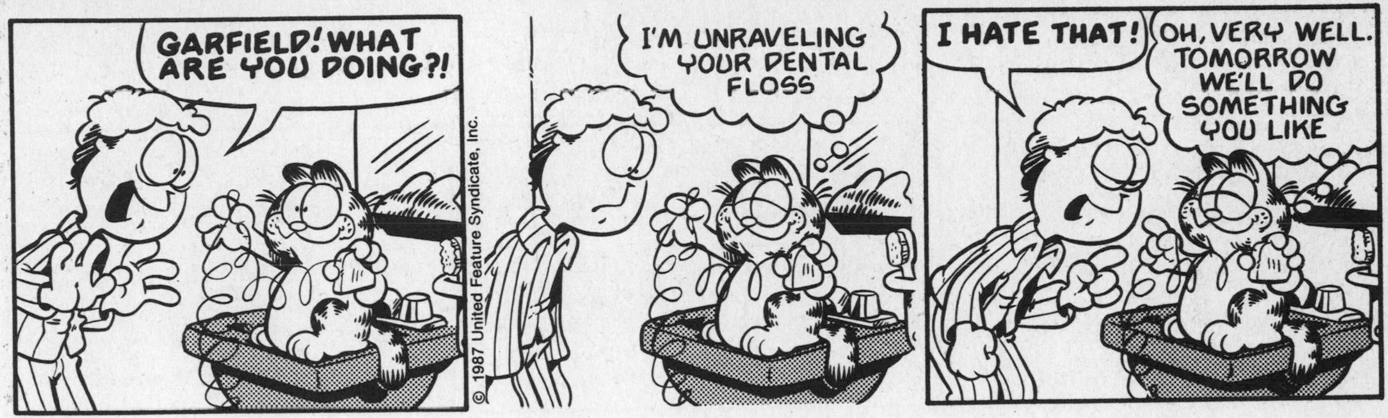
GARFIELD! WHAT ARE YOU DOING?!
© 1987 United Feature Syndicate, Inc.
I'M UNRAVELING YOUR DENTAL FLOSS
I HATE THAT!
OH, VERY WELL. TOMORROW WE'LL DO SOMETHING YOU LIKE

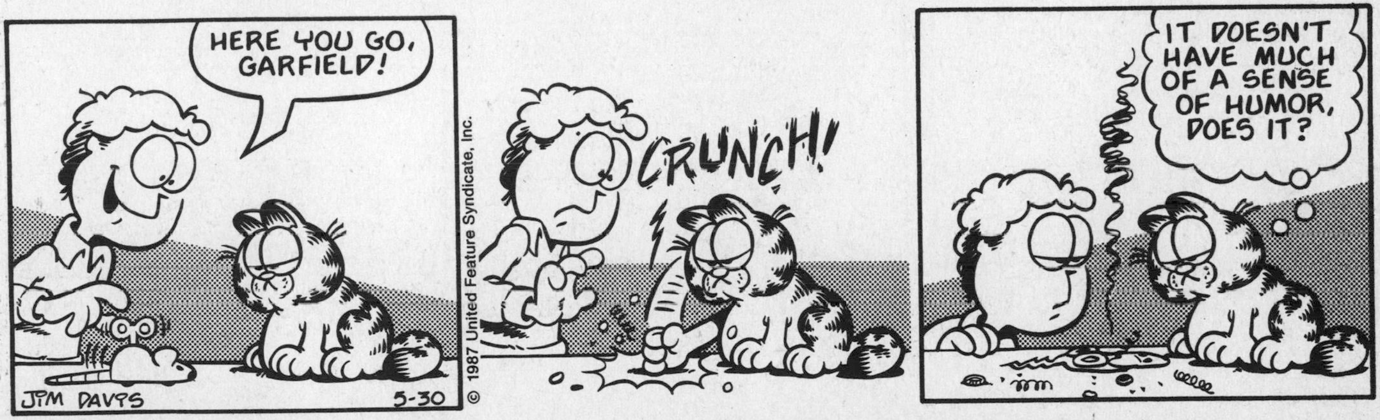
HERE YOU GO, GARFIELD!
JIM DAVIS
5-30
© 1987 United Feature Syndicate, Inc.
CRUNCH!
IT DOESN'T HAVE MUCH OF A SENSE OF HUMOR, DOES IT?

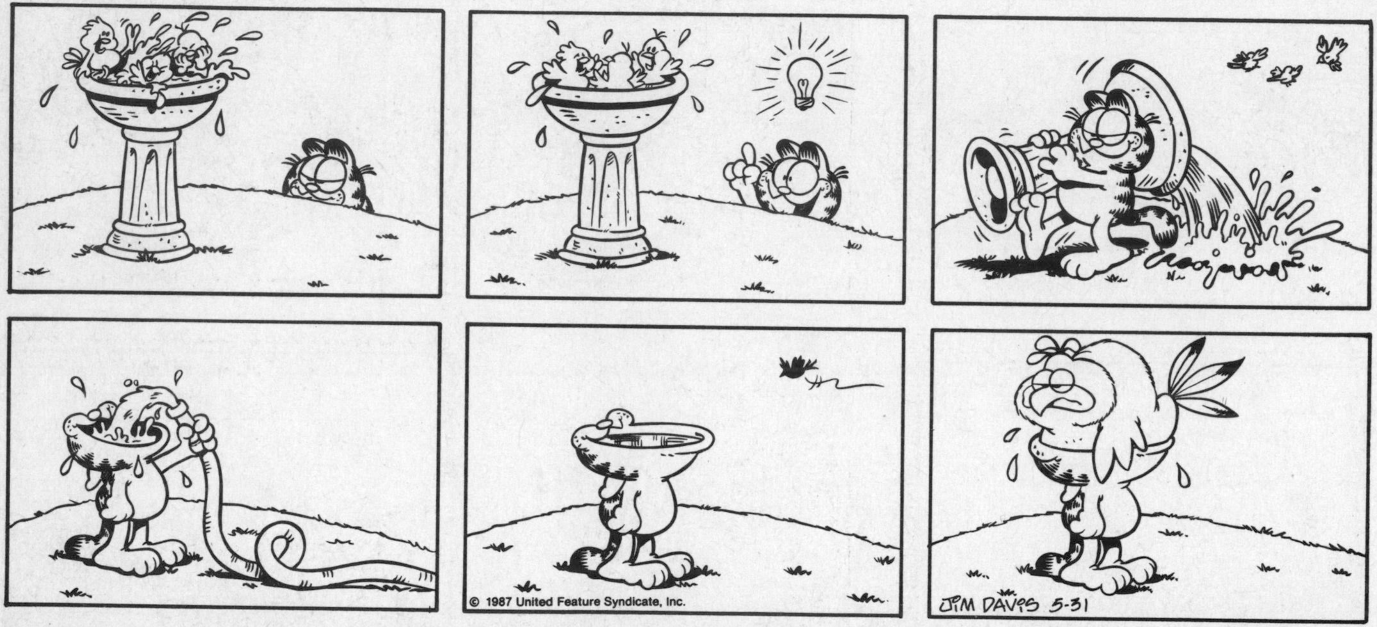

© 1987 United Feature Syndicate, Inc.
JIM DAVIS 5-31

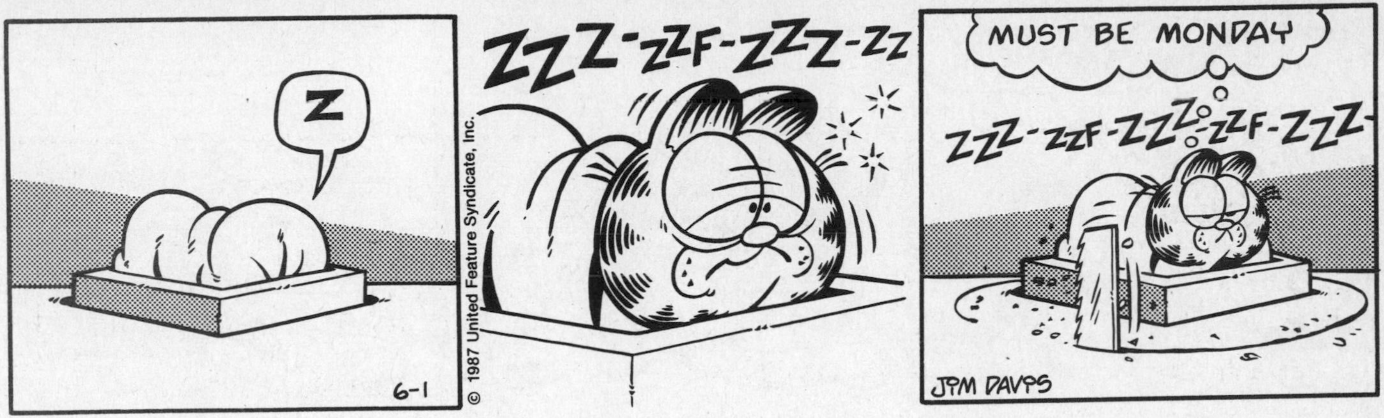
Z
ZZZ-ZZF-ZZZ-ZZ
6-1
© 1987 United Feature Syndicate, Inc.
MUST BE MONDAY
ZZZ-ZZF-ZZZ-ZZF-ZZZ-
JIM DAVIS

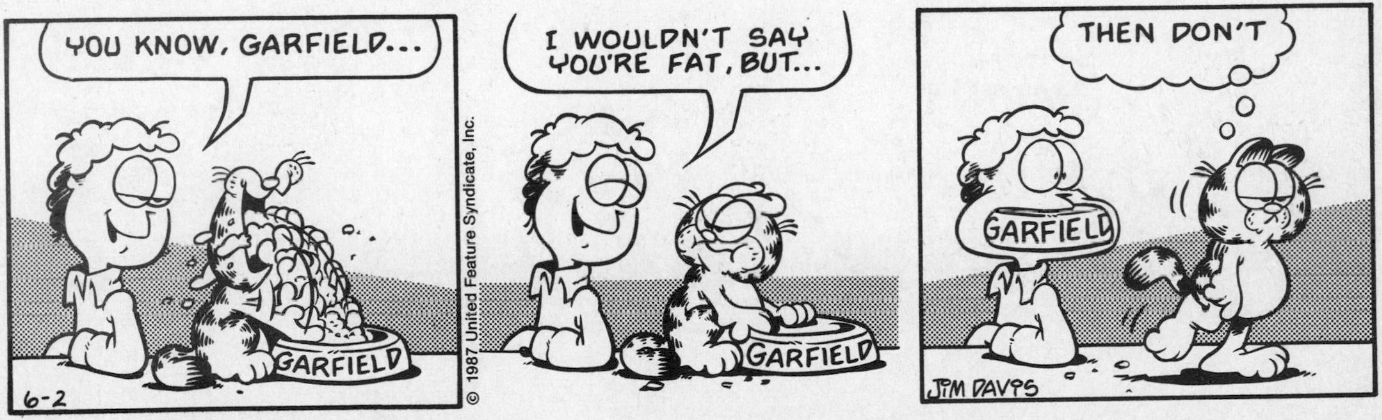
YOU KNOW, GARFIELD...
GARFIELD
6-2
© 1987 United Feature Syndicate, Inc.
I WOULDN'T SAY YOU'RE FAT, BUT...
GARFIELD
THEN DON'T
GARFIELD
JIM DAVIS

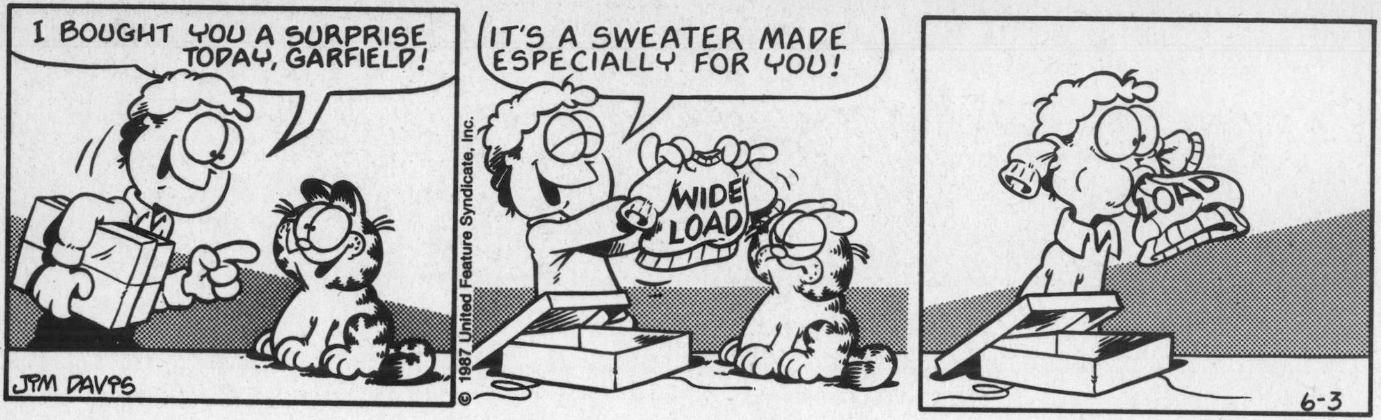
I BOUGHT YOU A SURPRISE TODAY, GARFIELD!
JIM DAVIS
© 1987 United Feature Syndicate, Inc.
IT'S A SWEATER MADE ESPECIALLY FOR YOU!
WIDE LOAD
LOAD
6-3

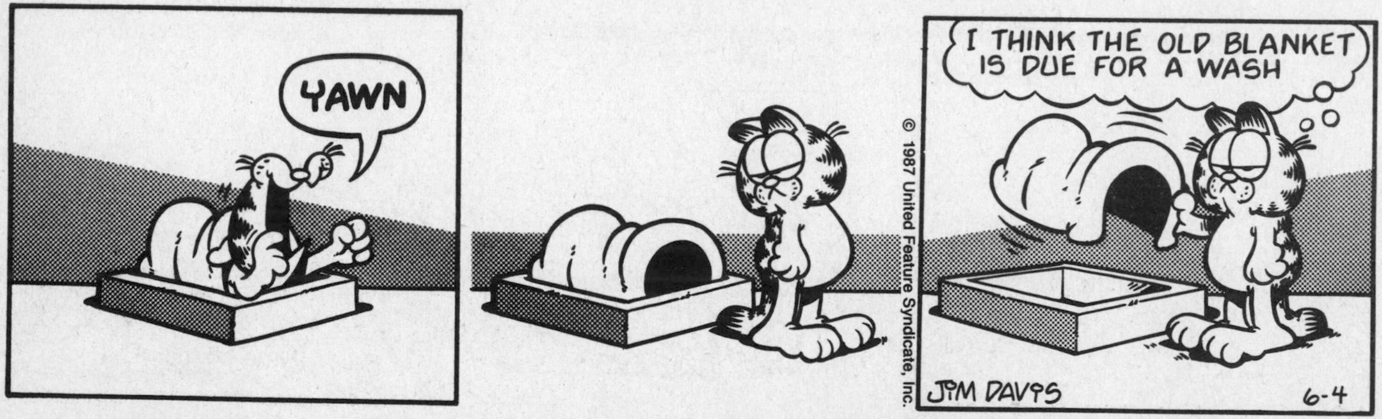
YAWN
© 1987 United Feature Syndicate, Inc.
I THINK THE OLD BLANKET IS DUE FOR A WASH
JIM DAVIS
6-4

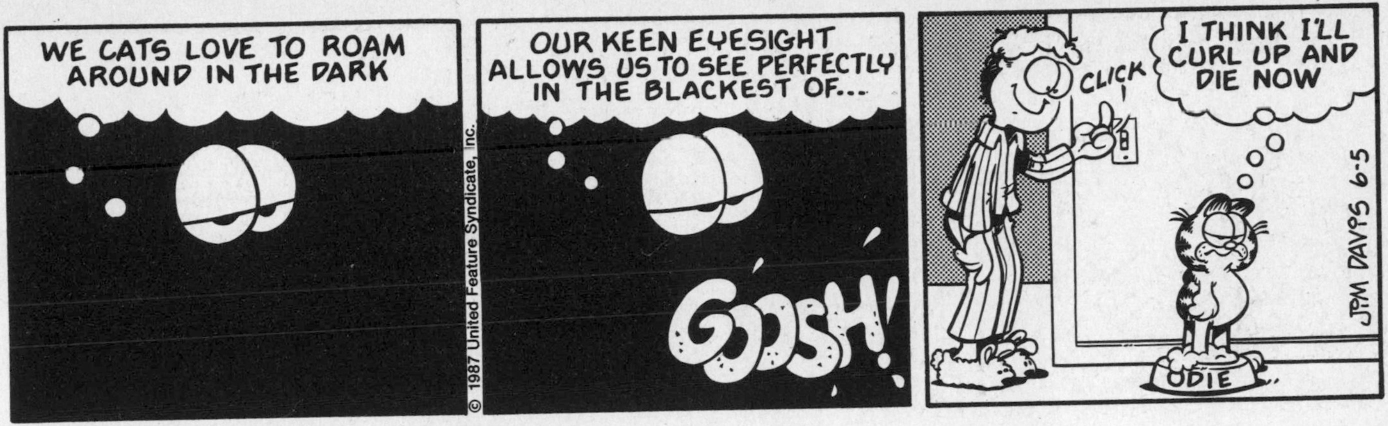
WE CATS LOVE TO ROAM AROUND IN THE DARK
© 1987 United Feature Syndicate, Inc.
OUR KEEN EYESIGHT ALLOWS US TO SEE PERFECTLY IN THE BLACKEST OF...
GOOSH!
CLICK
I THINK I'LL CURL UP AND DIE NOW
ODIE
JIM DAVIS 6-5

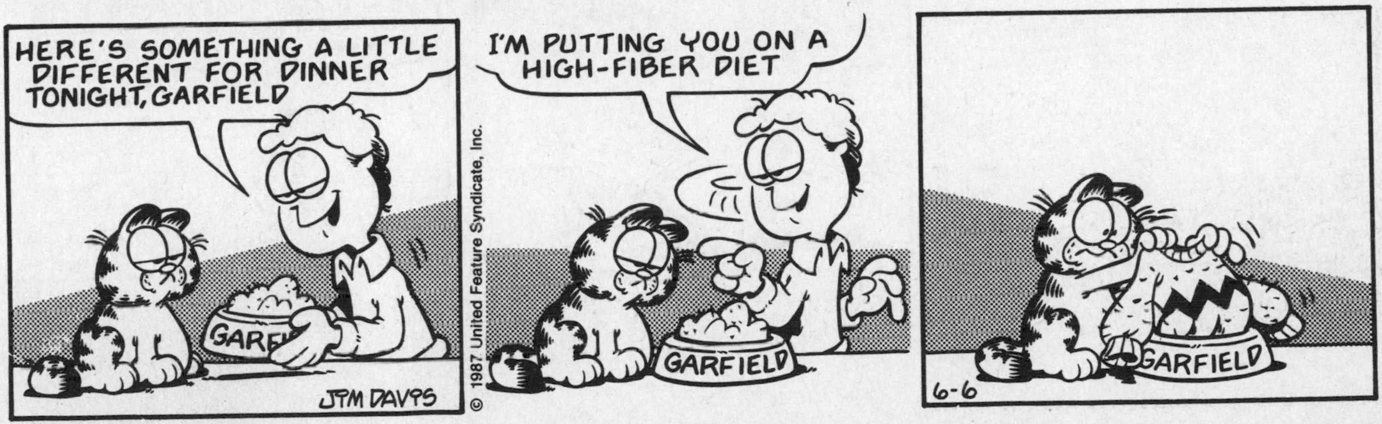
HERE'S SOMETHING A LITTLE DIFFERENT FOR DINNER TONIGHT, GARFIELD
GARFI
JIM DAVIS
© 1987 United Feature Syndicate, Inc.
I'M PUTTING YOU ON A HIGH-FIBER DIET
GARFIELD
GARFIELD
6-6

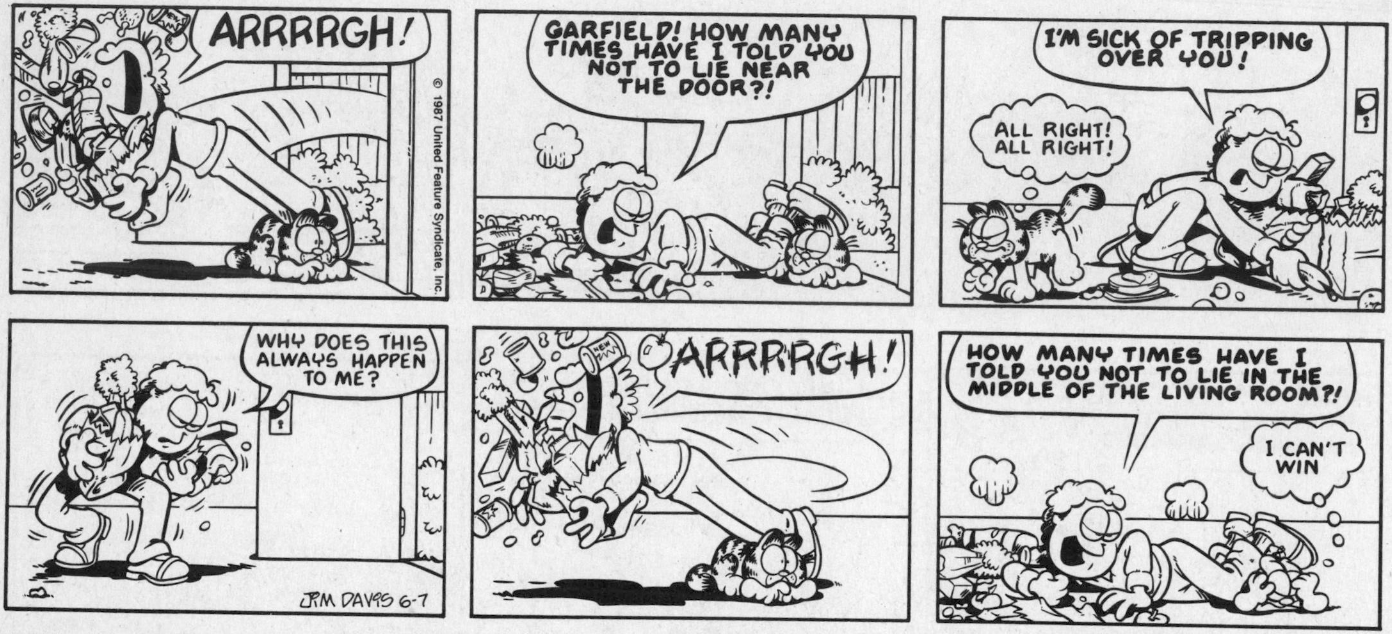
ARRRRGH!
© 1987 United Feature Syndicate, Inc.
GARFIELD! HOW MANY TIMES HAVE I TOLD YOU NOT TO LIE NEAR THE DOOR?!
I'M SICK OF TRIPPING OVER YOU!
ALL RIGHT! ALL RIGHT!
WHY DOES THIS ALWAYS HAPPEN TO ME?
JIM DAVIS 6-7
NEW
ARRRRGH!
HOW MANY TIMES HAVE I TOLD YOU NOT TO LIE IN THE MIDDLE OF THE LIVING ROOM?!
I CAN'T WIN

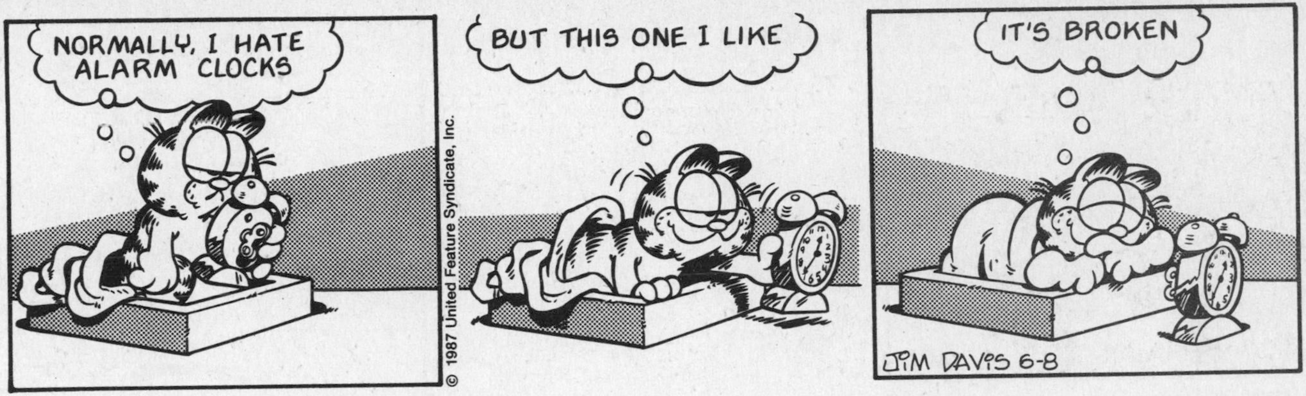
NORMALLY, I HATE ALARM CLOCKS
BUT THIS ONE I LIKE
IT'S BROKEN
© 1987 United Feature Syndicate, Inc.
JIM DAVIS 6-8

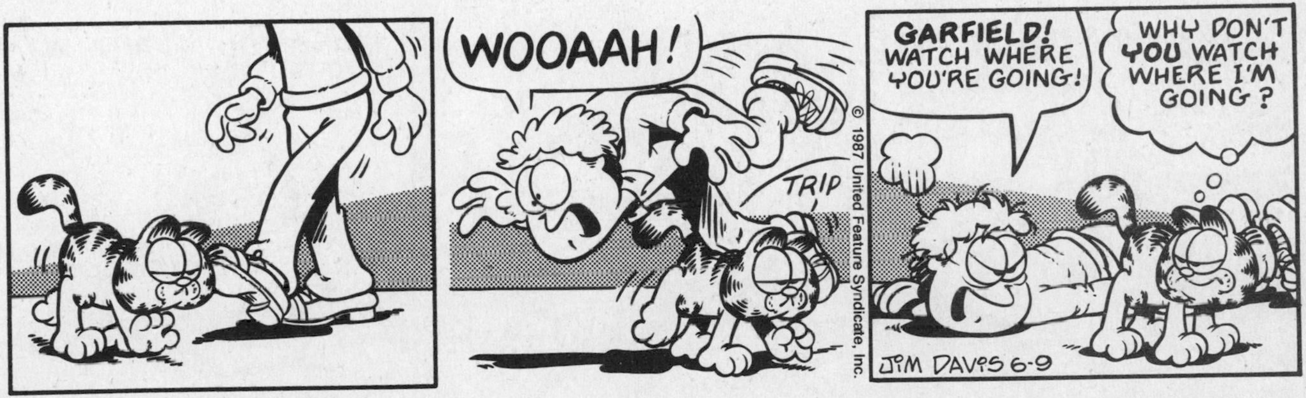
WOOAAH!
TRIP
GARFIELD! WATCH WHERE YOU'RE GOING!
WHY DON'T YOU WATCH WHERE I'M GOING?
© 1987 United Feature Syndicate, Inc.
JIM DAVIS 6-9

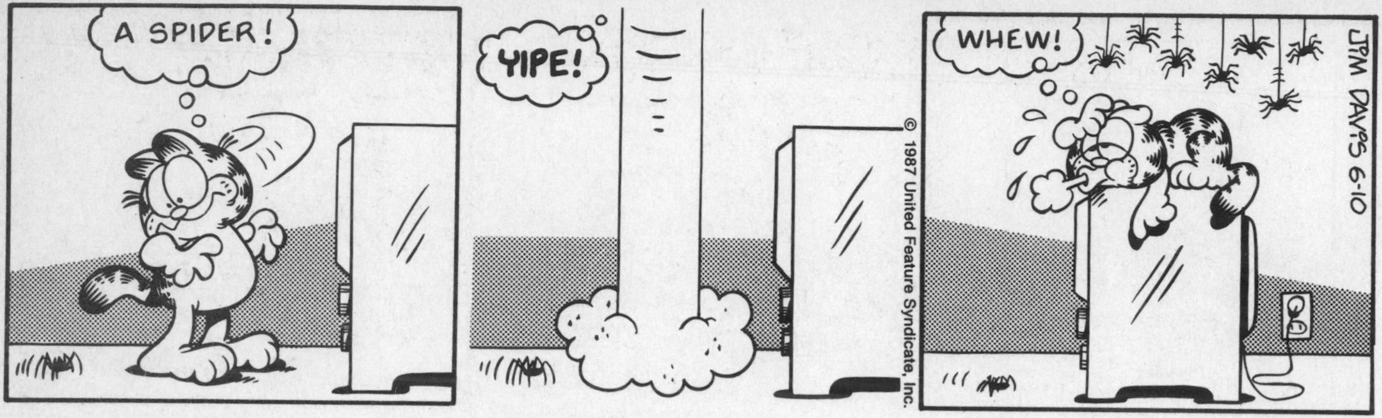
A SPIDER!
YIPE!
WHEW!
JIM DAVIS 6-10
© 1987 United Feature Syndicate, Inc.

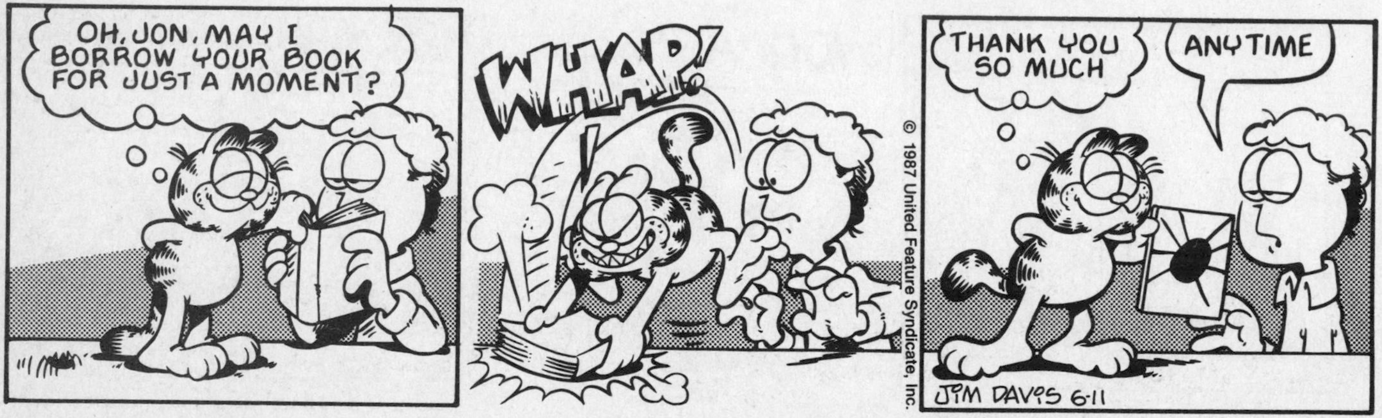
OH, JON, MAY I BORROW YOUR BOOK FOR JUST A MOMENT?
WHAP!
THANK YOU SO MUCH
ANYTIME
JIM DAVIS 6-11
© 1987 United Feature Syndicate, Inc.

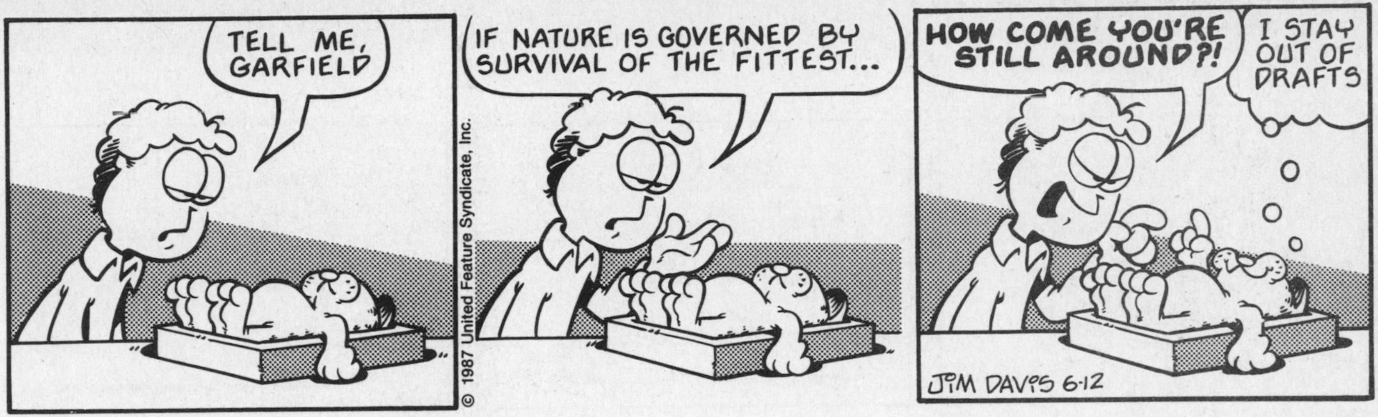
TELL ME, GARFIELD
IF NATURE IS GOVERNED BY SURVIVAL OF THE FITTEST...
HOW COME YOU'RE STILL AROUND?!
I STAY OUT OF DRAFTS
JIM DAVIS 6-12
© 1987 United Feature Syndicate, Inc.

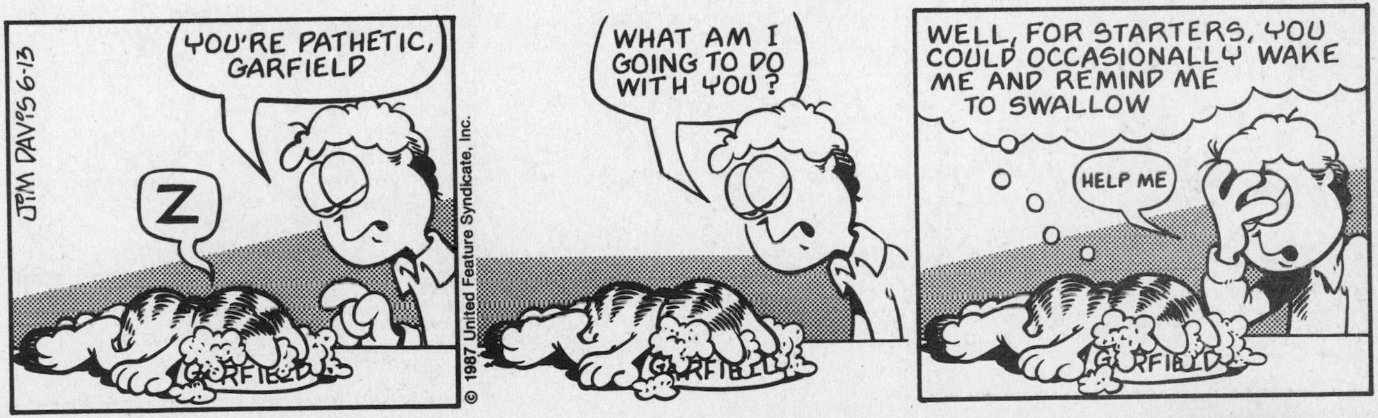
YOU'RE PATHETIC, GARFIELD
Z
GARFIELD
WHAT AM I GOING TO DO WITH YOU?
WELL, FOR STARTERS, YOU COULD OCCASIONALLY WAKE ME AND REMIND ME TO SWALLOW
HELP ME
JIM DAVIS 6-13
© 1987 United Feature Syndicate, Inc.

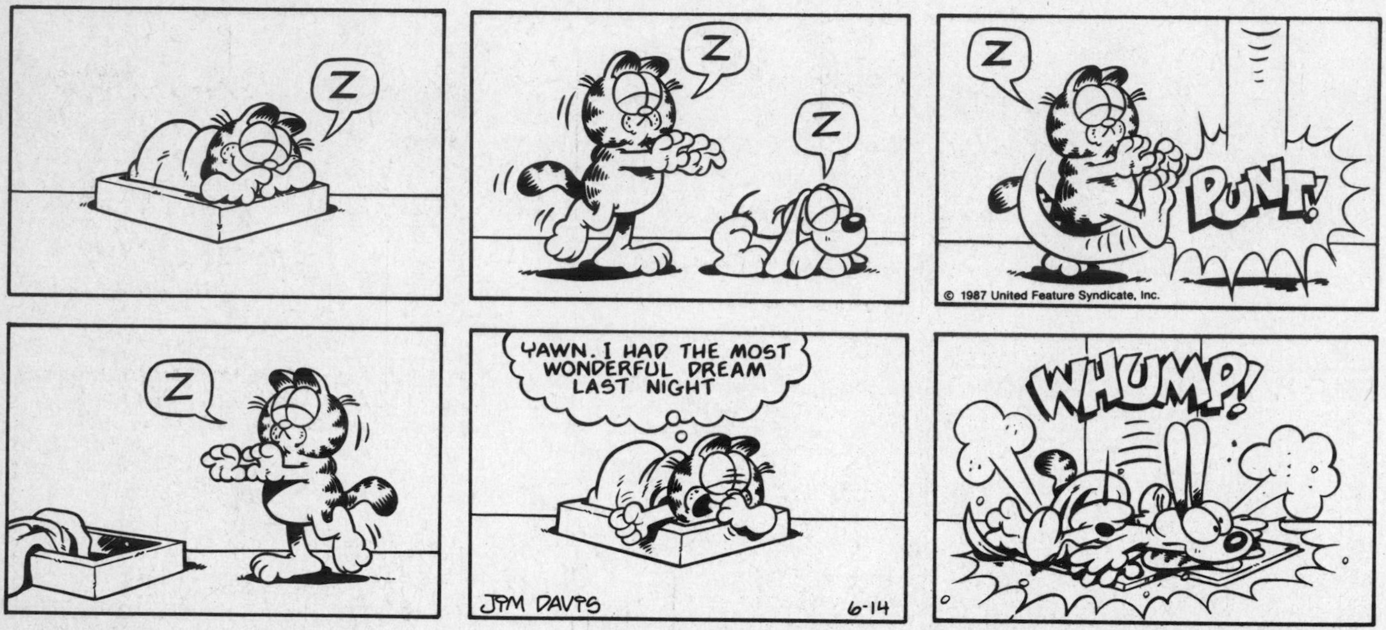
Z
Z
Z
Z
PUNT!
© 1987 United Feature Syndicate, Inc.
Z
YAWN. I HAD THE MOST WONDERFUL DREAM LAST NIGHT
JIM DAVIS
6-14
WHUMP!

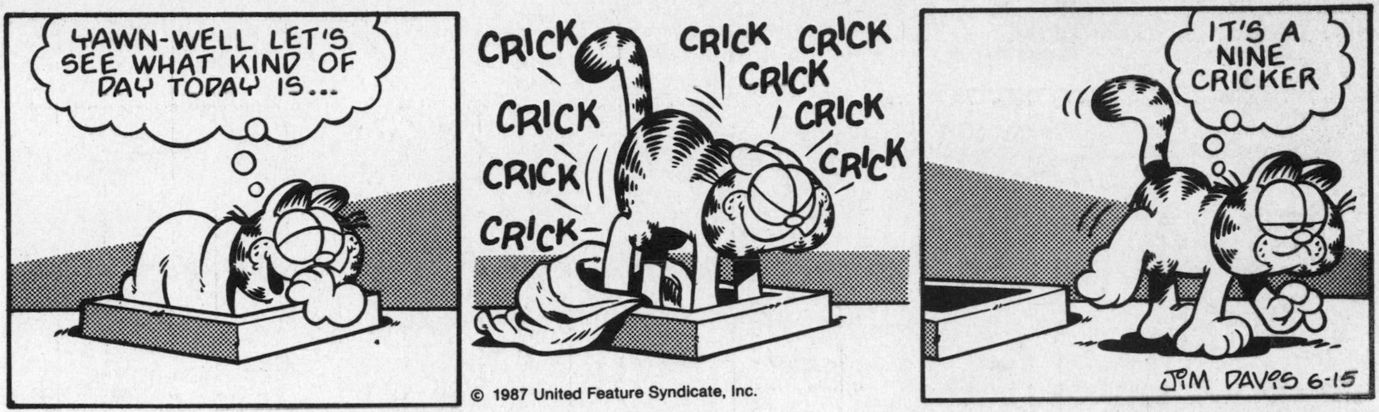
YAWN-WELL LET'S SEE WHAT KIND OF DAY TODAY IS...
CRICK CRICK CRICK CRICK CRICK CRICK CRICK CRICK CRICK
© 1987 United Feature Syndicate, Inc.
IT'S A NINE CRICKER
JIM DAVIS 6-15

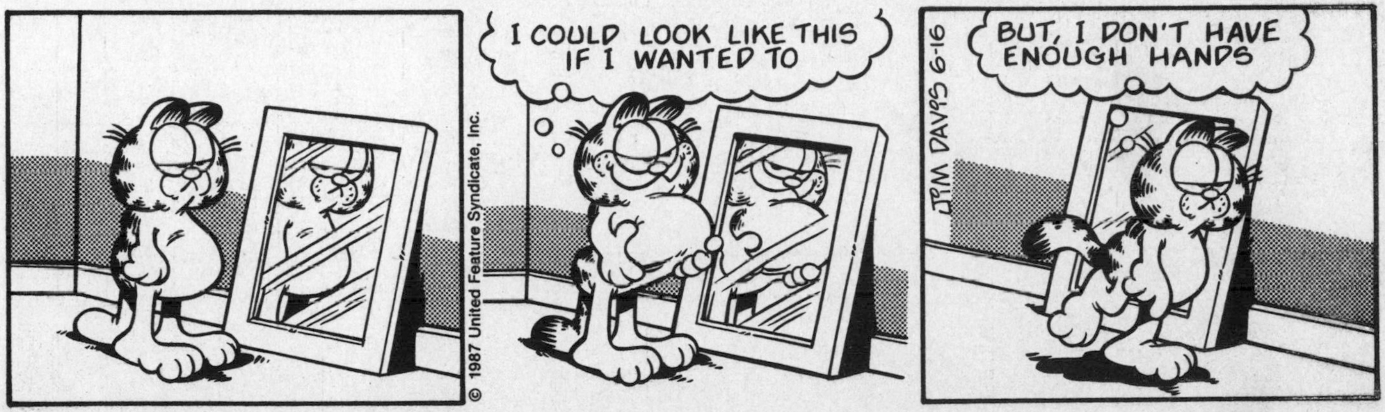
© 1987 United Feature Syndicate, Inc.
I COULD LOOK LIKE THIS IF I WANTED TO
JIM DAVIS 6-16
BUT, I DON'T HAVE ENOUGH HANDS

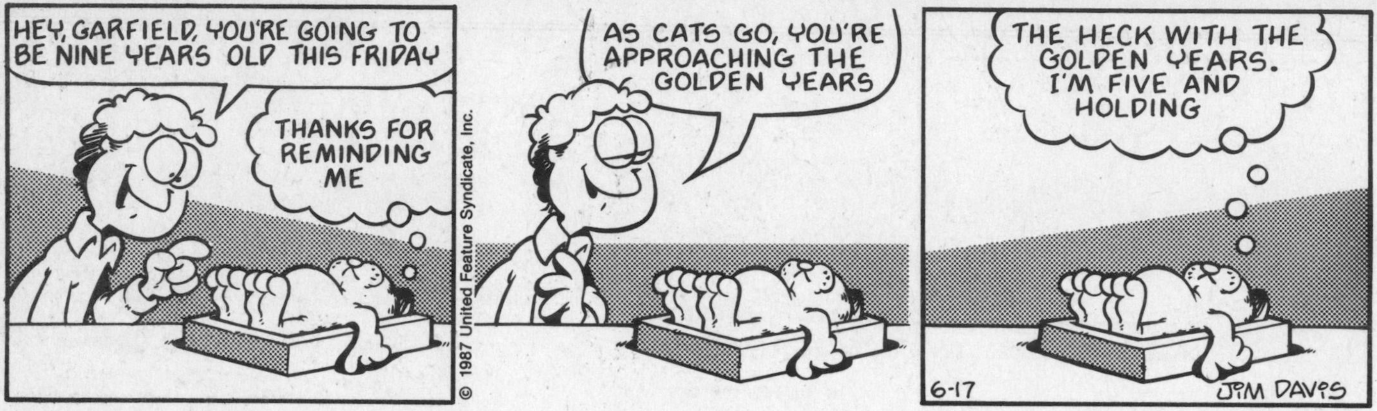
HEY, GARFIELD, YOU'RE GOING TO BE NINE YEARS OLD THIS FRIDAY
THANKS FOR REMINDING ME
AS CATS GO, YOU'RE APPROACHING THE GOLDEN YEARS
THE HECK WITH THE GOLDEN YEARS. I'M FIVE AND HOLDING
6-17
JIM DAVIS
© 1987 United Feature Syndicate, Inc.

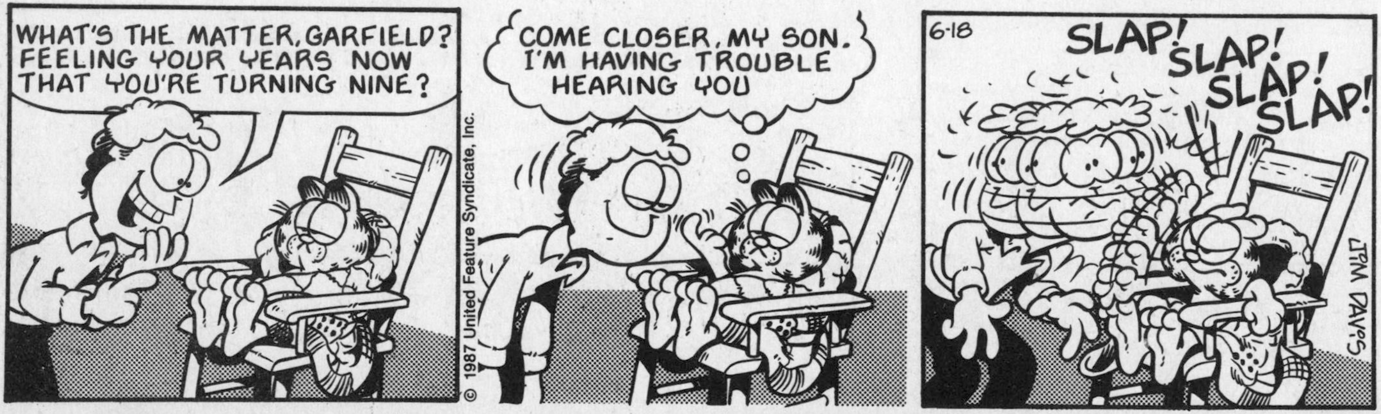
WHAT'S THE MATTER, GARFIELD? FEELING YOUR YEARS NOW THAT YOU'RE TURNING NINE?
COME CLOSER, MY SON. I'M HAVING TROUBLE HEARING YOU
6-18
SLAP! SLAP! SLAP! SLAP!
JIM DAVIS
© 1987 United Feature Syndicate, Inc.

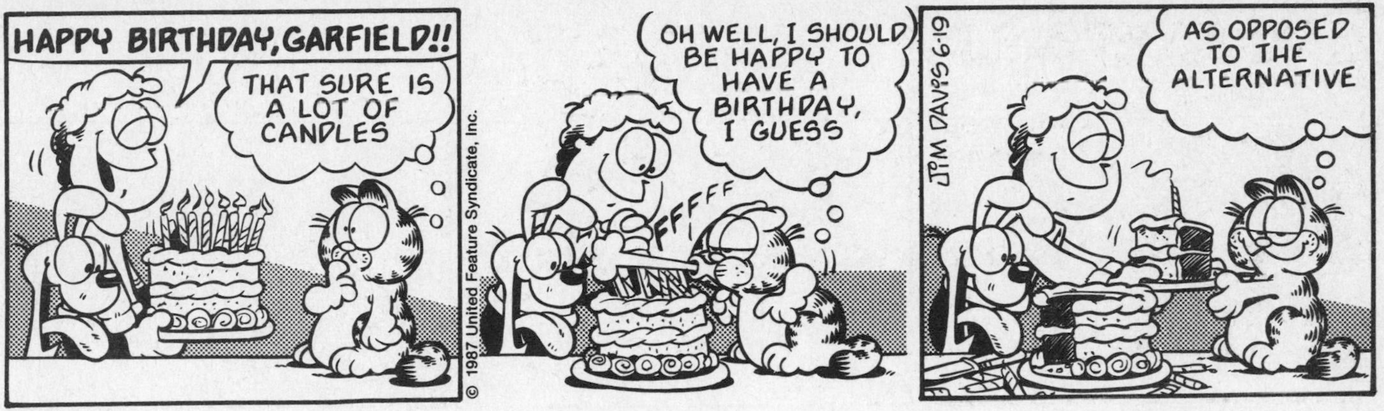
HAPPY BIRTHDAY, GARFIELD!!
THAT SURE IS A LOT OF CANDLES
FFFFFF
OH WELL, I SHOULD BE HAPPY TO HAVE A BIRTHDAY, I GUESS
JIM DAVIS 6-19
AS OPPOSED TO THE ALTERNATIVE

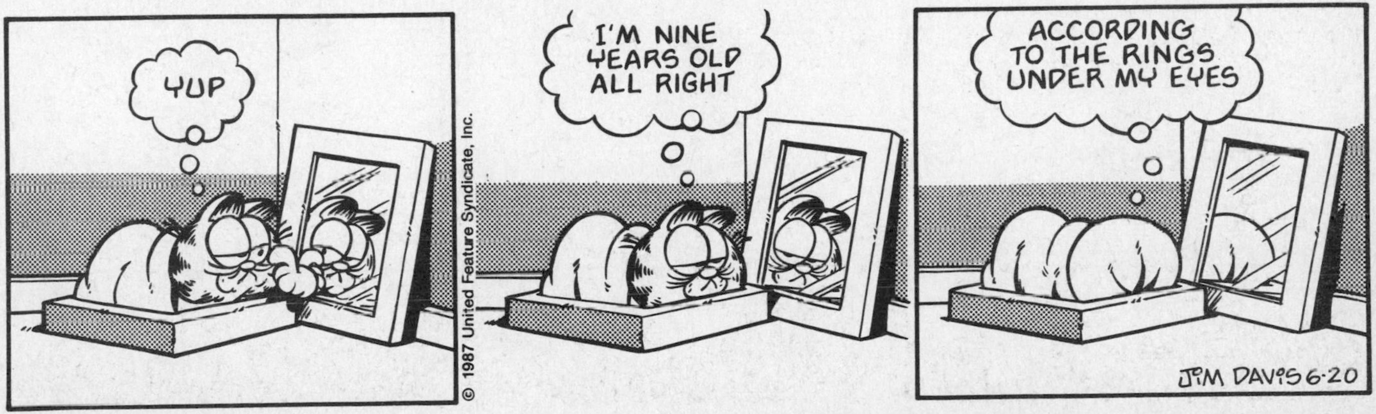
YUP
I'M NINE YEARS OLD ALL RIGHT
ACCORDING TO THE RINGS UNDER MY EYES
JIM DAVIS 6-20

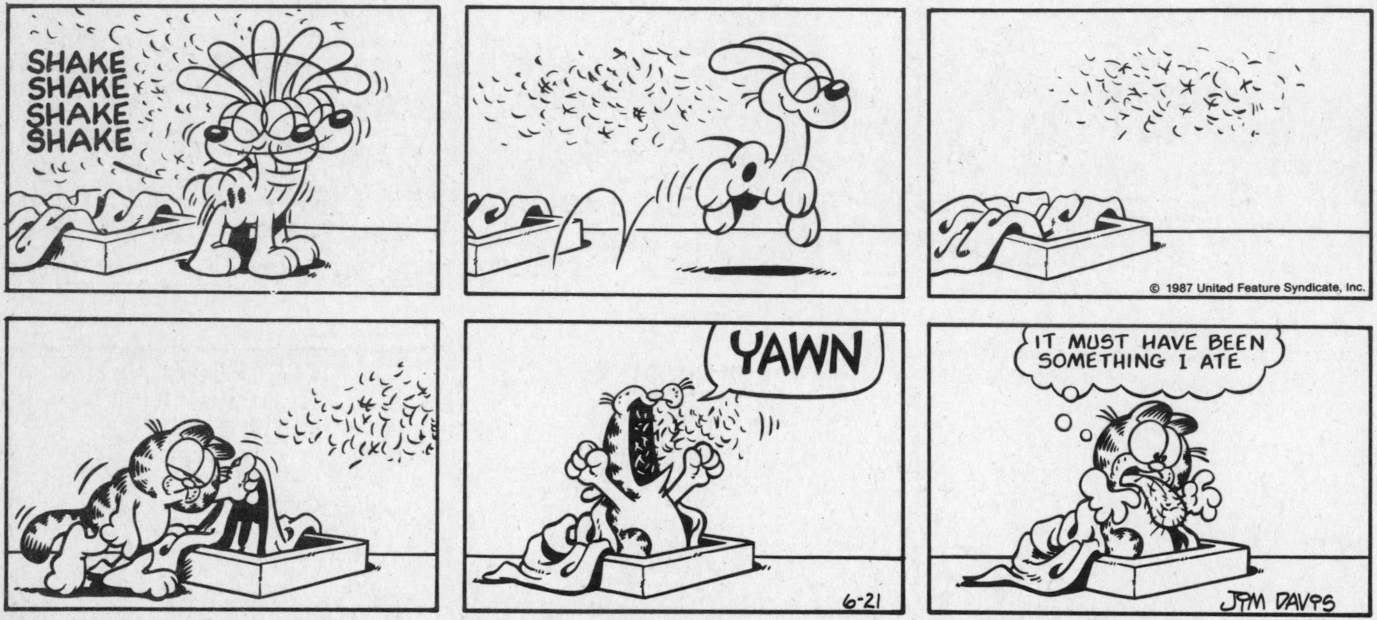
SHAKE
SHAKE
SHAKE
SHAKE
© 1987 United Feature Syndicate, Inc.
YAWN
6-21
IT MUST HAVE BEEN SOMETHING I ATE
JPM DAVIS

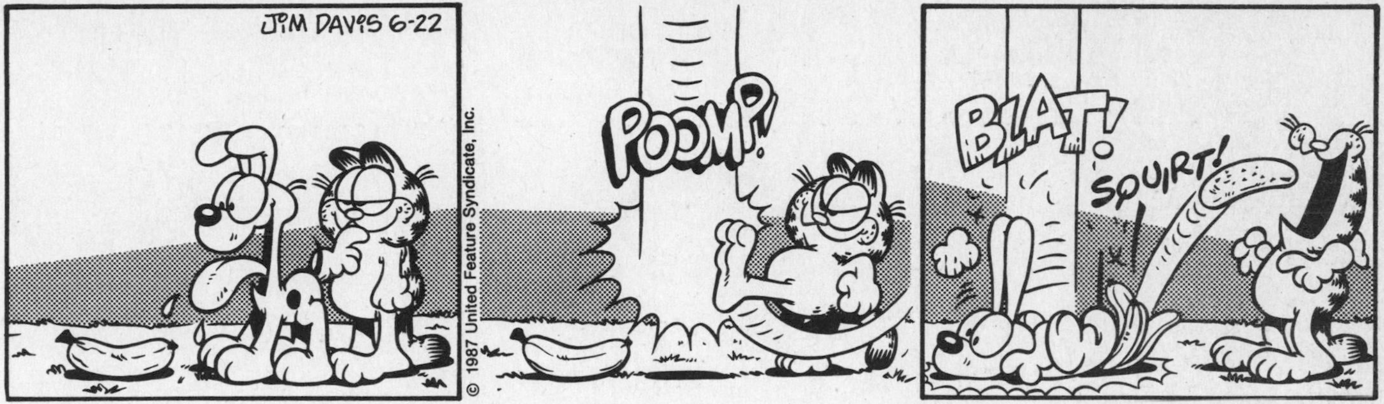
JIM DAVIS 6-22
© 1987 United Feature Syndicate, Inc.
POOMP!
BLAT!
SQUIRT!

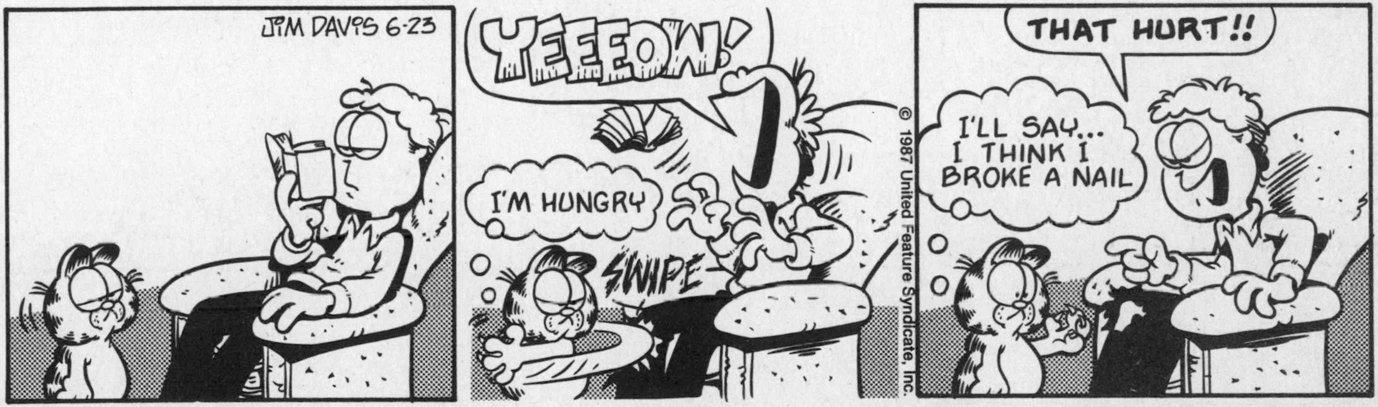
JIM DAVIS 6-23
I'M HUNGRY
YEEEOW!
SWIPE
© 1987 United Feature Syndicate, Inc.
THAT HURT!!
I'LL SAY... I THINK I BROKE A NAIL

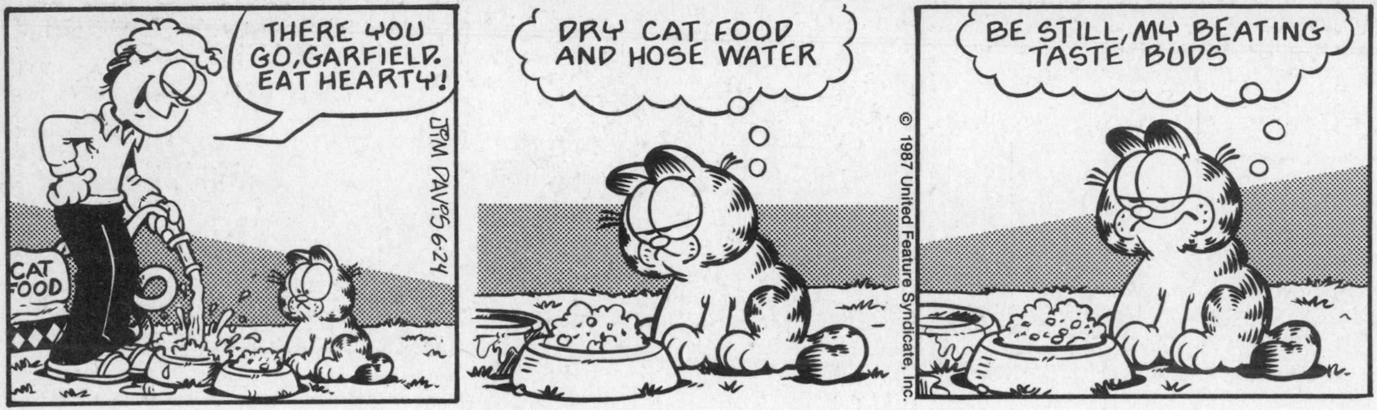
THERE YOU GO, GARFIELD. EAT HEARTY!
CAT FOOD
JIM DAVIS 6-24
DRY CAT FOOD AND HOSE WATER
© 1987 United Feature Syndicate, Inc.
BE STILL, MY BEATING TASTE BUDS

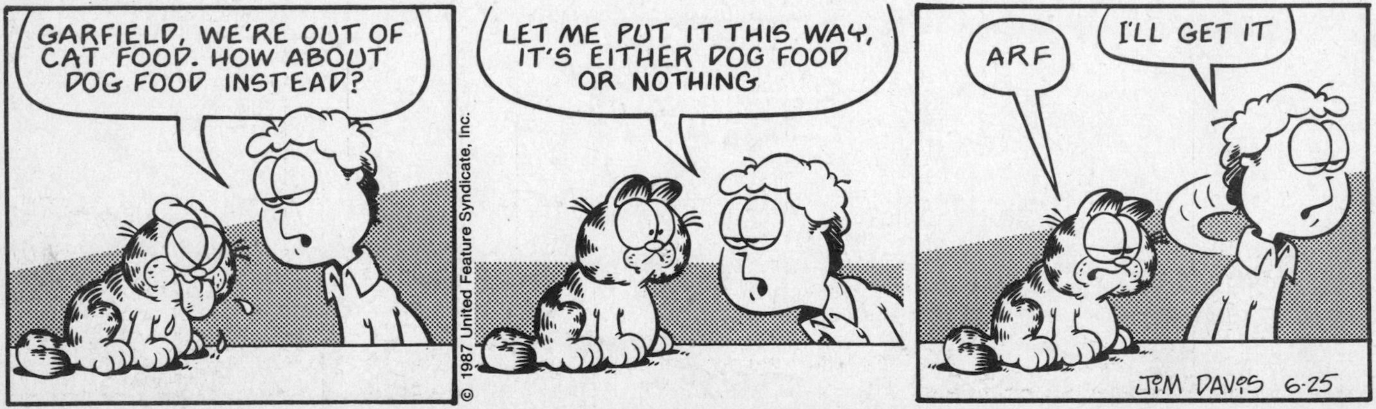
GARFIELD, WE'RE OUT OF CAT FOOD. HOW ABOUT DOG FOOD INSTEAD?
© 1987 United Feature Syndicate, Inc.
LET ME PUT IT THIS WAY, IT'S EITHER DOG FOOD OR NOTHING
ARF
I'LL GET IT
JIM DAVIS 6-25

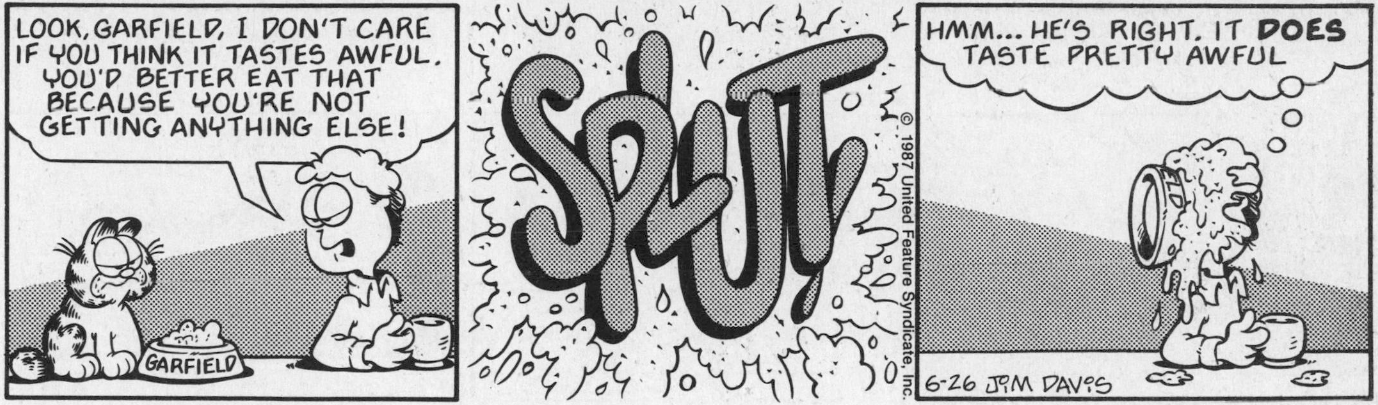
LOOK, GARFIELD, I DON'T CARE IF YOU THINK IT TASTES AWFUL. YOU'D BETTER EAT THAT BECAUSE YOU'RE NOT GETTING ANYTHING ELSE!
GARFIELD
SPLUT
© 1987 United Feature Syndicate, Inc.
HMM... HE'S RIGHT. IT **DOES** TASTE PRETTY AWFUL
6-26 JIM DAVIS

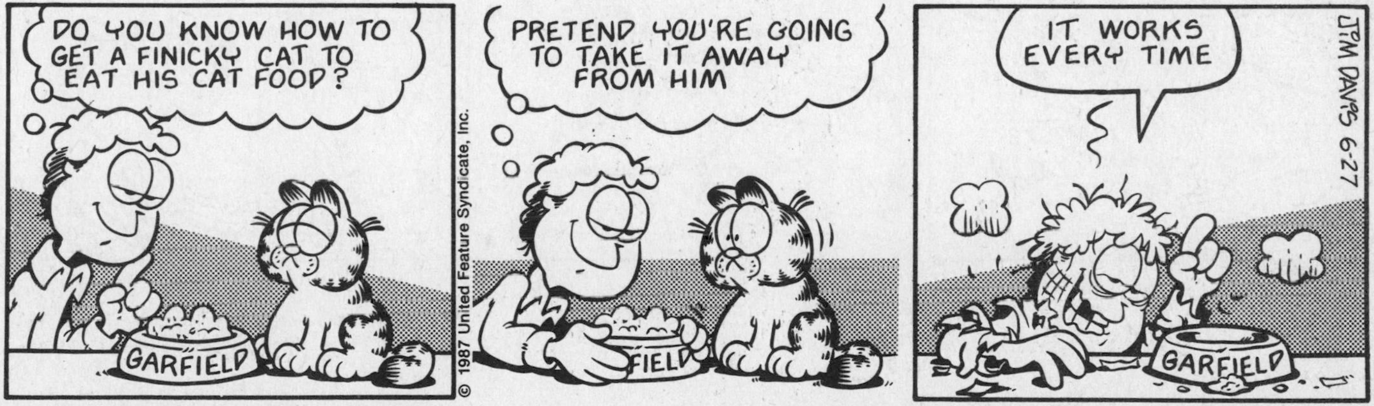
DO YOU KNOW HOW TO GET A FINICKY CAT TO EAT HIS CAT FOOD?
GARFIELD
© 1987 United Feature Syndicate, Inc.
PRETEND YOU'RE GOING TO TAKE IT AWAY FROM HIM
FIELD
IT WORKS EVERY TIME
GARFIELD
JIM DAVIS 6-27

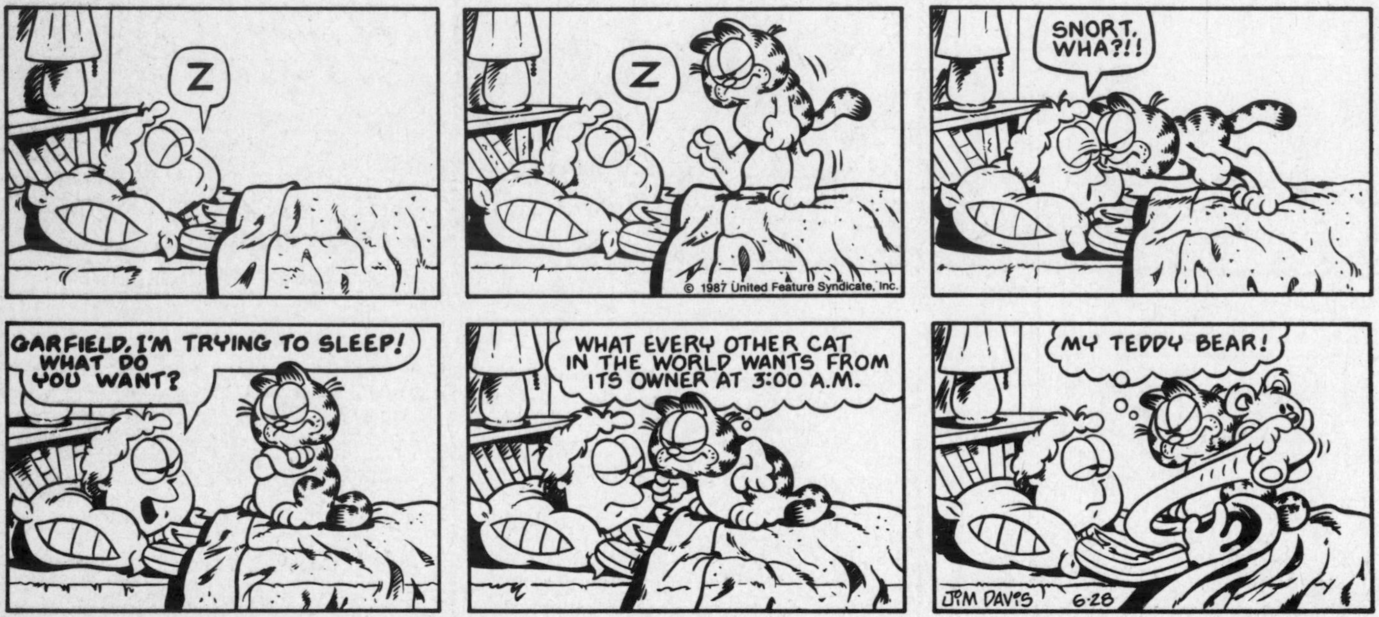
Z
Z
© 1987 United Feature Syndicate, Inc.
SNORT, WHA?!!
GARFIELD, I'M TRYING TO SLEEP! WHAT DO YOU WANT?
WHAT EVERY OTHER CAT IN THE WORLD WANTS FROM ITS OWNER AT 3:00 A.M.
MY TEDDY BEAR!
JIM DAVIS
6-28

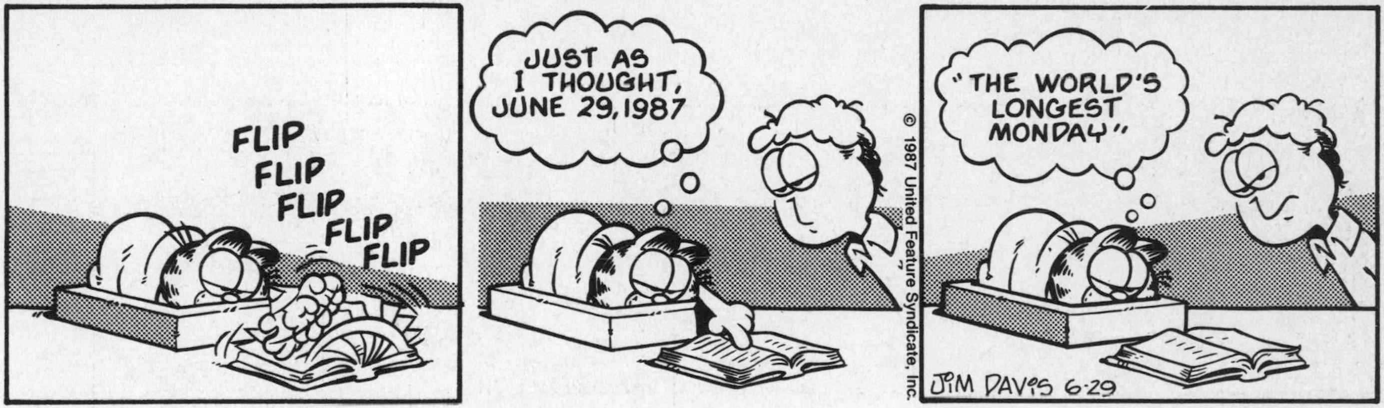
FLIP
FLIP
FLIP
FLIP
FLIP
JUST AS I THOUGHT, JUNE 29,1987
"THE WORLD'S LONGEST MONDAY"
JIM DAVIS 6-29

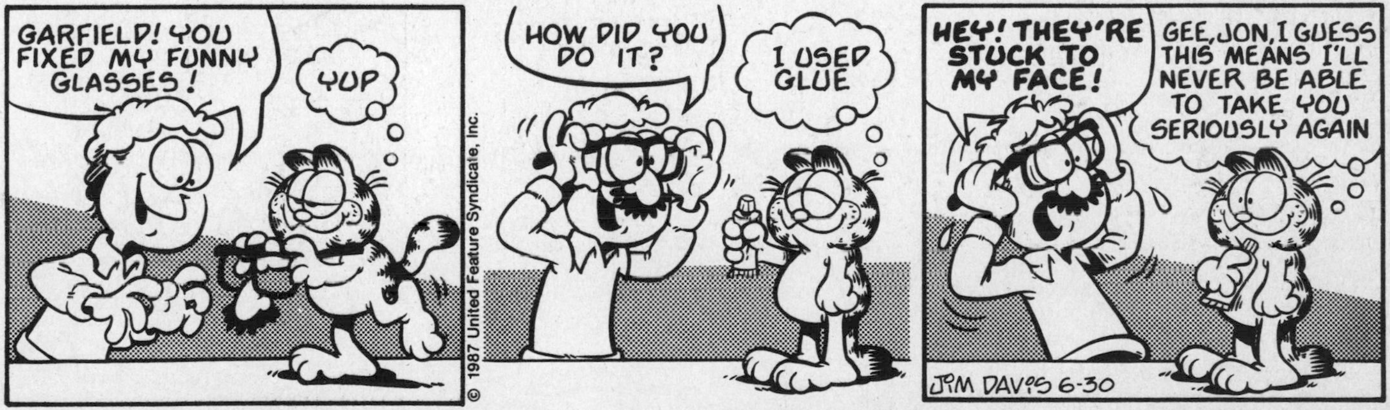
GARFIELD! YOU FIXED MY FUNNY GLASSES!
YUP
HOW DID YOU DO IT?
I USED GLUE
HEY! THEY'RE STUCK TO MY FACE!
GEE, JON, I GUESS THIS MEANS I'LL NEVER BE ABLE TO TAKE YOU SERIOUSLY AGAIN
JIM DAVIS 6-30

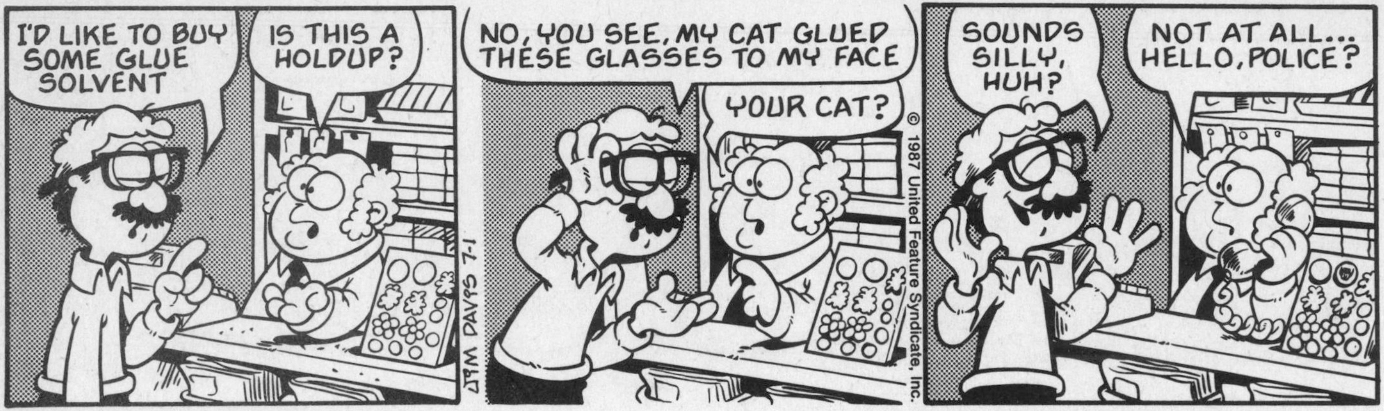
I'D LIKE TO BUY SOME GLUE SOLVENT
IS THIS A HOLDUP?
JIM DAVIS 7-1
NO, YOU SEE, MY CAT GLUED THESE GLASSES TO MY FACE
YOUR CAT?
© 1987 United Feature Syndicate, Inc.
SOUNDS SILLY, HUH?
NOT AT ALL... HELLO, POLICE?

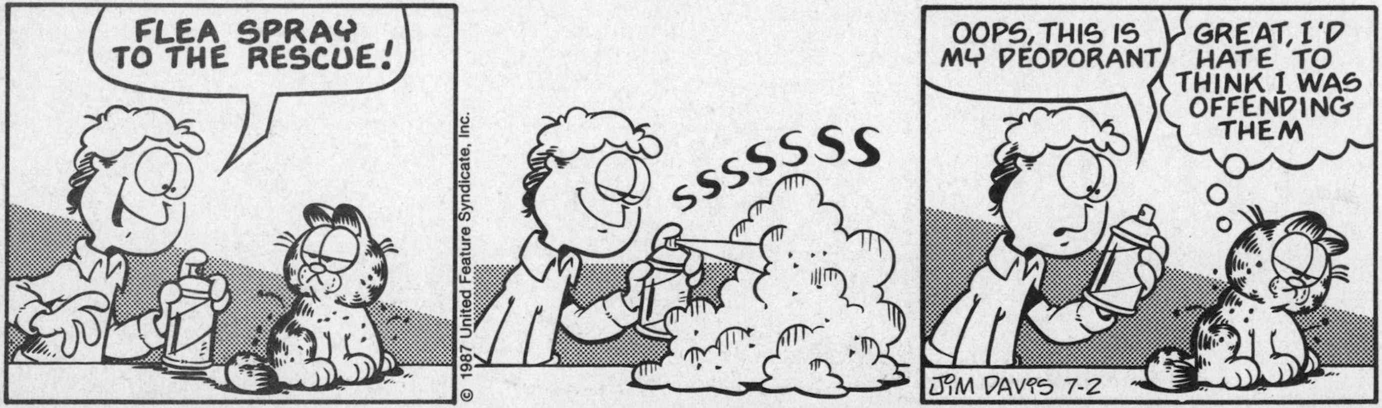
FLEA SPRAY TO THE RESCUE!
© 1987 United Feature Syndicate, Inc.
SSSSSSSS
OOPS, THIS IS MY DEODORANT
GREAT, I'D HATE TO THINK I WAS OFFENDING THEM
JIM DAVIS 7-2

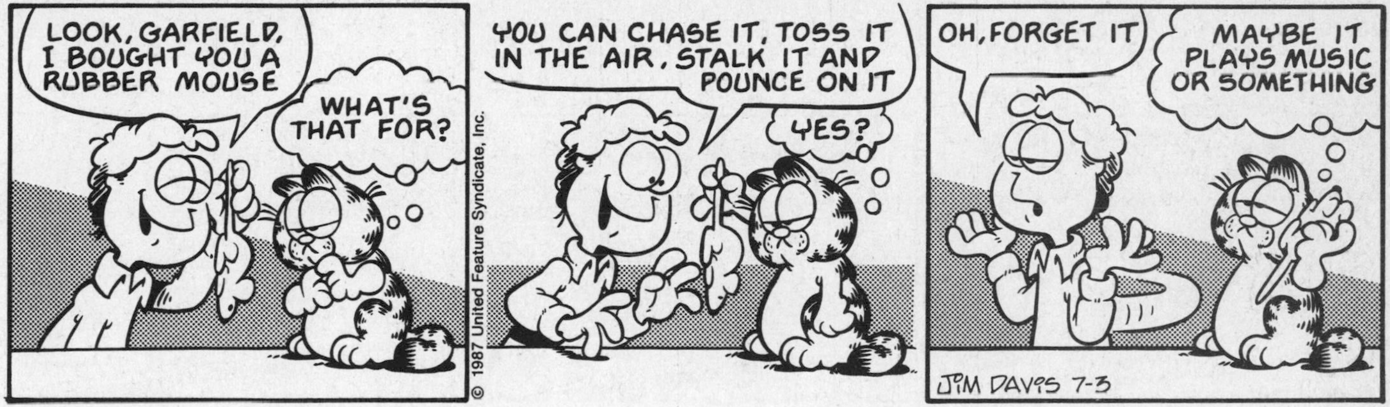
LOOK, GARFIELD, I BOUGHT YOU A RUBBER MOUSE
WHAT'S THAT FOR?
YOU CAN CHASE IT, TOSS IT IN THE AIR, STALK IT AND POUNCE ON IT
YES?
OH, FORGET IT
MAYBE IT PLAYS MUSIC OR SOMETHING
JIM DAVIS 7-3
© 1987 United Feature Syndicate, Inc.

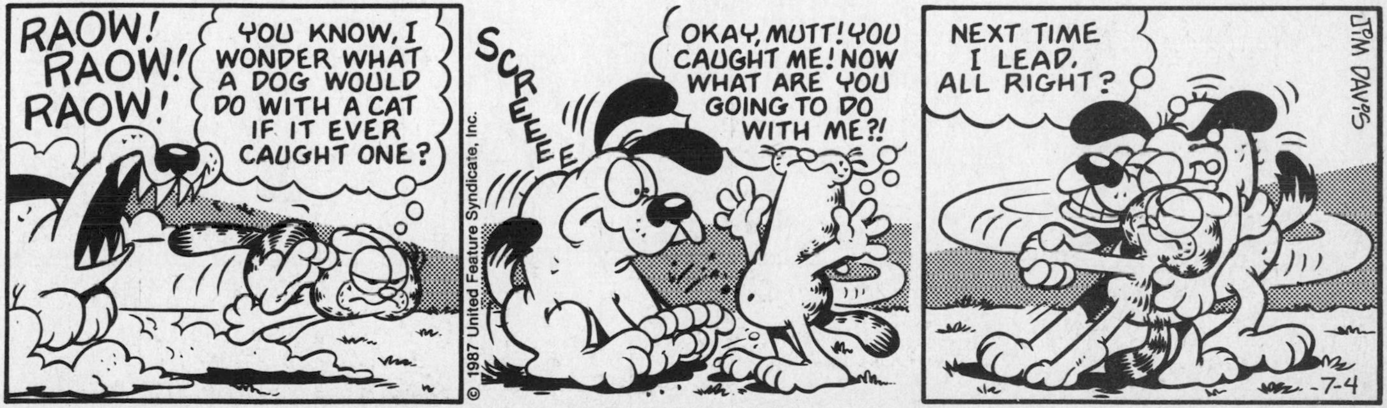
RAOW! RAOW! RAOW!
YOU KNOW, I WONDER WHAT A DOG WOULD DO WITH A CAT IF IT EVER CAUGHT ONE?
SCREEEE
OKAY, MUTT! YOU CAUGHT ME! NOW WHAT ARE YOU GOING TO DO WITH ME?!
NEXT TIME I LEAD, ALL RIGHT?
JIM DAVIS
7-4
© 1987 United Feature Syndicate, Inc.

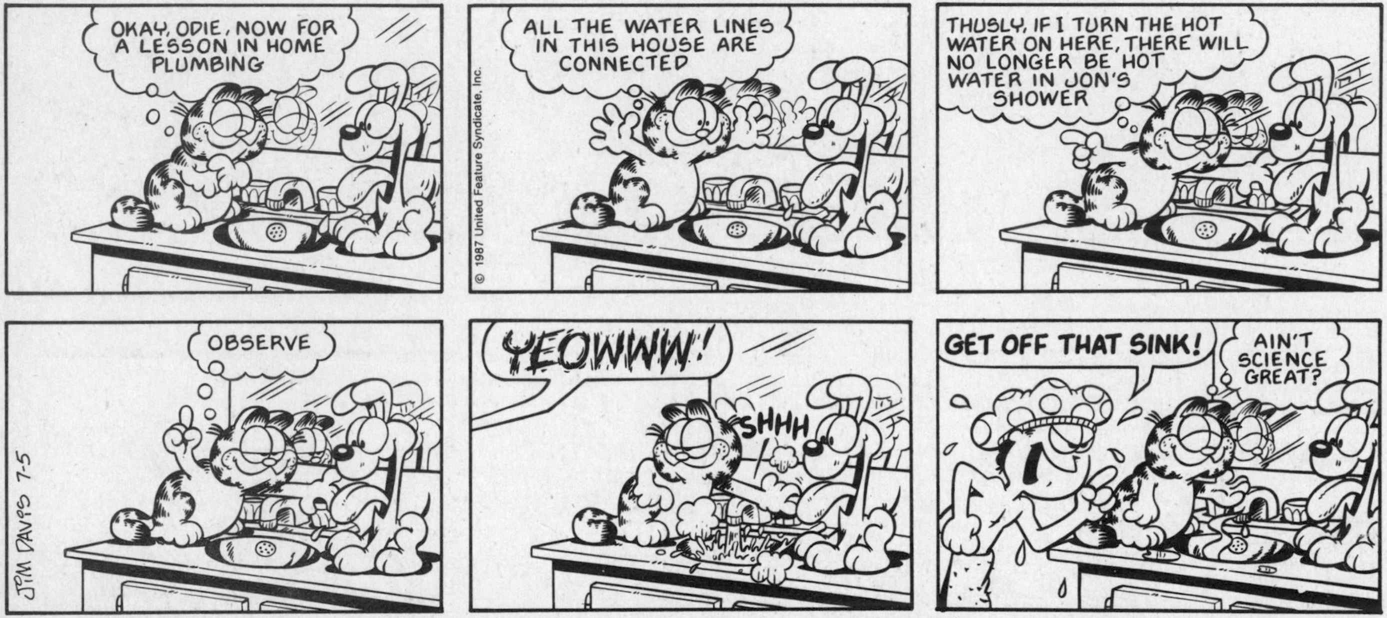

OKAY, ODIE, NOW FOR A LESSON IN HOME PLUMBING
ALL THE WATER LINES IN THIS HOUSE ARE CONNECTED
© 1987 United Feature Syndicate, Inc.
THUSLY, IF I TURN THE HOT WATER ON HERE, THERE WILL NO LONGER BE HOT WATER IN JON'S SHOWER
OBSERVE
JIM DAVIS 7-5
YEOWWW!
SHHH
GET OFF THAT SINK!
AIN'T SCIENCE GREAT?

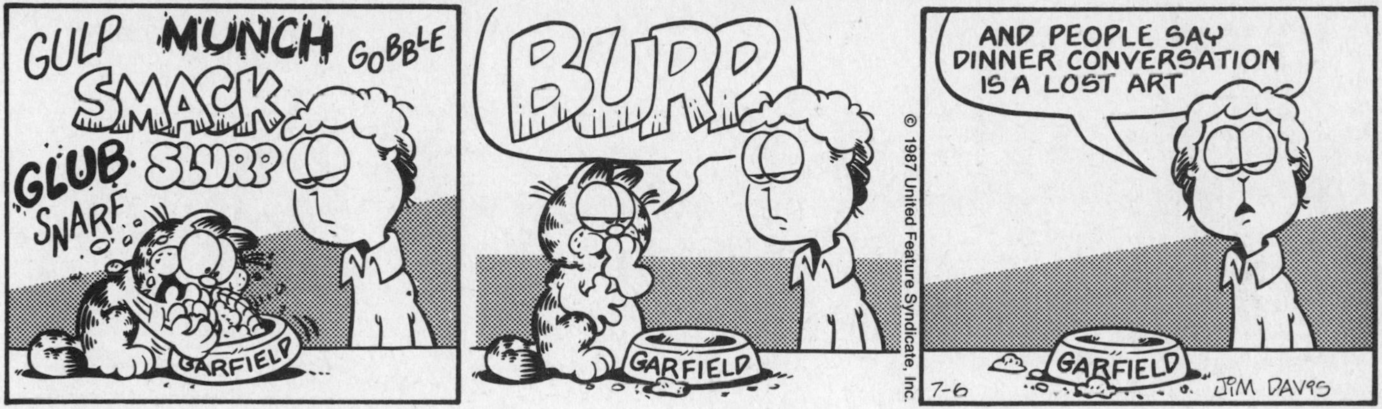
GULP
MUNCH
GOBBLE
SMACK
GLUB
SLURP
SNARF
GARFIELD
BURP
GARFIELD
© 1987 United Feature Syndicate, Inc.
AND PEOPLE SAY DINNER CONVERSATION IS A LOST ART
GARFIELD
7-6
JIM DAVIS

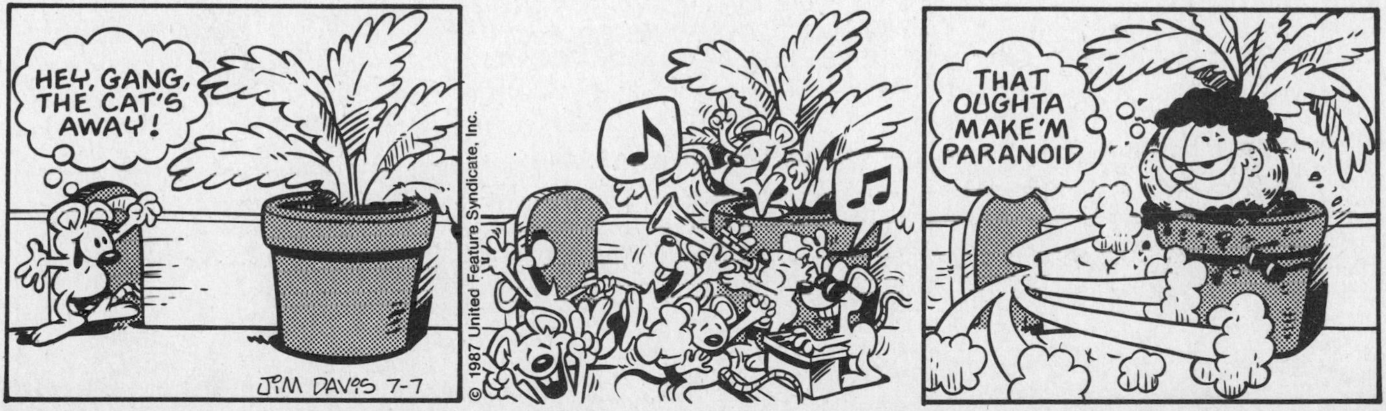
HEY, GANG, THE CAT'S AWAY!
JIM DAVIS 7-7
© 1987 United Feature Syndicate, Inc.
THAT OUGHTA MAKE'M PARANOID

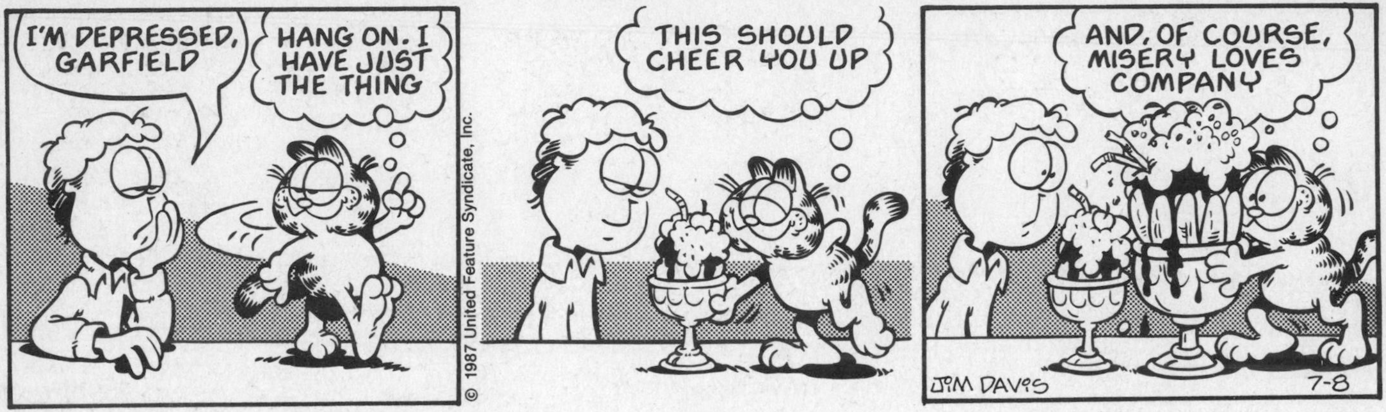
I'M DEPRESSED, GARFIELD
HANG ON. I HAVE JUST THE THING
© 1987 United Feature Syndicate, Inc.
THIS SHOULD CHEER YOU UP
AND, OF COURSE, MISERY LOVES COMPANY
JIM DAVIS
7-8

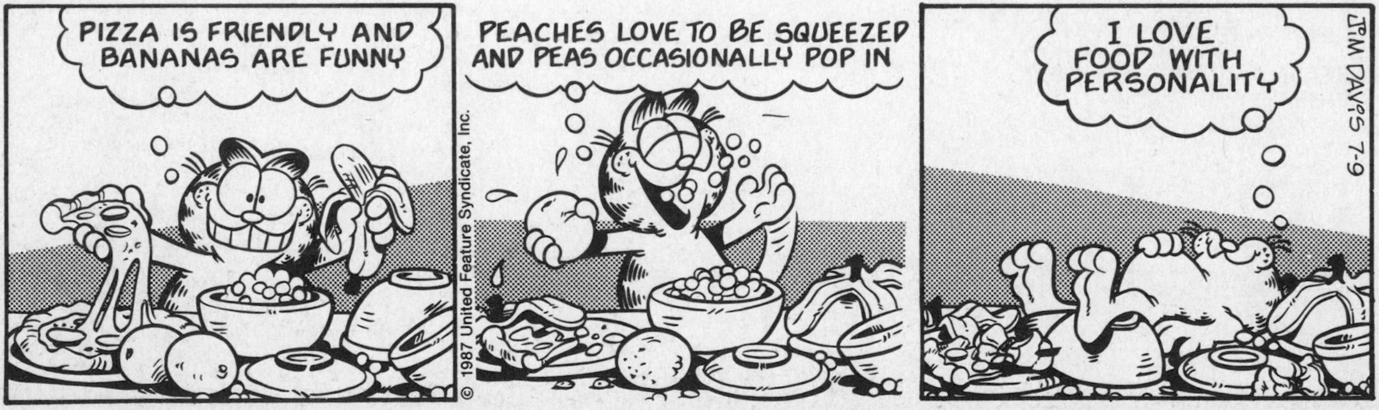
PIZZA IS FRIENDLY AND BANANAS ARE FUNNY
© 1987 United Feature Syndicate, Inc.
PEACHES LOVE TO BE SQUEEZED AND PEAS OCCASIONALLY POP IN
I LOVE FOOD WITH PERSONALITY
JIM DAVIS 7-9

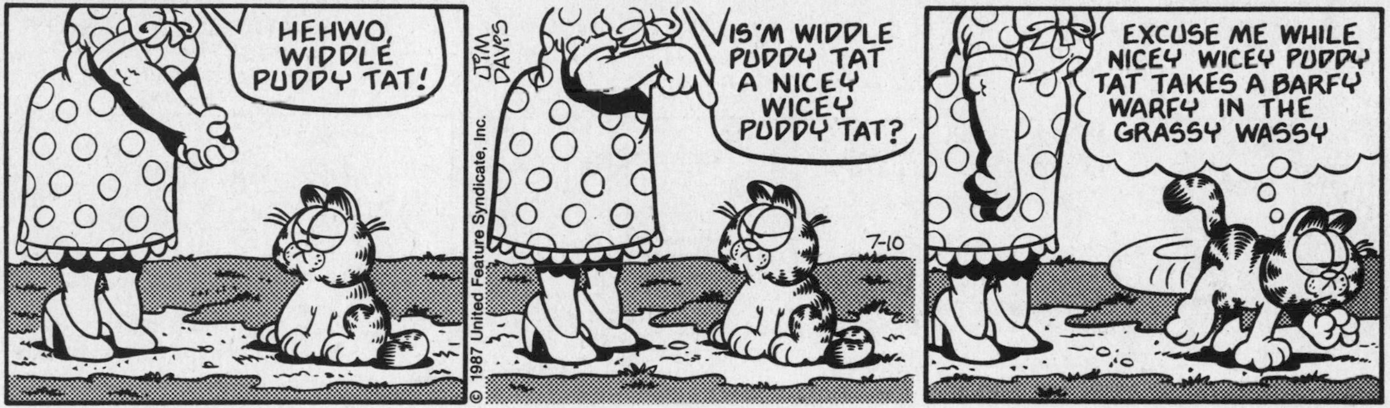
HEHWO, WIDDLE PUDDY TAT!
JIM DAVIS
© 1987 United Feature Syndicate, Inc.
IS'M WIDDLE PUDDY TAT A NICEY WICEY PUDDY TAT?
7-10
EXCUSE ME WHILE NICEY WICEY PUDDY TAT TAKES A BARFY WARFY IN THE GRASSY WASSY

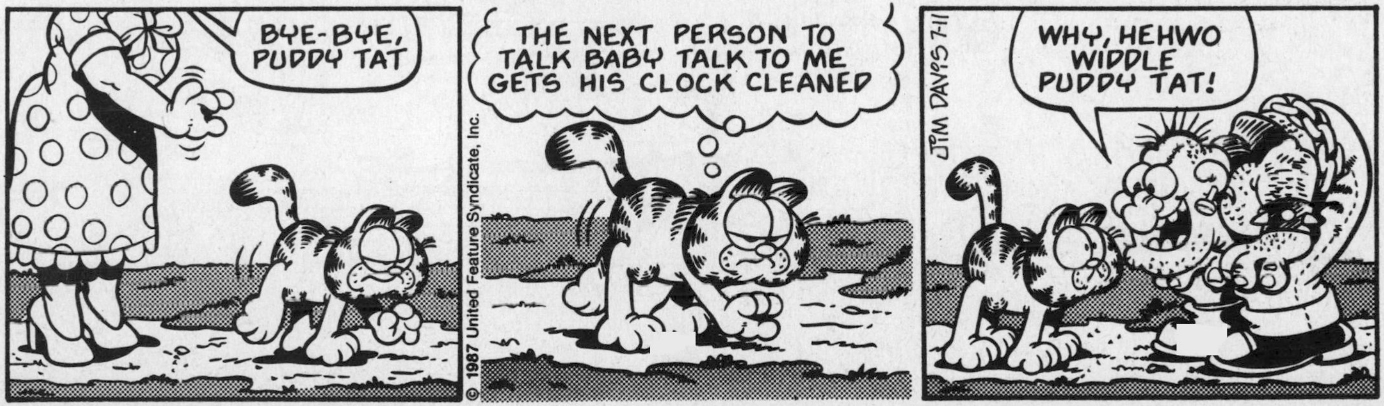
BYE-BYE, PUDDY TAT
© 1987 United Feature Syndicate, Inc.
THE NEXT PERSON TO TALK BABY TALK TO ME GETS HIS CLOCK CLEANED
JIM DAVIS 7-11
WHY, HEHWO WIDDLE PUDDY TAT!

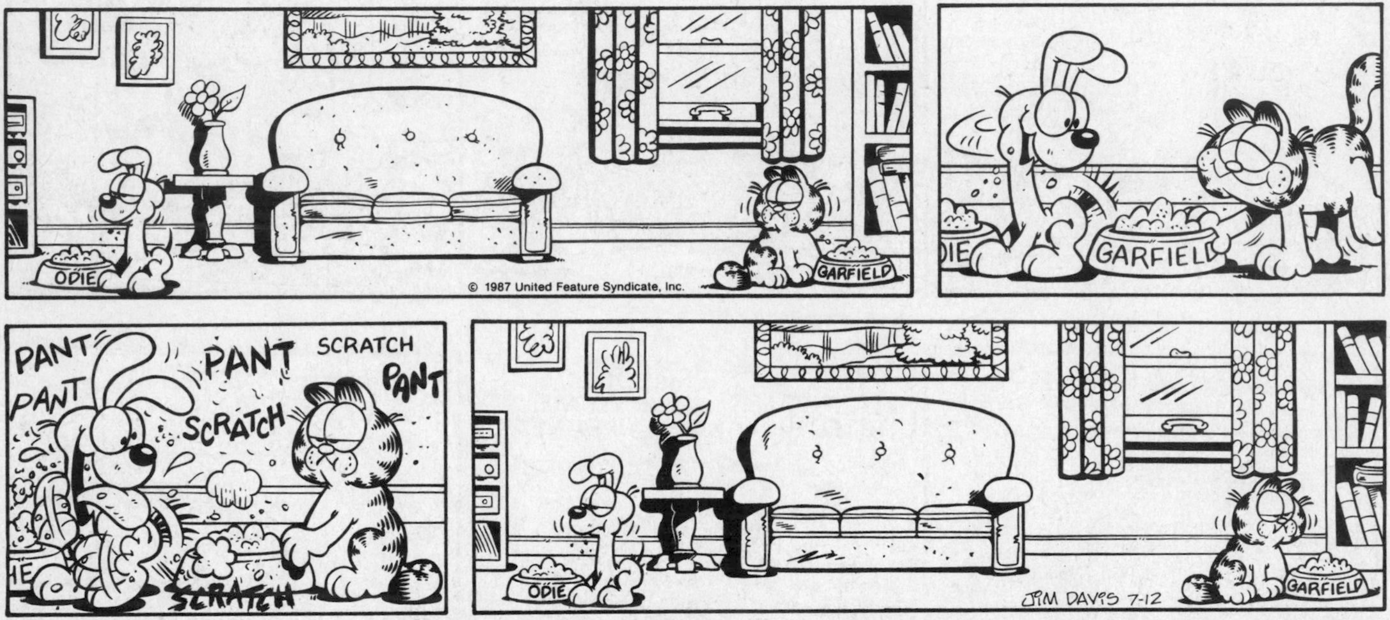

ODIE
GARFIELD
© 1987 United Feature Syndicate, Inc.
GARFIELD
PANT
PANT
PANT
SCRATCH
SCRATCH
PANT
SCRATCH
ODIE
GARFIELD
JIM DAVIS 7-12

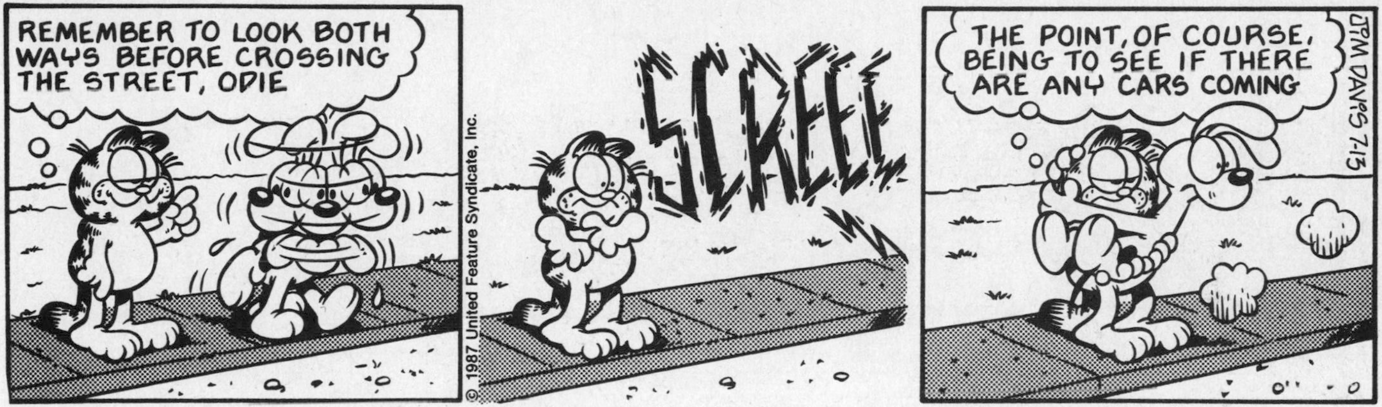
REMEMBER TO LOOK BOTH WAYS BEFORE CROSSING THE STREET, ODIE
© 1987 United Feature Syndicate, Inc.
SCREEE
THE POINT, OF COURSE, BEING TO SEE IF THERE ARE ANY CARS COMING
JIM DAVIS 7-13

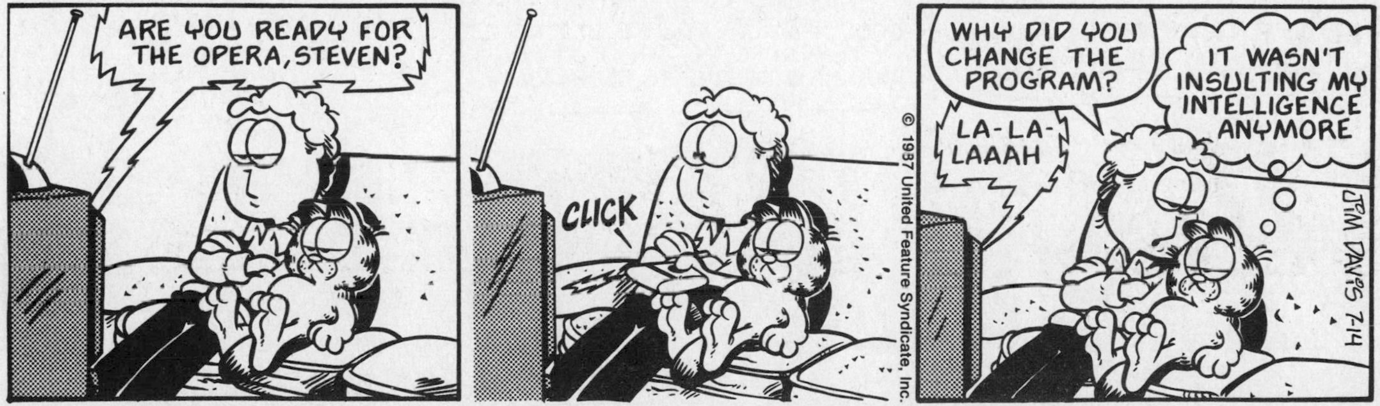
ARE YOU READY FOR THE OPERA, STEVEN?
CLICK
© 1987 United Feature Syndicate, Inc.
LA-LA-LAAAH
WHY DID YOU CHANGE THE PROGRAM?
IT WASN'T INSULTING MY INTELLIGENCE ANYMORE
JIM DAVIS 7-14

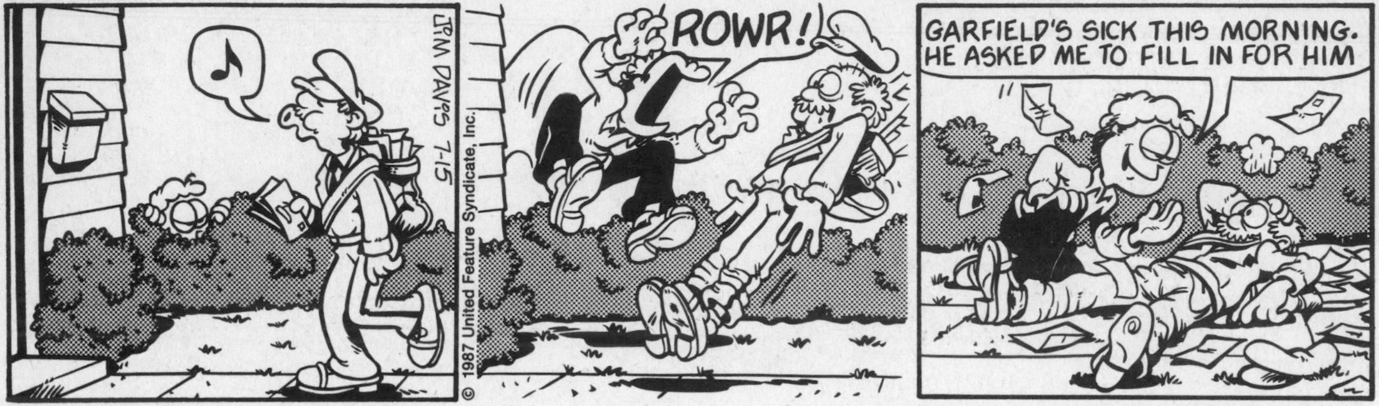
JIM DAVIS 7-15
© 1987 United Feature Syndicate, Inc.
ROWR!
GARFIELD'S SICK THIS MORNING. HE ASKED ME TO FILL IN FOR HIM

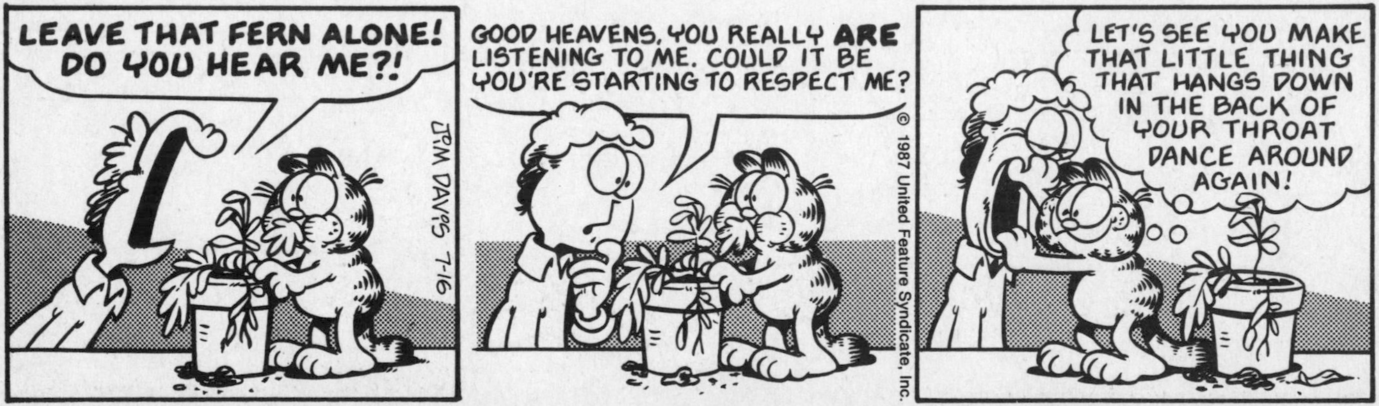
LEAVE THAT FERN ALONE! DO YOU HEAR ME?!
JIM DAVIS 7-16
GOOD HEAVENS, YOU REALLY ARE LISTENING TO ME. COULD IT BE YOU'RE STARTING TO RESPECT ME?
© 1987 United Feature Syndicate, Inc.
LET'S SEE YOU MAKE THAT LITTLE THING THAT HANGS DOWN IN THE BACK OF YOUR THROAT DANCE AROUND AGAIN!

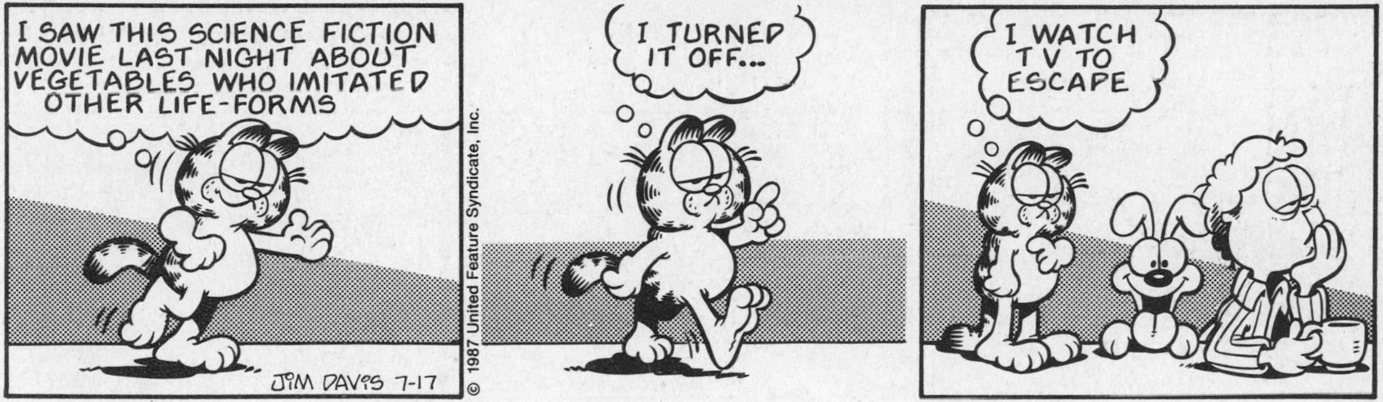
I SAW THIS SCIENCE FICTION MOVIE LAST NIGHT ABOUT VEGETABLES WHO IMITATED OTHER LIFE-FORMS
JIM DAVIS 7-17
I TURNED IT OFF...
I WATCH T V TO ESCAPE

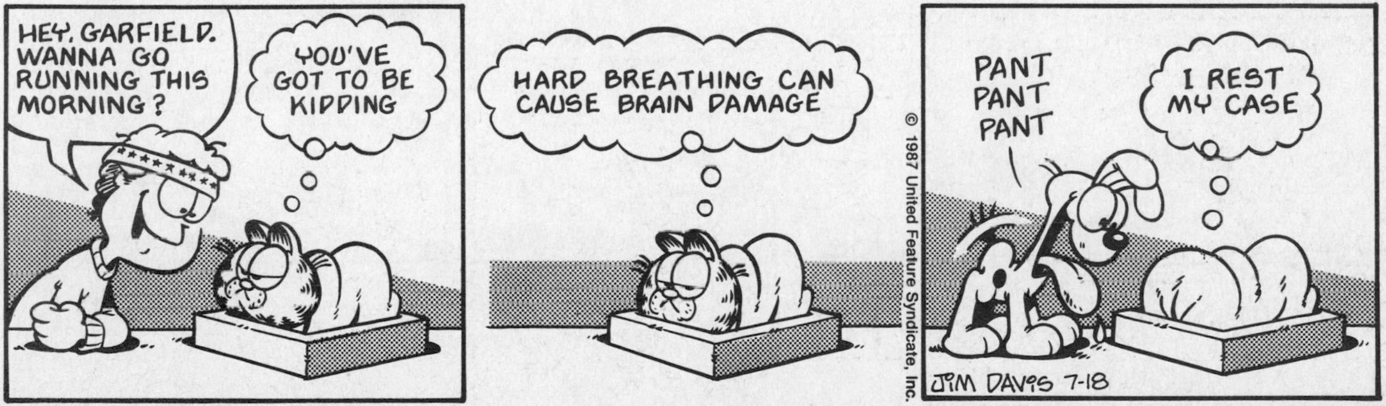
HEY, GARFIELD. WANNA GO RUNNING THIS MORNING?
YOU'VE GOT TO BE KIDDING
HARD BREATHING CAN CAUSE BRAIN DAMAGE
PANT PANT PANT
I REST MY CASE
JIM DAVIS 7-18

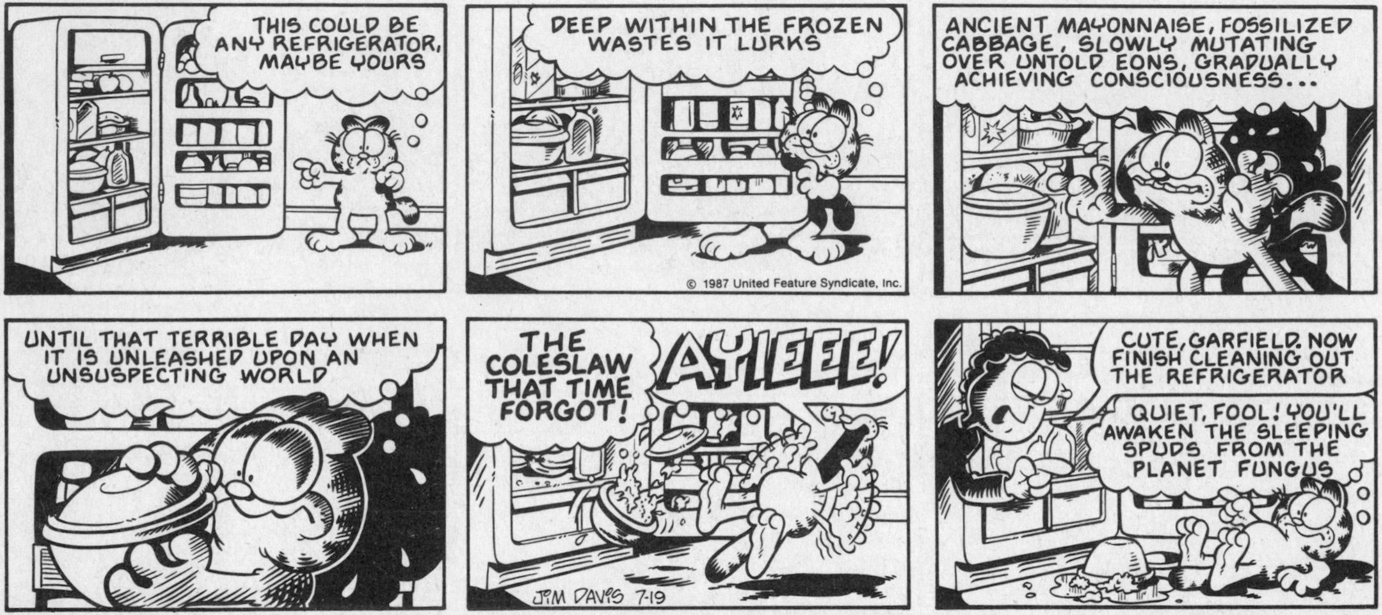
THIS COULD BE ANY REFRIGERATOR, MAYBE YOURS
DEEP WITHIN THE FROZEN WASTES IT LURKS
© 1987 United Feature Syndicate, Inc.
ANCIENT MAYONNAISE, FOSSILIZED CABBAGE, SLOWLY MUTATING OVER UNTOLD EONS, GRADUALLY ACHIEVING CONSCIOUSNESS...
UNTIL THAT TERRIBLE DAY WHEN IT IS UNLEASHED UPON AN UNSUSPECTING WORLD
THE COLESLAW THAT TIME FORGOT!
AYIEEE!
JIM DAVIS 7-19
CUTE, GARFIELD. NOW FINISH CLEANING OUT THE REFRIGERATOR
QUIET, FOOL! YOU'LL AWAKEN THE SLEEPING SPUDS FROM THE PLANET FUNGUS

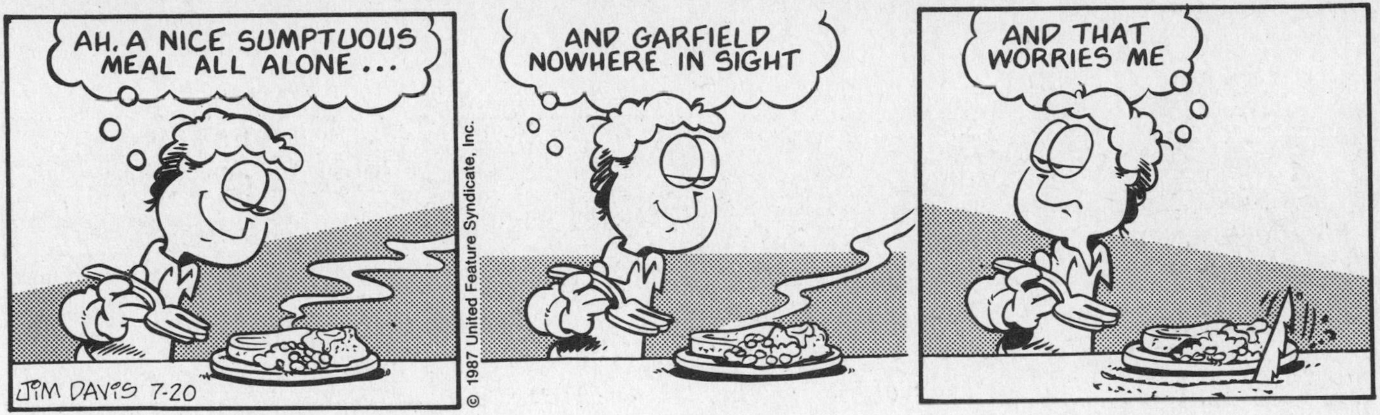
AH, A NICE SUMPTUOUS MEAL ALL ALONE...
JIM DAVIS 7-20
© 1987 United Feature Syndicate, Inc.
AND GARFIELD NOWHERE IN SIGHT
AND THAT WORRIES ME

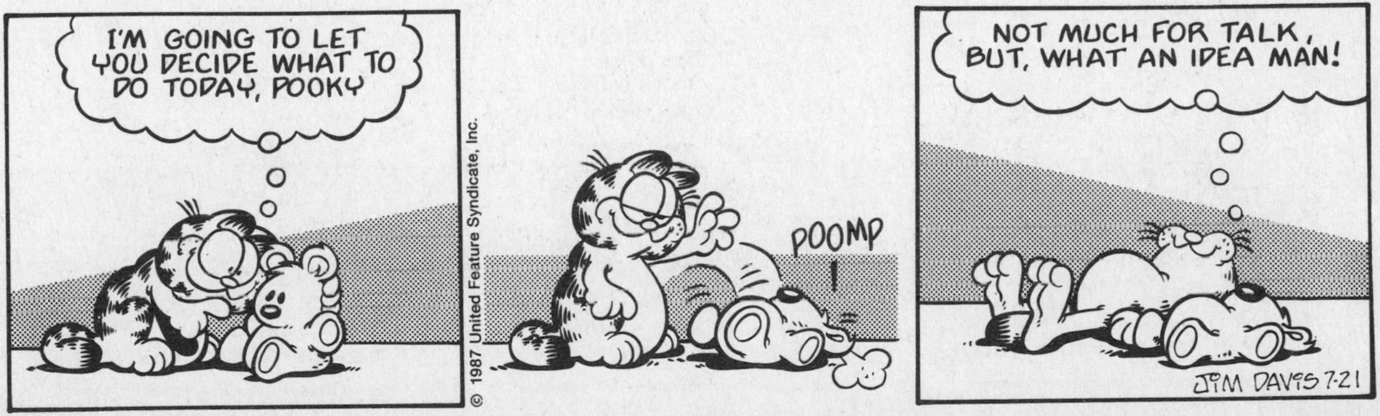
I'M GOING TO LET YOU DECIDE WHAT TO DO TODAY, POOKY
© 1987 United Feature Syndicate, Inc.
POOMP
!
NOT MUCH FOR TALK, BUT, WHAT AN IDEA MAN!
JIM DAVIS 7-21

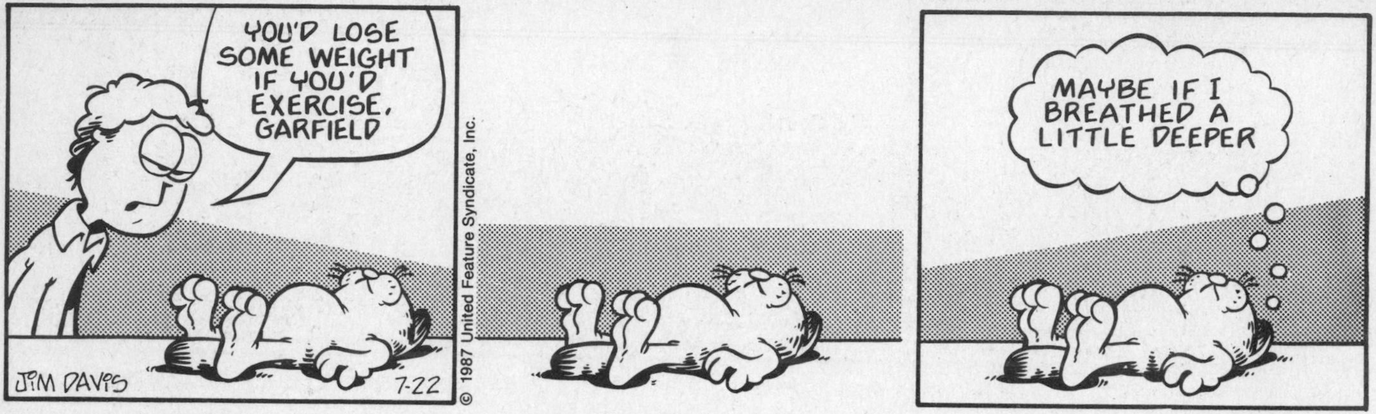
YOU'D LOSE SOME WEIGHT IF YOU'D EXERCISE, GARFIELD
JIM DAVIS 7-22
© 1987 United Feature Syndicate, Inc.
MAYBE IF I BREATHED A LITTLE DEEPER

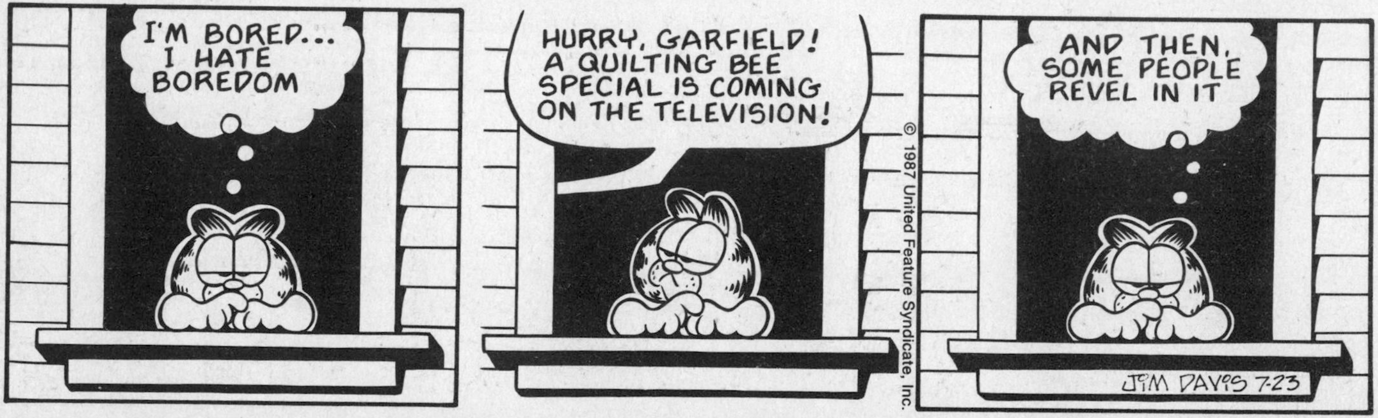
I'M BORED... I HATE BOREDOM
HURRY, GARFIELD! A QUILTING BEE SPECIAL IS COMING ON THE TELEVISION!
© 1987 United Feature Syndicate, Inc.
AND THEN, SOME PEOPLE REVEL IN IT
JIM DAVIS 7-23

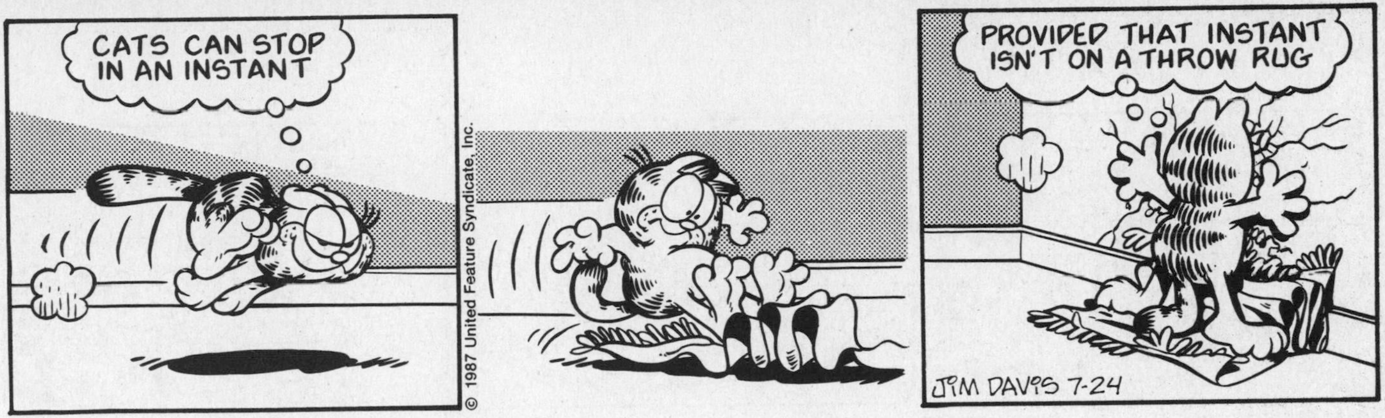
CATS CAN STOP IN AN INSTANT
© 1987 United Feature Syndicate, Inc.
PROVIDED THAT INSTANT ISN'T ON A THROW RUG
JIM DAVIS 7-24

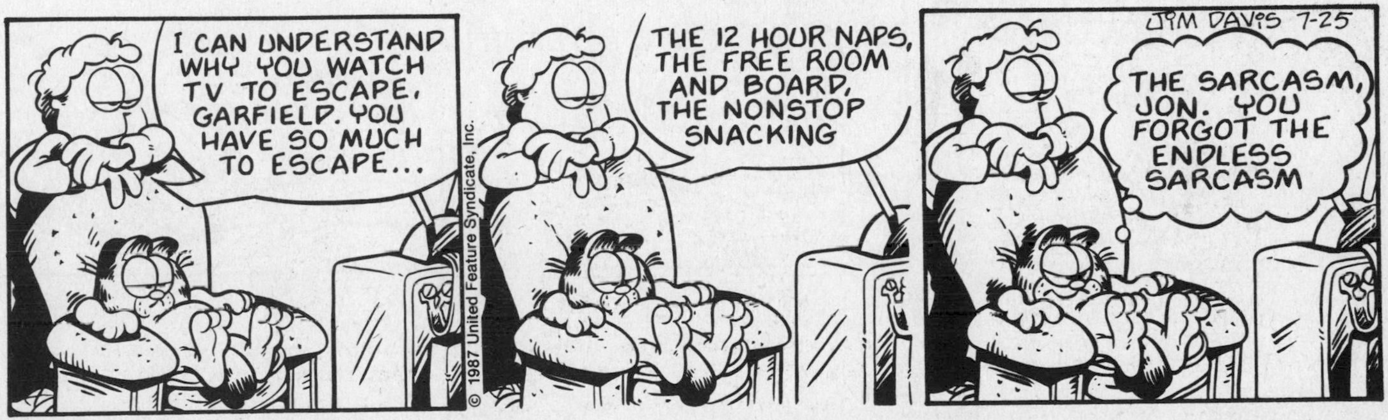
I CAN UNDERSTAND WHY YOU WATCH TV TO ESCAPE, GARFIELD. YOU HAVE SO MUCH TO ESCAPE...
© 1987 United Feature Syndicate, Inc.
THE 12 HOUR NAPS, THE FREE ROOM AND BOARD, THE NONSTOP SNACKING
JIM DAVIS 7-25
THE SARCASM, JON. YOU FORGOT THE ENDLESS SARCASM

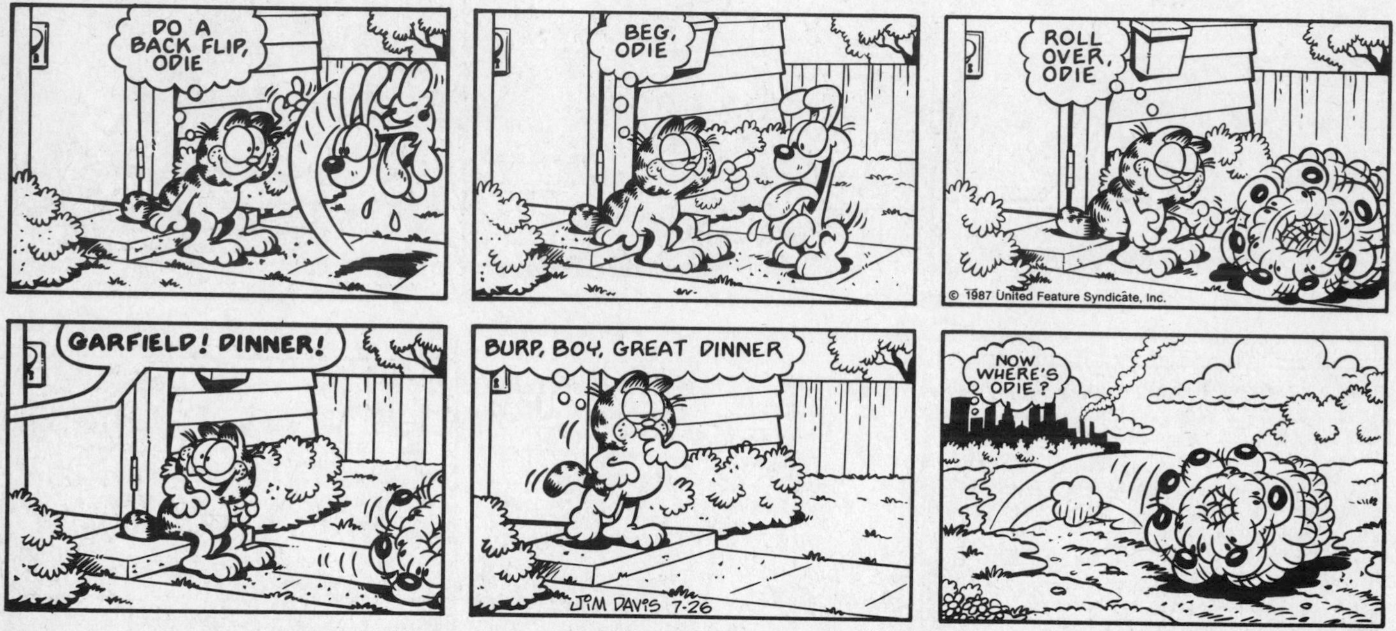
DO A BACK FLIP, ODIE
BEG, ODIE
ROLL OVER, ODIE
© 1987 United Feature Syndicate, Inc.
GARFIELD! DINNER!
BURP, BOY, GREAT DINNER
JIM DAVIS 7-26
NOW WHERE'S ODIE?

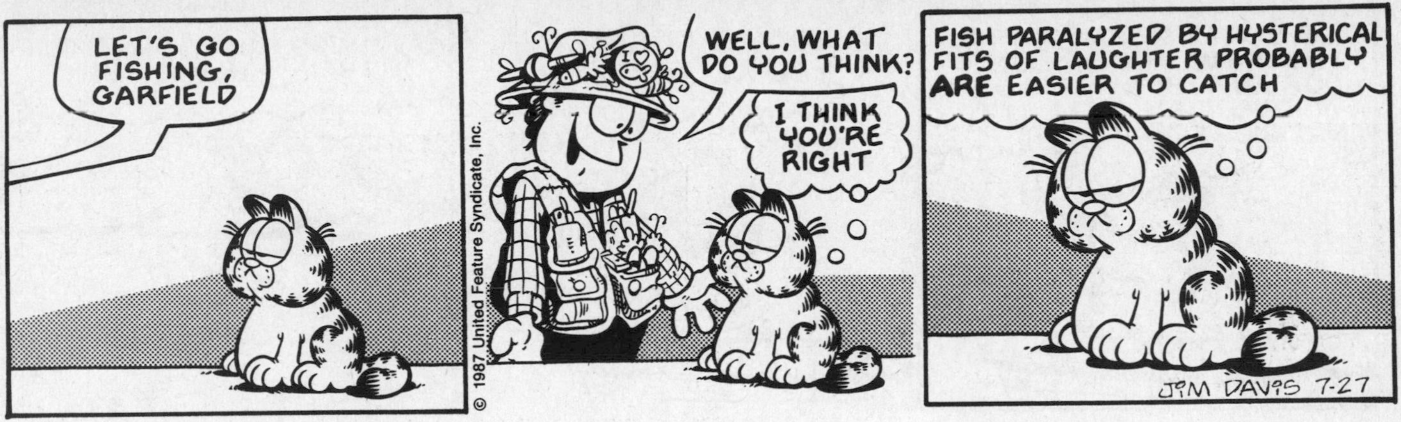
LET'S GO FISHING, GARFIELD
© 1987 United Feature Syndicate, Inc.
WELL, WHAT DO YOU THINK?
I THINK YOU'RE RIGHT
FISH PARALYZED BY HYSTERICAL FITS OF LAUGHTER PROBABLY ARE EASIER TO CATCH
JIM DAVIS 7-27

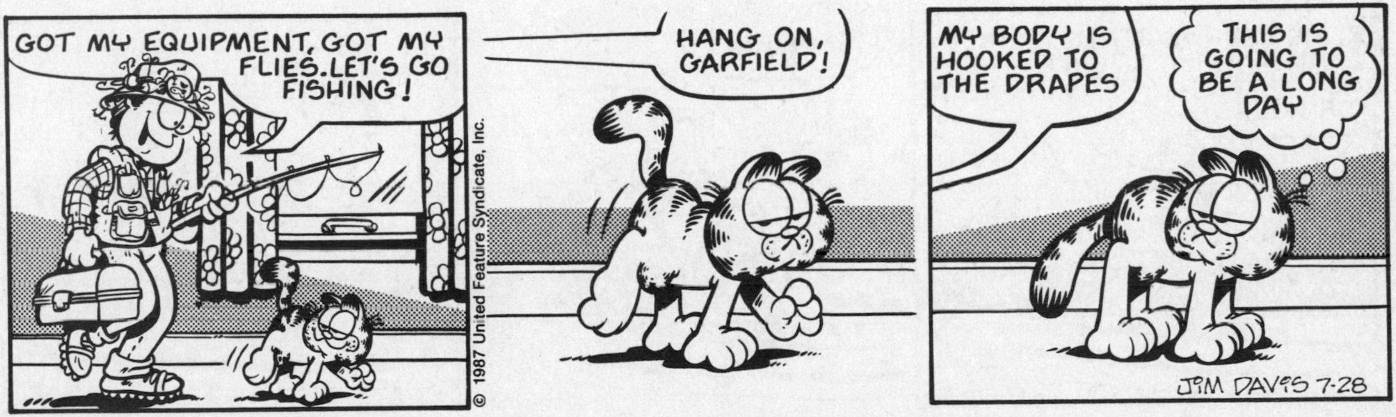
GOT MY EQUIPMENT, GOT MY FLIES. LET'S GO FISHING!
© 1987 United Feature Syndicate, Inc.
HANG ON, GARFIELD!
MY BODY IS HOOKED TO THE DRAPES
THIS IS GOING TO BE A LONG DAY
JIM DAVIS 7-28

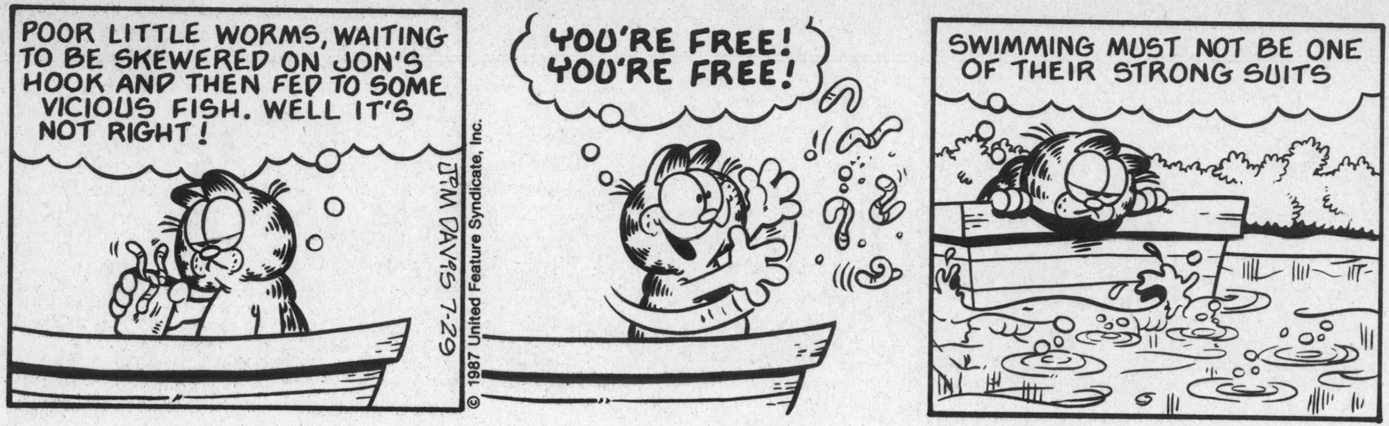
POOR LITTLE WORMS, WAITING TO BE SKEWERED ON JON'S HOOK AND THEN FED TO SOME VICIOUS FISH. WELL IT'S NOT RIGHT!
JIM DAVIS 7-29
© 1987 United Feature Syndicate, Inc.
YOU'RE FREE! YOU'RE FREE!
SWIMMING MUST NOT BE ONE OF THEIR STRONG SUITS

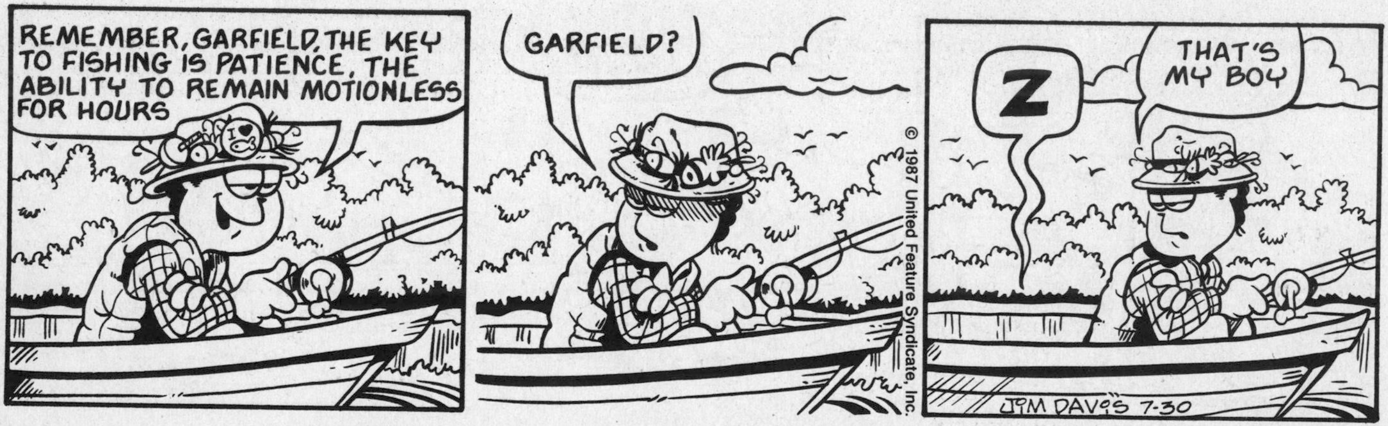
REMEMBER, GARFIELD, THE KEY TO FISHING IS PATIENCE, THE ABILITY TO REMAIN MOTIONLESS FOR HOURS
GARFIELD?
© 1987 United Feature Syndicate, Inc.
Z
THAT'S MY BOY
JIM DAVIS 7-30

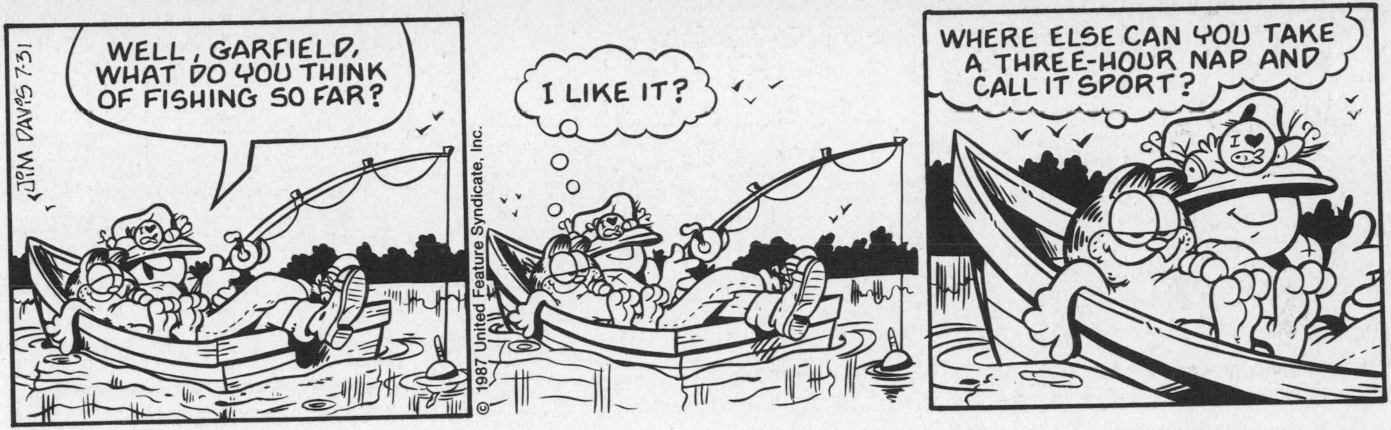
JIM DAVIS 7-31
WELL, GARFIELD, WHAT DO YOU THINK OF FISHING SO FAR?
I LIKE IT?
© 1987 United Feature Syndicate, Inc.
WHERE ELSE CAN YOU TAKE A THREE-HOUR NAP AND CALL IT SPORT?

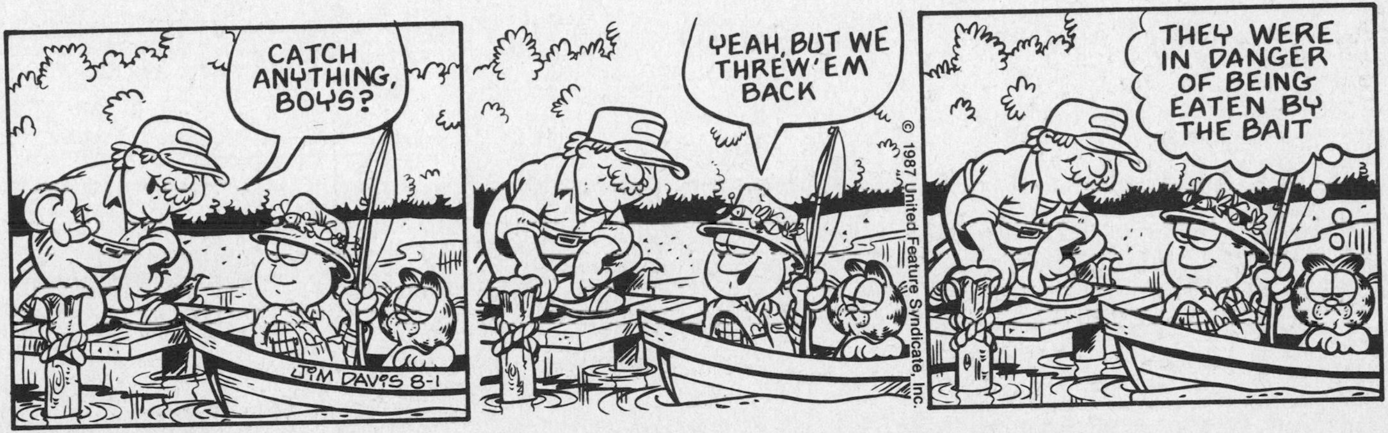
CATCH ANYTHING, BOYS?
JIM DAVIS 8-1
YEAH, BUT WE THREW'EM BACK
© 1987 United Feature Syndicate, Inc.
THEY WERE IN DANGER OF BEING EATEN BY THE BAIT

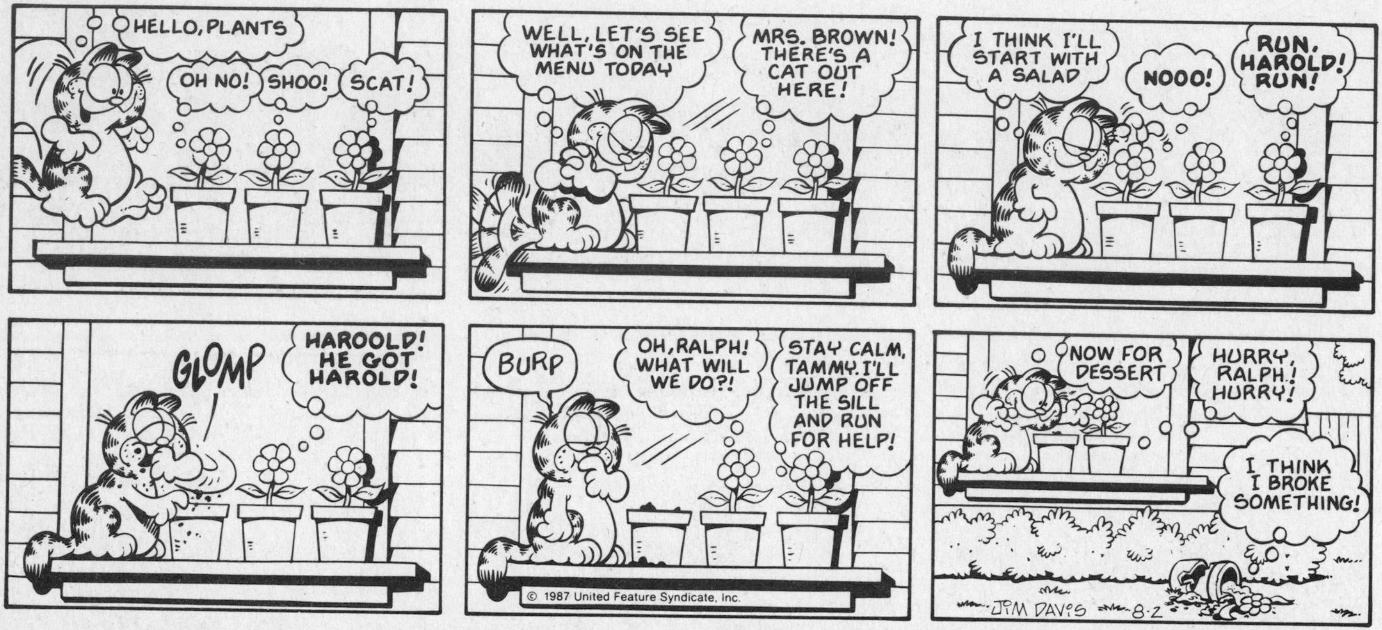
HELLO, PLANTS
OH NO!
SHOO!
SCAT!
WELL, LET'S SEE WHAT'S ON THE MENU TODAY
MRS. BROWN! THERE'S A CAT OUT HERE!
I THINK I'LL START WITH A SALAD
NOOO!
RUN, HAROLD! RUN!
GLOMP
HAROOLD! HE GOT HAROLD!
BURP
OH, RALPH! WHAT WILL WE DO?!
STAY CALM, TAMMY. I'LL JUMP OFF THE SILL AND RUN FOR HELP!
© 1987 United Feature Syndicate, Inc.
NOW FOR DESSERT
HURRY, RALPH! HURRY!
I THINK I BROKE SOMETHING!
JIM DAVIS 8-2

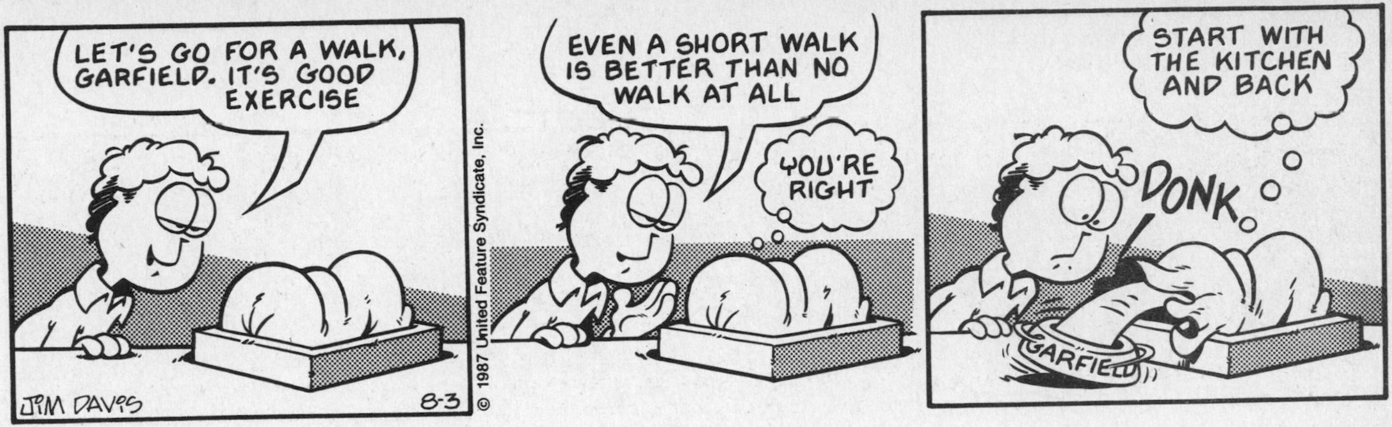
LET'S GO FOR A WALK, GARFIELD. IT'S GOOD EXERCISE
JIM DAVIS
8-3
© 1987 United Feature Syndicate, Inc.
EVEN A SHORT WALK IS BETTER THAN NO WALK AT ALL
YOU'RE RIGHT
START WITH THE KITCHEN AND BACK
DONK
GARFIELD

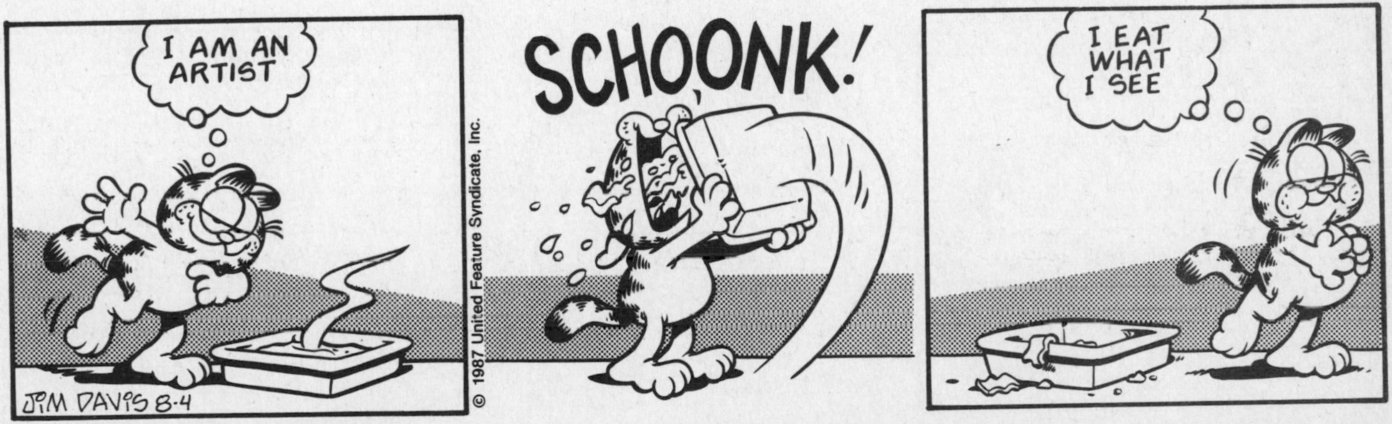
I AM AN ARTIST
JIM DAVIS 8-4
© 1987 United Feature Syndicate, Inc.
SCHOONK!
I EAT WHAT I SEE

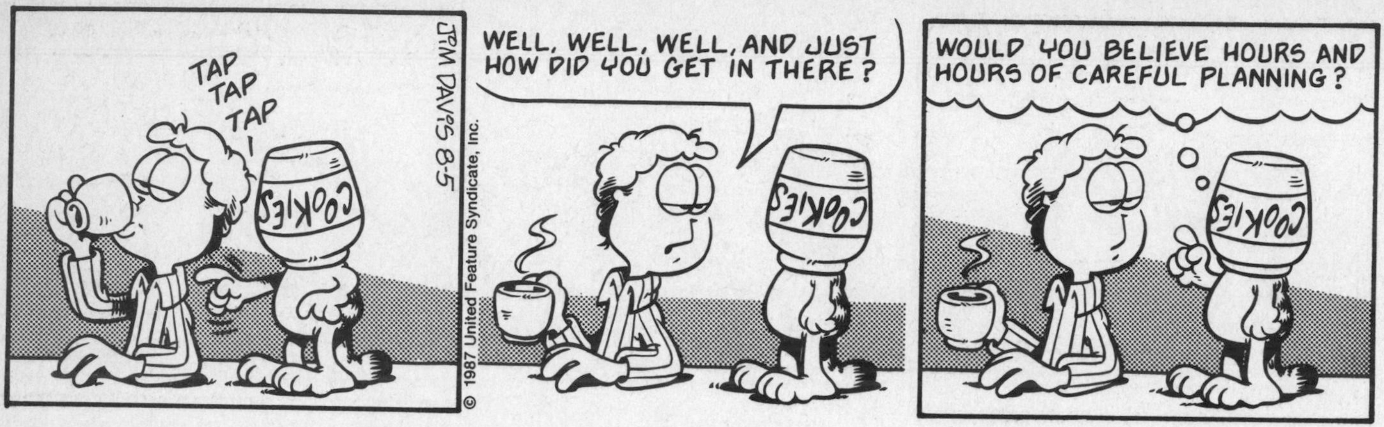
TAP
TAP
TAP
COOKIES
JIM DAVIS 8-5
© 1987 United Feature Syndicate, Inc.
WELL, WELL, WELL, AND JUST HOW DID YOU GET IN THERE?
COOKIES
WOULD YOU BELIEVE HOURS AND HOURS OF CAREFUL PLANNING?
COOKIES

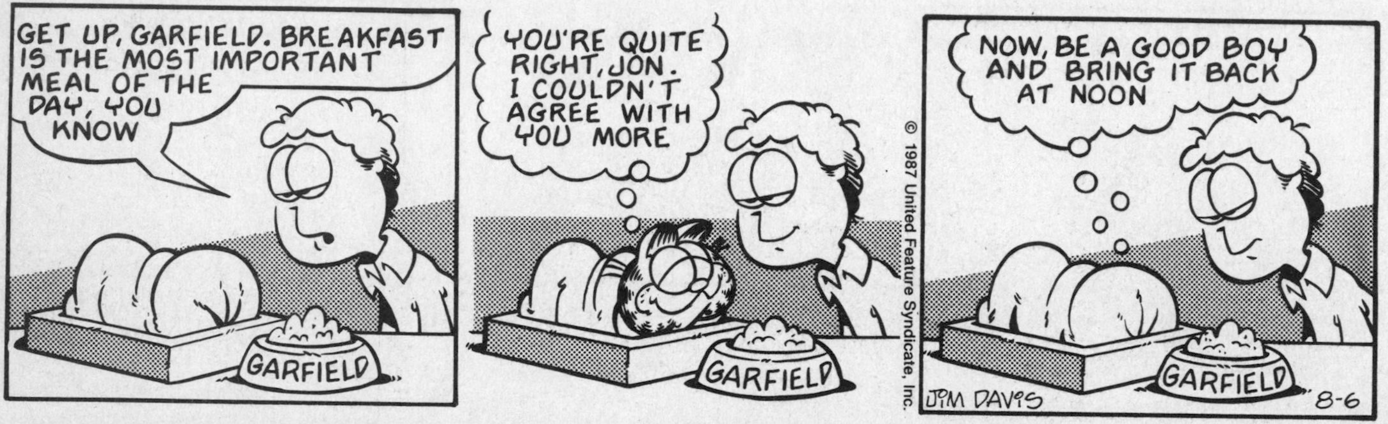
GET UP, GARFIELD. BREAKFAST IS THE MOST IMPORTANT MEAL OF THE DAY, YOU KNOW
GARFIELD
YOU'RE QUITE RIGHT, JON. I COULDN'T AGREE WITH YOU MORE
GARFIELD
© 1987 United Feature Syndicate, Inc.
NOW, BE A GOOD BOY AND BRING IT BACK AT NOON
GARFIELD
JIM DAVIS
8-6

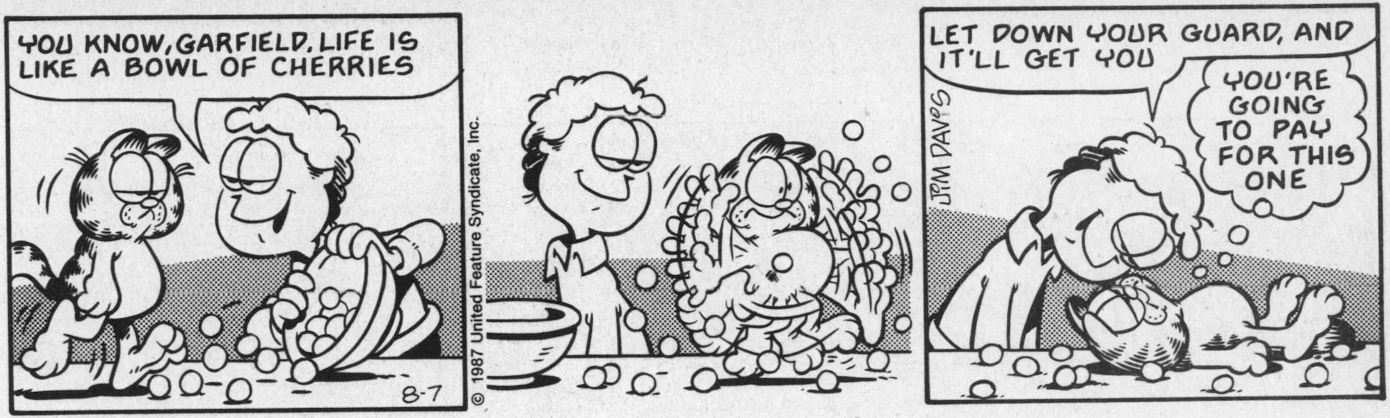
YOU KNOW, GARFIELD. LIFE IS LIKE A BOWL OF CHERRIES
LET DOWN YOUR GUARD, AND IT'LL GET YOU
YOU'RE GOING TO PAY FOR THIS ONE
8-7
© 1987 United Feature Syndicate, Inc.
JIM DAVIS

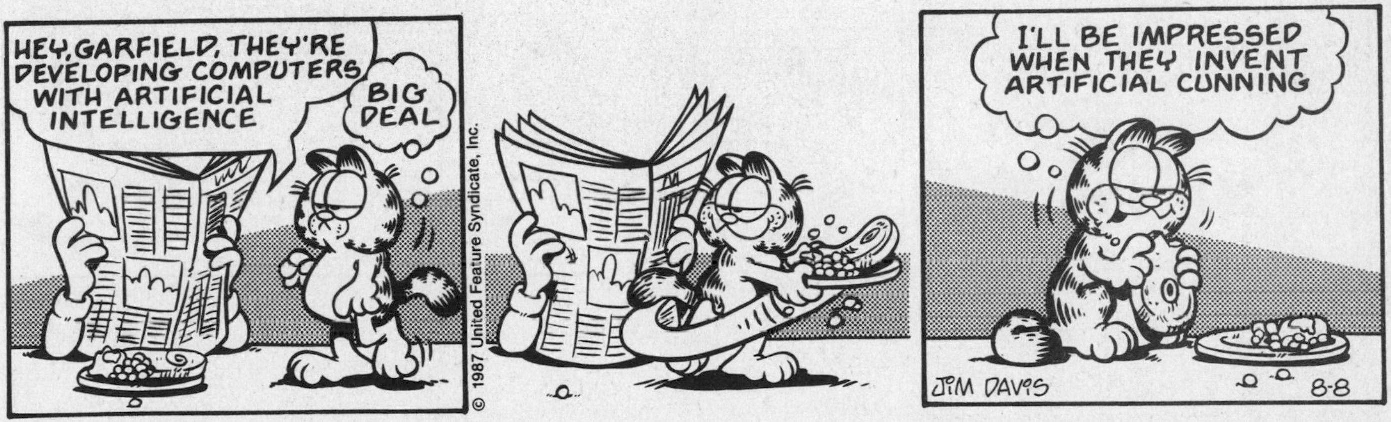
HEY, GARFIELD, THEY'RE DEVELOPING COMPUTERS WITH ARTIFICIAL INTELLIGENCE
BIG DEAL
I'LL BE IMPRESSED WHEN THEY INVENT ARTIFICIAL CUNNING
© 1987 United Feature Syndicate, Inc.
JIM DAVIS
8-8

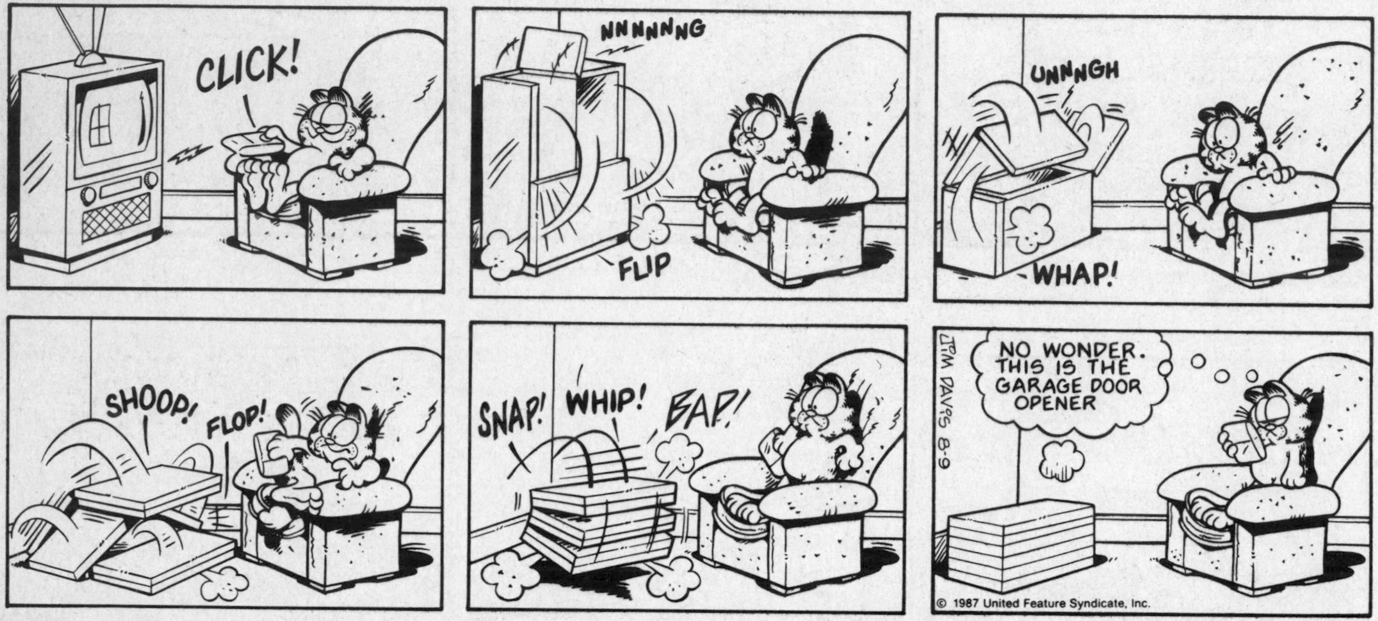
CLICK!
NNNNNNG
FLIP
UNNNGH
WHAP!
SHOOP!
FLOP!
SNAP!
WHIP!
BAP!
JIM DAVIS 8-9
NO WONDER. THIS IS THE GARAGE DOOR OPENER
© 1987 United Feature Syndicate, Inc.

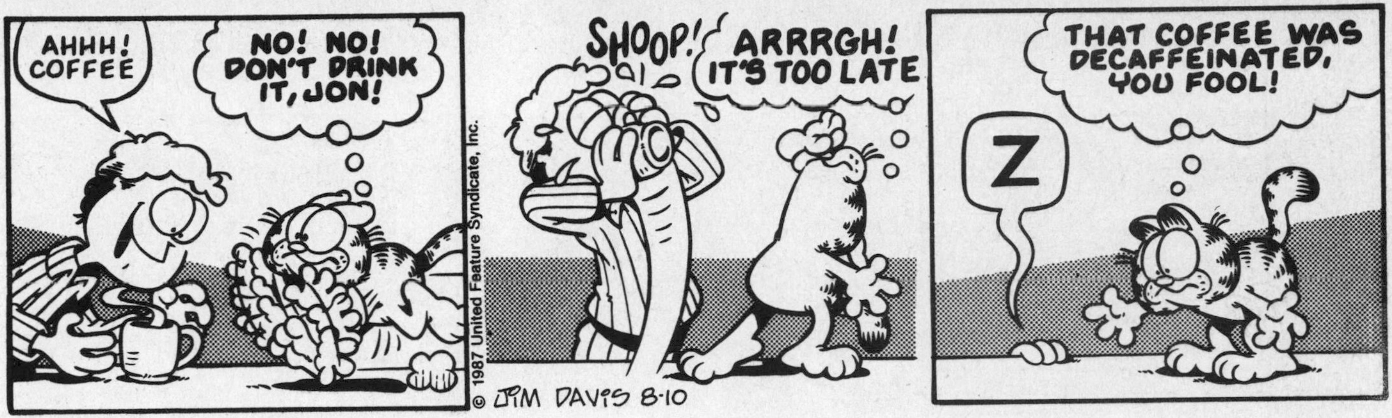
AHHH! COFFEE
NO! NO! DON'T DRINK IT, JON!
SHOOP!
ARRRGH! IT'S TOO LATE
Z
THAT COFFEE WAS DECAFFEINATED, YOU FOOL!
© 1987 United Feature Syndicate, Inc.
JIM DAVIS 8-10

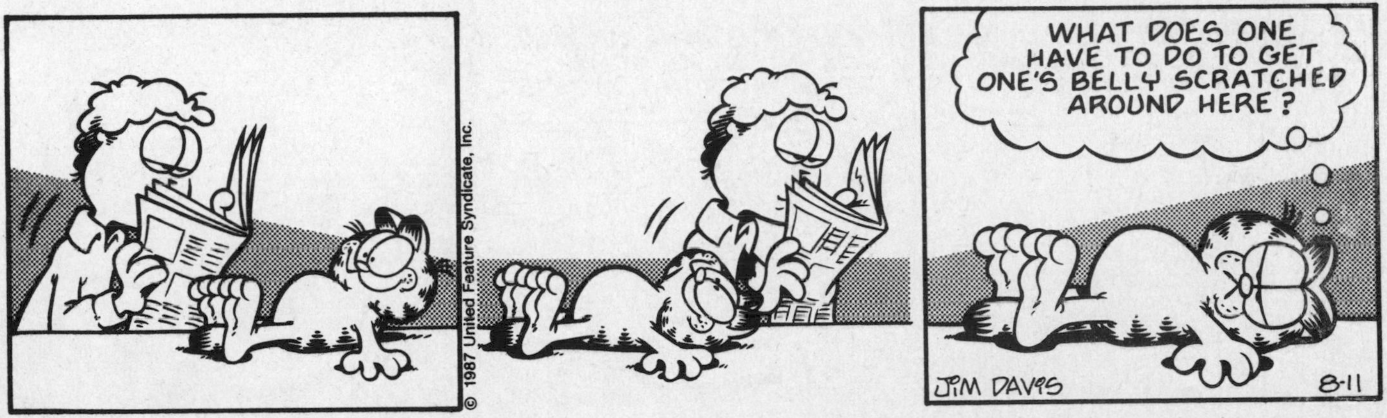
WHAT DOES ONE HAVE TO DO TO GET ONE'S BELLY SCRATCHED AROUND HERE?
© 1987 United Feature Syndicate, Inc.
JIM DAVIS
8-11

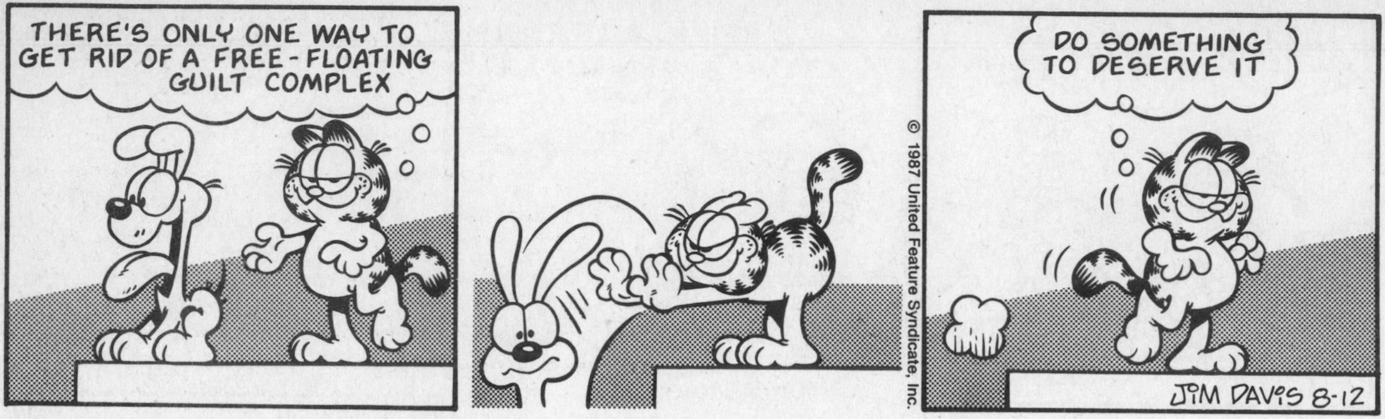
THERE'S ONLY ONE WAY TO GET RID OF A FREE-FLOATING GUILT COMPLEX
DO SOMETHING TO DESERVE IT
© 1987 United Feature Syndicate, Inc.
JIM DAVIS 8-12

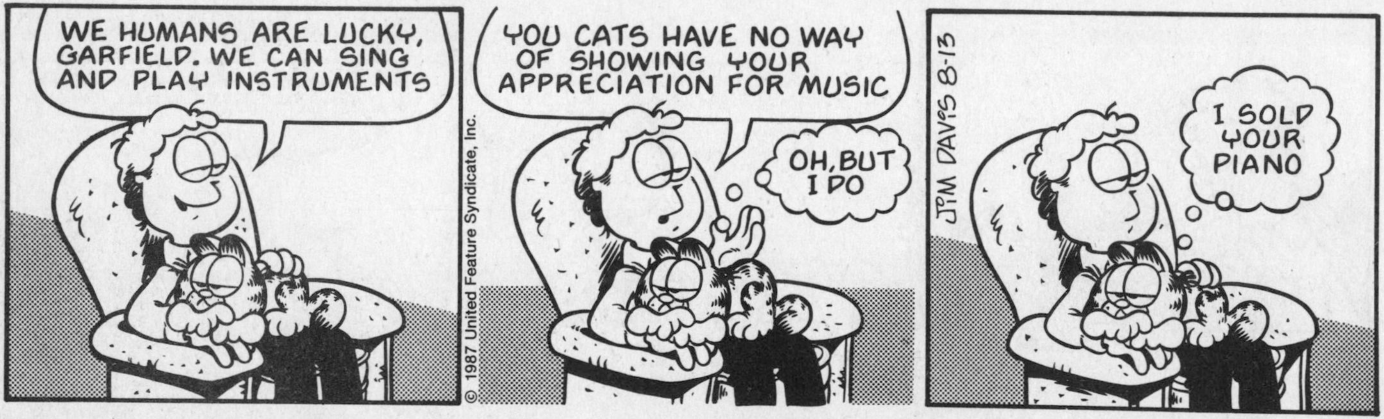
WE HUMANS ARE LUCKY, GARFIELD. WE CAN SING AND PLAY INSTRUMENTS
YOU CATS HAVE NO WAY OF SHOWING YOUR APPRECIATION FOR MUSIC
OH, BUT I DO
I SOLD YOUR PIANO
© 1987 United Feature Syndicate, Inc.
JIM DAVIS 8-13

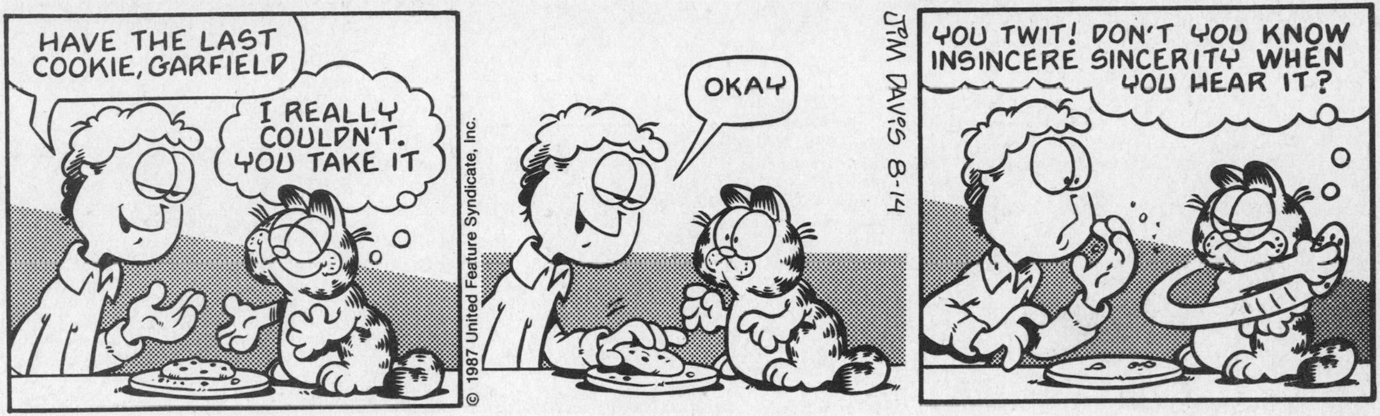
HAVE THE LAST COOKIE, GARFIELD
I REALLY COULDN'T. YOU TAKE IT
© 1987 United Feature Syndicate, Inc.
OKAY
JIM DAVIS 8-14
YOU TWIT! DON'T YOU KNOW INSINCERE SINCERITY WHEN YOU HEAR IT?

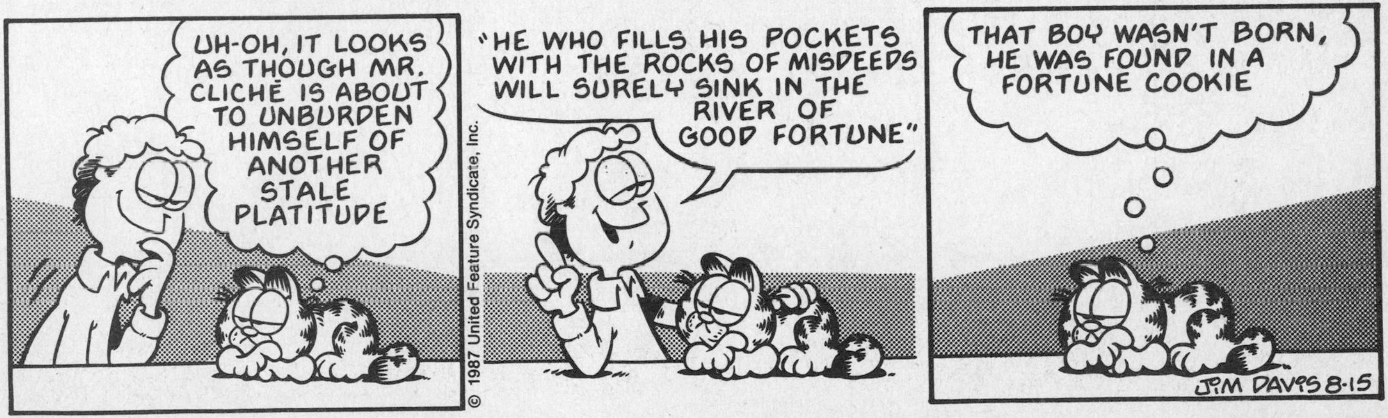
UH-OH, IT LOOKS AS THOUGH MR. CLICHÉ IS ABOUT TO UNBURDEN HIMSELF OF ANOTHER STALE PLATITUDE
© 1987 United Feature Syndicate, Inc.
"HE WHO FILLS HIS POCKETS WITH THE ROCKS OF MISDEEDS WILL SURELY SINK IN THE RIVER OF GOOD FORTUNE"
THAT BOY WASN'T BORN, HE WAS FOUND IN A FORTUNE COOKIE
JIM DAVIS 8-15

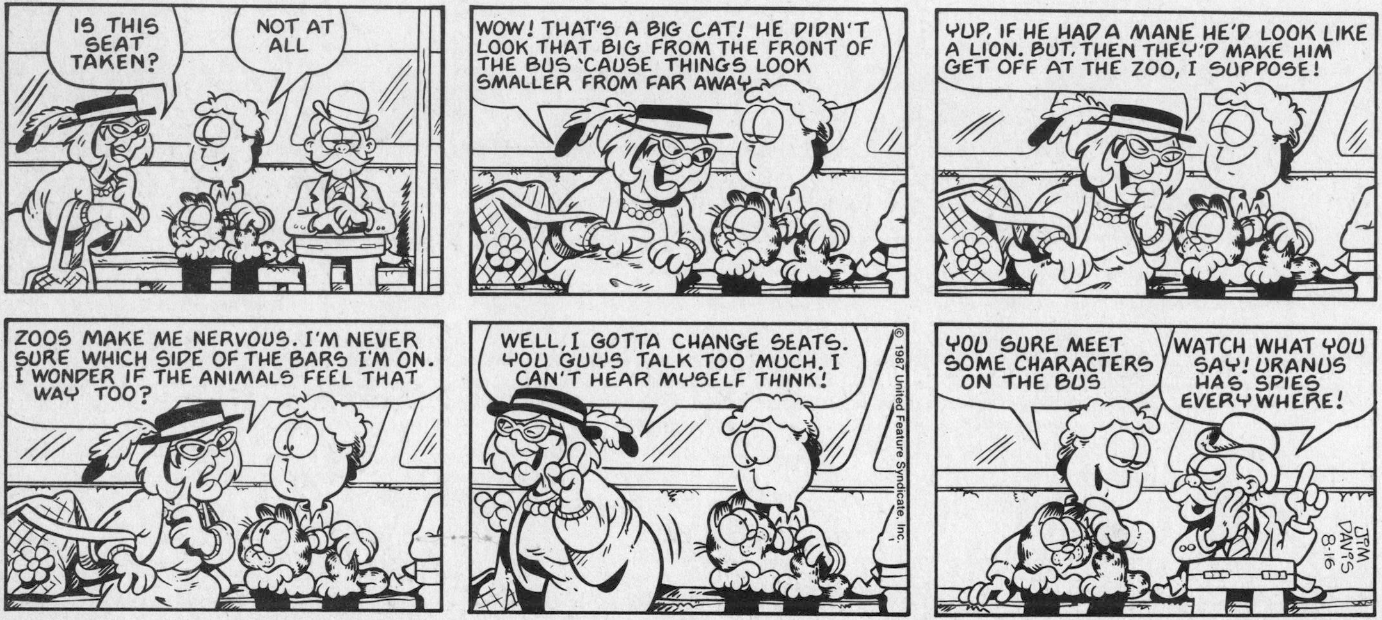
IS THIS SEAT TAKEN?
NOT AT ALL
WOW! THAT'S A BIG CAT! HE DIDN'T LOOK THAT BIG FROM THE FRONT OF THE BUS 'CAUSE THINGS LOOK SMALLER FROM FAR AWAY
YUP, IF HE HAD A MANE HE'D LOOK LIKE A LION. BUT, THEN THEY'D MAKE HIM GET OFF AT THE ZOO, I SUPPOSE!
ZOOS MAKE ME NERVOUS. I'M NEVER SURE WHICH SIDE OF THE BARS I'M ON. I WONDER IF THE ANIMALS FEEL THAT WAY TOO?
WELL, I GOTTA CHANGE SEATS. YOU GUYS TALK TOO MUCH. I CAN'T HEAR MYSELF THINK!
© 1987 United Feature Syndicate, Inc.
YOU SURE MEET SOME CHARACTERS ON THE BUS
WATCH WHAT YOU SAY! URANUS HAS SPIES EVERYWHERE!
JIM DAVIS 8-16

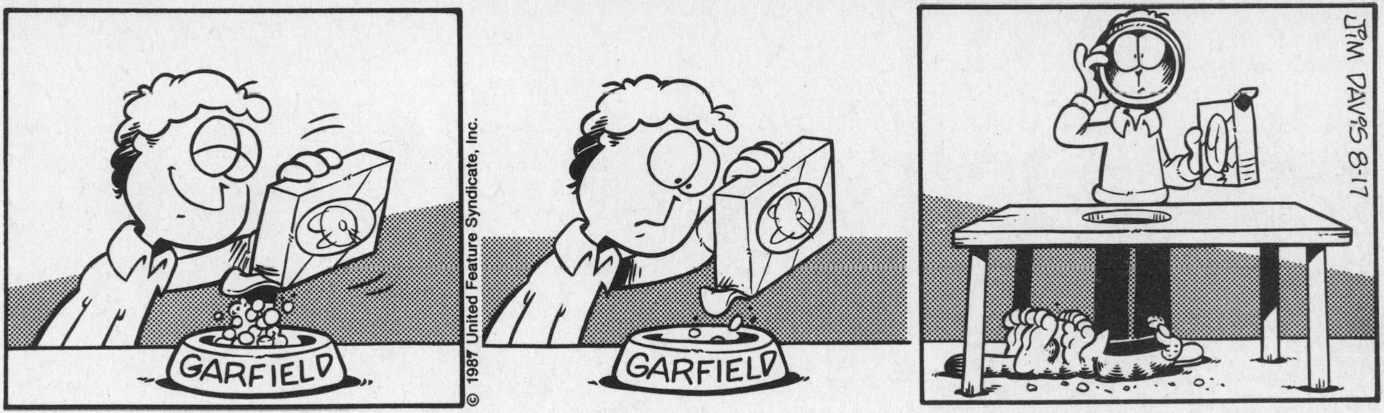
GARFIELD
© 1987 United Feature Syndicate, Inc.
GARFIELD
JIM DAVIS 8-17

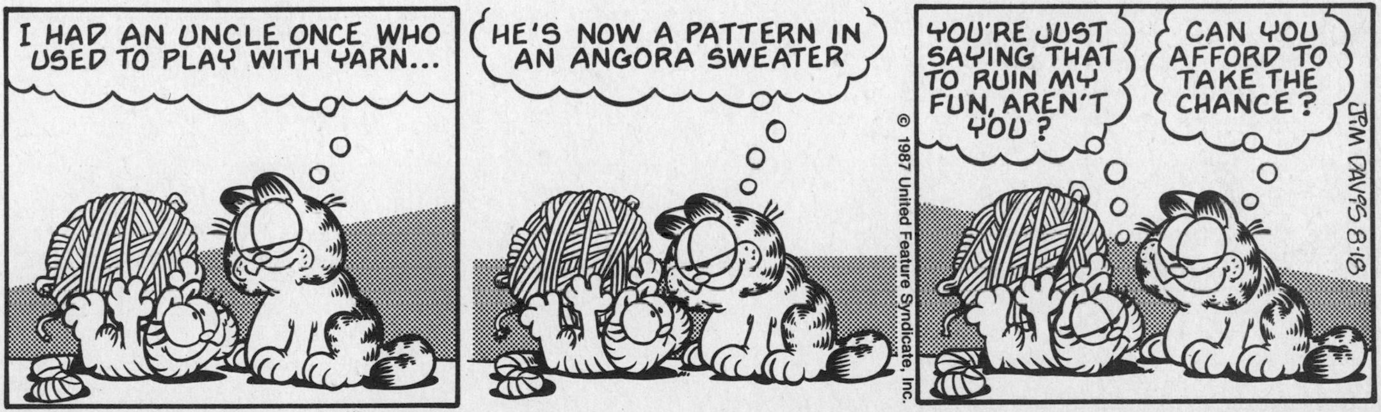
I HAD AN UNCLE ONCE WHO USED TO PLAY WITH YARN...
HE'S NOW A PATTERN IN AN ANGORA SWEATER
© 1987 United Feature Syndicate, Inc.
YOU'RE JUST SAYING THAT TO RUIN MY FUN, AREN'T YOU?
CAN YOU AFFORD TO TAKE THE CHANCE?
JIM DAVIS 8-18

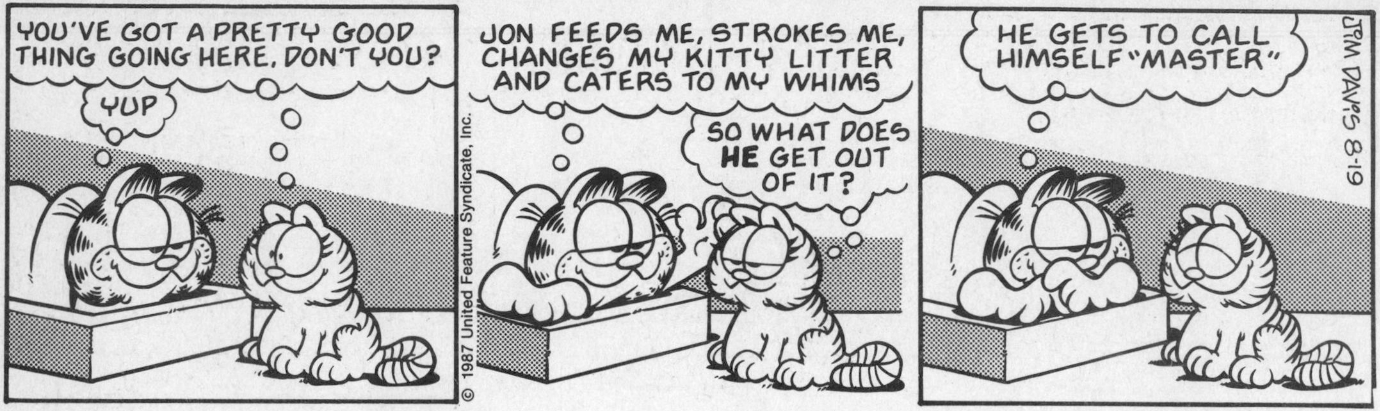
YOU'VE GOT A PRETTY GOOD THING GOING HERE, DON'T YOU?
YUP
JON FEEDS ME, STROKES ME, CHANGES MY KITTY LITTER AND CATERS TO MY WHIMS
SO WHAT DOES HE GET OUT OF IT?
HE GETS TO CALL HIMSELF "MASTER"
JIM DAVIS 8-19
© 1987 United Feature Syndicate, Inc.

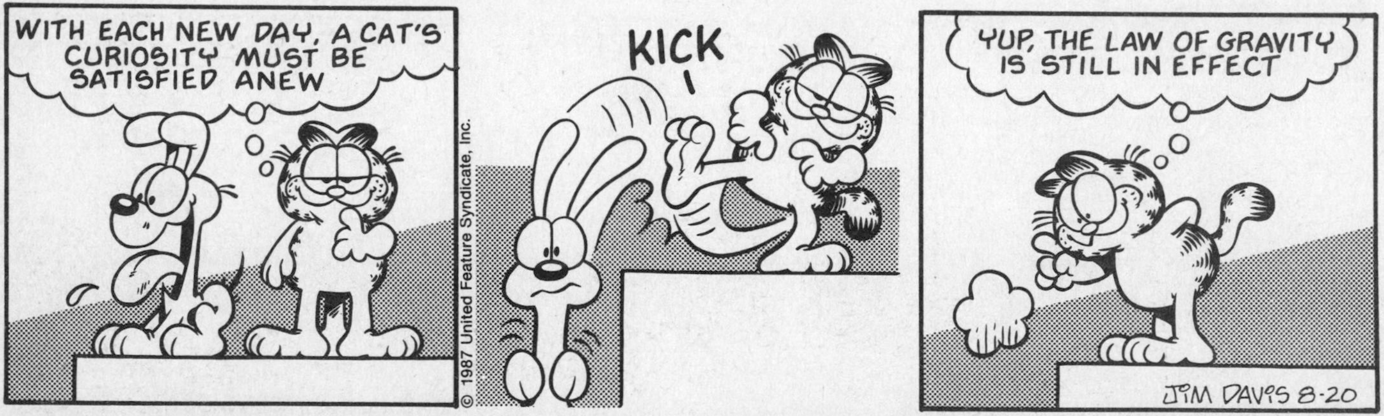
WITH EACH NEW DAY, A CAT'S CURIOSITY MUST BE SATISFIED ANEW
KICK
YUP, THE LAW OF GRAVITY IS STILL IN EFFECT
JIM DAVIS 8-20
© 1987 United Feature Syndicate, Inc.

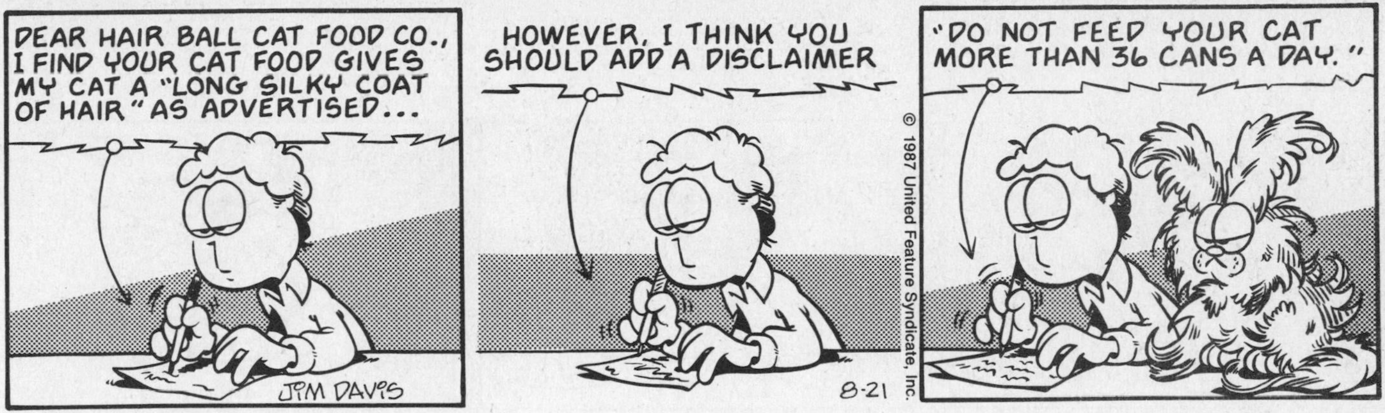
DEAR HAIR BALL CAT FOOD CO., I FIND YOUR CAT FOOD GIVES MY CAT A "LONG SILKY COAT OF HAIR" AS ADVERTISED...
JIM DAVIS
HOWEVER, I THINK YOU SHOULD ADD A DISCLAIMER
8-21
"DO NOT FEED YOUR CAT MORE THAN 36 CANS A DAY."

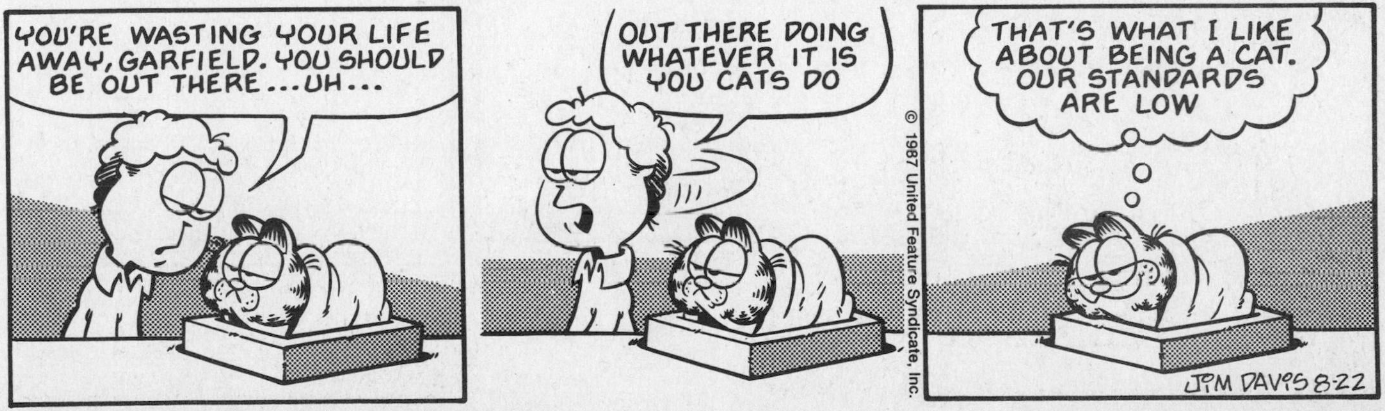
YOU'RE WASTING YOUR LIFE AWAY, GARFIELD. YOU SHOULD BE OUT THERE...UH...
OUT THERE DOING WHATEVER IT IS YOU CATS DO
THAT'S WHAT I LIKE ABOUT BEING A CAT. OUR STANDARDS ARE LOW
JIM DAVIS 8-22

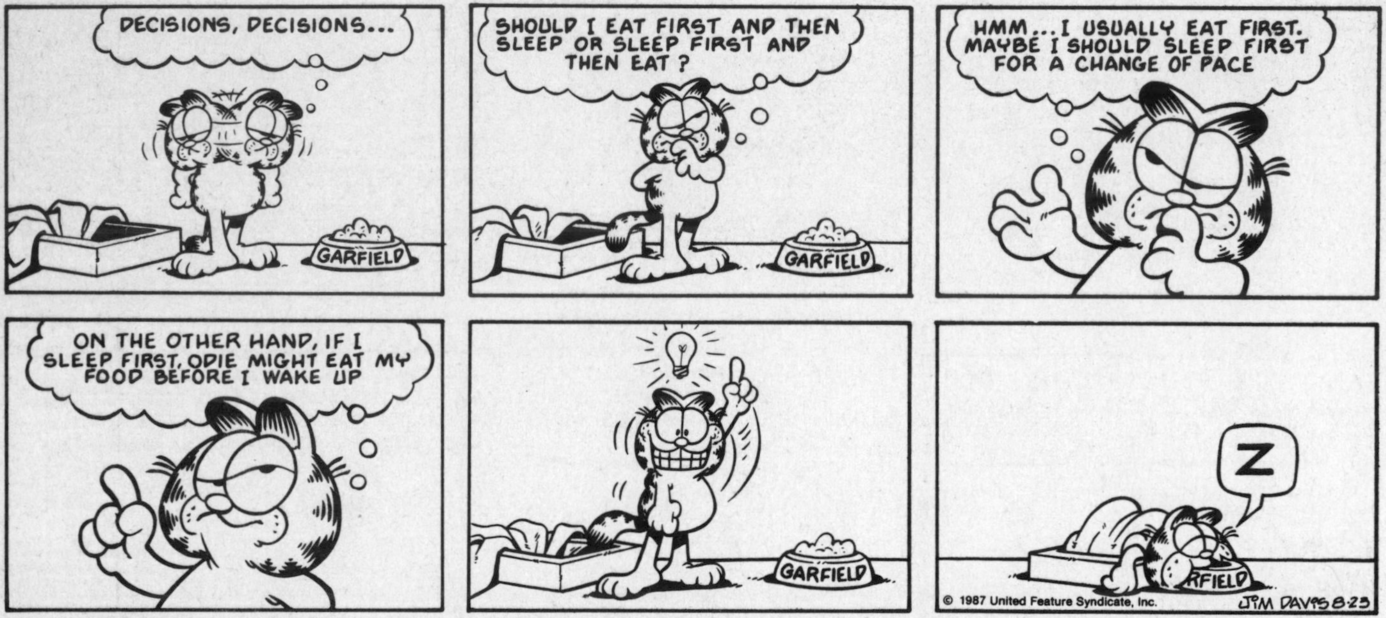
DECISIONS, DECISIONS...
GARFIELD
SHOULD I EAT FIRST AND THEN SLEEP OR SLEEP FIRST AND THEN EAT ?
GARFIELD
HMM... I USUALLY EAT FIRST. MAYBE I SHOULD SLEEP FIRST FOR A CHANGE OF PACE
ON THE OTHER HAND, IF I SLEEP FIRST, ODIE MIGHT EAT MY FOOD BEFORE I WAKE UP
GARFIELD
Z
RFIELD
© 1987 United Feature Syndicate, Inc.
JIM DAVIS 8-23

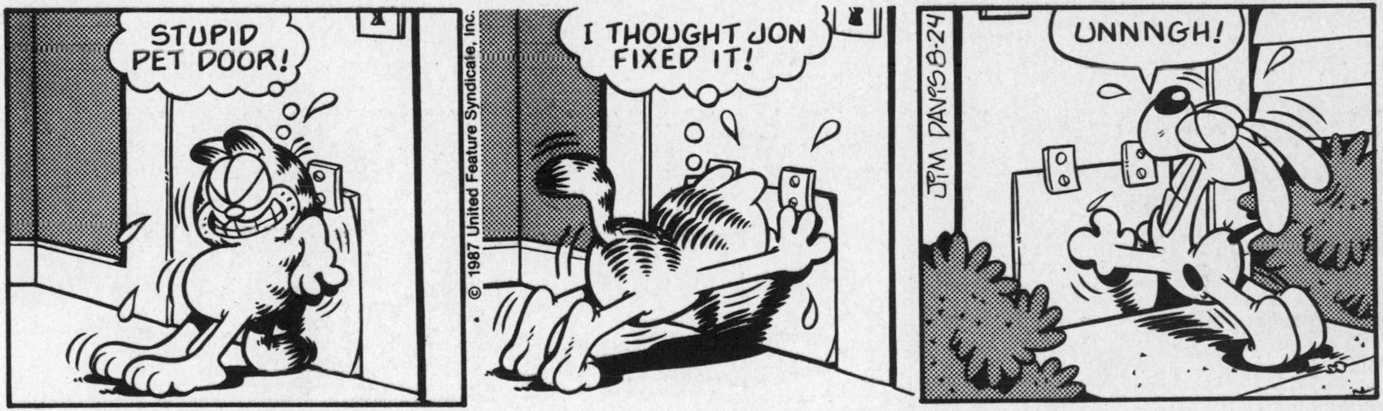
STUPID PET DOOR!
© 1987 United Feature Syndicate, Inc.
I THOUGHT JON FIXED IT!
JIM DAVIS 8-24
UNNNGH!

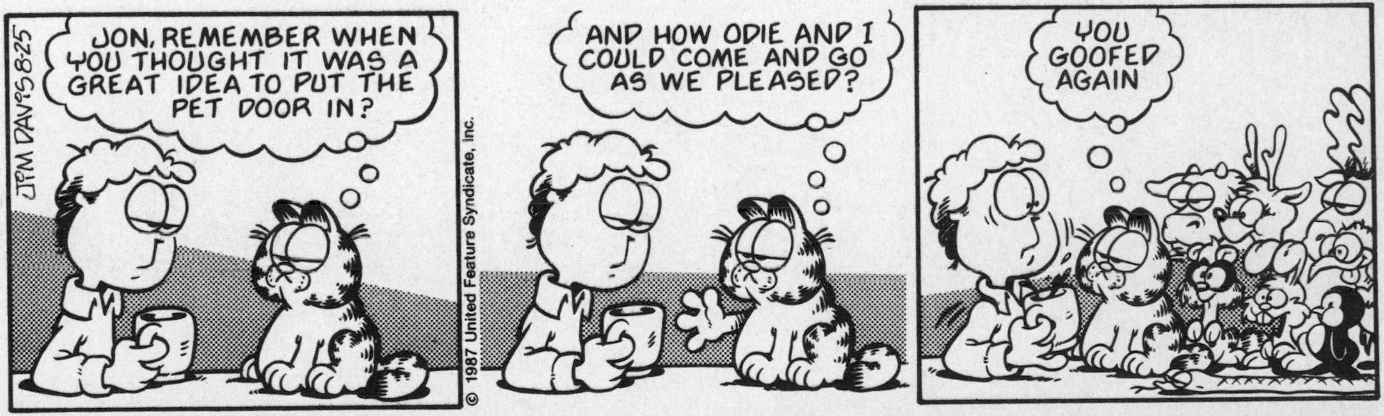
JIM DAVIS 8-25
JON, REMEMBER WHEN YOU THOUGHT IT WAS A GREAT IDEA TO PUT THE PET DOOR IN?
© 1987 United Feature Syndicate, Inc.
AND HOW ODIE AND I COULD COME AND GO AS WE PLEASED?
YOU GOOFED AGAIN

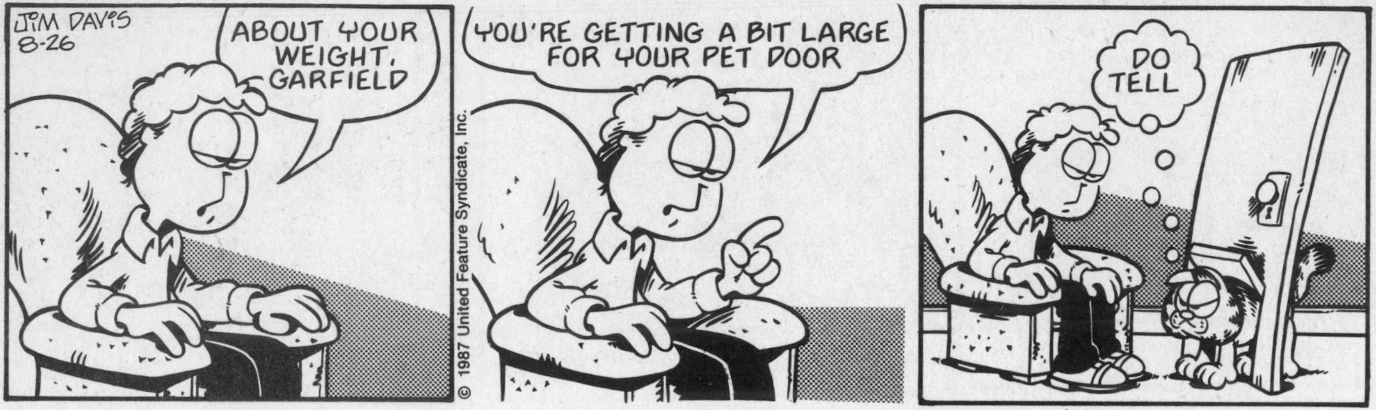
JIM DAVIS
8-26
ABOUT YOUR WEIGHT, GARFIELD
© 1987 United Feature Syndicate, Inc.
YOU'RE GETTING A BIT LARGE FOR YOUR PET DOOR
DO TELL

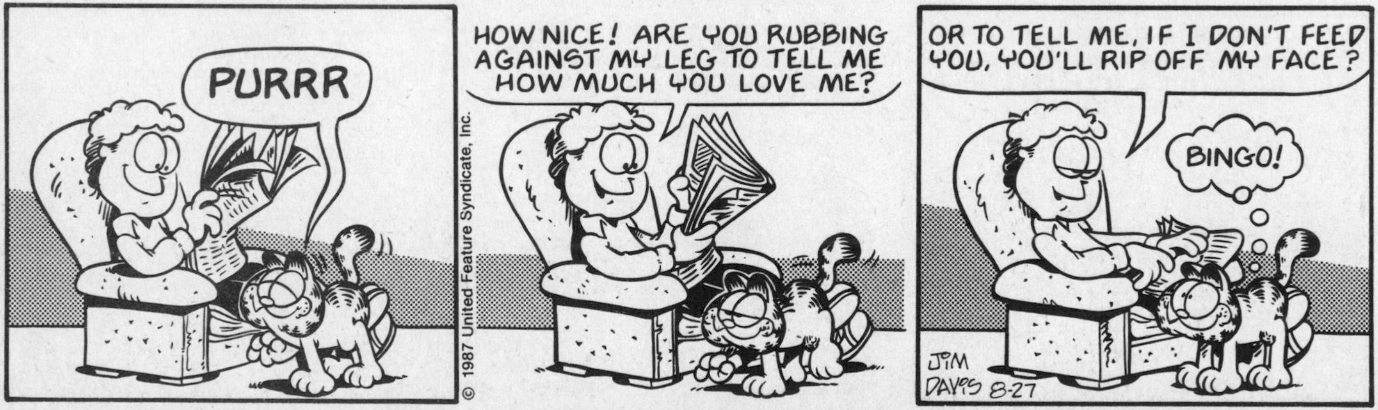
PURRR
© 1987 United Feature Syndicate, Inc.
HOW NICE! ARE YOU RUBBING AGAINST MY LEG TO TELL ME HOW MUCH YOU LOVE ME?
OR TO TELL ME, IF I DON'T FEED YOU, YOU'LL RIP OFF MY FACE?
BINGO!
JIM DAVIS 8-27

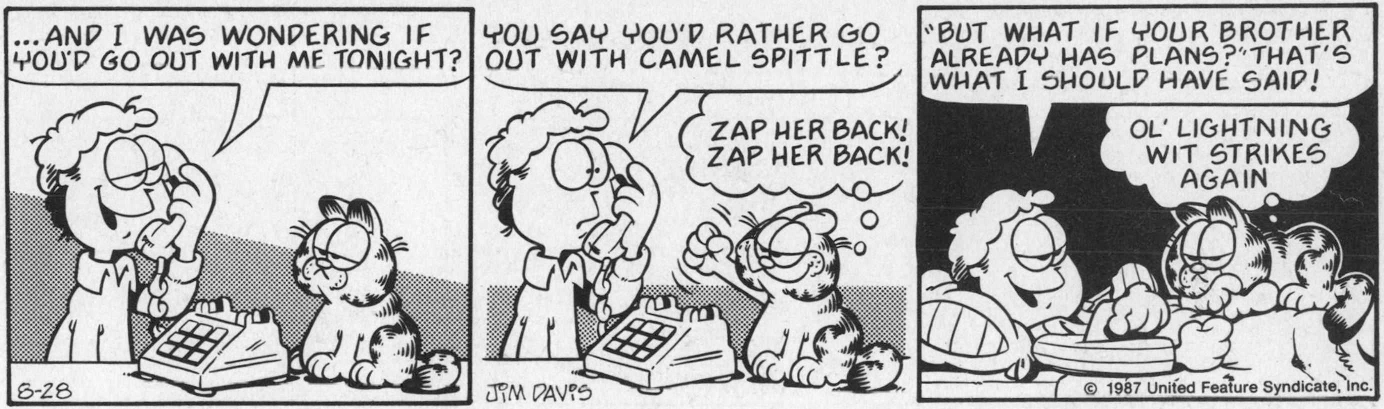
...AND I WAS WONDERING IF YOU'D GO OUT WITH ME TONIGHT?
8-28
YOU SAY YOU'D RATHER GO OUT WITH CAMEL SPITTLE?
ZAP HER BACK! ZAP HER BACK!
JIM DAVIS
"BUT WHAT IF YOUR BROTHER ALREADY HAS PLANS?" THAT'S WHAT I SHOULD HAVE SAID!
OL' LIGHTNING WIT STRIKES AGAIN
© 1987 United Feature Syndicate, Inc.

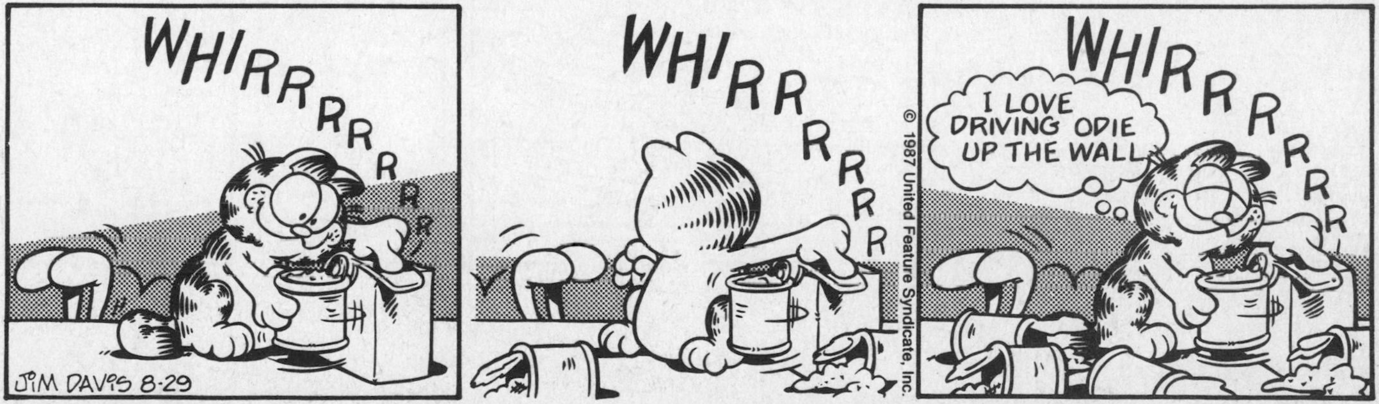
WHIRRRRRRRR
JIM DAVIS 8-29
WHIRRRRRRR
© 1987 United Feature Syndicate, Inc.
WHIRRRRRRR
I LOVE DRIVING ODIE UP THE WALL

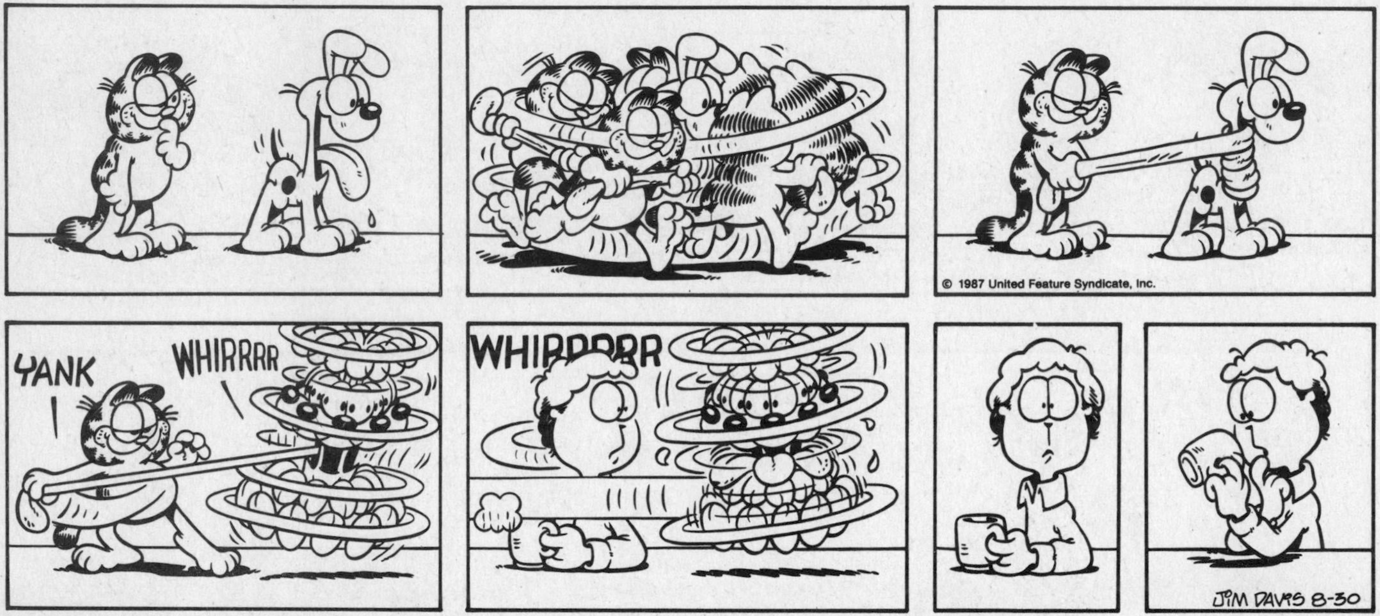
© 1987 United Feature Syndicate, Inc.
YANK
WHIRRRR
WHIRRRRR
JIM DAVIS 8-30

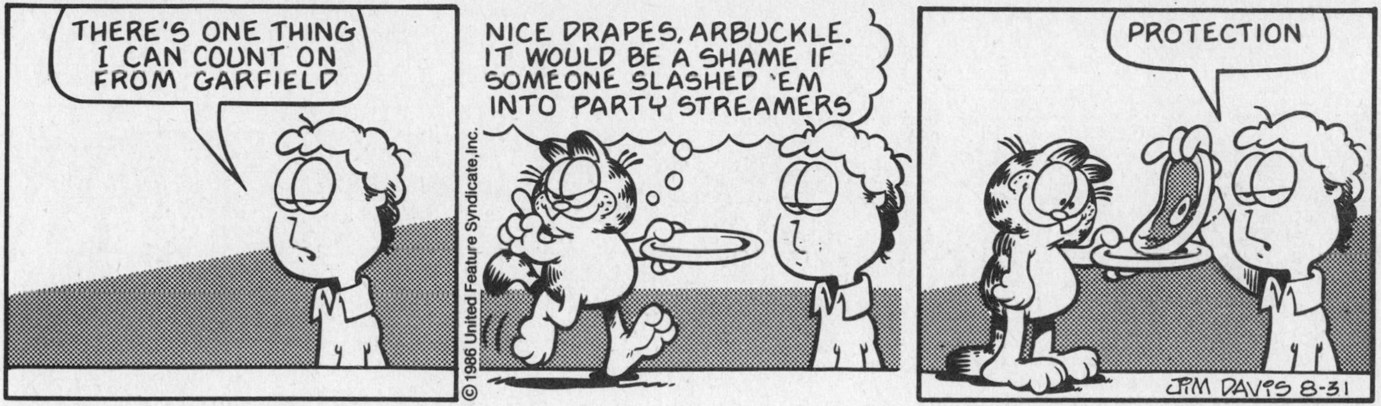
THERE'S ONE THING I CAN COUNT ON FROM GARFIELD
NICE DRAPES, ARBUCKLE. IT WOULD BE A SHAME IF SOMEONE SLASHED 'EM INTO PARTY STREAMERS
PROTECTION
JIM DAVIS 8-31

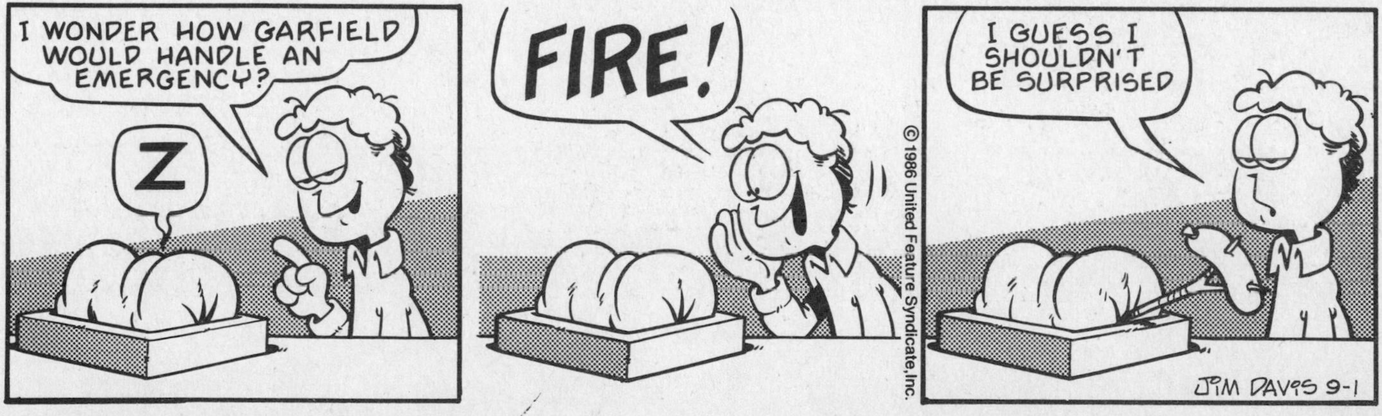
I WONDER HOW GARFIELD WOULD HANDLE AN EMERGENCY?
Z
FIRE!
I GUESS I SHOULDN'T BE SURPRISED
JIM DAVIS 9-1

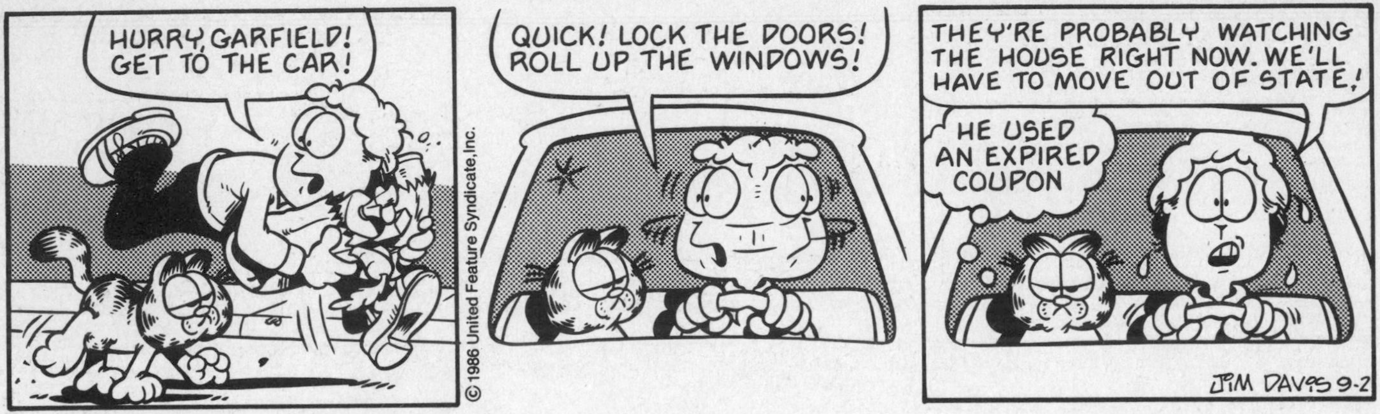
HURRY, GARFIELD! GET TO THE CAR!
QUICK! LOCK THE DOORS! ROLL UP THE WINDOWS!
THEY'RE PROBABLY WATCHING THE HOUSE RIGHT NOW. WE'LL HAVE TO MOVE OUT OF STATE!
HE USED AN EXPIRED COUPON
© 1986 United Feature Syndicate, Inc.
JIM DAVIS 9-2

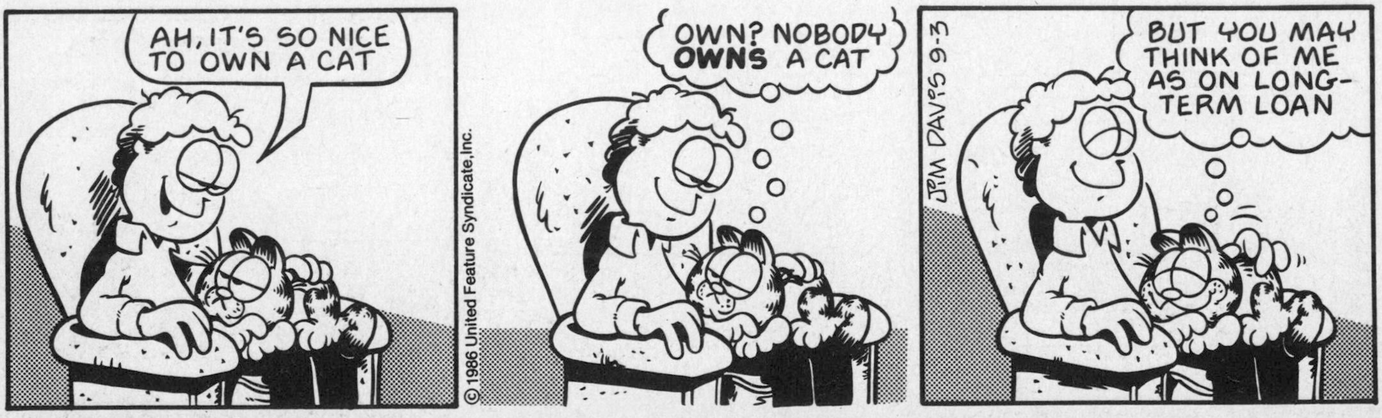
AH, IT'S SO NICE TO OWN A CAT
OWN? NOBODY **OWNS** A CAT
BUT YOU MAY THINK OF ME AS ON LONG-TERM LOAN
© 1986 United Feature Syndicate, Inc.
JIM DAVIS 9-3

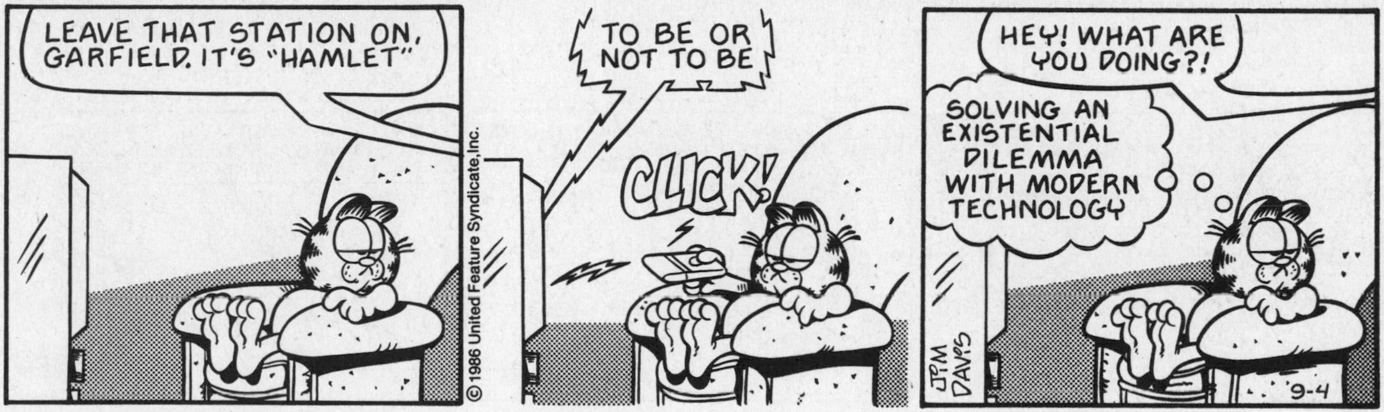
LEAVE THAT STATION ON, GARFIELD. IT'S "HAMLET"
© 1986 United Feature Syndicate, Inc.
TO BE OR NOT TO BE
CLICK!
HEY! WHAT ARE YOU DOING?!
SOLVING AN EXISTENTIAL DILEMMA WITH MODERN TECHNOLOGY
JIM DAVIS
9-4

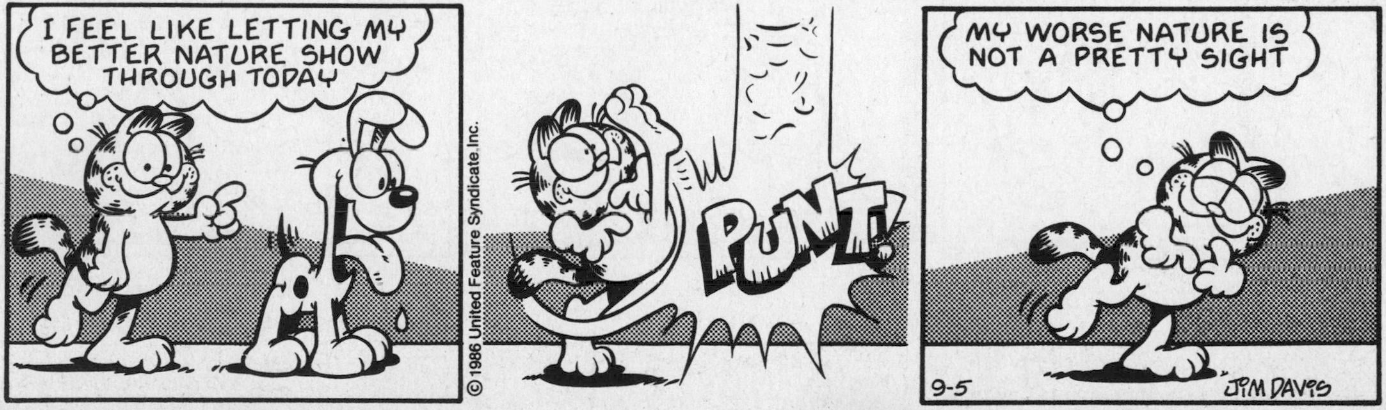
I FEEL LIKE LETTING MY BETTER NATURE SHOW THROUGH TODAY
© 1986 United Feature Syndicate, Inc.
PUNT!
MY WORSE NATURE IS NOT A PRETTY SIGHT
9-5
JIM DAVIS

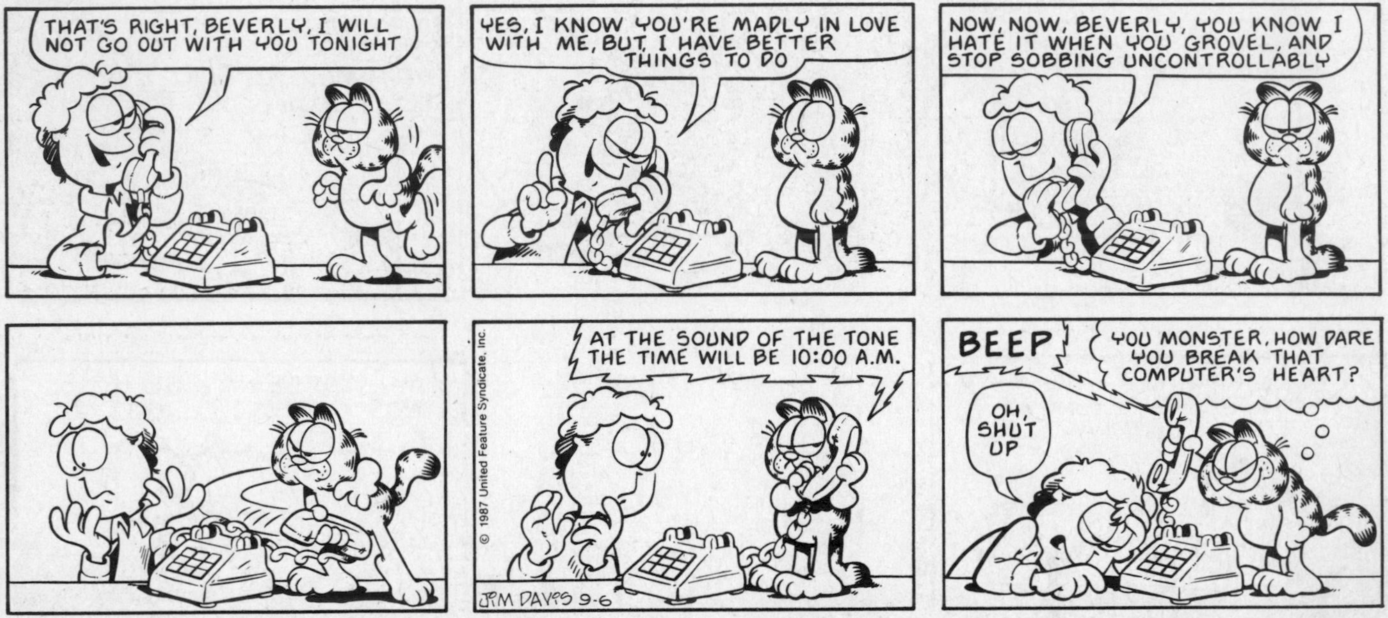

THAT'S RIGHT, BEVERLY, I WILL NOT GO OUT WITH YOU TONIGHT
YES, I KNOW YOU'RE MADLY IN LOVE WITH ME, BUT, I HAVE BETTER THINGS TO DO
NOW, NOW, BEVERLY, YOU KNOW I HATE IT WHEN YOU GROVEL, AND STOP SOBBING UNCONTROLLABLY
AT THE SOUND OF THE TONE THE TIME WILL BE 10:00 A.M.
BEEP
YOU MONSTER, HOW DARE YOU BREAK THAT COMPUTER'S HEART?
OH, SHUT UP
© 1987 United Feature Syndicate, Inc.
JIM DAVIS 9-6

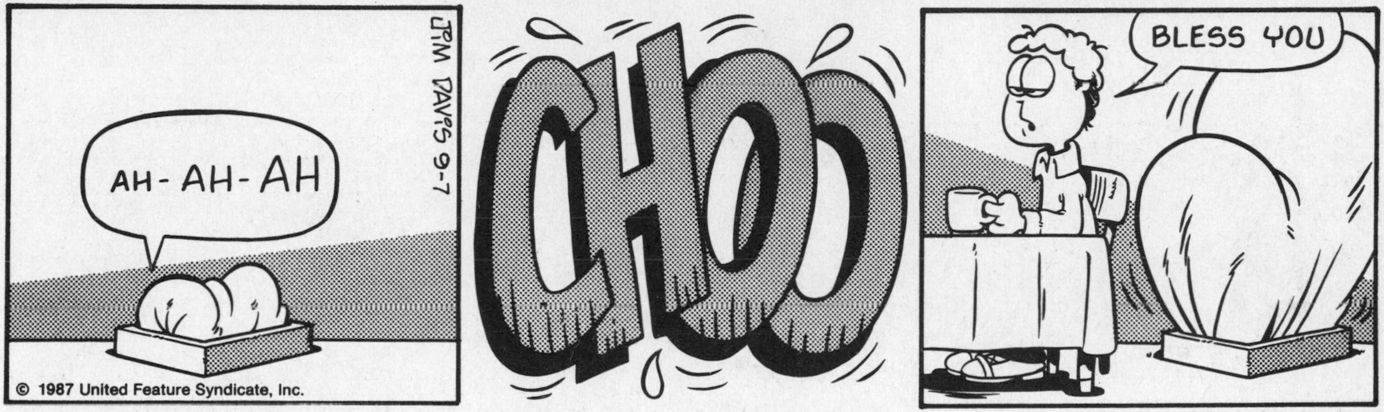
AH- AH- AH
JIM DAVIS 9-7
© 1987 United Feature Syndicate, Inc.
CHOO
BLESS YOU

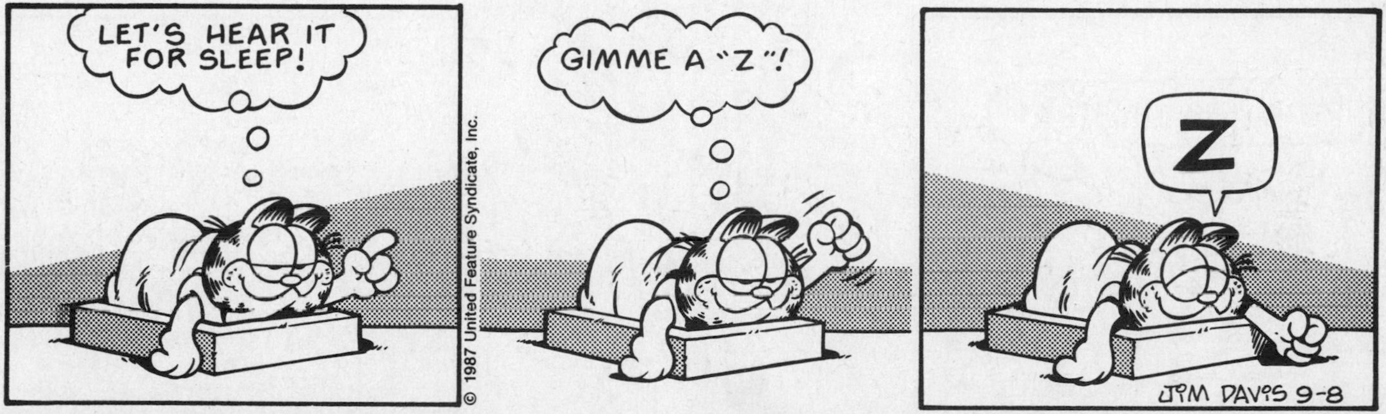
LET'S HEAR IT FOR SLEEP!
© 1987 United Feature Syndicate, Inc.
GIMME A "Z"!
Z
JIM DAVIS 9-8

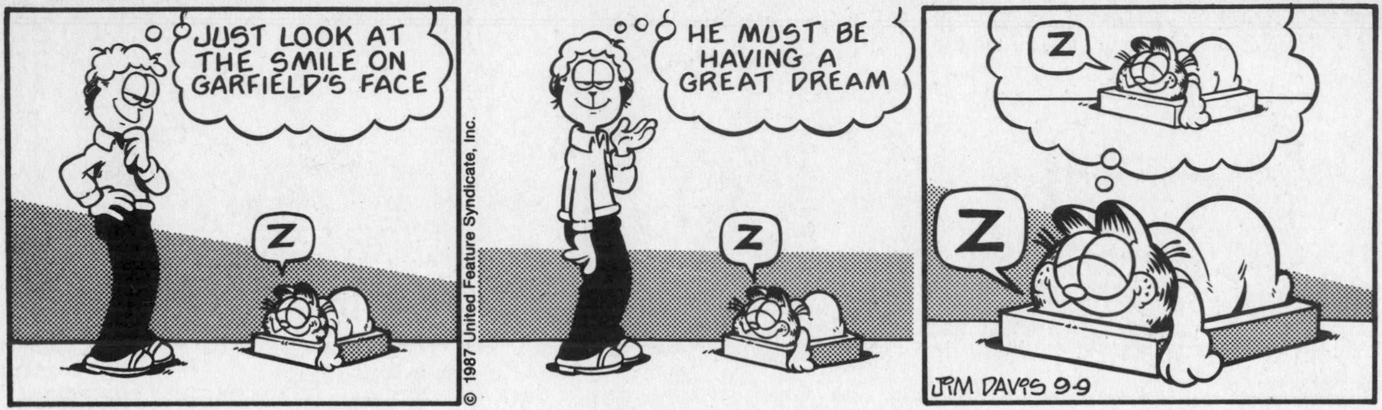
JUST LOOK AT THE SMILE ON GARFIELD'S FACE
Z
© 1987 United Feature Syndicate, Inc.
HE MUST BE HAVING A GREAT DREAM
Z
Z
Z
JIM DAVIS 9-9

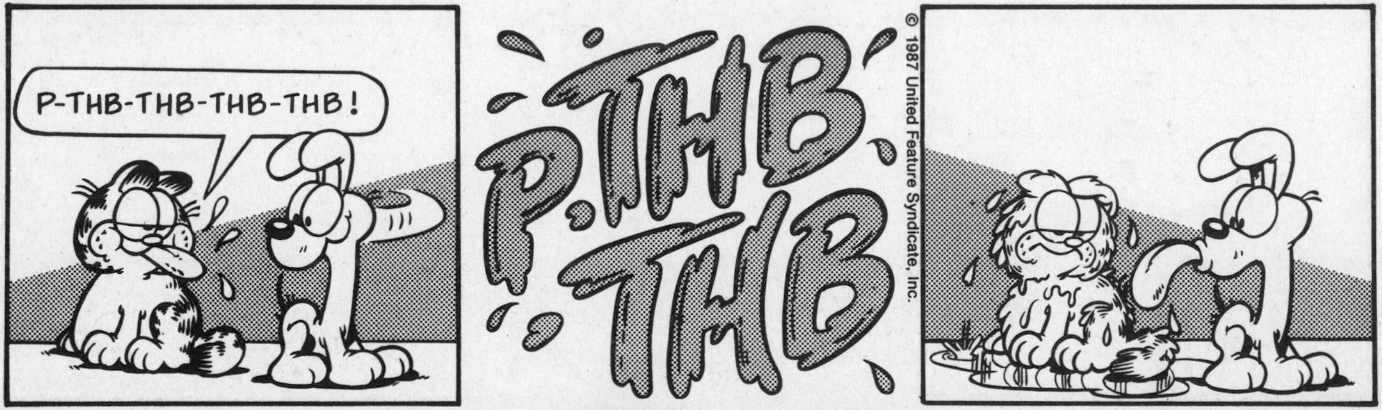
P-THB-THB-THB-THB!
P-THB THB
© 1987 United Feature Syndicate, Inc.

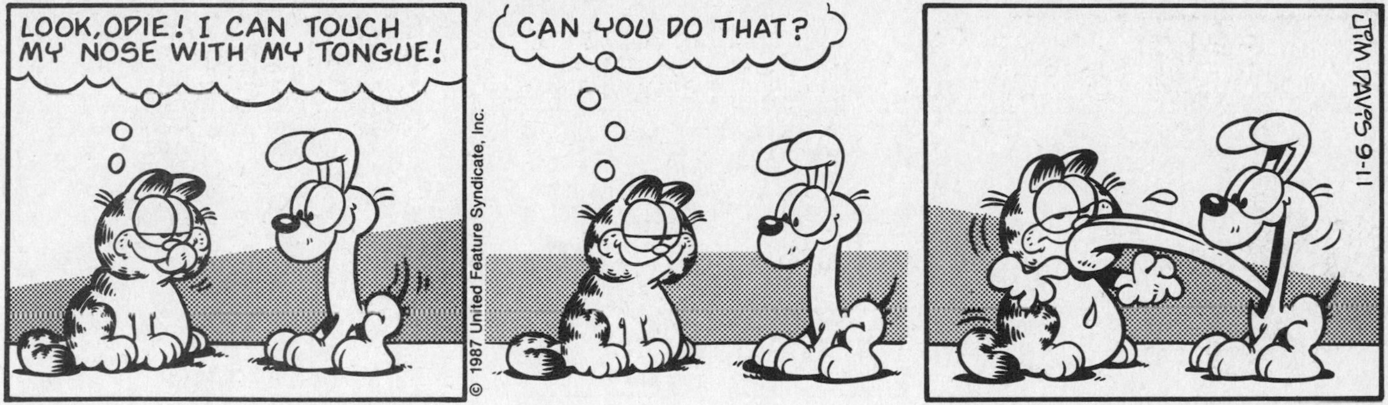
LOOK, ODIE! I CAN TOUCH MY NOSE WITH MY TONGUE!
CAN YOU DO THAT?
© 1987 United Feature Syndicate, Inc.
JIM DAVIS 9-11

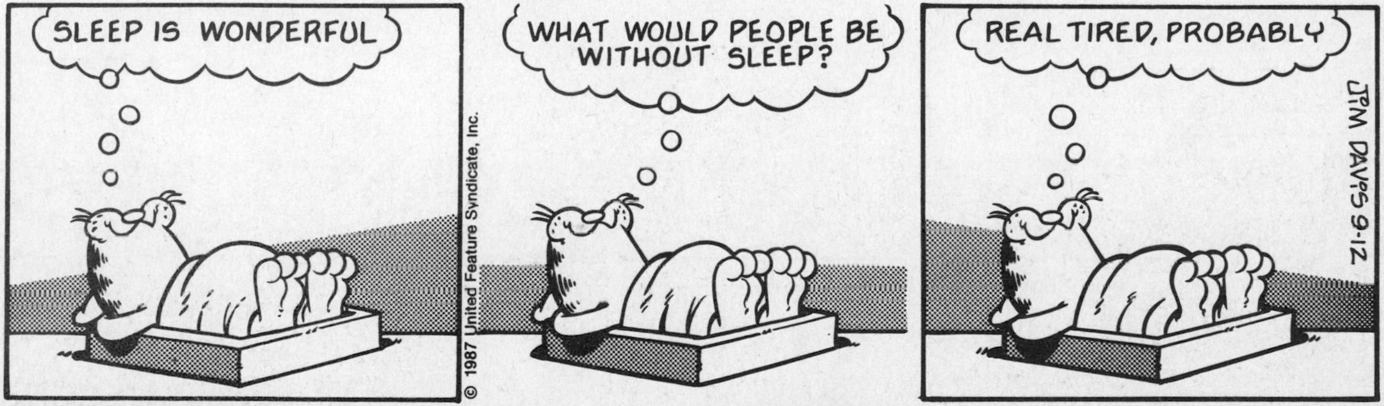
SLEEP IS WONDERFUL
WHAT WOULD PEOPLE BE WITHOUT SLEEP?
REAL TIRED, PROBABLY
© 1987 United Feature Syndicate, Inc.
JIM DAVIS 9-12

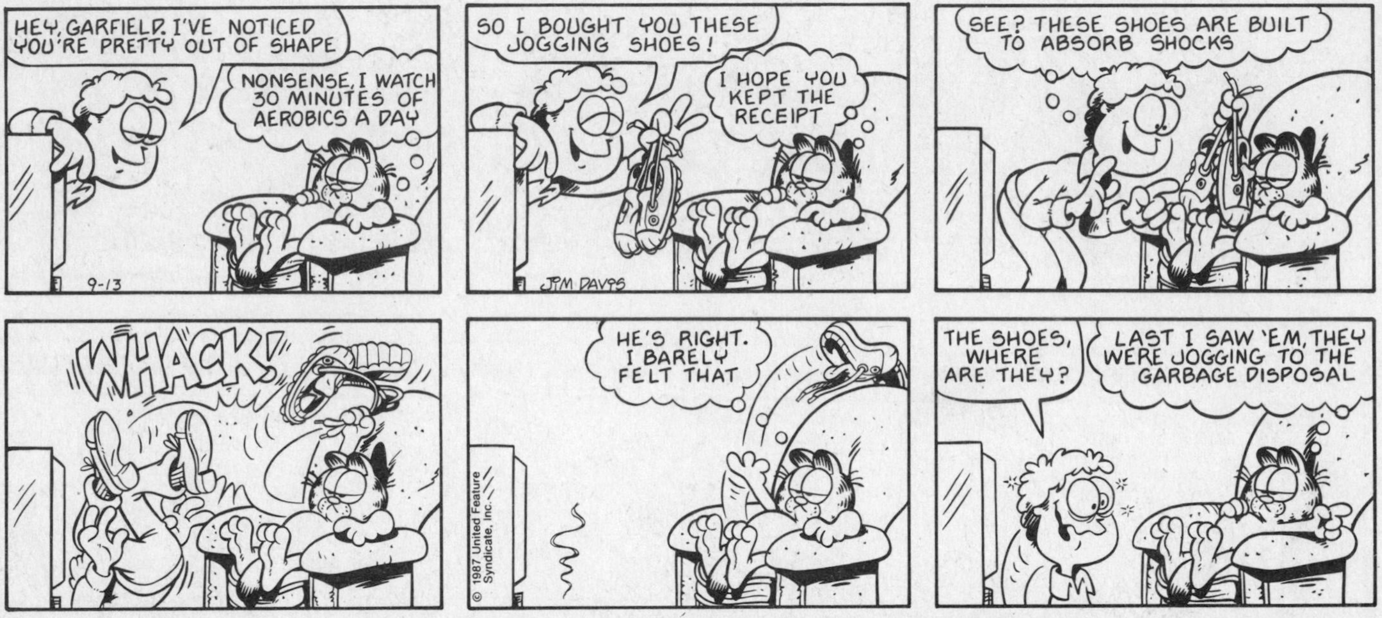
HEY, GARFIELD. I'VE NOTICED YOU'RE PRETTY OUT OF SHAPE
NONSENSE, I WATCH 30 MINUTES OF AEROBICS A DAY
9-13
SO I BOUGHT YOU THESE JOGGING SHOES!
I HOPE YOU KEPT THE RECEIPT
JIM DAVIS
SEE? THESE SHOES ARE BUILT TO ABSORB SHOCKS
WHACK!
© 1987 United Feature Syndicate, Inc.
HE'S RIGHT. I BARELY FELT THAT
THE SHOES, WHERE ARE THEY?
LAST I SAW 'EM, THEY WERE JOGGING TO THE GARBAGE DISPOSAL

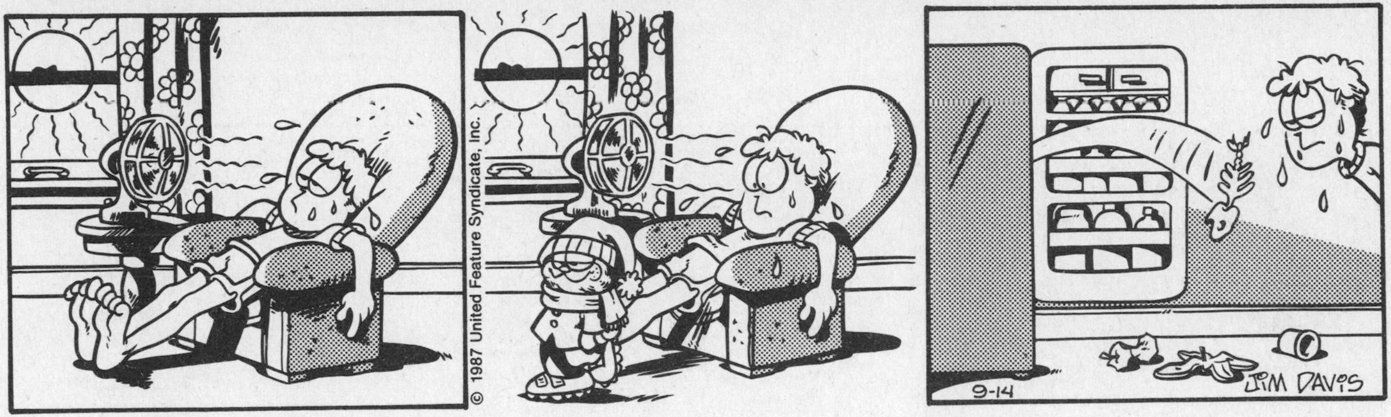
© 1987 United Feature Syndicate, Inc.
9-14
JIM DAVIS

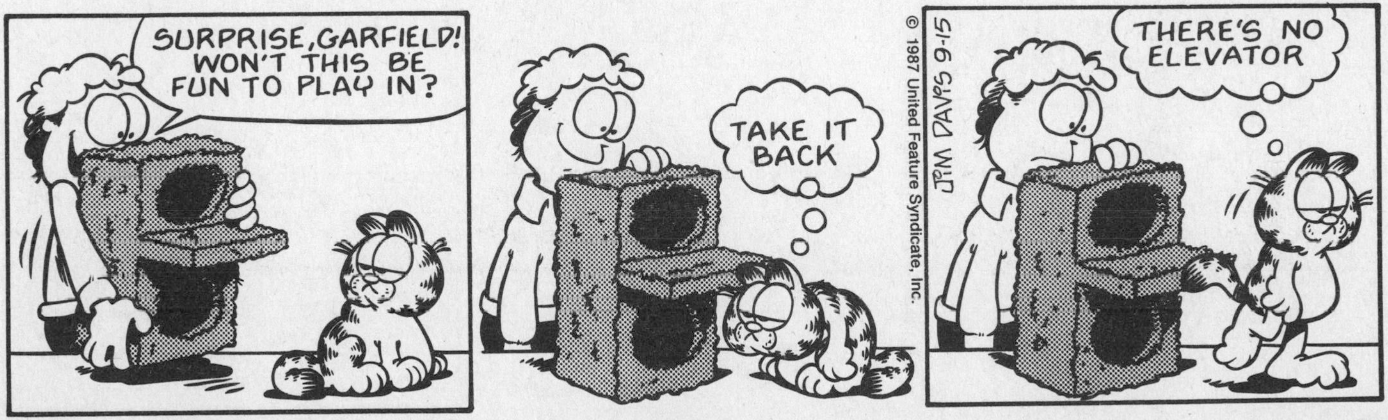
SURPRISE, GARFIELD! WON'T THIS BE FUN TO PLAY IN?
TAKE IT BACK
© 1987 United Feature Syndicate, Inc.
JIM DAVIS 9-15
THERE'S NO ELEVATOR

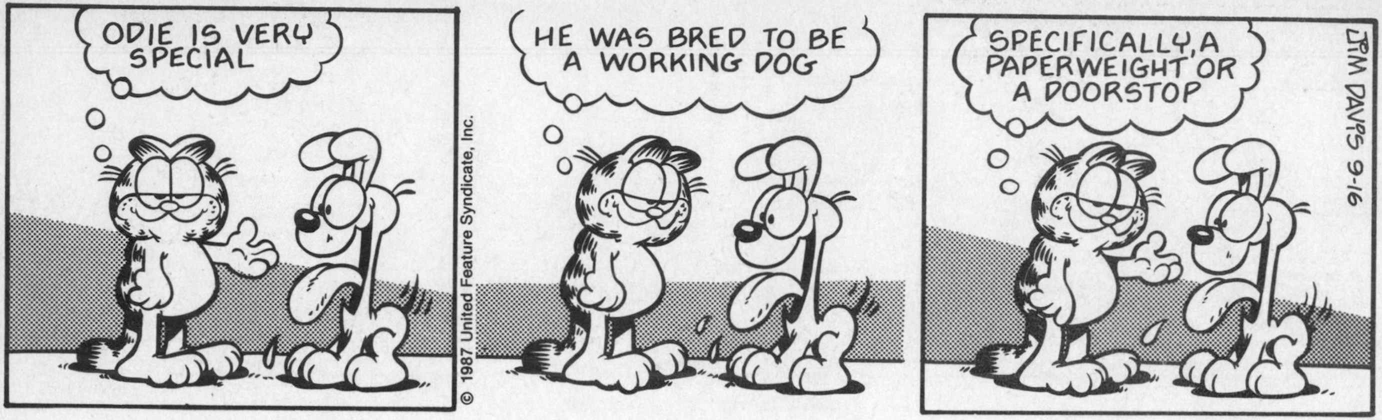
ODIE IS VERY SPECIAL
HE WAS BRED TO BE A WORKING DOG
SPECIFICALLY, A PAPERWEIGHT OR A DOORSTOP
JIM DAVIS 9-16
© 1987 United Feature Syndicate, Inc.

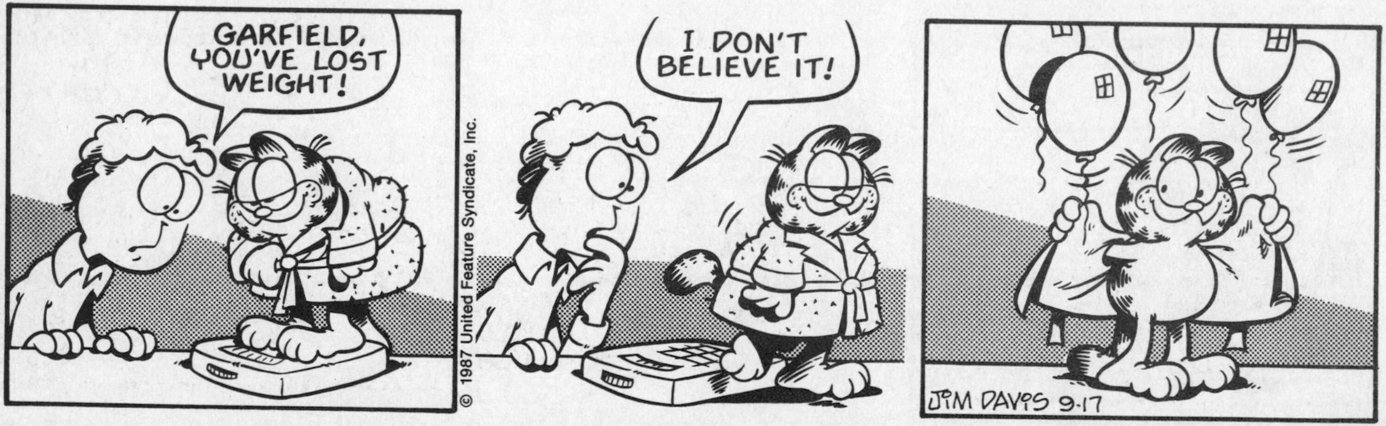
GARFIELD, YOU'VE LOST WEIGHT!
I DON'T BELIEVE IT!
JIM DAVIS 9-17
© 1987 United Feature Syndicate, Inc.

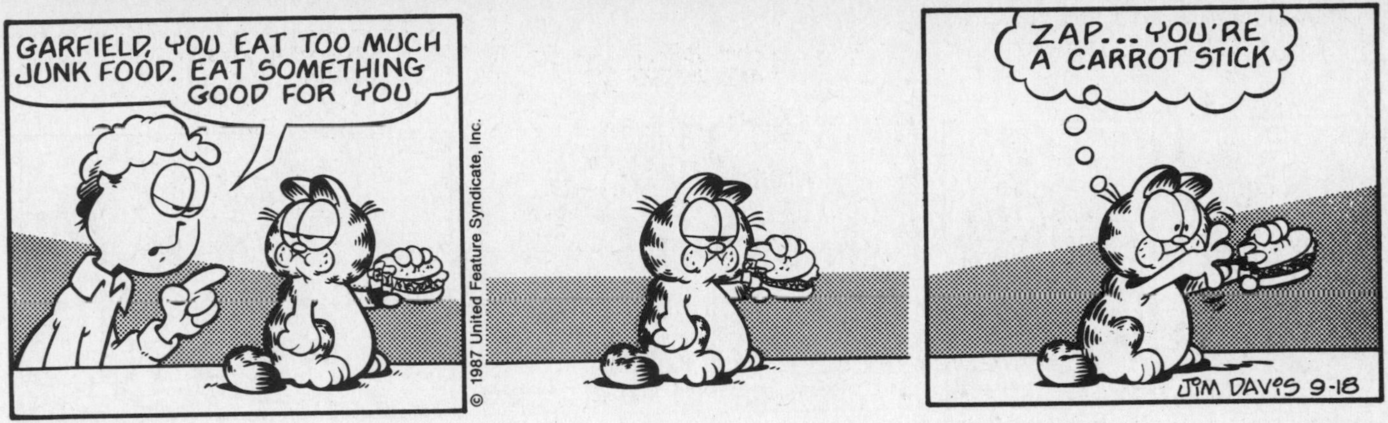
GARFIELD, YOU EAT TOO MUCH JUNK FOOD. EAT SOMETHING GOOD FOR YOU
ZAP... YOU'RE A CARROT STICK
JIM DAVIS 9-18

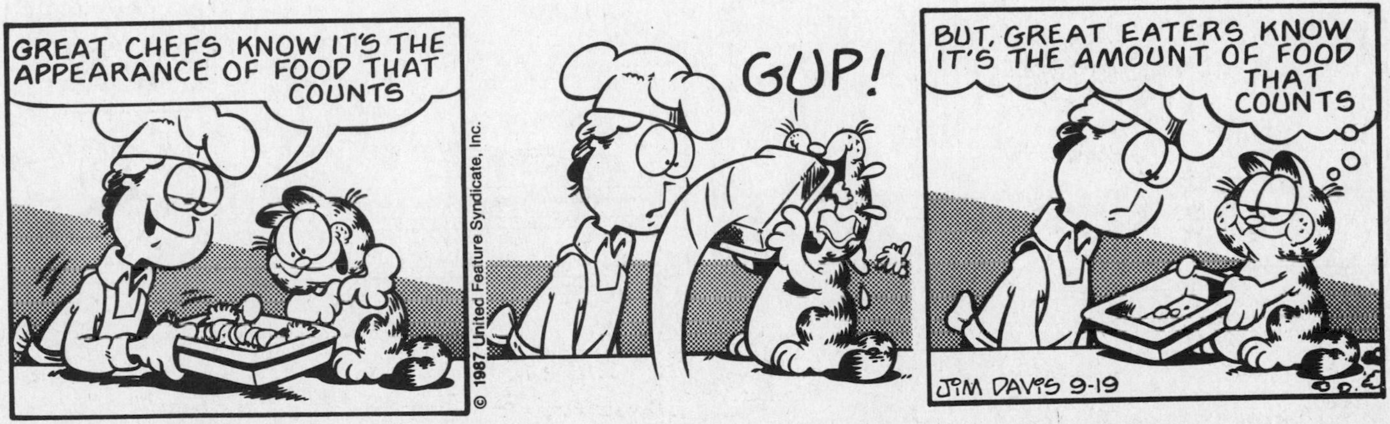
GREAT CHEFS KNOW IT'S THE APPEARANCE OF FOOD THAT COUNTS
GUP!
BUT, GREAT EATERS KNOW IT'S THE AMOUNT OF FOOD THAT COUNTS
JIM DAVIS 9-19

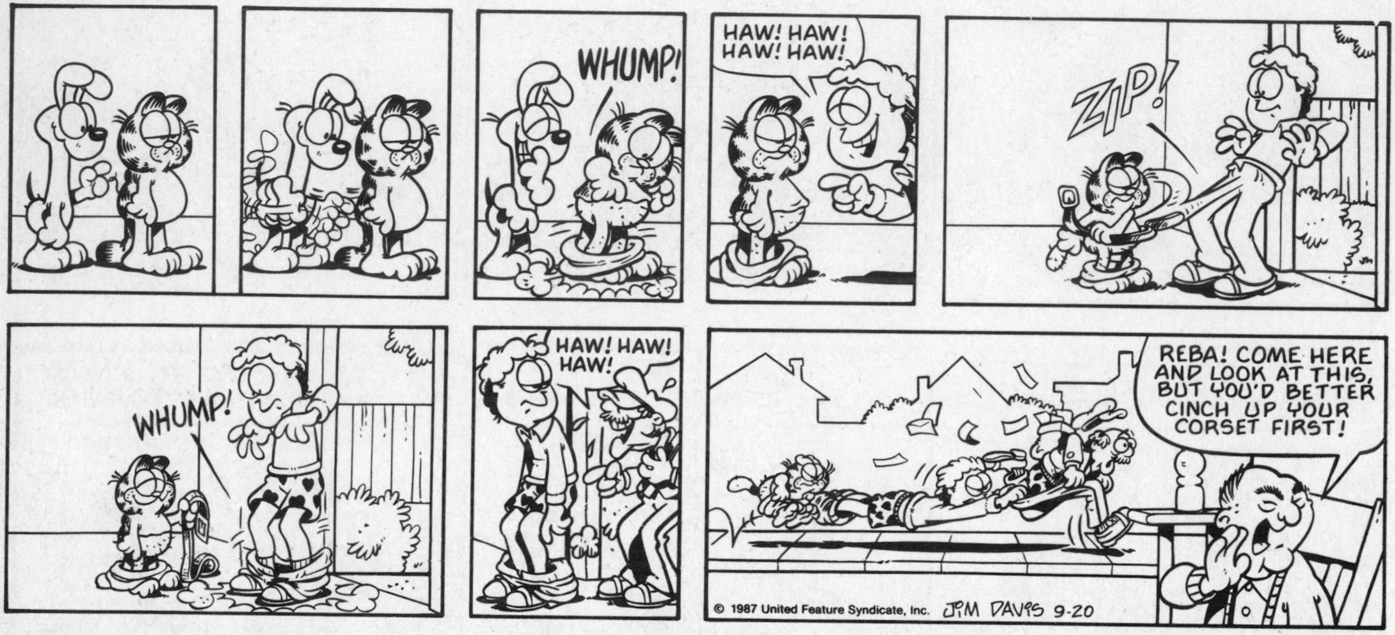
WHUMP!
HAW! HAW!
HAW! HAW!
ZIP!
WHUMP!
HAW! HAW!
HAW!
REBA! COME HERE AND LOOK AT THIS, BUT YOU'D BETTER CINCH UP YOUR CORSET FIRST!
© 1987 United Feature Syndicate, Inc.
JIM DAVIS 9-20

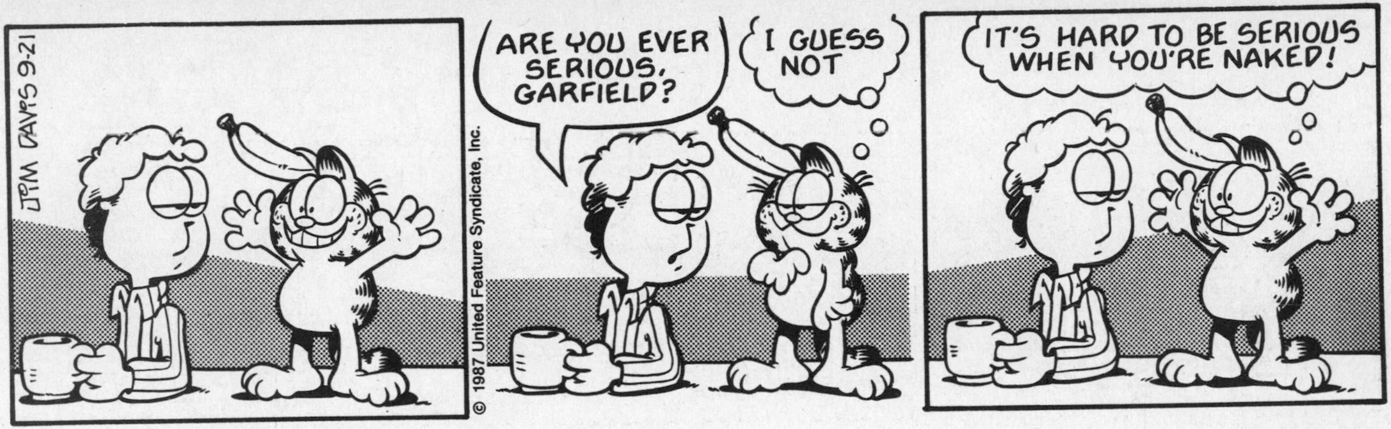
JIM DAVIS 9-21
ARE YOU EVER SERIOUS, GARFIELD?
I GUESS NOT
IT'S HARD TO BE SERIOUS WHEN YOU'RE NAKED!

© 1987 United Feature Syndicate, Inc.

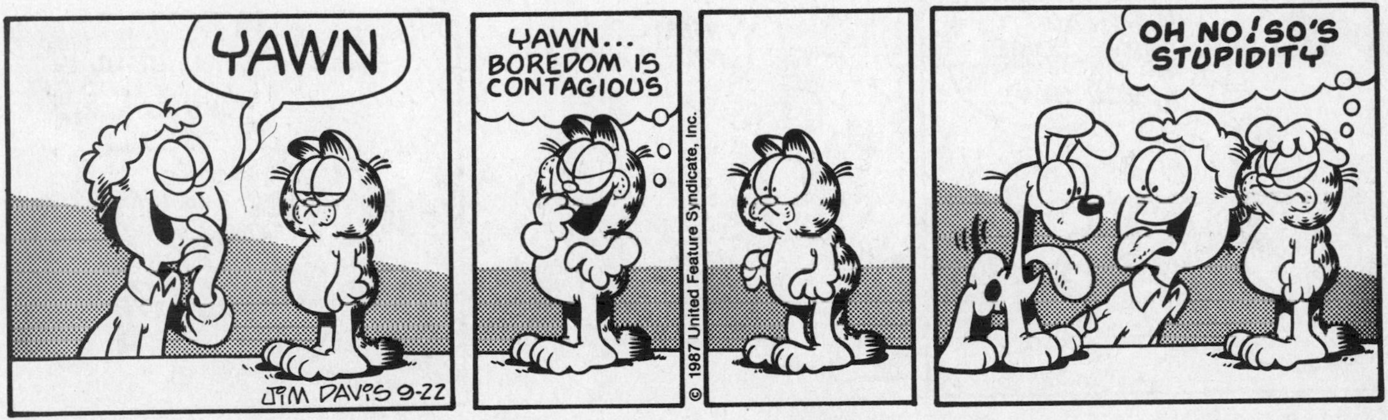
YAWN
JIM DAVIS 9-22
YAWN... BOREDOM IS CONTAGIOUS
OH NO! SO'S STUPIDITY

© 1987 United Feature Syndicate, Inc.

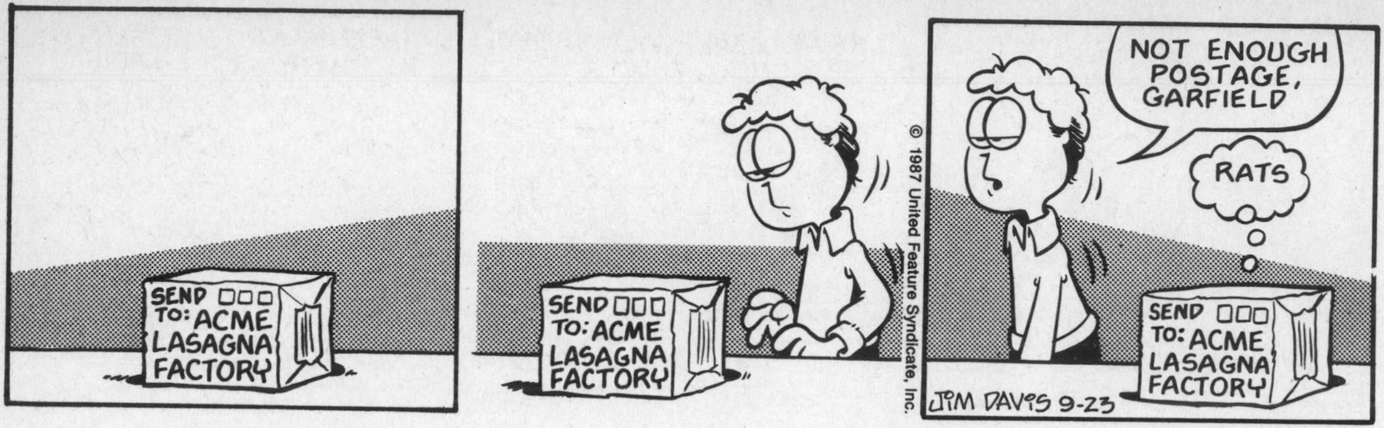
SEND TO: ACME LASAGNA FACTORY
SEND TO: ACME LASAGNA FACTORY
© 1987 United Feature Syndicate, Inc.
NOT ENOUGH POSTAGE, GARFIELD
RATS
SEND TO: ACME LASAGNA FACTORY
JIM DAVIS 9-23

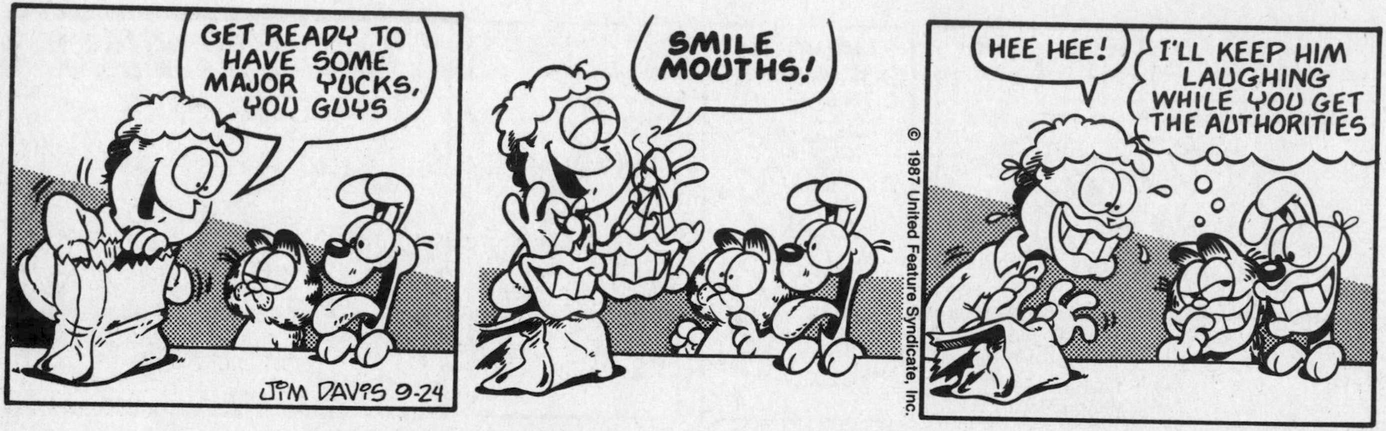
GET READY TO HAVE SOME MAJOR YUCKS, YOU GUYS
JIM DAVIS 9-24
SMILE MOUTHS!
© 1987 United Feature Syndicate, Inc.
HEE HEE!
I'LL KEEP HIM LAUGHING WHILE YOU GET THE AUTHORITIES

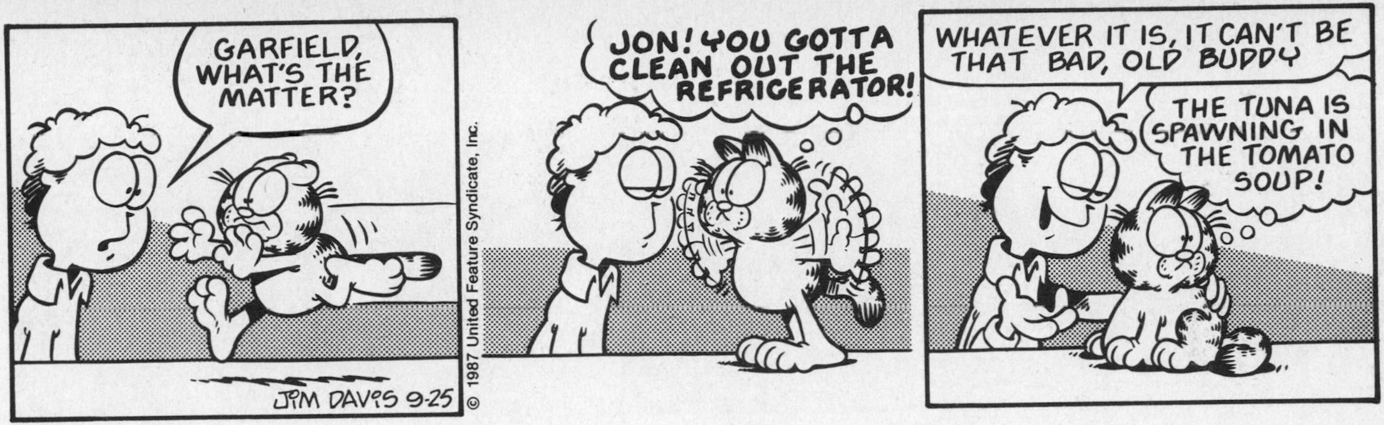
GARFIELD, WHAT'S THE MATTER?
JON! YOU GOTTA CLEAN OUT THE REFRIGERATOR!
WHATEVER IT IS, IT CAN'T BE THAT BAD, OLD BUDDY
THE TUNA IS SPAWNING IN THE TOMATO SOUP!
JIM DAVIS 9-25
© 1987 United Feature Syndicate, Inc.

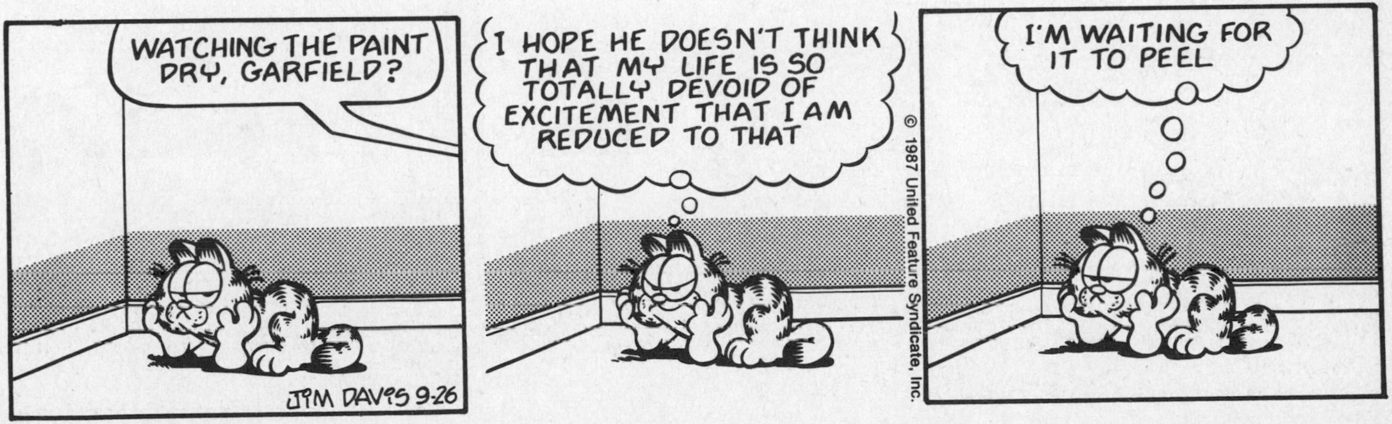
WATCHING THE PAINT DRY, GARFIELD?
I HOPE HE DOESN'T THINK THAT MY LIFE IS SO TOTALLY DEVOID OF EXCITEMENT THAT I AM REDUCED TO THAT
I'M WAITING FOR IT TO PEEL
JIM DAVIS 9-26
© 1987 United Feature Syndicate, Inc.

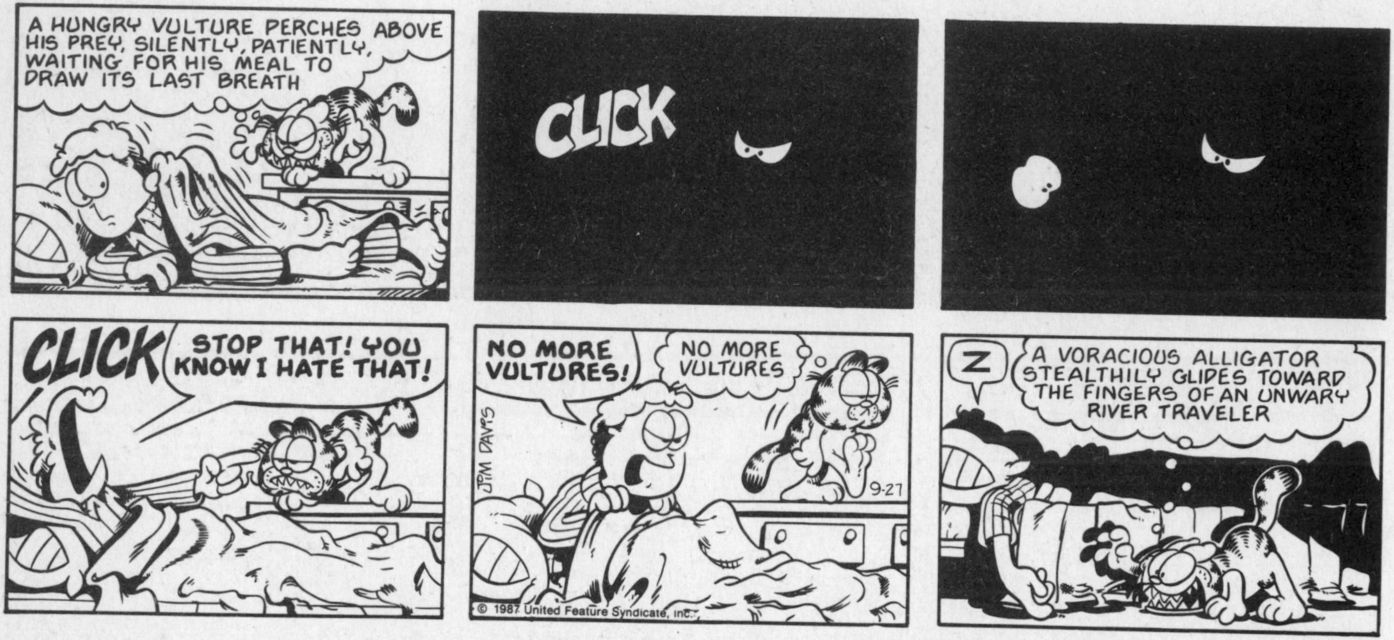
A HUNGRY VULTURE PERCHES ABOVE HIS PREY, SILENTLY, PATIENTLY, WAITING FOR HIS MEAL TO DRAW ITS LAST BREATH
CLICK
CLICK
STOP THAT! YOU KNOW I HATE THAT!
NO MORE VULTURES!
NO MORE VULTURES
JIM DAVIS
9-27
© 1987 United Feature Syndicate, Inc.
Z
A VORACIOUS ALLIGATOR STEALTHILY GLIDES TOWARD THE FINGERS OF AN UNWARY RIVER TRAVELER

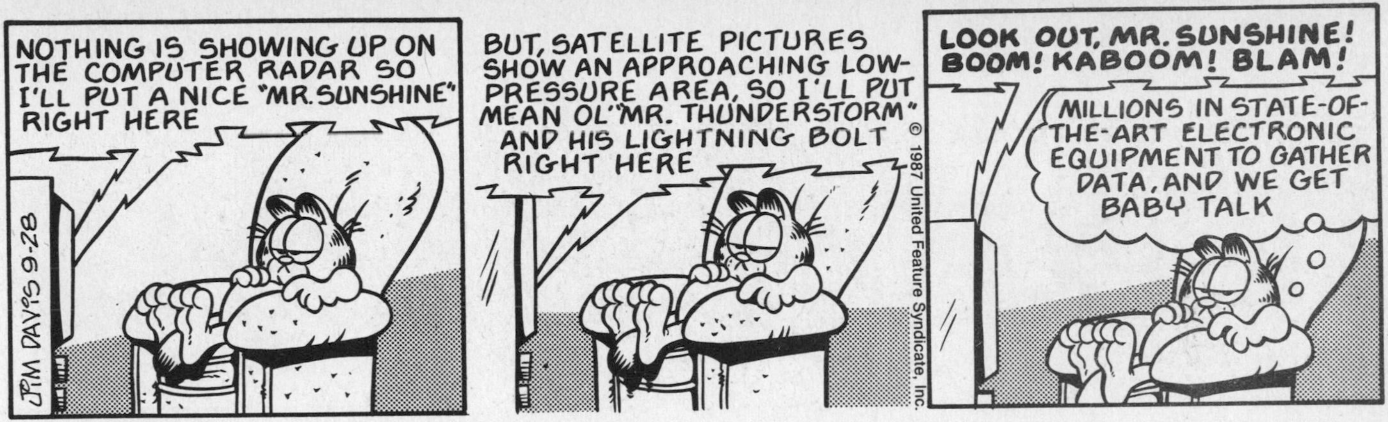
NOTHING IS SHOWING UP ON THE COMPUTER RADAR SO I'LL PUT A NICE "MR. SUNSHINE" RIGHT HERE
JIM DAVIS 9-28
BUT, SATELLITE PICTURES SHOW AN APPROACHING LOW-PRESSURE AREA, SO I'LL PUT MEAN OL' "MR. THUNDERSTORM" AND HIS LIGHTNING BOLT RIGHT HERE
© 1987 United Feature Syndicate, Inc.
LOOK OUT, MR. SUNSHINE! BOOM! KABOOM! BLAM!
MILLIONS IN STATE-OF-THE-ART ELECTRONIC EQUIPMENT TO GATHER DATA, AND WE GET BABY TALK

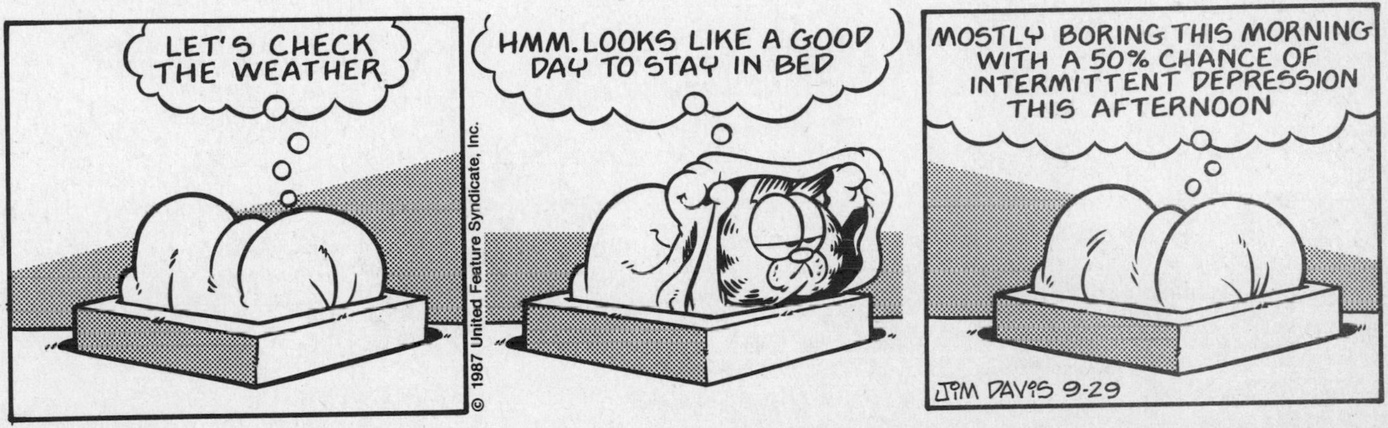
LET'S CHECK THE WEATHER
© 1987 United Feature Syndicate, Inc.
HMM. LOOKS LIKE A GOOD DAY TO STAY IN BED
MOSTLY BORING THIS MORNING WITH A 50% CHANCE OF INTERMITTENT DEPRESSION THIS AFTERNOON
JIM DAVIS 9-29

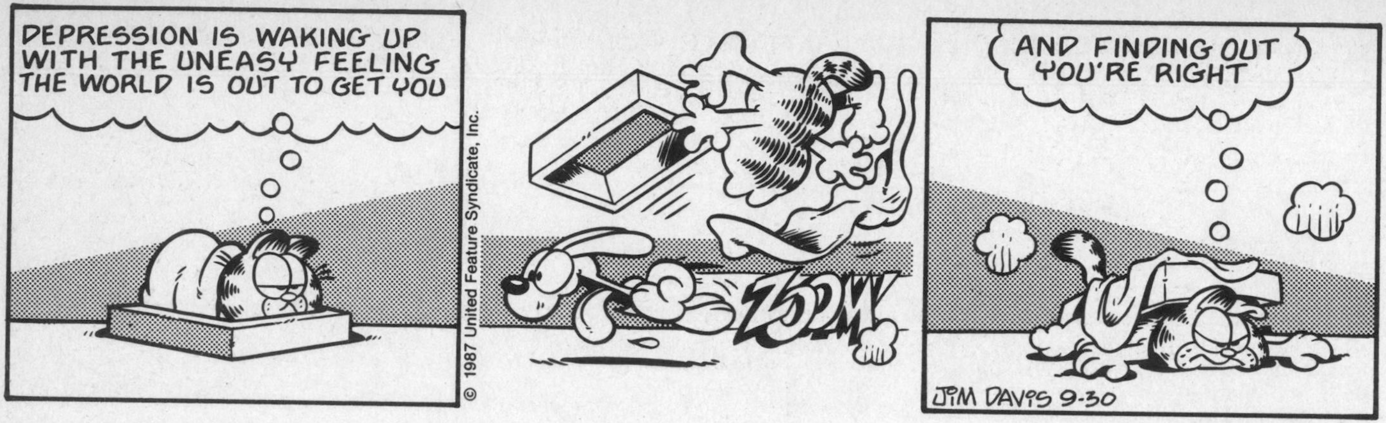
DEPRESSION IS WAKING UP WITH THE UNEASY FEELING THE WORLD IS OUT TO GET YOU
ZOOM
AND FINDING OUT YOU'RE RIGHT
JIM DAVIS 9-30

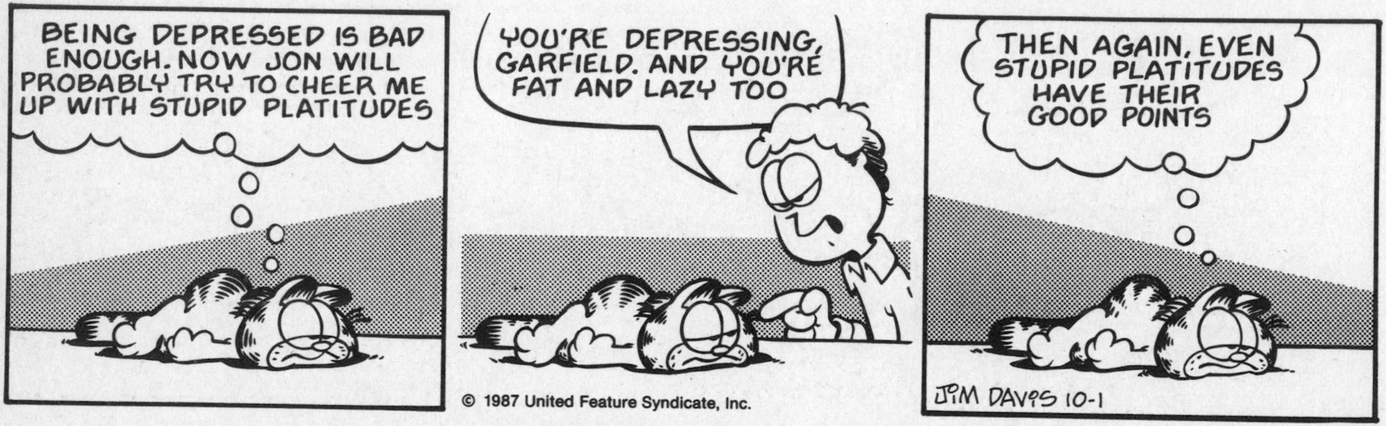
BEING DEPRESSED IS BAD ENOUGH. NOW JON WILL PROBABLY TRY TO CHEER ME UP WITH STUPID PLATITUDES
YOU'RE DEPRESSING, GARFIELD. AND YOU'RE FAT AND LAZY TOO
THEN AGAIN, EVEN STUPID PLATITUDES HAVE THEIR GOOD POINTS
JIM DAVIS 10-1

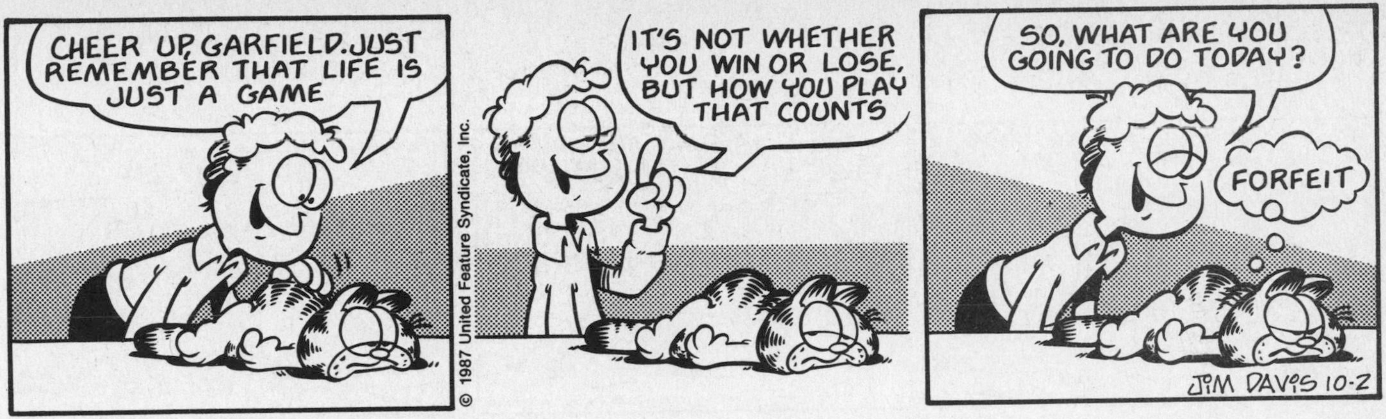
CHEER UP, GARFIELD. JUST REMEMBER THAT LIFE IS JUST A GAME
© 1987 United Feature Syndicate, Inc.
IT'S NOT WHETHER YOU WIN OR LOSE, BUT HOW YOU PLAY THAT COUNTS
SO, WHAT ARE YOU GOING TO DO TODAY?
FORFEIT
JIM DAVIS 10-2

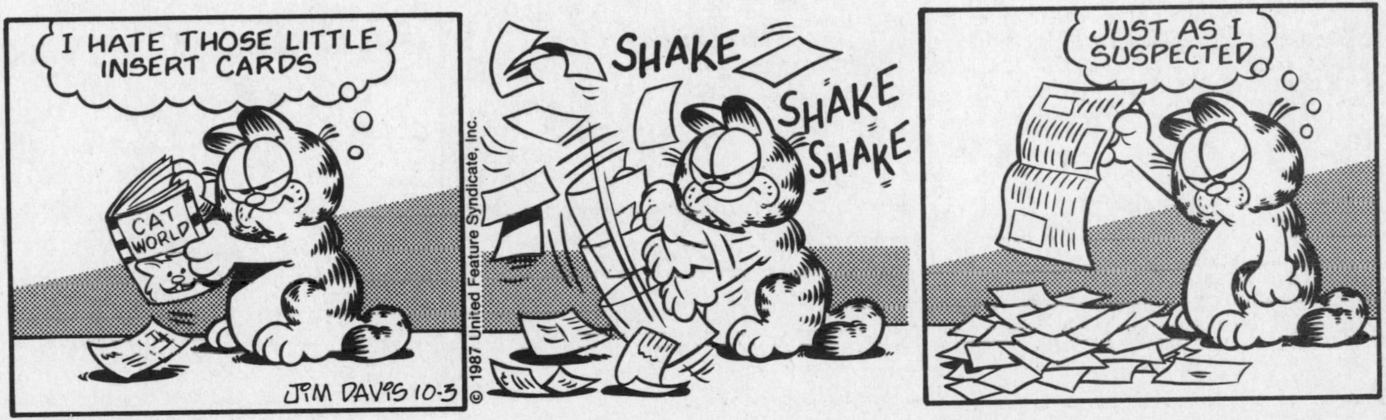
I HATE THOSE LITTLE INSERT CARDS
CAT WORLD
JIM DAVIS 10-3
© 1987 United Feature Syndicate, Inc.
SHAKE
SHAKE
SHAKE
JUST AS I SUSPECTED

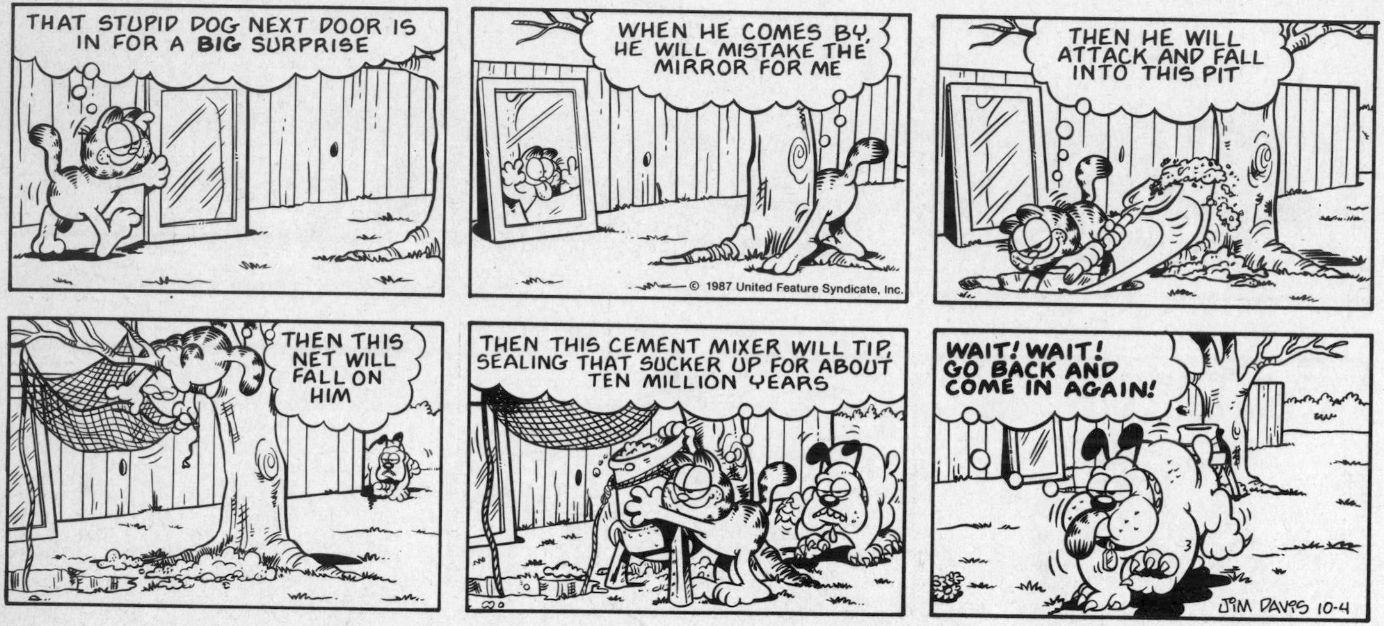
THAT STUPID DOG NEXT DOOR IS IN FOR A **BIG** SURPRISE
WHEN HE COMES BY, HE WILL MISTAKE THE MIRROR FOR ME
© 1987 United Feature Syndicate, Inc.
THEN HE WILL ATTACK AND FALL INTO THIS PIT
THEN THIS NET WILL FALL ON HIM
THEN THIS CEMENT MIXER WILL TIP, SEALING THAT SUCKER UP FOR ABOUT TEN MILLION YEARS
WAIT! WAIT! GO BACK AND COME IN AGAIN!
JIM DAVIS 10-4

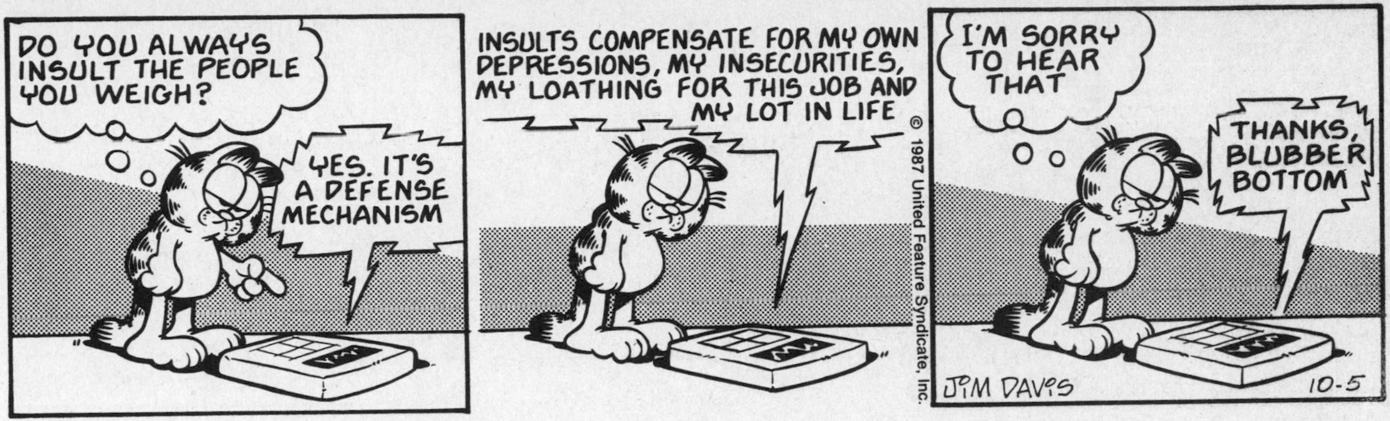
DO YOU ALWAYS INSULT THE PEOPLE YOU WEIGH?
YES. IT'S A DEFENSE MECHANISM
INSULTS COMPENSATE FOR MY OWN DEPRESSIONS, MY INSECURITIES, MY LOATHING FOR THIS JOB AND MY LOT IN LIFE
I'M SORRY TO HEAR THAT
THANKS, BLUBBER BOTTOM
© 1987 United Feature Syndicate, Inc.
JIM DAVIS 10-5

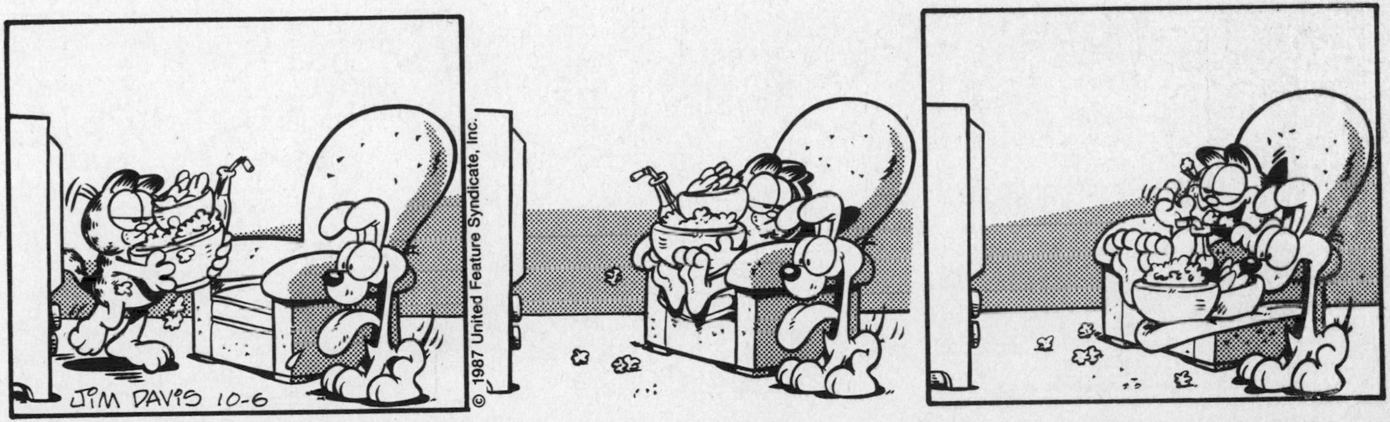
JIM DAVIS 10-6
© 1987 United Feature Syndicate, Inc.

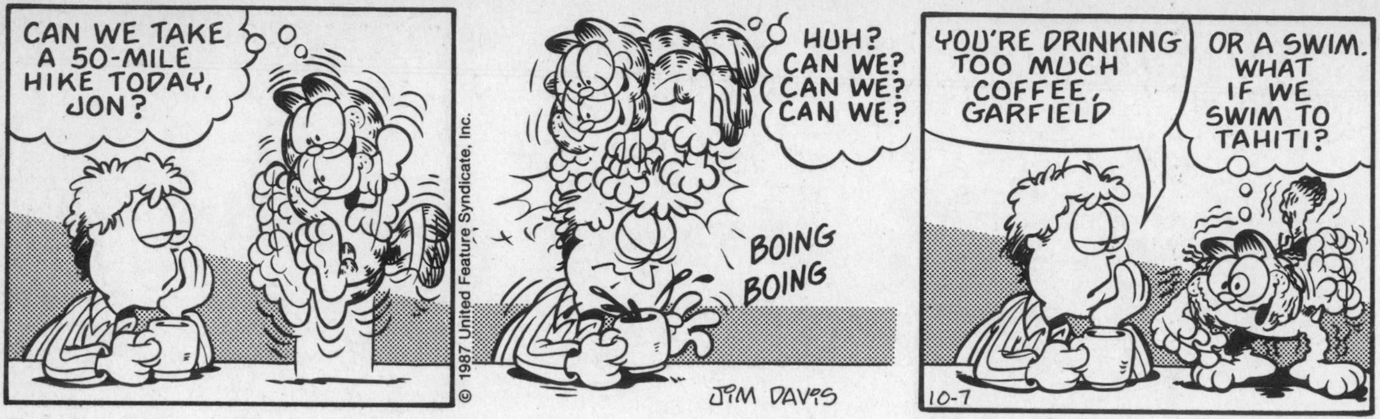
CAN WE TAKE A 50-MILE HIKE TODAY, JON?
© 1987 United Feature Syndicate, Inc.
HUH? CAN WE? CAN WE? CAN WE?
BOING BOING
JIM DAVIS
YOU'RE DRINKING TOO MUCH COFFEE, GARFIELD
OR A SWIM. WHAT IF WE SWIM TO TAHITI?
10-7

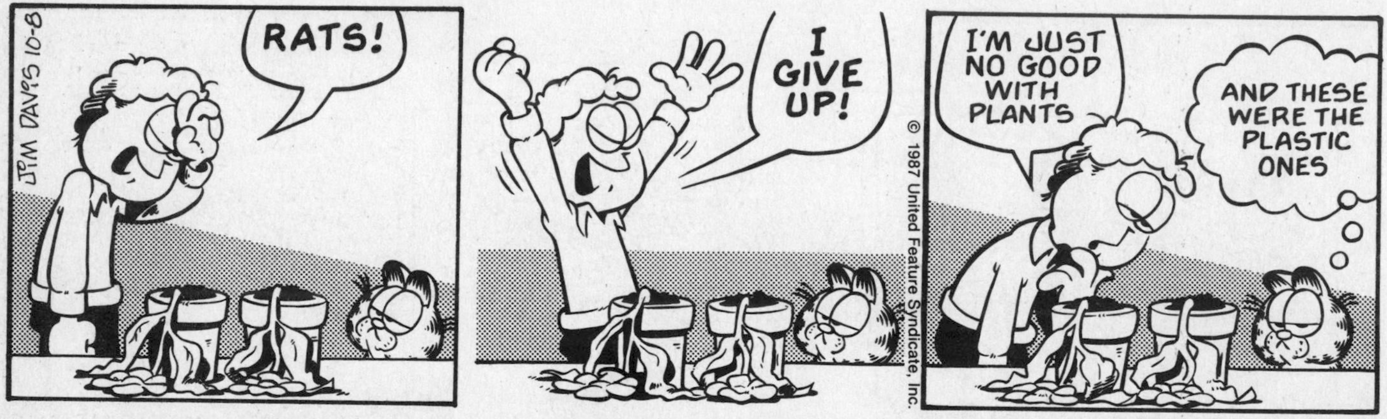
JIM DAVIS 10-8
RATS!
I GIVE UP!
© 1987 United Feature Syndicate, Inc.
I'M JUST NO GOOD WITH PLANTS
AND THESE WERE THE PLASTIC ONES

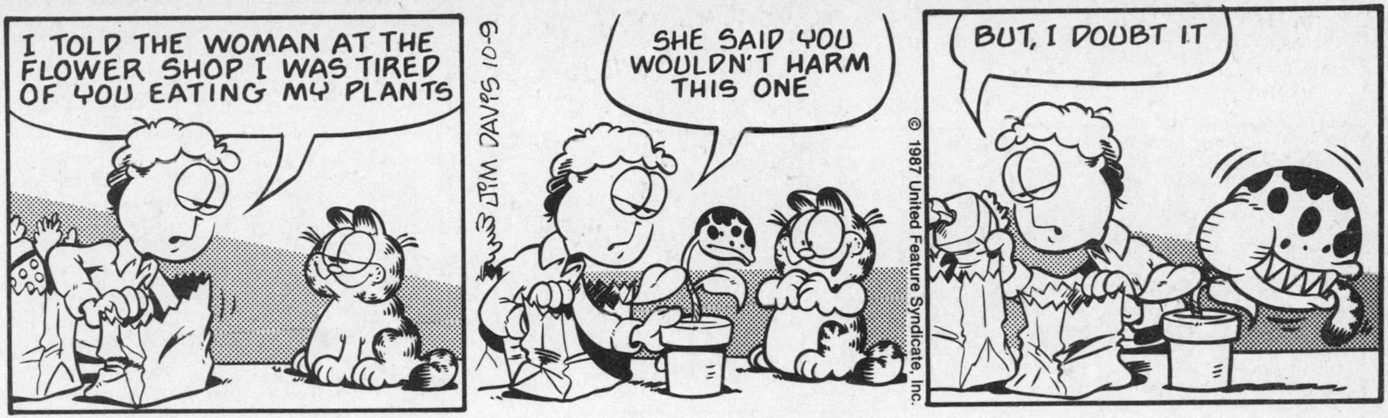
I TOLD THE WOMAN AT THE FLOWER SHOP I WAS TIRED OF YOU EATING MY PLANTS
JIM DAVIS 10-9
SHE SAID YOU WOULDN'T HARM THIS ONE
© 1987 United Feature Syndicate, Inc.
BUT, I DOUBT IT

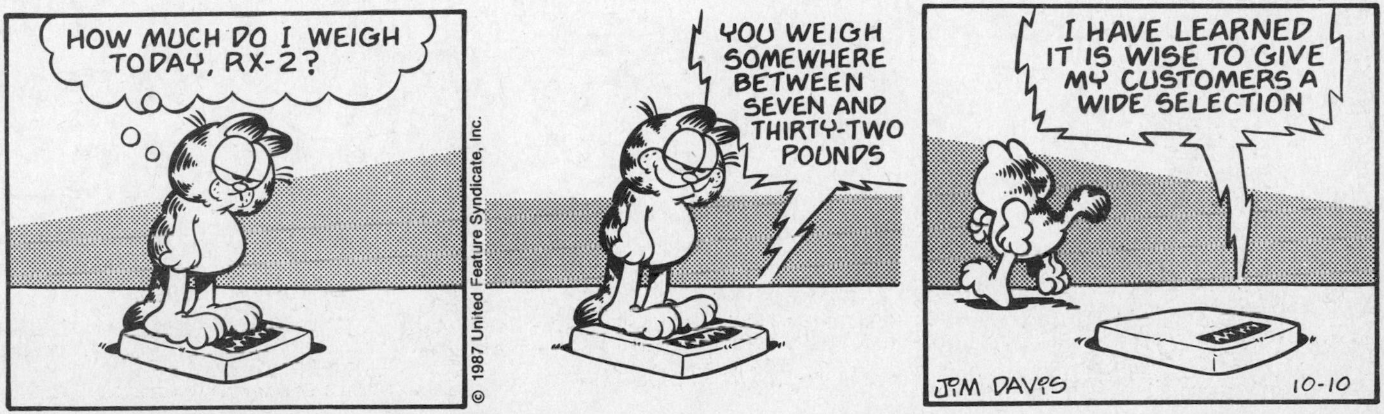
HOW MUCH DO I WEIGH TODAY, RX-2?
© 1987 United Feature Syndicate, Inc.
YOU WEIGH SOMEWHERE BETWEEN SEVEN AND THIRTY-TWO POUNDS
I HAVE LEARNED IT IS WISE TO GIVE MY CUSTOMERS A WIDE SELECTION
JIM DAVIS
10-10

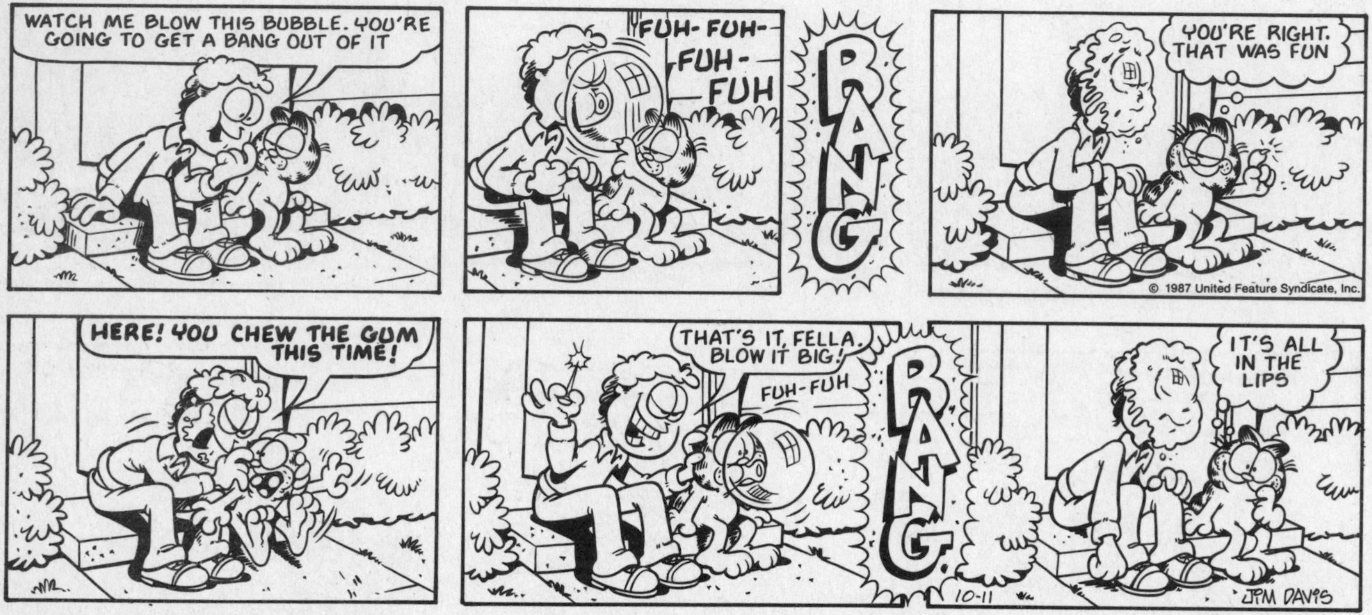

WATCH ME BLOW THIS BUBBLE. YOU'RE GOING TO GET A BANG OUT OF IT
FUH- FUH- FUH- FUH
BANG
YOU'RE RIGHT. THAT WAS FUN
© 1987 United Feature Syndicate, Inc.
HERE! YOU CHEW THE GUM THIS TIME!
THAT'S IT, FELLA. BLOW IT BIG!
FUH-FUH
BANG.
IT'S ALL IN THE LIPS
10-11
JIM DAVIS

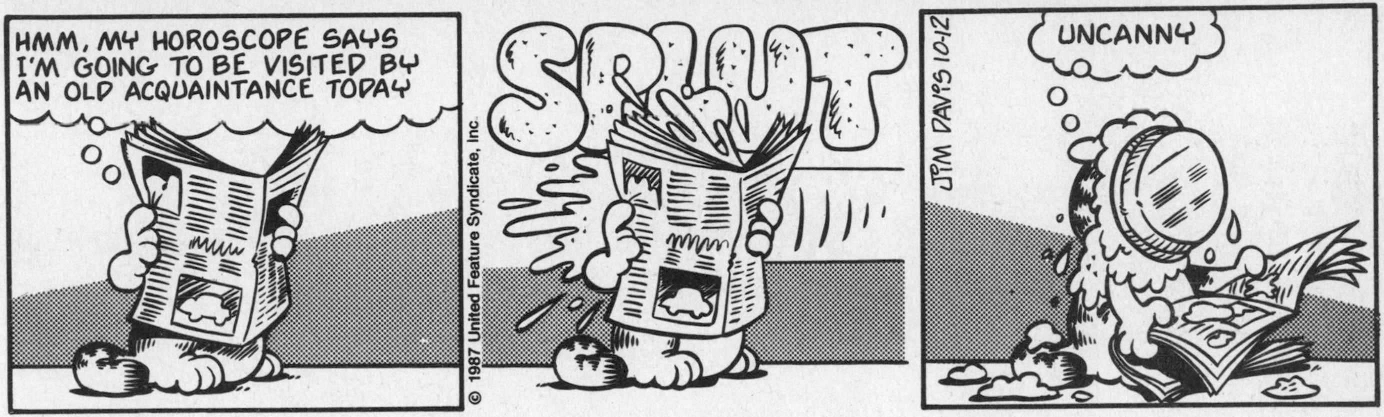
HMM, MY HOROSCOPE SAYS I'M GOING TO BE VISITED BY AN OLD ACQUAINTANCE TODAY
SPLUT
JIM DAVIS 10-12
UNCANNY

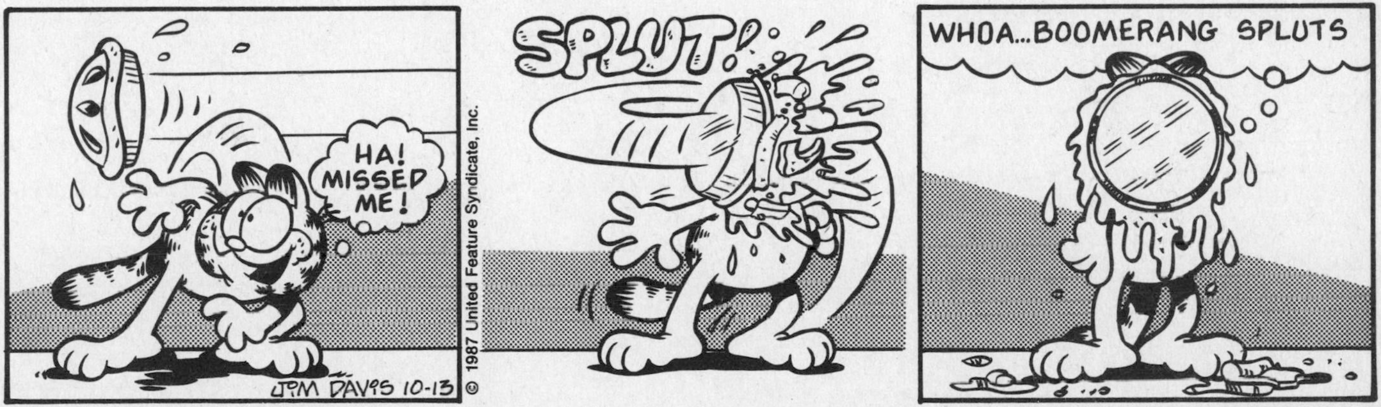
HA! MISSED ME!
JIM DAVIS 10-13
SPLUT!
WHOA...BOOMERANG SPLUTS

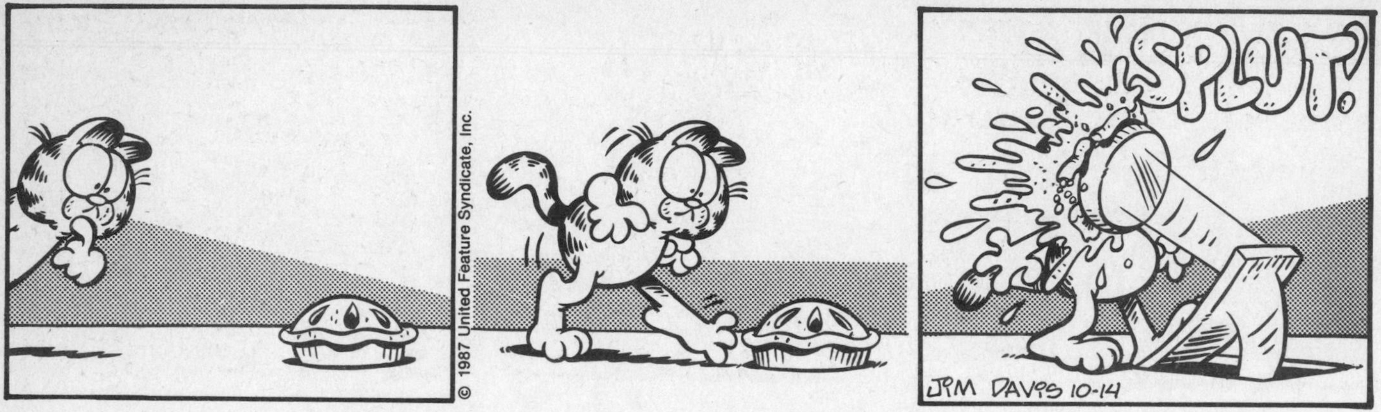
© 1987 United Feature Syndicate, Inc.
SPLUT!
JIM DAVIS 10-14

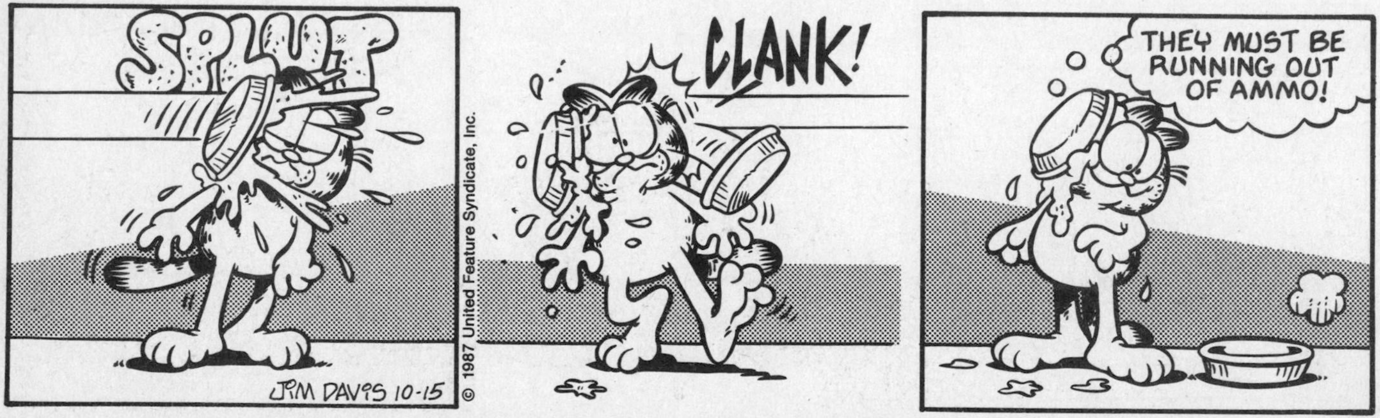
SPLUT
JIM DAVIS 10-15
© 1987 United Feature Syndicate, Inc.
CLANK!
THEY MUST BE RUNNING OUT OF AMMO!

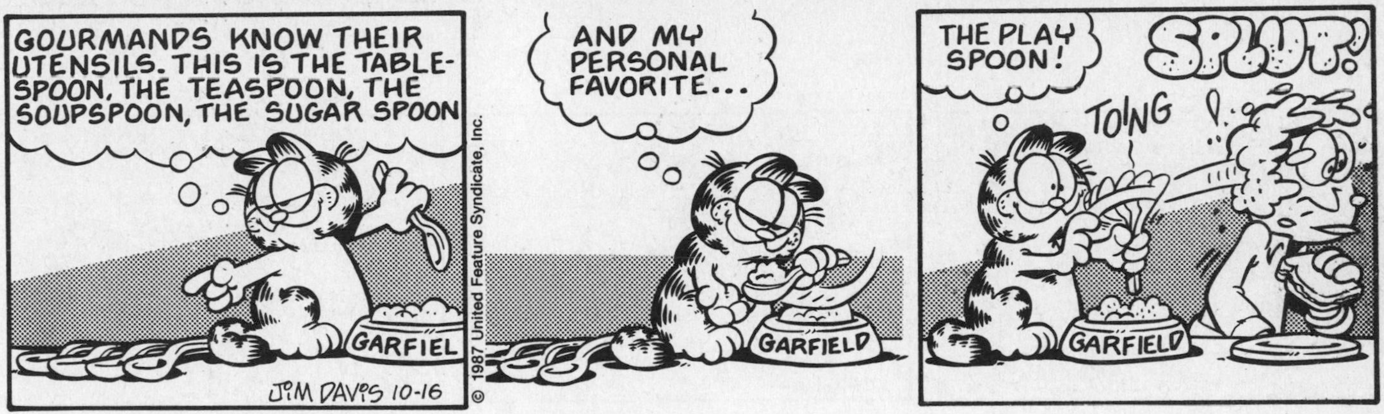
GOURMANDS KNOW THEIR UTENSILS. THIS IS THE TABLESPOON, THE TEASPOON, THE SOUPSPOON, THE SUGAR SPOON
GARFIEL
JIM DAVIS 10-16
© 1987 United Feature Syndicate, Inc.
AND MY PERSONAL FAVORITE...
GARFIELD
THE PLAY SPOON!
SPLUT!
TOING
GARFIELD

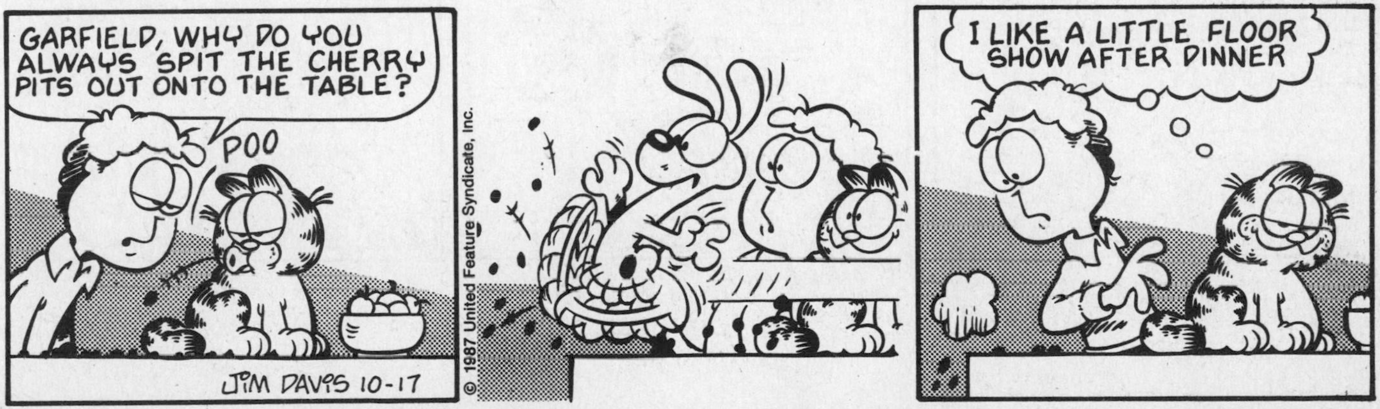
GARFIELD, WHY DO YOU ALWAYS SPIT THE CHERRY PITS OUT ONTO THE TABLE?
POO
JIM DAVIS 10-17
© 1987 United Feature Syndicate, Inc.
I LIKE A LITTLE FLOOR SHOW AFTER DINNER

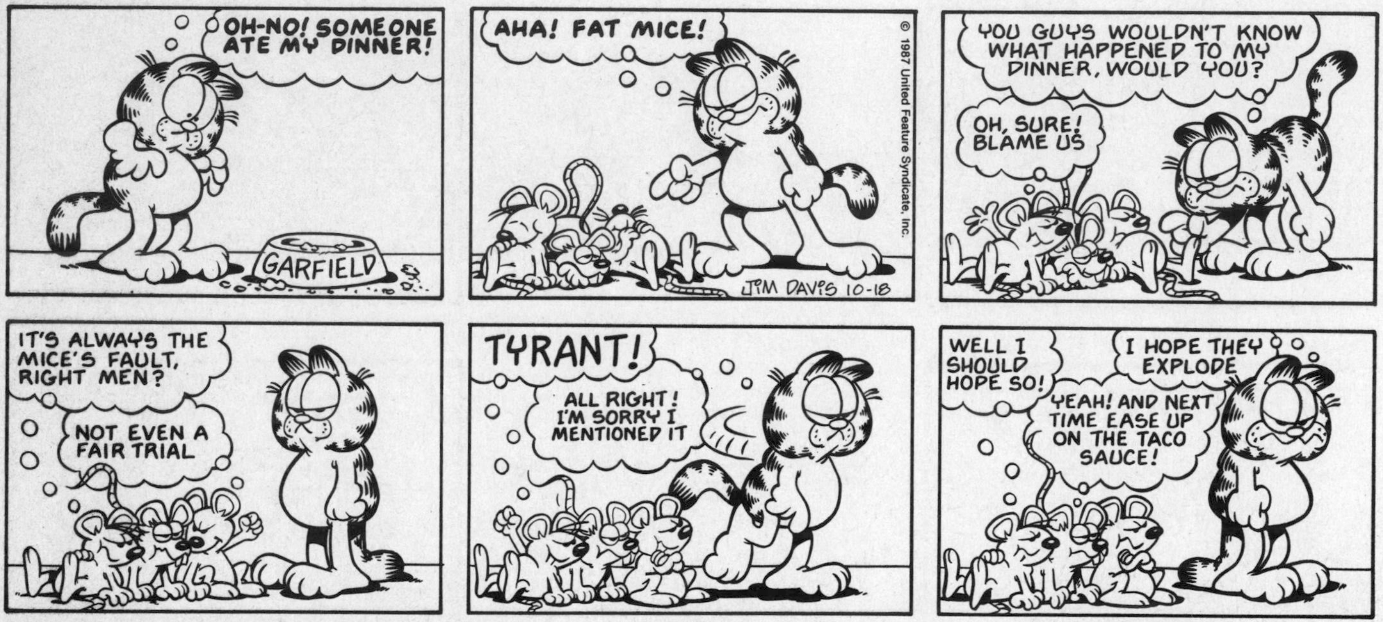

OH-NO! SOMEONE ATE MY DINNER!
GARFIELD
AHA! FAT MICE!
© 1987 United Feature Syndicate, Inc.
JIM DAVIS 10-18
YOU GUYS WOULDN'T KNOW WHAT HAPPENED TO MY DINNER, WOULD YOU?
OH, SURE! BLAME US
IT'S ALWAYS THE MICE'S FAULT, RIGHT MEN?
NOT EVEN A FAIR TRIAL
TYRANT!
ALL RIGHT! I'M SORRY I MENTIONED IT
WELL I SHOULD HOPE SO!
I HOPE THEY EXPLODE
YEAH! AND NEXT TIME EASE UP ON THE TACO SAUCE!

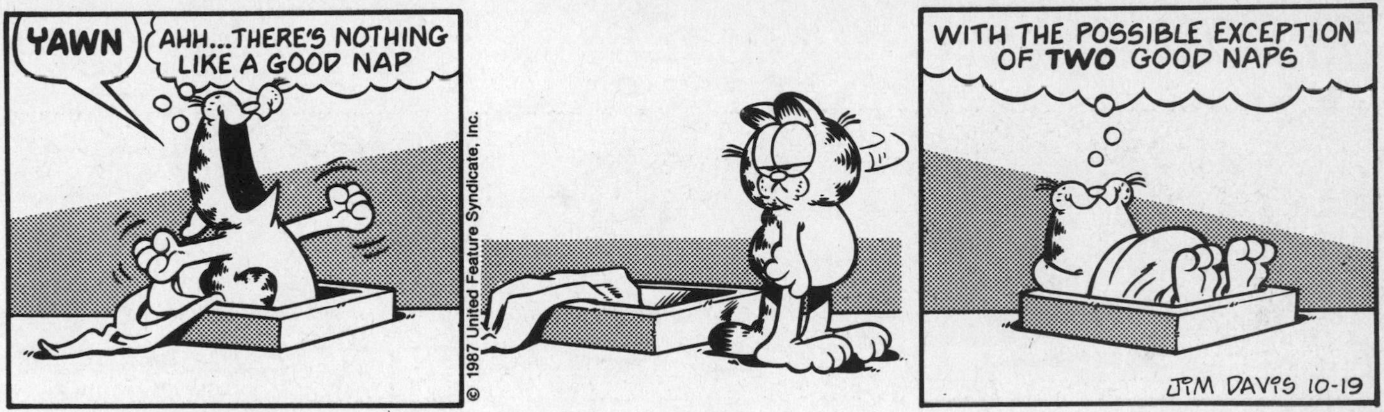
YAWN
AHH...THERE'S NOTHING LIKE A GOOD NAP
WITH THE POSSIBLE EXCEPTION OF **TWO** GOOD NAPS
© 1987 United Feature Syndicate, Inc.
JIM DAVIS 10-19

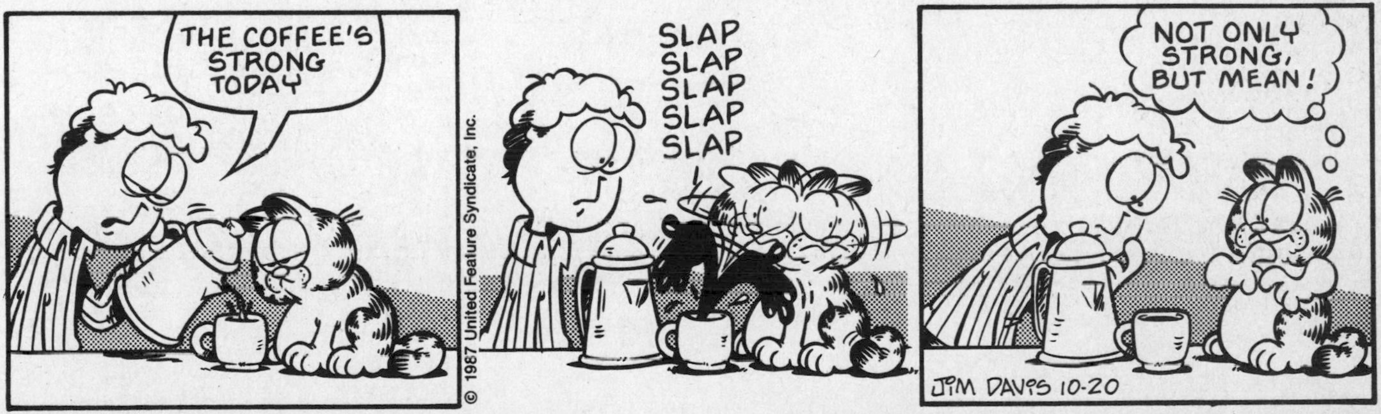
THE COFFEE'S STRONG TODAY
SLAP SLAP SLAP SLAP SLAP
NOT ONLY STRONG, BUT MEAN!
© 1987 United Feature Syndicate, Inc.
JIM DAVIS 10-20

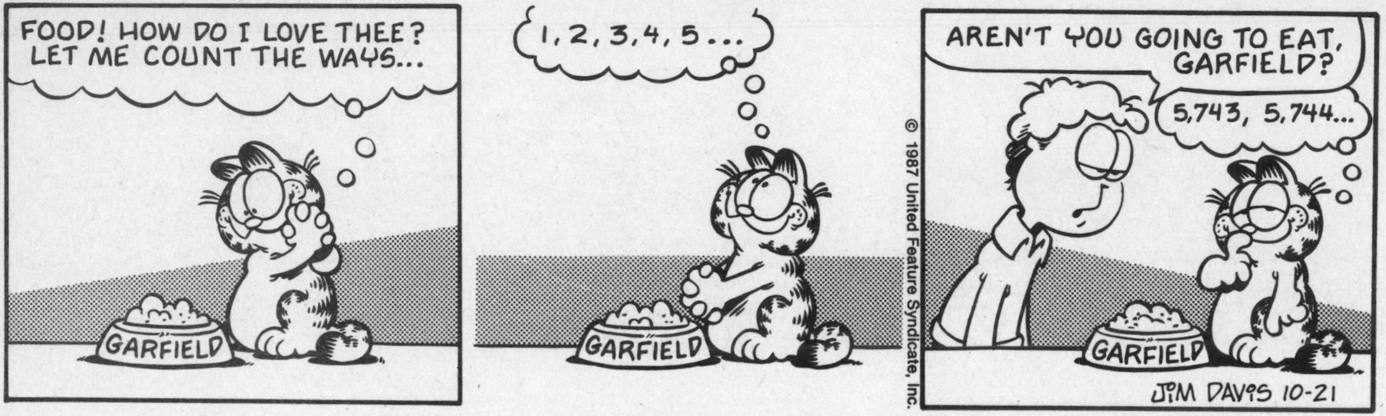
FOOD! HOW DO I LOVE THEE? LET ME COUNT THE WAYS...
GARFIELD
1, 2, 3, 4, 5 . . .
GARFIELD
© 1987 United Feature Syndicate, Inc.
AREN'T YOU GOING TO EAT, GARFIELD?
5,743, 5,744...
GARFIELD
JIM DAVIS 10-21

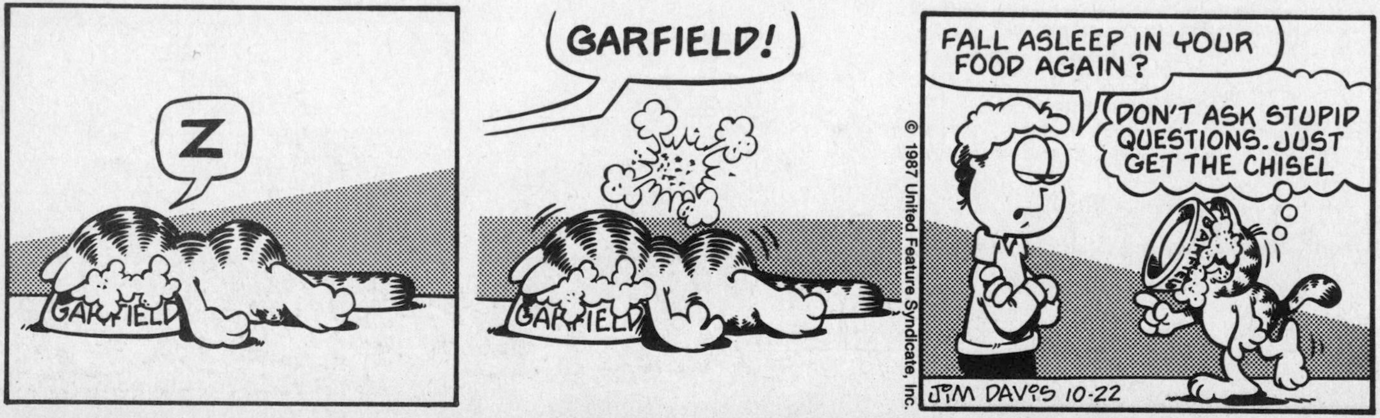
Z
GARFIELD
GARFIELD!
GARFIELD
© 1987 United Feature Syndicate, Inc.
FALL ASLEEP IN YOUR FOOD AGAIN?
DON'T ASK STUPID QUESTIONS. JUST GET THE CHISEL
JIM DAVIS 10-22

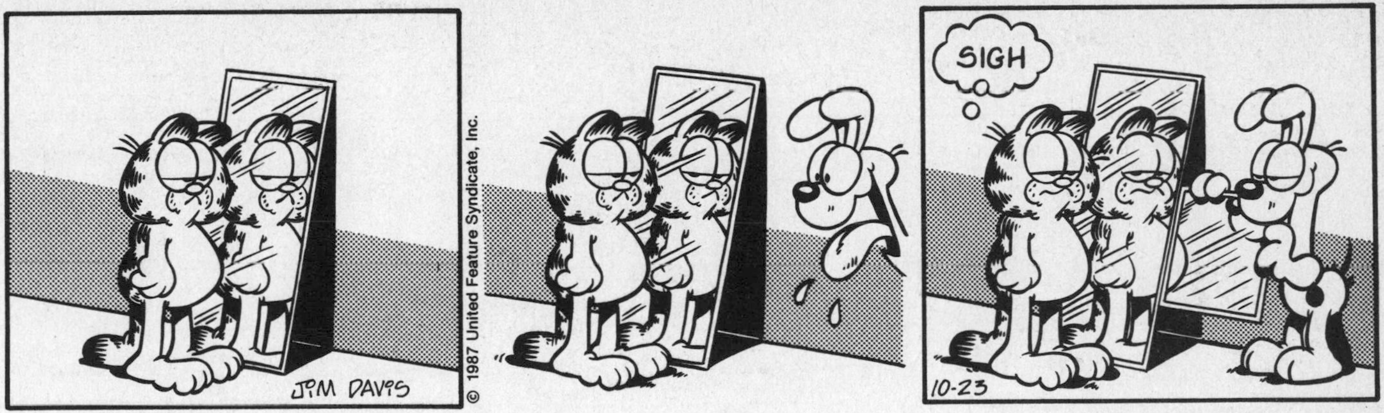
SIGH
JIM DAVIS
© 1987 United Feature Syndicate, Inc.
10-23

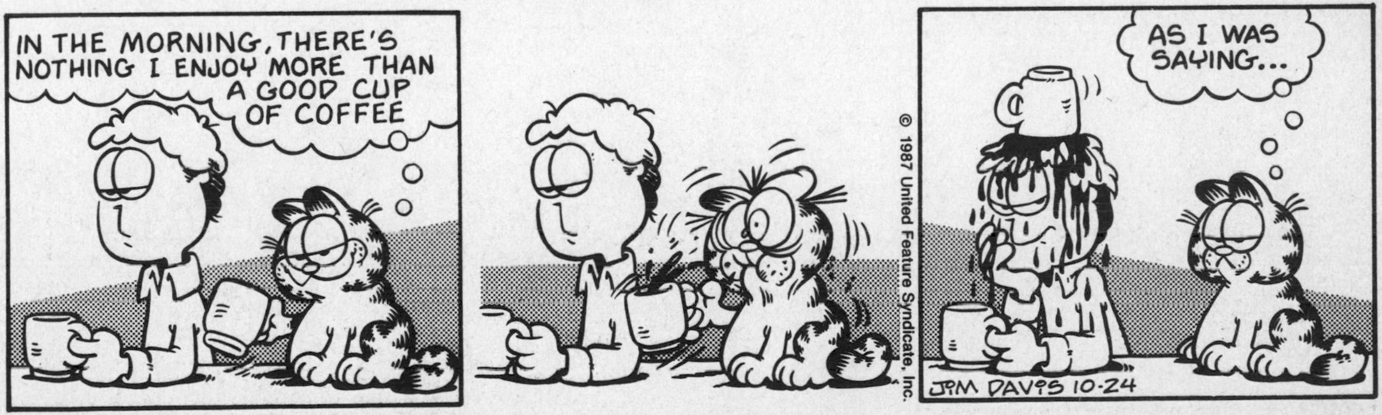
IN THE MORNING, THERE'S NOTHING I ENJOY MORE THAN A GOOD CUP OF COFFEE
AS I WAS SAYING...
© 1987 United Feature Syndicate, Inc.
JIM DAVIS 10-24

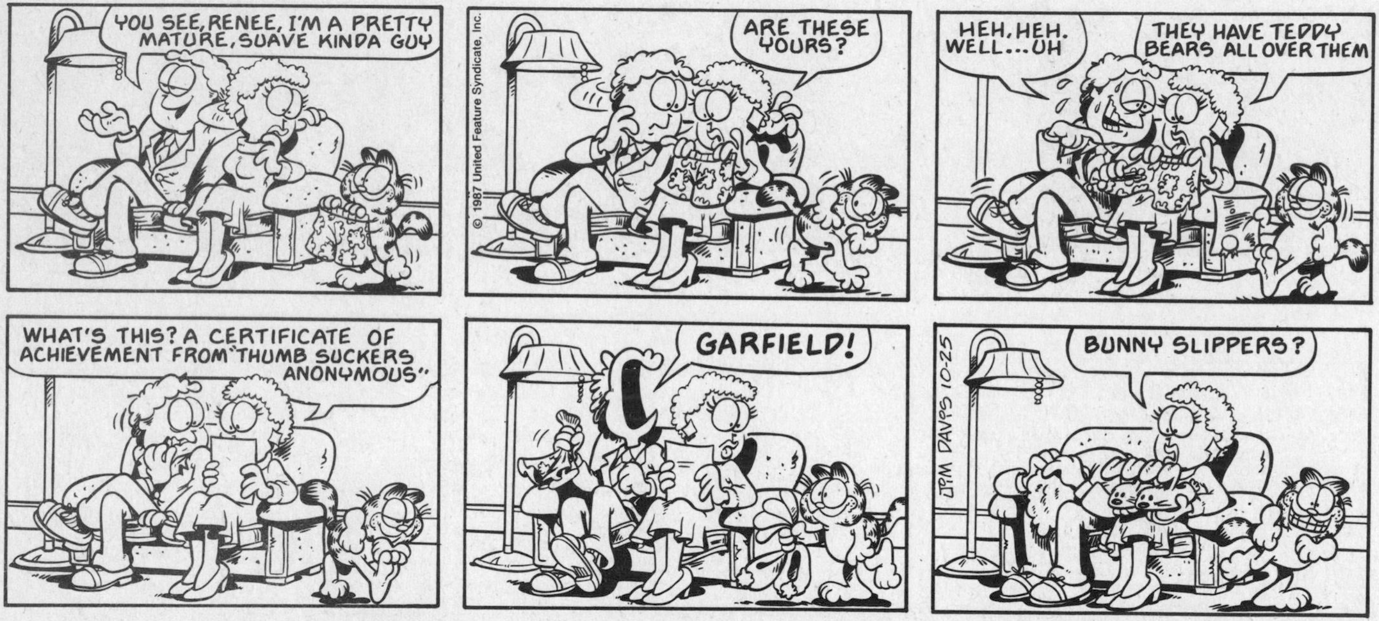
YOU SEE, RENEE, I'M A PRETTY MATURE, SUAVE KINDA GUY
© 1987 United Feature Syndicate, Inc.
ARE THESE YOURS?
HEH, HEH. WELL...UH
THEY HAVE TEDDY BEARS ALL OVER THEM
WHAT'S THIS? A CERTIFICATE OF ACHIEVEMENT FROM "THUMB SUCKERS ANONYMOUS"
GARFIELD!
JPM DAVPS 10-25
BUNNY SLIPPERS?

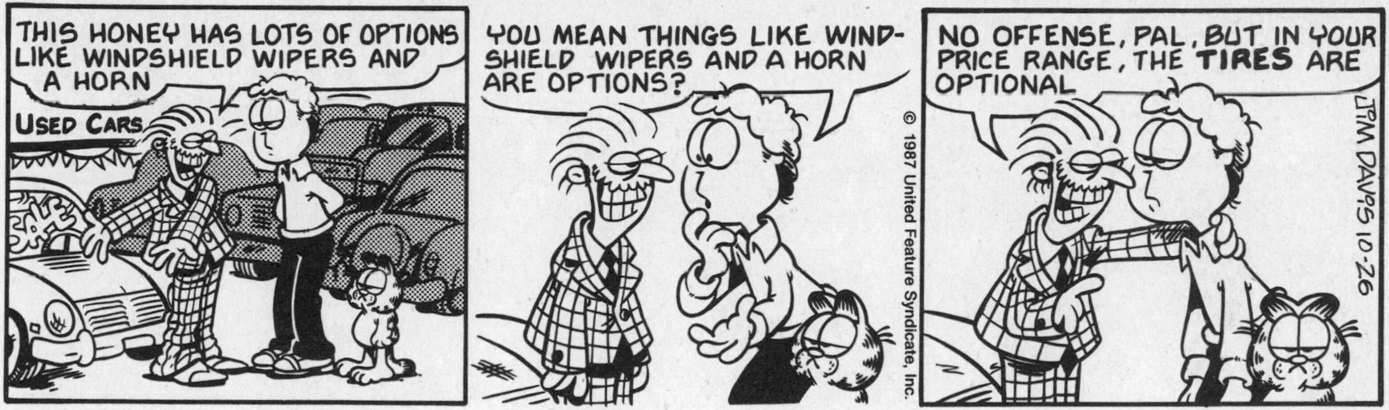
THIS HONEY HAS LOTS OF OPTIONS LIKE WINDSHIELD WIPERS AND A HORN
USED CARS
YOU MEAN THINGS LIKE WIND-SHIELD WIPERS AND A HORN ARE OPTIONS?
NO OFFENSE, PAL, BUT IN YOUR PRICE RANGE, THE **TIRES** ARE OPTIONAL
JIM DAVIS 10-26
© 1987 United Feature Syndicate, Inc.

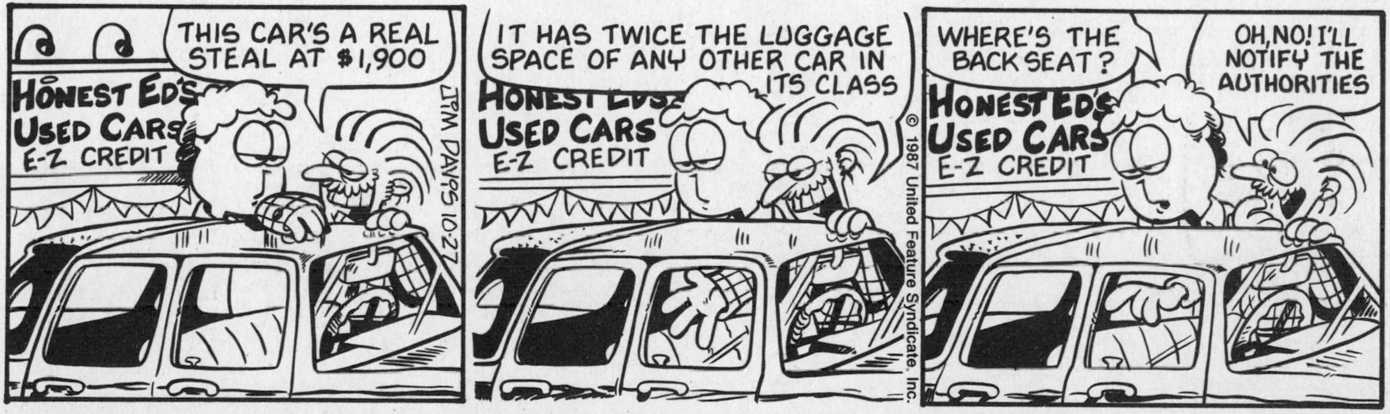
HONEST ED'S USED CARS E-Z CREDIT
THIS CAR'S A REAL STEAL AT $1,900
JIM DAVIS 10-27
IT HAS TWICE THE LUGGAGE SPACE OF ANY OTHER CAR IN ITS CLASS
WHERE'S THE BACK SEAT?
OH, NO! I'LL NOTIFY THE AUTHORITIES
© 1987 United Feature Syndicate, Inc.

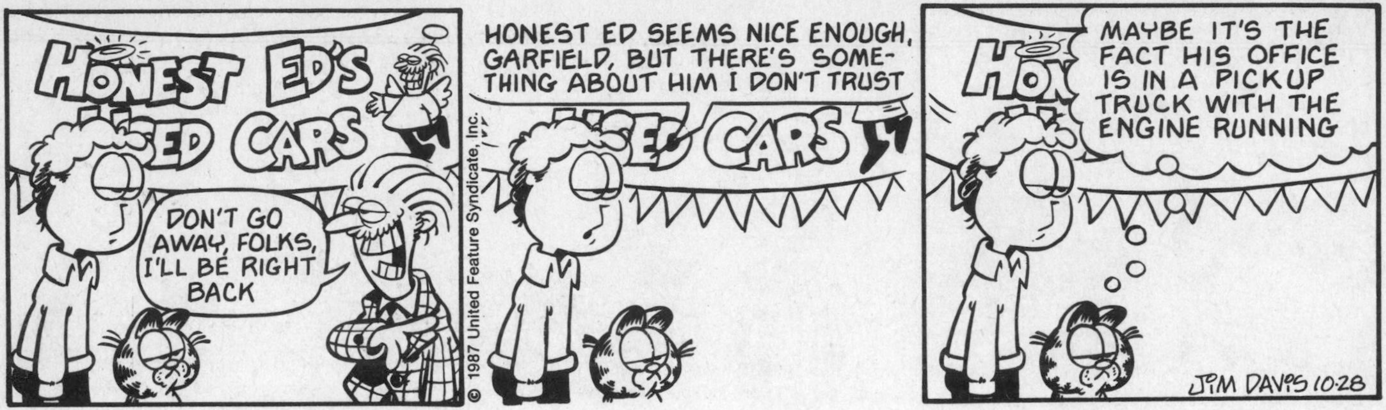
HONEST ED'S USED CARS
DON'T GO AWAY, FOLKS, I'LL BE RIGHT BACK
© 1987 United Feature Syndicate, Inc.
HONEST ED SEEMS NICE ENOUGH, GARFIELD, BUT THERE'S SOMETHING ABOUT HIM I DON'T TRUST
MAYBE IT'S THE FACT HIS OFFICE IS IN A PICKUP TRUCK WITH THE ENGINE RUNNING
JIM DAVIS 10-28

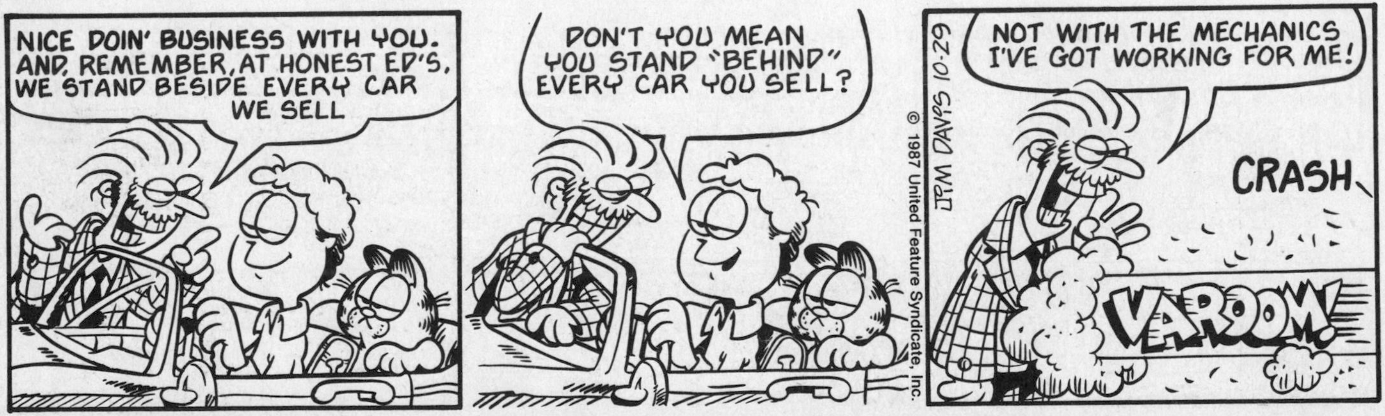
NICE DOIN' BUSINESS WITH YOU. AND, REMEMBER, AT HONEST ED'S, WE STAND BESIDE EVERY CAR WE SELL
DON'T YOU MEAN YOU STAND "BEHIND" EVERY CAR YOU SELL?
© 1987 United Feature Syndicate, Inc.
JIM DAVIS 10-29
NOT WITH THE MECHANICS I'VE GOT WORKING FOR ME!
CRASH
VAROOM!

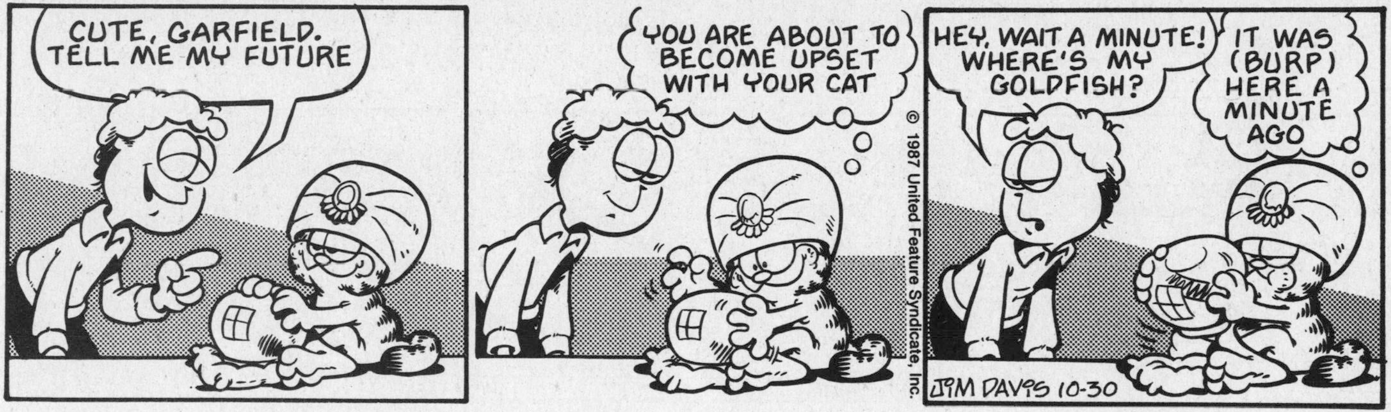
CUTE, GARFIELD. TELL ME MY FUTURE
YOU ARE ABOUT TO BECOME UPSET WITH YOUR CAT
HEY, WAIT A MINUTE! WHERE'S MY GOLDFISH?
IT WAS (BURP) HERE A MINUTE AGO
© 1987 United Feature Syndicate, Inc.
JIM DAVIS 10-30

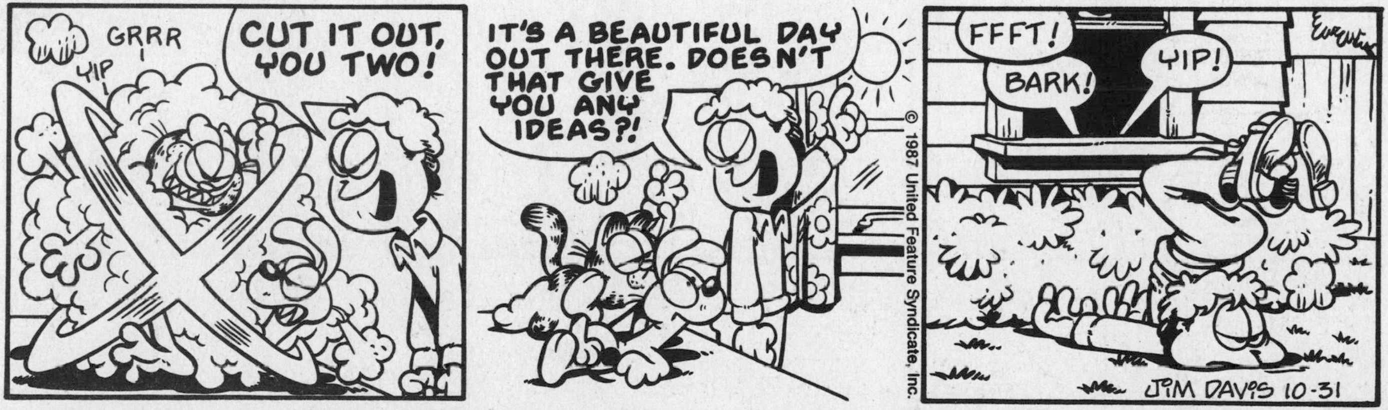
GRRR
YIP
CUT IT OUT, YOU TWO!
IT'S A BEAUTIFUL DAY OUT THERE. DOESN'T THAT GIVE YOU ANY IDEAS?!
FFFT!
BARK!
YIP!
© 1987 United Feature Syndicate, Inc.
JIM DAVIS 10-31

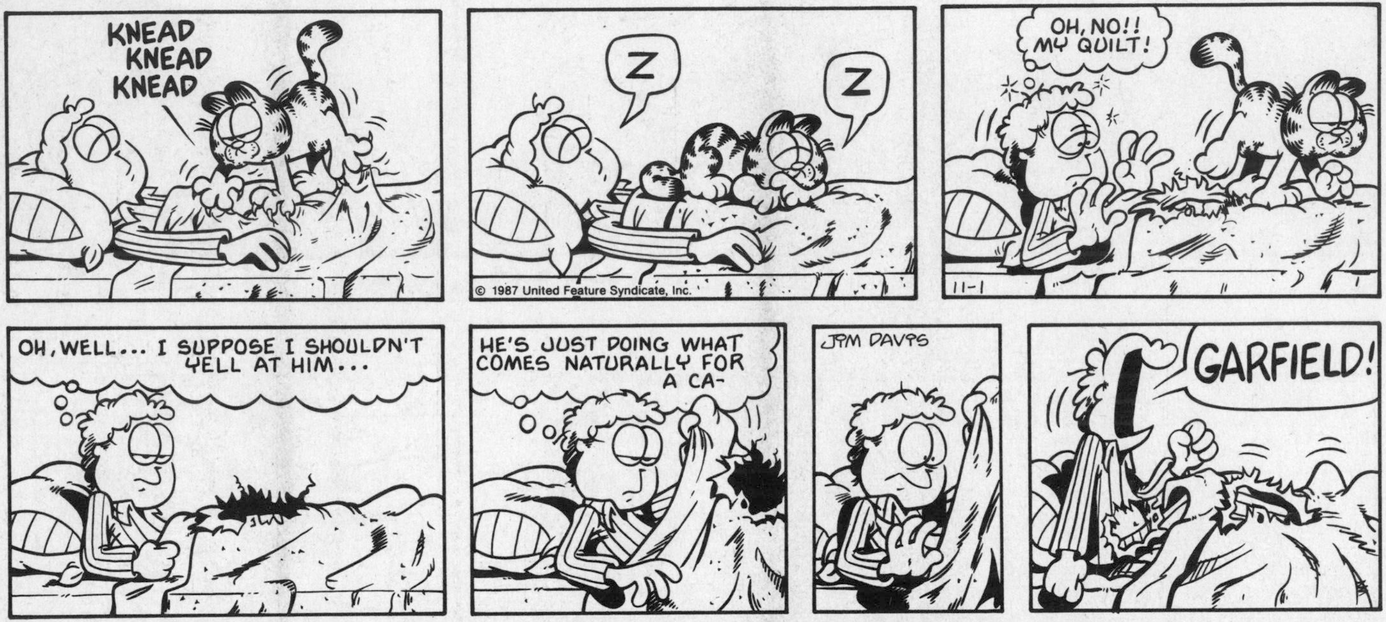
KNEAD
KNEAD
KNEAD
Z
Z
© 1987 United Feature Syndicate, Inc.
OH, NO!! MY QUILT!
11-1
OH, WELL... I SUPPOSE I SHOULDN'T YELL AT HIM...
HE'S JUST DOING WHAT COMES NATURALLY FOR A CA-
JIM DAVIS
GARFIELD!

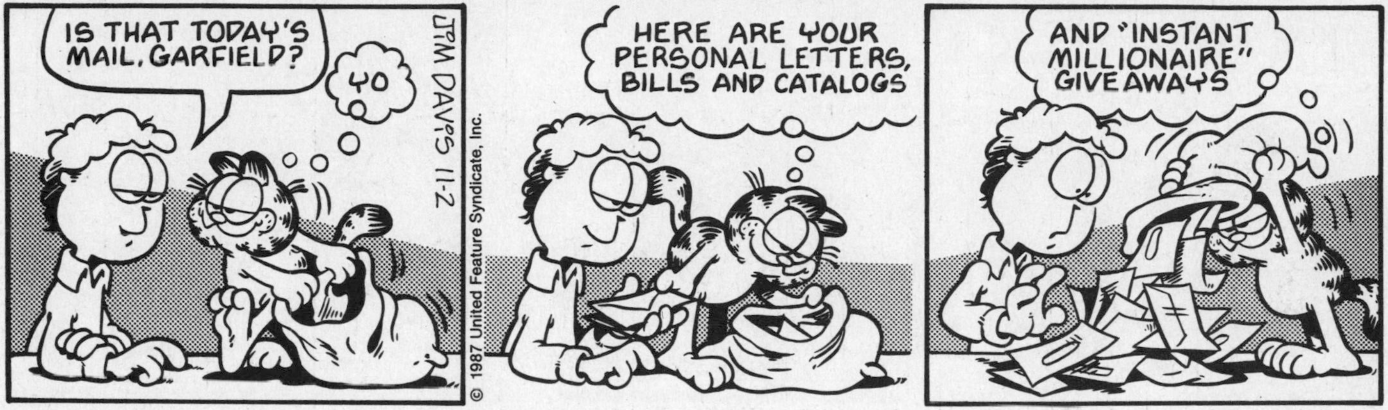
IS THAT TODAY'S MAIL, GARFIELD?
YO
JIM DAVIS 11-2
© 1987 United Feature Syndicate, Inc.
HERE ARE YOUR PERSONAL LETTERS, BILLS AND CATALOGS
AND "INSTANT MILLIONAIRE" GIVEAWAYS

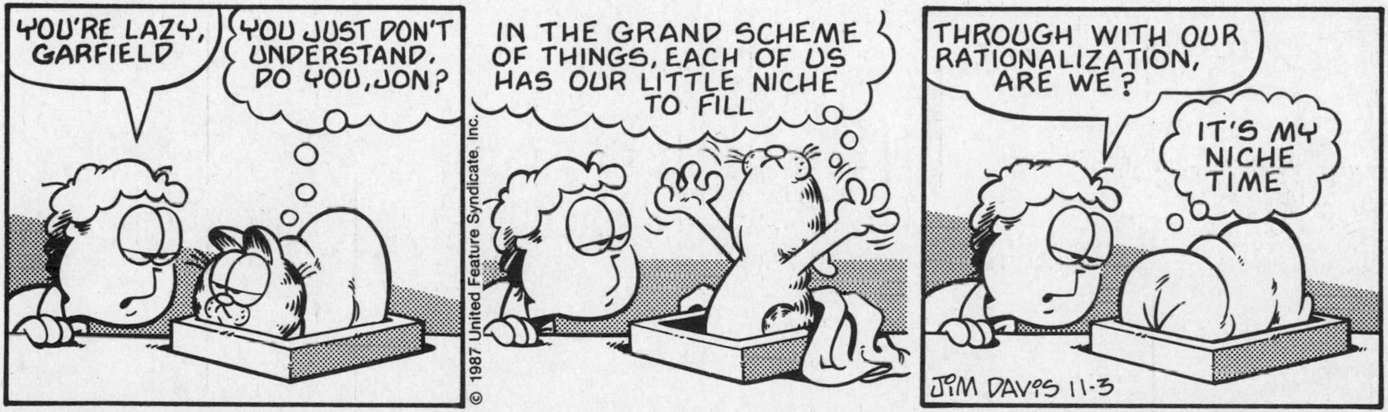
YOU'RE LAZY, GARFIELD
YOU JUST DON'T UNDERSTAND, DO YOU, JON?
© 1987 United Feature Syndicate, Inc.
IN THE GRAND SCHEME OF THINGS, EACH OF US HAS OUR LITTLE NICHE TO FILL
THROUGH WITH OUR RATIONALIZATION, ARE WE?
IT'S MY NICHE TIME
JIM DAVIS 11-3

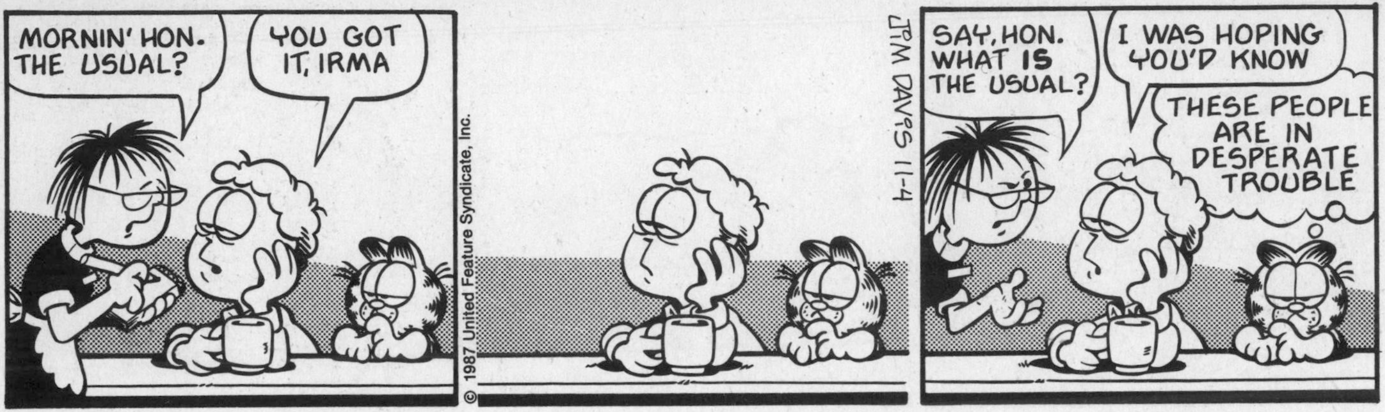
MORNIN' HON. THE USUAL?
YOU GOT IT, IRMA
JIM DAVIS 11-4
SAY, HON. WHAT **IS** THE USUAL?
I WAS HOPING YOU'D KNOW
THESE PEOPLE ARE IN DESPERATE TROUBLE

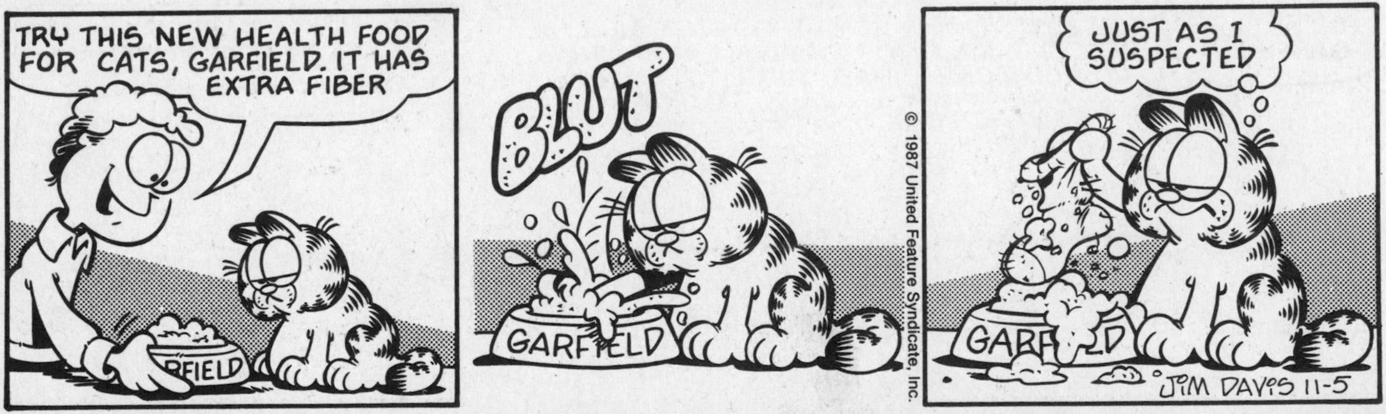
TRY THIS NEW HEALTH FOOD FOR CATS, GARFIELD. IT HAS EXTRA FIBER
RFIELD
BLUT
GARFIELD
JUST AS I SUSPECTED
GARF LD
JIM DAVIS 11-5

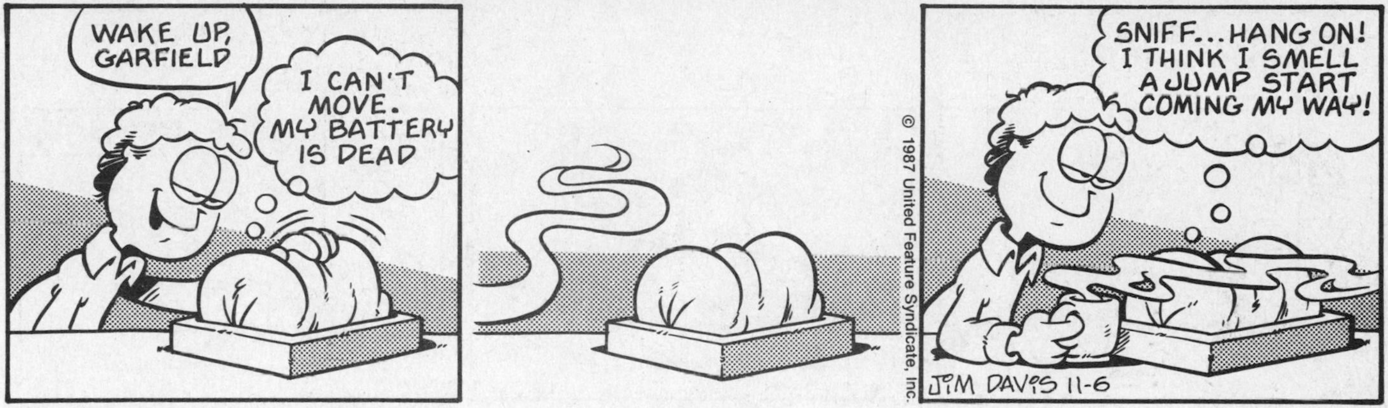
WAKE UP, GARFIELD
I CAN'T MOVE. MY BATTERY IS DEAD
SNIFF...HANG ON! I THINK I SMELL A JUMP START COMING MY WAY!
JIM DAVIS 11-6
© 1987 United Feature Syndicate, Inc.

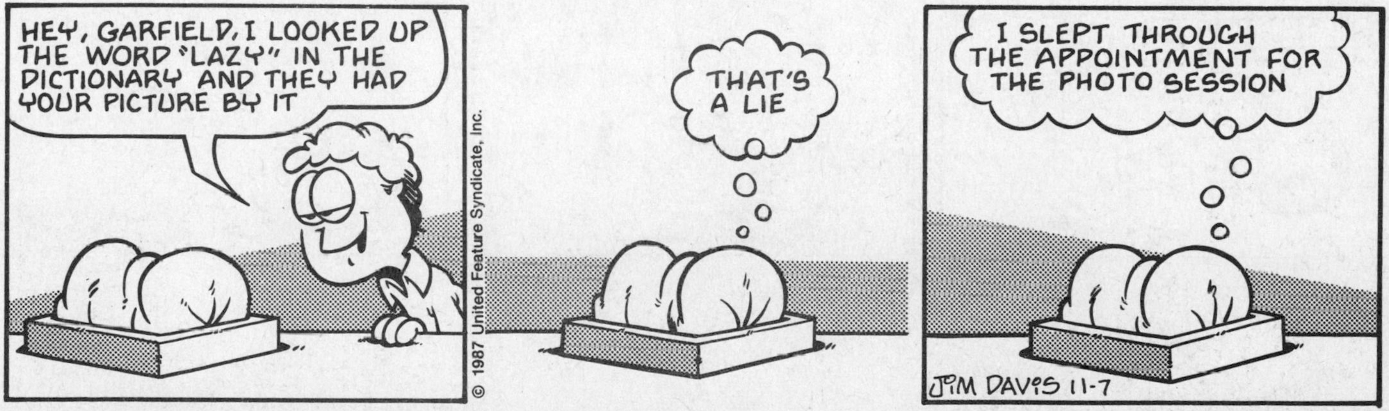
HEY, GARFIELD, I LOOKED UP THE WORD "LAZY" IN THE DICTIONARY AND THEY HAD YOUR PICTURE BY IT
THAT'S A LIE
I SLEPT THROUGH THE APPOINTMENT FOR THE PHOTO SESSION
JIM DAVIS 11-7
© 1987 United Feature Syndicate, Inc.

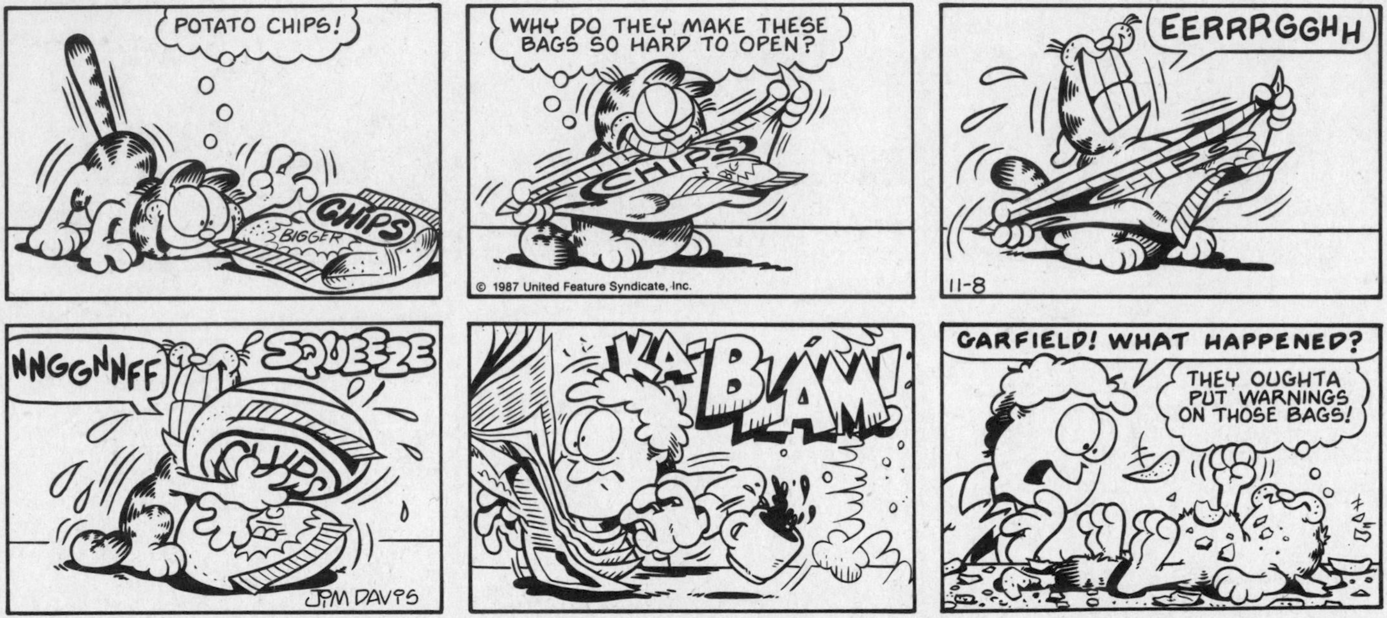

POTATO CHIPS!
CHIPS
BIGGER
WHY DO THEY MAKE THESE BAGS SO HARD TO OPEN?
CHIPS
© 1987 United Feature Syndicate, Inc.
EERRRGGHH
11-8
NNGGNNFF
SQUEEZE
JIM DAVIS
KA-BLAM!
GARFIELD! WHAT HAPPENED?
THEY OUGHTA PUT WARNINGS ON THOSE BAGS!

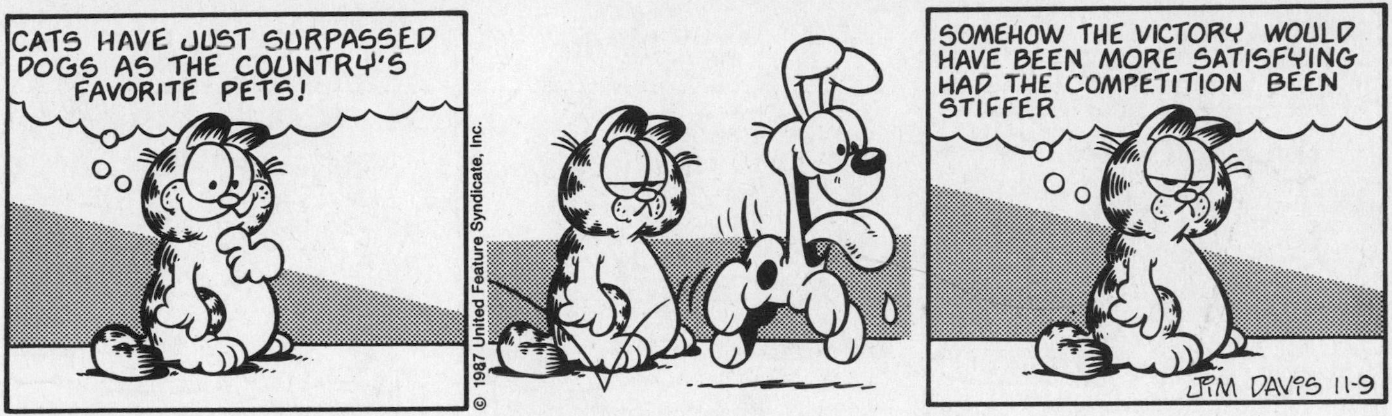
CATS HAVE JUST SURPASSED DOGS AS THE COUNTRY'S FAVORITE PETS!
© 1987 United Feature Syndicate, Inc.
SOMEHOW THE VICTORY WOULD HAVE BEEN MORE SATISFYING HAD THE COMPETITION BEEN STIFFER
JIM DAVIS 11-9

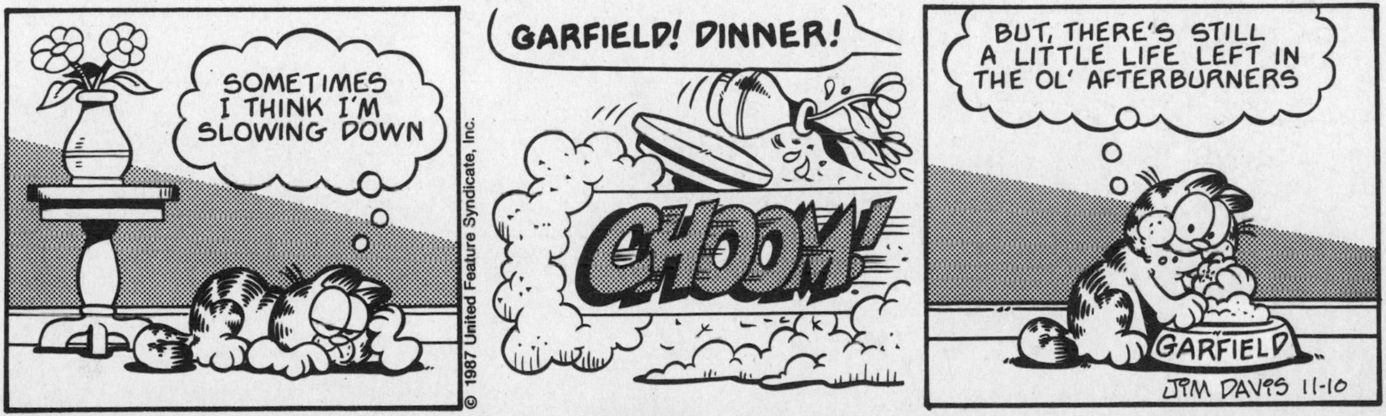
SOMETIMES I THINK I'M SLOWING DOWN
© 1987 United Feature Syndicate, Inc.
GARFIELD! DINNER!
CHOOM!
BUT, THERE'S STILL A LITTLE LIFE LEFT IN THE OL' AFTERBURNERS
GARFIELD
JIM DAVIS 11-10

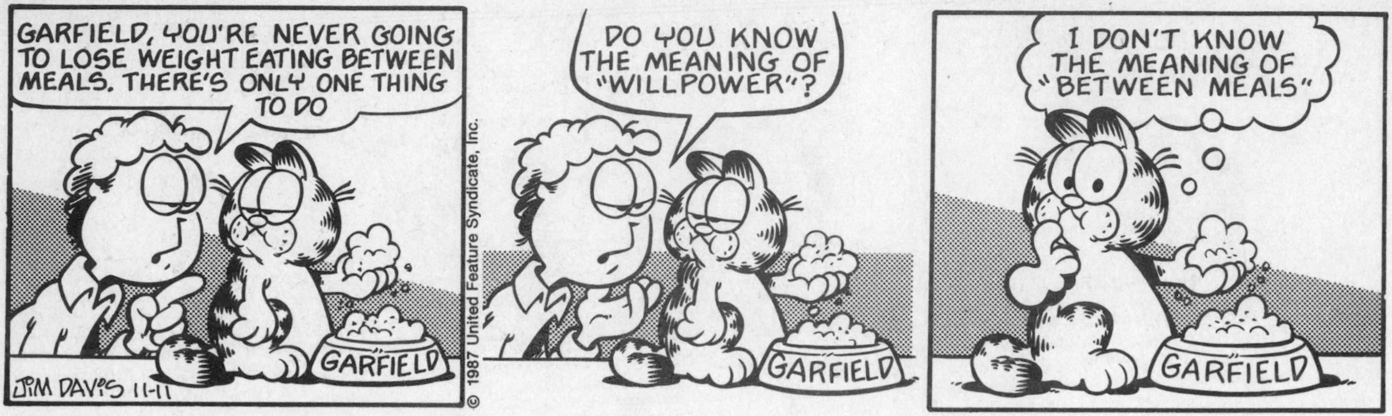
GARFIELD, YOU'RE NEVER GOING TO LOSE WEIGHT EATING BETWEEN MEALS. THERE'S ONLY ONE THING TO DO
GARFIELD
JIM DAVIS 11-11
DO YOU KNOW THE MEANING OF "WILLPOWER"?
GARFIELD
I DON'T KNOW THE MEANING OF "BETWEEN MEALS"
GARFIELD

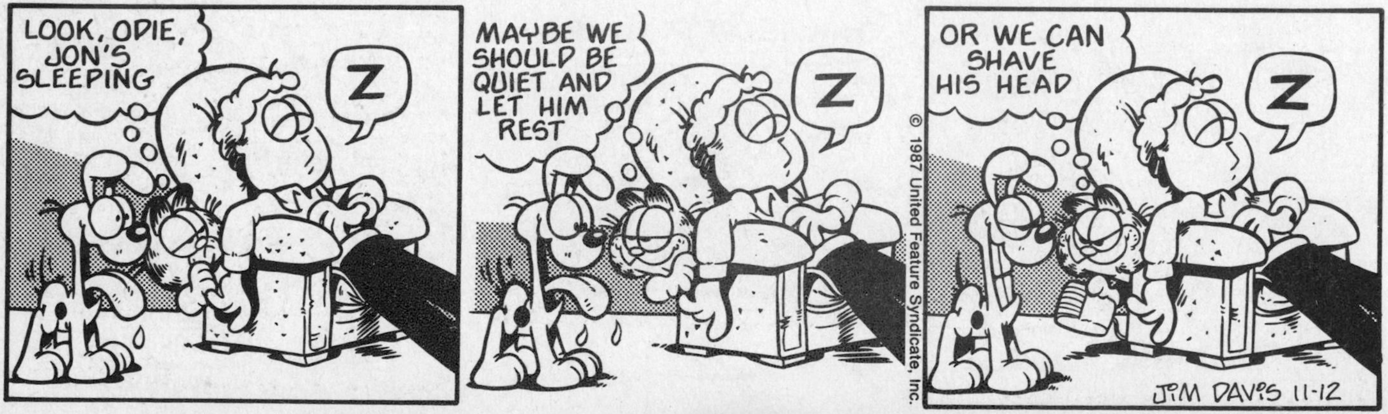
LOOK, ODIE, JON'S SLEEPING
Z
MAYBE WE SHOULD BE QUIET AND LET HIM REST
Z
OR WE CAN SHAVE HIS HEAD
Z
JIM DAVIS 11-12

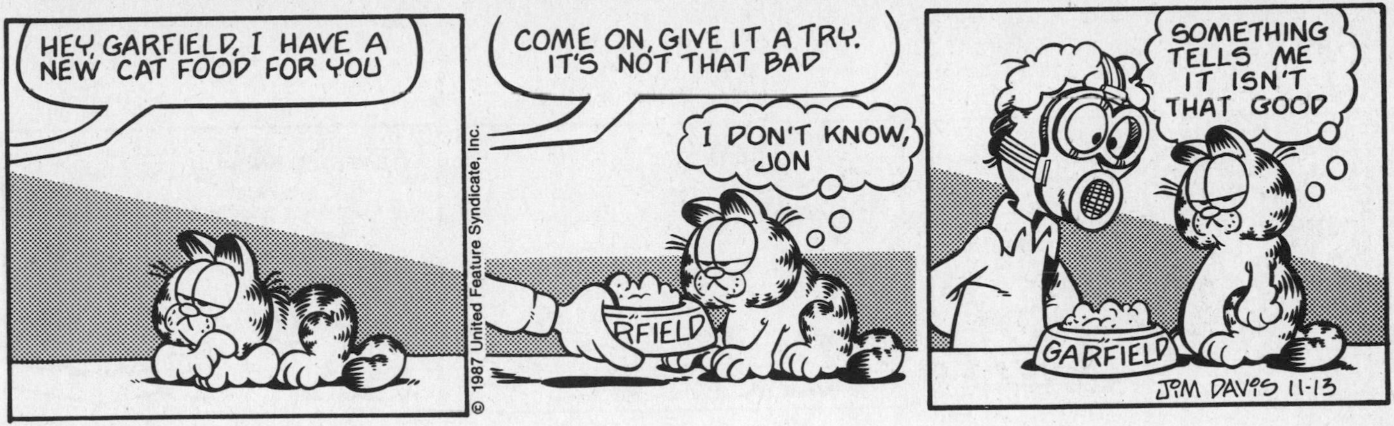
HEY, GARFIELD, I HAVE A NEW CAT FOOD FOR YOU
COME ON, GIVE IT A TRY. IT'S NOT THAT BAD
I DON'T KNOW, JON
RFIELD
SOMETHING TELLS ME IT ISN'T THAT GOOD
GARFIELD
JIM DAVIS 11-13
© 1987 United Feature Syndicate, Inc.

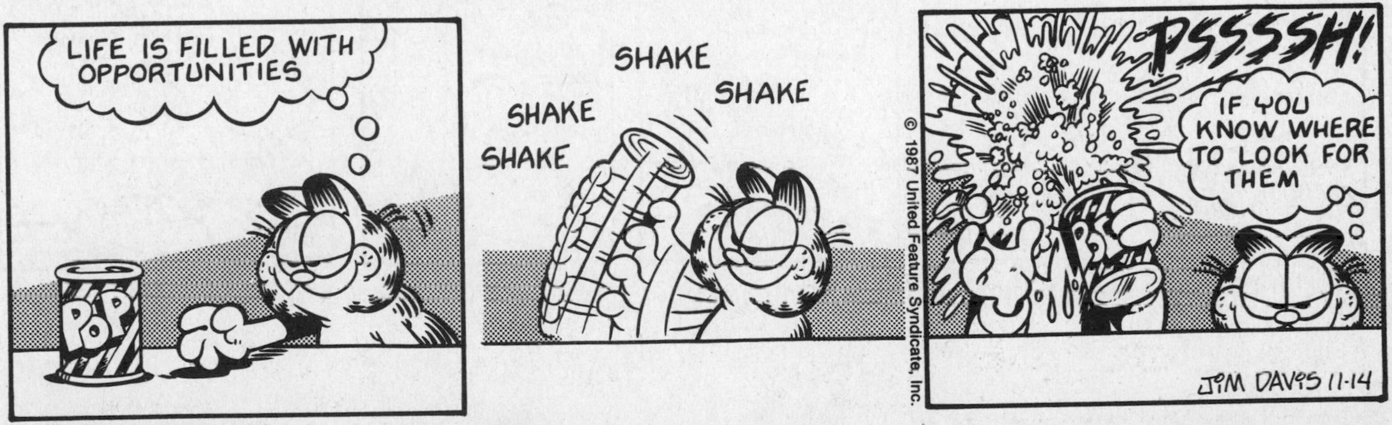
LIFE IS FILLED WITH OPPORTUNITIES
POP
SHAKE
SHAKE
SHAKE
SHAKE
PSSSSH!
IF YOU KNOW WHERE TO LOOK FOR THEM
JIM DAVIS 11-14
© 1987 United Feature Syndicate, Inc.

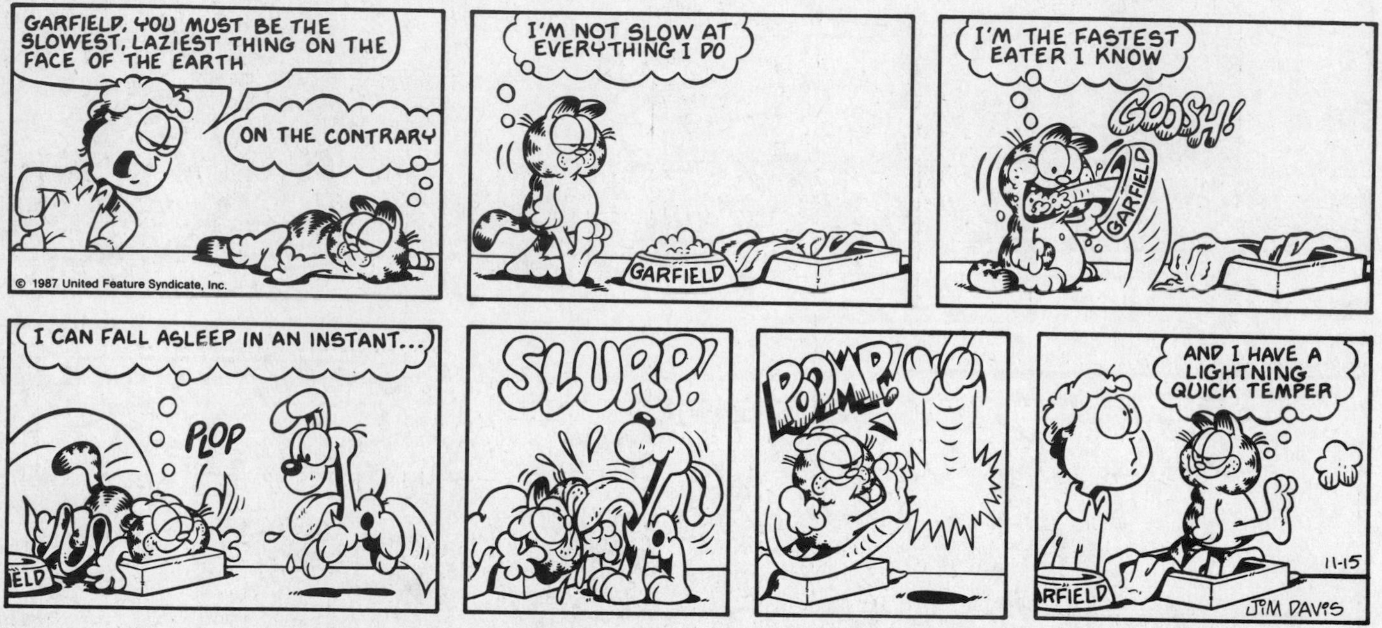
GARFIELD, YOU MUST BE THE SLOWEST, LAZIEST THING ON THE FACE OF THE EARTH
ON THE CONTRARY
© 1987 United Feature Syndicate, Inc.
I'M NOT SLOW AT EVERYTHING I DO
GARFIELD
I'M THE FASTEST EATER I KNOW
GOOSH!
GARFIELD
I CAN FALL ASLEEP IN AN INSTANT...
PLOP
SLURP!
POMP!
AND I HAVE A LIGHTNING QUICK TEMPER
11-15
JIM DAVIS

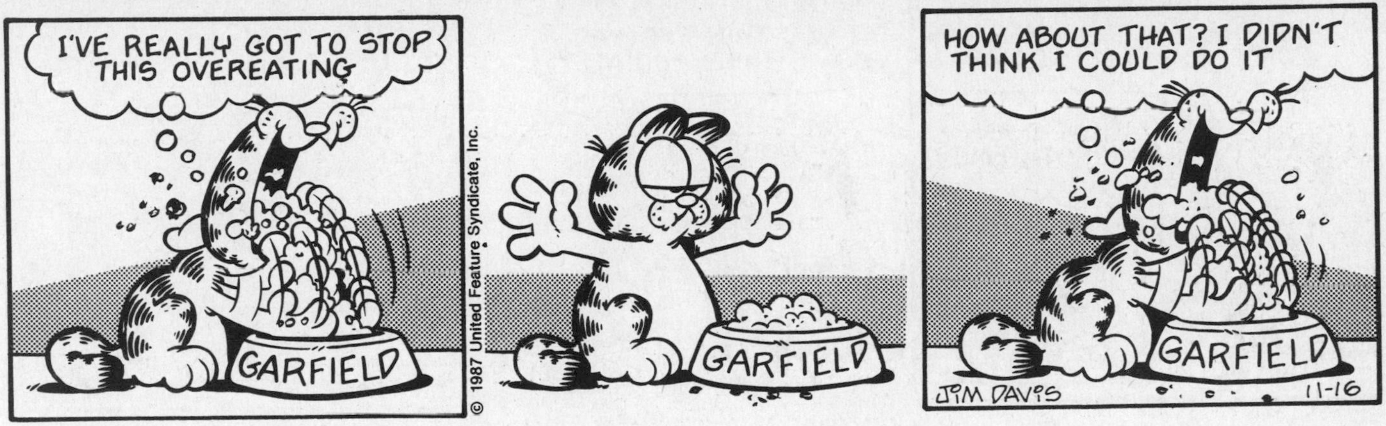
I'VE REALLY GOT TO STOP THIS OVEREATING
GARFIELD
© 1987 United Feature Syndicate, Inc.
GARFIELD
HOW ABOUT THAT? I DIDN'T THINK I COULD DO IT
GARFIELD
JIM DAVIS 11-16

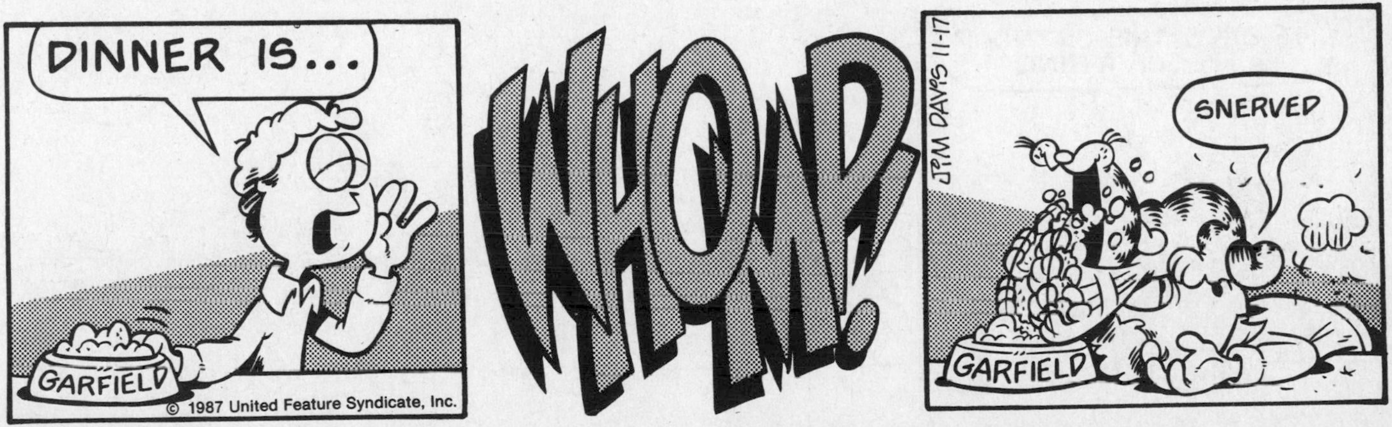
DINNER IS...
GARFIELD
© 1987 United Feature Syndicate, Inc.
WHOMP!
JIM DAVIS 11-17
SNERVED
GARFIELD

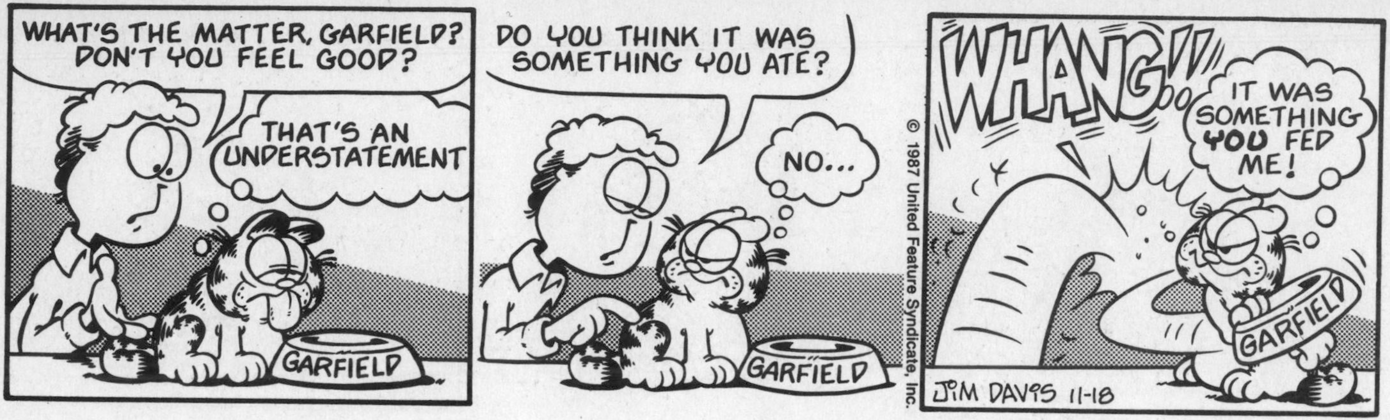
WHAT'S THE MATTER, GARFIELD? DON'T YOU FEEL GOOD?
THAT'S AN UNDERSTATEMENT
GARFIELD
DO YOU THINK IT WAS SOMETHING YOU ATE?
NO...
GARFIELD
© 1987 United Feature Syndicate, Inc.
WHANG!!
IT WAS SOMETHING **YOU** FED ME!
GARFIELD
JIM DAVIS 11-18

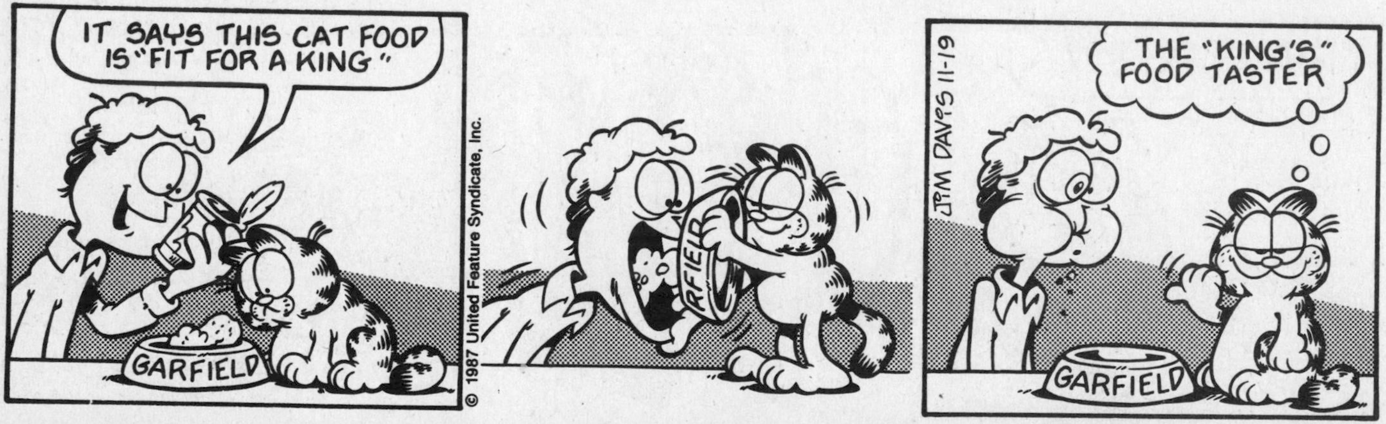
IT SAYS THIS CAT FOOD IS "FIT FOR A KING"
GARFIELD
© 1987 United Feature Syndicate, Inc.
JIM DAVIS 11-19
THE "KING'S" FOOD TASTER
GARFIELD

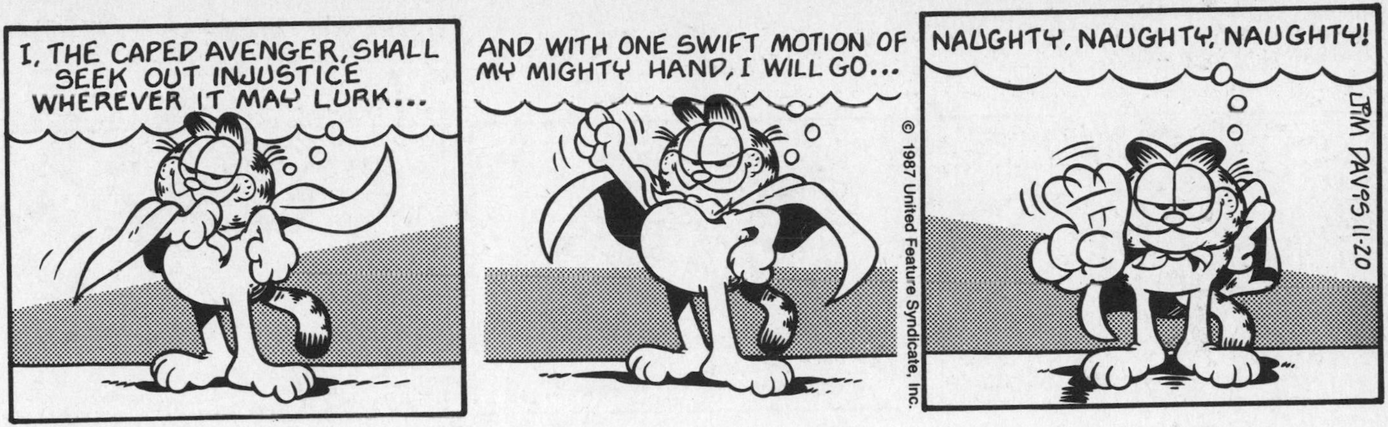
I, THE CAPED AVENGER, SHALL SEEK OUT INJUSTICE WHEREVER IT MAY LURK...
AND WITH ONE SWIFT MOTION OF MY MIGHTY HAND, I WILL GO...
© 1987 United Feature Syndicate, Inc.
NAUGHTY, NAUGHTY, NAUGHTY!
JIM DAVIS 11-20

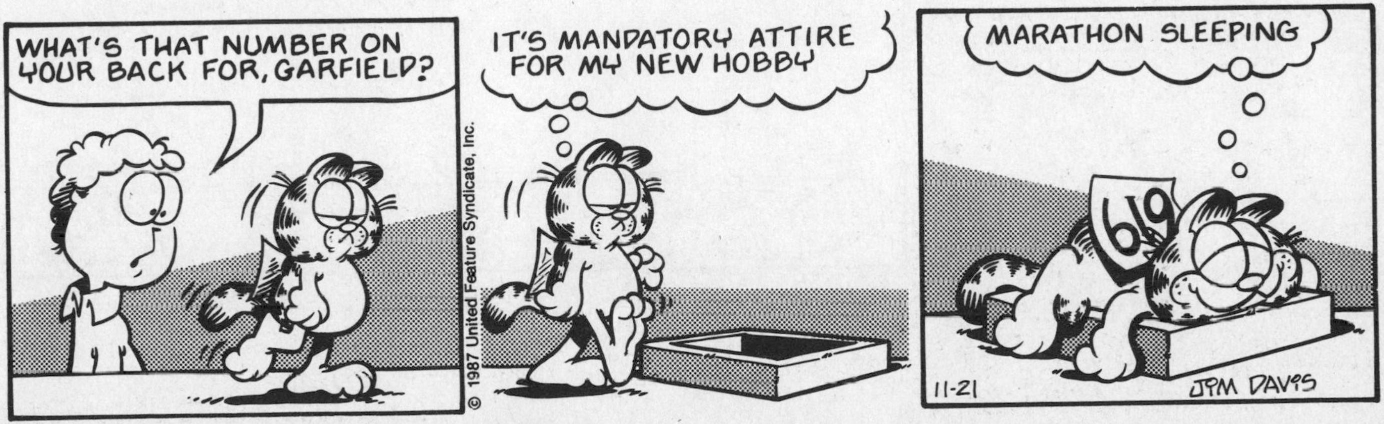
WHAT'S THAT NUMBER ON YOUR BACK FOR, GARFIELD?
© 1987 United Feature Syndicate, Inc.
IT'S MANDATORY ATTIRE FOR MY NEW HOBBY
MARATHON SLEEPING
619
11-21
JIM DAVIS

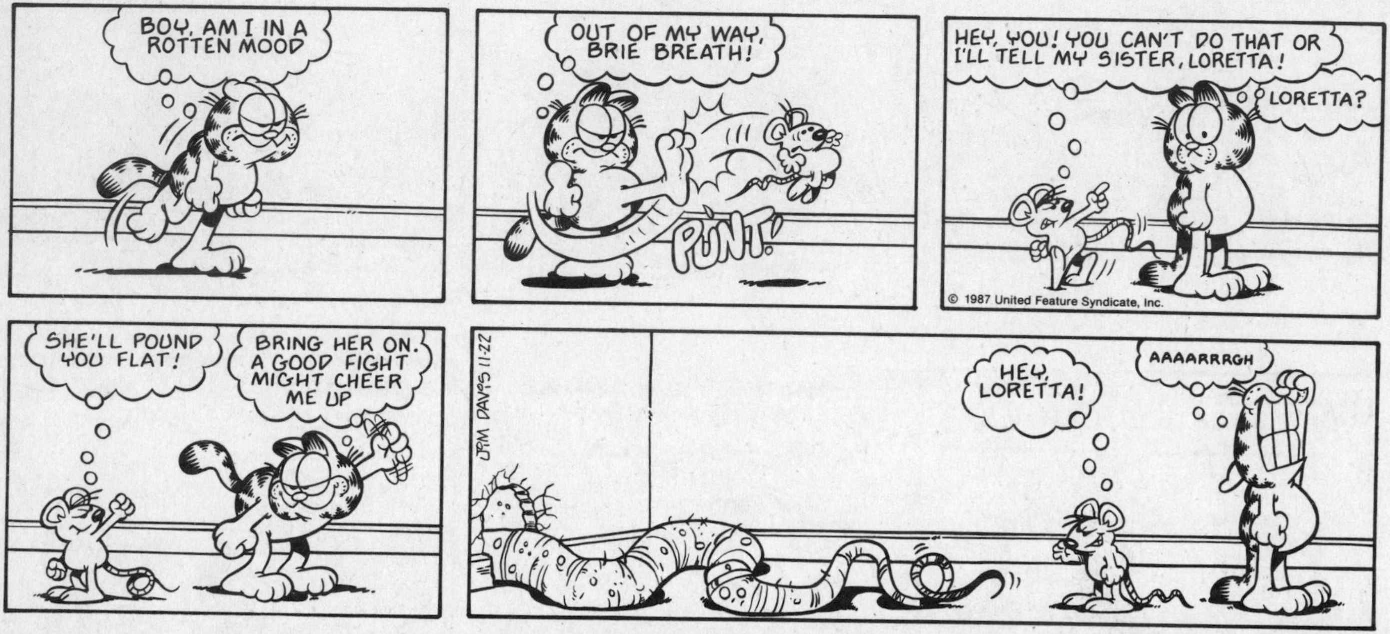
BOY, AM I IN A ROTTEN MOOD
OUT OF MY WAY, BRIE BREATH!
PUNT!
HEY, YOU! YOU CAN'T DO THAT OR I'LL TELL MY SISTER, LORETTA!
LORETTA?
© 1987 United Feature Syndicate, Inc.
SHE'LL POUND YOU FLAT!
BRING HER ON. A GOOD FIGHT MIGHT CHEER ME UP
JIM DAVIS 11-22
HEY, LORETTA!
AAAARRRGH

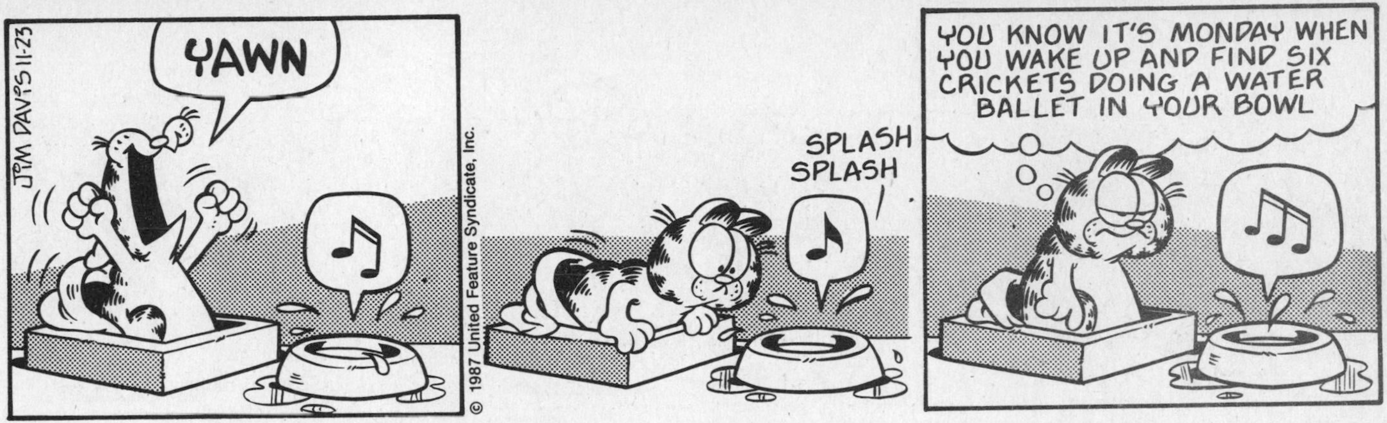

JIM DAVIS 11-23
YAWN
SPLASH
SPLASH
YOU KNOW IT'S MONDAY WHEN YOU WAKE UP AND FIND SIX CRICKETS DOING A WATER BALLET IN YOUR BOWL

© 1987 United Feature Syndicate, Inc.

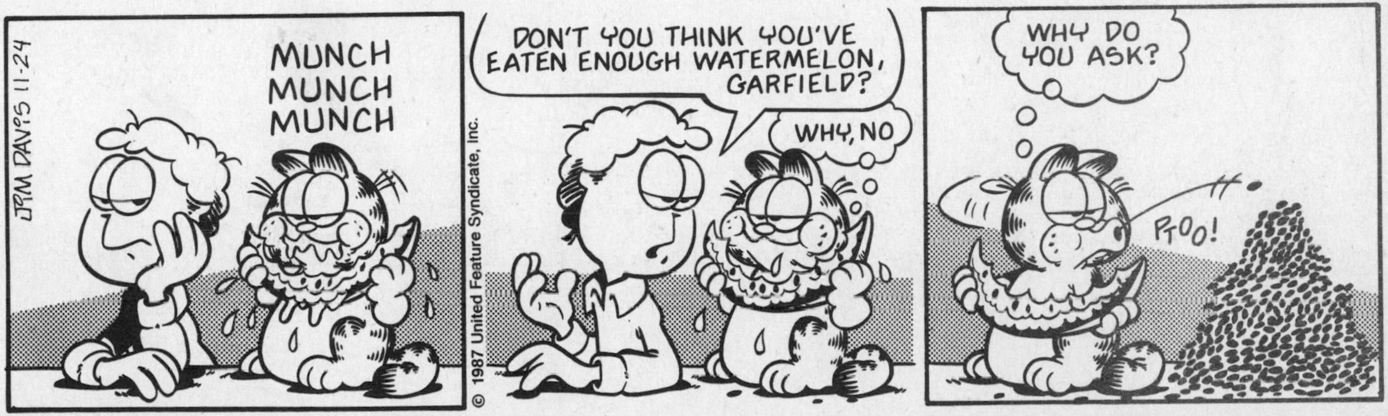

JIM DAVIS 11-24
MUNCH
MUNCH
MUNCH
DON'T YOU THINK YOU'VE EATEN ENOUGH WATERMELON, GARFIELD?
WHY, NO
WHY DO YOU ASK?
PTOO!

© 1987 United Feature Syndicate, Inc.

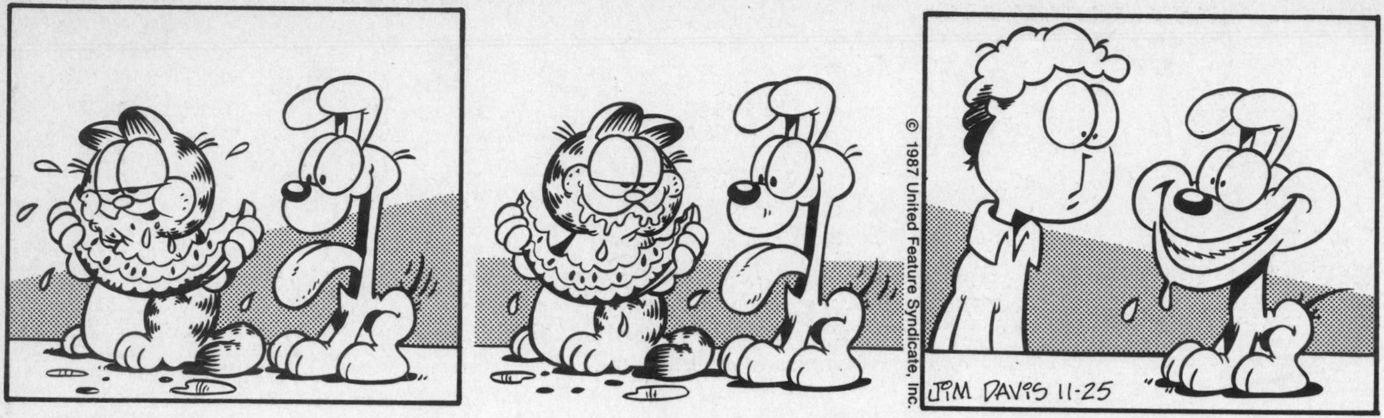
© 1987 United Feature Syndicate, Inc.
JIM DAVIS 11-25

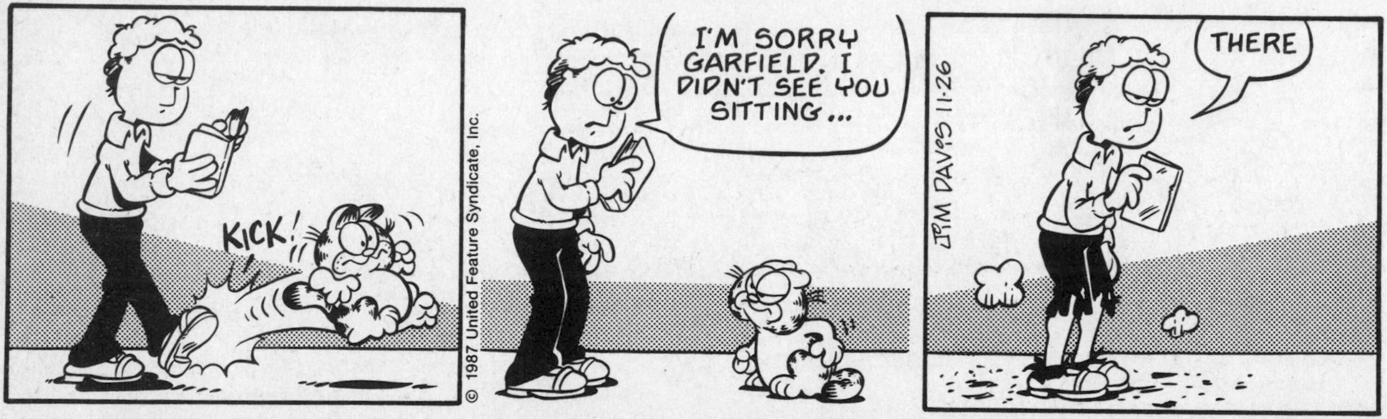
KICK!
© 1987 United Feature Syndicate, Inc.
I'M SORRY GARFIELD. I DIDN'T SEE YOU SITTING...
JIM DAVIS 11-26
THERE

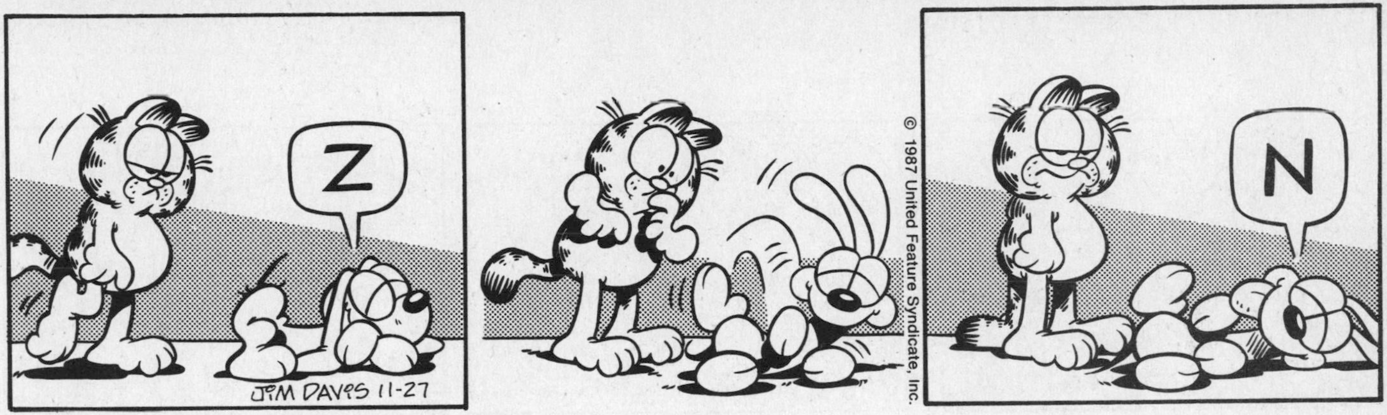
Z
N
JIM DAVIS 11-27
© 1987 United Feature Syndicate, Inc.

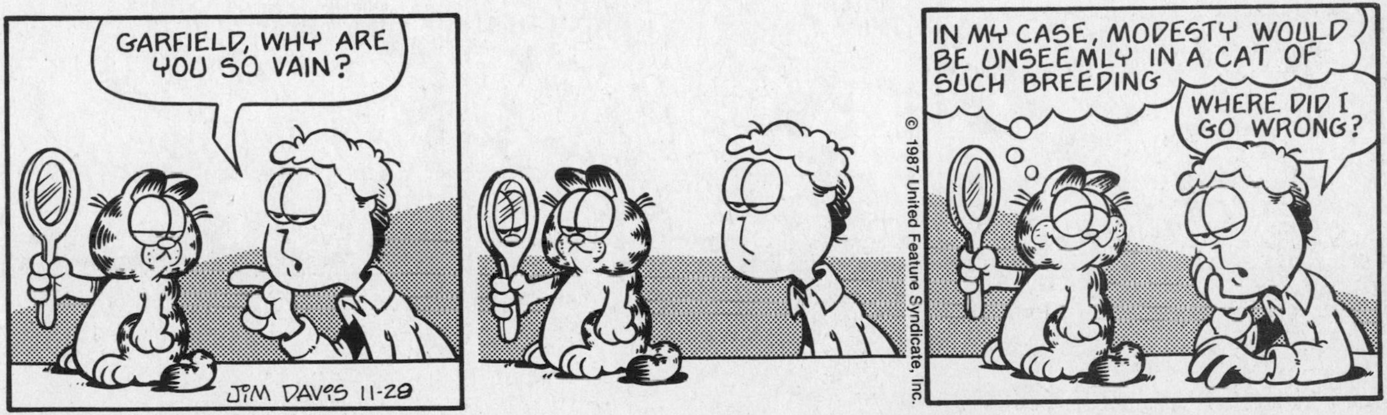
GARFIELD, WHY ARE YOU SO VAIN?
IN MY CASE, MODESTY WOULD BE UNSEEMLY IN A CAT OF SUCH BREEDING
WHERE DID I GO WRONG?
JIM DAVIS 11-28
© 1987 United Feature Syndicate, Inc.

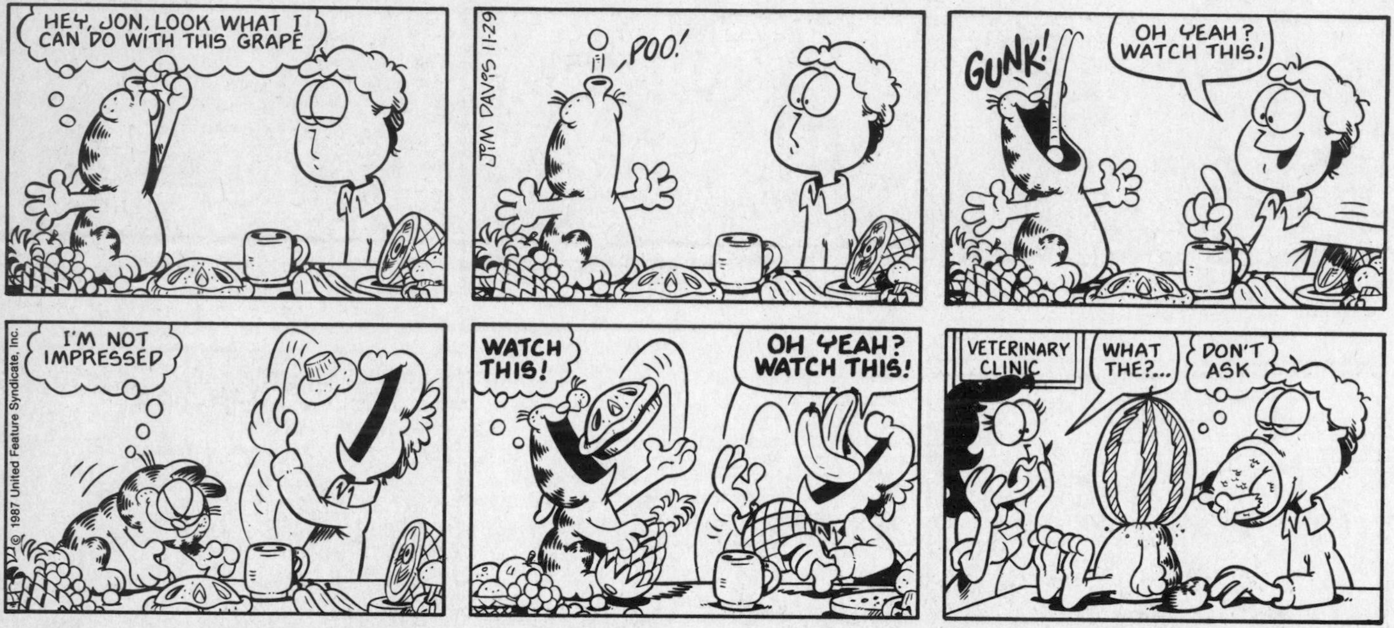
HEY, JON, LOOK WHAT I CAN DO WITH THIS GRAPE
JIM DAVIS 11-29
POO!
GUNK!
OH YEAH? WATCH THIS!
© 1987 United Feature Syndicate, Inc.
I'M NOT IMPRESSED
WATCH THIS!
OH YEAH? WATCH THIS!
VETERINARY CLINIC
WHAT THE?...
DON'T ASK

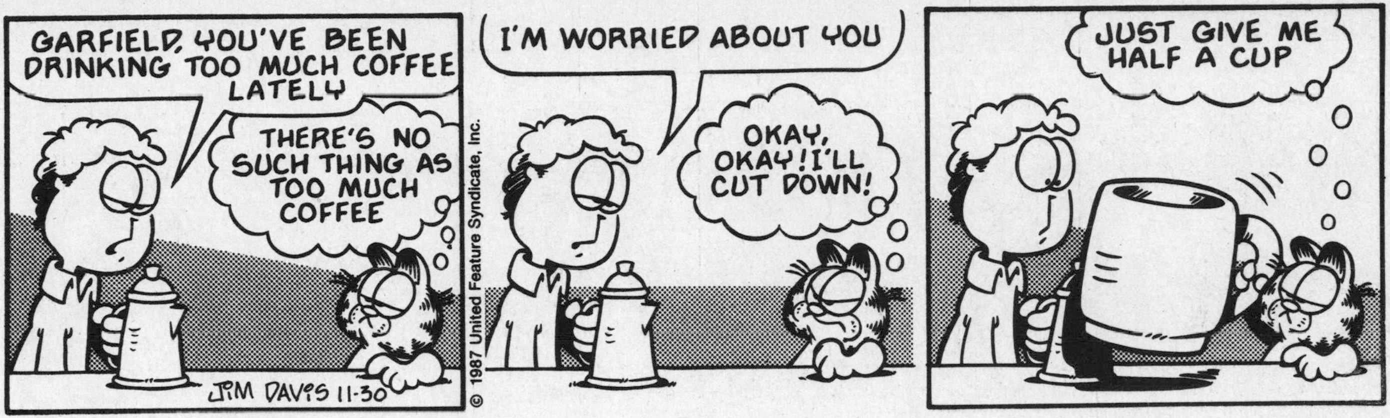
GARFIELD, YOU'VE BEEN DRINKING TOO MUCH COFFEE LATELY
THERE'S NO SUCH THING AS TOO MUCH COFFEE
JIM DAVIS 11-30
I'M WORRIED ABOUT YOU
OKAY, OKAY! I'LL CUT DOWN!
JUST GIVE ME HALF A CUP

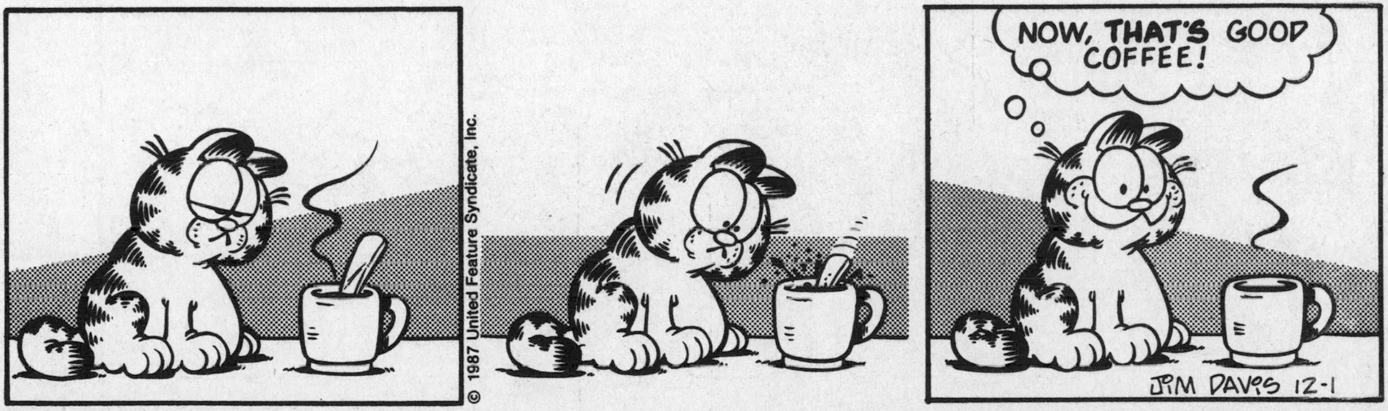
NOW, THAT'S GOOD COFFEE!
JIM DAVIS 12-1

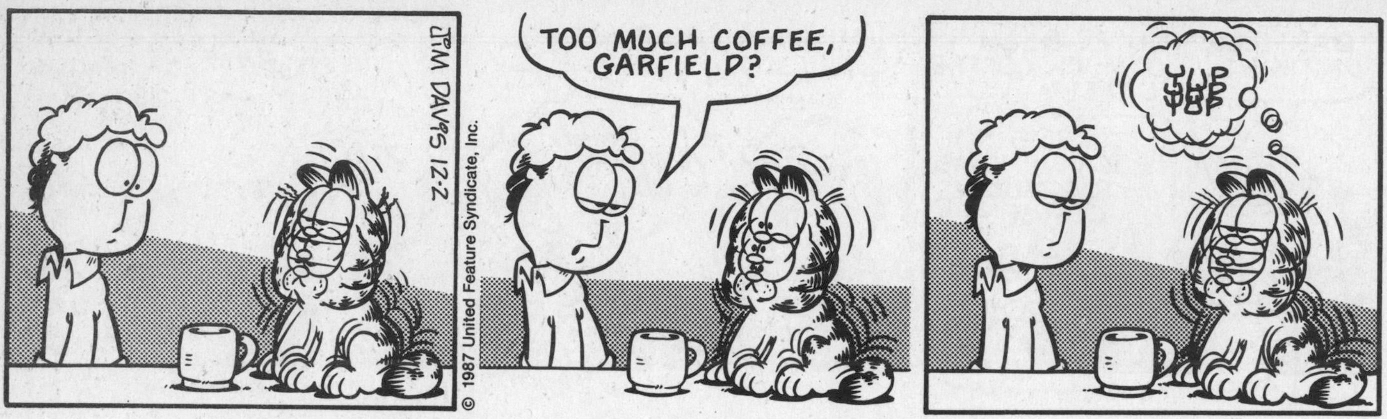
JIM DAVIS 12-2
© 1987 United Feature Syndicate, Inc.
TOO MUCH COFFEE, GARFIELD?
YUP YUP YUP

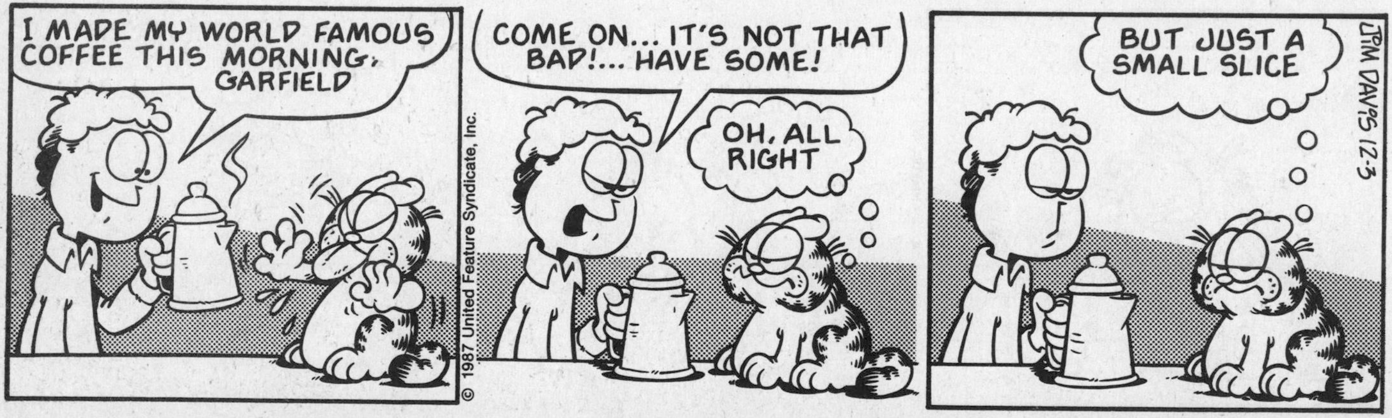
I MADE MY WORLD FAMOUS COFFEE THIS MORNING, GARFIELD
© 1987 United Feature Syndicate, Inc.
COME ON... IT'S NOT THAT BAD!... HAVE SOME!
OH, ALL RIGHT
BUT JUST A SMALL SLICE
JIM DAVIS 12-3

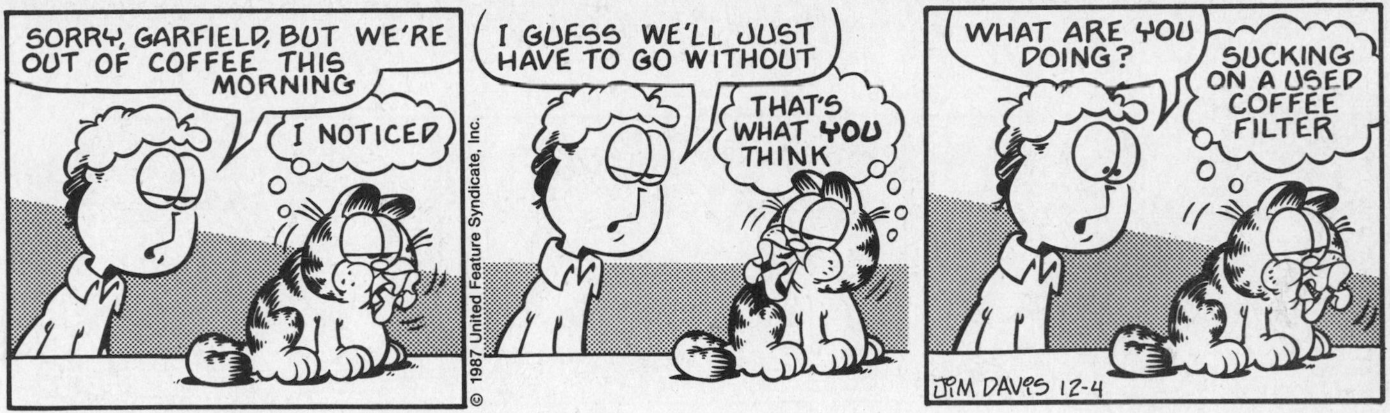
SORRY, GARFIELD, BUT WE'RE OUT OF COFFEE THIS MORNING
I NOTICED
I GUESS WE'LL JUST HAVE TO GO WITHOUT
THAT'S WHAT **YOU** THINK
WHAT ARE YOU DOING?
SUCKING ON A USED COFFEE FILTER
JIM DAVIS 12-4
© 1987 United Feature Syndicate, Inc.

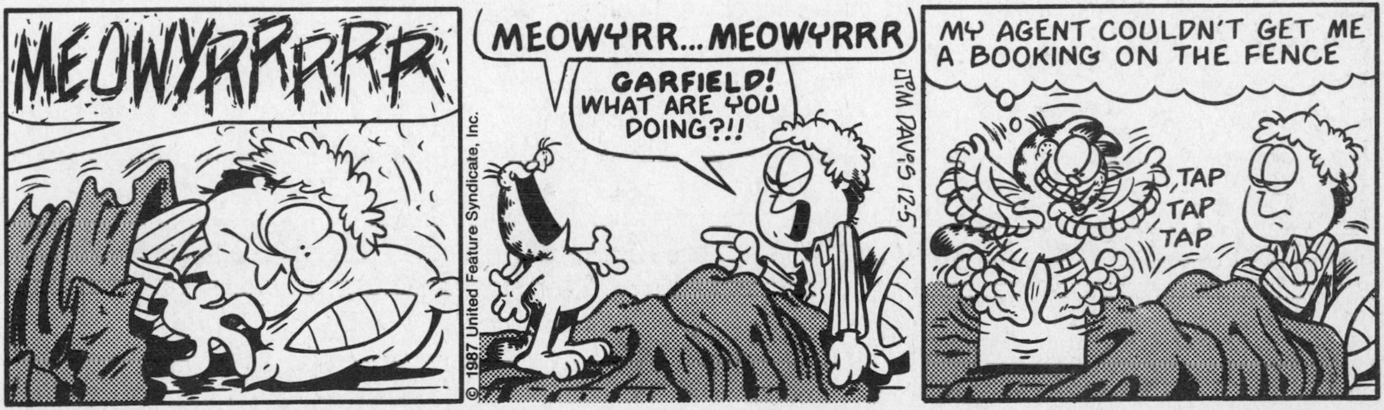
MEOWYRRRRR
MEOWYRR... MEOWYRRR
GARFIELD! WHAT ARE YOU DOING?!!
MY AGENT COULDN'T GET ME A BOOKING ON THE FENCE
TAP
TAP
TAP
JIM DAVIS 12-5
© 1987 United Feature Syndicate, Inc.

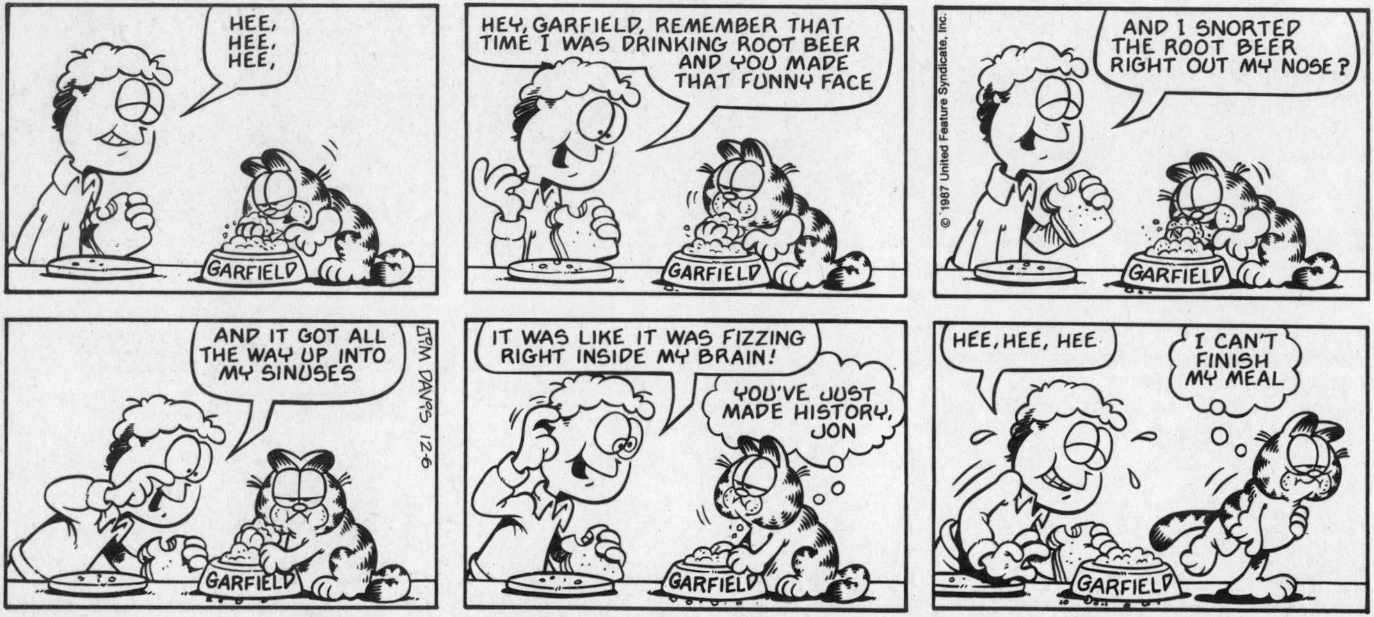
HEE, HEE, HEE,
HEY, GARFIELD, REMEMBER THAT TIME I WAS DRINKING ROOT BEER AND YOU MADE THAT FUNNY FACE
© 1987 United Feature Syndicate, Inc.
AND I SNORTED THE ROOT BEER RIGHT OUT MY NOSE?
AND IT GOT ALL THE WAY UP INTO MY SINUSES
JIM DAVIS 12-6
IT WAS LIKE IT WAS FIZZING RIGHT INSIDE MY BRAIN!
YOU'VE JUST MADE HISTORY, JON
HEE, HEE, HEE
I CAN'T FINISH MY MEAL
GARFIELD

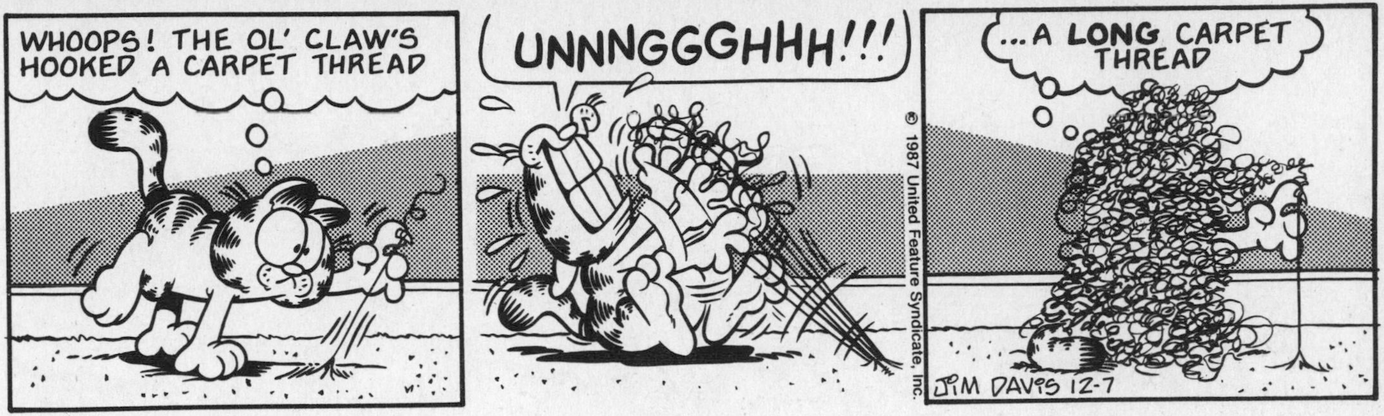
WHOOPS! THE OL' CLAW'S HOOKED A CARPET THREAD
UNNNGGGHHH!!!
...A LONG CARPET THREAD
© 1987 United Feature Syndicate, Inc.
JIM DAVIS 12-7

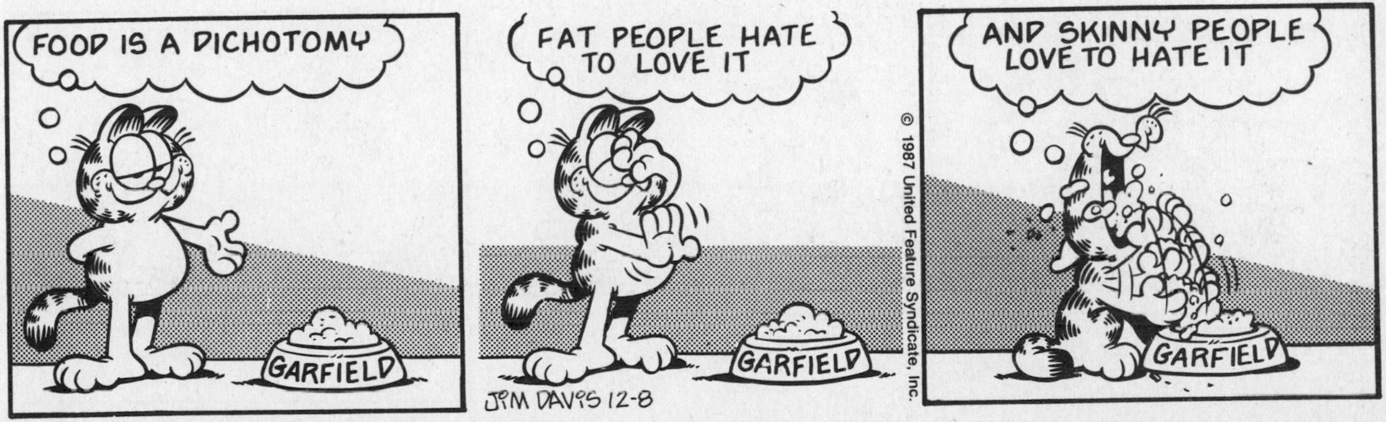
FOOD IS A DICHOTOMY
FAT PEOPLE HATE TO LOVE IT
AND SKINNY PEOPLE LOVE TO HATE IT
GARFIELD
GARFIELD
GARFIELD
© 1987 United Feature Syndicate, Inc.
JIM DAVIS 12-8

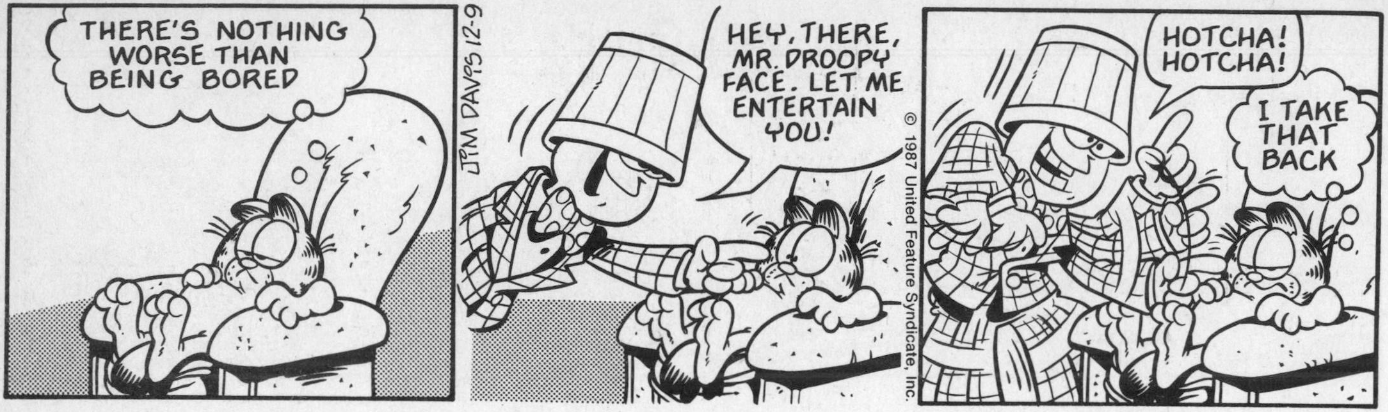
THERE'S NOTHING WORSE THAN BEING BORED
JIM DAVIS 12-9
HEY, THERE, MR. DROOPY FACE. LET ME ENTERTAIN YOU!
© 1987 United Feature Syndicate, Inc.
HOTCHA! HOTCHA!
I TAKE THAT BACK

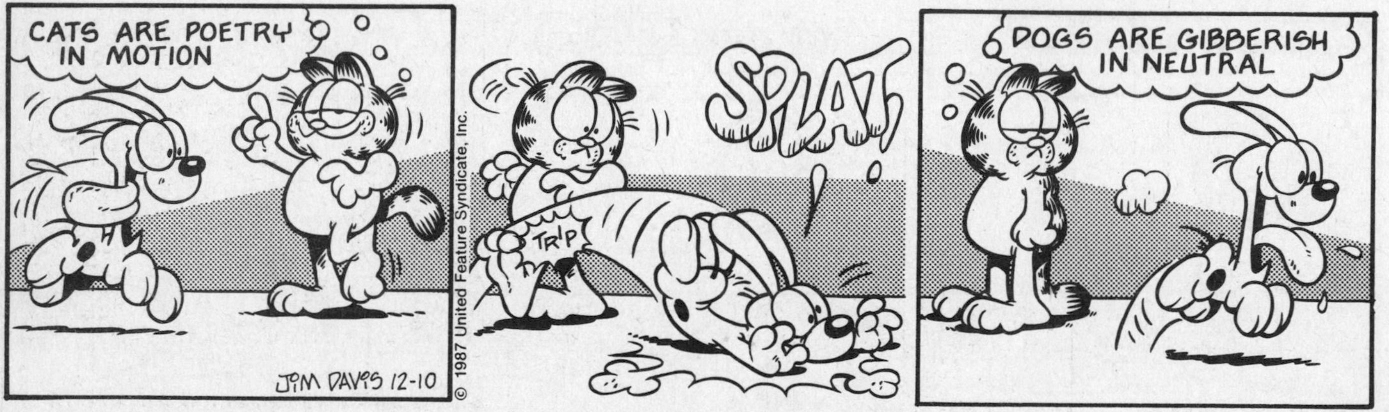
CATS ARE POETRY IN MOTION
JIM DAVIS 12-10
© 1987 United Feature Syndicate, Inc.
SPLAT
TRIP
DOGS ARE GIBBERISH IN NEUTRAL

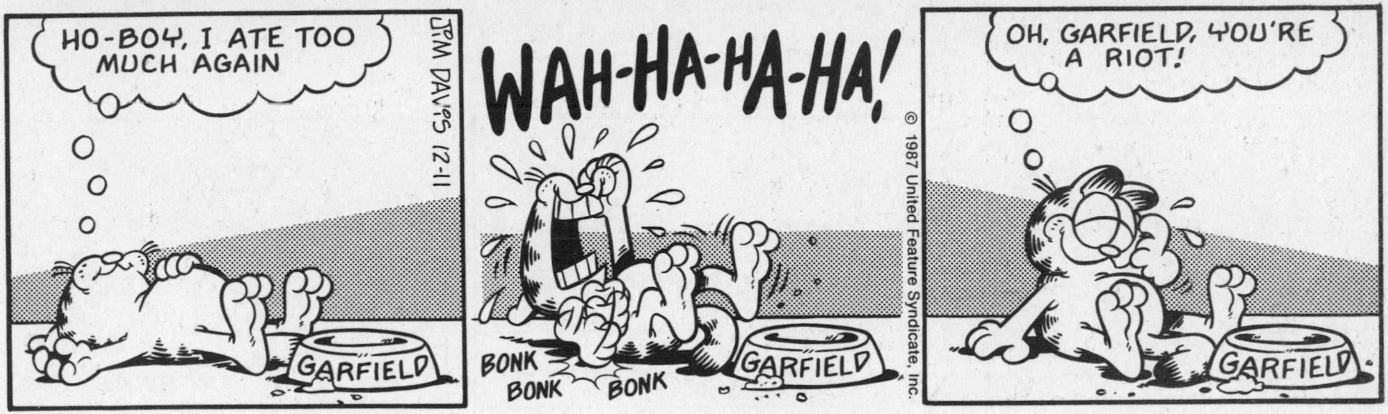
HO-BOY, I ATE TOO MUCH AGAIN
JIM DAVIS 12-11
WAH-HA-HA-HA!
BONK
BONK
BONK
GARFIELD
© 1987 United Feature Syndicate, Inc.
OH, GARFIELD, YOU'RE A RIOT!
GARFIELD

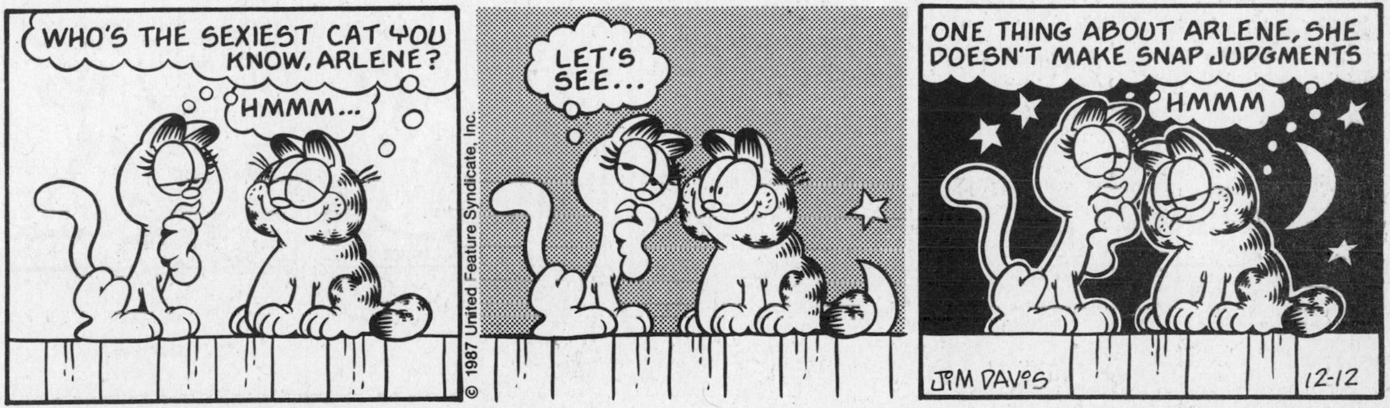
WHO'S THE SEXIEST CAT YOU KNOW, ARLENE?
HMMM...
© 1987 United Feature Syndicate, Inc.
LET'S SEE...
ONE THING ABOUT ARLENE, SHE DOESN'T MAKE SNAP JUDGMENTS
HMMM
JIM DAVIS
12-12

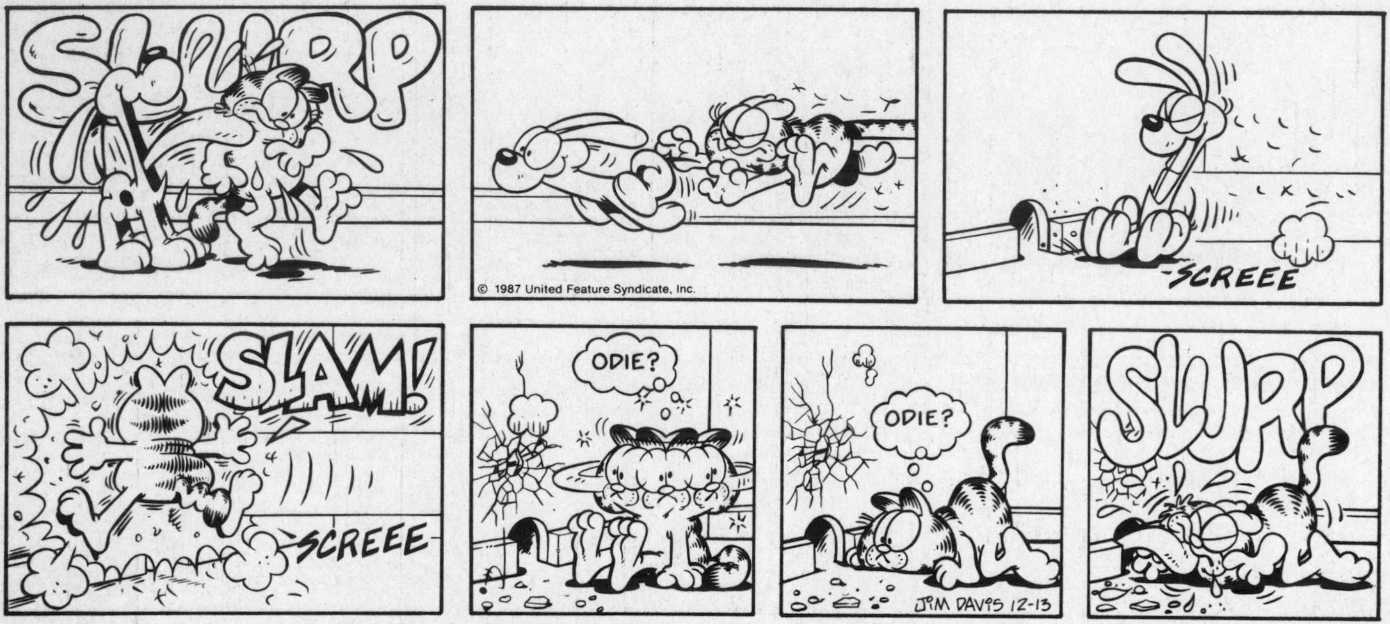
SLURP
© 1987 United Feature Syndicate, Inc.
SCREEE
SLAM!
SCREEE
ODIE?
ODIE?
JIM DAVIS 12-13
SLURP

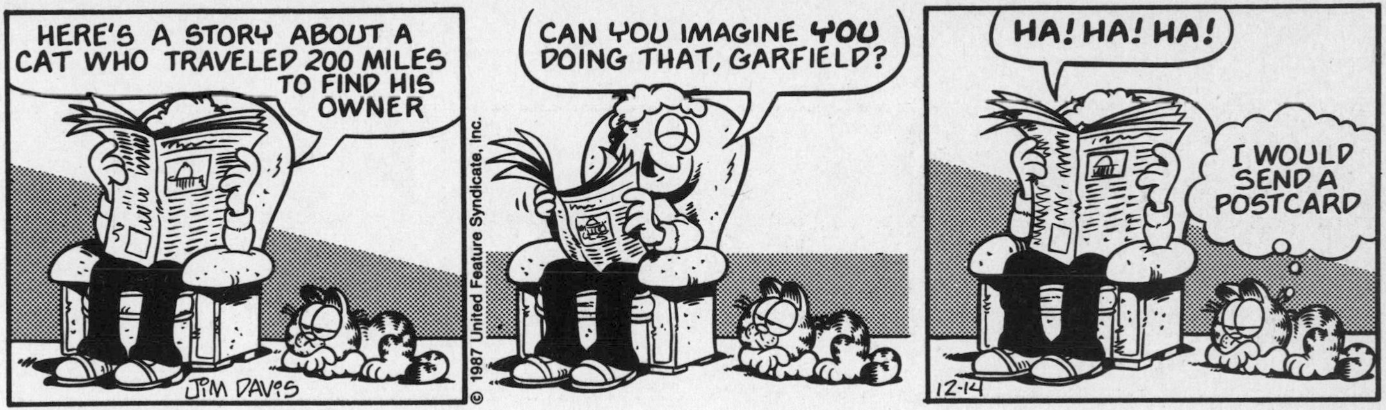
HERE'S A STORY ABOUT A CAT WHO TRAVELED 200 MILES TO FIND HIS OWNER
CAN YOU IMAGINE YOU DOING THAT, GARFIELD?
HA! HA! HA!
I WOULD SEND A POSTCARD
JIM DAVIS
© 1987 United Feature Syndicate, Inc.
12-14

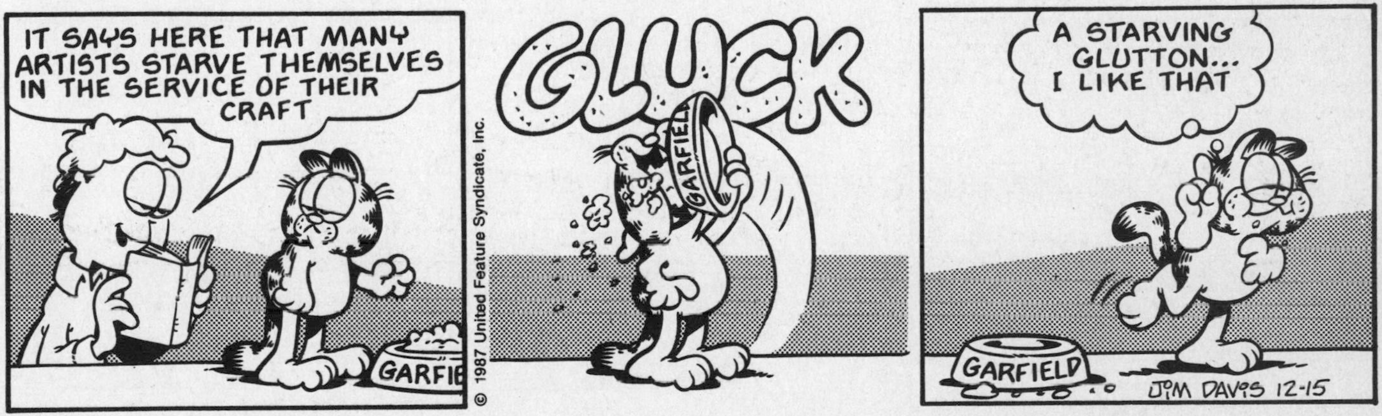
IT SAYS HERE THAT MANY ARTISTS STARVE THEMSELVES IN THE SERVICE OF THEIR CRAFT
GARFIE
GLUCK
GARFIELD
A STARVING GLUTTON... I LIKE THAT
GARFIELD
JIM DAVIS 12-15
© 1987 United Feature Syndicate, Inc.

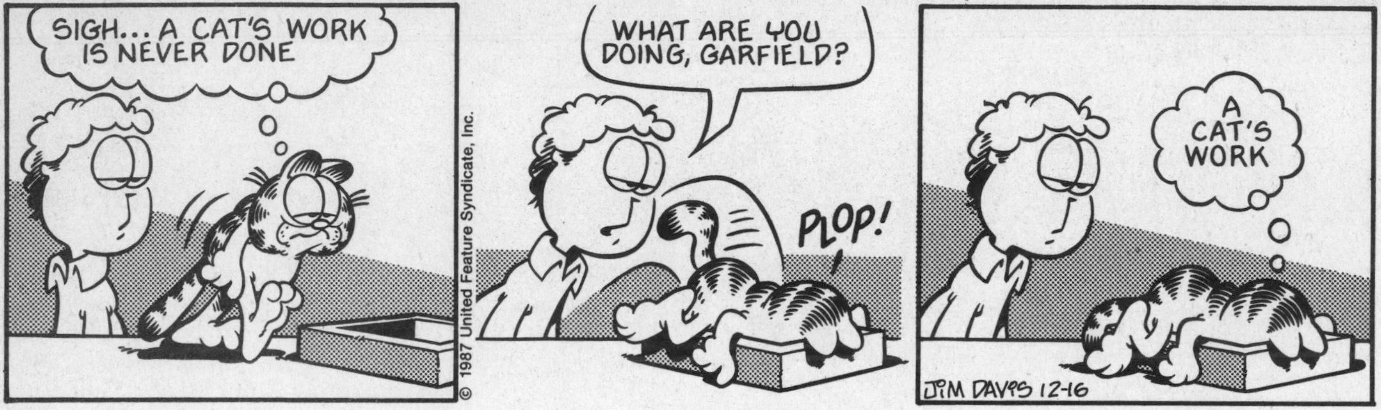
SIGH... A CAT'S WORK IS NEVER DONE
© 1987 United Feature Syndicate, Inc.
WHAT ARE YOU DOING, GARFIELD?
PLOP!
A CAT'S WORK
JIM DAVIS 12-16

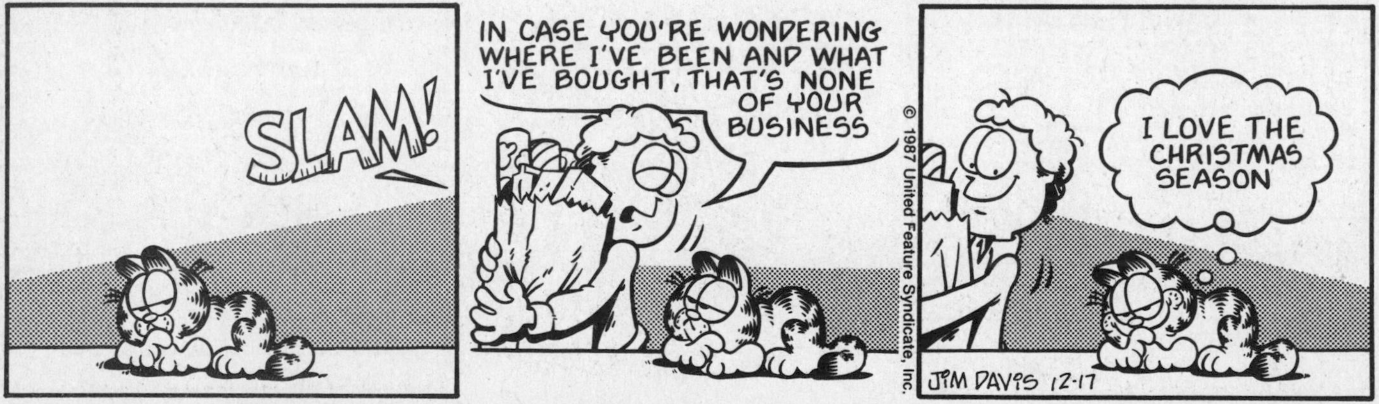
SLAM!
IN CASE YOU'RE WONDERING WHERE I'VE BEEN AND WHAT I'VE BOUGHT, THAT'S NONE OF YOUR BUSINESS
© 1987 United Feature Syndicate, Inc.
I LOVE THE CHRISTMAS SEASON
JIM DAVIS 12-17

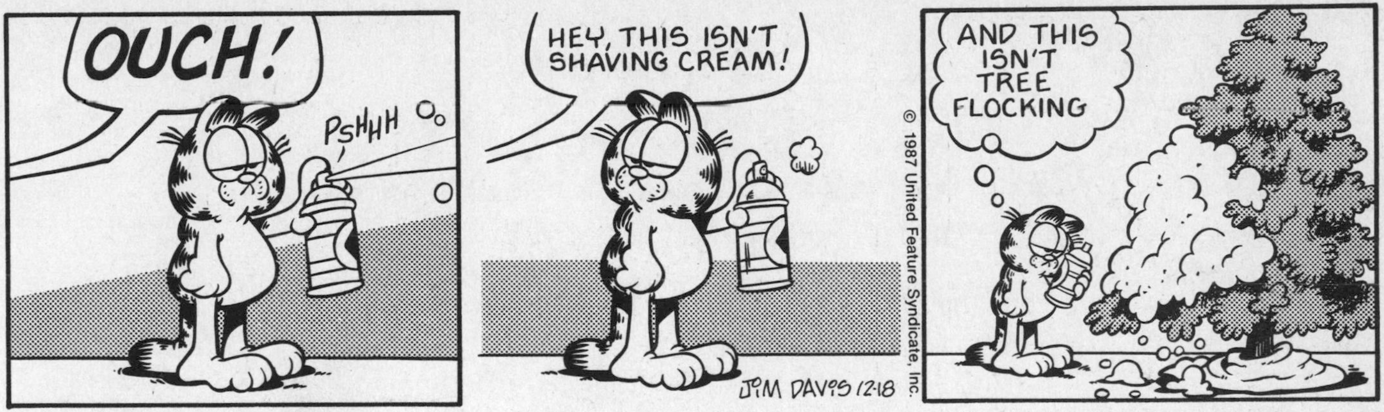
OUCH!
PSHHH
HEY, THIS ISN'T SHAVING CREAM!
AND THIS ISN'T TREE FLOCKING
JIM DAVIS 12-18
© 1987 United Feature Syndicate, Inc.

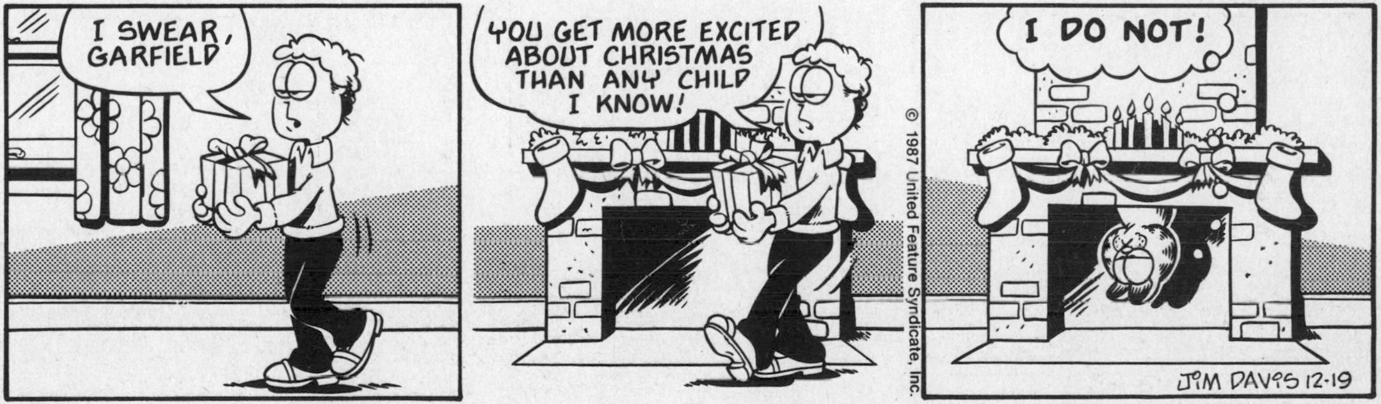
I SWEAR, GARFIELD
YOU GET MORE EXCITED ABOUT CHRISTMAS THAN ANY CHILD I KNOW!
I DO NOT!
JIM DAVIS 12-19
© 1987 United Feature Syndicate, Inc.

THE GARFIELD WORKOUT

DO THESE EXERCISES EVERY DAY, AND YOU'LL SOON BE IN THE SAME SHAPE AS GARFIELD!

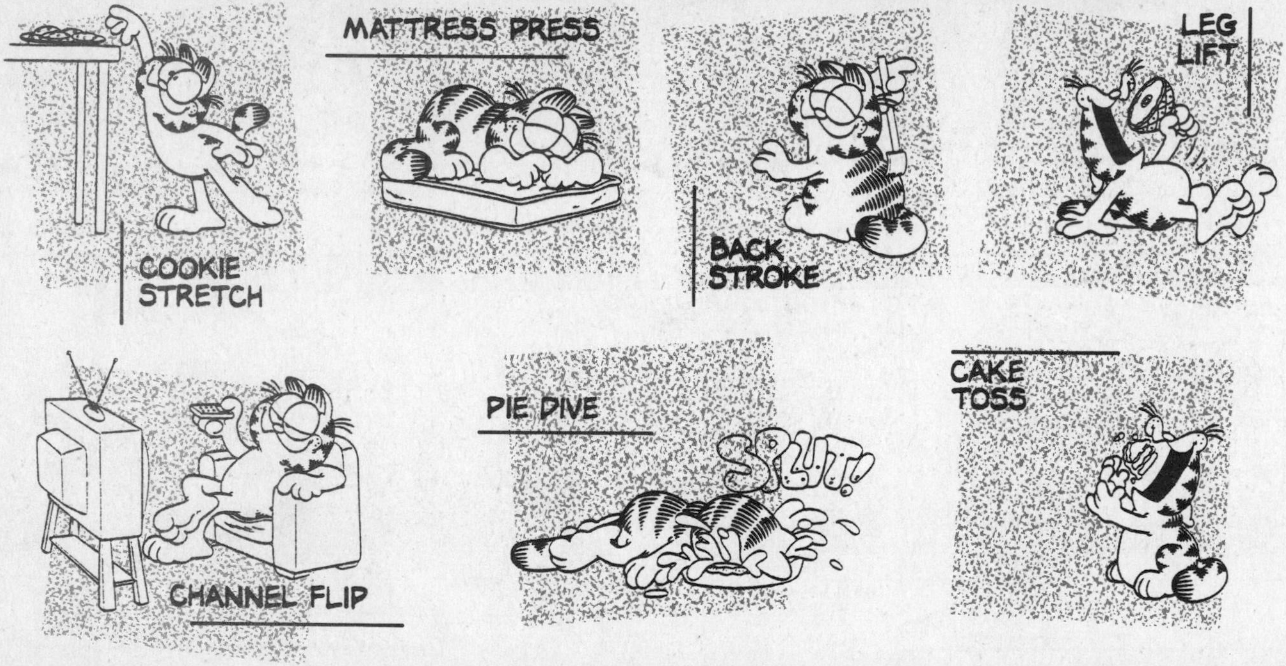

COOKIE STRETCH
MATTRESS PRESS
BACK STROKE
LEG LIFT
CHANNEL FLIP
PIE DIVE
SPLUT!
CAKE TOSS

Garfield chews the fat

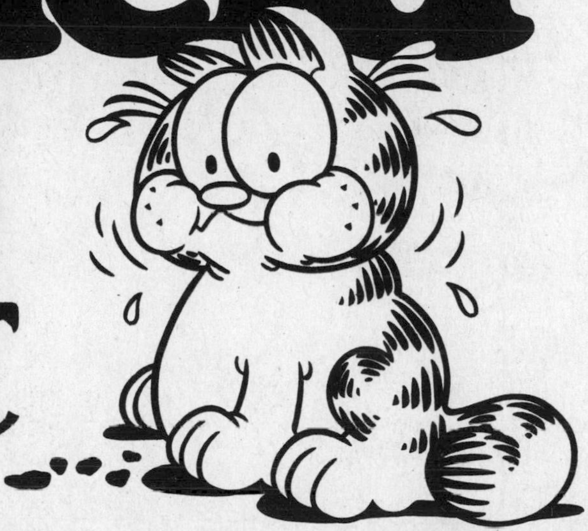

BY: JIM DAVIS

Garfield impressions

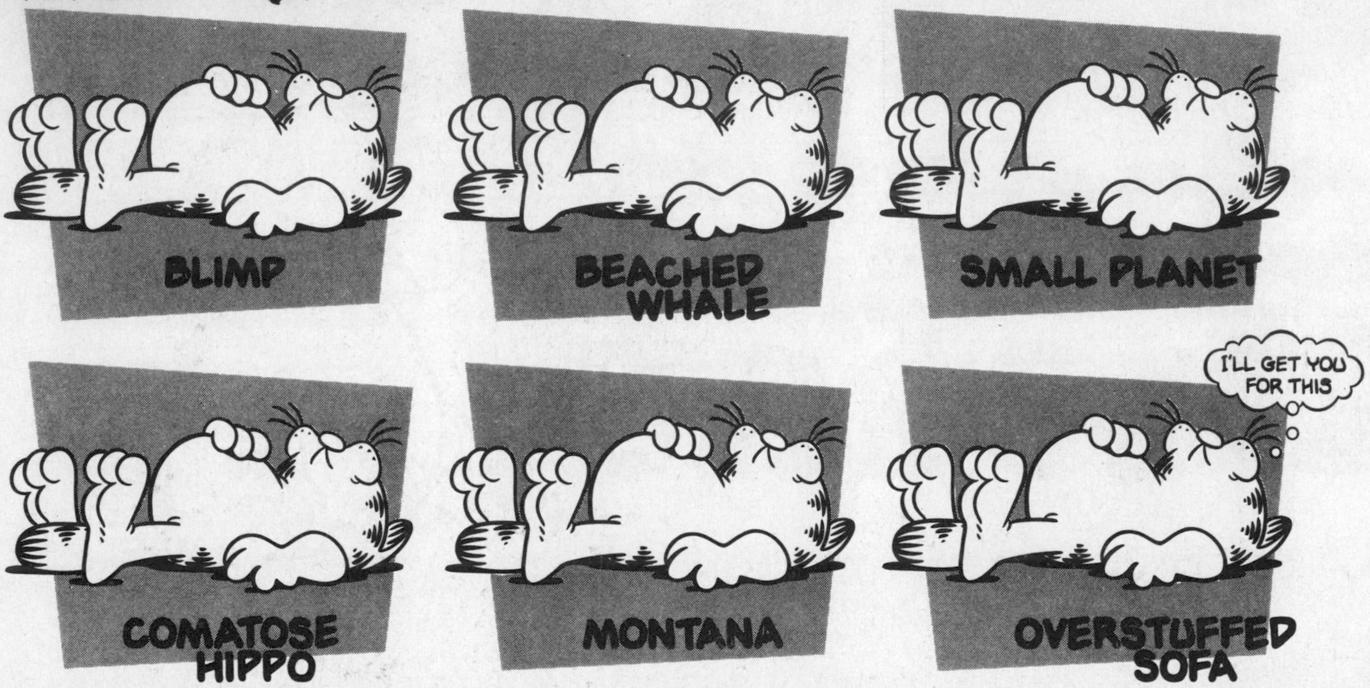

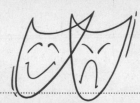

BLIMP
BEACHED WHALE
SMALL PLANET
I'LL GET YOU FOR THIS
COMATOSE HIPPO
MONTANA
OVERSTUFFED SOFA

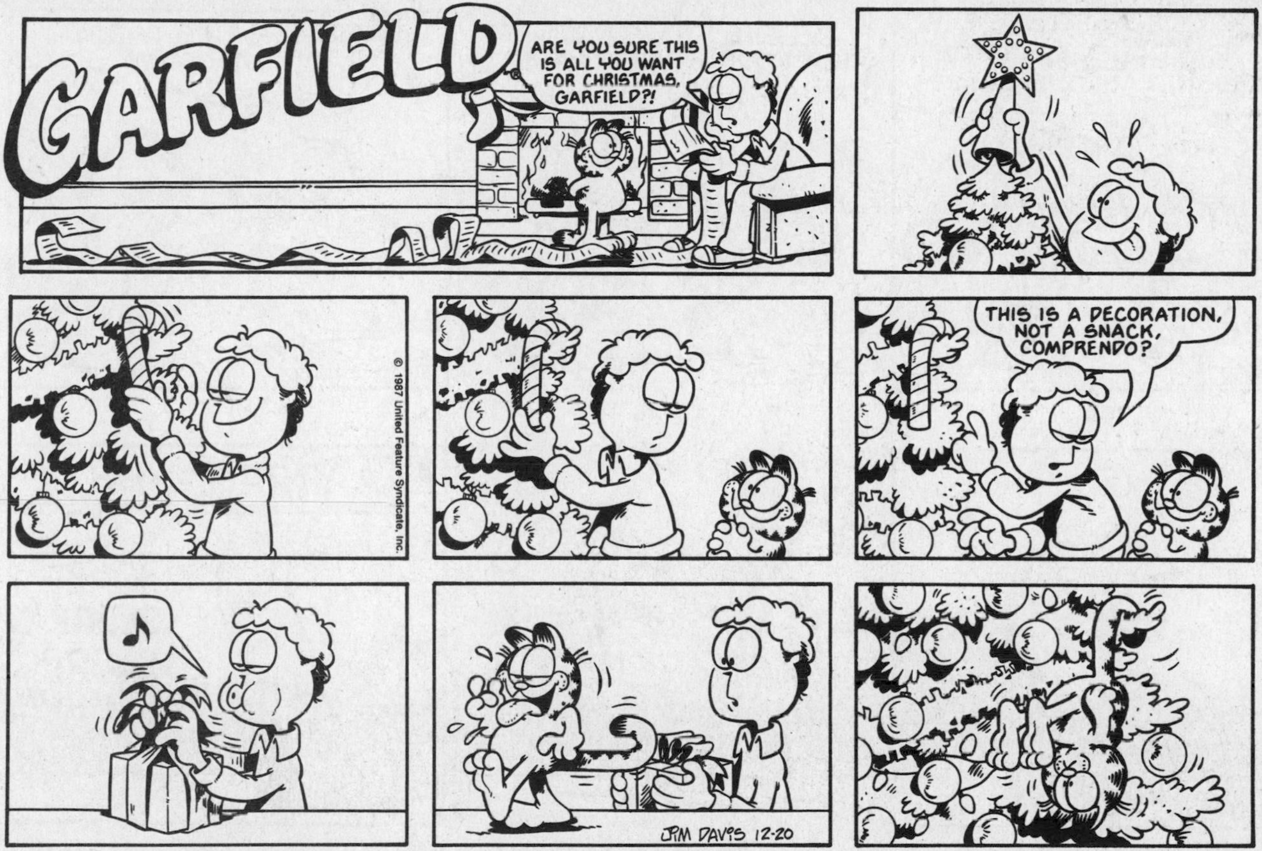
GARFIELD
ARE YOU SURE THIS IS ALL YOU WANT FOR CHRISTMAS, GARFIELD?!
© 1987 United Feature Syndicate, Inc.
THIS IS A DECORATION, NOT A SNACK, COMPRENDO?
♪
JIM DAVIS 12-20

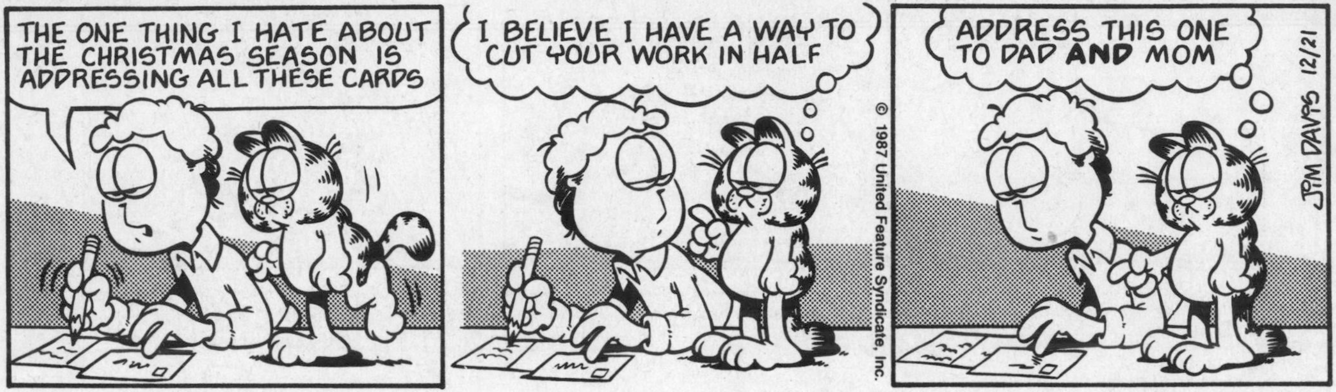
THE ONE THING I HATE ABOUT THE CHRISTMAS SEASON IS ADDRESSING ALL THESE CARDS
I BELIEVE I HAVE A WAY TO CUT YOUR WORK IN HALF
ADDRESS THIS ONE TO DAD **AND** MOM
JIM DAVIS 12/21
© 1987 United Feature Syndicate, Inc.

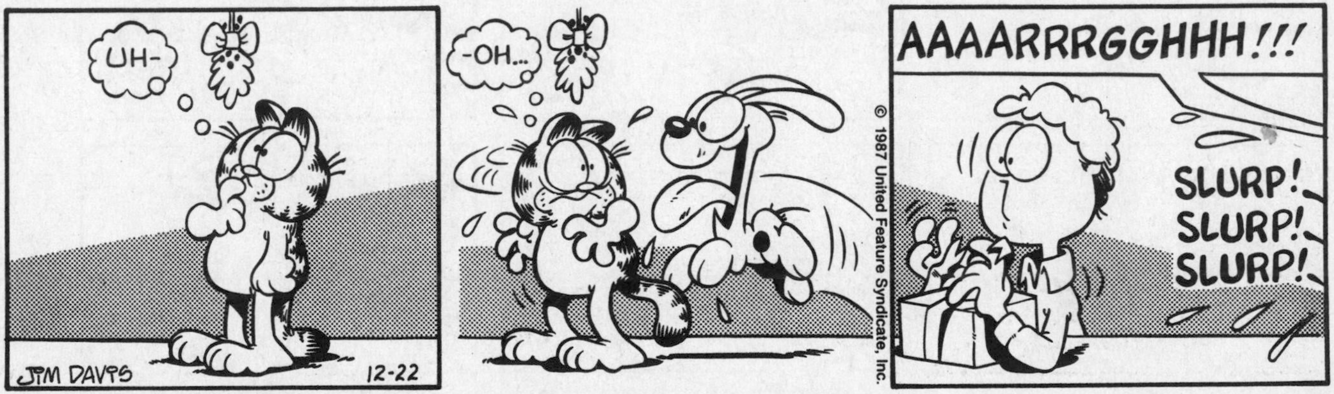
UH-
JIM DAVIS 12-22
-OH...
© 1987 United Feature Syndicate, Inc.
AAAARRRGGHHH!!!
SLURP!
SLURP!
SLURP!

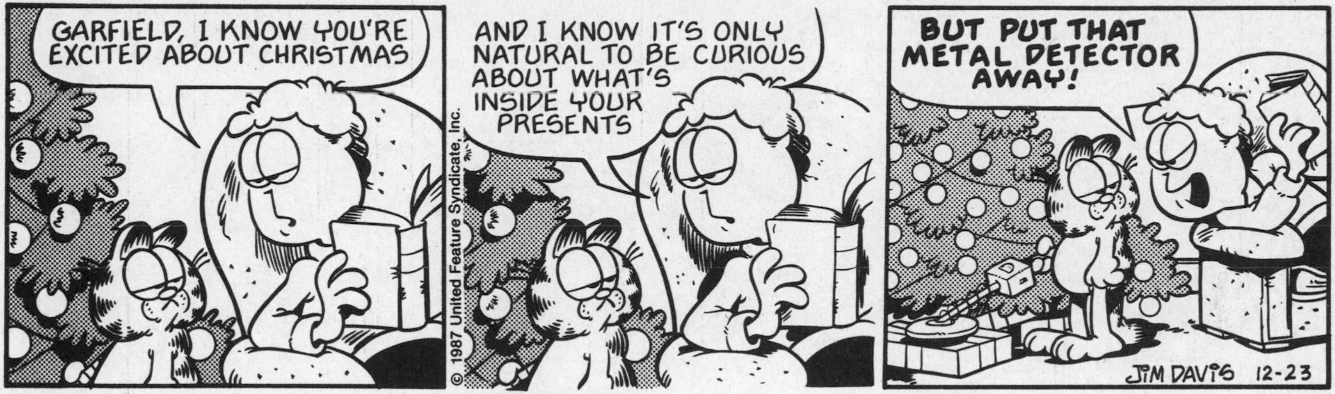
GARFIELD, I KNOW YOU'RE EXCITED ABOUT CHRISTMAS
AND I KNOW IT'S ONLY NATURAL TO BE CURIOUS ABOUT WHAT'S INSIDE YOUR PRESENTS
© 1987 United Feature Syndicate, Inc.
BUT PUT THAT METAL DETECTOR AWAY!
JIM DAVIS 12-23

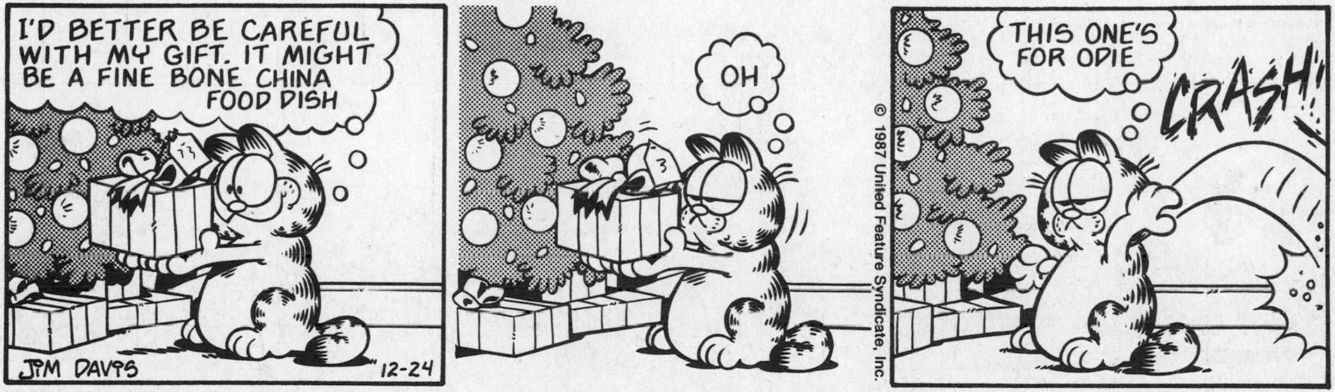
I'D BETTER BE CAREFUL WITH MY GIFT. IT MIGHT BE A FINE BONE CHINA FOOD DISH
JIM DAVIS 12-24
OH
© 1987 United Feature Syndicate, Inc.
THIS ONE'S FOR ODIE
CRASH!

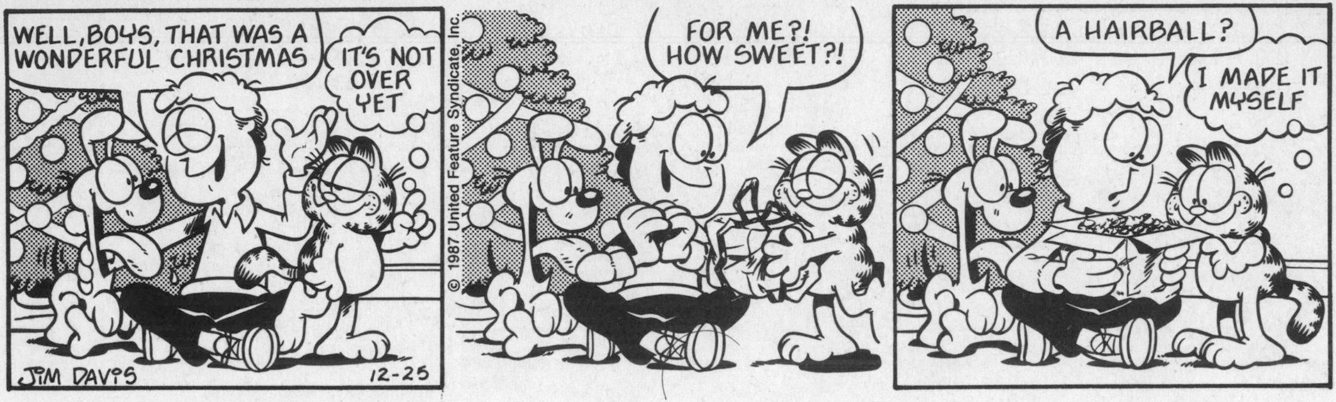
WELL, BOYS, THAT WAS A WONDERFUL CHRISTMAS
IT'S NOT OVER YET
JIM DAVIS
12-25
© 1987 United Feature Syndicate, Inc.
FOR ME?! HOW SWEET?!
A HAIRBALL?
I MADE IT MYSELF

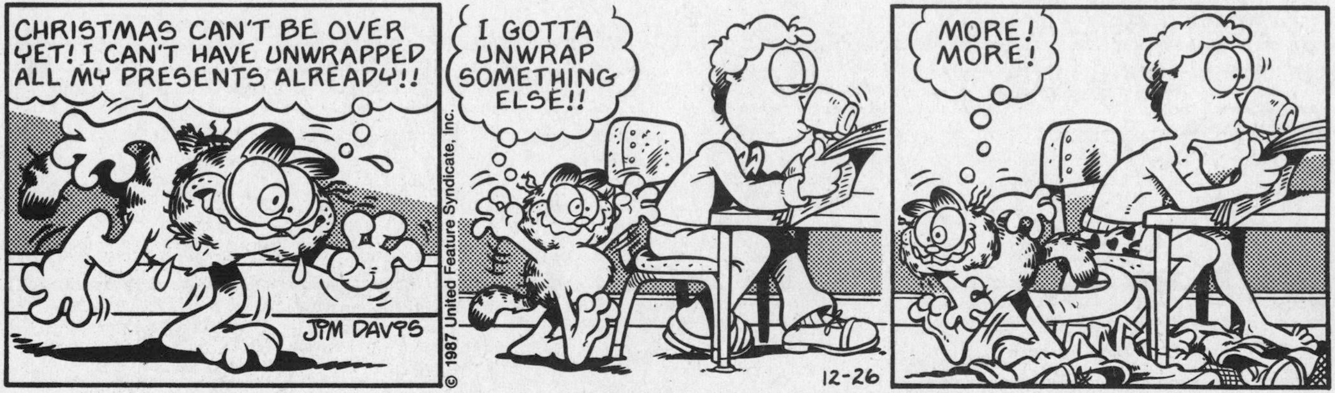
CHRISTMAS CAN'T BE OVER YET! I CAN'T HAVE UNWRAPPED ALL MY PRESENTS ALREADY!!
JIM DAVIS
© 1987 United Feature Syndicate, Inc.
I GOTTA UNWRAP SOMETHING ELSE!!
12-26
MORE! MORE!

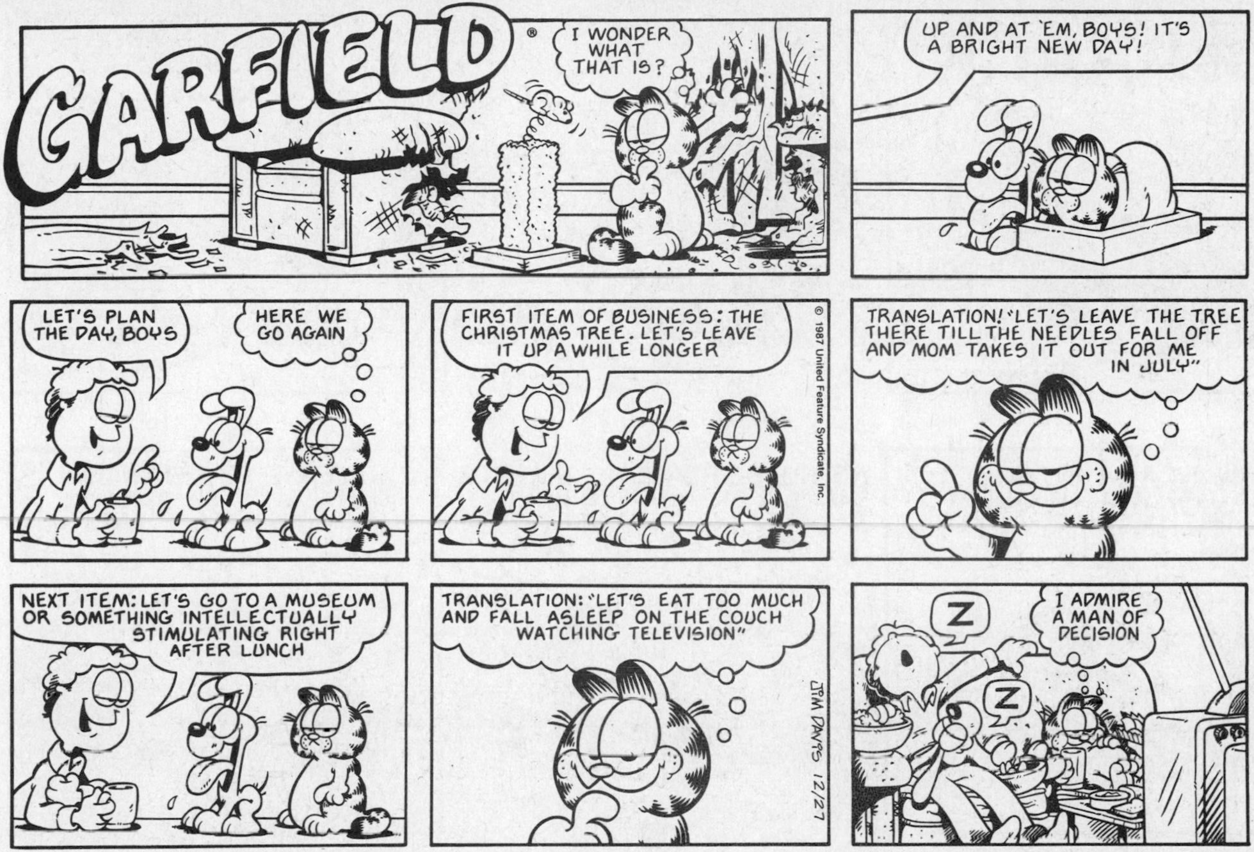
GARFIELD®
I WONDER WHAT THAT IS?
UP AND AT 'EM, BOYS! IT'S A BRIGHT NEW DAY!
LET'S PLAN THE DAY, BOYS
HERE WE GO AGAIN
FIRST ITEM OF BUSINESS: THE CHRISTMAS TREE. LET'S LEAVE IT UP A WHILE LONGER
© 1987 United Feature Syndicate, Inc.
TRANSLATION! "LET'S LEAVE THE TREE THERE TILL THE NEEDLES FALL OFF AND MOM TAKES IT OUT FOR ME IN JULY"
NEXT ITEM: LET'S GO TO A MUSEUM OR SOMETHING INTELLECTUALLY STIMULATING RIGHT AFTER LUNCH
TRANSLATION: "LET'S EAT TOO MUCH AND FALL ASLEEP ON THE COUCH WATCHING TELEVISION"
JIM DAVIS 12/27
Z
Z
I ADMIRE A MAN OF DECISION

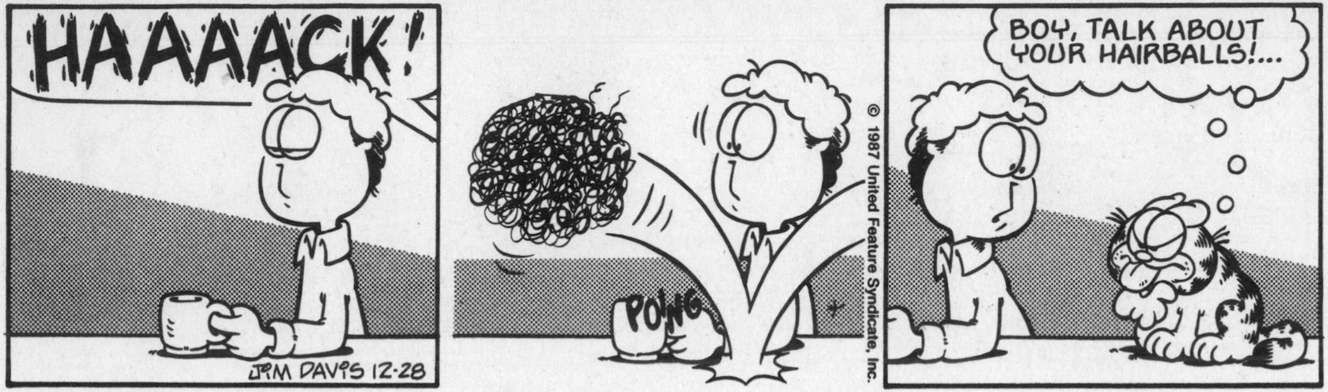
HAAAACK!
JIM DAVIS 12-28
POING
© 1987 United Feature Syndicate, Inc.
BOY, TALK ABOUT YOUR HAIRBALLS!...

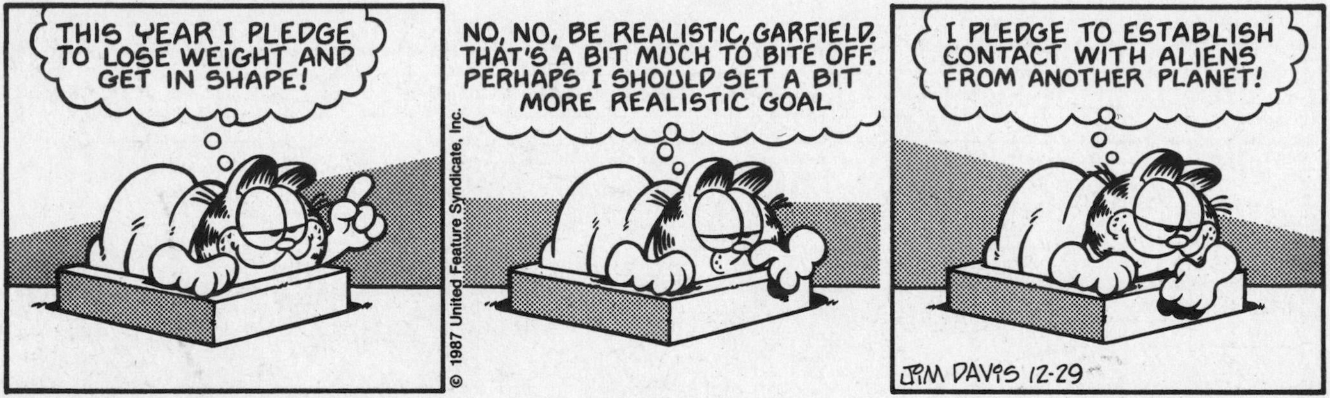
THIS YEAR I PLEDGE TO LOSE WEIGHT AND GET IN SHAPE!
© 1987 United Feature Syndicate, Inc.
NO, NO, BE REALISTIC, GARFIELD. THAT'S A BIT MUCH TO BITE OFF. PERHAPS I SHOULD SET A BIT MORE REALISTIC GOAL
I PLEDGE TO ESTABLISH CONTACT WITH ALIENS FROM ANOTHER PLANET!
JIM DAVIS 12-29

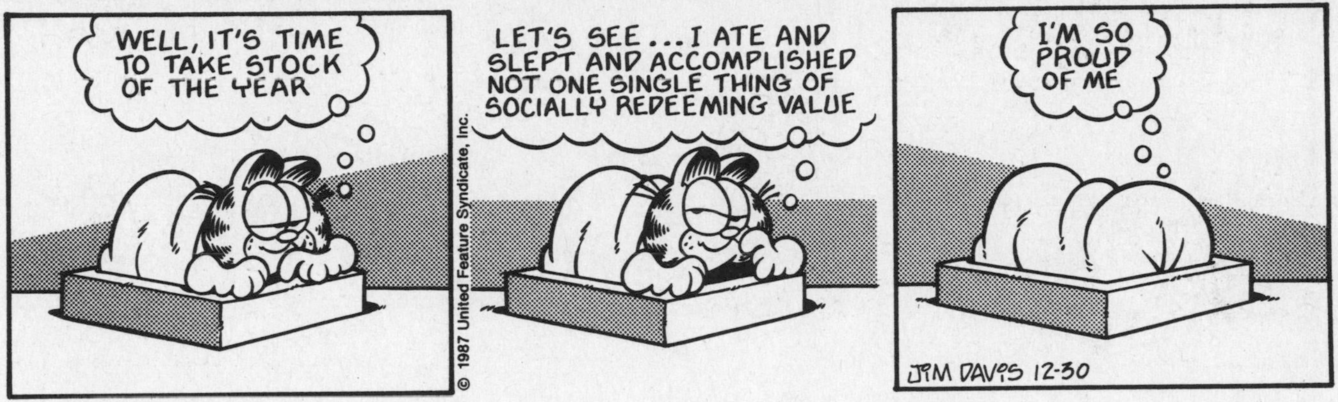
WELL, IT'S TIME TO TAKE STOCK OF THE YEAR
© 1987 United Feature Syndicate, Inc.
LET'S SEE... I ATE AND SLEPT AND ACCOMPLISHED NOT ONE SINGLE THING OF SOCIALLY REDEEMING VALUE
I'M SO PROUD OF ME
JIM DAVIS 12-30

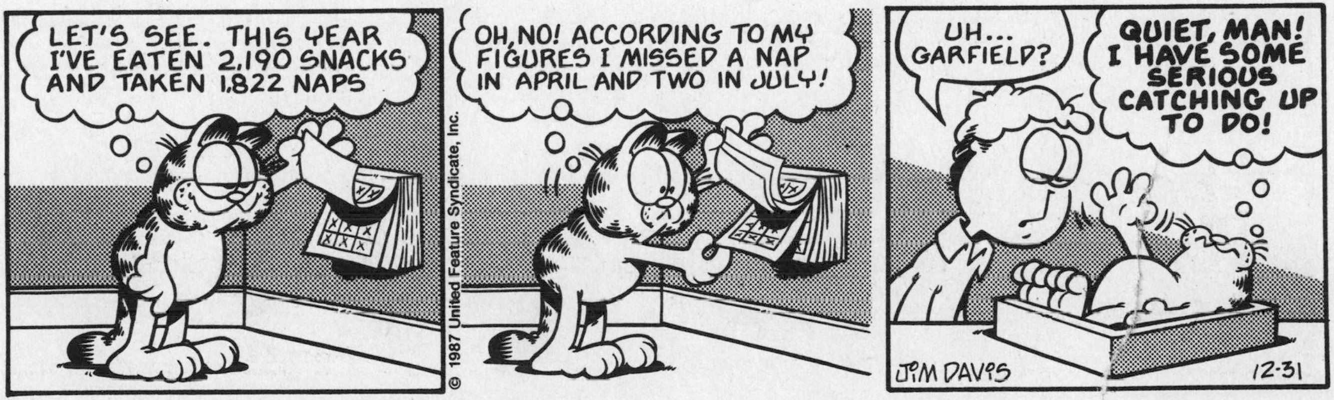
LET'S SEE. THIS YEAR I'VE EATEN 2,190 SNACKS AND TAKEN 1,822 NAPS
© 1987 United Feature Syndicate, Inc.
OH, NO! ACCORDING TO MY FIGURES I MISSED A NAP IN APRIL AND TWO IN JULY!
UH... GARFIELD?
QUIET, MAN! I HAVE SOME SERIOUS CATCHING UP TO DO!
JIM DAVIS
12-31

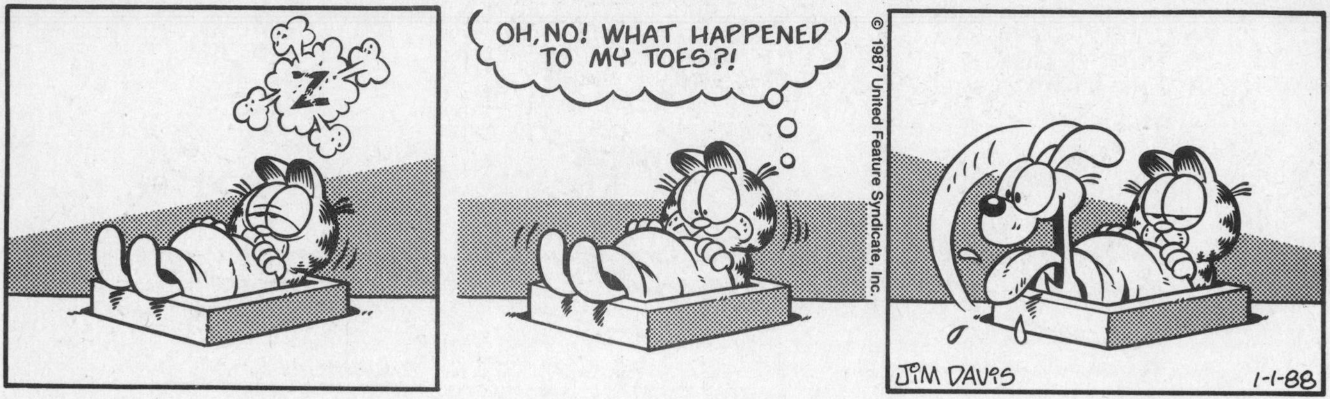
OH, NO! WHAT HAPPENED TO MY TOES?!
© 1987 United Feature Syndicate, Inc.
JIM DAVIS
1-1-88

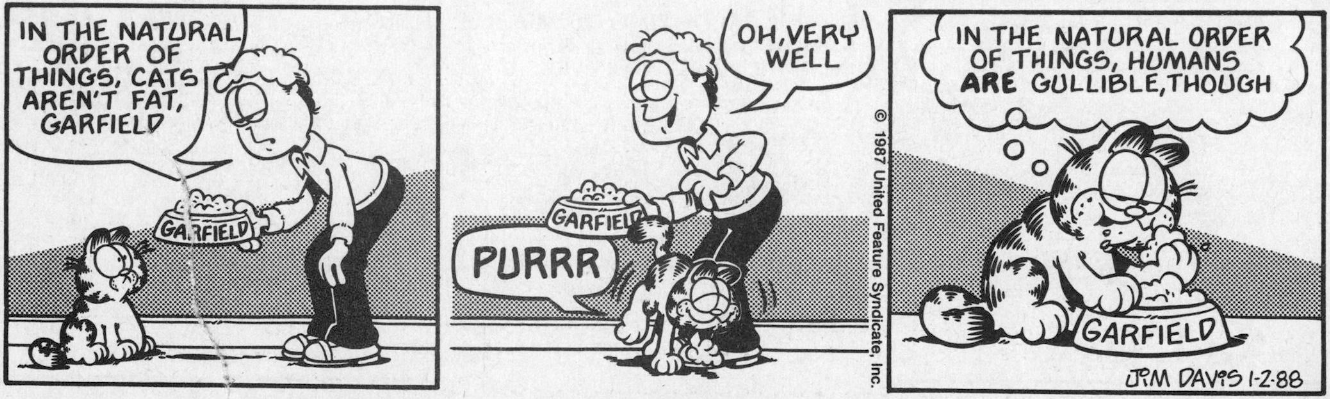
IN THE NATURAL ORDER OF THINGS, CATS AREN'T FAT, GARFIELD
GARFIELD
OH, VERY WELL
GARFIELD
PURRR
© 1987 United Feature Syndicate, Inc.
IN THE NATURAL ORDER OF THINGS, HUMANS **ARE** GULLIBLE, THOUGH
GARFIELD
JIM DAVIS 1-2-88

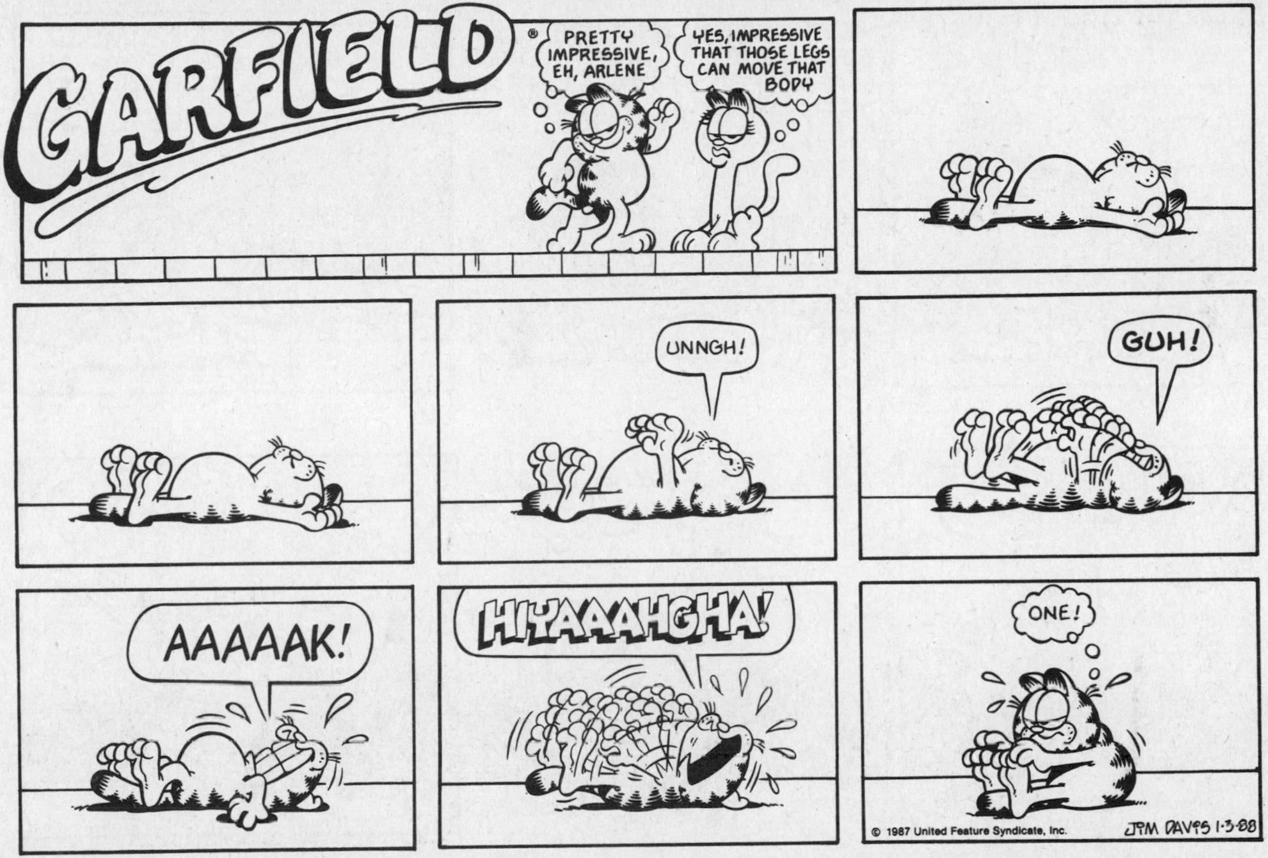
GARFIELD®
PRETTY IMPRESSIVE, EH, ARLENE
YES, IMPRESSIVE THAT THOSE LEGS CAN MOVE THAT BODY
UNNGH!
GUH!
AAAAAK!
HIYAAAHGHA!
ONE!
© 1987 United Feature Syndicate, Inc.
JIM DAVIS 1-3-88

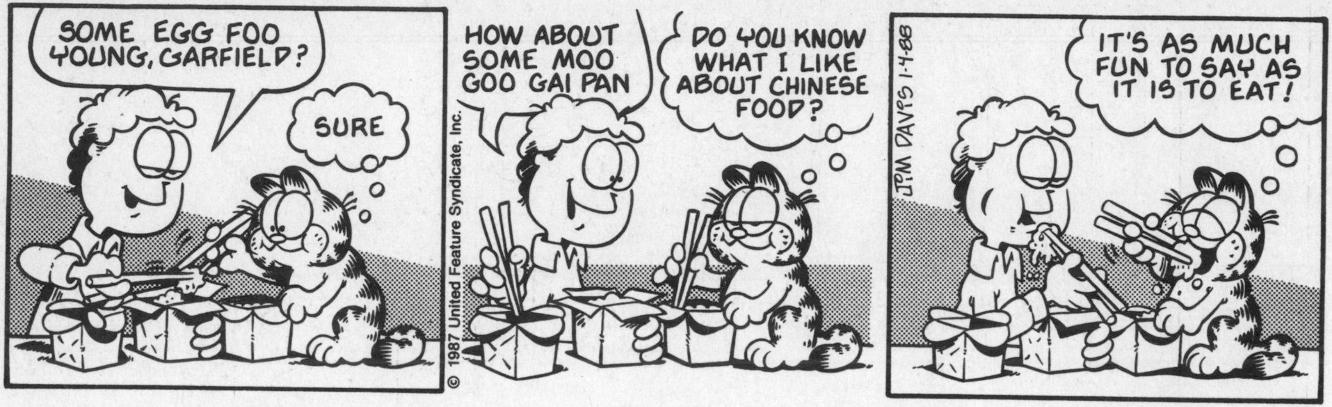
SOME EGG FOO YOUNG, GARFIELD?
SURE
HOW ABOUT SOME MOO GOO GAI PAN
DO YOU KNOW WHAT I LIKE ABOUT CHINESE FOOD?
IT'S AS MUCH FUN TO SAY AS IT IS TO EAT!
JPM DAVPS 1-4-88
© 1987 United Feature Syndicate, Inc.

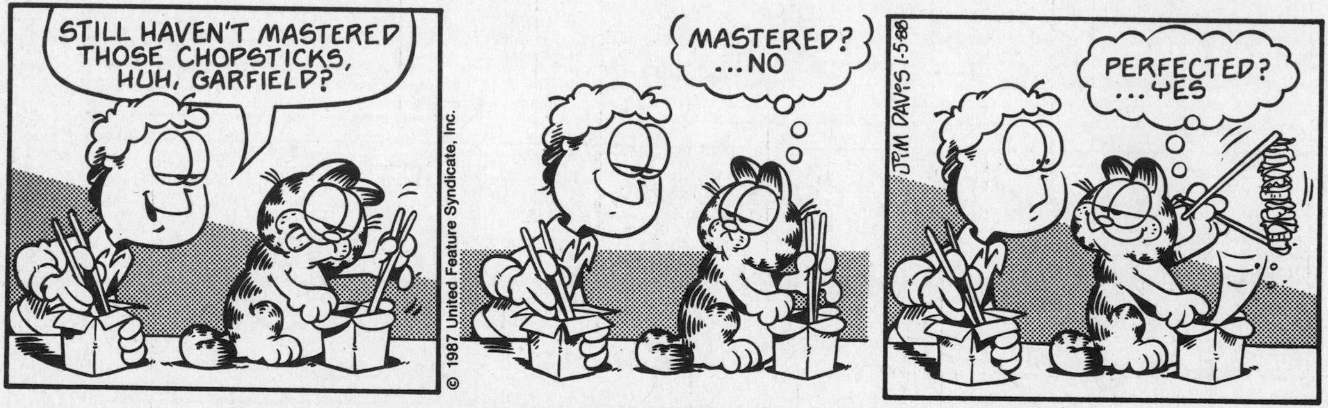
STILL HAVEN'T MASTERED THOSE CHOPSTICKS, HUH, GARFIELD?
MASTERED? ...NO
PERFECTED? ...YES
JPM DAVPS 1-5-88
© 1987 United Feature Syndicate, Inc.

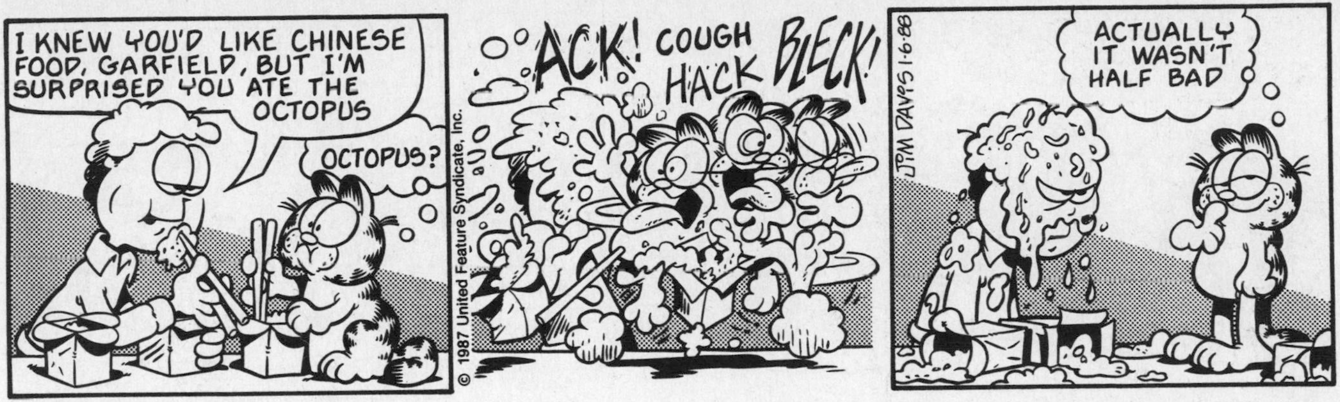
I KNEW YOU'D LIKE CHINESE FOOD, GARFIELD, BUT I'M SURPRISED YOU ATE THE OCTOPUS
OCTOPUS?
© 1987 United Feature Syndicate, Inc.
ACK! COUGH
HACK BLECK!
JIM DAVIS 1-6-88
ACTUALLY IT WASN'T HALF BAD

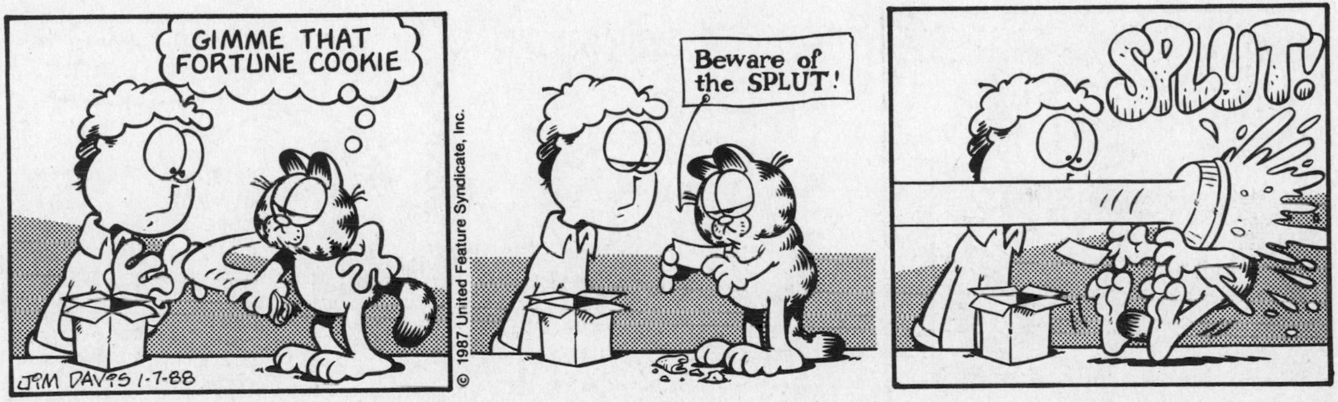
GIMME THAT FORTUNE COOKIE
JIM DAVIS 1-7-88
© 1987 United Feature Syndicate, Inc.
Beware of the SPLUT!
SPLUT!

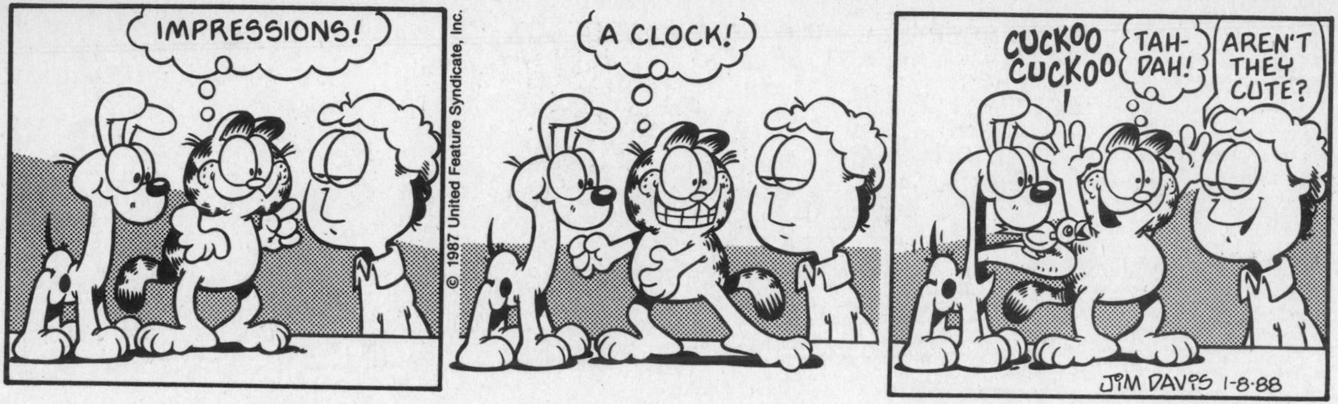
IMPRESSIONS!
© 1987 United Feature Syndicate, Inc.
A CLOCK!
CUCKOO CUCKOO
TAH-DAH!
AREN'T THEY CUTE?
JIM DAVIS 1-8-88

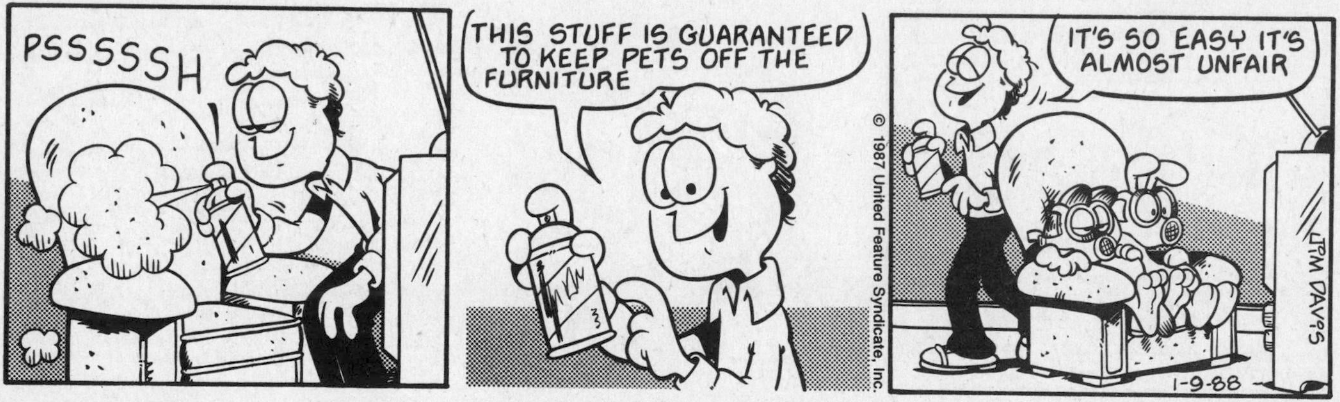
PSSSSSSH
THIS STUFF IS GUARANTEED TO KEEP PETS OFF THE FURNITURE
© 1987 United Feature Syndicate, Inc.
IT'S SO EASY IT'S ALMOST UNFAIR
JIM DAVIS
1-9-88

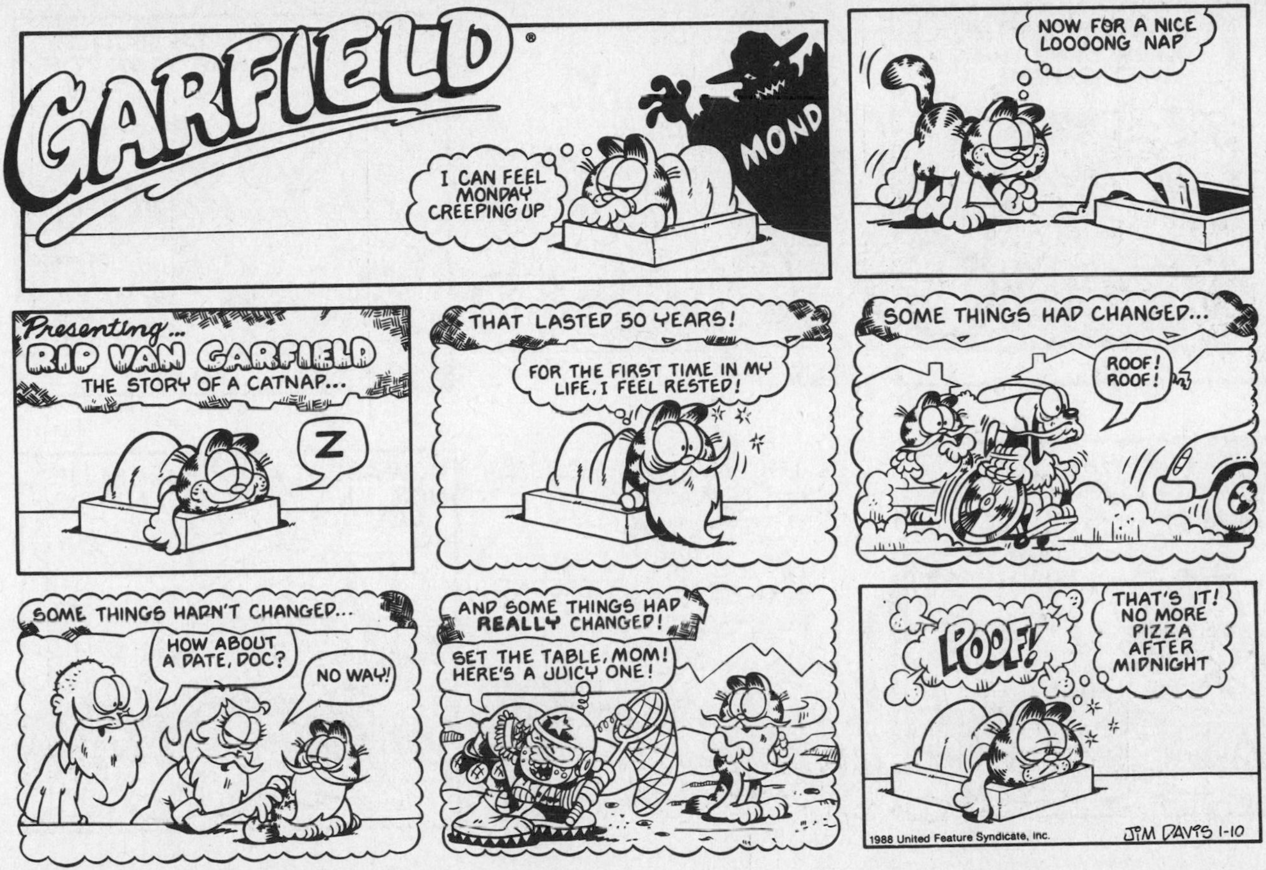
GARFIELD®
MOND
I CAN FEEL MONDAY CREEPING UP
NOW FOR A NICE LOOOONG NAP
Presenting... RIP VAN GARFIELD
THE STORY OF A CATNAP...
Z
THAT LASTED 50 YEARS!
FOR THE FIRST TIME IN MY LIFE, I FEEL RESTED!
SOME THINGS HAD CHANGED...
ROOF! ROOF!
SOME THINGS HADN'T CHANGED...
HOW ABOUT A DATE, DOC?
NO WAY!
AND SOME THINGS HAD **REALLY** CHANGED!
SET THE TABLE, MOM! HERE'S A JUICY ONE!
POOF!
THAT'S IT! NO MORE PIZZA AFTER MIDNIGHT
1988 United Feature Syndicate, Inc.
JIM DAVIS 1-10

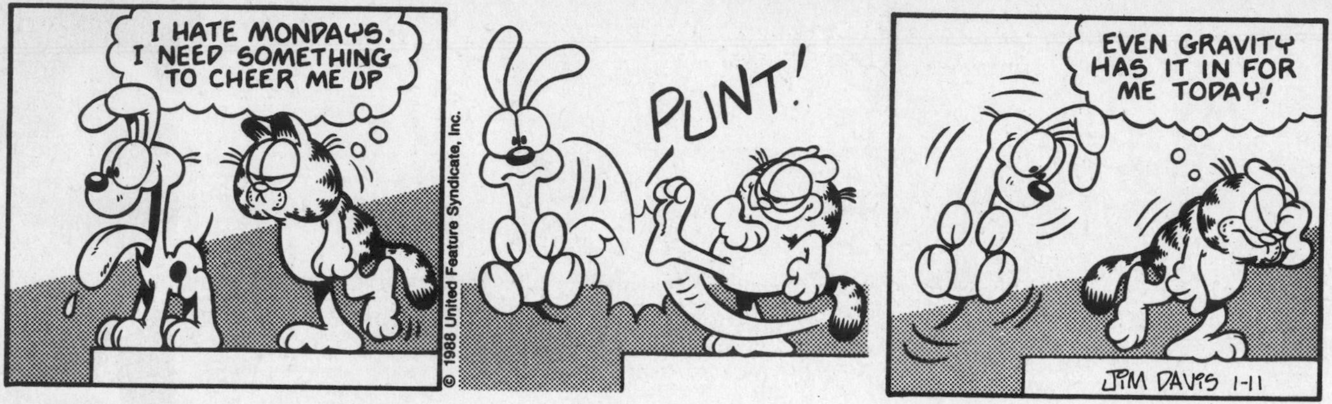
I HATE MONDAYS. I NEED SOMETHING TO CHEER ME UP
PUNT!
EVEN GRAVITY HAS IT IN FOR ME TODAY!
JIM DAVIS 1-11
© 1988 United Feature Syndicate, Inc.

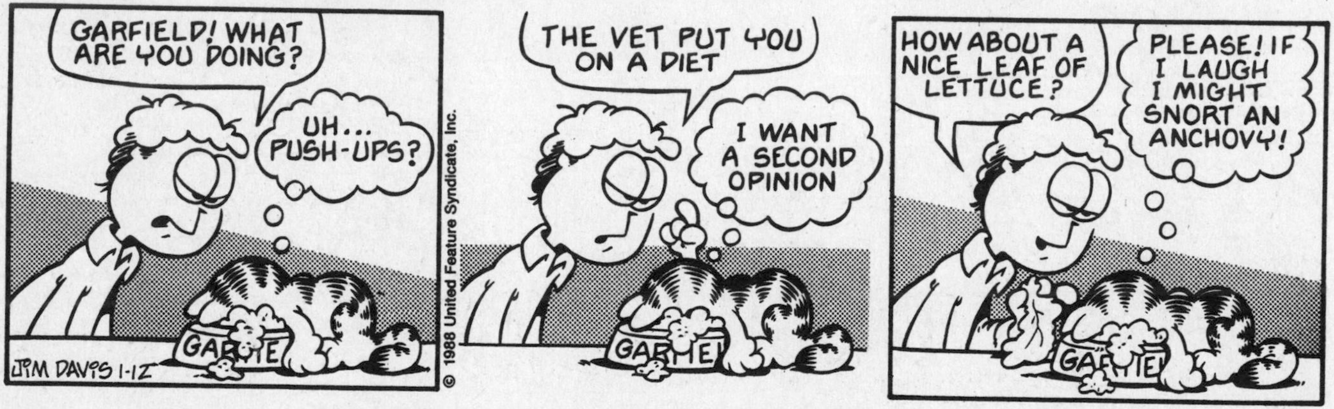
GARFIELD! WHAT ARE YOU DOING?
UH... PUSH-UPS?
THE VET PUT YOU ON A DIET
I WANT A SECOND OPINION
HOW ABOUT A NICE LEAF OF LETTUCE?
PLEASE! IF I LAUGH I MIGHT SNORT AN ANCHOVY!
JIM DAVIS 1-12
© 1988 United Feature Syndicate, Inc.

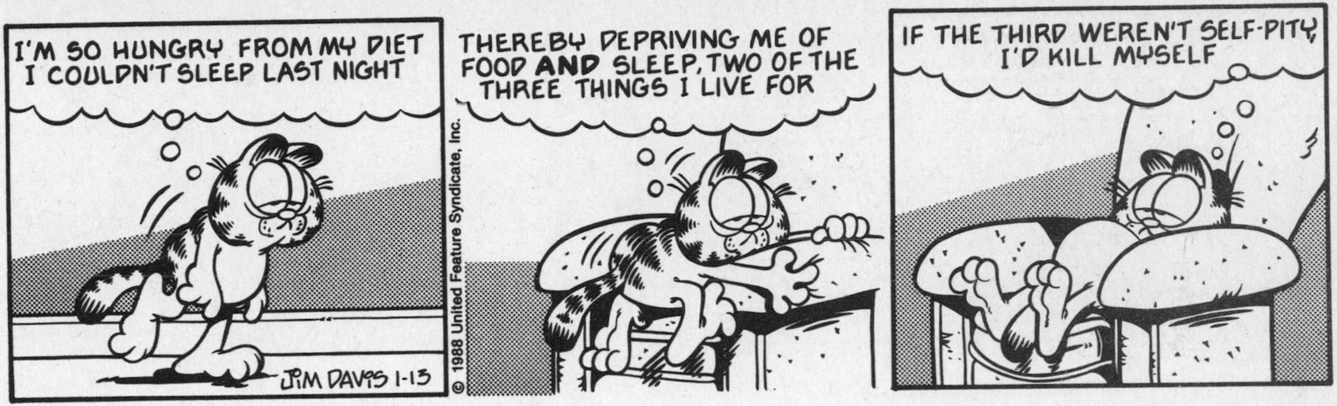
I'M SO HUNGRY FROM MY DIET I COULDN'T SLEEP LAST NIGHT
JIM DAVIS 1-13
© 1988 United Feature Syndicate, Inc.
THEREBY DEPRIVING ME OF FOOD **AND** SLEEP, TWO OF THE THREE THINGS I LIVE FOR
IF THE THIRD WEREN'T SELF-PITY, I'D KILL MYSELF

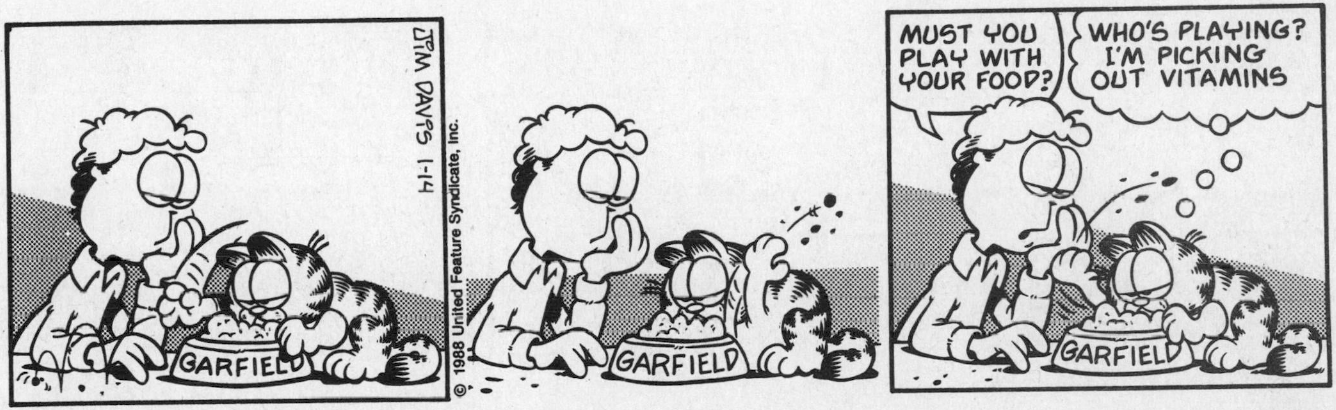
GARFIELD
JIM DAVIS 1-14
© 1988 United Feature Syndicate, Inc.
GARFIELD
MUST YOU PLAY WITH YOUR FOOD?
WHO'S PLAYING? I'M PICKING OUT VITAMINS
GARFIELD

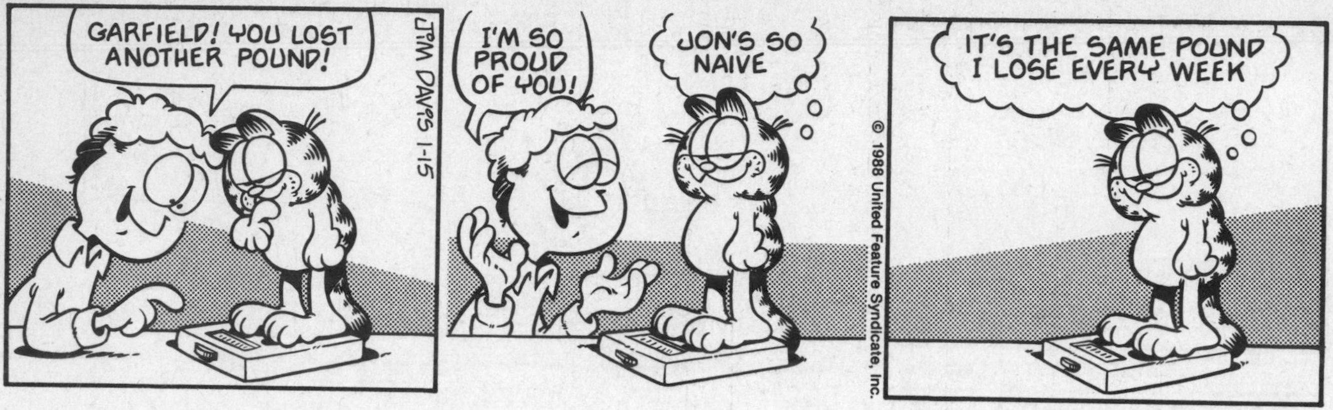
GARFIELD! YOU LOST ANOTHER POUND!
JIM DAVIS 1-15
I'M SO PROUD OF YOU!
JON'S SO NAIVE
© 1988 United Feature Syndicate, Inc.
IT'S THE SAME POUND I LOSE EVERY WEEK

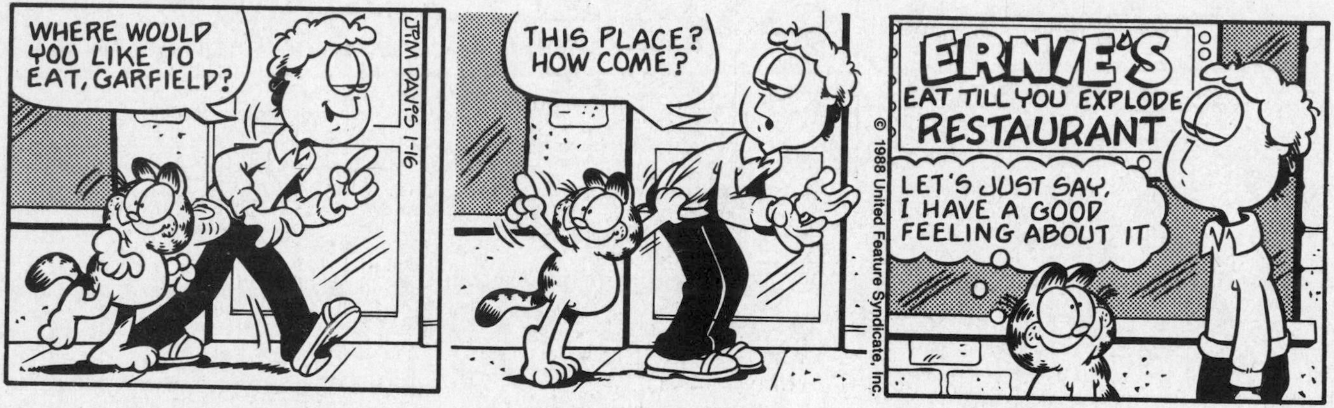
WHERE WOULD YOU LIKE TO EAT, GARFIELD?
JIM DAVIS 1-16
THIS PLACE? HOW COME?
© 1988 United Feature Syndicate, Inc.
ERNIE'S
EAT TILL YOU EXPLODE
RESTAURANT
LET'S JUST SAY, I HAVE A GOOD FEELING ABOUT IT

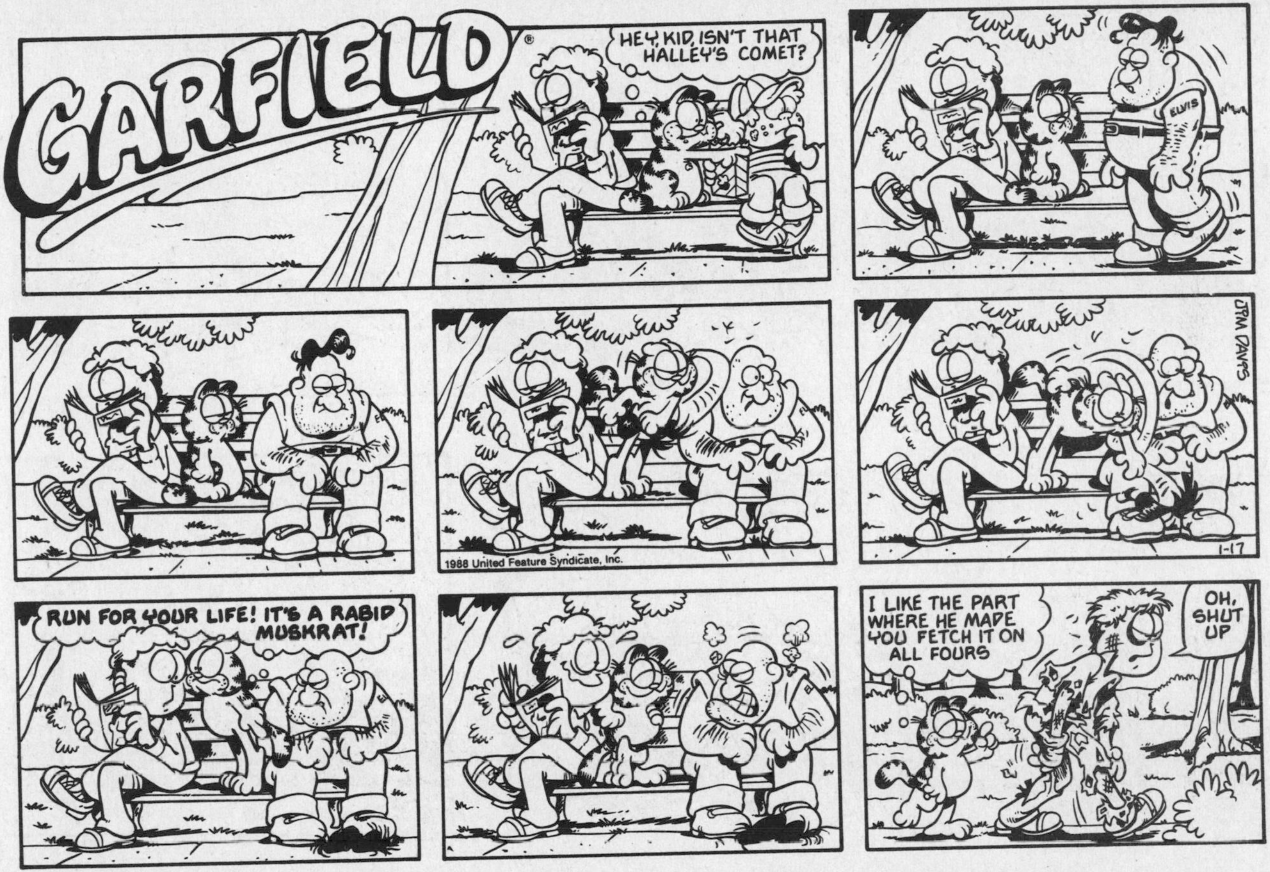
GARFIELD
HEY, KID, ISN'T THAT HALLEY'S COMET?
ELVIS
JIM DAVIS
1988 United Feature Syndicate, Inc.
1-17
RUN FOR YOUR LIFE! IT'S A RABID MUSKRAT!
I LIKE THE PART WHERE HE MADE YOU FETCH IT ON ALL FOURS
OH, SHUT UP

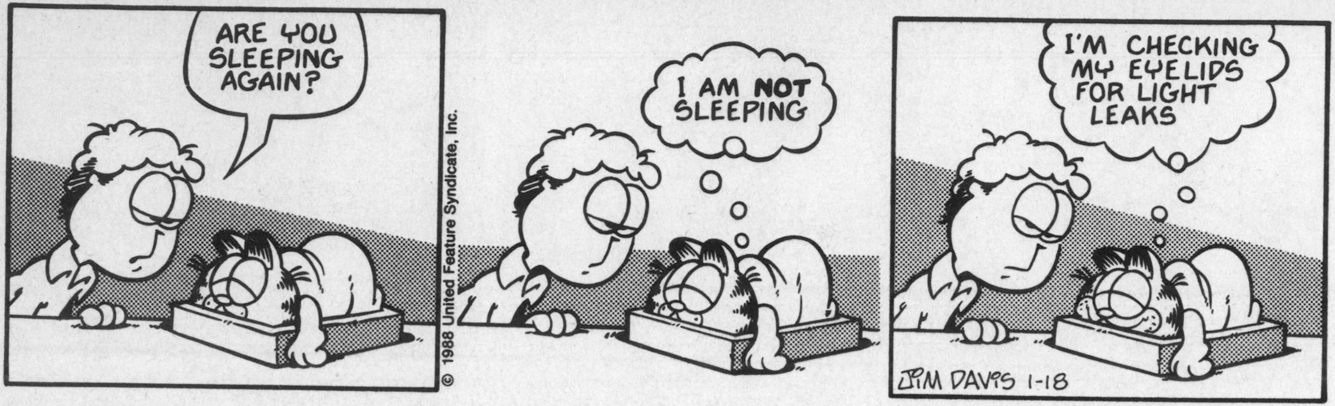
ARE YOU SLEEPING AGAIN?
I AM NOT SLEEPING
© 1988 United Feature Syndicate, Inc.
I'M CHECKING MY EYELIDS FOR LIGHT LEAKS
JIM DAVIS 1-18

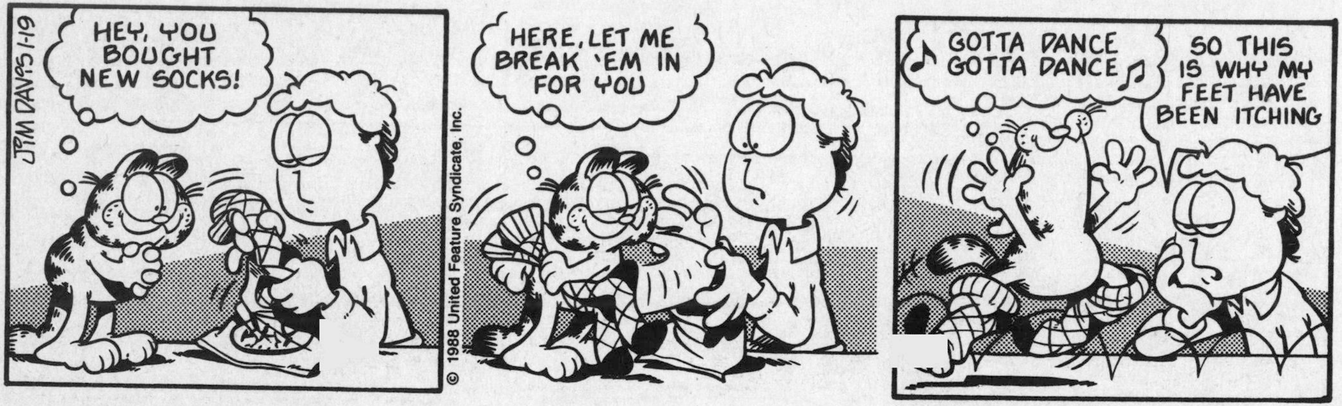
JIM DAVIS 1-19
HEY, YOU BOUGHT NEW SOCKS!
© 1988 United Feature Syndicate, Inc.
HERE, LET ME BREAK 'EM IN FOR YOU
♪ GOTTA DANCE GOTTA DANCE ♪
SO THIS IS WHY MY FEET HAVE BEEN ITCHING

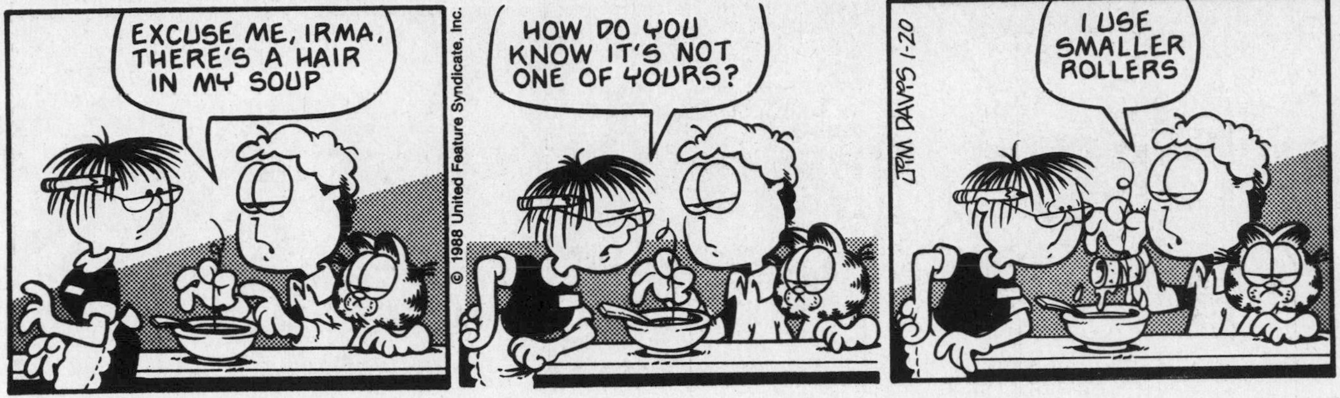
EXCUSE ME, IRMA. THERE'S A HAIR IN MY SOUP
© 1988 United Feature Syndicate, Inc.
HOW DO YOU KNOW IT'S NOT ONE OF YOURS?
JPM DAVPS 1-20
I USE SMALLER ROLLERS

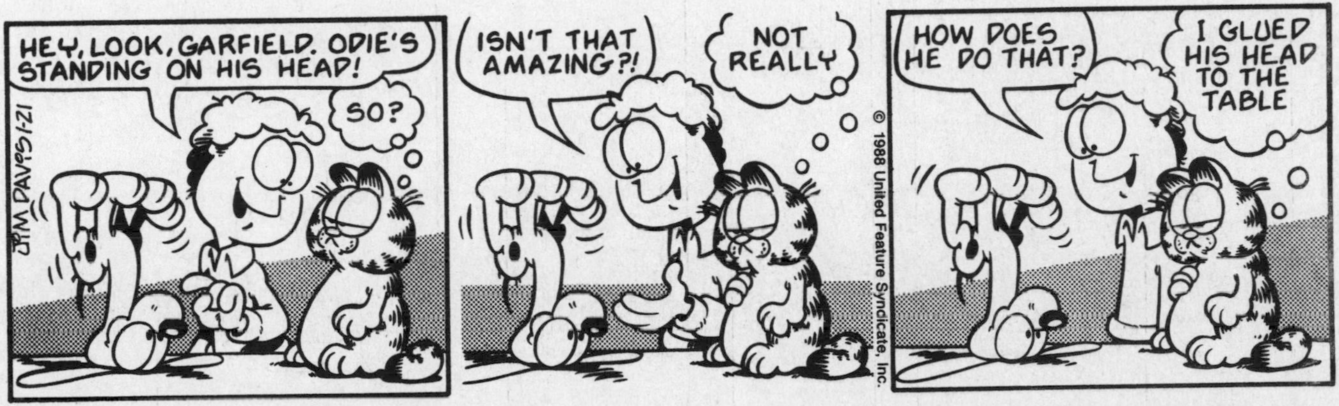
HEY, LOOK, GARFIELD. ODIE'S STANDING ON HIS HEAD!
SO?
JPM DAVPS 1-21
ISN'T THAT AMAZING?!
NOT REALLY
© 1988 United Feature Syndicate, Inc.
HOW DOES HE DO THAT?
I GLUED HIS HEAD TO THE TABLE

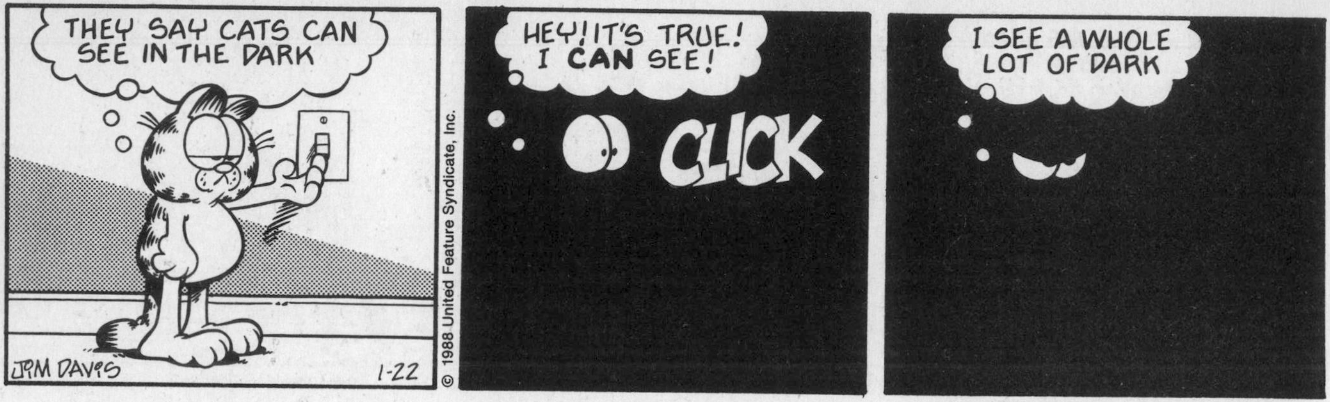
THEY SAY CATS CAN SEE IN THE DARK
JIM DAVIS
1-22
© 1988 United Feature Syndicate, Inc.
HEY! IT'S TRUE! I CAN SEE!
CLICK
I SEE A WHOLE LOT OF DARK

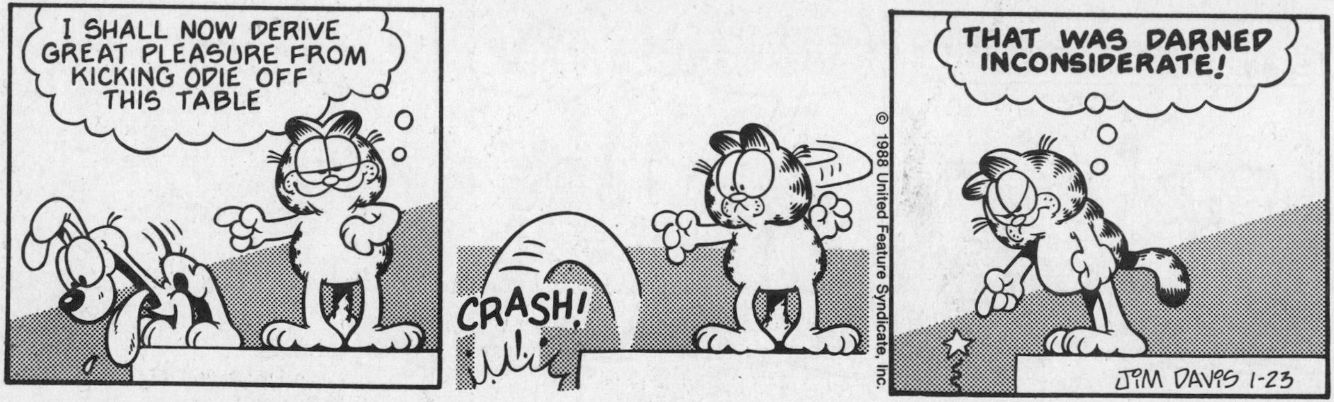
I SHALL NOW DERIVE GREAT PLEASURE FROM KICKING ODIE OFF THIS TABLE
CRASH!
© 1988 United Feature Syndicate, Inc.
THAT WAS DARNED INCONSIDERATE!
JIM DAVIS 1-23

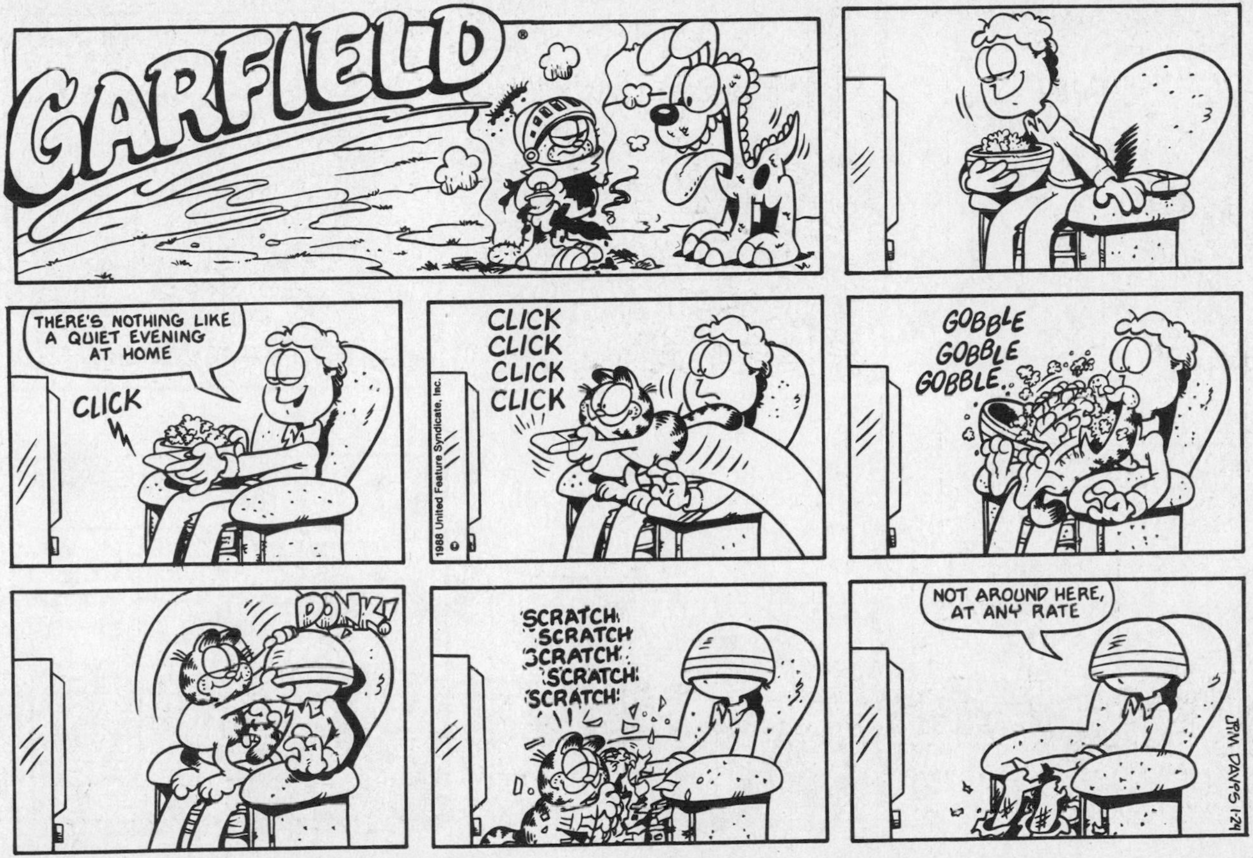
GARFIELD
THERE'S NOTHING LIKE A QUIET EVENING AT HOME
CLICK
CLICK CLICK CLICK CLICK
© 1988 United Feature Syndicate, Inc.
GOBBLE GOBBLE GOBBLE GOBBLE...
DONK!
SCRATCH! SCRATCH! SCRATCH! SCRATCH! SCRATCH!
NOT AROUND HERE, AT ANY RATE
JPM DAVIS 1-24

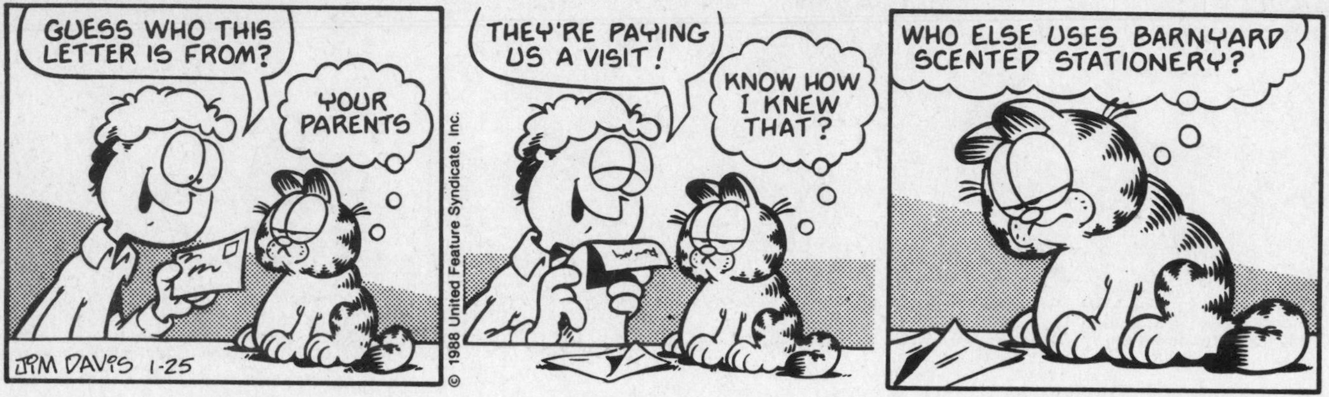
GUESS WHO THIS LETTER IS FROM?
YOUR PARENTS
JIM DAVIS 1-25
THEY'RE PAYING US A VISIT!
KNOW HOW I KNEW THAT?
WHO ELSE USES BARNYARD SCENTED STATIONERY?
© 1988 United Feature Syndicate, Inc.

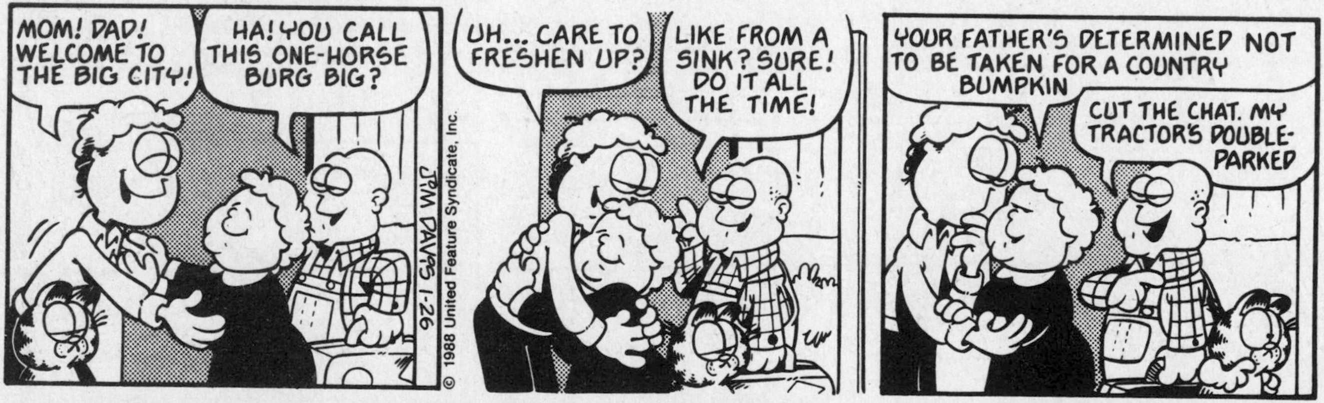
MOM! DAD! WELCOME TO THE BIG CITY!
HA! YOU CALL THIS ONE-HORSE BURG BIG?
JIM DAVIS 1-26
UH... CARE TO FRESHEN UP?
LIKE FROM A SINK? SURE! DO IT ALL THE TIME!
YOUR FATHER'S DETERMINED NOT TO BE TAKEN FOR A COUNTRY BUMPKIN
CUT THE CHAT. MY TRACTOR'S DOUBLE-PARKED
© 1988 United Feature Syndicate, Inc.

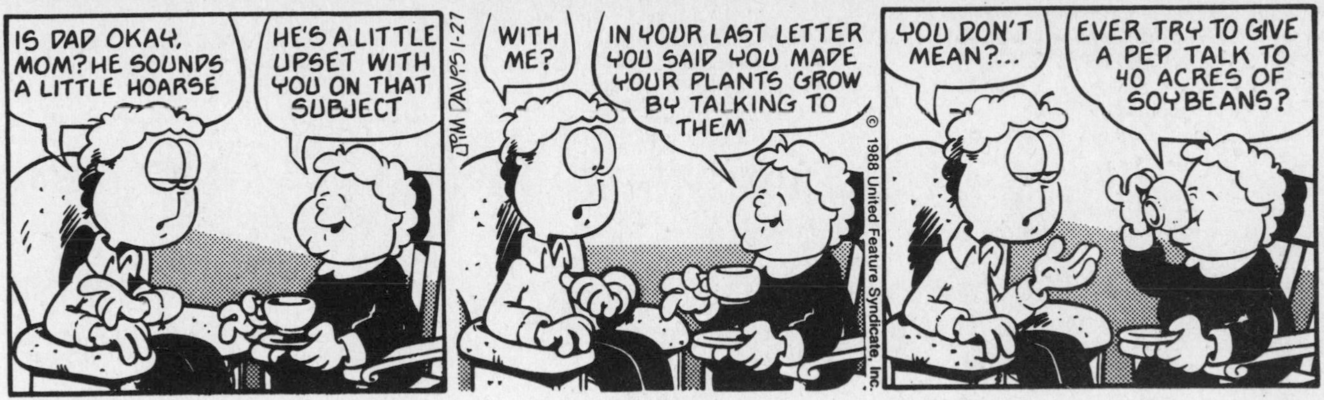
IS DAD OKAY, MOM? HE SOUNDS A LITTLE HOARSE
HE'S A LITTLE UPSET WITH YOU ON THAT SUBJECT
JIM DAVIS 1-27
WITH ME?
IN YOUR LAST LETTER YOU SAID YOU MADE YOUR PLANTS GROW BY TALKING TO THEM
© 1988 United Feature Syndicate, Inc.
YOU DON'T MEAN?...
EVER TRY TO GIVE A PEP TALK TO 40 ACRES OF SOYBEANS?

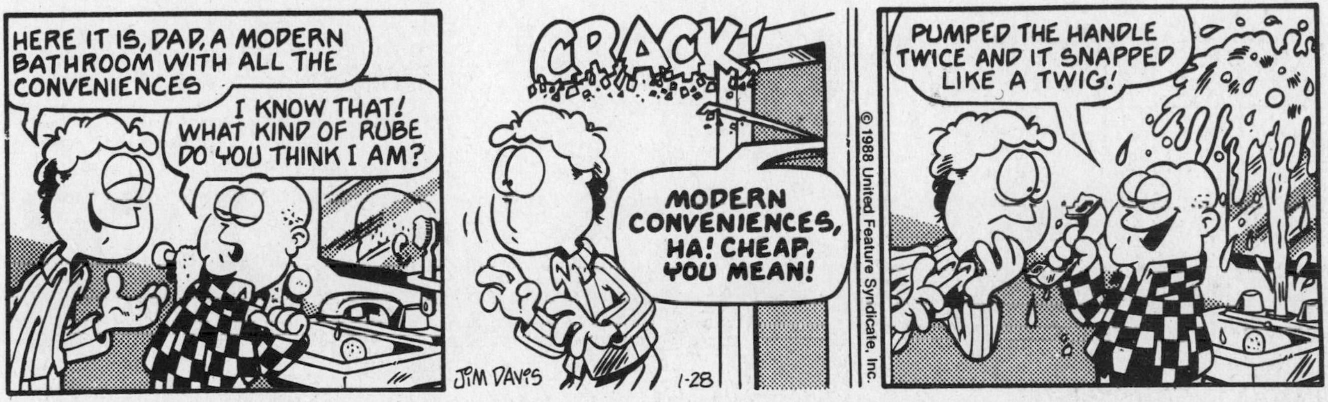
HERE IT IS, DAD, A MODERN BATHROOM WITH ALL THE CONVENIENCES
I KNOW THAT! WHAT KIND OF RUBE DO YOU THINK I AM?
CRACK!
MODERN CONVENIENCES, HA! CHEAP, YOU MEAN!
JIM DAVIS
1-28
© 1988 United Feature Syndicate, Inc.
PUMPED THE HANDLE TWICE AND IT SNAPPED LIKE A TWIG!

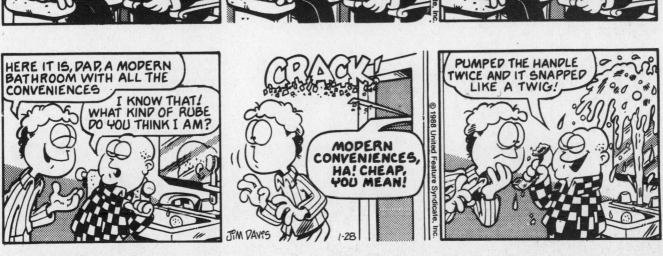

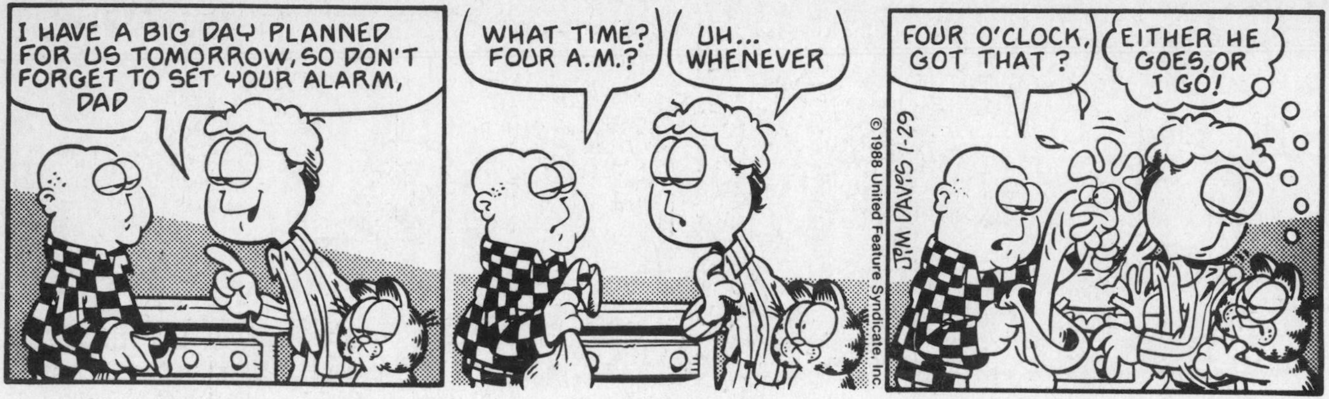
I HAVE A BIG DAY PLANNED FOR US TOMORROW, SO DON'T FORGET TO SET YOUR ALARM, DAD
WHAT TIME? FOUR A.M.?
UH... WHENEVER
FOUR O'CLOCK, GOT THAT?
EITHER HE GOES, OR I GO!
JIM DAVIS 1-29
© 1988 United Feature Syndicate, Inc.

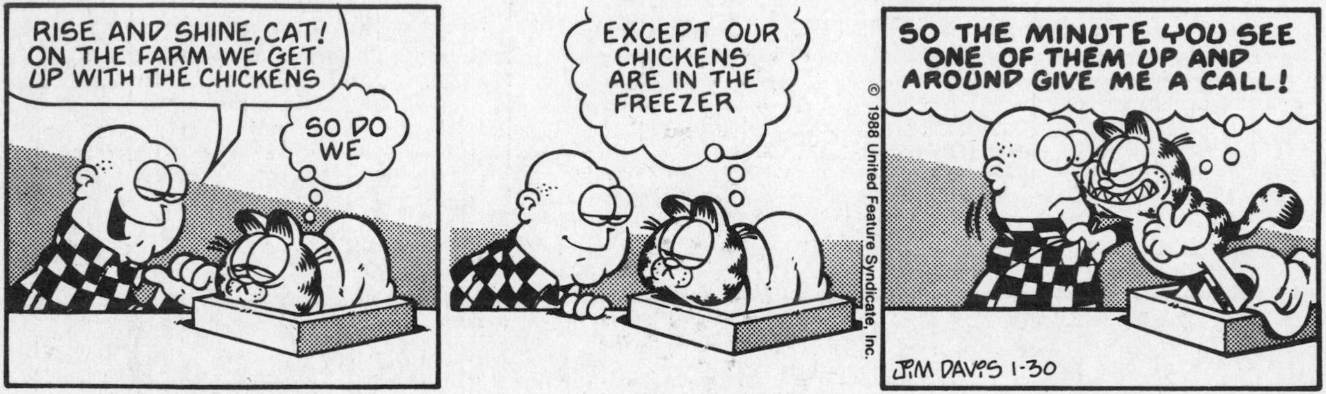
RISE AND SHINE, CAT! ON THE FARM WE GET UP WITH THE CHICKENS
SO DO WE
EXCEPT OUR CHICKENS ARE IN THE FREEZER
SO THE MINUTE YOU SEE ONE OF THEM UP AND AROUND GIVE ME A CALL!
JIM DAVIS 1-30
© 1988 United Feature Syndicate, Inc.

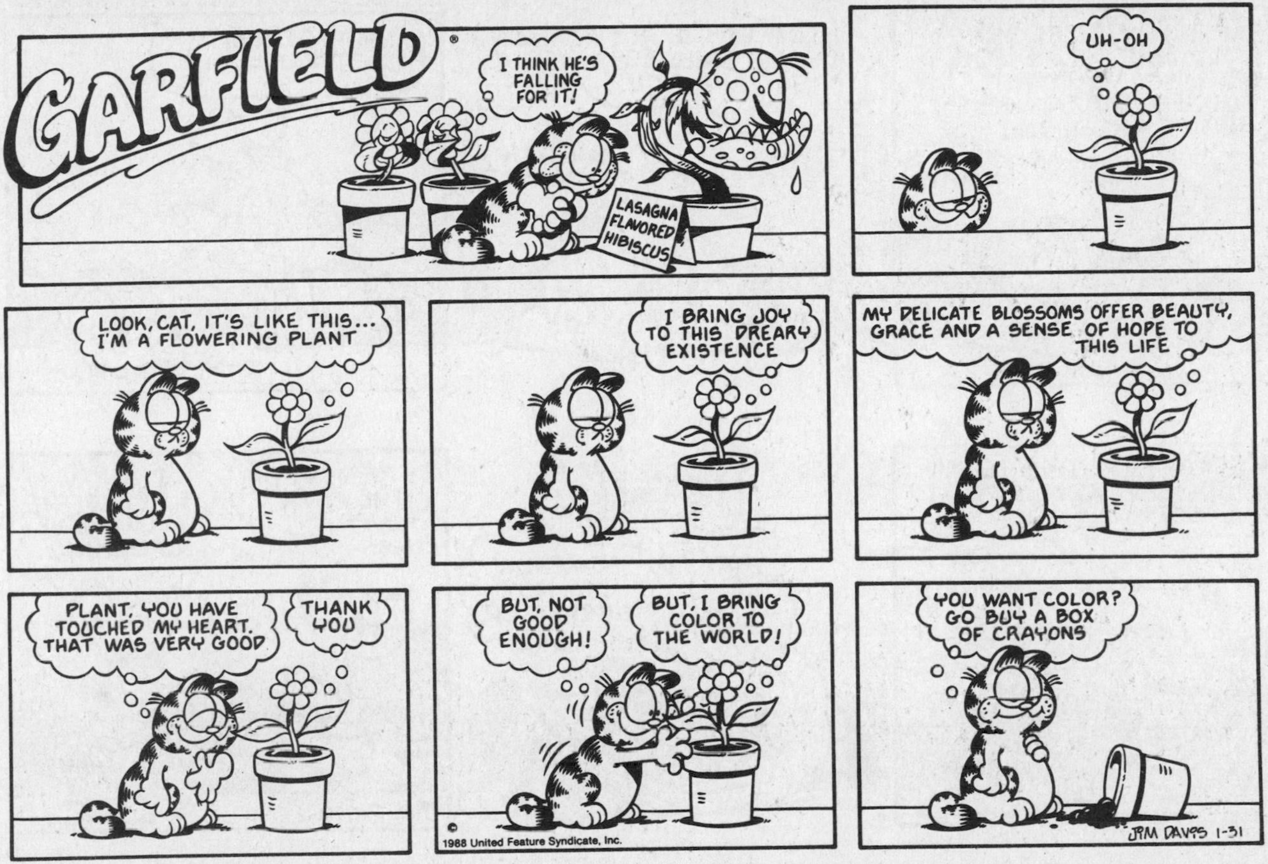
GARFIELD®
I THINK HE'S FALLING FOR IT!
LASAGNA FLAVORED HIBISCUS
UH-OH
LOOK, CAT, IT'S LIKE THIS... I'M A FLOWERING PLANT
I BRING JOY TO THIS DREARY EXISTENCE
MY DELICATE BLOSSOMS OFFER BEAUTY, GRACE AND A SENSE OF HOPE TO THIS LIFE
PLANT, YOU HAVE TOUCHED MY HEART. THAT WAS VERY GOOD
THANK YOU
BUT, I BRING COLOR TO THE WORLD!
BUT, NOT GOOD ENOUGH!
YOU WANT COLOR? GO BUY A BOX OF CRAYONS
© 1988 United Feature Syndicate, Inc.
JPM DAVIS 1-31

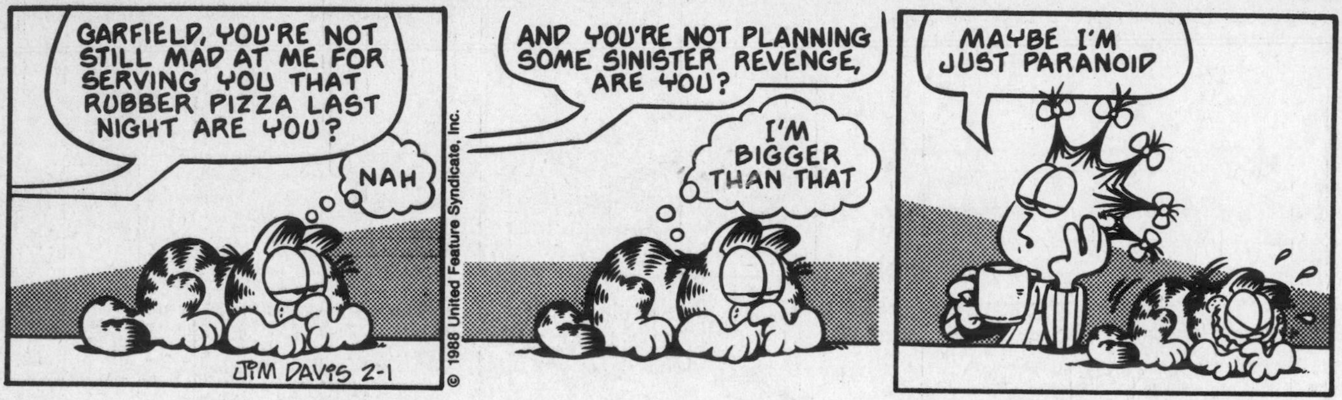
GARFIELD, YOU'RE NOT STILL MAD AT ME FOR SERVING YOU THAT RUBBER PIZZA LAST NIGHT ARE YOU?
NAH
AND YOU'RE NOT PLANNING SOME SINISTER REVENGE, ARE YOU?
I'M BIGGER THAN THAT
MAYBE I'M JUST PARANOID
JIM DAVIS 2-1
© 1988 United Feature Syndicate, Inc.

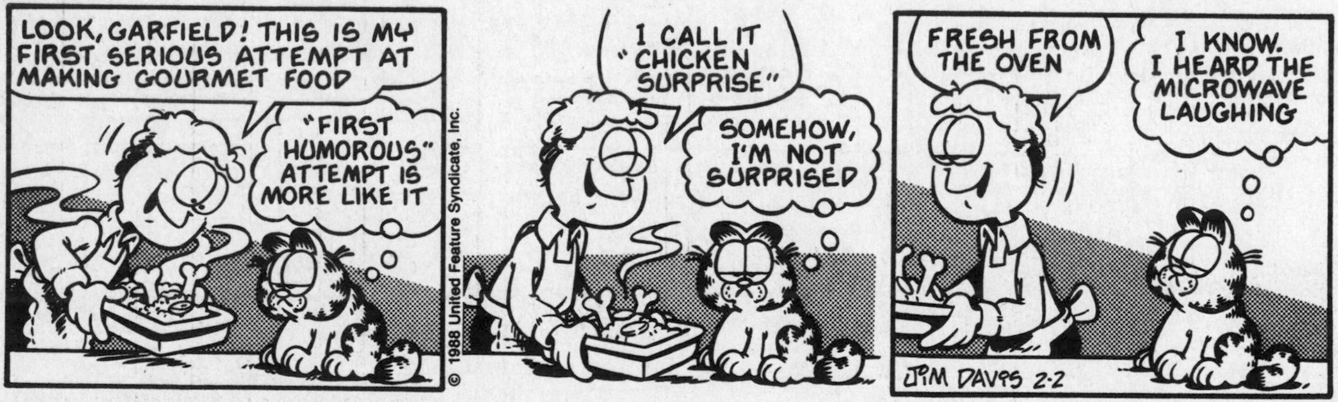
LOOK, GARFIELD! THIS IS MY FIRST SERIOUS ATTEMPT AT MAKING GOURMET FOOD
"FIRST HUMOROUS" ATTEMPT IS MORE LIKE IT
I CALL IT "CHICKEN SURPRISE"
SOMEHOW, I'M NOT SURPRISED
FRESH FROM THE OVEN
I KNOW. I HEARD THE MICROWAVE LAUGHING
JIM DAVIS 2-2
© 1988 United Feature Syndicate, Inc.

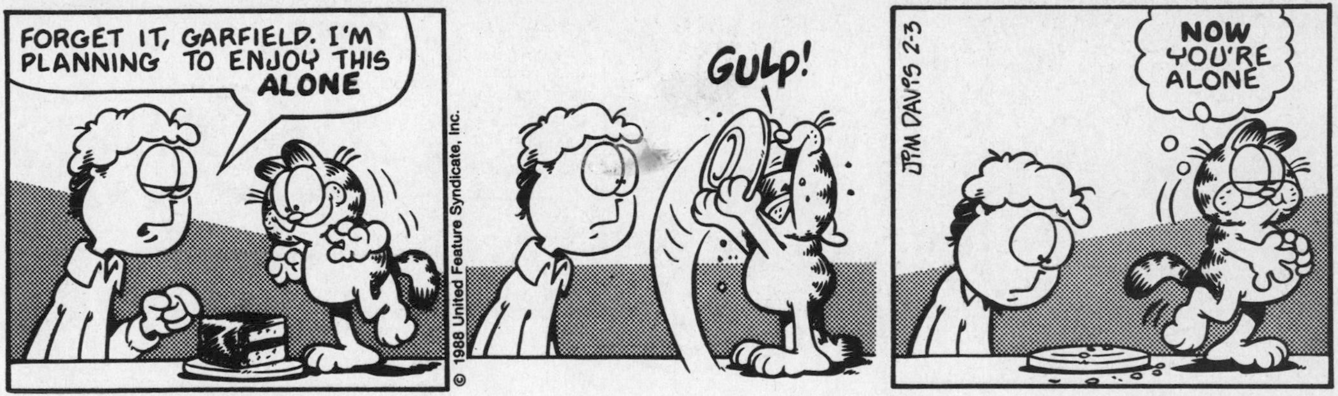
FORGET IT, GARFIELD. I'M PLANNING TO ENJOY THIS ALONE
© 1988 United Feature Syndicate, Inc.
GULP!
NOW YOU'RE ALONE

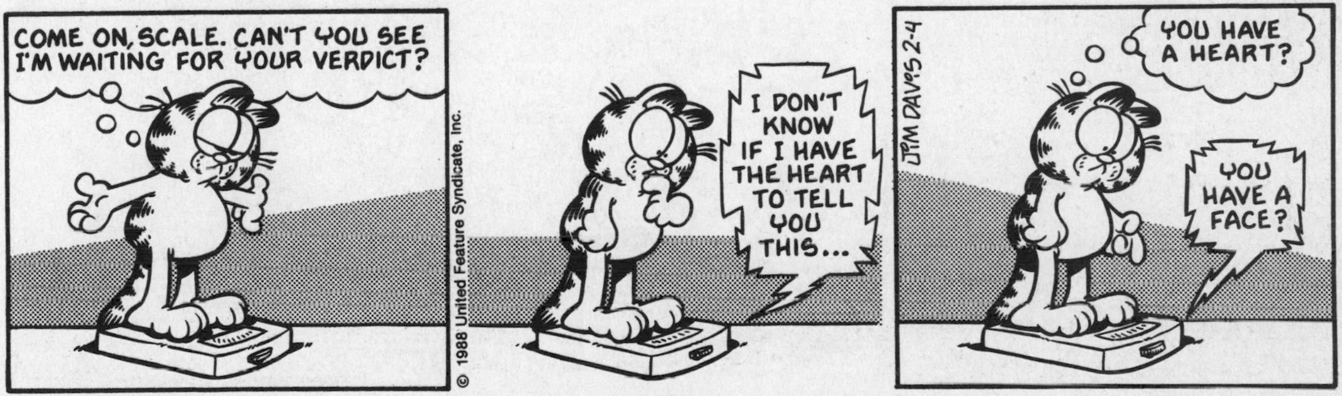
COME ON, SCALE. CAN'T YOU SEE I'M WAITING FOR YOUR VERDICT?
© 1988 United Feature Syndicate, Inc.
I DON'T KNOW IF I HAVE THE HEART TO TELL YOU THIS...
YOU HAVE A HEART?
YOU HAVE A FACE?

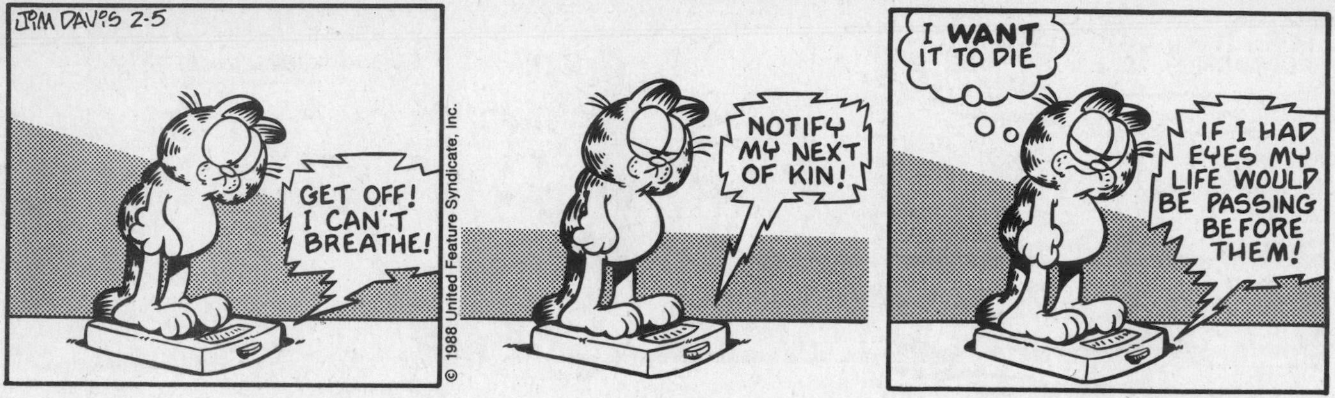
JIM DAVIS 2-5
GET OFF! I CAN'T BREATHE!
NOTIFY MY NEXT OF KIN!
I WANT IT TO DIE
IF I HAD EYES MY LIFE WOULD BE PASSING BEFORE THEM!

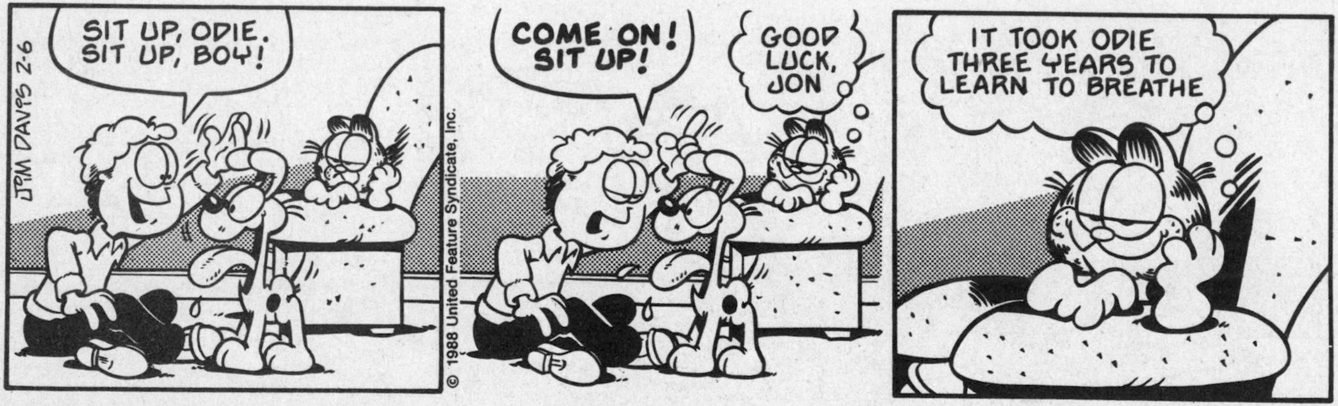
JIM DAVIS 2-6
SIT UP, ODIE. SIT UP, BOY!
COME ON! SIT UP!
GOOD LUCK, JON
IT TOOK ODIE THREE YEARS TO LEARN TO BREATHE

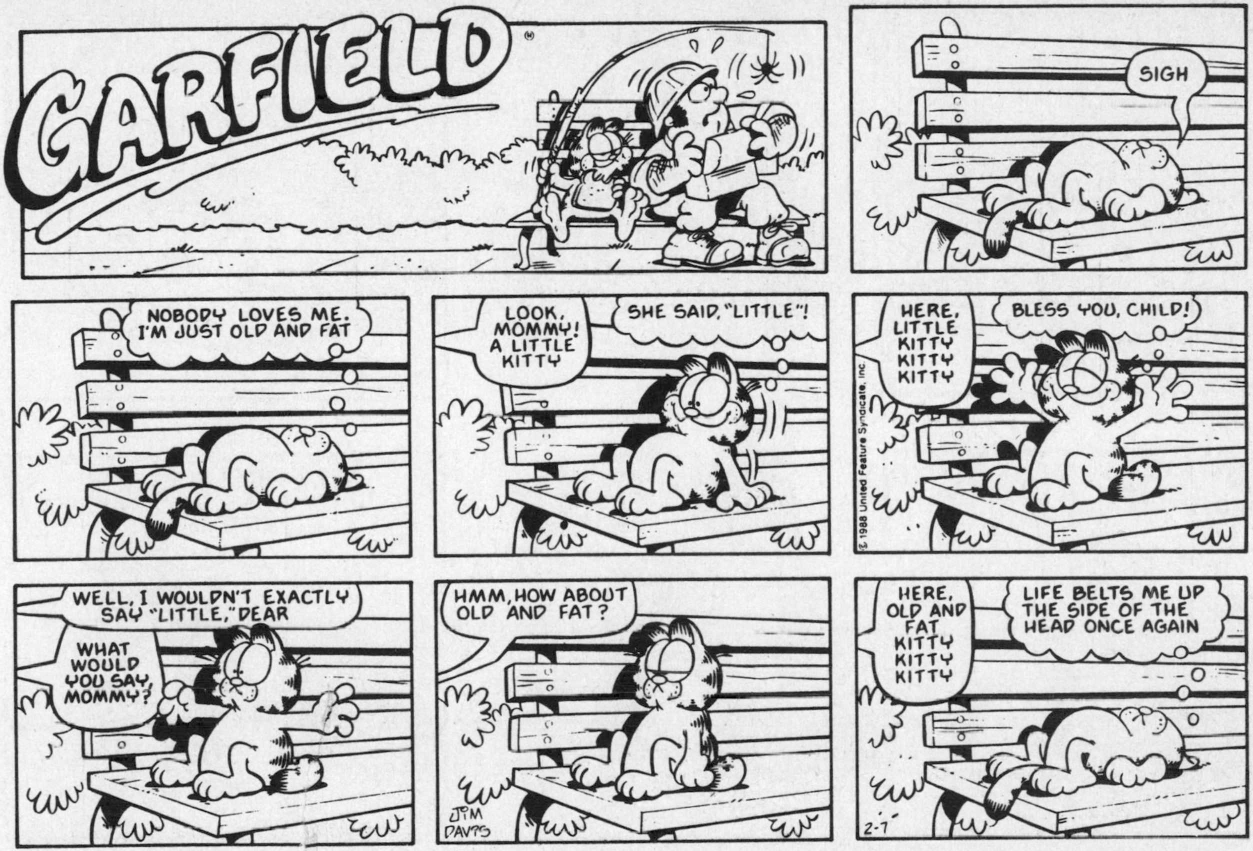
GARFIELD
SIGH
NOBODY LOVES ME. I'M JUST OLD AND FAT
LOOK, MOMMY! A LITTLE KITTY
SHE SAID, "LITTLE"!
HERE, LITTLE KITTY KITTY KITTY
BLESS YOU, CHILD!
© 1988 United Feature Syndicate, Inc.
WELL, I WOULDN'T EXACTLY SAY "LITTLE," DEAR
WHAT WOULD YOU SAY, MOMMY?
HMM, HOW ABOUT OLD AND FAT?
JIM DAVIS
HERE, OLD AND FAT KITTY KITTY KITTY
LIFE BELTS ME UP THE SIDE OF THE HEAD ONCE AGAIN
2-7

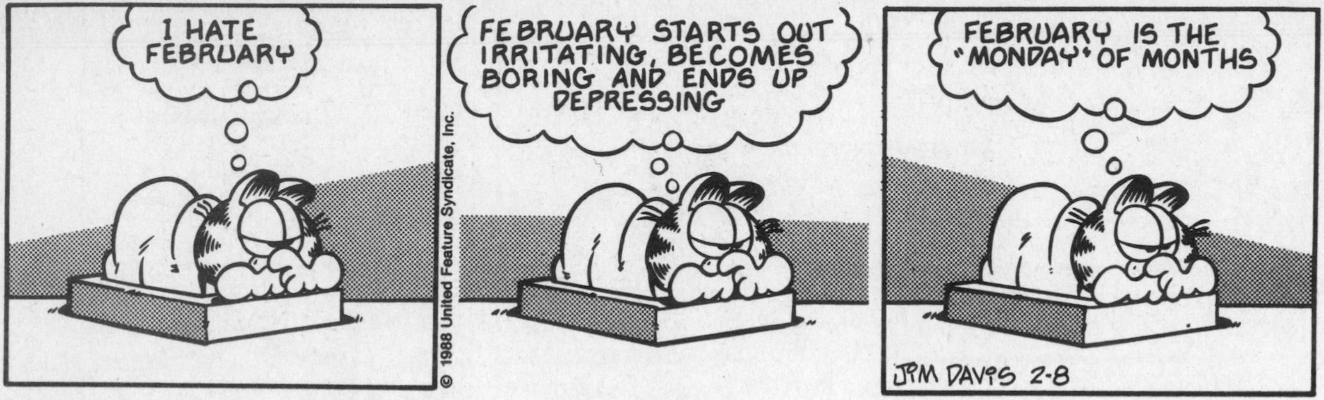
I HATE FEBRUARY
FEBRUARY STARTS OUT IRRITATING, BECOMES BORING AND ENDS UP DEPRESSING
FEBRUARY IS THE "MONDAY" OF MONTHS
JIM DAVIS 2-8
© 1988 United Feature Syndicate, Inc.

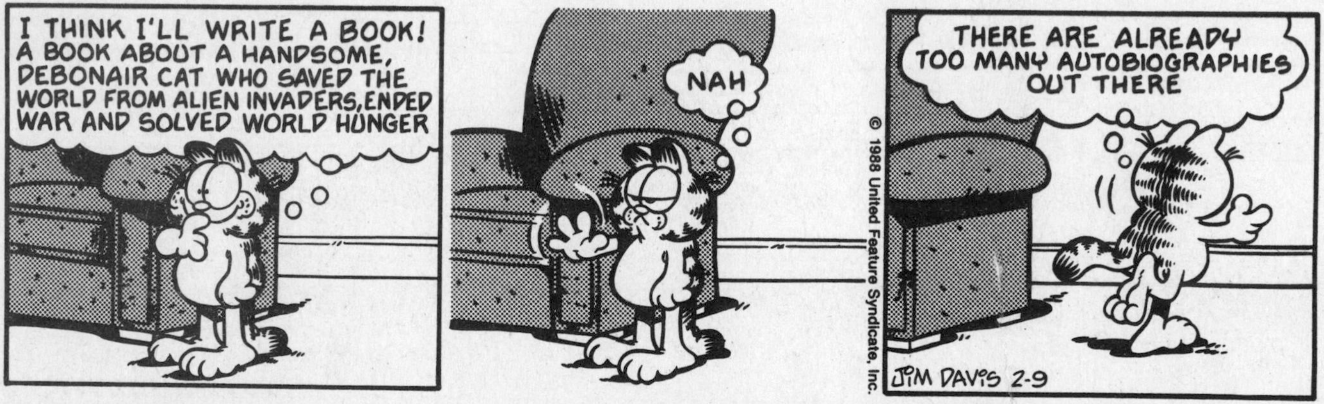
I THINK I'LL WRITE A BOOK! A BOOK ABOUT A HANDSOME, DEBONAIR CAT WHO SAVED THE WORLD FROM ALIEN INVADERS, ENDED WAR AND SOLVED WORLD HUNGER
NAH
THERE ARE ALREADY TOO MANY AUTOBIOGRAPHIES OUT THERE
JIM DAVIS 2-9
© 1988 United Feature Syndicate, Inc.

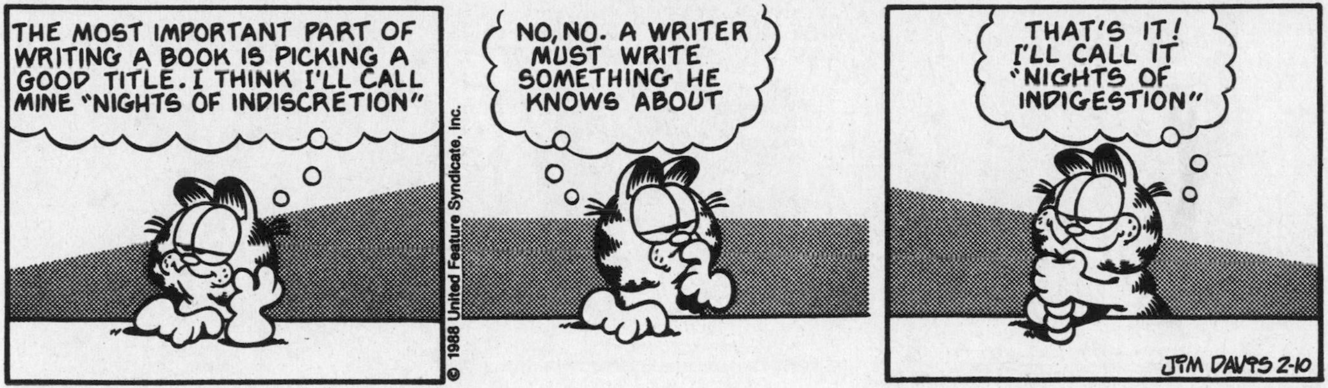
THE MOST IMPORTANT PART OF WRITING A BOOK IS PICKING A GOOD TITLE. I THINK I'LL CALL MINE "NIGHTS OF INDISCRETION"
© 1988 United Feature Syndicate, Inc.
NO, NO. A WRITER MUST WRITE SOMETHING HE KNOWS ABOUT
THAT'S IT! I'LL CALL IT "NIGHTS OF INDIGESTION"
JIM DAVIS 2-10

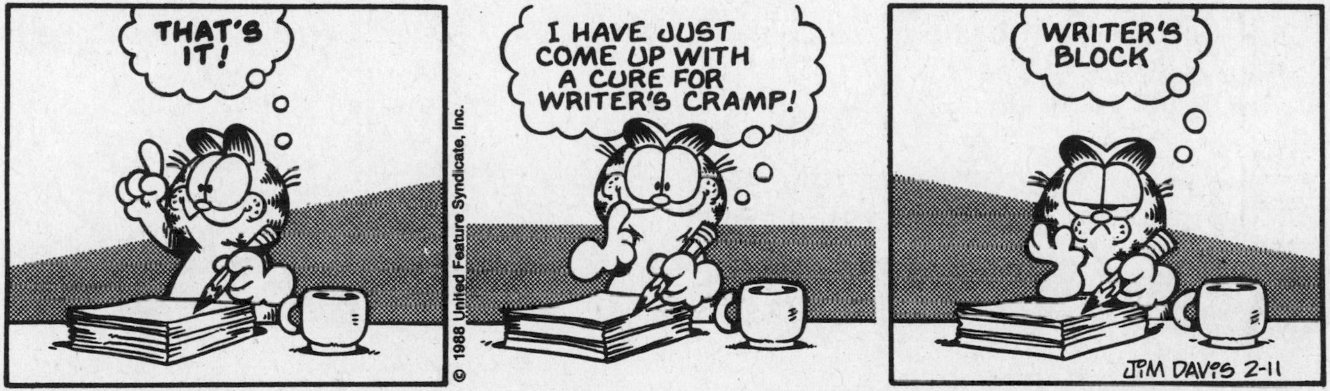
THAT'S IT!
© 1988 United Feature Syndicate, Inc.
I HAVE JUST COME UP WITH A CURE FOR WRITER'S CRAMP!
WRITER'S BLOCK
JIM DAVIS 2-11

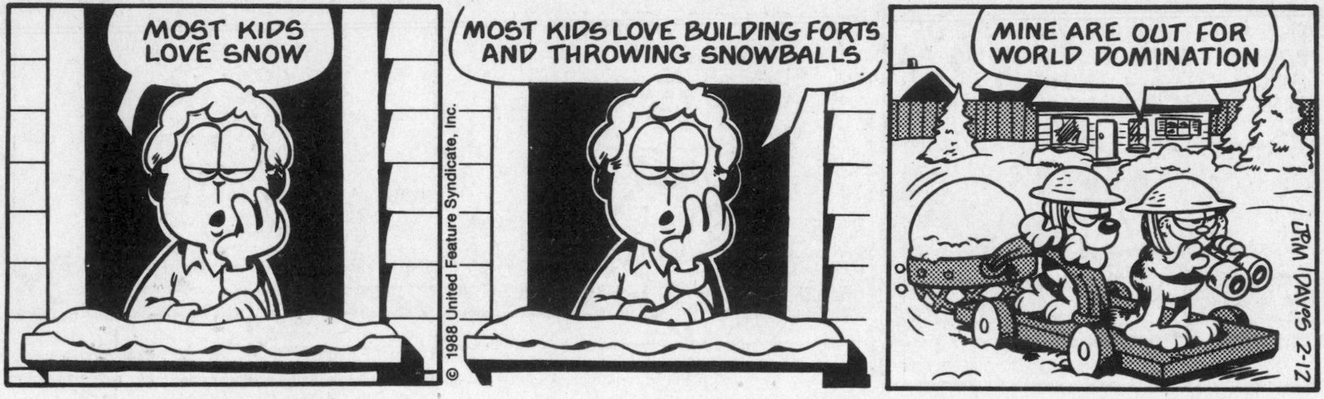
MOST KIDS LOVE SNOW
MOST KIDS LOVE BUILDING FORTS AND THROWING SNOWBALLS
MINE ARE OUT FOR WORLD DOMINATION
© 1988 United Feature Syndicate, Inc.
JIM DAVIS 2-12

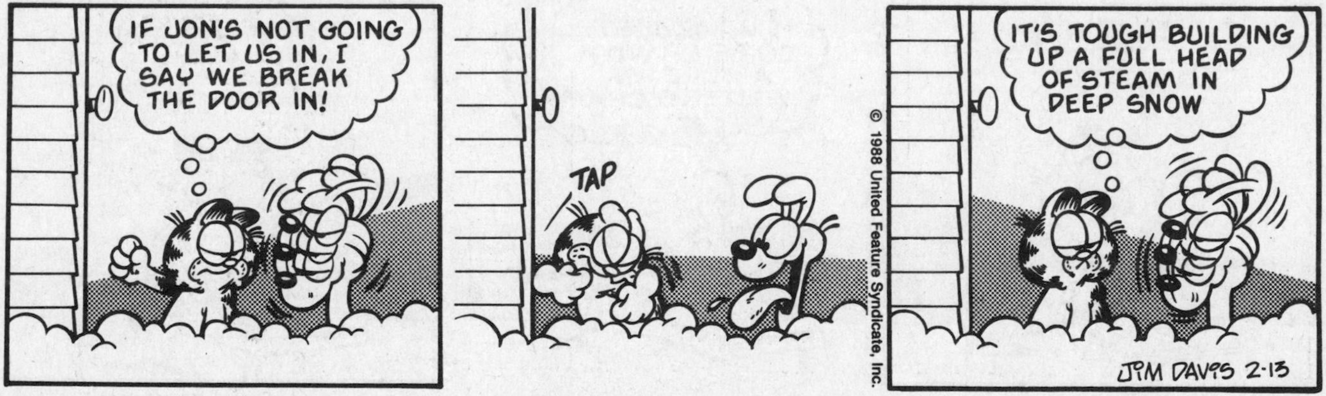
IF JON'S NOT GOING TO LET US IN, I SAY WE BREAK THE DOOR IN!
TAP
IT'S TOUGH BUILDING UP A FULL HEAD OF STEAM IN DEEP SNOW
© 1988 United Feature Syndicate, Inc.
JIM DAVIS 2-13

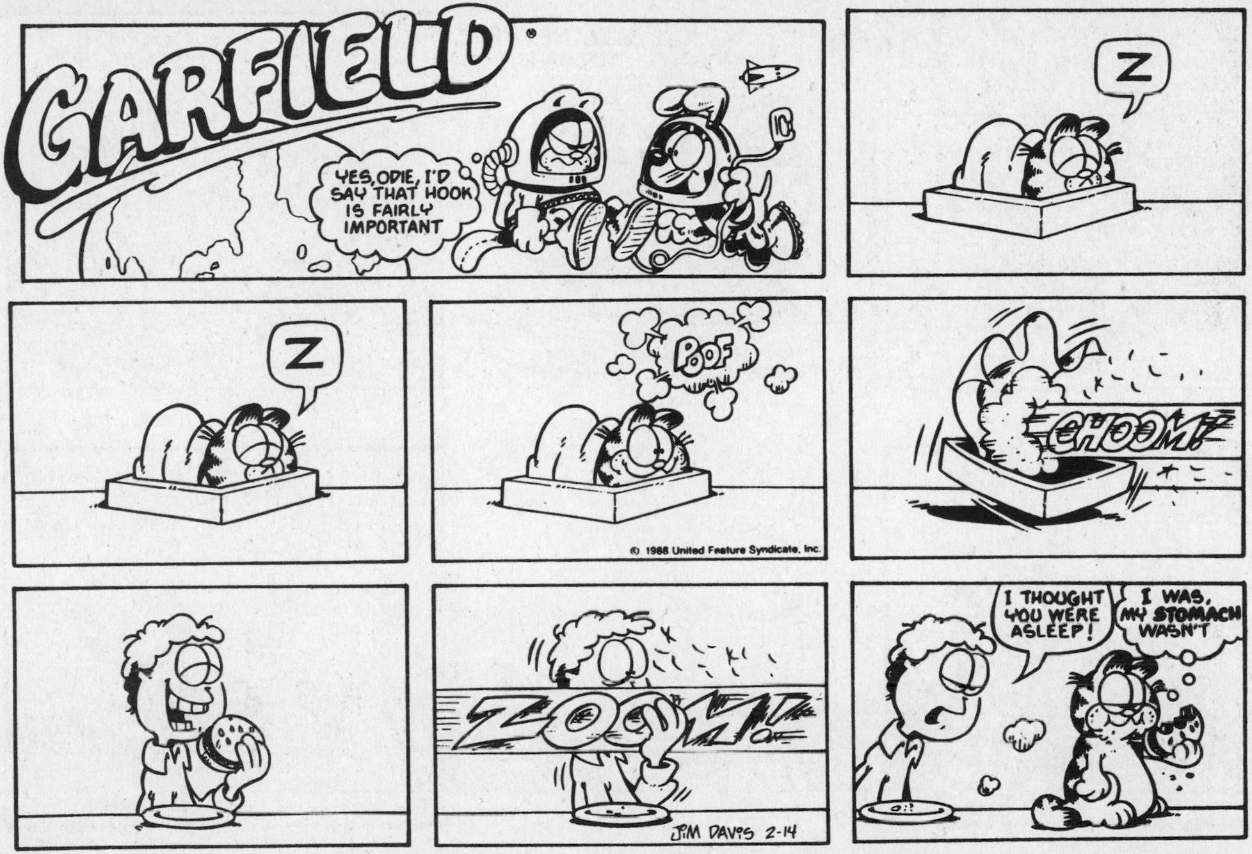
GARFIELD
YES, ODIE, I'D SAY THAT HOOK IS FAIRLY IMPORTANT
Z
Z
POOF
CHOOM!
ZOOM!
I THOUGHT YOU WERE ASLEEP!
I WAS, MY STOMACH WASN'T
JIM DAVIS 2-14

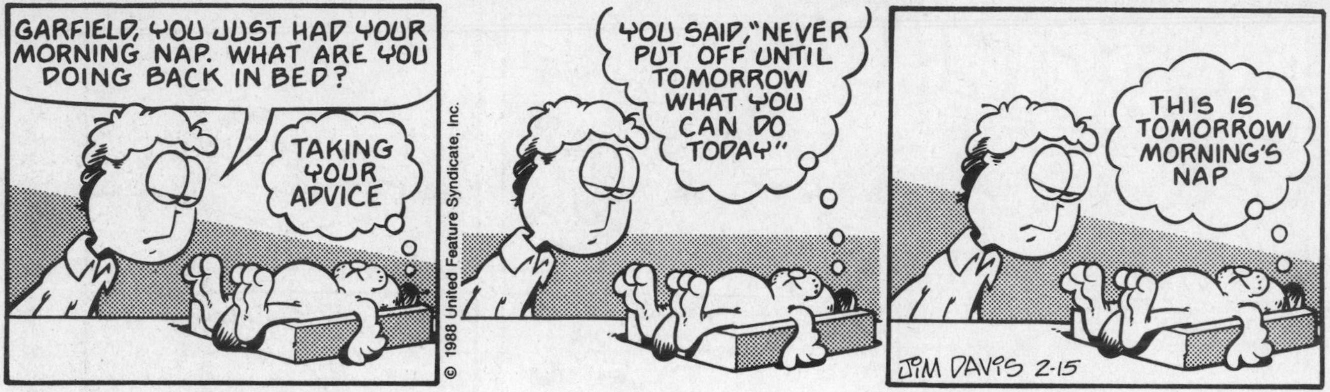
GARFIELD, YOU JUST HAD YOUR MORNING NAP. WHAT ARE YOU DOING BACK IN BED?
TAKING YOUR ADVICE
YOU SAID, "NEVER PUT OFF UNTIL TOMORROW WHAT YOU CAN DO TODAY"
THIS IS TOMORROW MORNING'S NAP
JIM DAVIS 2-15
© 1988 United Feature Syndicate, Inc.

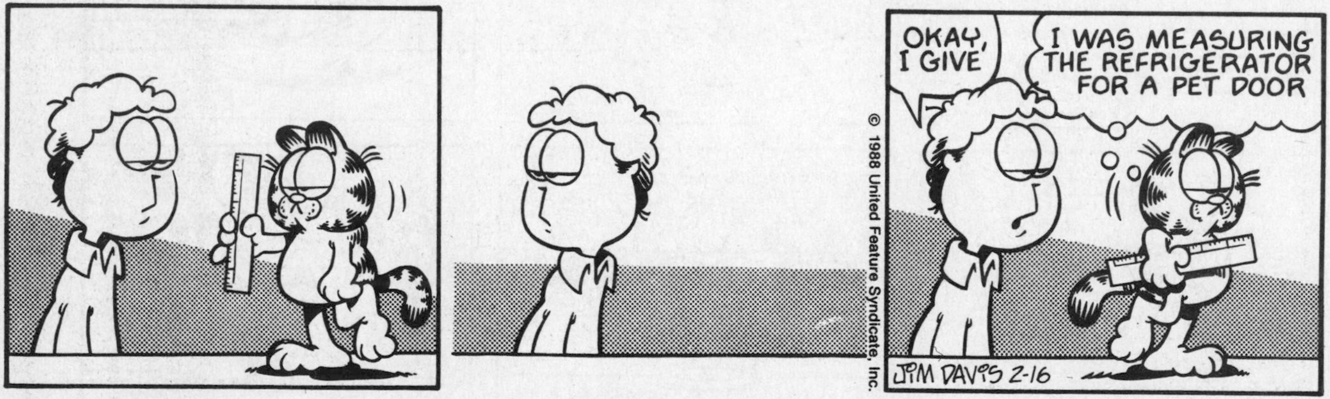
OKAY, I GIVE
I WAS MEASURING THE REFRIGERATOR FOR A PET DOOR
JIM DAVIS 2-16
© 1988 United Feature Syndicate, Inc.

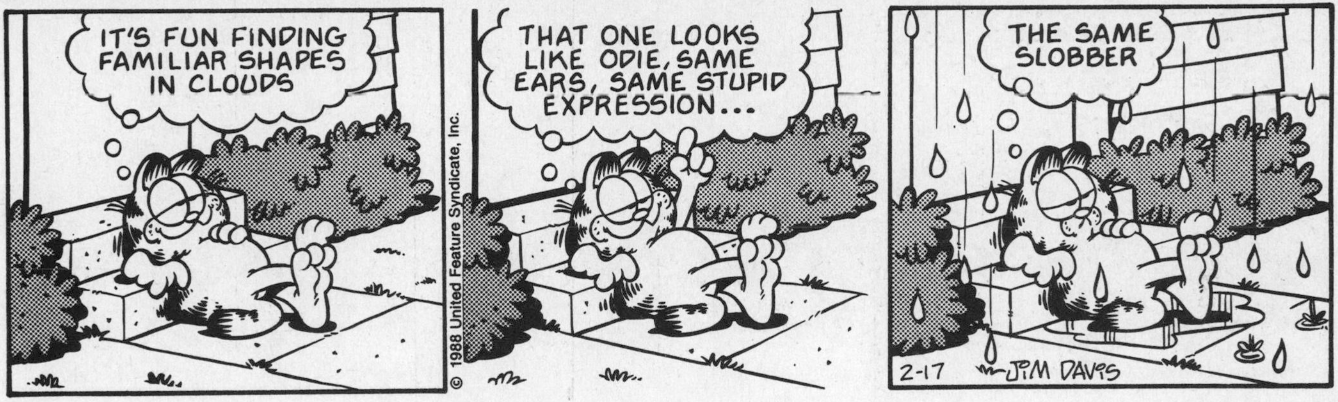
IT'S FUN FINDING FAMILIAR SHAPES IN CLOUDS
THAT ONE LOOKS LIKE ODIE, SAME EARS, SAME STUPID EXPRESSION...
THE SAME SLOBBER
2-17
JIM DAVIS

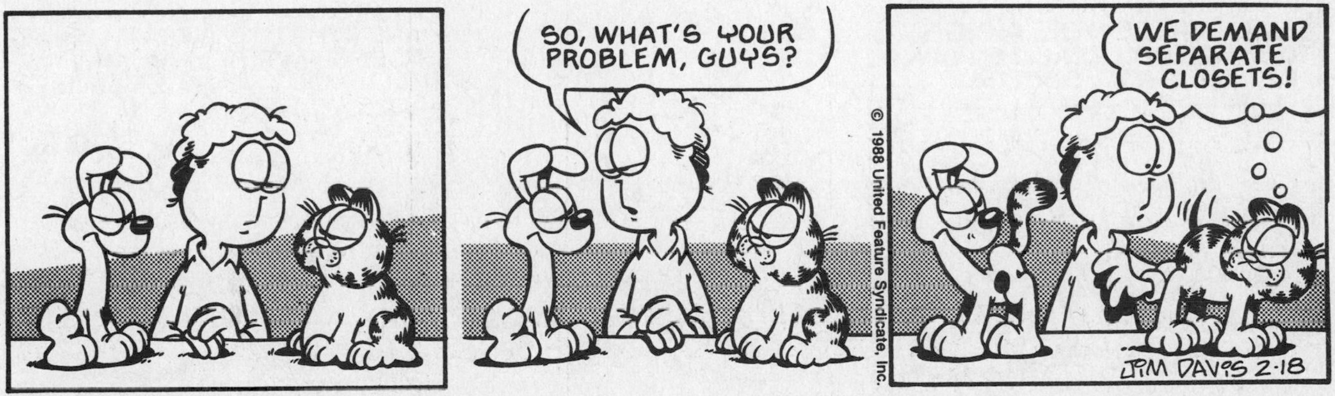
SO, WHAT'S YOUR PROBLEM, GUYS?
WE DEMAND SEPARATE CLOSETS!
JIM DAVIS 2-18

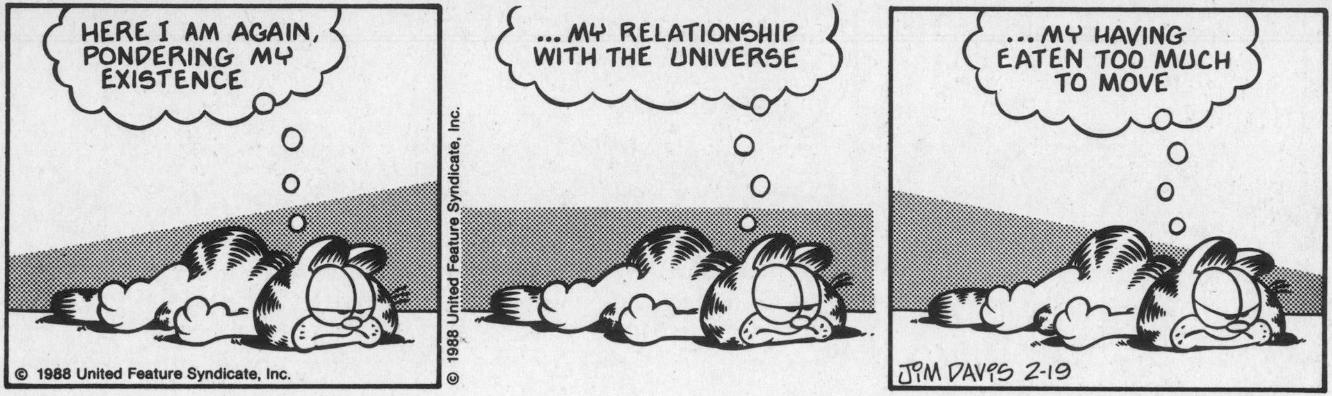
HERE I AM AGAIN, PONDERING MY EXISTENCE
© 1988 United Feature Syndicate, Inc.
... MY RELATIONSHIP WITH THE UNIVERSE
© 1988 United Feature Syndicate, Inc.
... MY HAVING EATEN TOO MUCH TO MOVE
JIM DAVIS 2-19

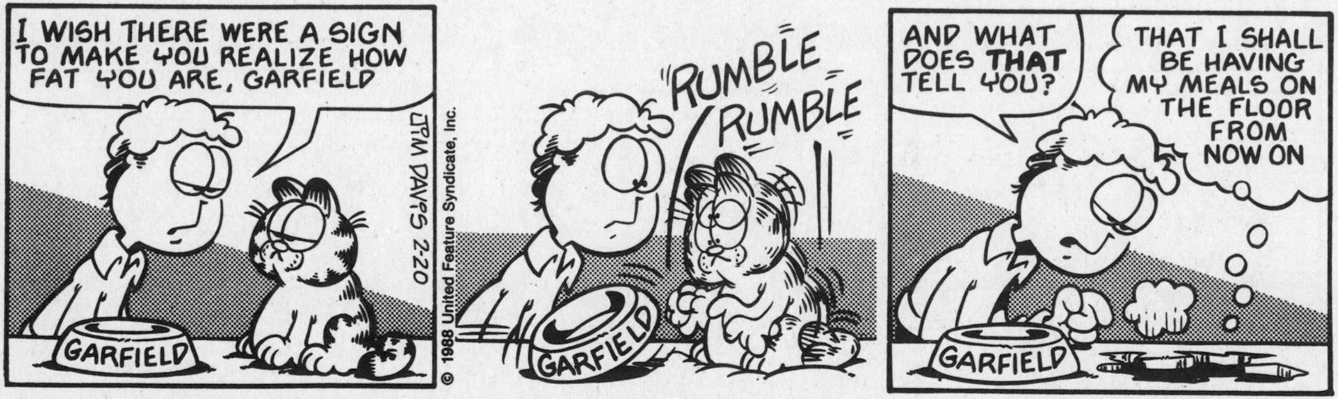
I WISH THERE WERE A SIGN TO MAKE YOU REALIZE HOW FAT YOU ARE, GARFIELD
GARFIELD
JIM DAVIS 2-20
© 1988 United Feature Syndicate, Inc.
RUMBLE RUMBLE
GARFIELD
AND WHAT DOES **THAT** TELL YOU?
THAT I SHALL BE HAVING MY MEALS ON THE FLOOR FROM NOW ON
GARFIELD

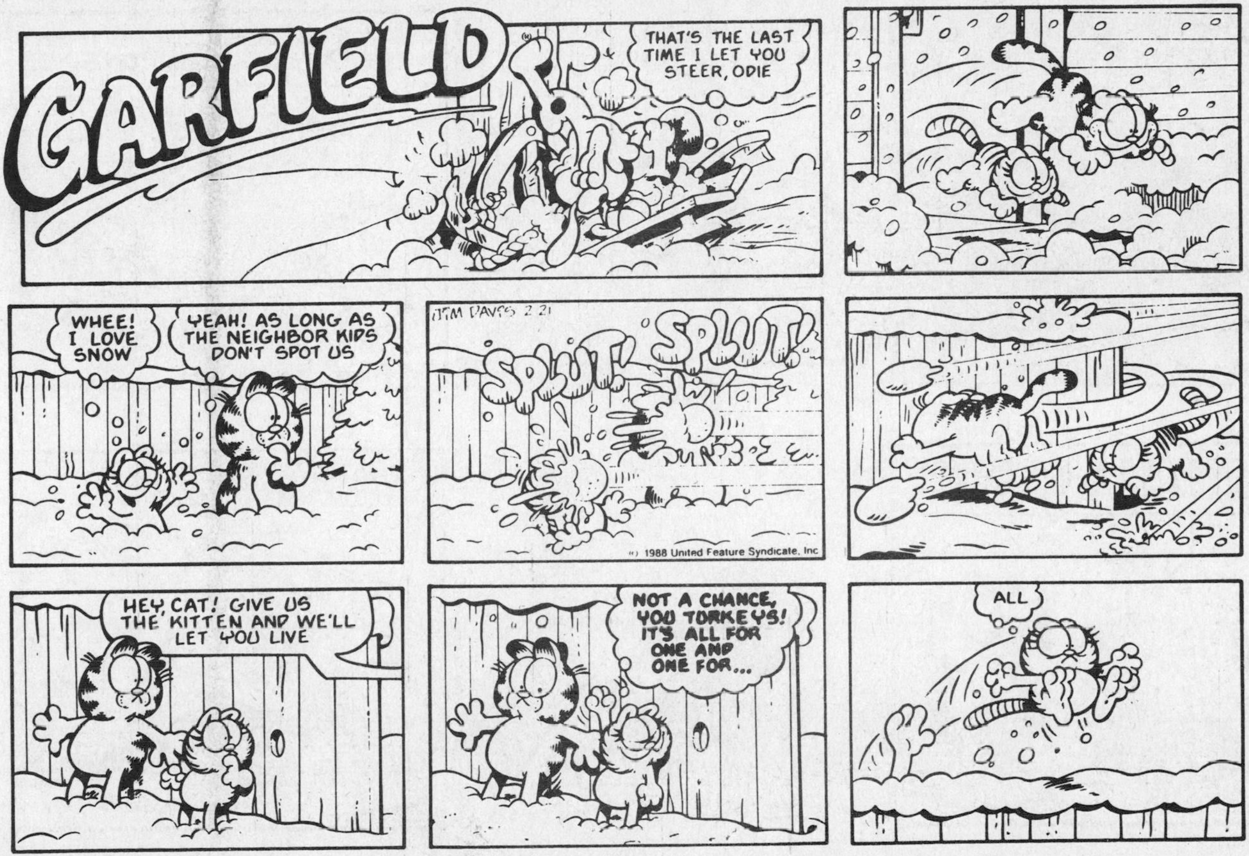
GARFIELD
THAT'S THE LAST TIME I LET YOU STEER, ODIE
WHEE! I LOVE SNOW
YEAH! AS LONG AS THE NEIGHBOR KIDS DON'T SPOT US
JIM DAVIS 2.21
SPLUT! SPLUT!
© 1988 United Feature Syndicate, Inc
HEY CAT! GIVE US THE KITTEN AND WE'LL LET YOU LIVE
NOT A CHANCE, YOU TURKEYS! IT'S ALL FOR ONE AND ONE FOR...
ALL

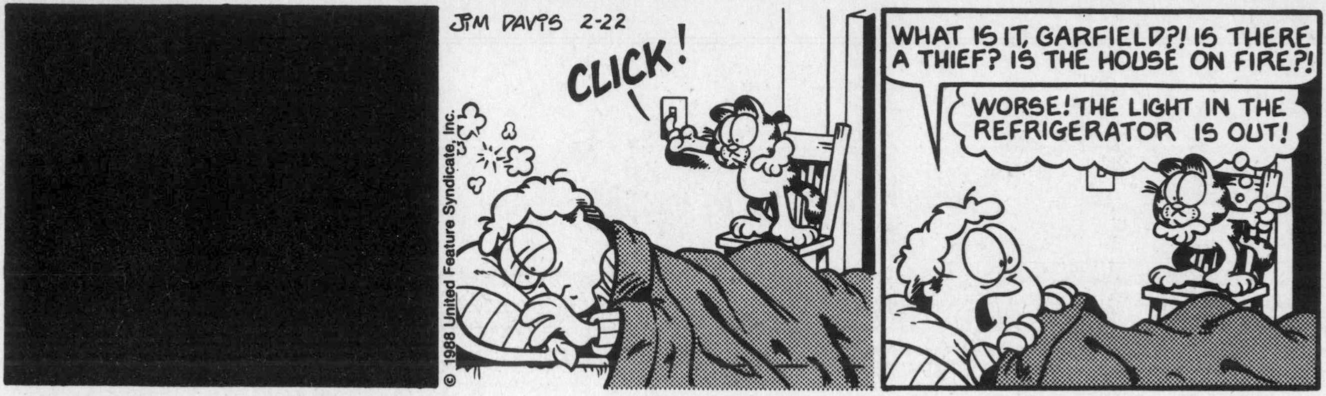
JIM DAVIS 2-22
© 1988 United Feature Syndicate, Inc.
CLICK!
WHAT IS IT, GARFIELD?! IS THERE A THIEF? IS THE HOUSE ON FIRE?!
WORSE! THE LIGHT IN THE REFRIGERATOR IS OUT!

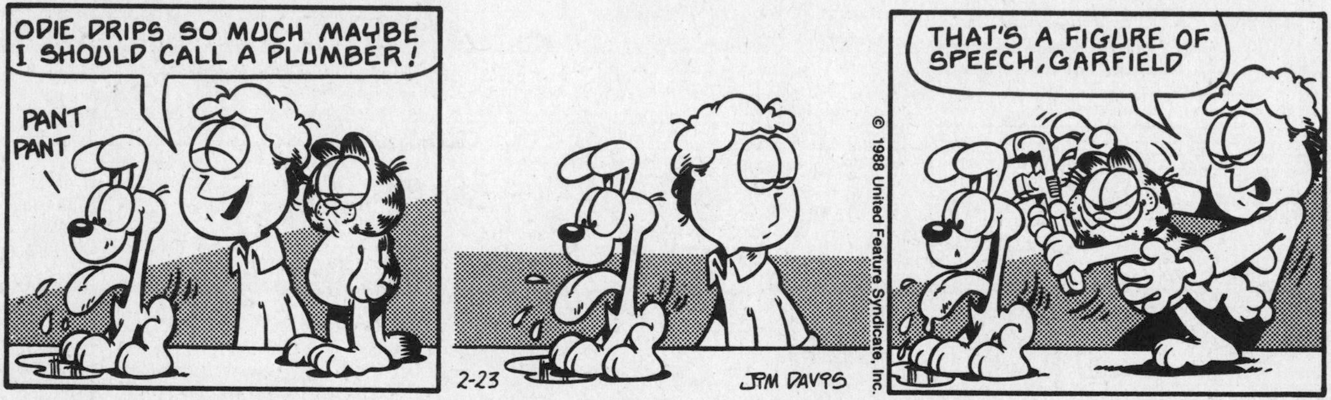
ODIE DRIPS SO MUCH MAYBE I SHOULD CALL A PLUMBER!
PANT PANT
2-23
JIM DAVIS
© 1988 United Feature Syndicate, Inc.
THAT'S A FIGURE OF SPEECH, GARFIELD

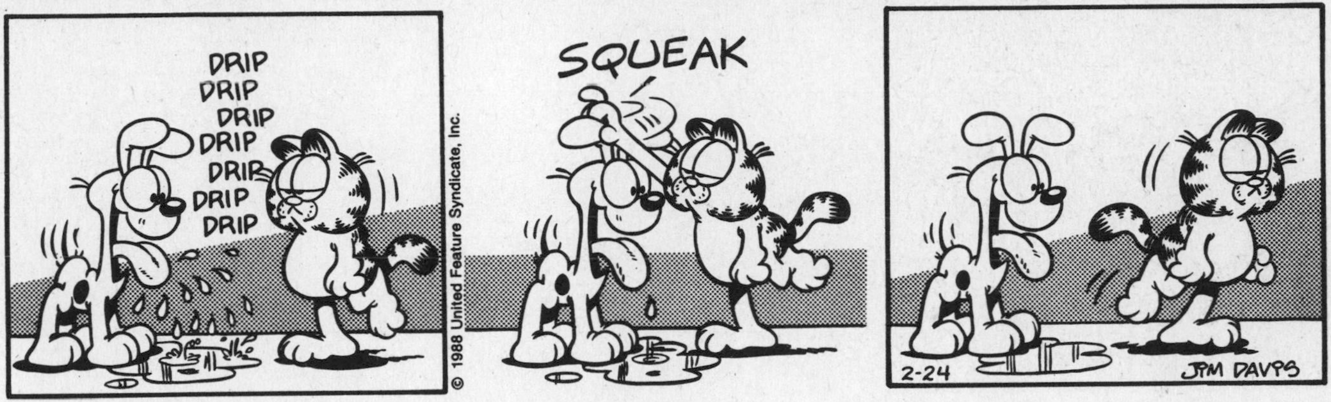
DRIP
DRIP
DRIP
DRIP
DRIP
DRIP
DRIP
© 1988 United Feature Syndicate, Inc.
SQUEAK
2-24
JIM DAVIS

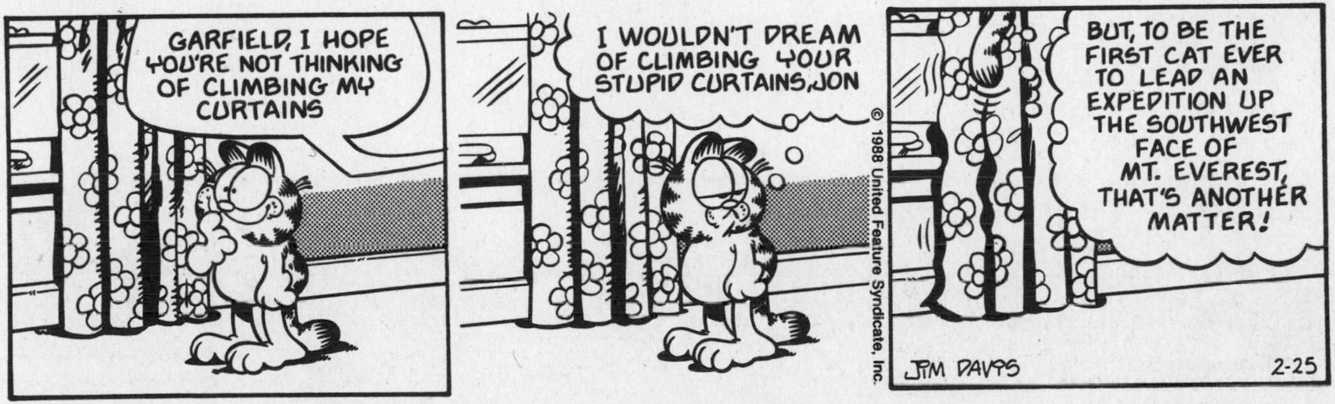
GARFIELD, I HOPE YOU'RE NOT THINKING OF CLIMBING MY CURTAINS
I WOULDN'T DREAM OF CLIMBING YOUR STUPID CURTAINS, JON
© 1988 United Feature Syndicate, Inc.
BUT, TO BE THE FIRST CAT EVER TO LEAD AN EXPEDITION UP THE SOUTHWEST FACE OF MT. EVEREST, THAT'S ANOTHER MATTER!
JIM DAVIS
2-25

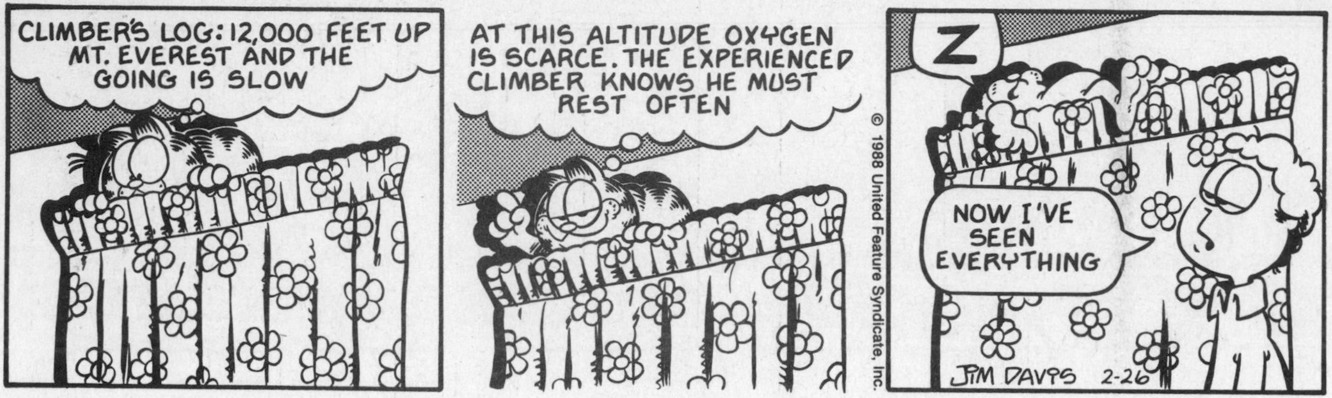
CLIMBER'S LOG: 12,000 FEET UP MT. EVEREST AND THE GOING IS SLOW
AT THIS ALTITUDE OXYGEN IS SCARCE. THE EXPERIENCED CLIMBER KNOWS HE MUST REST OFTEN
© 1988 United Feature Syndicate, Inc.
Z
NOW I'VE SEEN EVERYTHING
JIM DAVIS 2-26

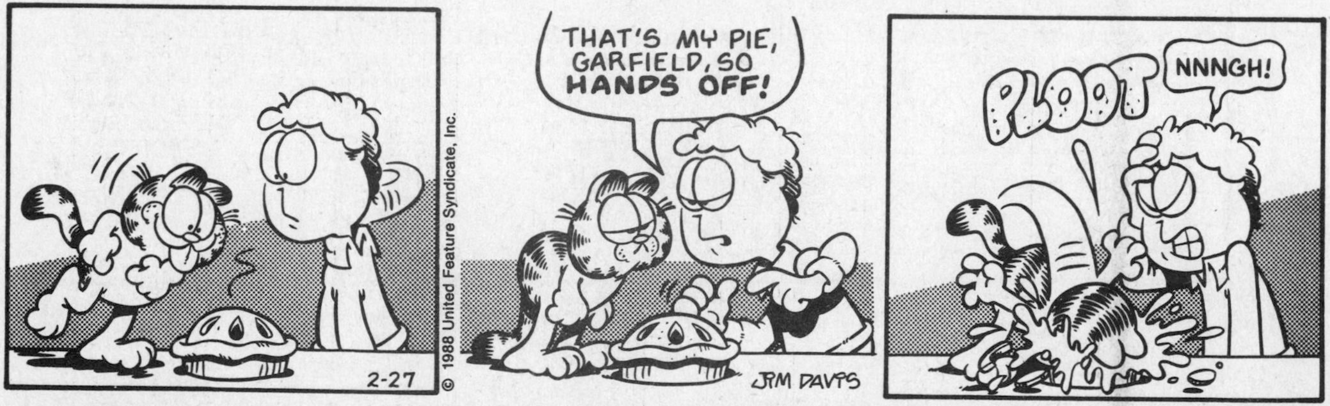
2-27
© 1988 United Feature Syndicate, Inc.
THAT'S MY PIE, GARFIELD, SO **HANDS OFF!**
JIM DAVIS
PLOOT
NNNGH!

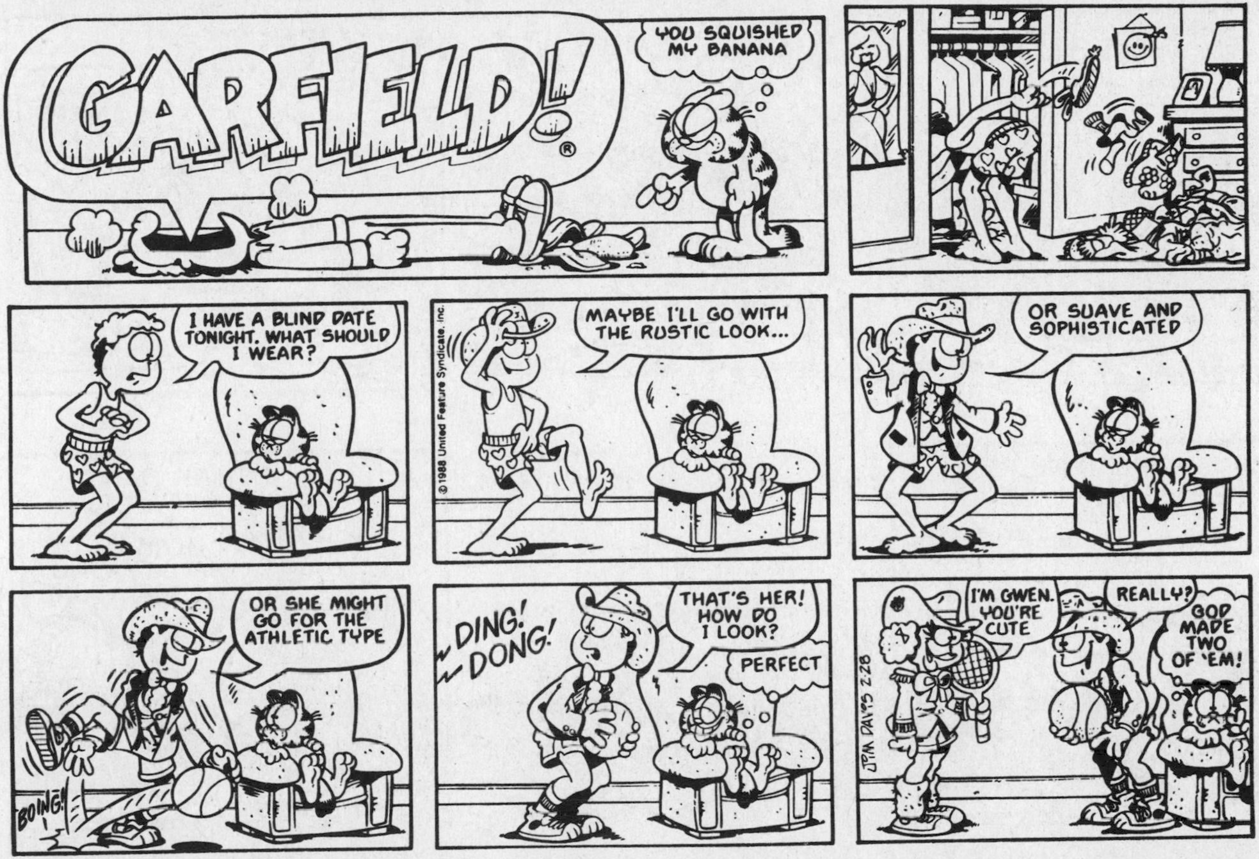
GARFIELD!
YOU SQUISHED MY BANANA
© 1988 United Feature Syndicate, Inc.
I HAVE A BLIND DATE TONIGHT. WHAT SHOULD I WEAR?
MAYBE I'LL GO WITH THE RUSTIC LOOK...
OR SUAVE AND SOPHISTICATED
OR SHE MIGHT GO FOR THE ATHLETIC TYPE
BOING!
DING! DONG!
THAT'S HER! HOW DO I LOOK?
PERFECT
JPM DAVIS 2-28
I'M GWEN. YOU'RE CUTE
REALLY?
GOD MADE TWO OF 'EM!

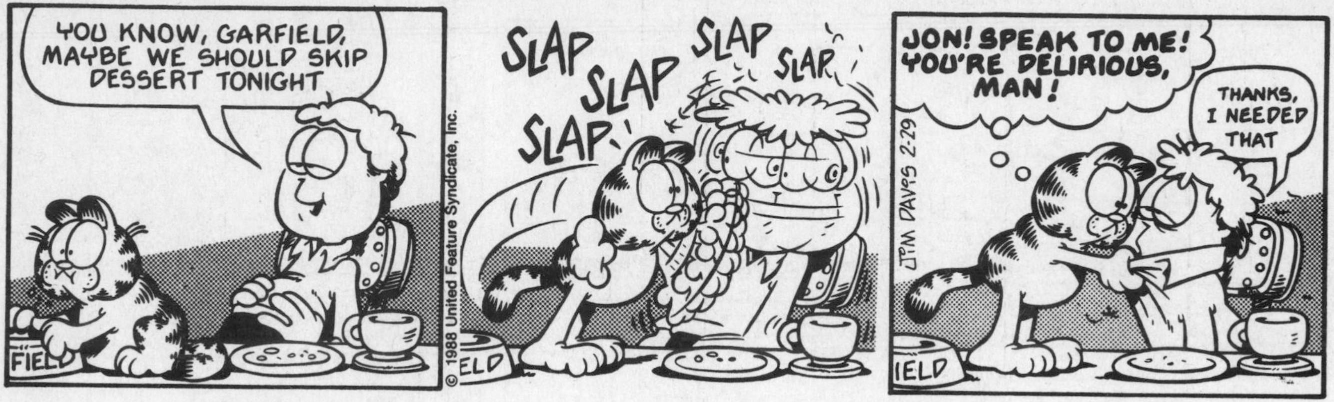
YOU KNOW, GARFIELD, MAYBE WE SHOULD SKIP DESSERT TONIGHT
FIELD
© 1988 United Feature Syndicate, Inc.
SLAP SLAP SLAP SLAP SLAP
ELD
JIM DAVIS 2-29
JON! SPEAK TO ME! YOU'RE DELIRIOUS, MAN!
THANKS, I NEEDED THAT
IELD

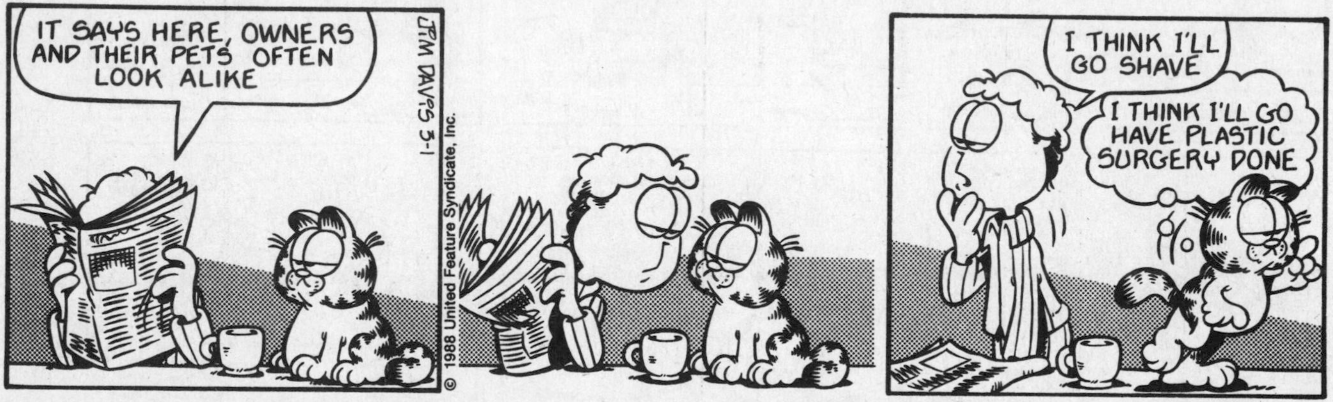
IT SAYS HERE, OWNERS AND THEIR PETS OFTEN LOOK ALIKE
JIM DAVIS 3-1
© 1988 United Feature Syndicate, Inc.
I THINK I'LL GO SHAVE
I THINK I'LL GO HAVE PLASTIC SURGERY DONE

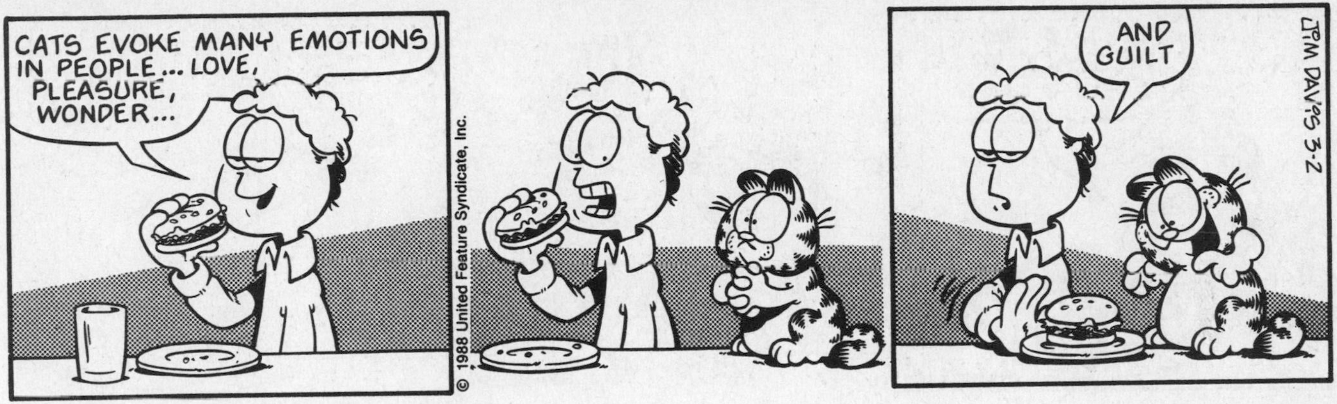
CATS EVOKE MANY EMOTIONS IN PEOPLE... LOVE, PLEASURE, WONDER...
© 1988 United Feature Syndicate, Inc.
AND GUILT
JIM DAVIS 3-2

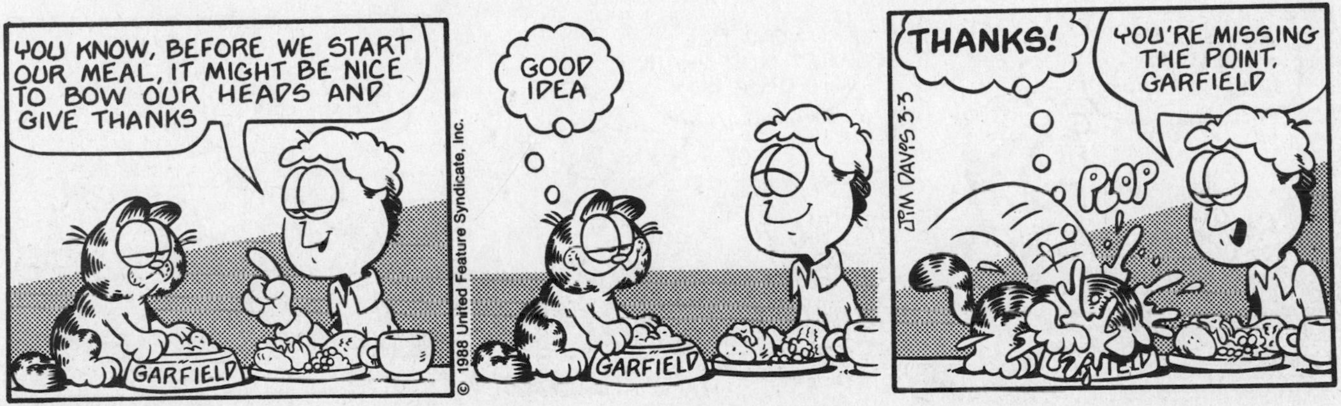
YOU KNOW, BEFORE WE START OUR MEAL, IT MIGHT BE NICE TO BOW OUR HEADS AND GIVE THANKS
GARFIELD
© 1988 United Feature Syndicate, Inc.
GOOD IDEA
GARFIELD
THANKS!
YOU'RE MISSING THE POINT, GARFIELD
PLOP
JIM DAVIS 3-3

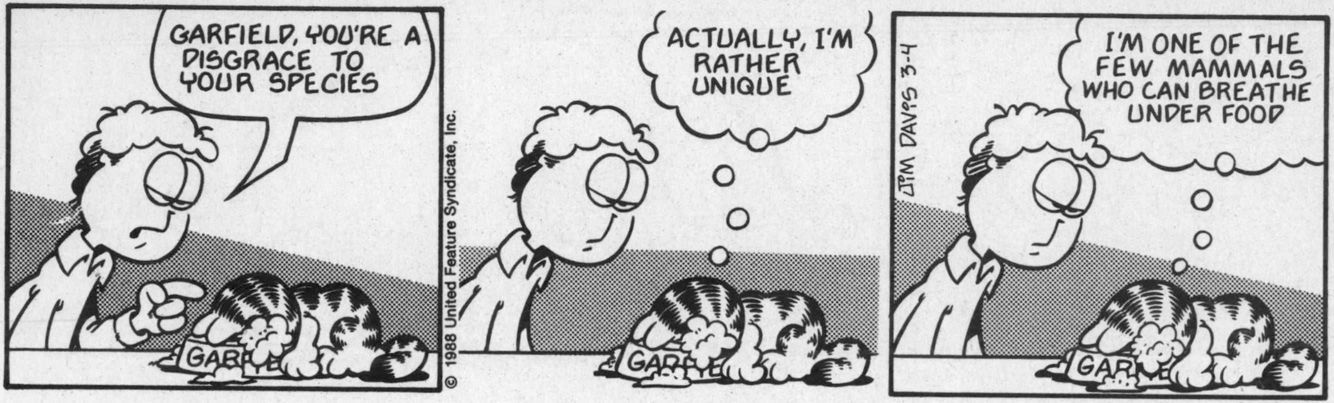
GARFIELD, YOU'RE A DISGRACE TO YOUR SPECIES
GAR
© 1988 United Feature Syndicate, Inc.
ACTUALLY, I'M RATHER UNIQUE
JIM DAVIS 3-4
I'M ONE OF THE FEW MAMMALS WHO CAN BREATHE UNDER FOOD

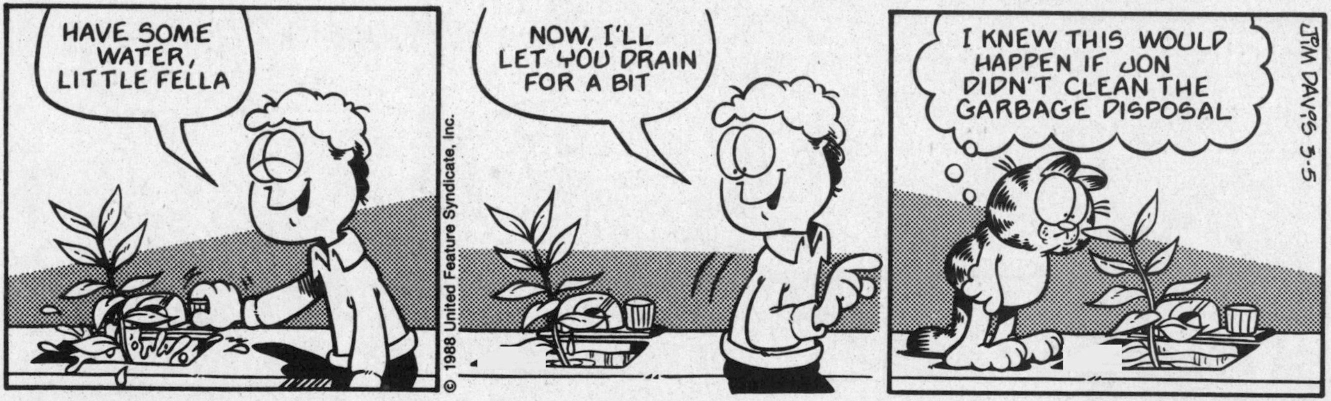
HAVE SOME WATER, LITTLE FELLA
© 1988 United Feature Syndicate, Inc.
NOW, I'LL LET YOU DRAIN FOR A BIT
I KNEW THIS WOULD HAPPEN IF JON DIDN'T CLEAN THE GARBAGE DISPOSAL
JIM DAVIS 3-5

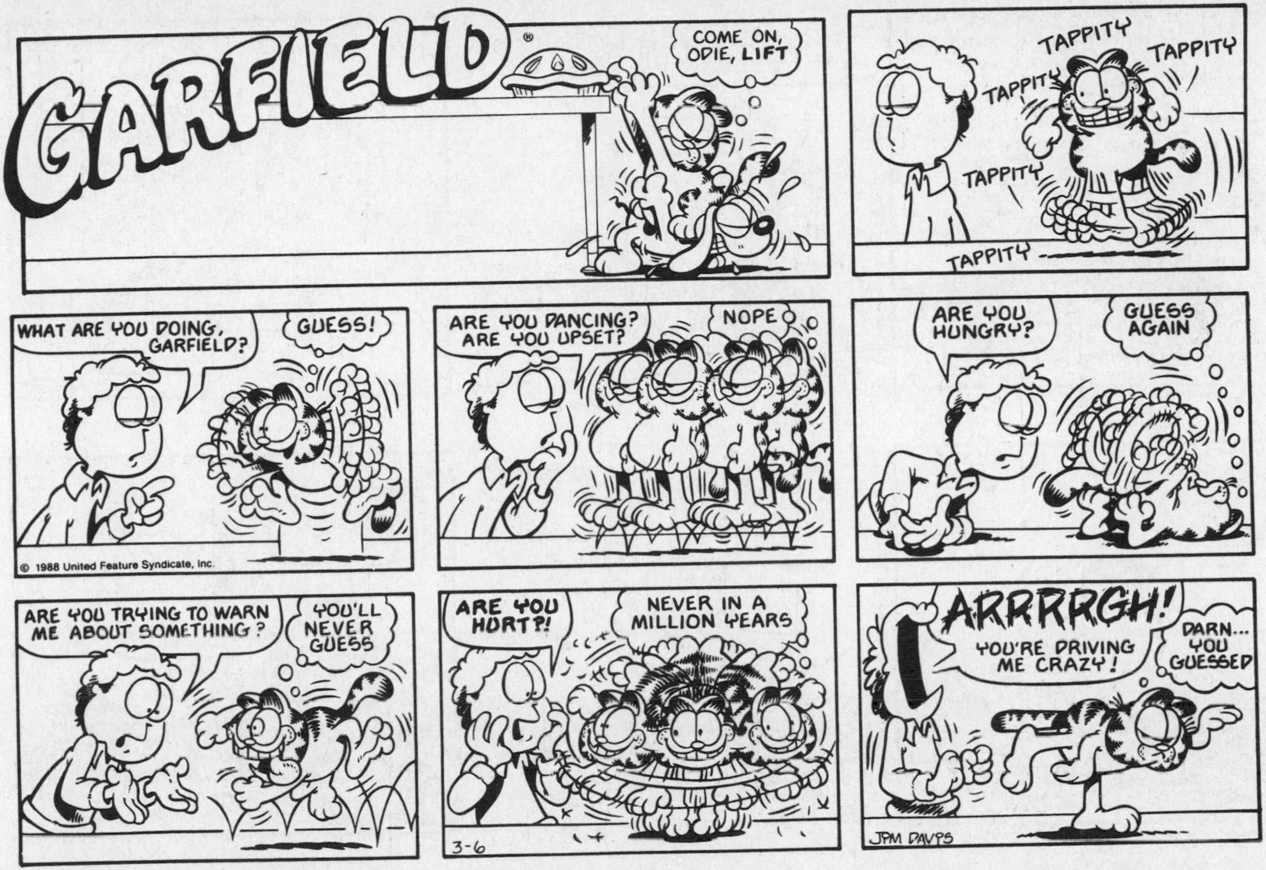
GARFIELD®
COME ON, ODIE, LIFT
TAPPITY TAPPITY TAPPITY TAPPITY TAPPITY TAPPITY
WHAT ARE YOU DOING, GARFIELD?
GUESS!
© 1988 United Feature Syndicate, Inc.
ARE YOU DANCING? ARE YOU UPSET?
NOPE
ARE YOU HUNGRY?
GUESS AGAIN
ARE YOU TRYING TO WARN ME ABOUT SOMETHING?
YOU'LL NEVER GUESS
ARE YOU HURT?!
NEVER IN A MILLION YEARS
3-6
ARRRRGH! YOU'RE DRIVING ME CRAZY!
DARN... YOU GUESSED
JPM DAVPS

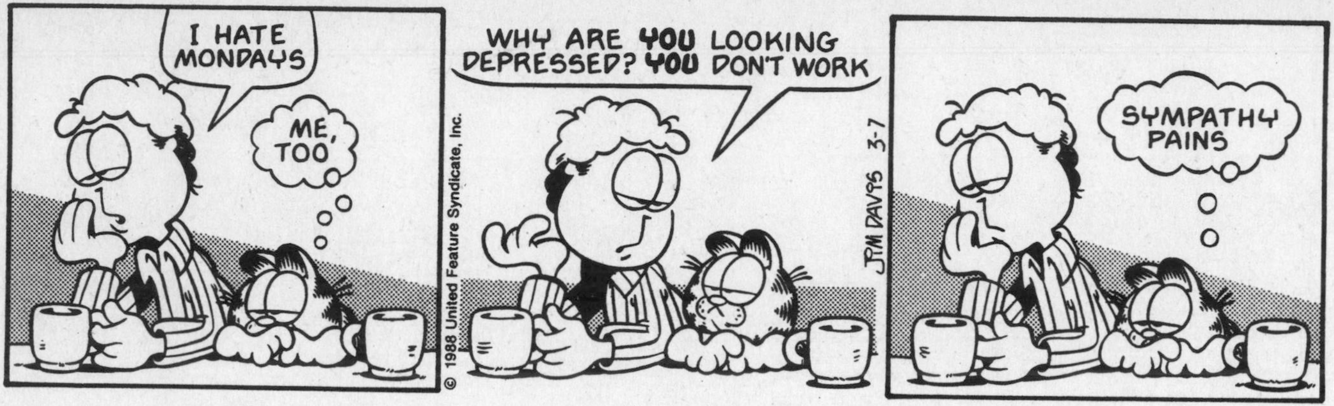
I HATE MONDAYS
ME, TOO
WHY ARE YOU LOOKING DEPRESSED? YOU DON'T WORK
SYMPATHY PAINS
© 1988 United Feature Syndicate, Inc.
JIM DAVIS 3-7

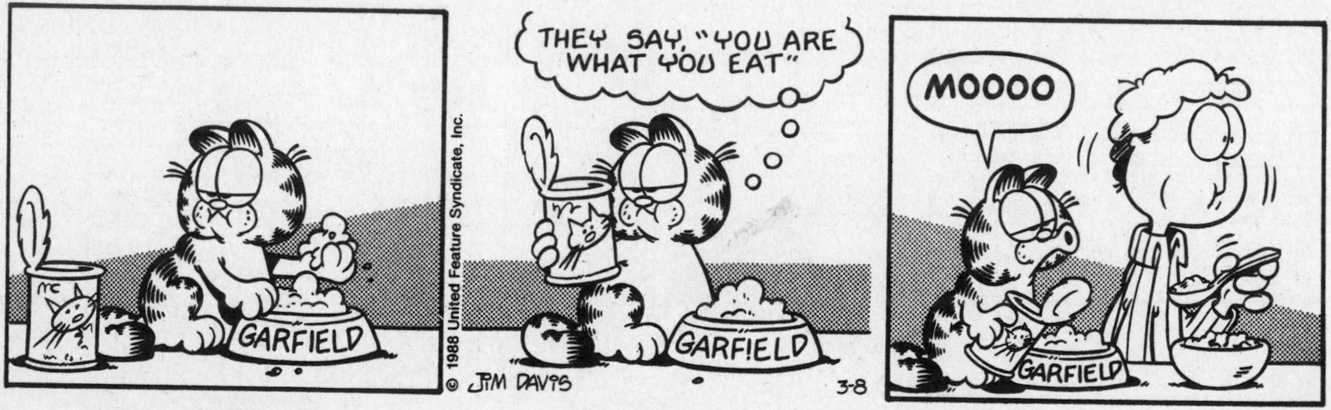
THEY SAY, "YOU ARE WHAT YOU EAT"
MOOOO
GARFIELD
© 1988 United Feature Syndicate, Inc.
JIM DAVIS
3-8

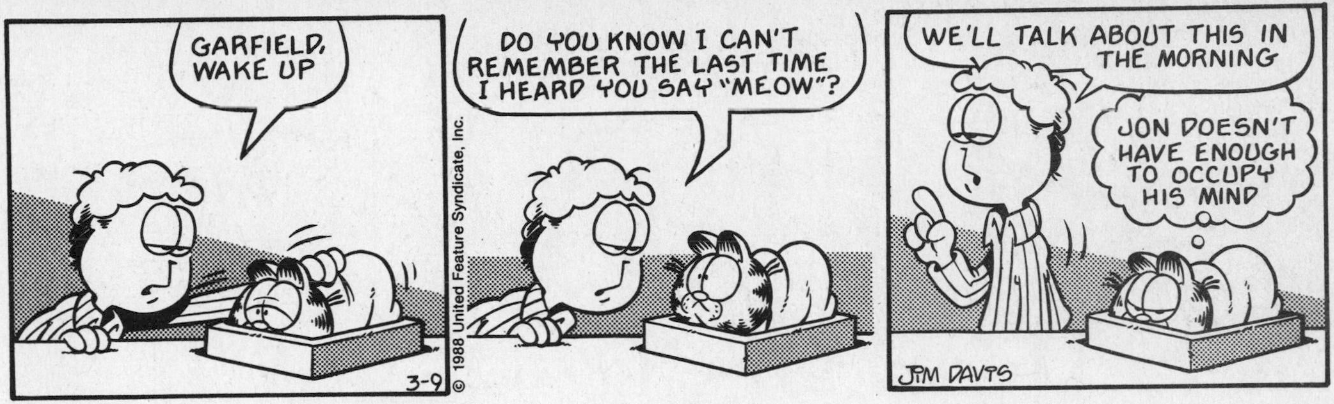
GARFIELD, WAKE UP
3-9
© 1988 United Feature Syndicate, Inc.
DO YOU KNOW I CAN'T REMEMBER THE LAST TIME I HEARD YOU SAY "MEOW"?
WE'LL TALK ABOUT THIS IN THE MORNING
JON DOESN'T HAVE ENOUGH TO OCCUPY HIS MIND
JIM DAVIS

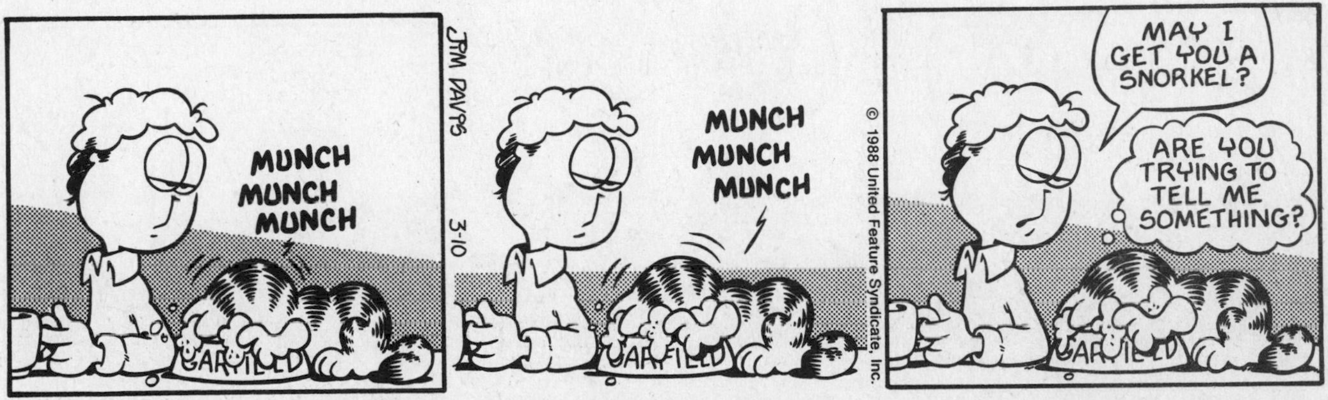
MUNCH MUNCH MUNCH
JIM DAVIS
3-10
MUNCH MUNCH MUNCH
© 1988 United Feature Syndicate, Inc.
MAY I GET YOU A SNORKEL?
ARE YOU TRYING TO TELL ME SOMETHING?

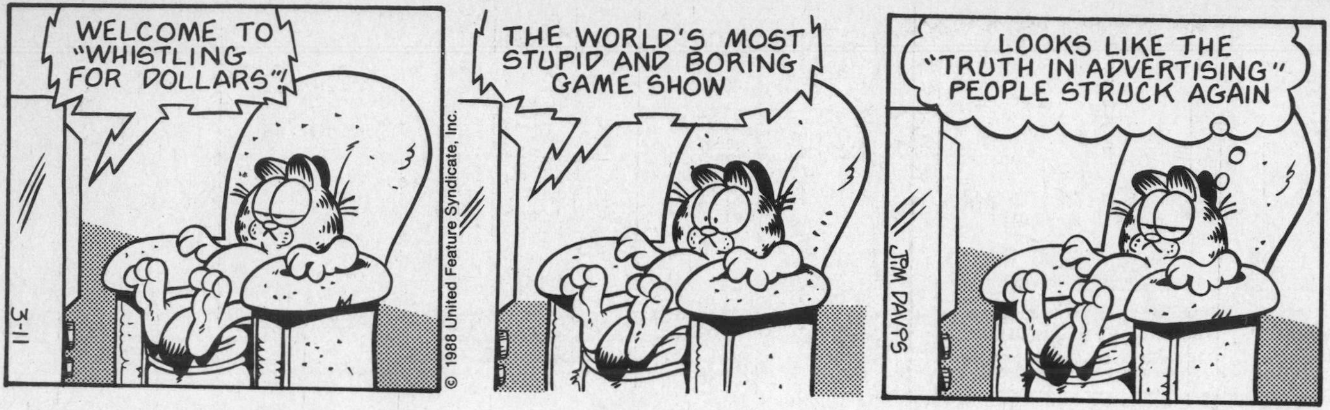
WELCOME TO "WHISTLING FOR DOLLARS"!
THE WORLD'S MOST STUPID AND BORING GAME SHOW
LOOKS LIKE THE "TRUTH IN ADVERTISING" PEOPLE STRUCK AGAIN
3-11
JIM DAVIS

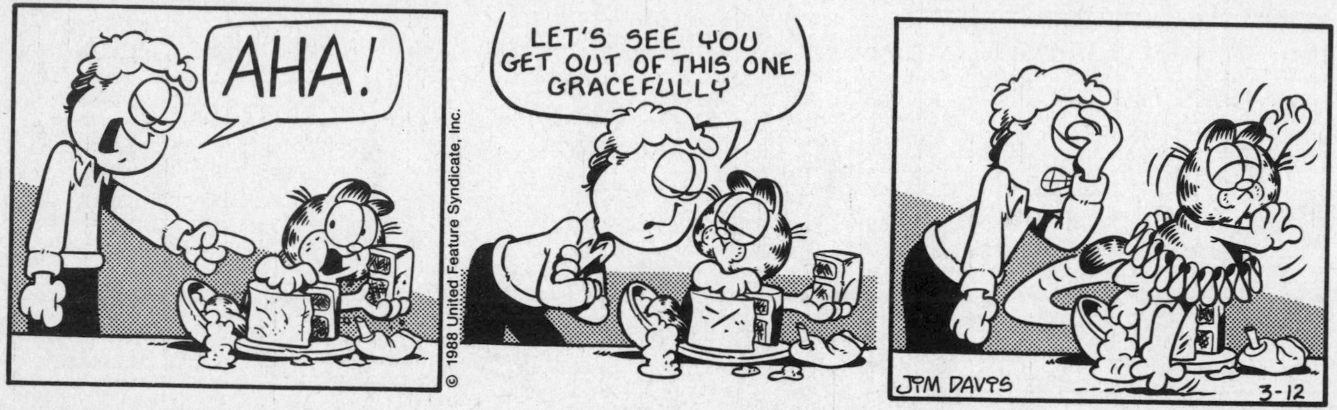
AHA!
LET'S SEE YOU GET OUT OF THIS ONE GRACEFULLY
JIM DAVIS
3-12

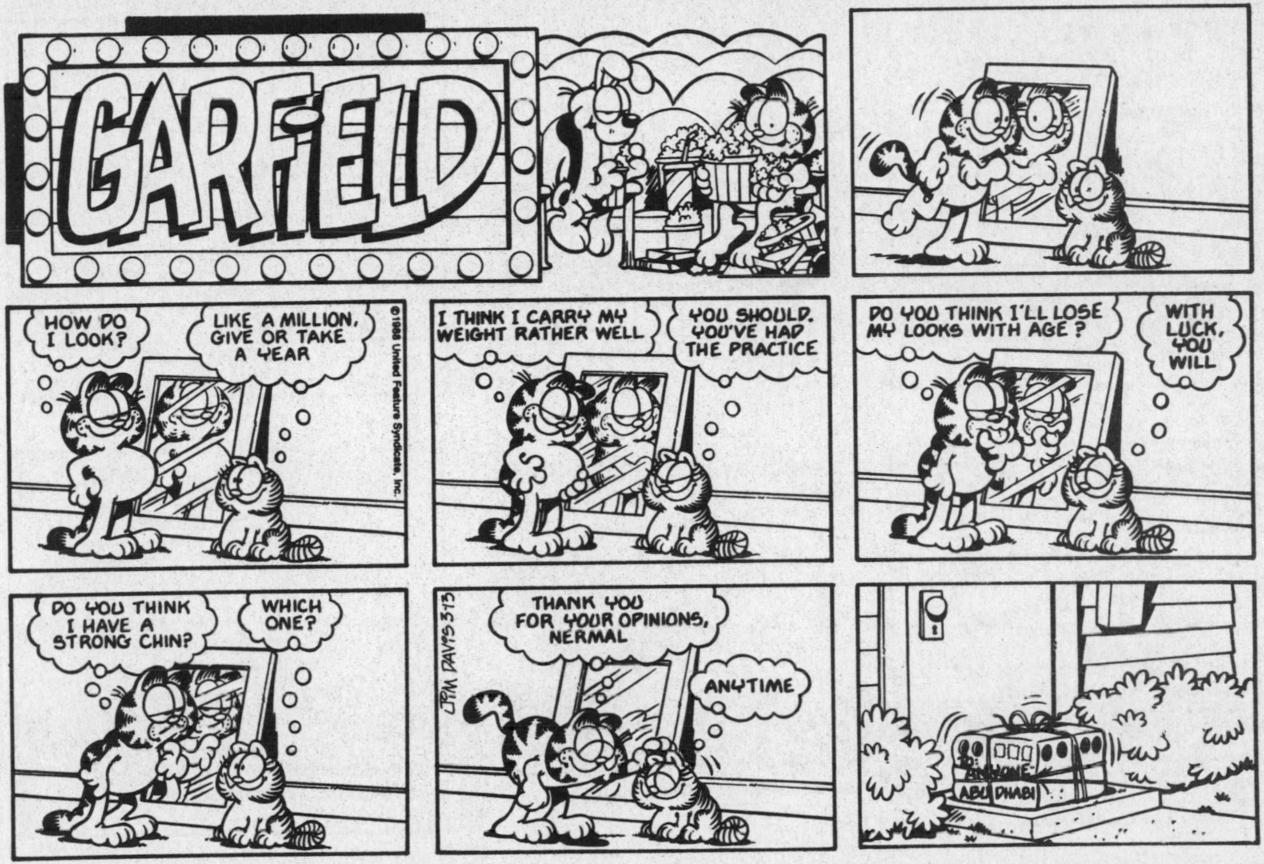
GARFIELD
HOW DO I LOOK?
LIKE A MILLION, GIVE OR TAKE A YEAR
© 1988 United Feature Syndicate, Inc.
I THINK I CARRY MY WEIGHT RATHER WELL
YOU SHOULD. YOU'VE HAD THE PRACTICE
DO YOU THINK I'LL LOSE MY LOOKS WITH AGE?
WITH LUCK, YOU WILL
DO YOU THINK I HAVE A STRONG CHIN?
WHICH ONE?
JPM DAVIS 3-13
THANK YOU FOR YOUR OPINIONS, NERMAL
ANYTIME
TO: ANYONE
ABU DHABI

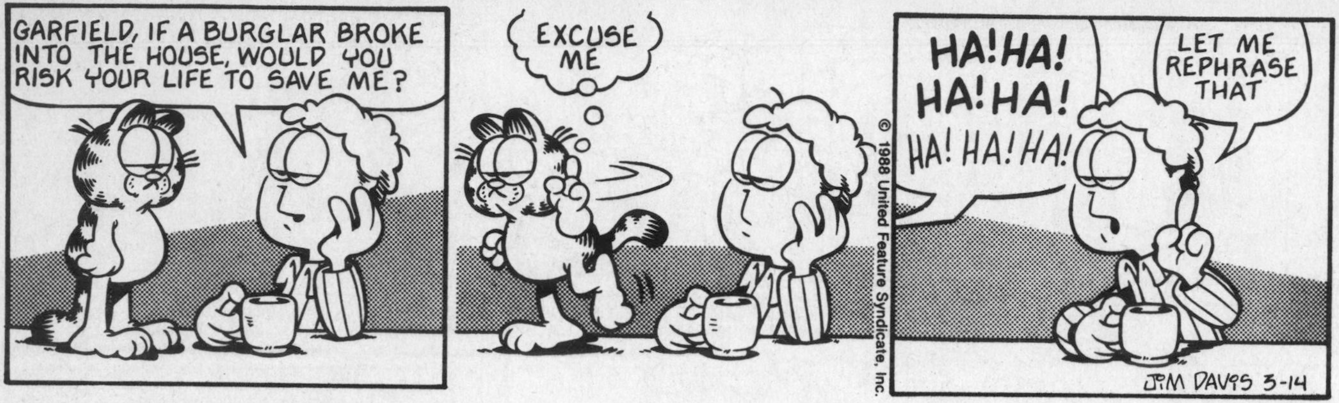
GARFIELD, IF A BURGLAR BROKE INTO THE HOUSE, WOULD YOU RISK YOUR LIFE TO SAVE ME?
EXCUSE ME
HA! HA! HA! HA! HA! HA! HA!
LET ME REPHRASE THAT
© 1988 United Feature Syndicate, Inc.
JIM DAVIS 3-14

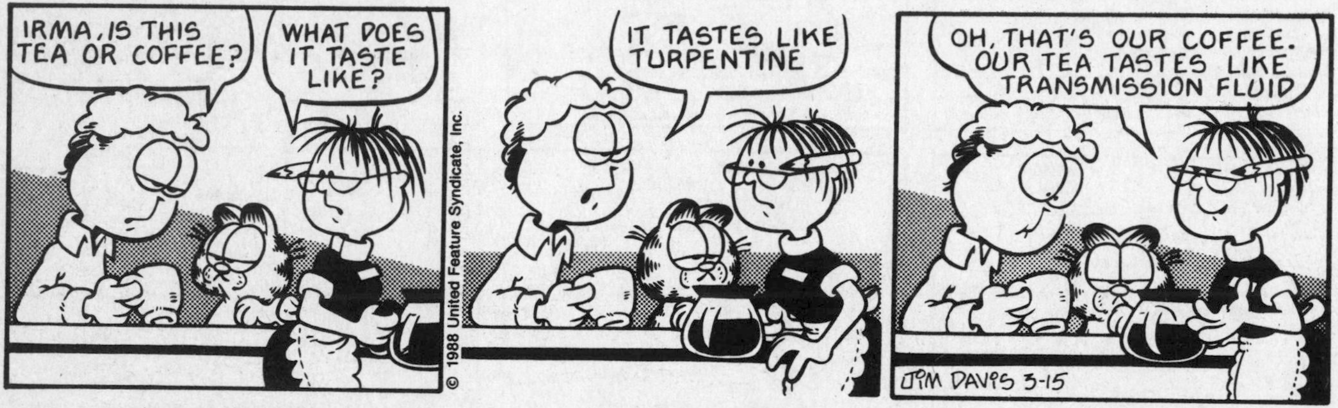
IRMA, IS THIS TEA OR COFFEE?
WHAT DOES IT TASTE LIKE?
© 1988 United Feature Syndicate, Inc.
IT TASTES LIKE TURPENTINE
OH, THAT'S OUR COFFEE. OUR TEA TASTES LIKE TRANSMISSION FLUID
JIM DAVIS 3-15

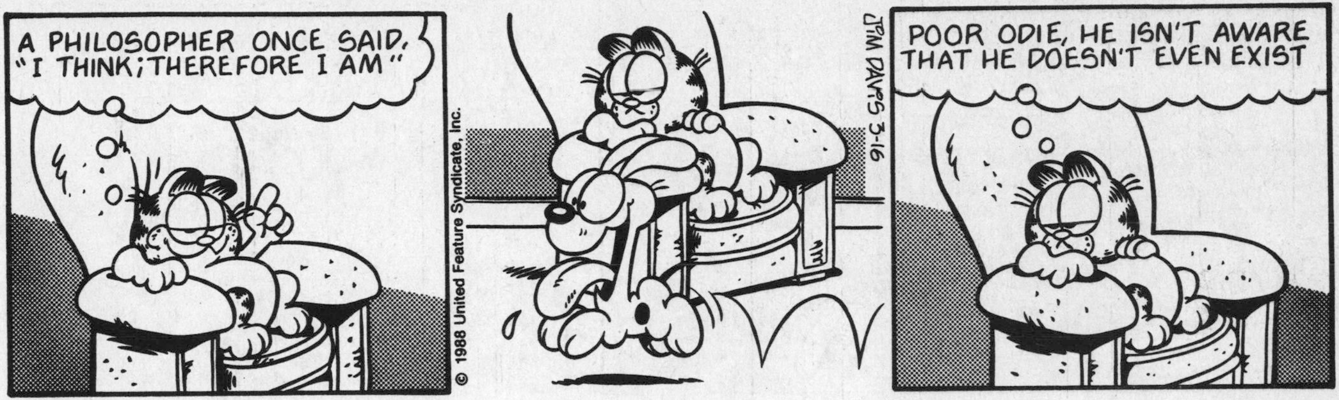
A PHILOSOPHER ONCE SAID, "I THINK; THEREFORE I AM"
POOR ODIE, HE ISN'T AWARE THAT HE DOESN'T EVEN EXIST
© 1988 United Feature Syndicate, Inc.
JIM DAVIS 3-16

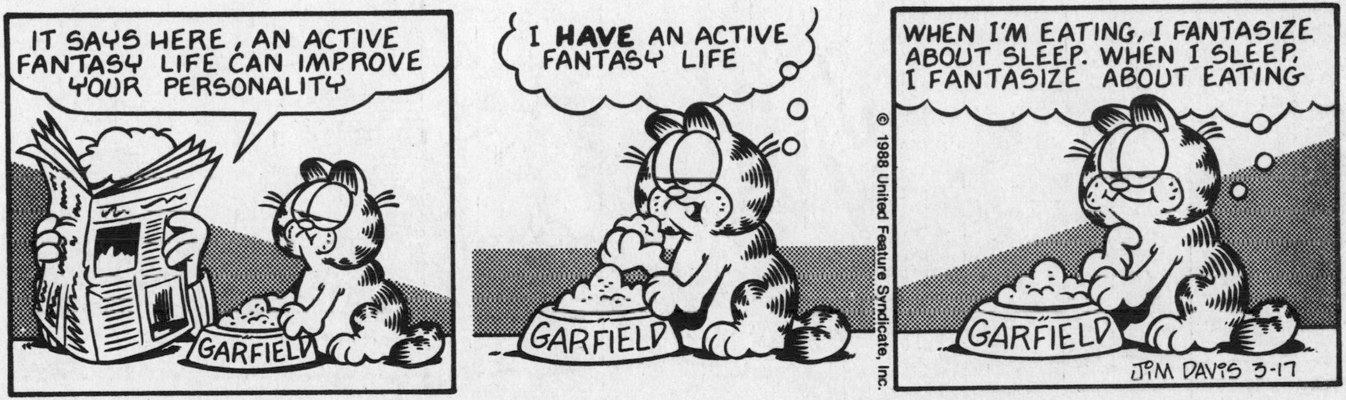
IT SAYS HERE, AN ACTIVE FANTASY LIFE CAN IMPROVE YOUR PERSONALITY
GARFIELD
I **HAVE** AN ACTIVE FANTASY LIFE
GARFIELD
WHEN I'M EATING, I FANTASIZE ABOUT SLEEP. WHEN I SLEEP, I FANTASIZE ABOUT EATING
GARFIELD
© 1988 United Feature Syndicate, Inc.
JIM DAVIS 3-17

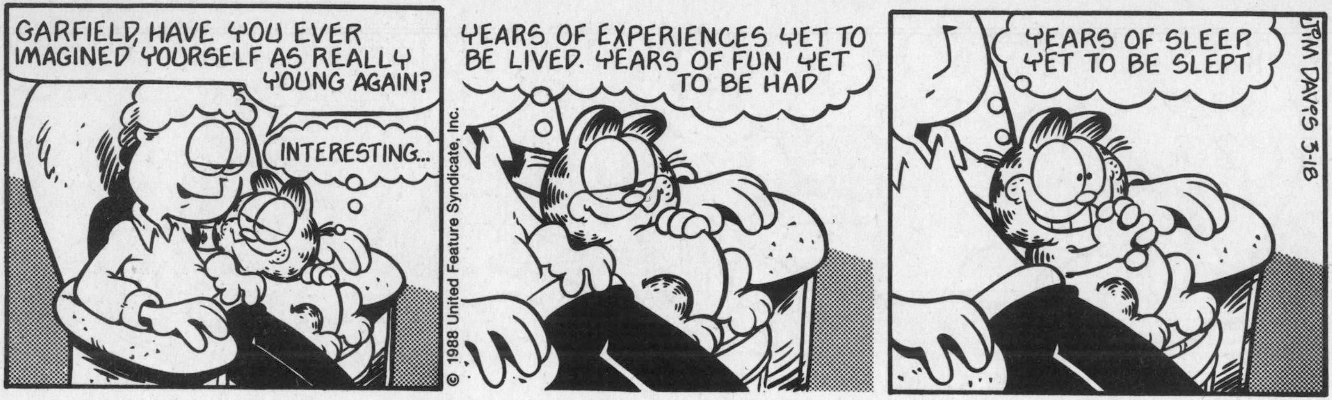
GARFIELD, HAVE YOU EVER IMAGINED YOURSELF AS REALLY YOUNG AGAIN?
INTERESTING...
© 1988 United Feature Syndicate, Inc.
YEARS OF EXPERIENCES YET TO BE LIVED. YEARS OF FUN YET TO BE HAD
YEARS OF SLEEP YET TO BE SLEPT
JIM DAVIS 3-18

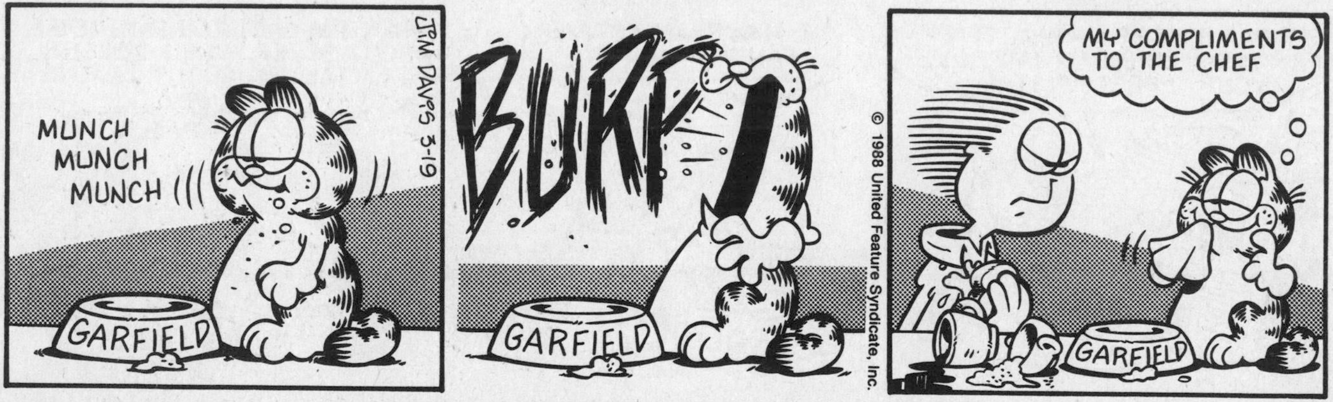
MUNCH
MUNCH
MUNCH
GARFIELD
JIM DAVIS 3-19
BURP
GARFIELD
© 1988 United Feature Syndicate, Inc.
MY COMPLIMENTS TO THE CHEF
GARFIELD

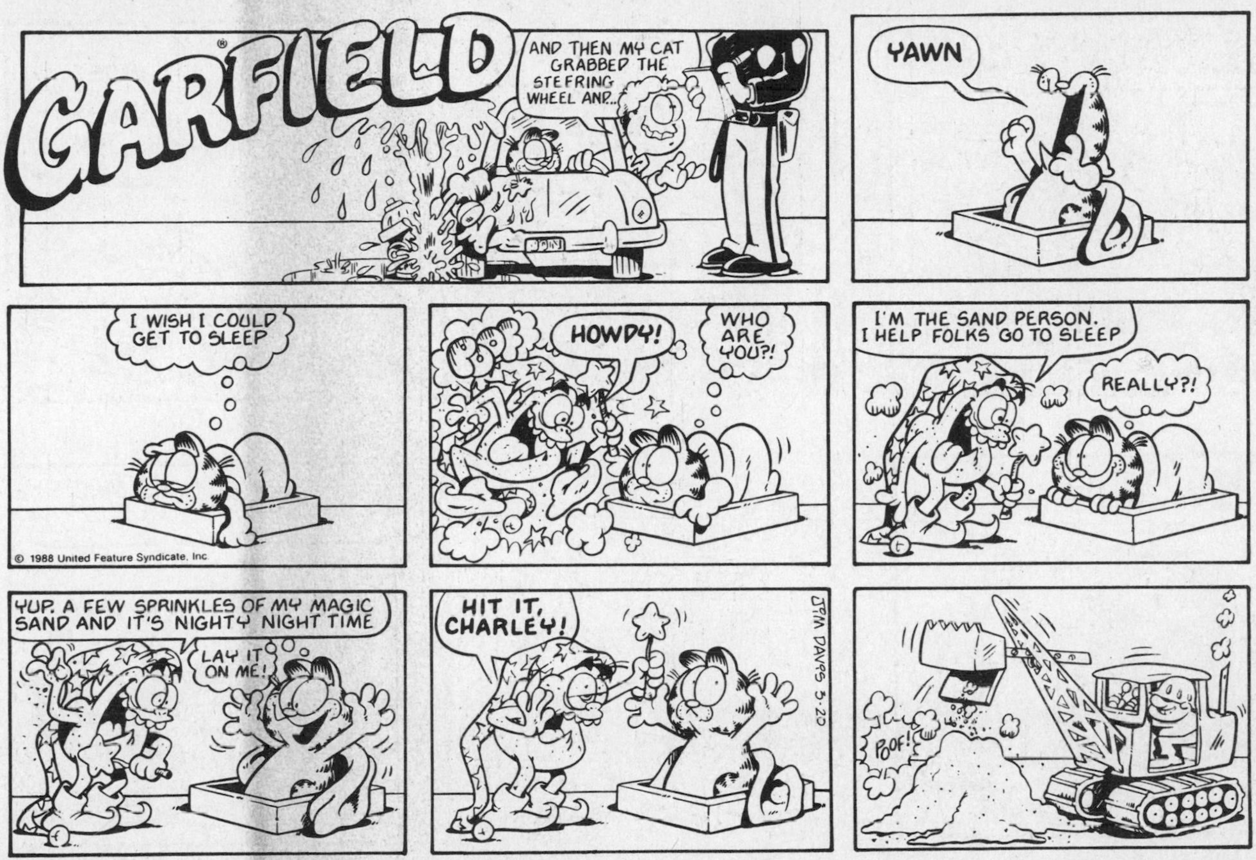
GARFIELD
AND THEN MY CAT GRABBED THE STEERING WHEEL AND...
JOHN
YAWN
I WISH I COULD GET TO SLEEP
© 1988 United Feature Syndicate, Inc.
POOF
HOWDY!
WHO ARE YOU?!
I'M THE SAND PERSON. I HELP FOLKS GO TO SLEEP
REALLY?!
YUP. A FEW SPRINKLES OF MY MAGIC SAND AND IT'S NIGHTY NIGHT TIME
LAY IT ON ME!
HIT IT, CHARLEY!
JIM DAVIS 3-20
POOF!

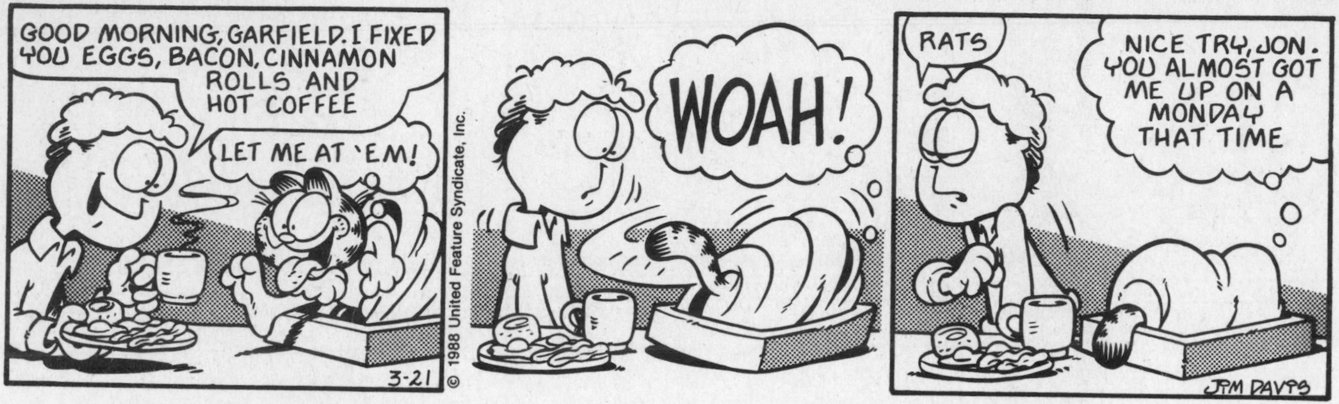
GOOD MORNING, GARFIELD. I FIXED YOU EGGS, BACON, CINNAMON ROLLS AND HOT COFFEE
LET ME AT 'EM!
3-21
WOAH!
RATS
NICE TRY, JON. YOU ALMOST GOT ME UP ON A MONDAY THAT TIME
JIM DAVIS

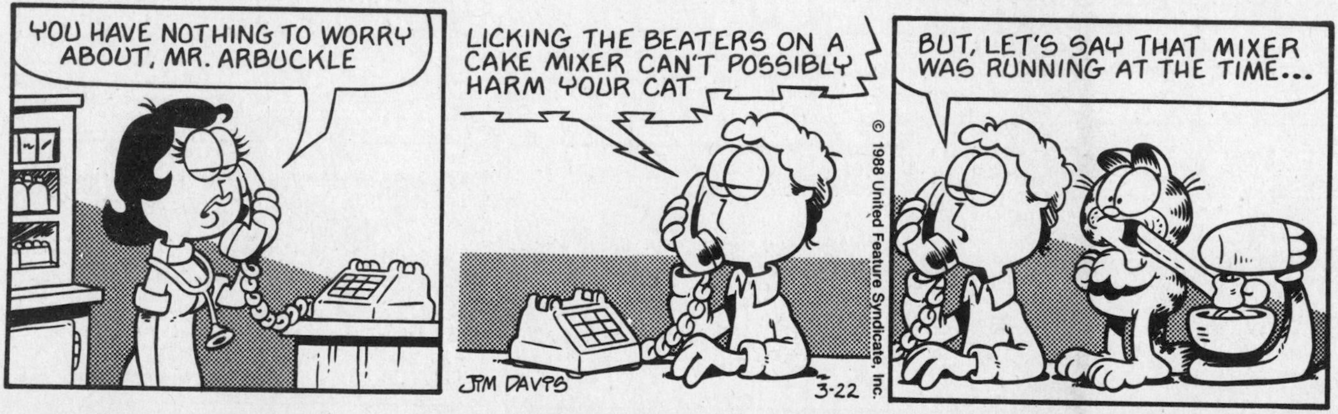
YOU HAVE NOTHING TO WORRY ABOUT, MR. ARBUCKLE
LICKING THE BEATERS ON A CAKE MIXER CAN'T POSSIBLY HARM YOUR CAT
JIM DAVIS
3-22
BUT, LET'S SAY THAT MIXER WAS RUNNING AT THE TIME...

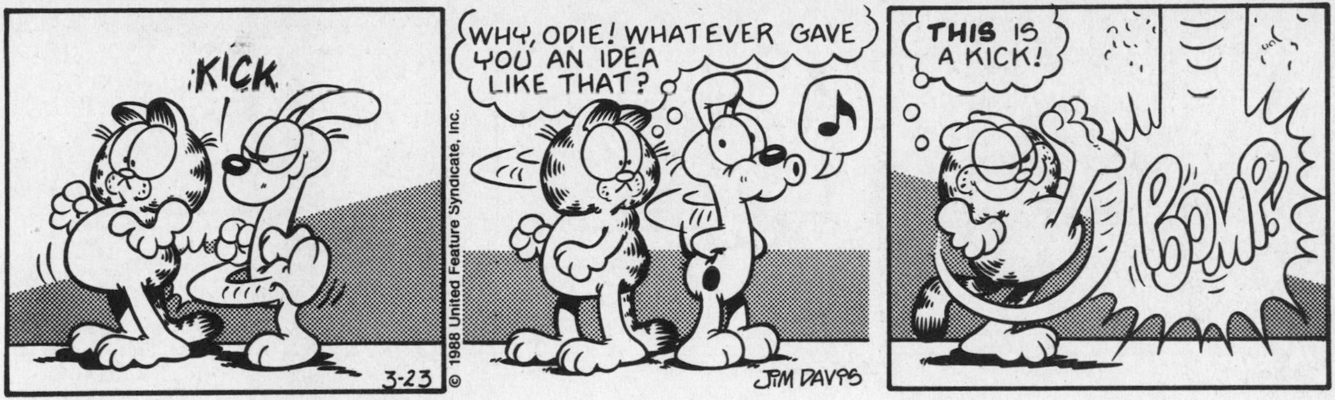
KICK
WHY, ODIE! WHATEVER GAVE YOU AN IDEA LIKE THAT?
THIS IS A KICK!
BOMP!
3-23
© 1988 United Feature Syndicate, Inc.
JIM DAVIS

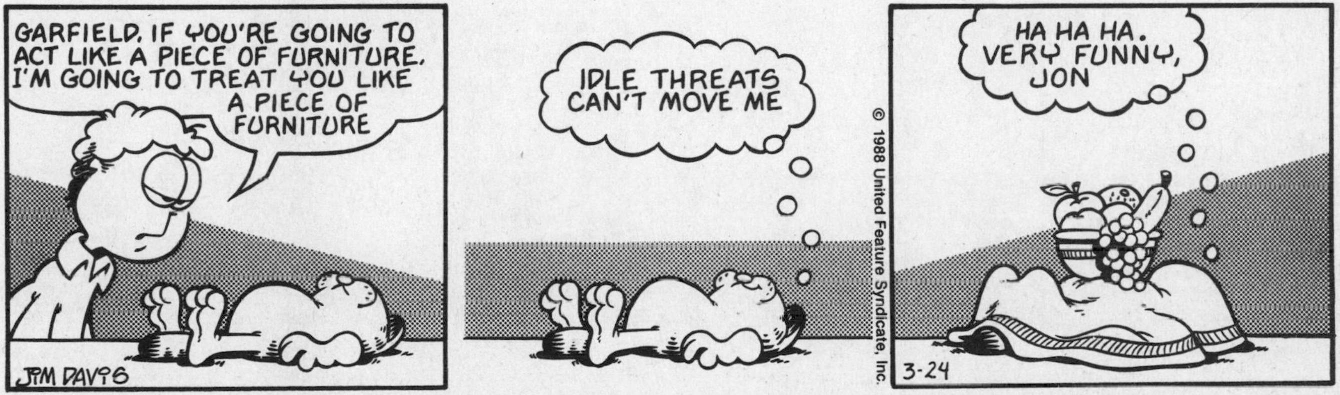
GARFIELD, IF YOU'RE GOING TO ACT LIKE A PIECE OF FURNITURE, I'M GOING TO TREAT YOU LIKE A PIECE OF FURNITURE
IDLE THREATS CAN'T MOVE ME
HA HA HA. VERY FUNNY, JON
JIM DAVIS
© 1988 United Feature Syndicate, Inc.
3-24

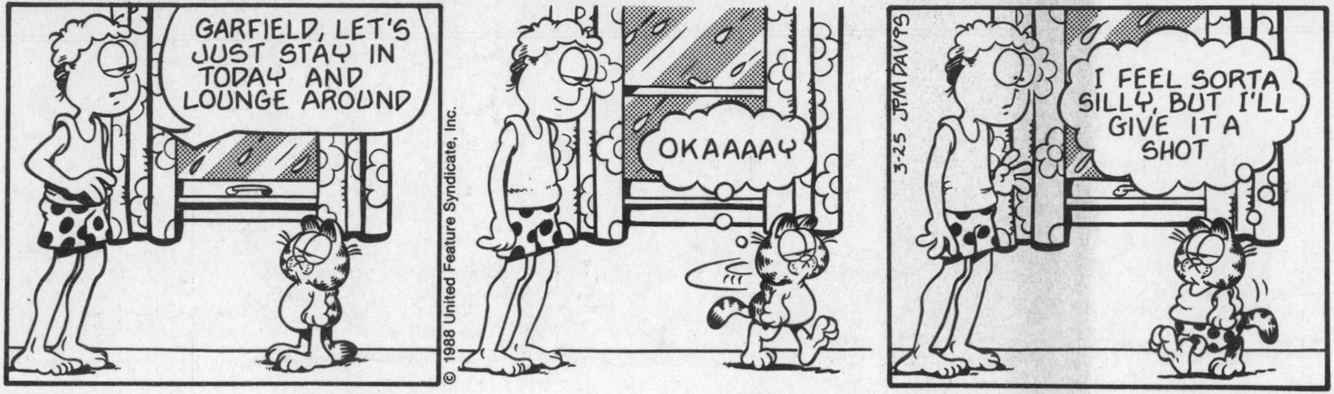
GARFIELD, LET'S JUST STAY IN TODAY AND LOUNGE AROUND
OKAAAAY
I FEEL SORTA SILLY, BUT I'LL GIVE IT A SHOT
JIM DAVIS
3-25
© 1988 United Feature Syndicate, Inc.

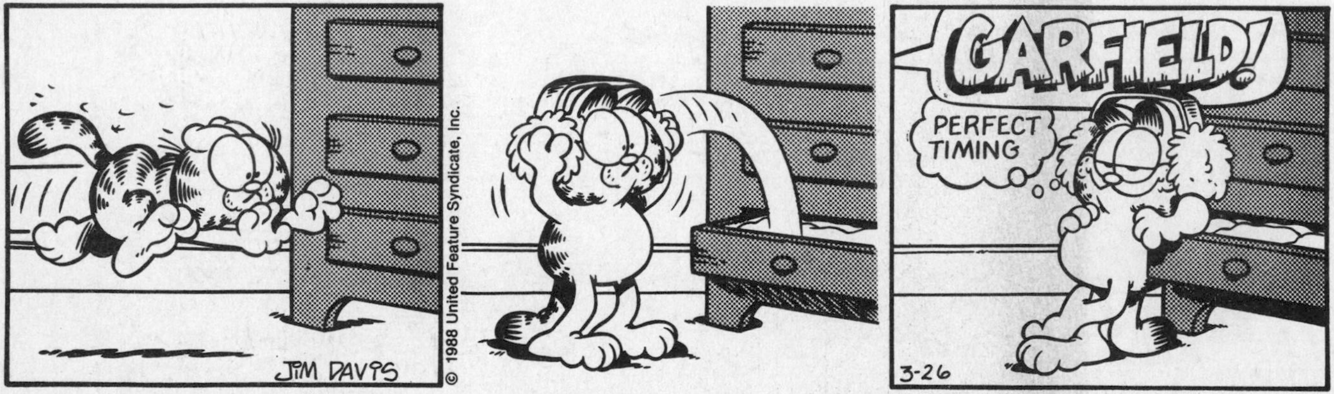
JIM DAVIS
© 1988 United Feature Syndicate, Inc.
GARFIELD!
PERFECT TIMING
3-26

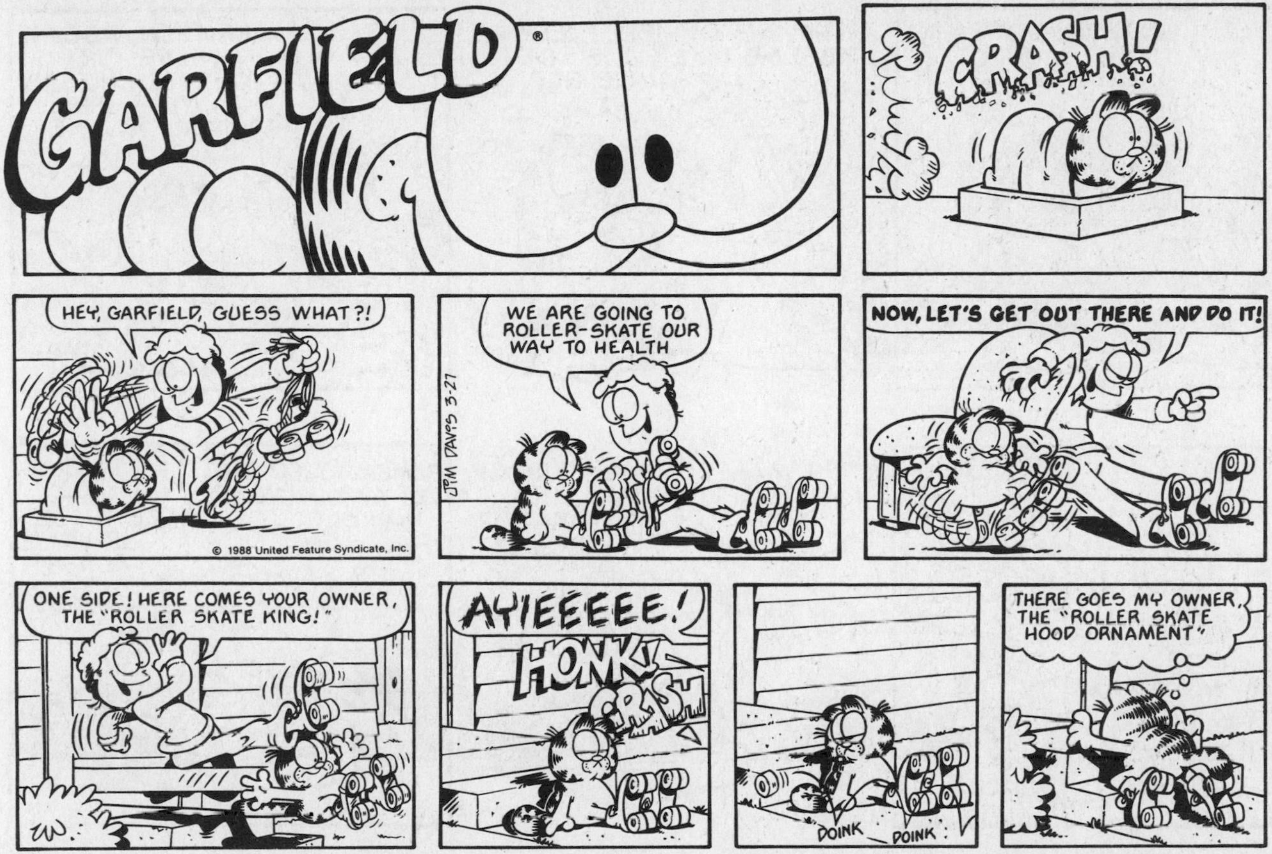
GARFIELD®
CRASH!
HEY, GARFIELD, GUESS WHAT?!
© 1988 United Feature Syndicate, Inc.
JIM DAVIS 3-27
WE ARE GOING TO ROLLER-SKATE OUR WAY TO HEALTH
NOW, LET'S GET OUT THERE AND DO IT!
ONE SIDE! HERE COMES YOUR OWNER, THE "ROLLER SKATE KING!"
AYIEEEEEE!
HONK!
CRASH
DOINK
DOINK
THERE GOES MY OWNER, THE "ROLLER SKATE HOOD ORNAMENT"

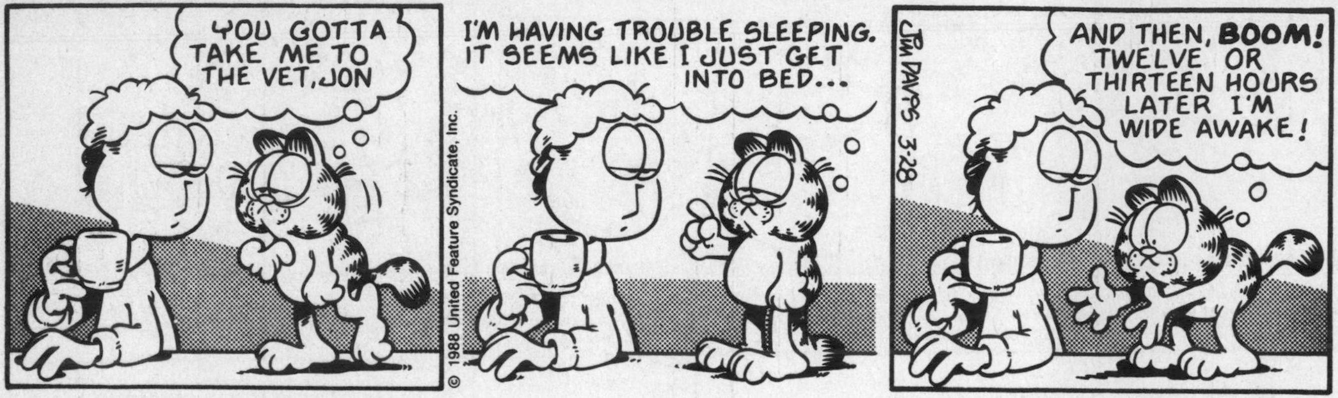
YOU GOTTA TAKE ME TO THE VET, JON
I'M HAVING TROUBLE SLEEPING. IT SEEMS LIKE I JUST GET INTO BED...
© 1988 United Feature Syndicate, Inc.
JIM DAVIS 3-28
AND THEN, **BOOM!** TWELVE OR THIRTEEN HOURS LATER I'M WIDE AWAKE!

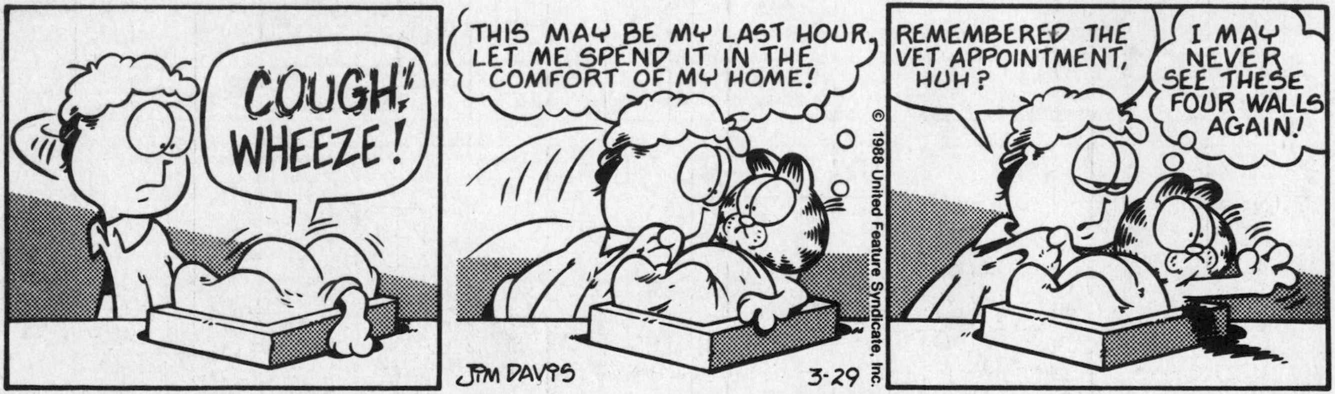
COUGH! WHEEZE!
THIS MAY BE MY LAST HOUR, LET ME SPEND IT IN THE COMFORT OF MY HOME!
JIM DAVIS
3-29
© 1988 United Feature Syndicate, Inc.
REMEMBERED THE VET APPOINTMENT, HUH?
I MAY NEVER SEE THESE FOUR WALLS AGAIN!

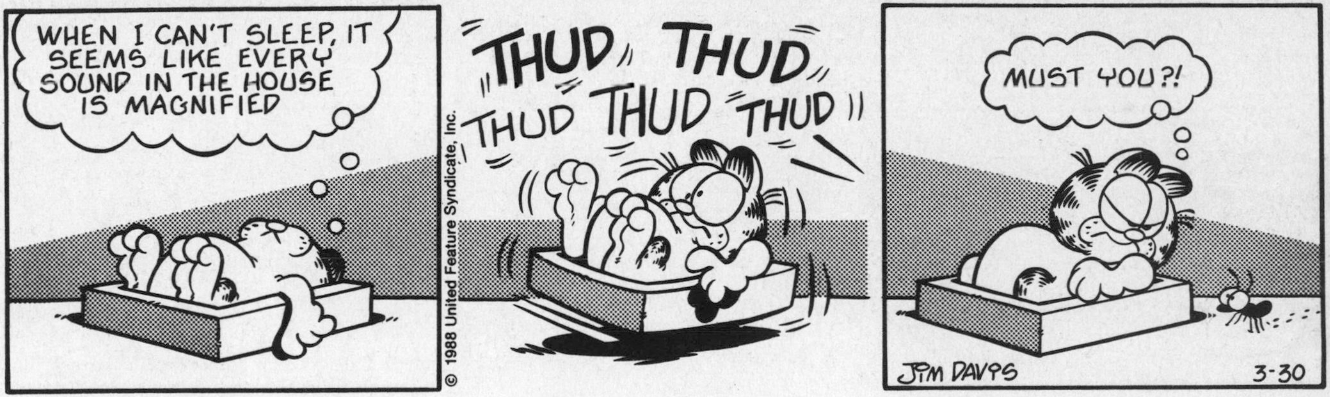
WHEN I CAN'T SLEEP, IT SEEMS LIKE EVERY SOUND IN THE HOUSE IS MAGNIFIED
THUD THUD
THUD THUD THUD
© 1988 United Feature Syndicate, Inc.
MUST YOU?!
JIM DAVIS
3-30

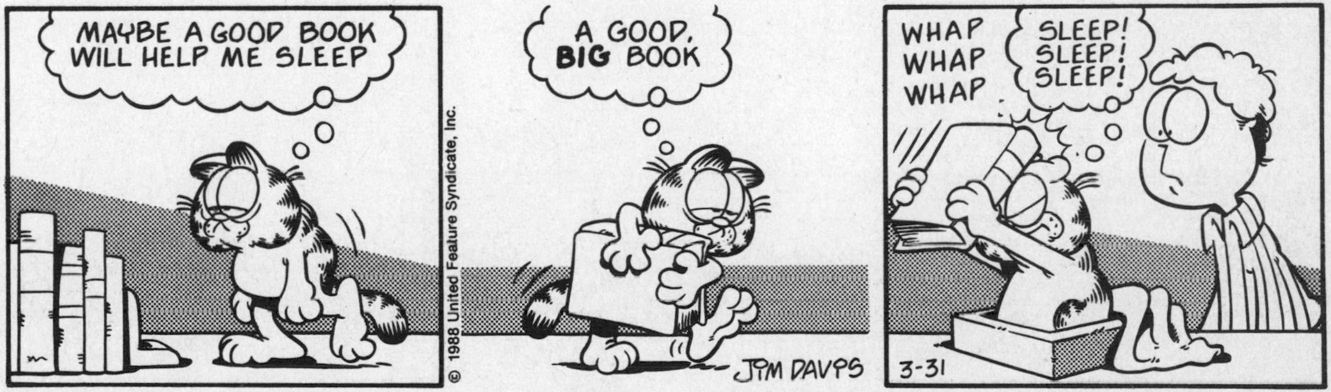
MAYBE A GOOD BOOK WILL HELP ME SLEEP
© 1988 United Feature Syndicate, Inc.
A GOOD, **BIG** BOOK
JIM DAVIS
WHAP WHAP WHAP
SLEEP! SLEEP! SLEEP!
3-31

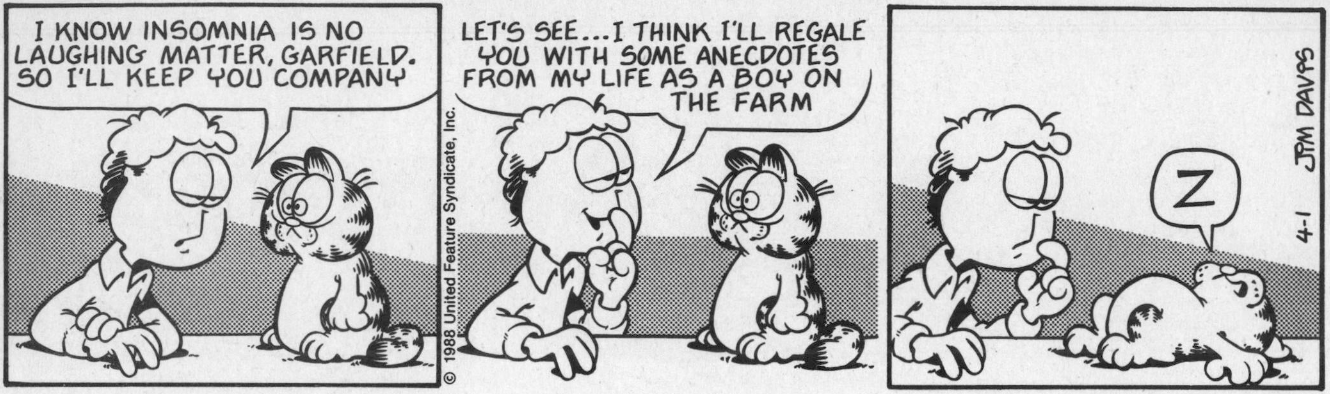
I KNOW INSOMNIA IS NO LAUGHING MATTER, GARFIELD. SO I'LL KEEP YOU COMPANY
© 1988 United Feature Syndicate, Inc.
LET'S SEE... I THINK I'LL REGALE YOU WITH SOME ANECDOTES FROM MY LIFE AS A BOY ON THE FARM
Z
JIM DAVIS
4-1

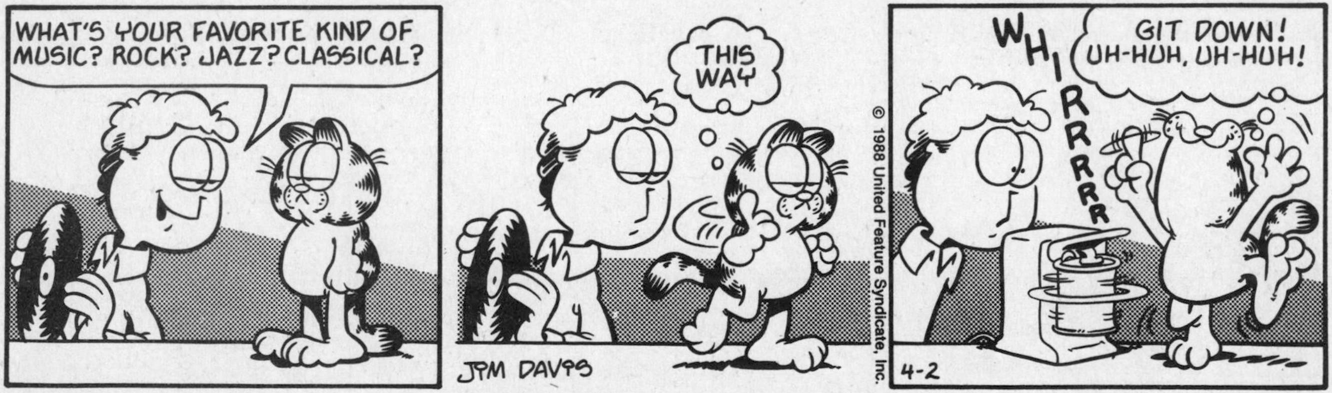
WHAT'S YOUR FAVORITE KIND OF MUSIC? ROCK? JAZZ? CLASSICAL?
THIS WAY
JIM DAVIS
© 1988 United Feature Syndicate, Inc.
WHIRRRRR
GIT DOWN! UH-HUH, UH-HUH!
4-2

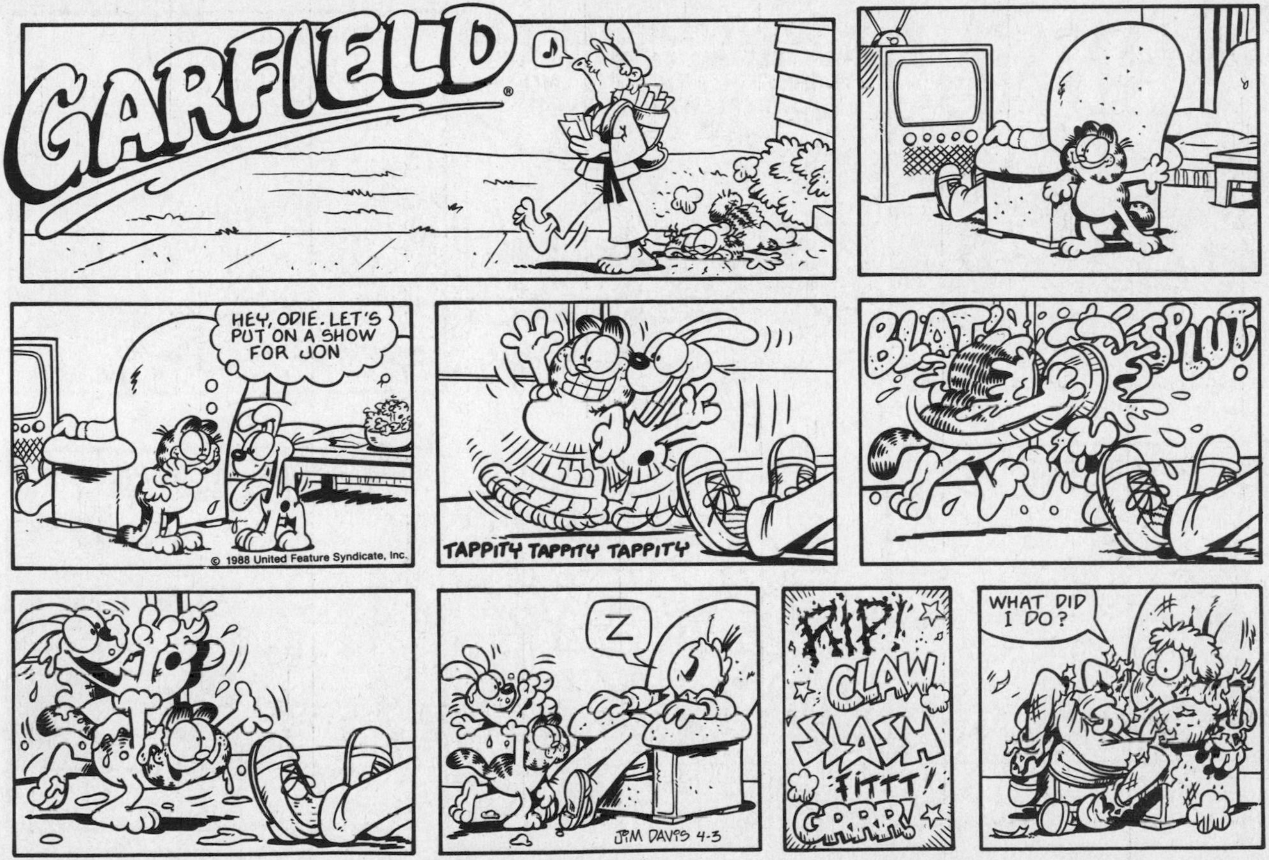

GARFIELD®
HEY, ODIE. LET'S PUT ON A SHOW FOR JON
© 1988 United Feature Syndicate, Inc.
TAPPITY TAPPITY TAPPITY
BLAT
SPLUT
Z
JIM DAVIS 4-3
RIP!
CLAW
SLASH
FTTTT!
GRRR!
WHAT DID I DO?

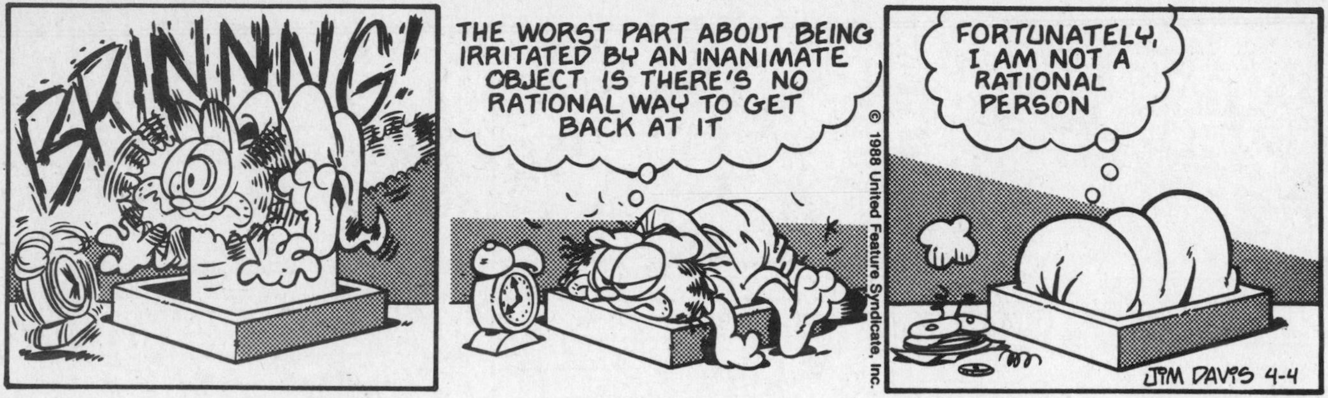
BRINNNG!
THE WORST PART ABOUT BEING IRRITATED BY AN INANIMATE OBJECT IS THERE'S NO RATIONAL WAY TO GET BACK AT IT
© 1988 United Feature Syndicate, Inc.
FORTUNATELY, I AM NOT A RATIONAL PERSON
JIM DAVIS 4-4

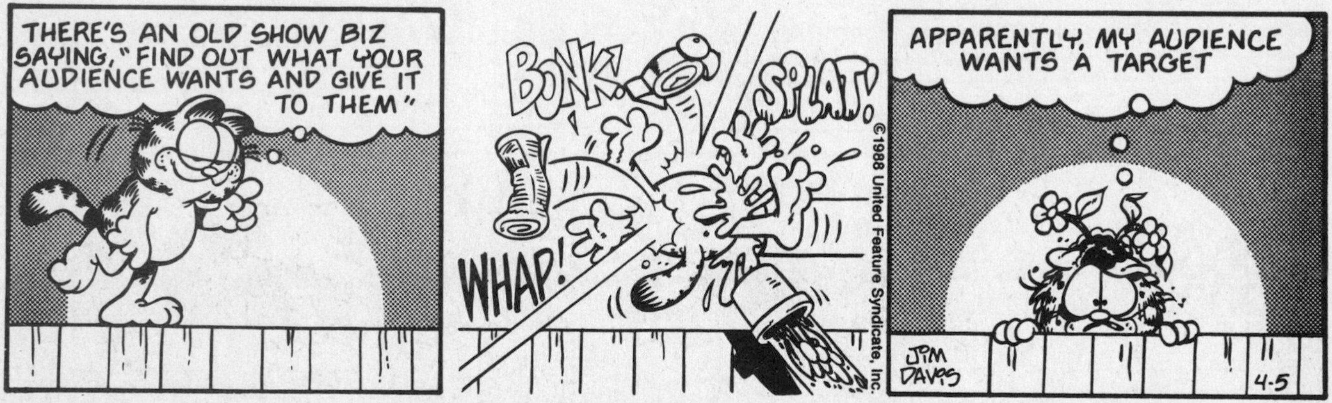
THERE'S AN OLD SHOW BIZ SAYING, "FIND OUT WHAT YOUR AUDIENCE WANTS AND GIVE IT TO THEM"
BONK!
SPLAT!
WHAP!
©1988 United Feature Syndicate, Inc.
APPARENTLY, MY AUDIENCE WANTS A TARGET
JIM DAVIS
4-5

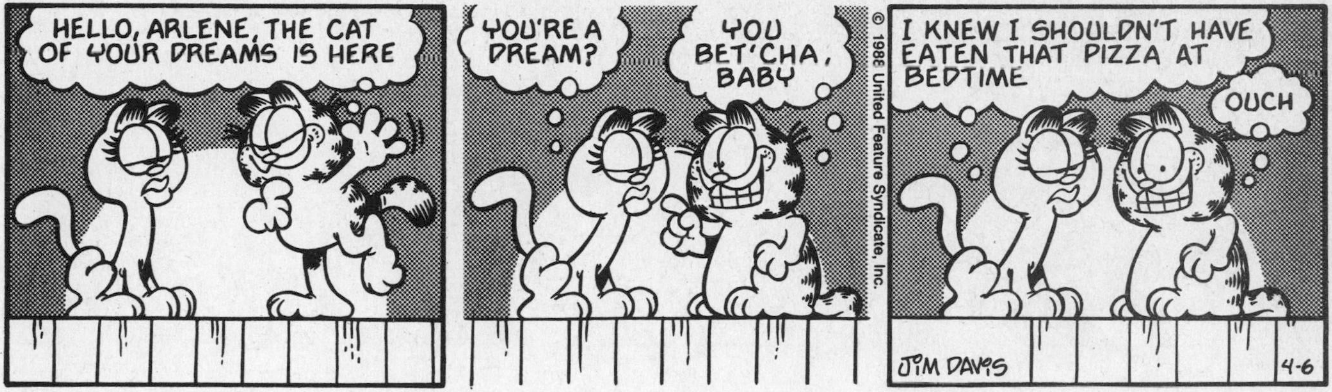
HELLO, ARLENE, THE CAT OF YOUR DREAMS IS HERE
YOU'RE A DREAM?
YOU BET'CHA, BABY
© 1988 United Feature Syndicate, Inc.
I KNEW I SHOULDN'T HAVE EATEN THAT PIZZA AT BEDTIME
OUCH
JIM DAVIS
4-6

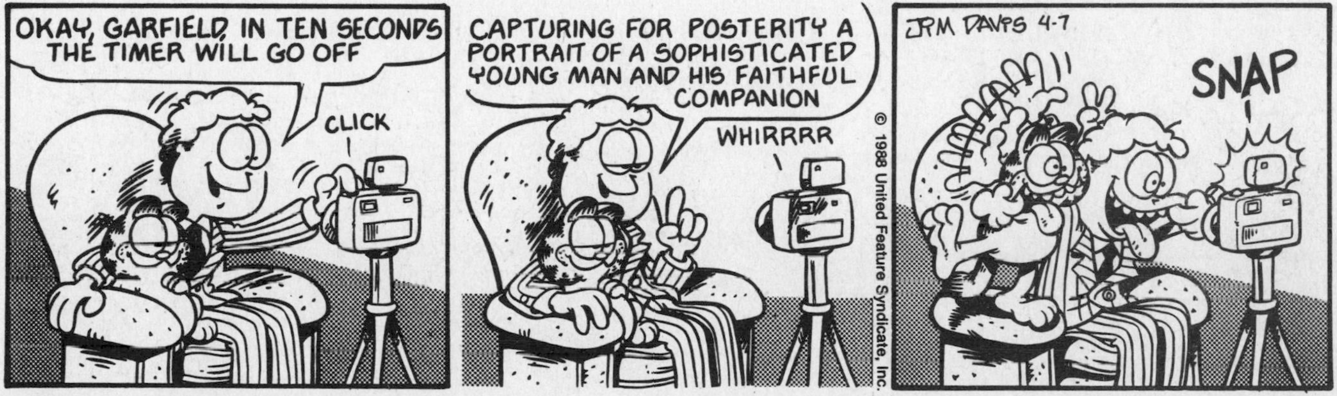
OKAY, GARFIELD, IN TEN SECONDS THE TIMER WILL GO OFF
CLICK
CAPTURING FOR POSTERITY A PORTRAIT OF A SOPHISTICATED YOUNG MAN AND HIS FAITHFUL COMPANION
WHIRRRR
© 1988 United Feature Syndicate, Inc.
JIM DAVIS 4-7
SNAP

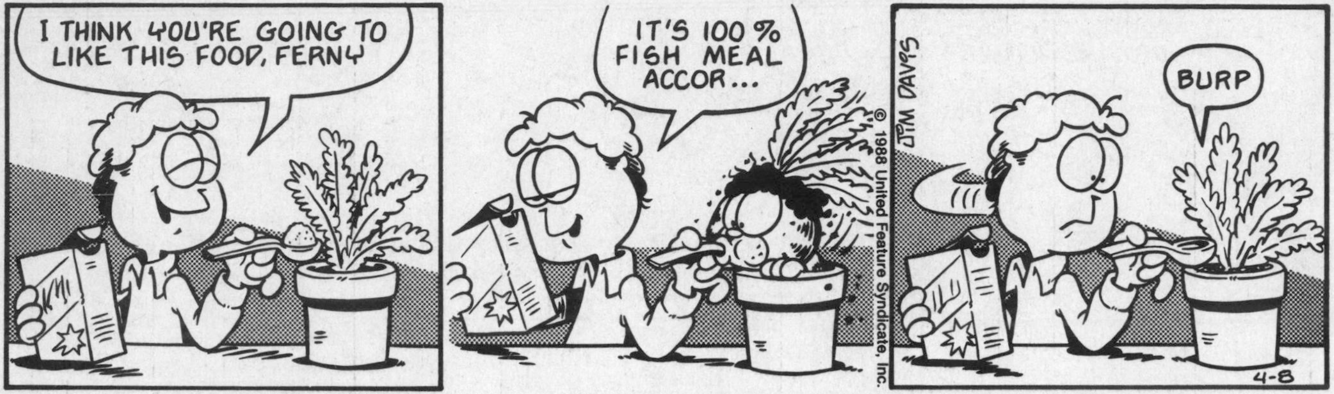
I THINK YOU'RE GOING TO LIKE THIS FOOD, FERNY
IT'S 100% FISH MEAL ACCOR...
BURP
© 1988 United Feature Syndicate, Inc.
JIM DAVIS
4-8

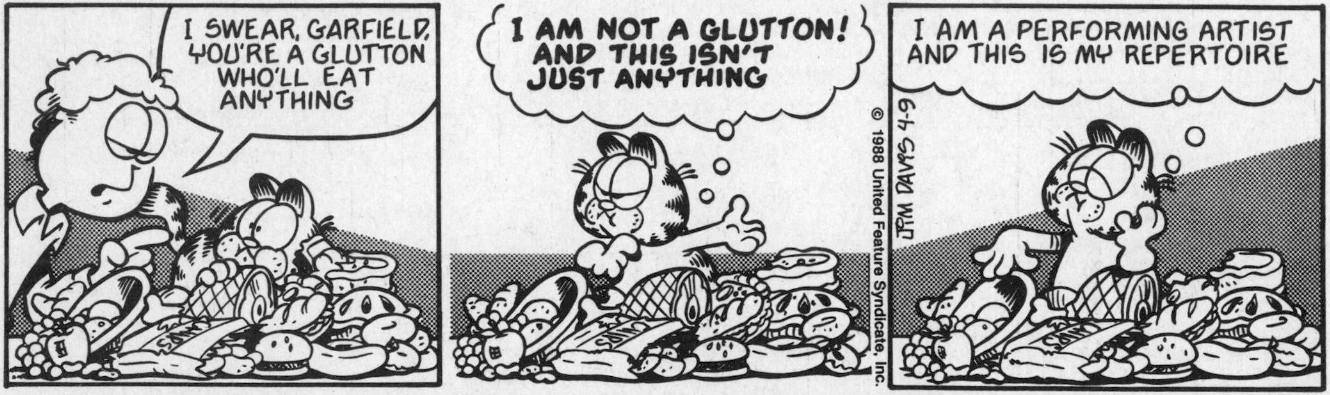
I SWEAR, GARFIELD, YOU'RE A GLUTTON WHO'LL EAT ANYTHING
I AM NOT A GLUTTON! AND THIS ISN'T JUST ANYTHING
I AM A PERFORMING ARTIST AND THIS IS MY REPERTOIRE
© 1988 United Feature Syndicate, Inc.
JIM DAVIS 4-9

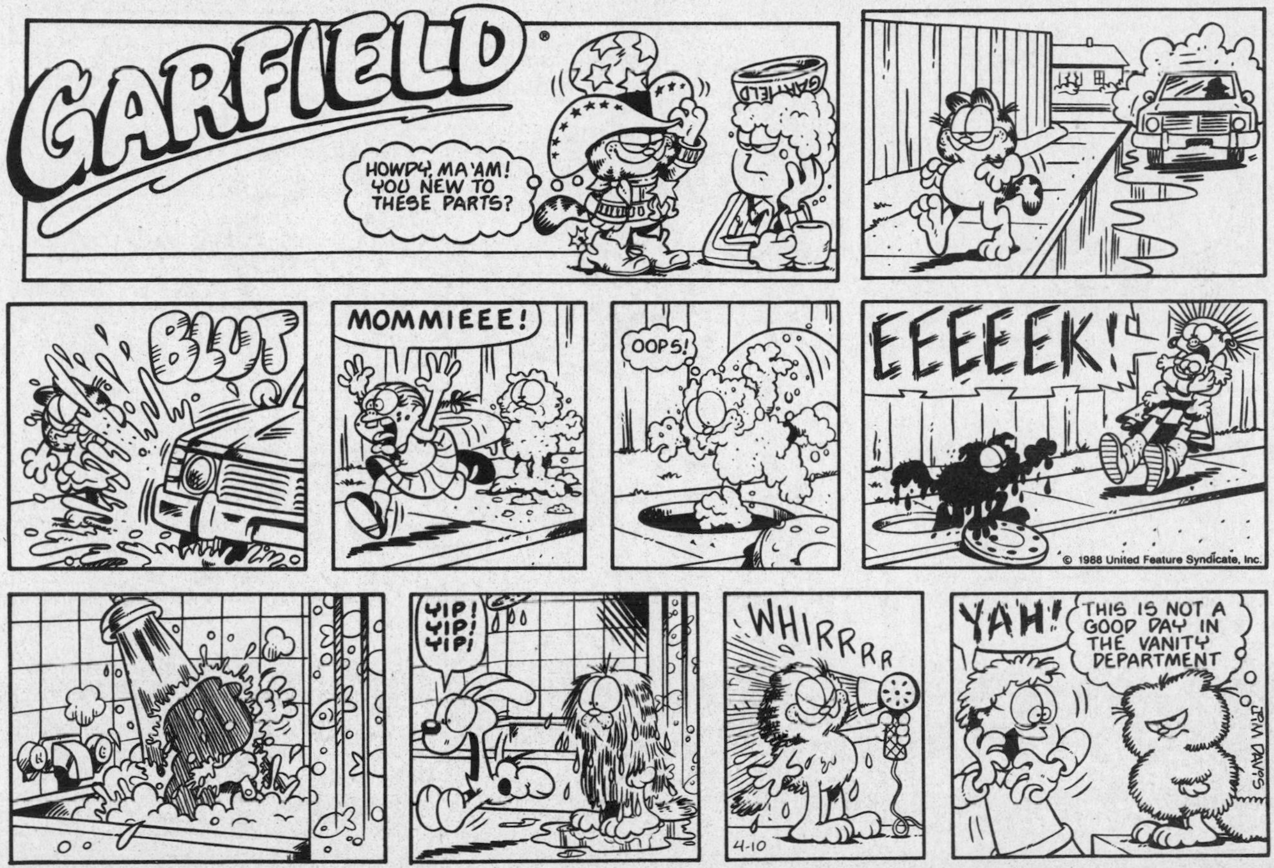
GARFIELD®
HOWDY, MA'AM! YOU NEW TO THESE PARTS?
GARFIELD
BLUT
MOMMIEEE!
OOPS!
EEEEEK!
© 1988 United Feature Syndicate, Inc.
YIP! YIP! YIP!
WHIRRRRR
4-10
YAH!
THIS IS NOT A GOOD DAY IN THE VANITY DEPARTMENT
JIM DAVIS

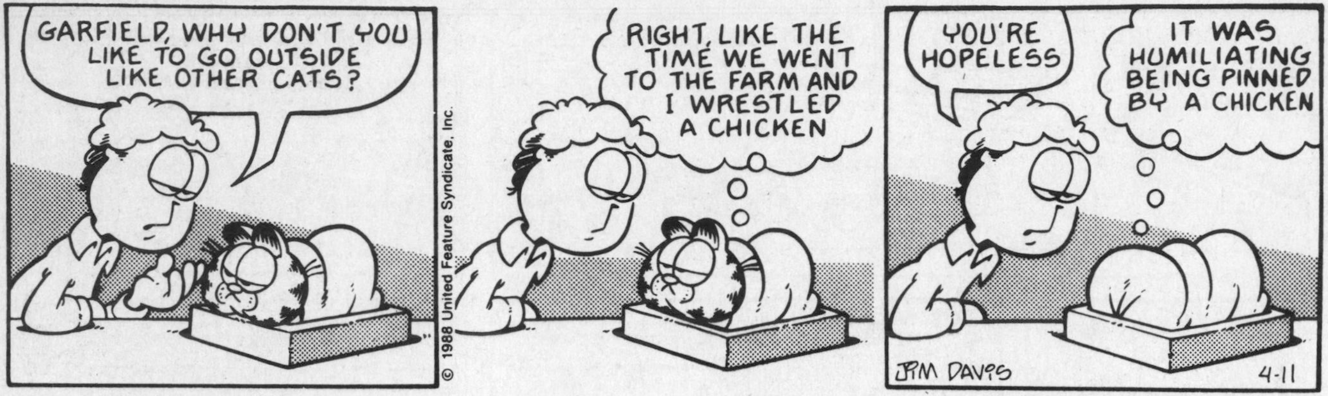
GARFIELD, WHY DON'T YOU LIKE TO GO OUTSIDE LIKE OTHER CATS?
RIGHT, LIKE THE TIME WE WENT TO THE FARM AND I WRESTLED A CHICKEN
YOU'RE HOPELESS
IT WAS HUMILIATING BEING PINNED BY A CHICKEN
© 1988 United Feature Syndicate, Inc.
JIM DAVIS
4-11

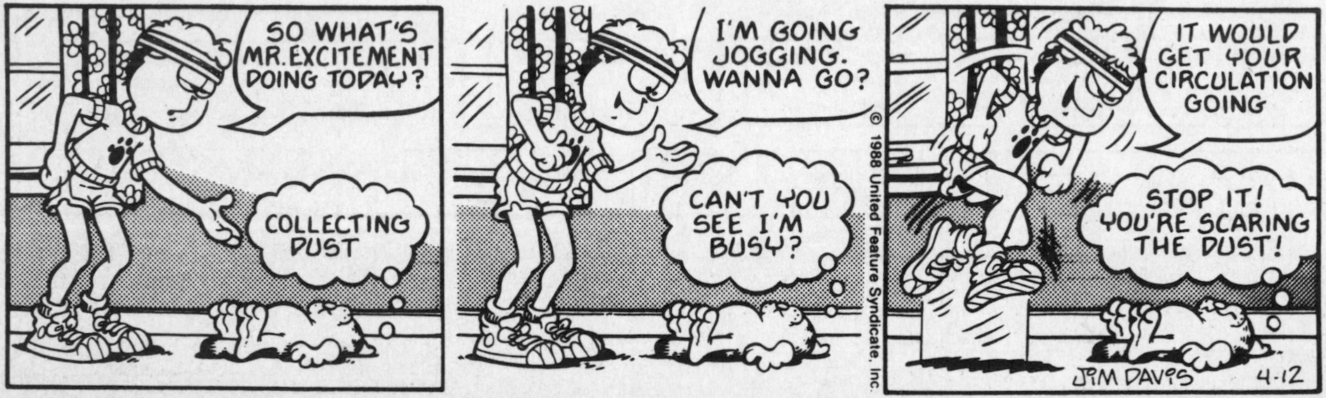
SO WHAT'S MR. EXCITEMENT DOING TODAY?
COLLECTING DUST
I'M GOING JOGGING. WANNA GO?
CAN'T YOU SEE I'M BUSY?
IT WOULD GET YOUR CIRCULATION GOING
STOP IT! YOU'RE SCARING THE DUST!
© 1988 United Feature Syndicate, Inc.
JIM DAVIS
4-12

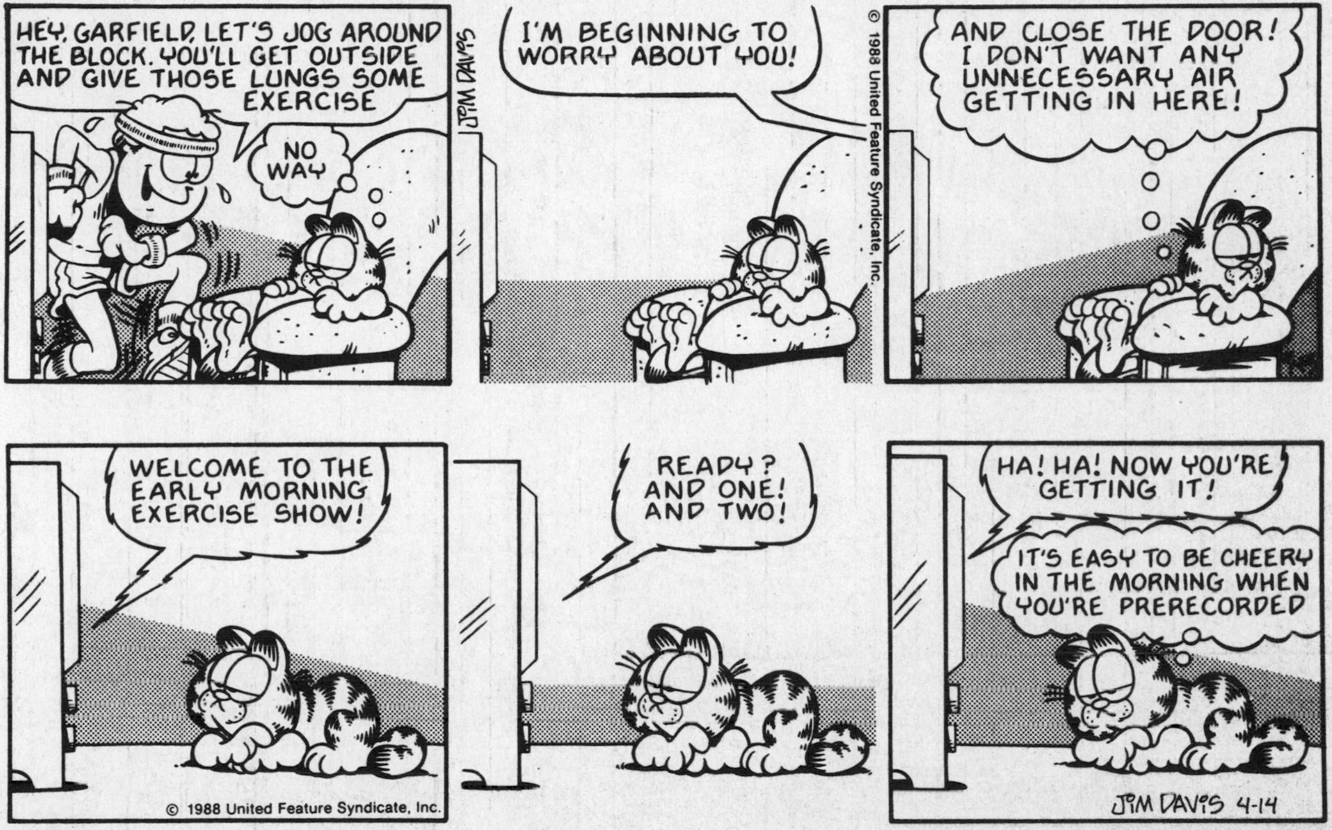
HEY, GARFIELD, LET'S JOG AROUND THE BLOCK. YOU'LL GET OUTSIDE AND GIVE THOSE LUNGS SOME EXERCISE
NO WAY
JIM DAVIS
I'M BEGINNING TO WORRY ABOUT YOU!
© 1988 United Feature Syndicate, Inc.
AND CLOSE THE DOOR! I DON'T WANT ANY UNNECESSARY AIR GETTING IN HERE!
WELCOME TO THE EARLY MORNING EXERCISE SHOW!
READY? AND ONE! AND TWO!
HA! HA! NOW YOU'RE GETTING IT!
IT'S EASY TO BE CHEERY IN THE MORNING WHEN YOU'RE PRERECORDED
© 1988 United Feature Syndicate, Inc.
JIM DAVIS 4-14

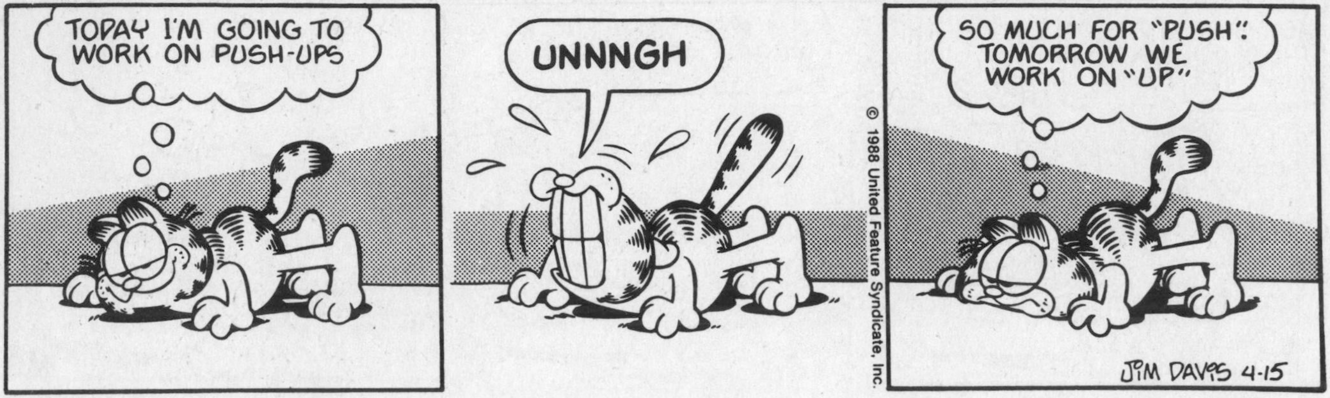
TODAY I'M GOING TO WORK ON PUSH-UPS
UNNNGH
SO MUCH FOR "PUSH". TOMORROW WE WORK ON "UP"
JIM DAVIS 4-15
© 1988 United Feature Syndicate, Inc.

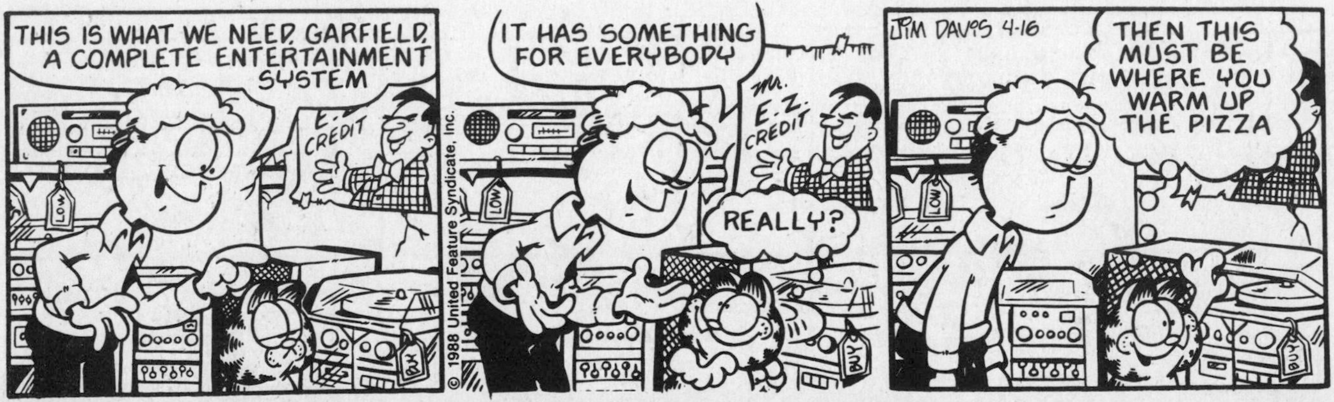
THIS IS WHAT WE NEED, GARFIELD. A COMPLETE ENTERTAINMENT SYSTEM
CREDIT
LOW
IT HAS SOMETHING FOR EVERYBODY
E.Z. CREDIT
REALLY?
JIM DAVIS 4-16
THEN THIS MUST BE WHERE YOU WARM UP THE PIZZA
© 1988 United Feature Syndicate, Inc.

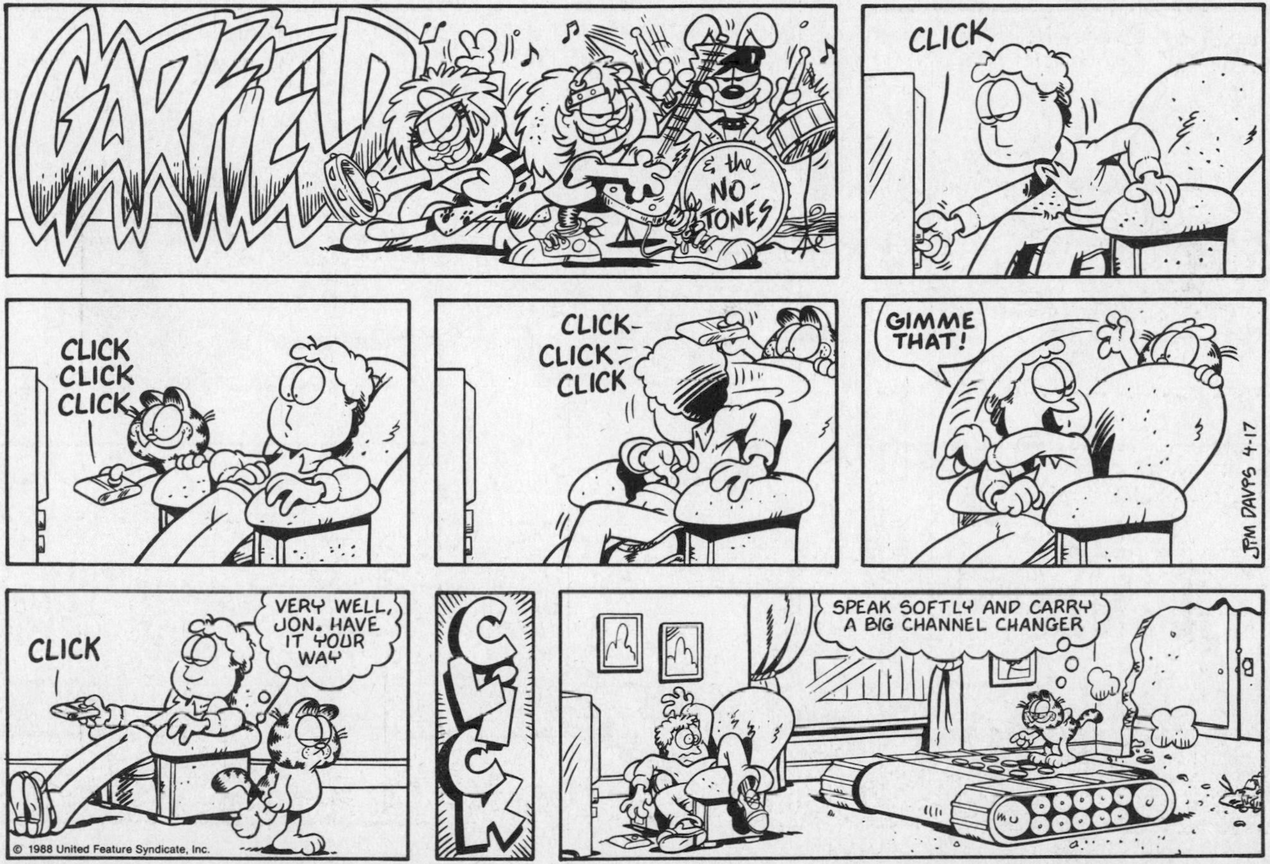
GARFIELD
& the NO-TONES
CLICK
CLICK
CLICK
CLICK
CLICK-
CLICK-
CLICK
GIMME THAT!
JIM DAVIS 4-17
CLICK
VERY WELL, JON. HAVE IT YOUR WAY
CLICK
SPEAK SOFTLY AND CARRY A BIG CHANNEL CHANGER

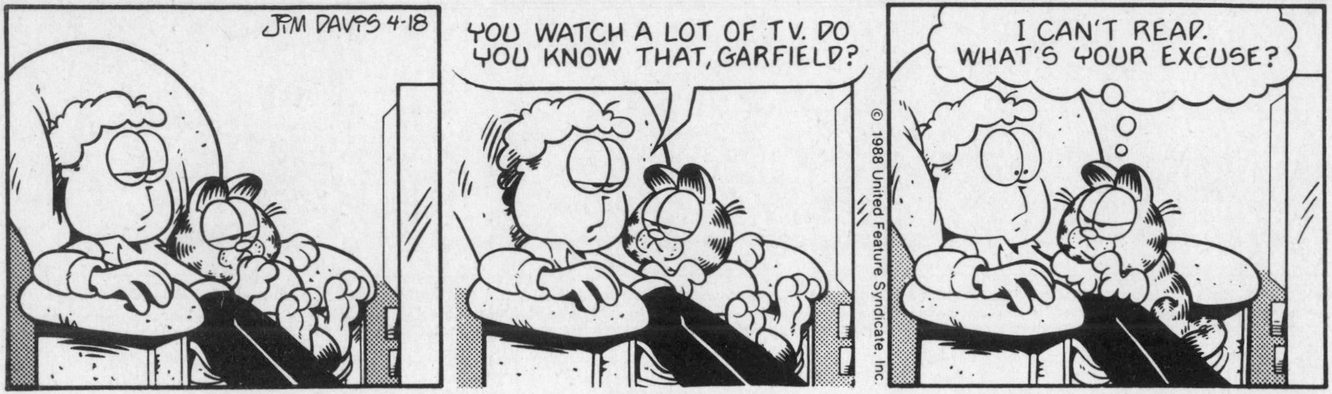
JIM DAVIS 4-18
YOU WATCH A LOT OF T.V. DO YOU KNOW THAT, GARFIELD?
I CAN'T READ. WHAT'S YOUR EXCUSE?
© 1988 United Feature Syndicate, Inc.

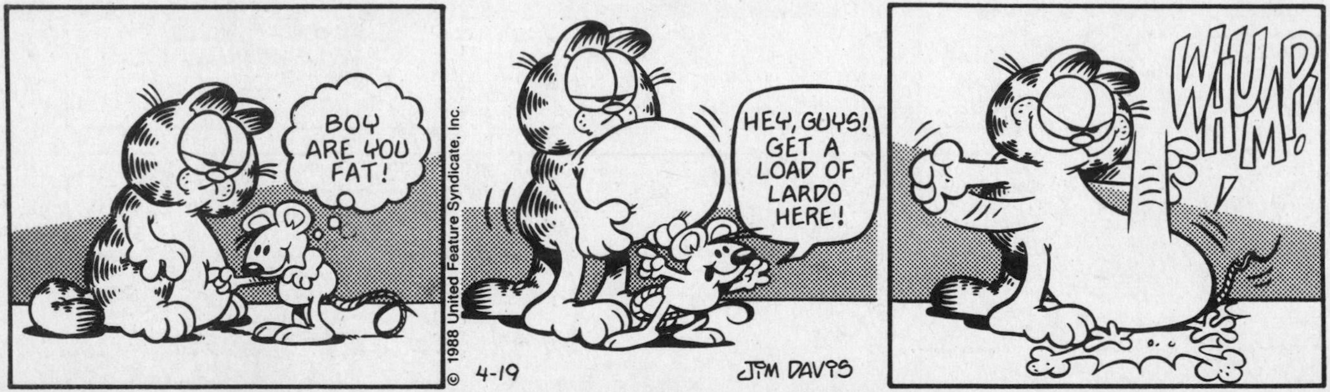
BOY ARE YOU FAT!
© 1988 United Feature Syndicate, Inc.
HEY, GUYS! GET A LOAD OF LARDO HERE!
4-19
JIM DAVIS
WHUMP!

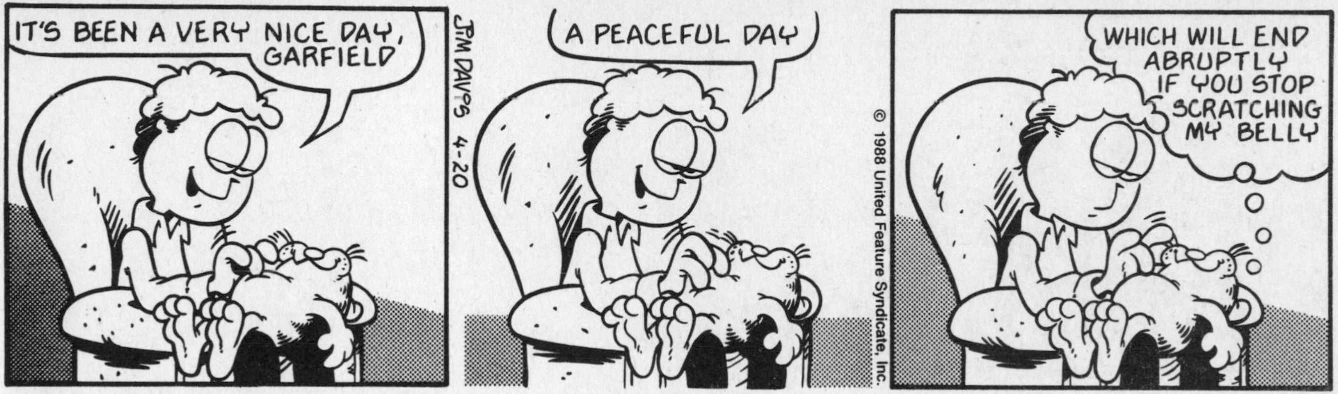
IT'S BEEN A VERY NICE DAY, GARFIELD
JIM DAVIS 4-20
A PEACEFUL DAY
© 1988 United Feature Syndicate, Inc.
WHICH WILL END ABRUPTLY IF YOU STOP SCRATCHING MY BELLY

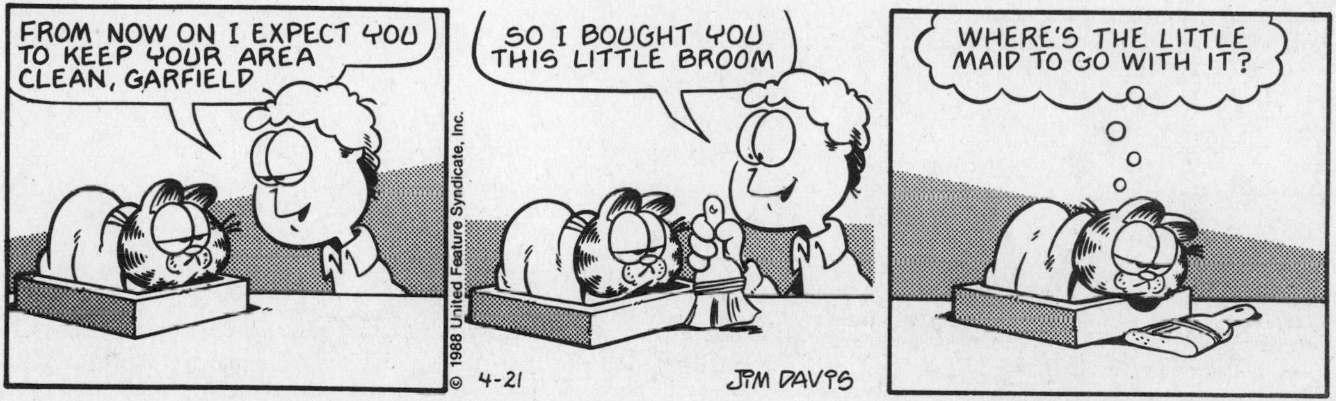
FROM NOW ON I EXPECT YOU TO KEEP YOUR AREA CLEAN, GARFIELD
© 1988 United Feature Syndicate, Inc.
SO I BOUGHT YOU THIS LITTLE BROOM
4-21
JIM DAVIS
WHERE'S THE LITTLE MAID TO GO WITH IT?

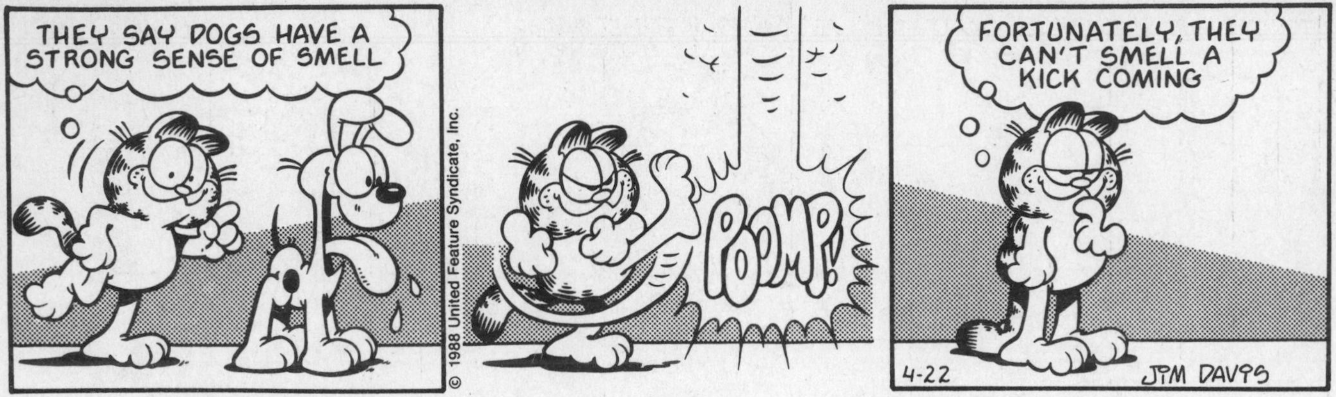
THEY SAY DOGS HAVE A STRONG SENSE OF SMELL
© 1988 United Feature Syndicate, Inc.
POOMP!
FORTUNATELY, THEY CAN'T SMELL A KICK COMING
4-22
JIM DAVIS

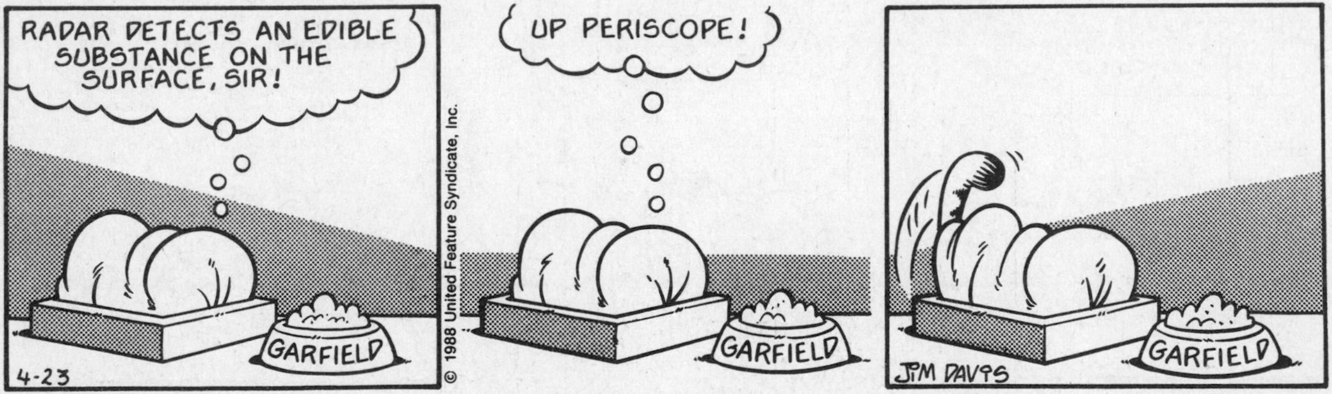
RADAR DETECTS AN EDIBLE SUBSTANCE ON THE SURFACE, SIR!
4-23
GARFIELD
© 1988 United Feature Syndicate, Inc.
UP PERISCOPE!
GARFIELD
JIM DAVIS
GARFIELD

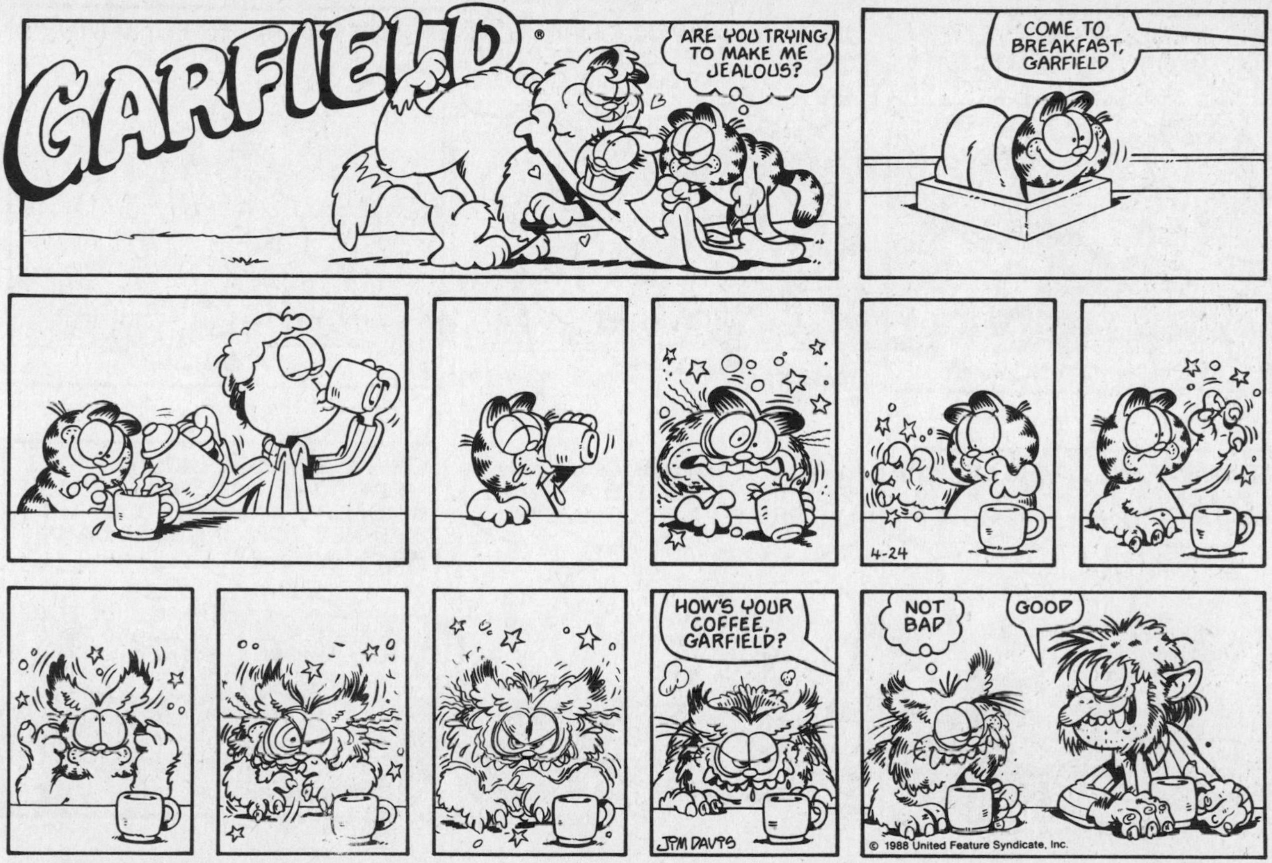
GARFIELD®
ARE YOU TRYING TO MAKE ME JEALOUS?
COME TO BREAKFAST, GARFIELD
4-24
HOW'S YOUR COFFEE, GARFIELD?
NOT BAD
GOOD
JIM DAVIS
© 1988 United Feature Syndicate, Inc.

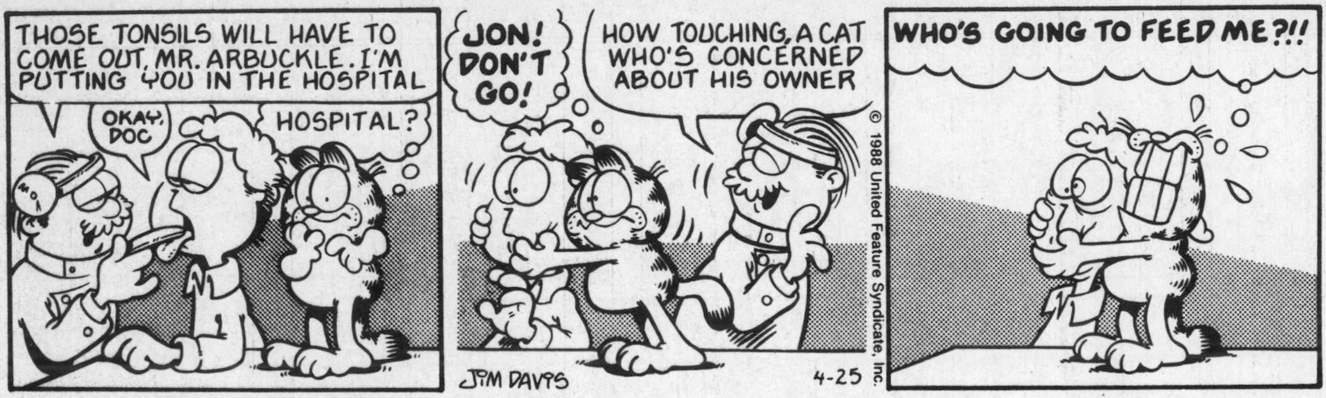
THOSE TONSILS WILL HAVE TO COME OUT, MR. ARBUCKLE. I'M PUTTING YOU IN THE HOSPITAL
OKAY, DOC
HOSPITAL?
JON! DON'T GO!
HOW TOUCHING, A CAT WHO'S CONCERNED ABOUT HIS OWNER
WHO'S GOING TO FEED ME?!!
JIM DAVIS 4-25
© 1988 United Feature Syndicate, Inc.

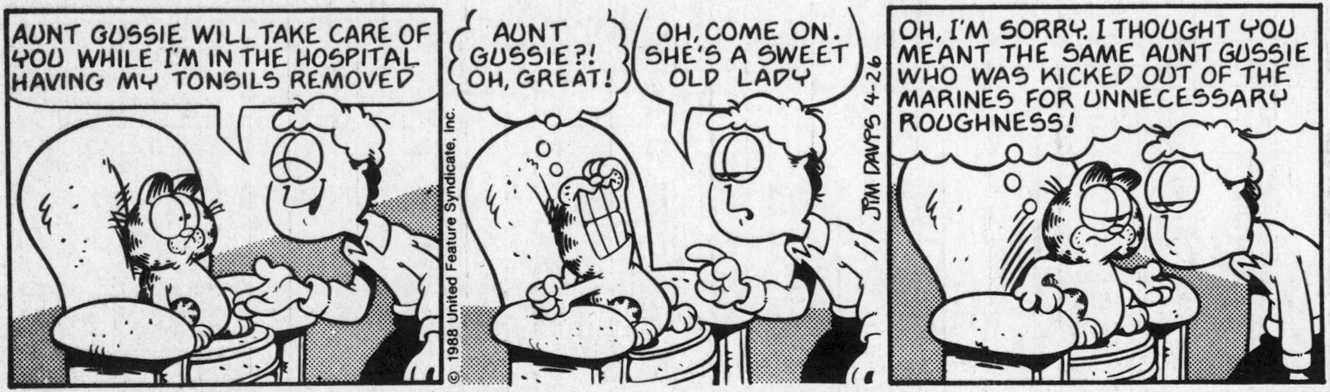
AUNT GUSSIE WILL TAKE CARE OF YOU WHILE I'M IN THE HOSPITAL HAVING MY TONSILS REMOVED
AUNT GUSSIE?! OH, GREAT!
OH, COME ON. SHE'S A SWEET OLD LADY
OH, I'M SORRY. I THOUGHT YOU MEANT THE SAME AUNT GUSSIE WHO WAS KICKED OUT OF THE MARINES FOR UNNECESSARY ROUGHNESS!
JIM DAVIS 4-26
© 1988 United Feature Syndicate, Inc.

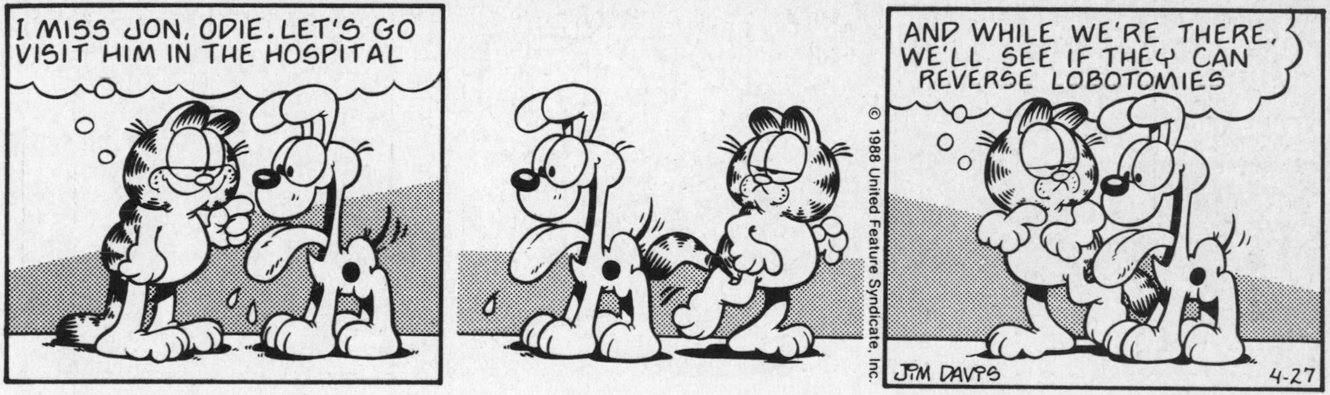
I MISS JON, ODIE. LET'S GO VISIT HIM IN THE HOSPITAL
AND WHILE WE'RE THERE, WE'LL SEE IF THEY CAN REVERSE LOBOTOMIES
© 1988 United Feature Syndicate, Inc.
JIM DAVIS
4-27

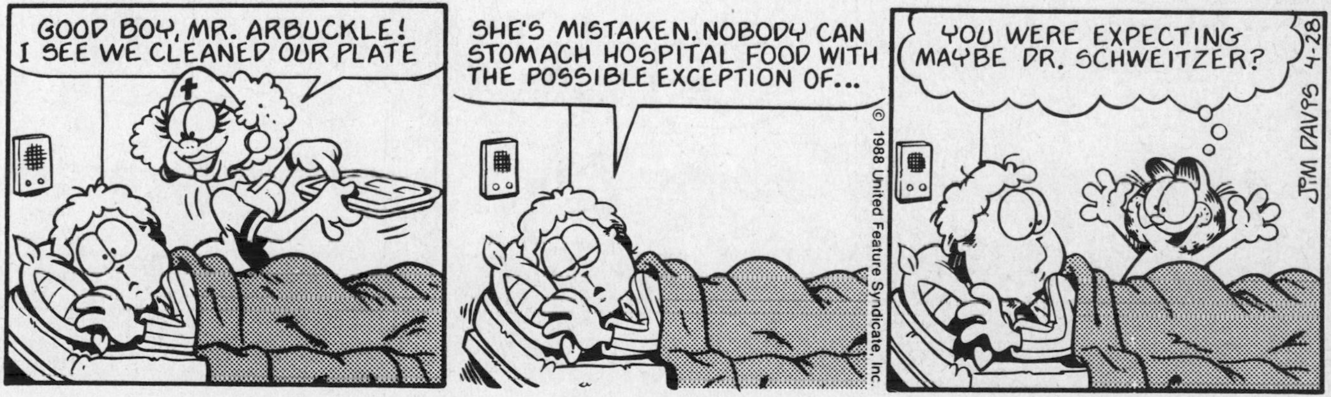
GOOD BOY, MR. ARBUCKLE! I SEE WE CLEANED OUR PLATE
SHE'S MISTAKEN. NOBODY CAN STOMACH HOSPITAL FOOD WITH THE POSSIBLE EXCEPTION OF...
YOU WERE EXPECTING MAYBE DR. SCHWEITZER?
© 1988 United Feature Syndicate, Inc.
JIM DAVIS
4-28

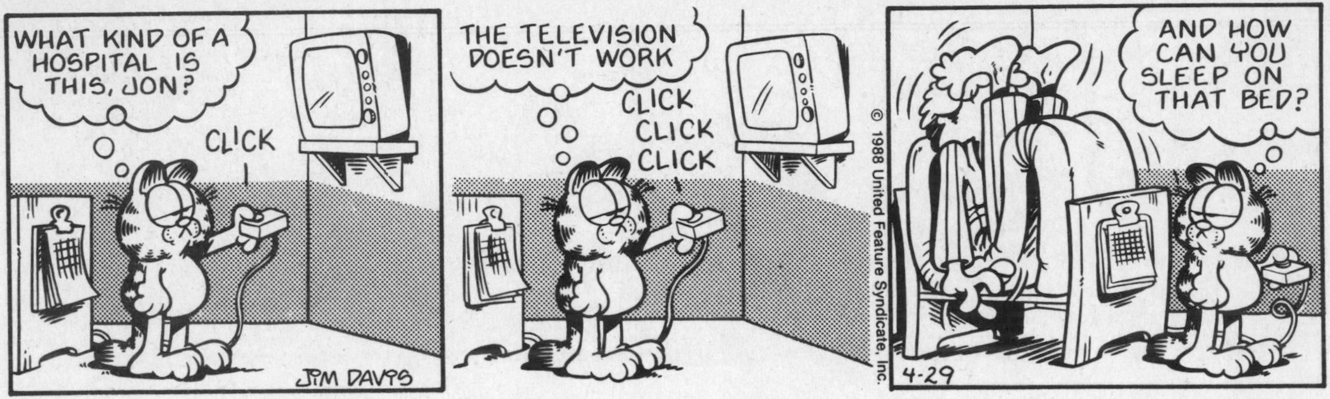
WHAT KIND OF A HOSPITAL IS THIS, JON?
CLICK
JIM DAVIS
THE TELEVISION DOESN'T WORK
CLICK CLICK CLICK
© 1988 United Feature Syndicate, Inc.
AND HOW CAN YOU SLEEP ON THAT BED?
4-29

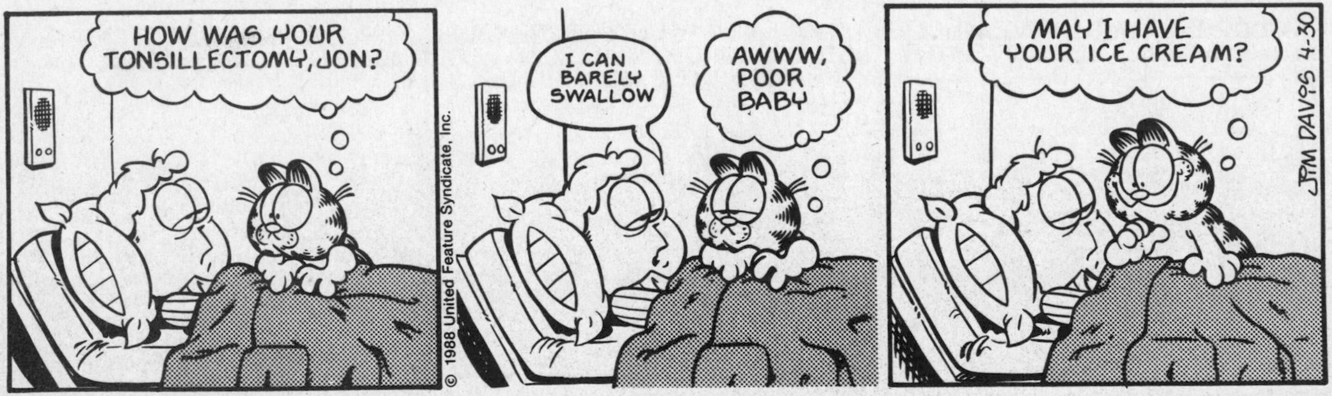
HOW WAS YOUR TONSILLECTOMY, JON?
© 1988 United Feature Syndicate, Inc.
I CAN BARELY SWALLOW
AWWW, POOR BABY
MAY I HAVE YOUR ICE CREAM?
JIM DAVIS 4-30

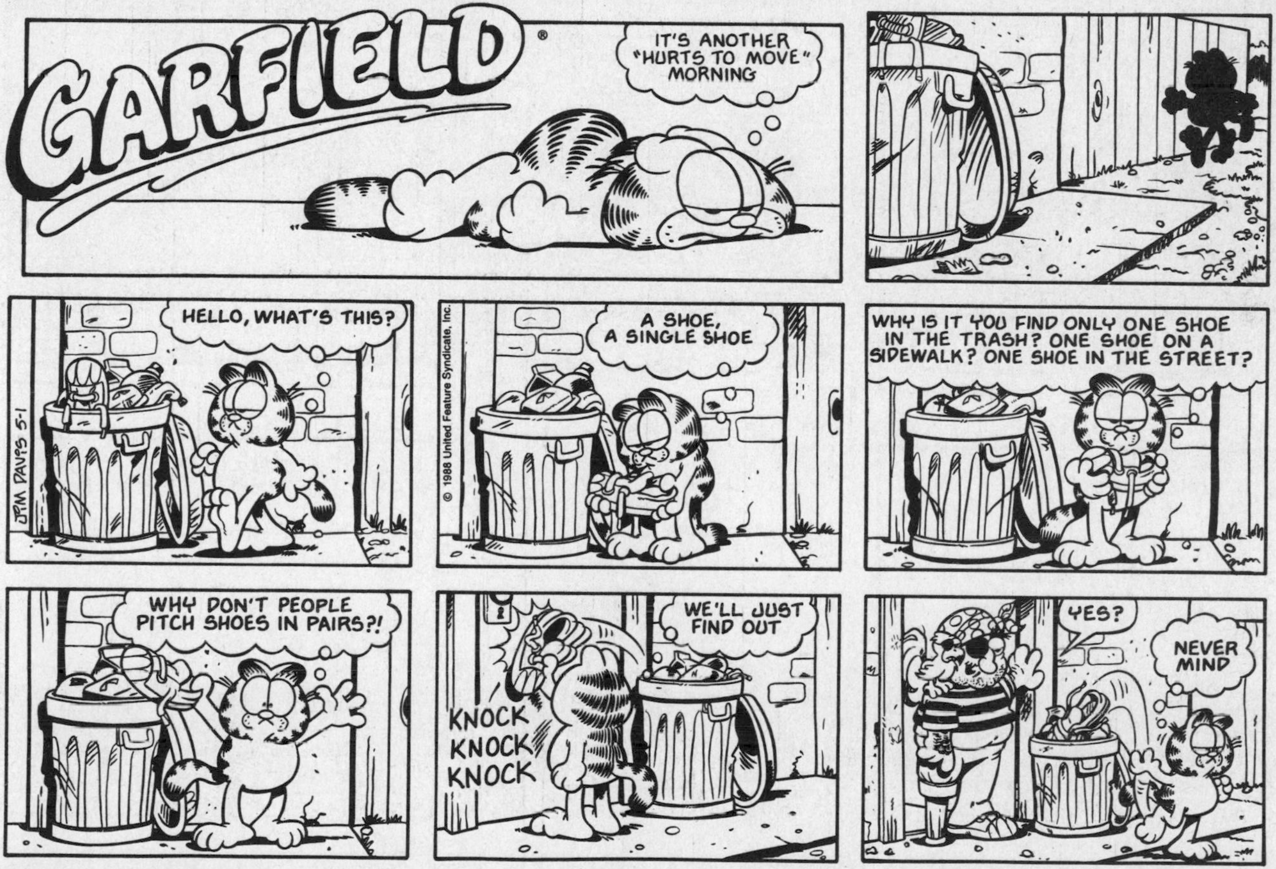
GARFIELD®
IT'S ANOTHER "HURTS TO MOVE" MORNING
HELLO, WHAT'S THIS?
JIM DAVIS 5-1
© 1988 United Feature Syndicate, Inc.
A SHOE, A SINGLE SHOE
WHY IS IT YOU FIND ONLY ONE SHOE IN THE TRASH? ONE SHOE ON A SIDEWALK? ONE SHOE IN THE STREET?
WHY DON'T PEOPLE PITCH SHOES IN PAIRS?!
KNOCK KNOCK KNOCK
WE'LL JUST FIND OUT
YES?
NEVER MIND

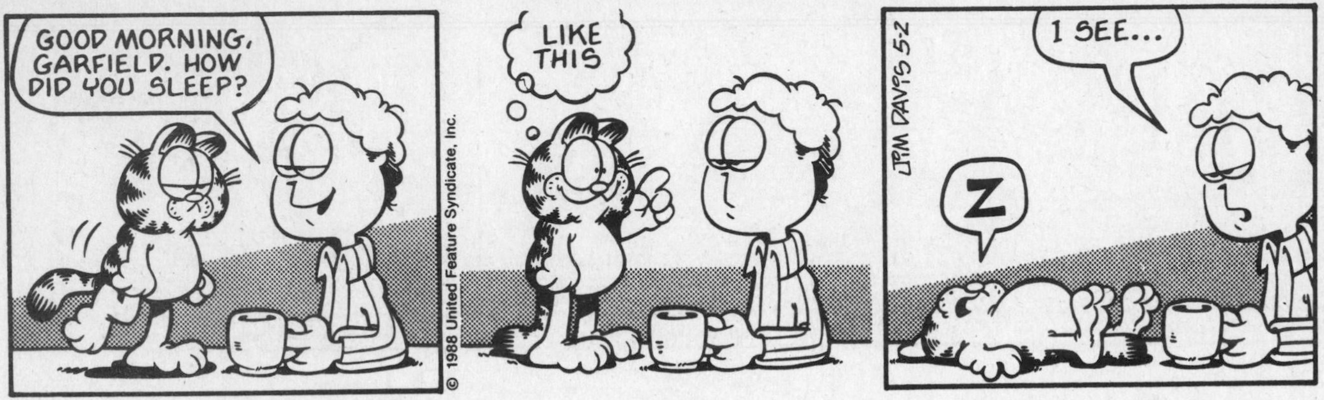
GOOD MORNING, GARFIELD. HOW DID YOU SLEEP?
LIKE THIS
Z
I SEE...
© 1988 United Feature Syndicate, Inc.
JIM DAVIS 5-2

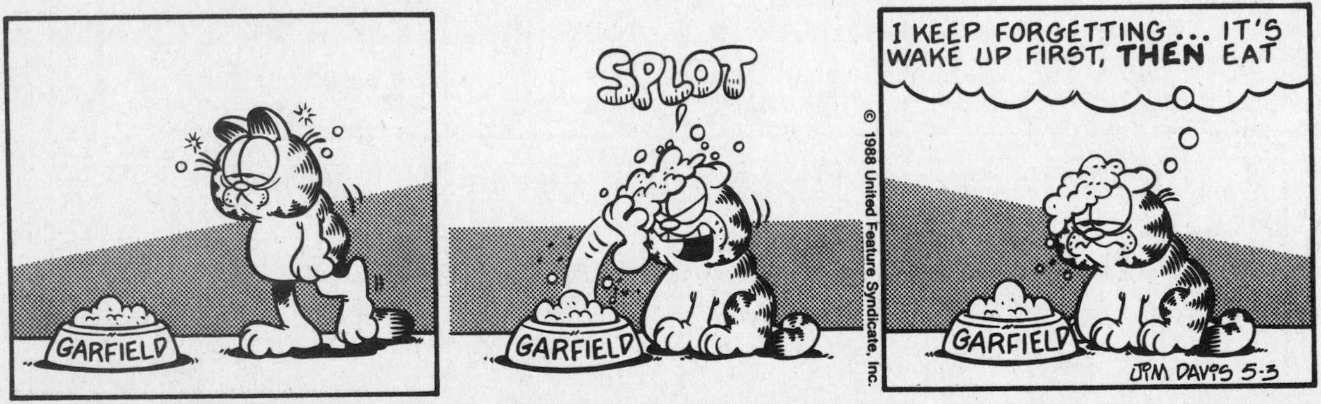
GARFIELD
SPLOT
GARFIELD
I KEEP FORGETTING ... IT'S WAKE UP FIRST, THEN EAT
GARFIELD
© 1988 United Feature Syndicate, Inc.
JIM DAVIS 5-3

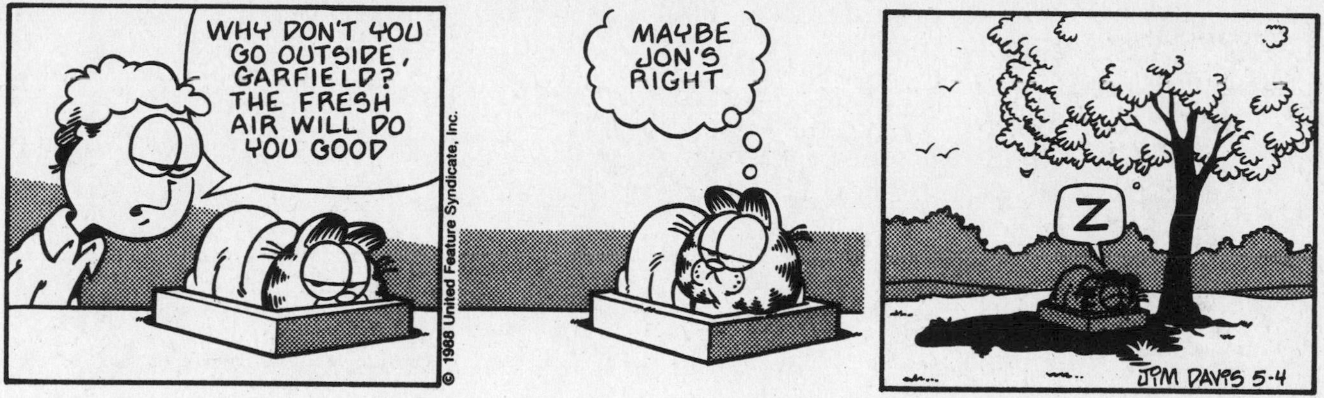
WHY DON'T YOU GO OUTSIDE, GARFIELD? THE FRESH AIR WILL DO YOU GOOD
© 1988 United Feature Syndicate, Inc.
MAYBE JON'S RIGHT
Z
JIM DAVIS 5-4

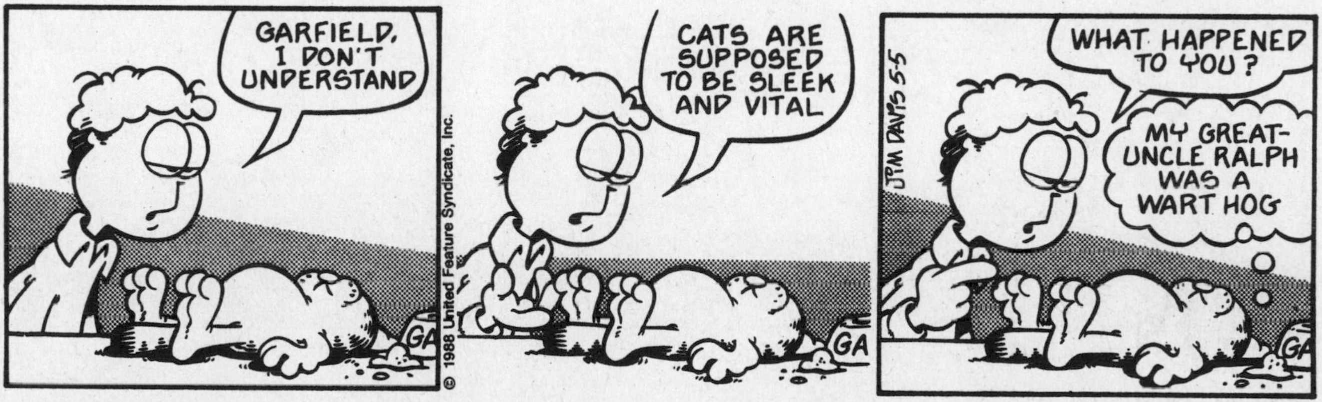
GARFIELD, I DON'T UNDERSTAND
© 1988 United Feature Syndicate, Inc.
CATS ARE SUPPOSED TO BE SLEEK AND VITAL
JIM DAVIS 5-5
WHAT HAPPENED TO YOU?
MY GREAT-UNCLE RALPH WAS A WART HOG

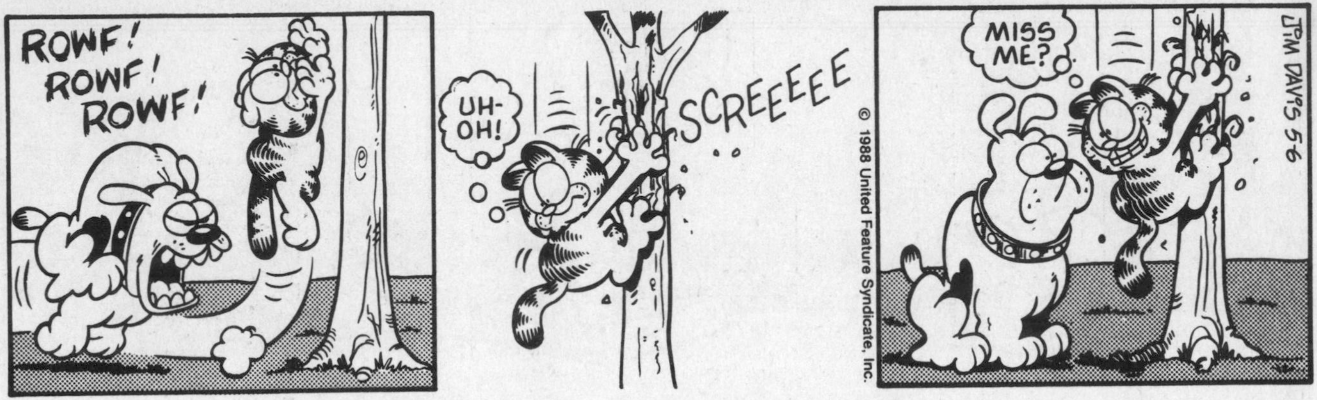
ROWF! ROWF! ROWF!
UH-OH!
SCREEEEEE
MISS ME?
JIM DAVIS 5-6
© 1988 United Feature Syndicate, Inc.

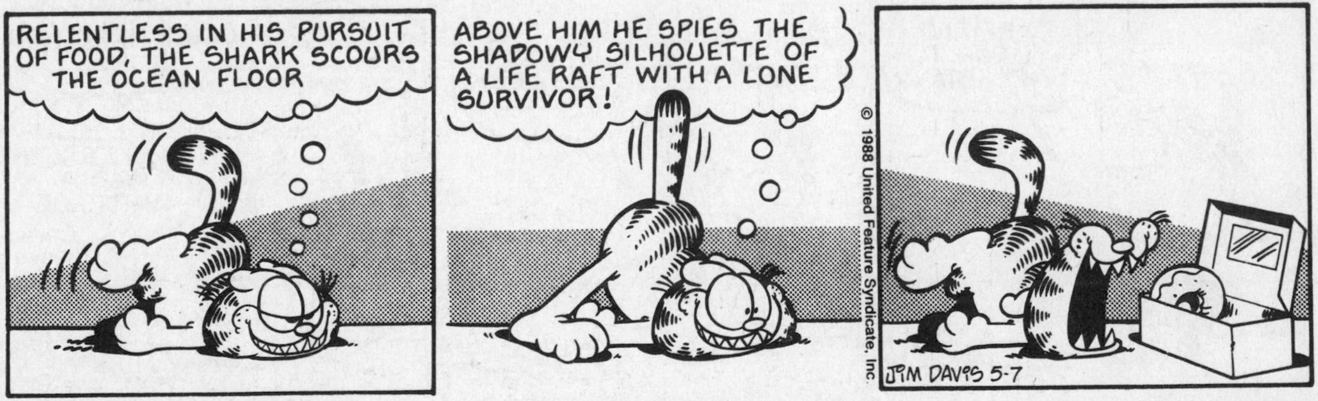
RELENTLESS IN HIS PURSUIT OF FOOD, THE SHARK SCOURS THE OCEAN FLOOR
ABOVE HIM HE SPIES THE SHADOWY SILHOUETTE OF A LIFE RAFT WITH A LONE SURVIVOR!
© 1988 United Feature Syndicate, Inc.
JIM DAVIS 5-7

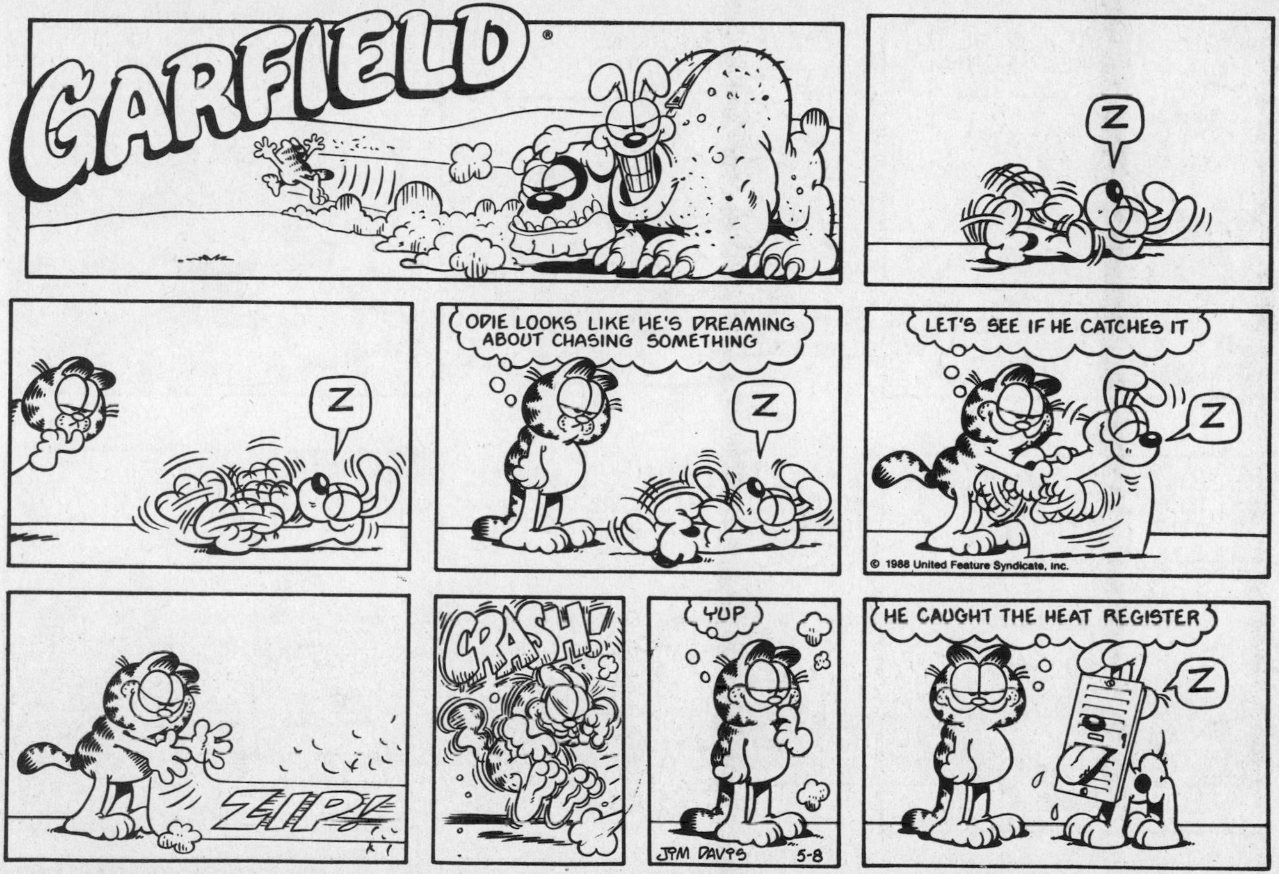
GARFIELD®
Z
Z
ODIE LOOKS LIKE HE'S DREAMING ABOUT CHASING SOMETHING
Z
LET'S SEE IF HE CATCHES IT
Z
© 1988 United Feature Syndicate, Inc.
ZIP!
CRASH!
YUP
JIM DAVIS 5-8
HE CAUGHT THE HEAT REGISTER
Z

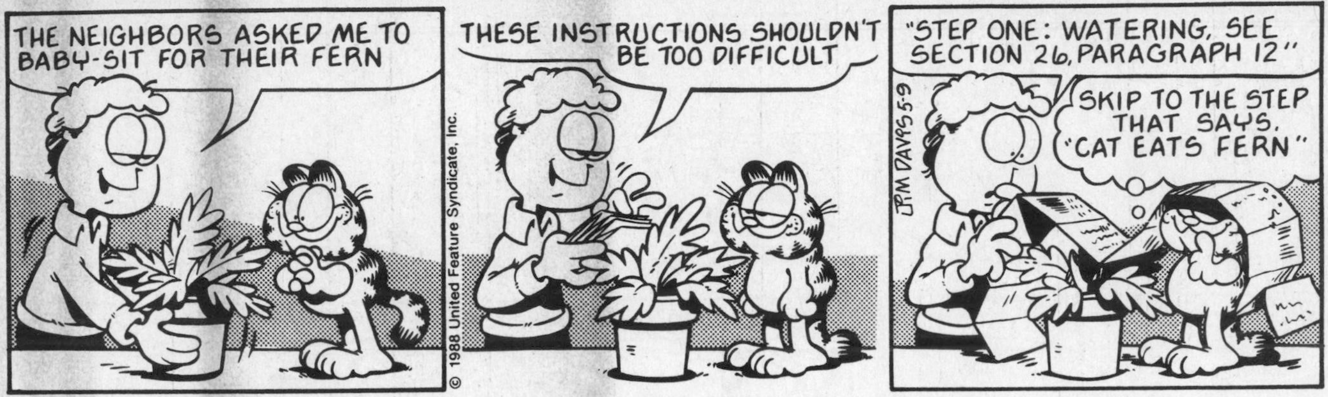
THE NEIGHBORS ASKED ME TO BABY-SIT FOR THEIR FERN
© 1988 United Feature Syndicate, Inc.
THESE INSTRUCTIONS SHOULDN'T BE TOO DIFFICULT
"STEP ONE: WATERING, SEE SECTION 26, PARAGRAPH 12"
JIM DAVIS 5-9
SKIP TO THE STEP THAT SAYS, "CAT EATS FERN"

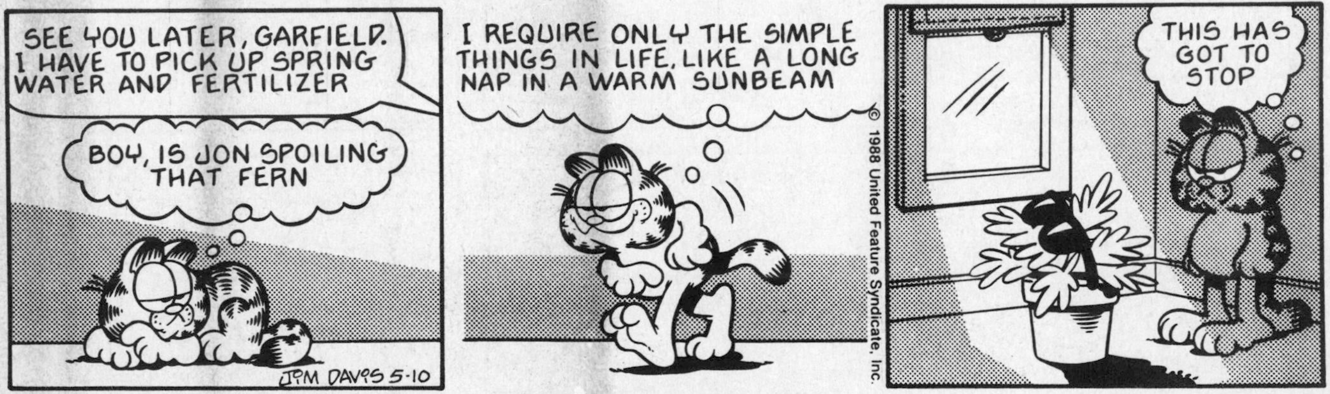
SEE YOU LATER, GARFIELD. I HAVE TO PICK UP SPRING WATER AND FERTILIZER
BOY, IS JON SPOILING THAT FERN
JIM DAVIS 5-10
I REQUIRE ONLY THE SIMPLE THINGS IN LIFE, LIKE A LONG NAP IN A WARM SUNBEAM
© 1988 United Feature Syndicate, Inc.
THIS HAS GOT TO STOP

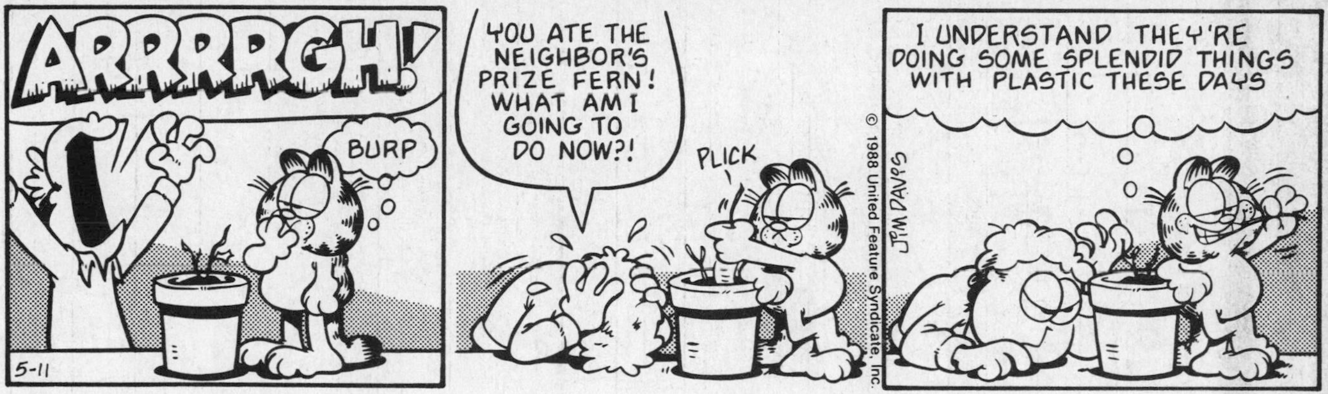
ARRRRGH!
BURP
5-11
YOU ATE THE NEIGHBOR'S PRIZE FERN! WHAT AM I GOING TO DO NOW?!
PLICK
© 1988 United Feature Syndicate, Inc.
JPM DAVPS
I UNDERSTAND THEY'RE DOING SOME SPLENDID THINGS WITH PLASTIC THESE DAYS

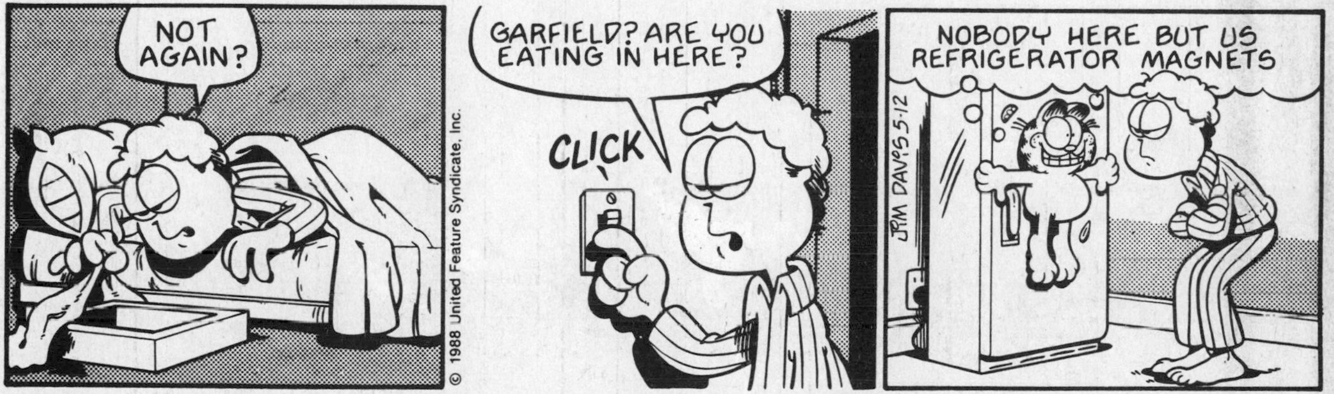
NOT AGAIN?
© 1988 United Feature Syndicate, Inc.
GARFIELD? ARE YOU EATING IN HERE?
CLICK
NOBODY HERE BUT US REFRIGERATOR MAGNETS
JPM DAVPS 5-12

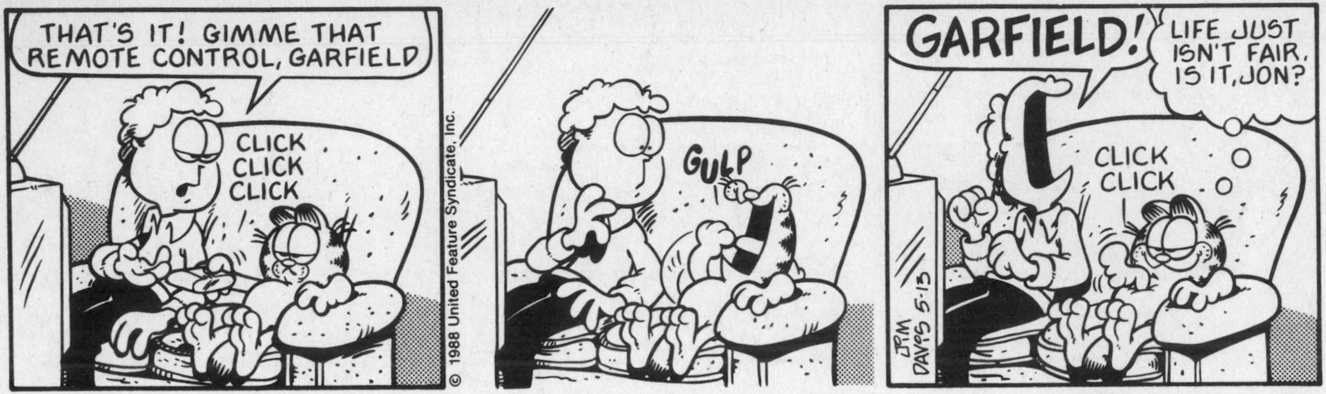
THAT'S IT! GIMME THAT REMOTE CONTROL, GARFIELD
CLICK CLICK CLICK
© 1988 United Feature Syndicate, Inc.
GULP
GARFIELD!
LIFE JUST ISN'T FAIR, IS IT, JON?
CLICK CLICK
JIM DAVIS 5-13

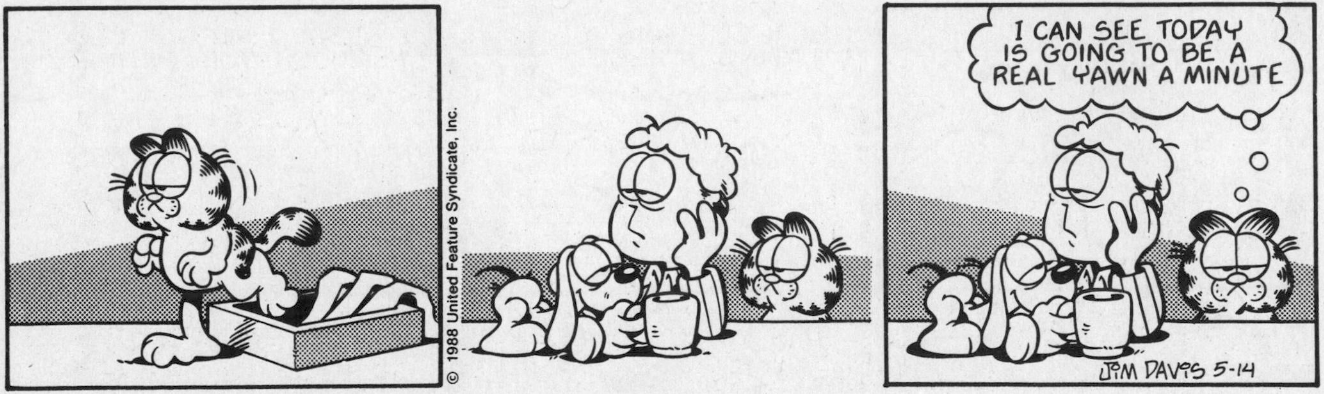
© 1988 United Feature Syndicate, Inc.
I CAN SEE TODAY IS GOING TO BE A REAL YAWN A MINUTE
JIM DAVIS 5-14

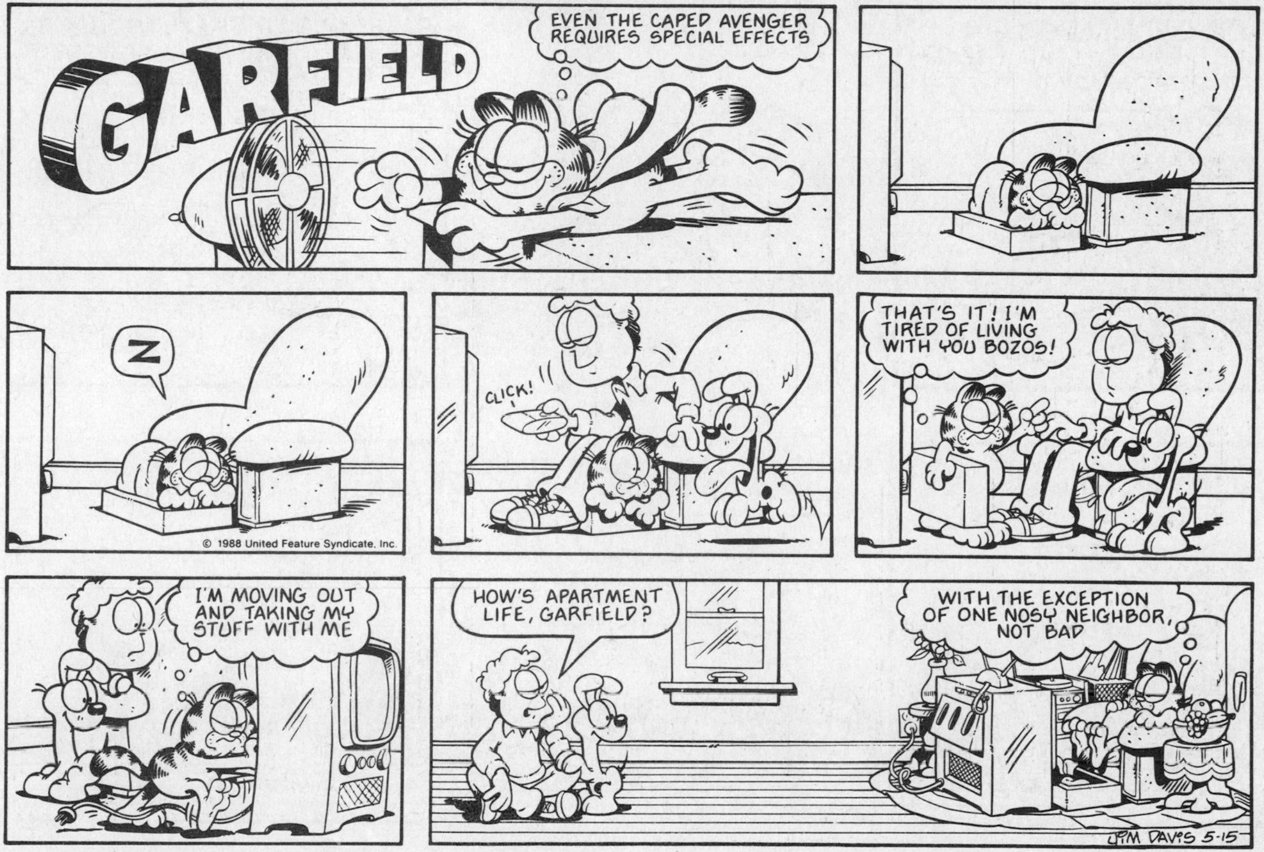
GARFIELD
EVEN THE CAPED AVENGER REQUIRES SPECIAL EFFECTS
Z
© 1988 United Feature Syndicate, Inc.
CLICK!
THAT'S IT! I'M TIRED OF LIVING WITH YOU BOZOS!
I'M MOVING OUT AND TAKING MY STUFF WITH ME
HOW'S APARTMENT LIFE, GARFIELD?
WITH THE EXCEPTION OF ONE NOSY NEIGHBOR, NOT BAD
JIM DAVIS 5-15

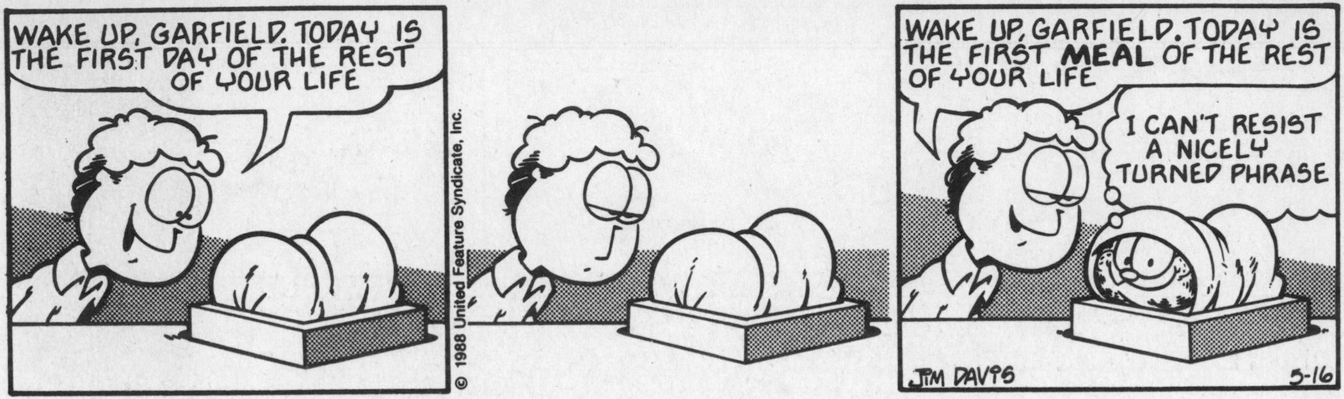
WAKE UP, GARFIELD. TODAY IS THE FIRST DAY OF THE REST OF YOUR LIFE
WAKE UP, GARFIELD. TODAY IS THE FIRST MEAL OF THE REST OF YOUR LIFE
I CAN'T RESIST A NICELY TURNED PHRASE
JIM DAVIS
5-16
© 1988 United Feature Syndicate, Inc.

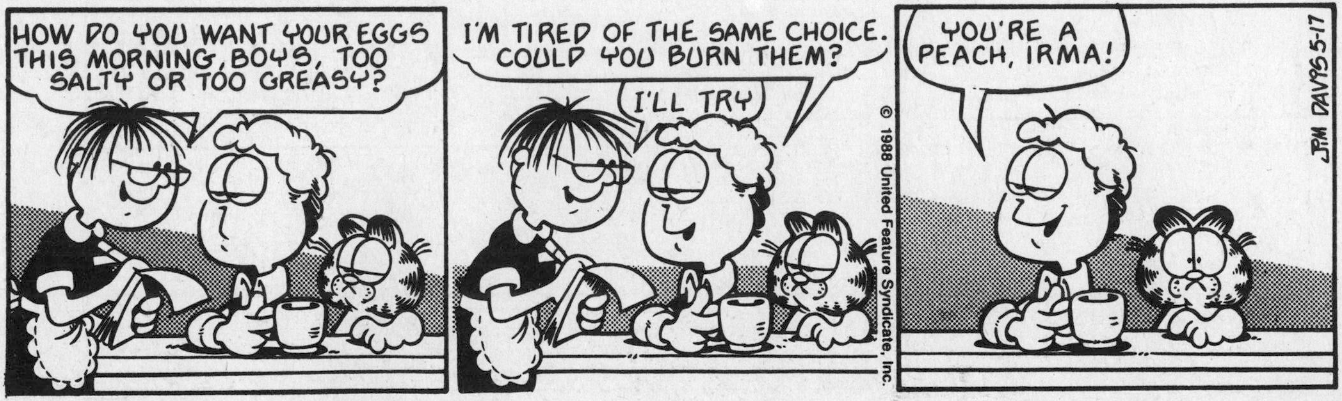
HOW DO YOU WANT YOUR EGGS THIS MORNING, BOYS, TOO SALTY OR TOO GREASY?
I'M TIRED OF THE SAME CHOICE. COULD YOU BURN THEM?
I'LL TRY
YOU'RE A PEACH, IRMA!
JIM DAVIS 5-17
© 1988 United Feature Syndicate, Inc.

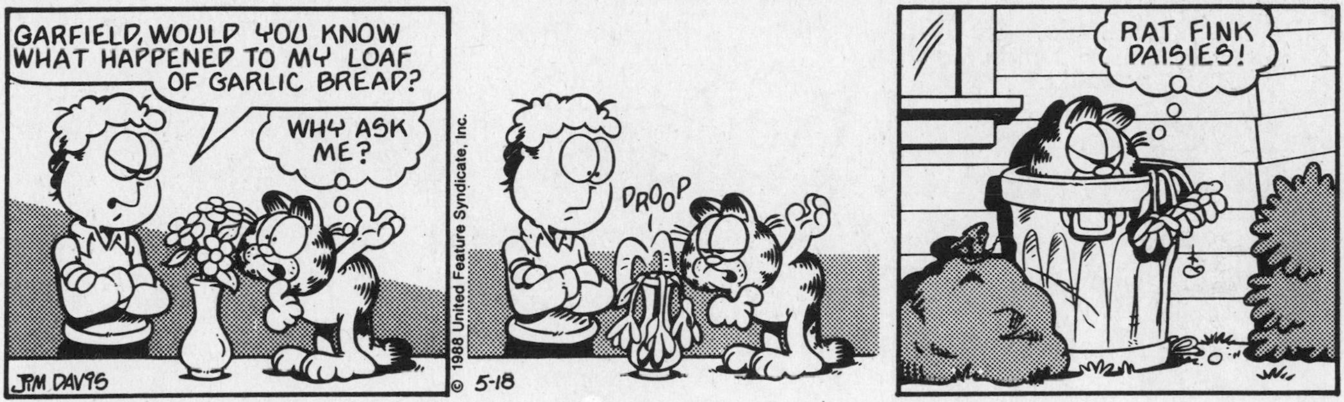
GARFIELD, WOULD YOU KNOW WHAT HAPPENED TO MY LOAF OF GARLIC BREAD?
WHY ASK ME?
JIM DAVIS
© 1988 United Feature Syndicate, Inc.
5-18
DROOP
RAT FINK DAISIES!

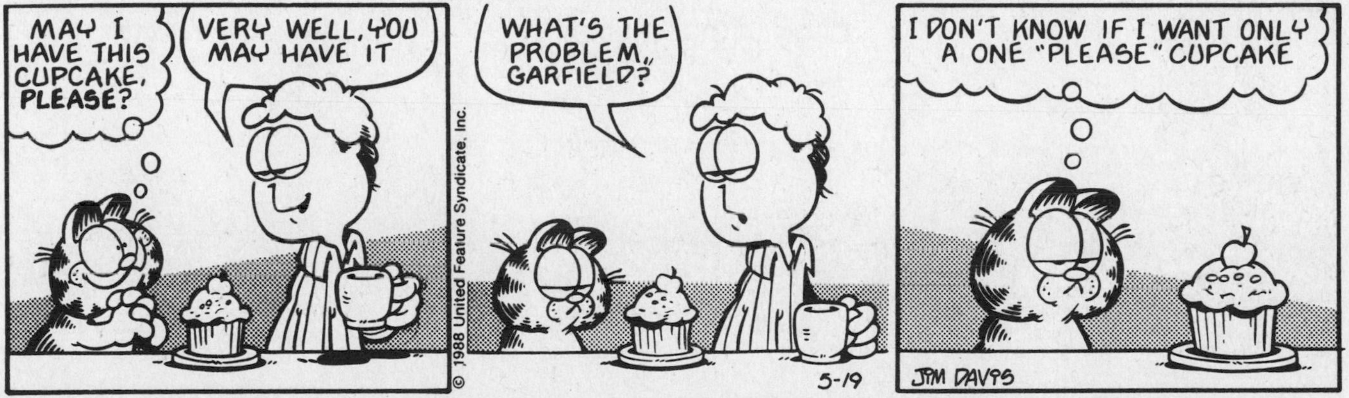
MAY I HAVE THIS CUPCAKE, **PLEASE**?
VERY WELL, YOU MAY HAVE IT
© 1988 United Feature Syndicate, Inc.
WHAT'S THE PROBLEM, GARFIELD?
5-19
I DON'T KNOW IF I WANT ONLY A ONE "PLEASE" CUPCAKE
JIM DAVIS

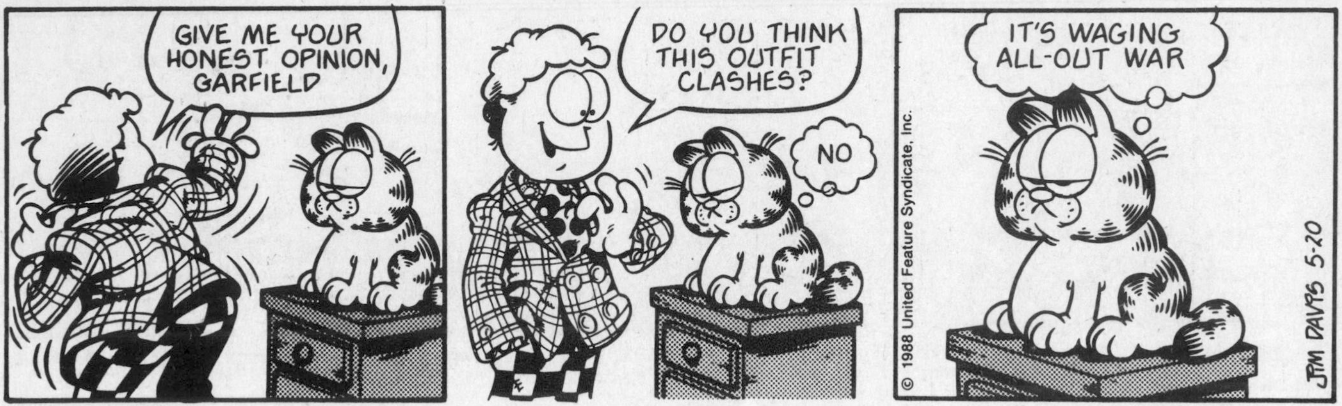
GIVE ME YOUR HONEST OPINION, GARFIELD
DO YOU THINK THIS OUTFIT CLASHES?
NO
IT'S WAGING ALL-OUT WAR
JIM DAVIS 5-20

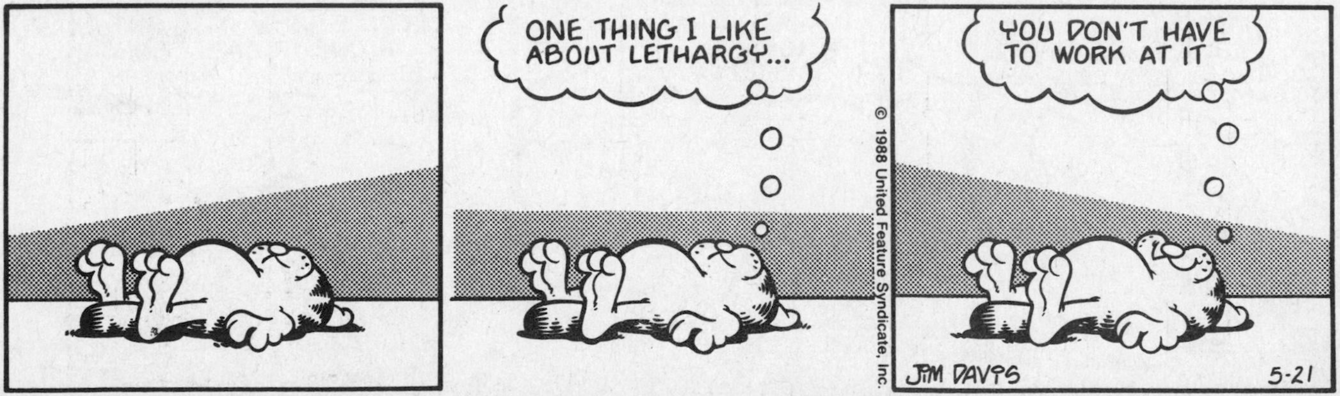
ONE THING I LIKE ABOUT LETHARGY...
YOU DON'T HAVE TO WORK AT IT
JIM DAVIS
5-21

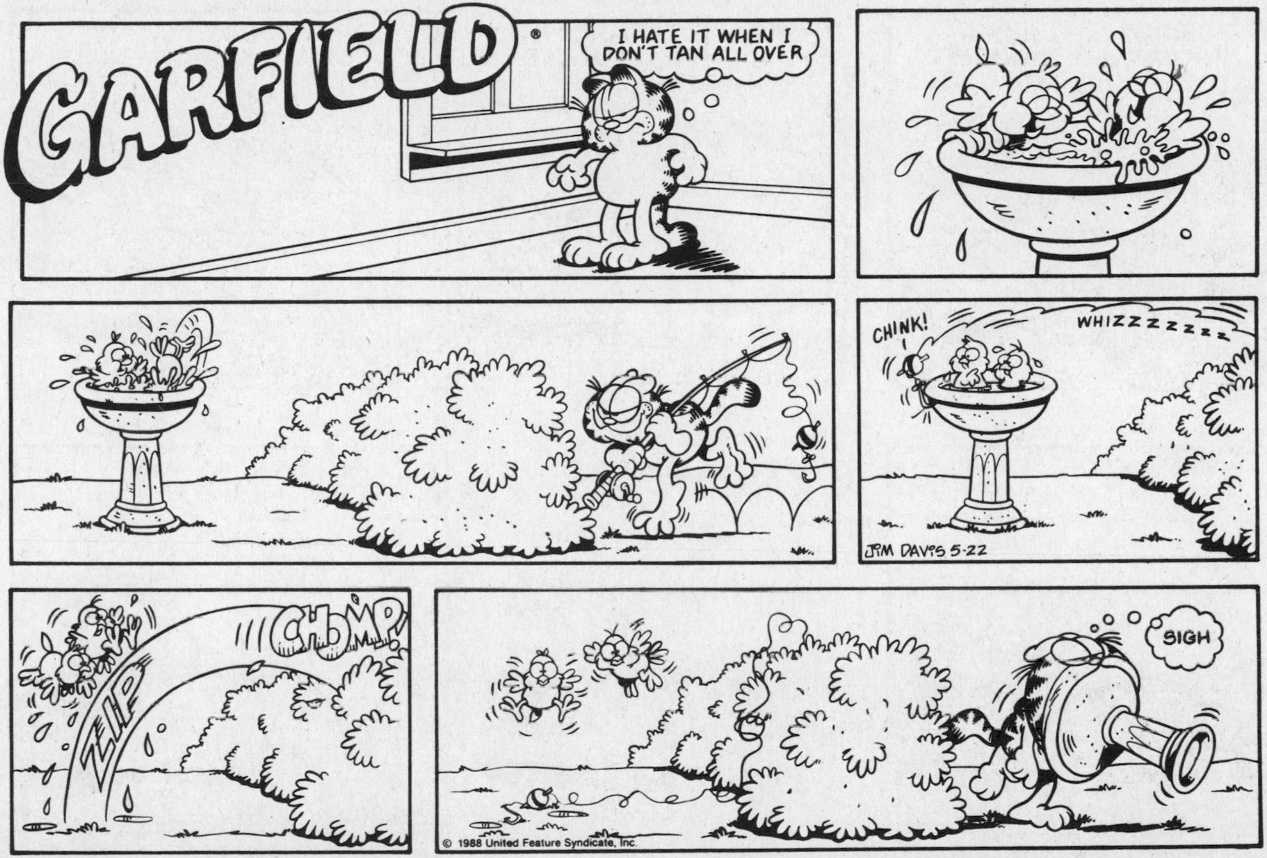
GARFIELD®
I HATE IT WHEN I DON'T TAN ALL OVER
CHINK!
WHIZZZZZZZ
JIM DAVIS 5-22
ZIP
CHOMP!
SIGH
© 1988 United Feature Syndicate, Inc.

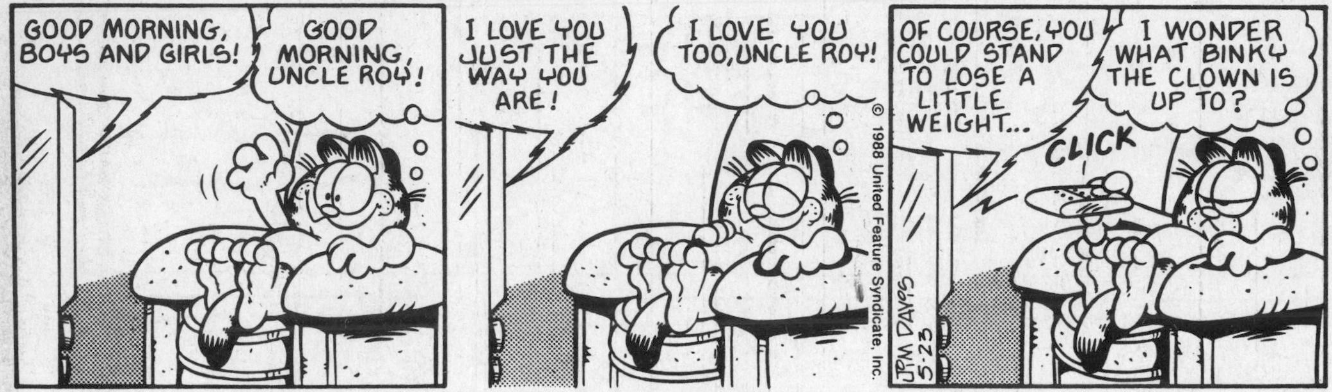
GOOD MORNING, BOYS AND GIRLS!
GOOD MORNING, UNCLE ROY!
I LOVE YOU JUST THE WAY YOU ARE!
I LOVE YOU TOO, UNCLE ROY!
OF COURSE, YOU COULD STAND TO LOSE A LITTLE WEIGHT...
CLICK
I WONDER WHAT BINKY THE CLOWN IS UP TO?
© 1988 United Feature Syndicate, Inc.
JPM DAVPS 5-23

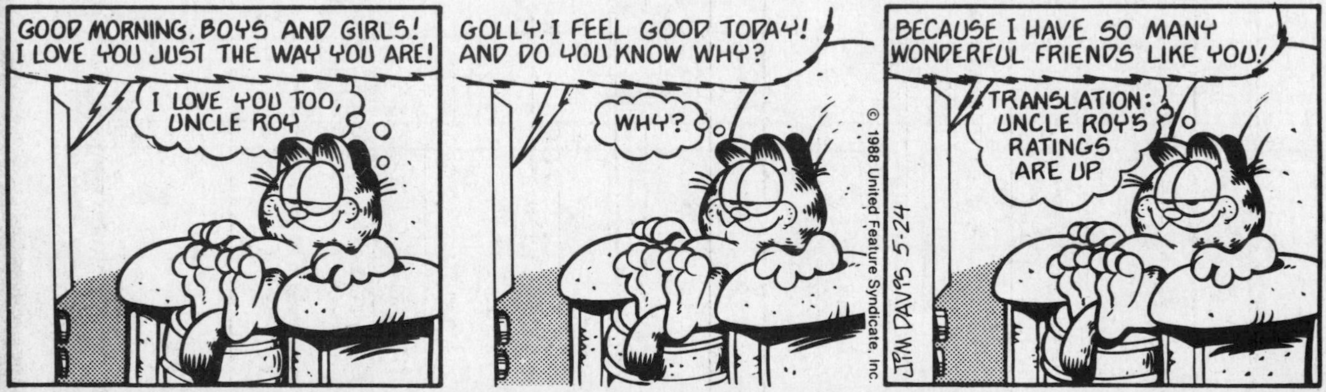
GOOD MORNING, BOYS AND GIRLS! I LOVE YOU JUST THE WAY YOU ARE!
I LOVE YOU TOO, UNCLE ROY
GOLLY, I FEEL GOOD TODAY! AND DO YOU KNOW WHY?
WHY?
BECAUSE I HAVE SO MANY WONDERFUL FRIENDS LIKE YOU!
TRANSLATION: UNCLE ROY'S RATINGS ARE UP
© 1988 United Feature Syndicate, Inc.
JPM DAVPS 5-24

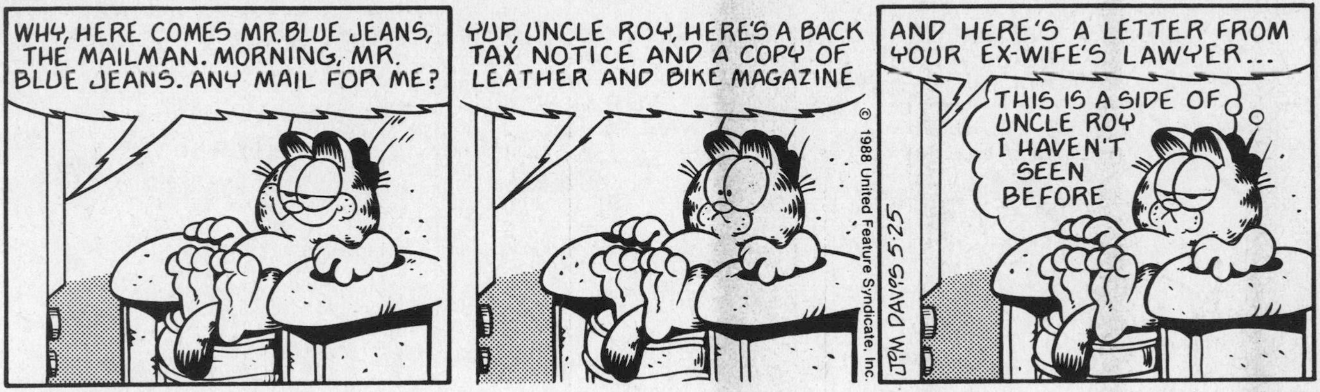
WHY, HERE COMES MR. BLUE JEANS, THE MAILMAN. MORNING, MR. BLUE JEANS. ANY MAIL FOR ME?
YUP, UNCLE ROY, HERE'S A BACK TAX NOTICE AND A COPY OF LEATHER AND BIKE MAGAZINE
© 1988 United Feature Syndicate, Inc.
AND HERE'S A LETTER FROM YOUR EX-WIFE'S LAWYER...
THIS IS A SIDE OF UNCLE ROY I HAVEN'T SEEN BEFORE
JPM DAVIS 5-25

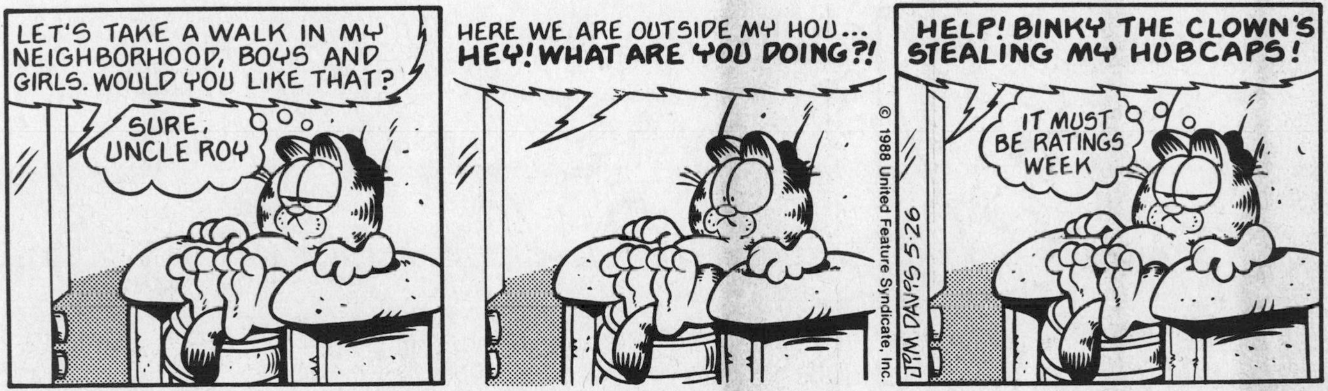
LET'S TAKE A WALK IN MY NEIGHBORHOOD, BOYS AND GIRLS. WOULD YOU LIKE THAT?
SURE, UNCLE ROY
HERE WE ARE OUTSIDE MY HOU... **HEY! WHAT ARE YOU DOING?!**
© 1988 United Feature Syndicate, Inc.
HELP! BINKY THE CLOWN'S STEALING MY HUBCAPS!
IT MUST BE RATINGS WEEK
JPM DAVIS 5-26

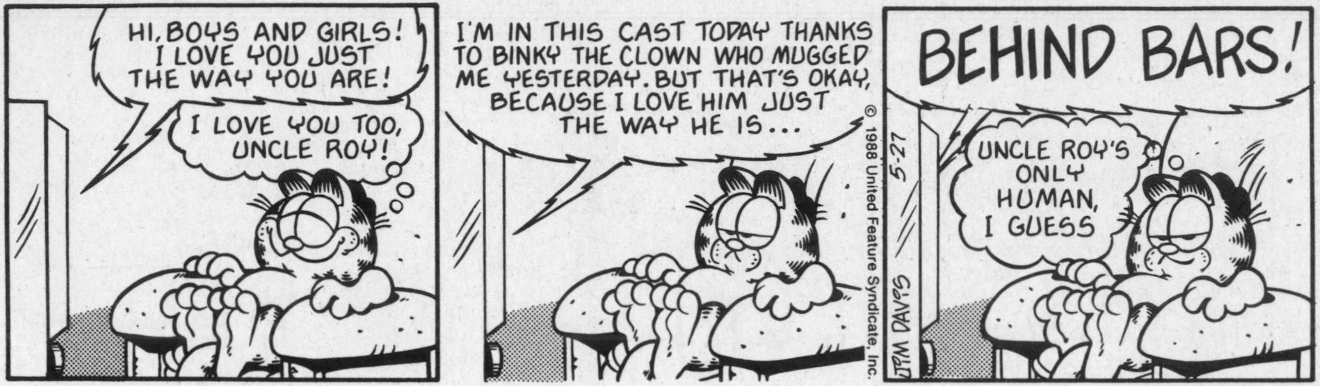
HI, BOYS AND GIRLS! I LOVE YOU JUST THE WAY YOU ARE!
I LOVE YOU TOO, UNCLE ROY!
I'M IN THIS CAST TODAY THANKS TO BINKY THE CLOWN WHO MUGGED ME YESTERDAY. BUT THAT'S OKAY, BECAUSE I LOVE HIM JUST THE WAY HE IS...
© 1988 United Feature Syndicate, Inc.
5-27
JIM DAVIS
BEHIND BARS!
UNCLE ROY'S ONLY HUMAN, I GUESS

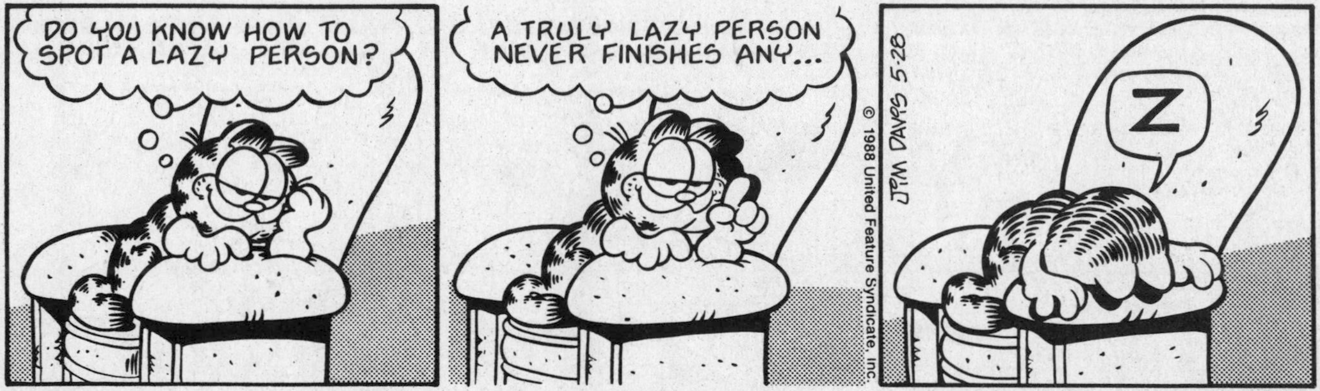
DO YOU KNOW HOW TO SPOT A LAZY PERSON?
A TRULY LAZY PERSON NEVER FINISHES ANY...
© 1988 United Feature Syndicate, Inc.
JIM DAVIS 5-28
Z

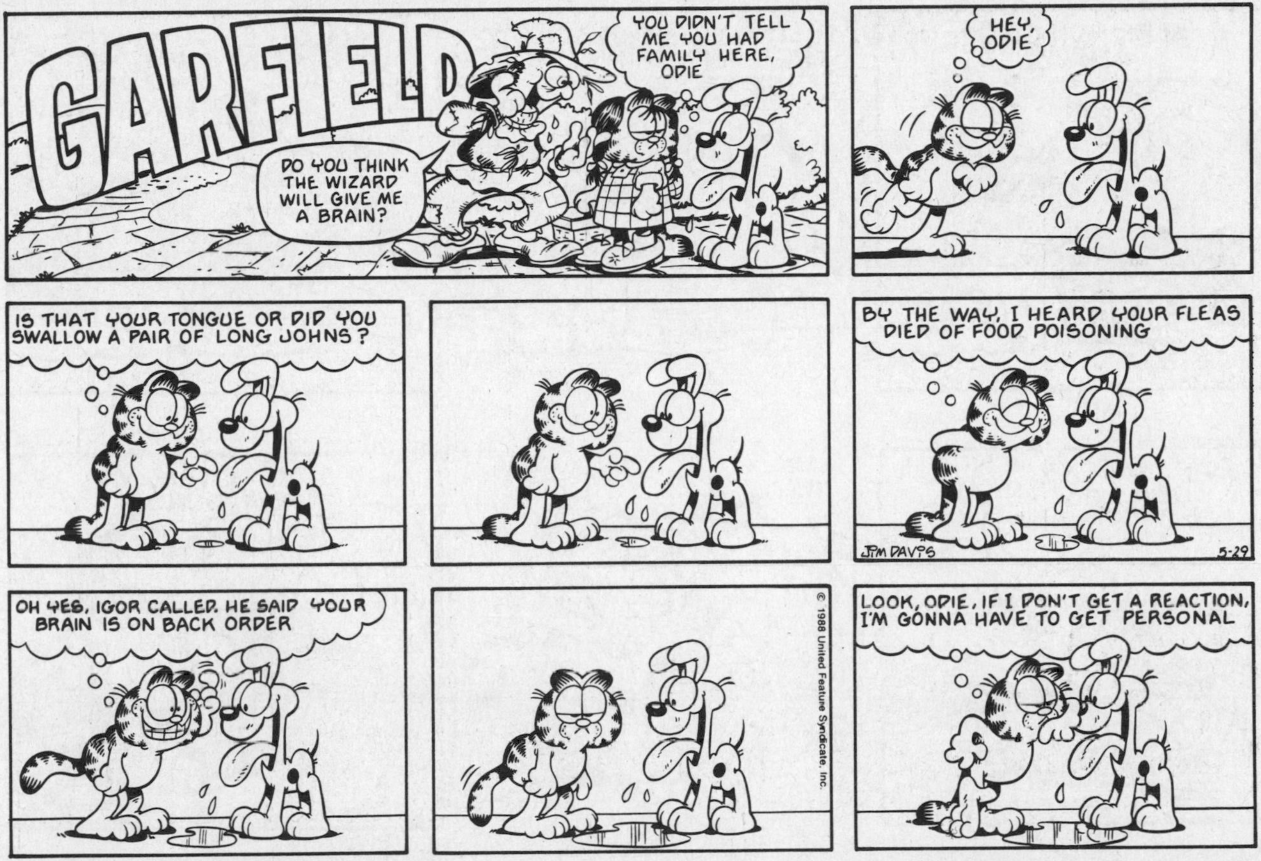
GARFIELD
DO YOU THINK THE WIZARD WILL GIVE ME A BRAIN?
YOU DIDN'T TELL ME YOU HAD FAMILY HERE, ODIE
HEY, ODIE
IS THAT YOUR TONGUE OR DID YOU SWALLOW A PAIR OF LONG JOHNS?
BY THE WAY, I HEARD YOUR FLEAS DIED OF FOOD POISONING
JIM DAVIS
5-29
OH YES, IGOR CALLED. HE SAID YOUR BRAIN IS ON BACK ORDER
LOOK, ODIE, IF I DON'T GET A REACTION, I'M GONNA HAVE TO GET PERSONAL

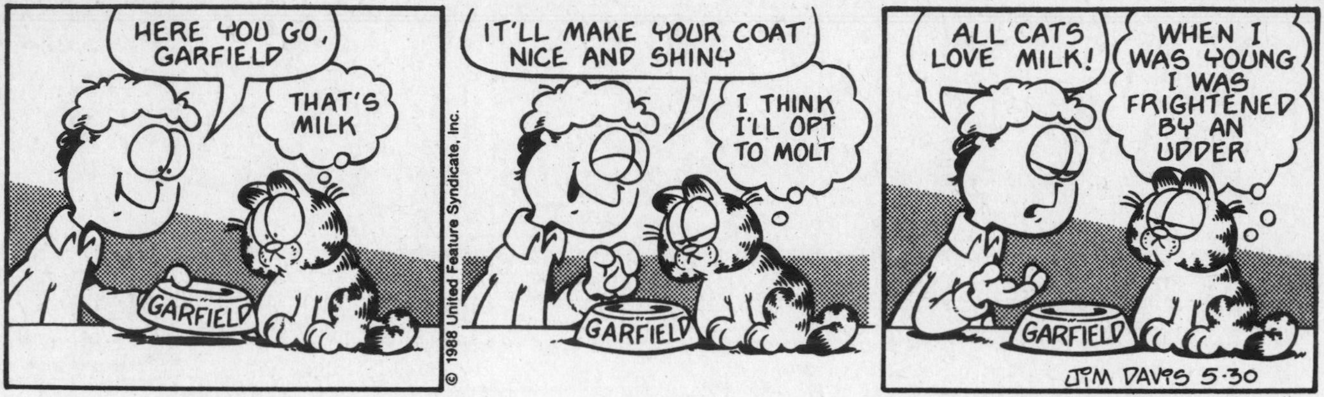
HERE YOU GO, GARFIELD
THAT'S MILK
IT'LL MAKE YOUR COAT NICE AND SHINY
I THINK I'LL OPT TO MOLT
ALL CATS LOVE MILK!
WHEN I WAS YOUNG I WAS FRIGHTENED BY AN UDDER
GARFIELD
GARFIELD
GARFIELD
JIM DAVIS 5-30
© 1988 United Feature Syndicate, Inc.

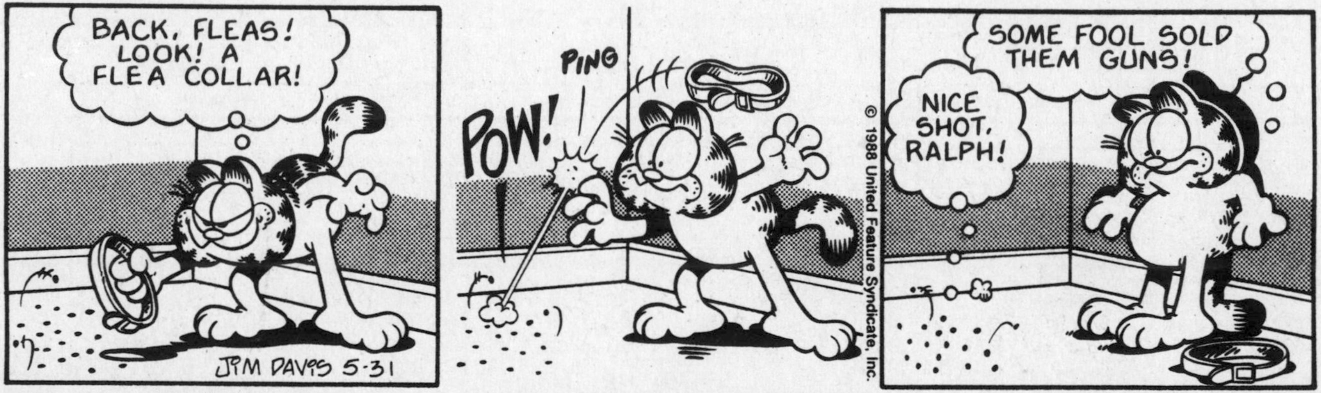
BACK, FLEAS! LOOK! A FLEA COLLAR!
JIM DAVIS 5-31
PING
POW!
SOME FOOL SOLD THEM GUNS!
NICE SHOT, RALPH!
© 1988 United Feature Syndicate, Inc.

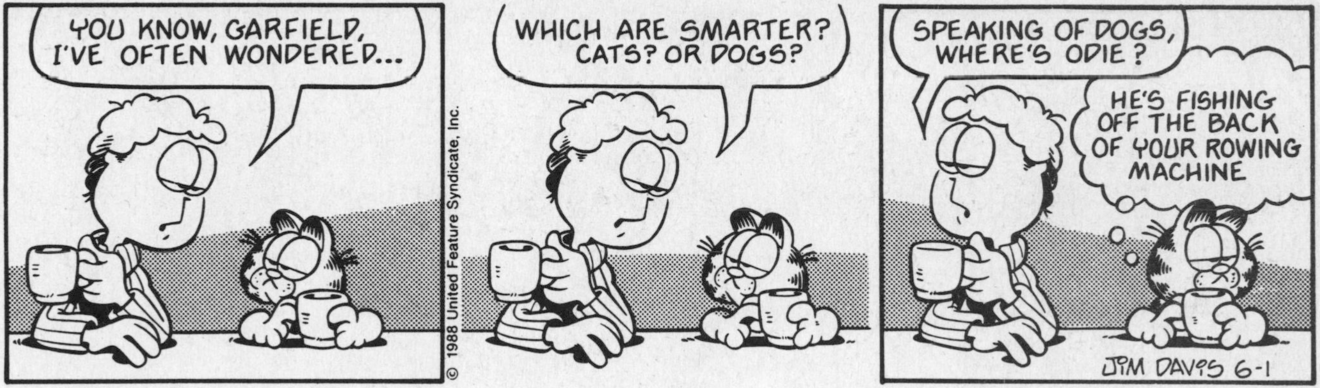
YOU KNOW, GARFIELD, I'VE OFTEN WONDERED...
WHICH ARE SMARTER? CATS? OR DOGS?
SPEAKING OF DOGS, WHERE'S ODIE ?
HE'S FISHING OFF THE BACK OF YOUR ROWING MACHINE
JIM DAVIS 6-1
© 1988 United Feature Syndicate, Inc.

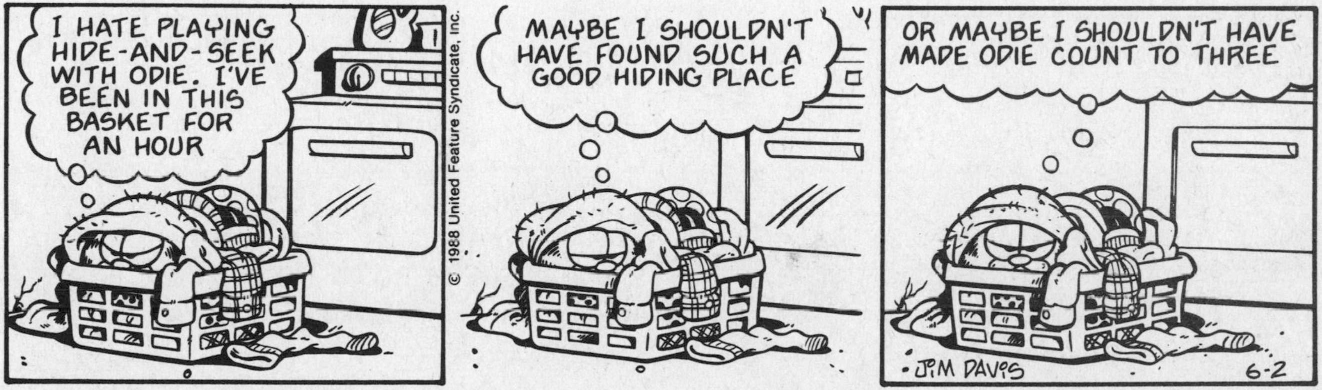
I HATE PLAYING HIDE-AND-SEEK WITH ODIE. I'VE BEEN IN THIS BASKET FOR AN HOUR
MAYBE I SHOULDN'T HAVE FOUND SUCH A GOOD HIDING PLACE
OR MAYBE I SHOULDN'T HAVE MADE ODIE COUNT TO THREE
JIM DAVIS 6-2
© 1988 United Feature Syndicate, Inc.

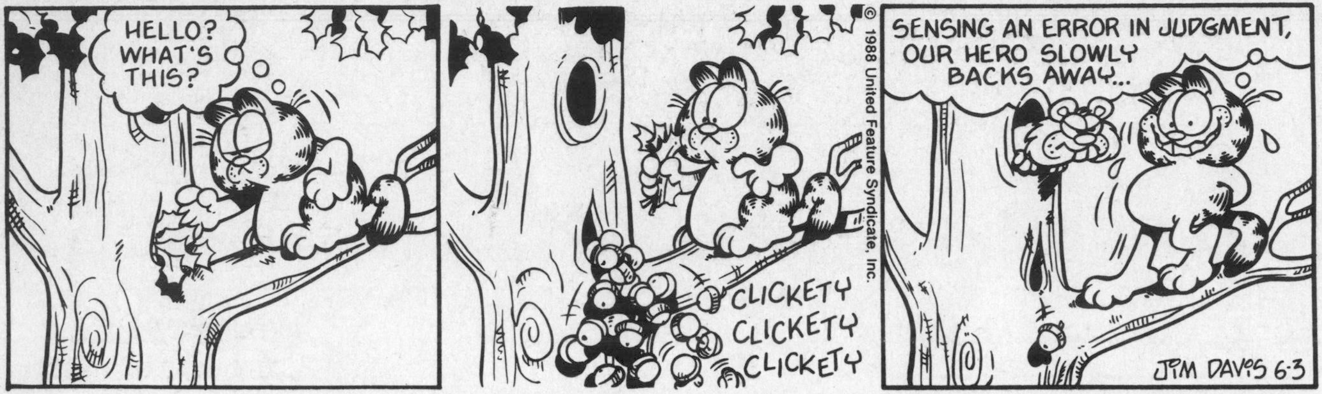
HELLO? WHAT'S THIS?
CLICKETY
CLICKETY
CLICKETY
© 1988 United Feature Syndicate, Inc.
SENSING AN ERROR IN JUDGMENT, OUR HERO SLOWLY BACKS AWAY...
JIM DAVIS 6-3

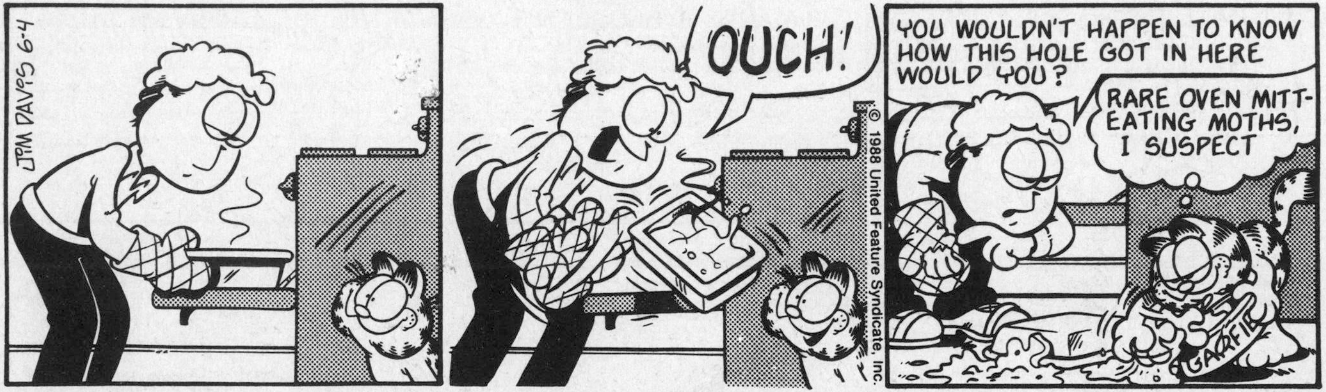
JIM DAVIS 6-4
OUCH!
© 1988 United Feature Syndicate, Inc.
YOU WOULDN'T HAPPEN TO KNOW HOW THIS HOLE GOT IN HERE WOULD YOU?
RARE OVEN MITT-EATING MOTHS, I SUSPECT

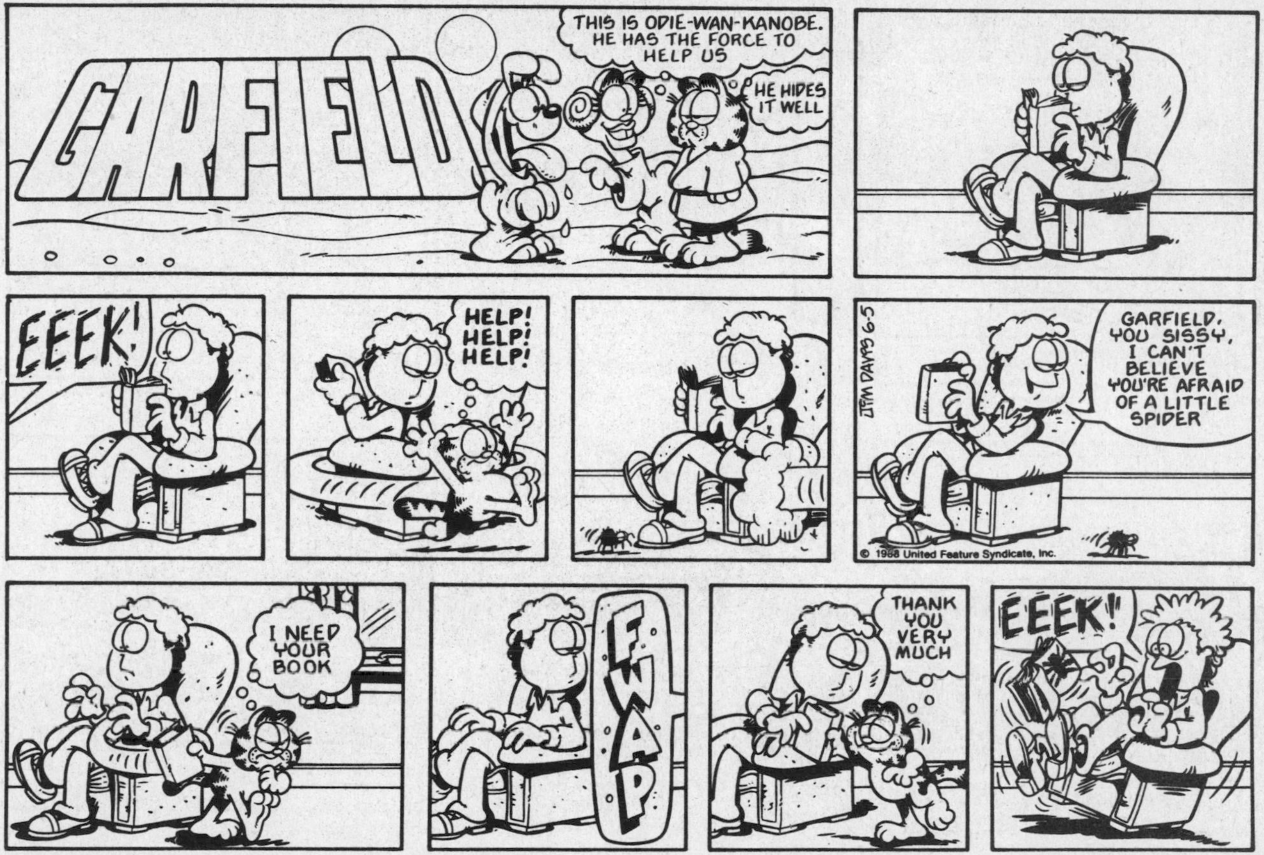
GARFIELD
THIS IS ODIE-WAN-KANOBE. HE HAS THE FORCE TO HELP US
HE HIDES IT WELL
EEEK!
HELP! HELP! HELP!
JIM DAVIS 6-5
GARFIELD, YOU SISSY, I CAN'T BELIEVE YOU'RE AFRAID OF A LITTLE SPIDER
© 1988 United Feature Syndicate, Inc.
I NEED YOUR BOOK
FWAP
THANK YOU VERY MUCH
EEEK!

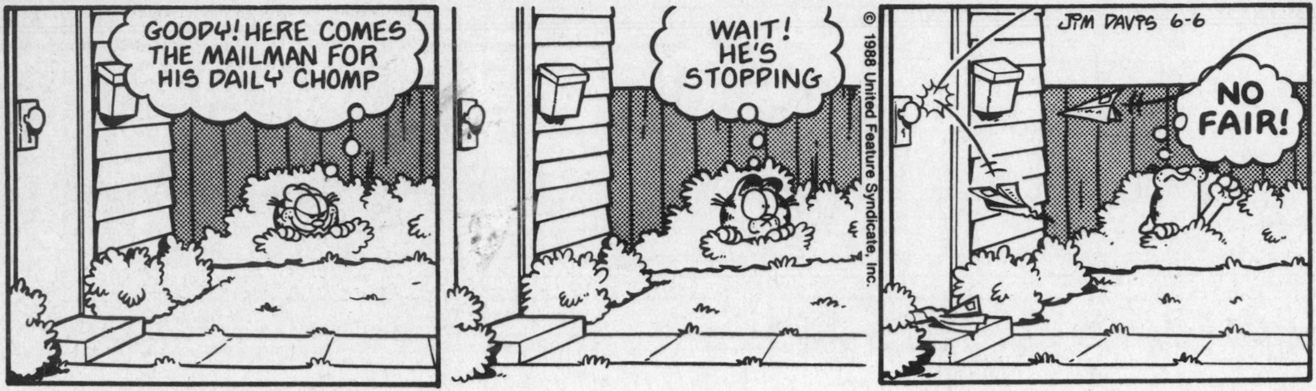
GOODY! HERE COMES THE MAILMAN FOR HIS DAILY CHOMP
WAIT! HE'S STOPPING
© 1988 United Feature Syndicate, Inc.
JIM DAVIS 6-6
NO FAIR!

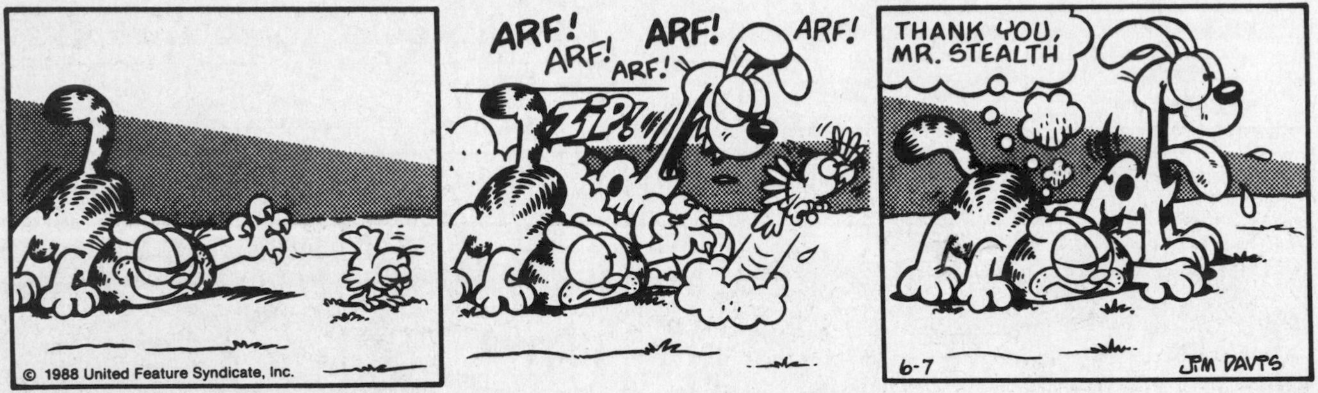
© 1988 United Feature Syndicate, Inc.
ARF! ARF! ARF! ARF! ARF!
ZIP!
THANK YOU, MR. STEALTH
6-7
JIM DAVIS

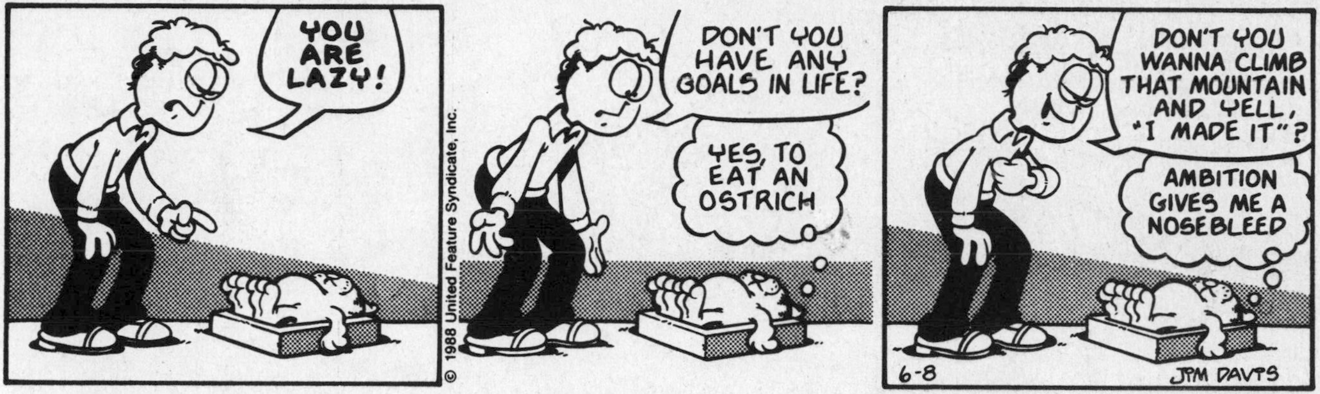
YOU ARE LAZY!
DON'T YOU HAVE ANY GOALS IN LIFE?
YES, TO EAT AN OSTRICH
DON'T YOU WANNA CLIMB THAT MOUNTAIN AND YELL, "I MADE IT"?
AMBITION GIVES ME A NOSEBLEED
© 1988 United Feature Syndicate, Inc.
6-8
JIM DAVIS

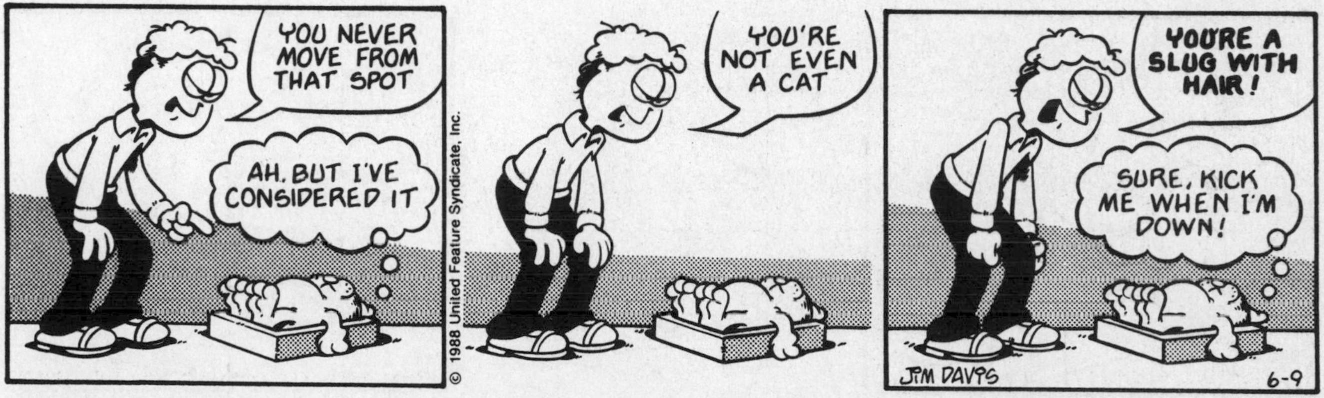
YOU NEVER MOVE FROM THAT SPOT
AH. BUT I'VE CONSIDERED IT
YOU'RE NOT EVEN A CAT
YOU'RE A SLUG WITH HAIR!
SURE, KICK ME WHEN I'M DOWN!
© 1988 United Feature Syndicate, Inc.
JIM DAVIS
6-9

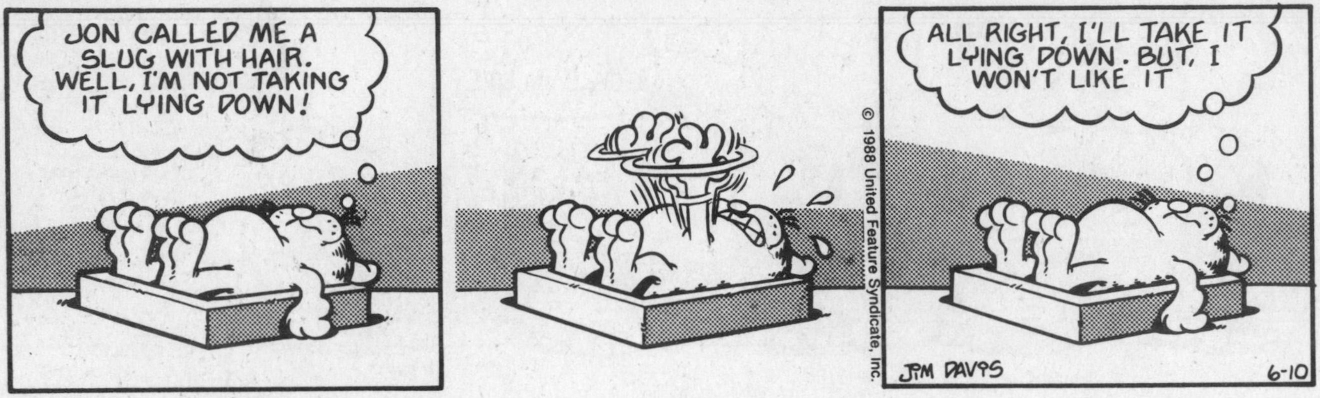
JON CALLED ME A SLUG WITH HAIR. WELL, I'M NOT TAKING IT LYING DOWN!
ALL RIGHT, I'LL TAKE IT LYING DOWN. BUT, I WON'T LIKE IT
© 1988 United Feature Syndicate, Inc.
JIM DAVIS
6-10

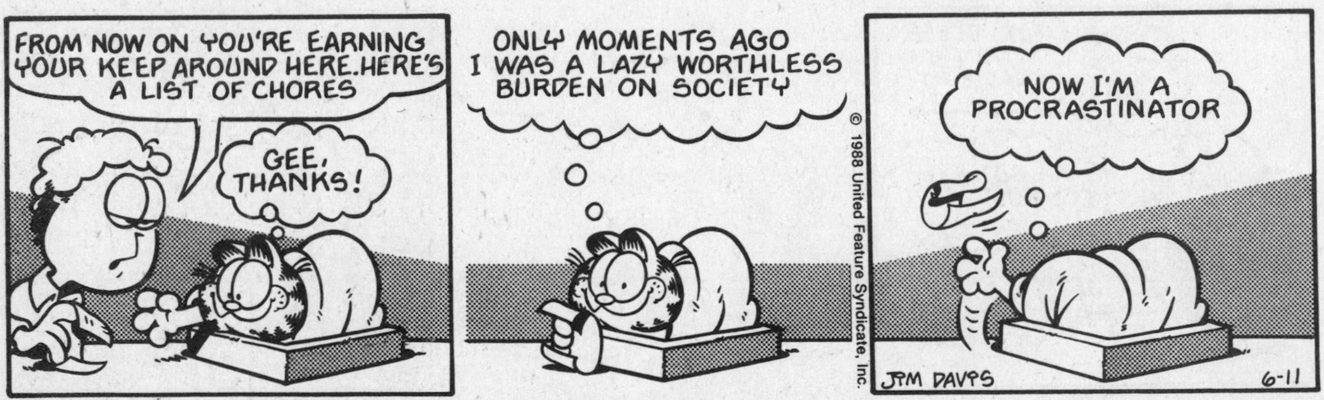
FROM NOW ON YOU'RE EARNING YOUR KEEP AROUND HERE. HERE'S A LIST OF CHORES
GEE, THANKS!
ONLY MOMENTS AGO I WAS A LAZY WORTHLESS BURDEN ON SOCIETY
NOW I'M A PROCRASTINATOR
© 1988 United Feature Syndicate, Inc.
JIM DAVIS
6-11

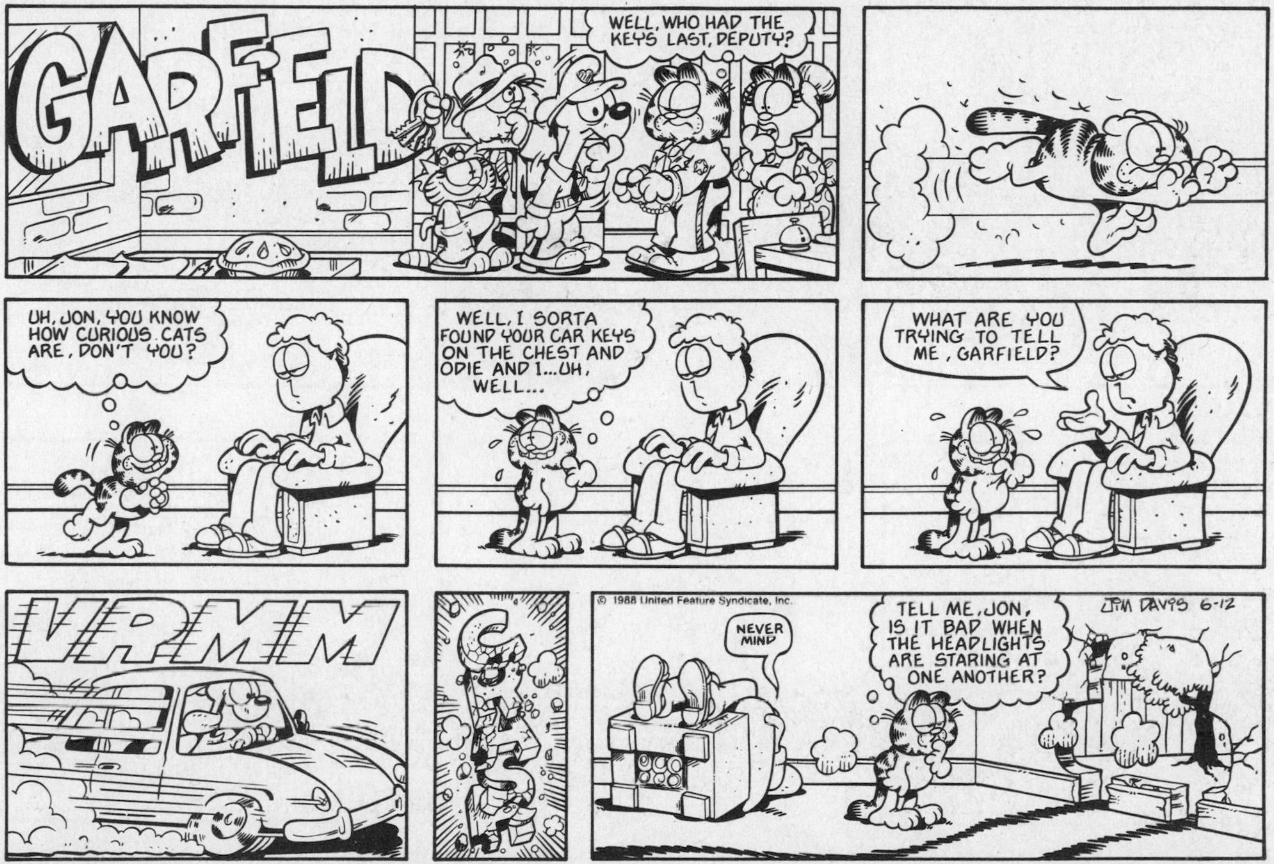
GARFIELD
WELL, WHO HAD THE KEYS LAST, DEPUTY?
UH, JON, YOU KNOW HOW CURIOUS CATS ARE, DON'T YOU?
WELL, I SORTA FOUND YOUR CAR KEYS ON THE CHEST AND ODIE AND I...UH, WELL...
WHAT ARE YOU TRYING TO TELL ME, GARFIELD?
VRMMM
© 1988 United Feature Syndicate, Inc.
NEVER MIND
TELL ME, JON, IS IT BAD WHEN THE HEADLIGHTS ARE STARING AT ONE ANOTHER?
JIM DAVIS 6-12

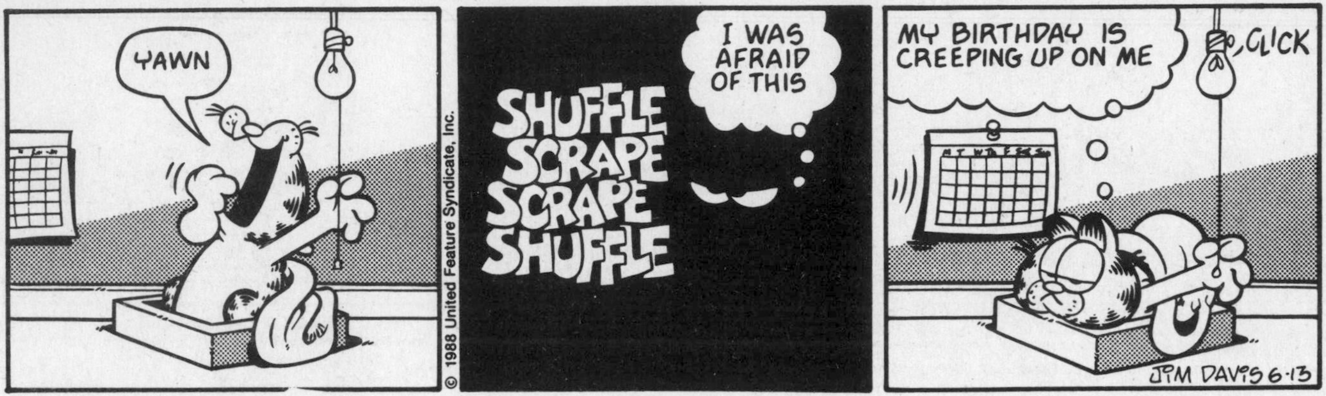
YAWN
SHUFFLE SCRAPE SCRAPE SHUFFLE
I WAS AFRAID OF THIS
MY BIRTHDAY IS CREEPING UP ON ME
CLICK
JIM DAVIS 6-13

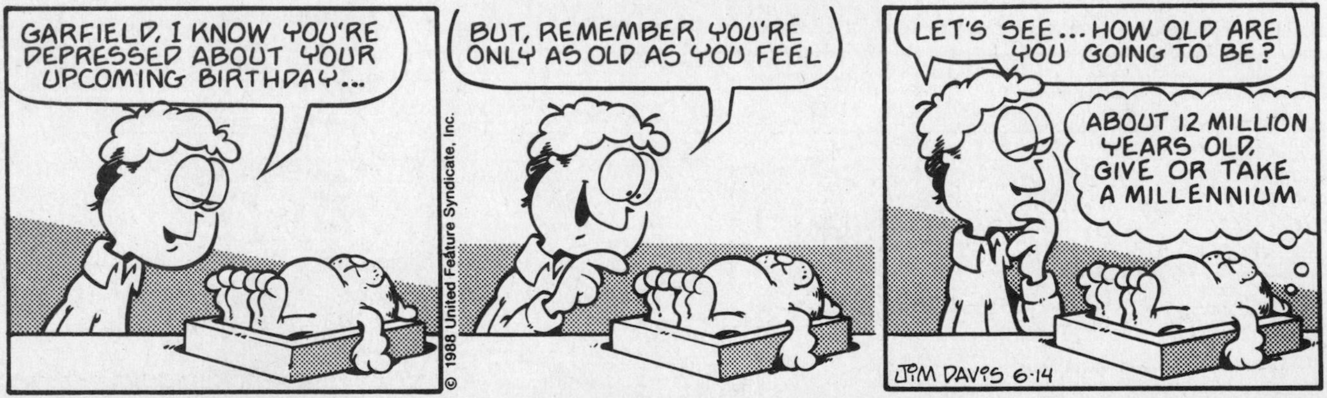
GARFIELD, I KNOW YOU'RE DEPRESSED ABOUT YOUR UPCOMING BIRTHDAY...
BUT, REMEMBER YOU'RE ONLY AS OLD AS YOU FEEL
LET'S SEE... HOW OLD ARE YOU GOING TO BE?
ABOUT 12 MILLION YEARS OLD, GIVE OR TAKE A MILLENNIUM
JIM DAVIS 6-14

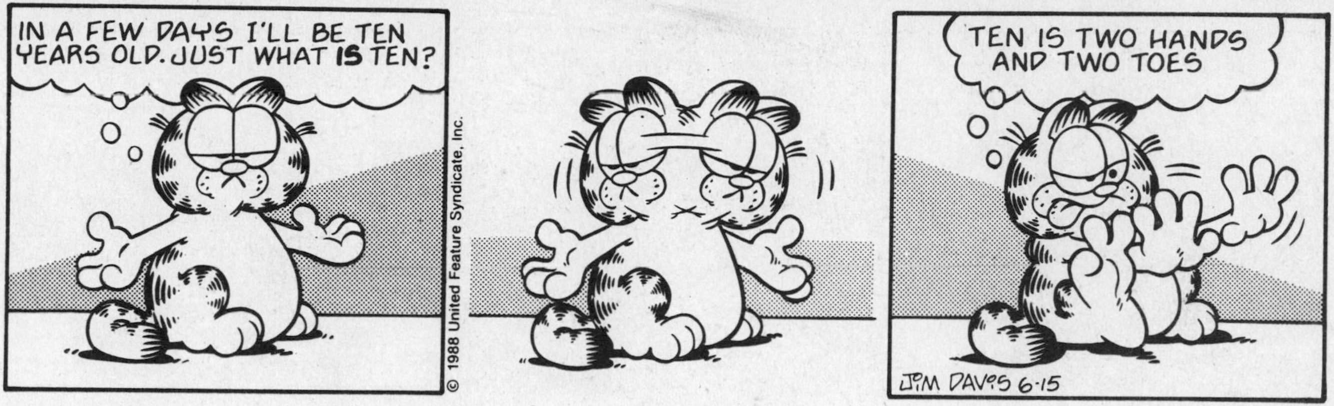
IN A FEW DAYS I'LL BE TEN YEARS OLD. JUST WHAT **IS** TEN?
TEN IS TWO HANDS AND TWO TOES
JIM DAVIS 6-15
© 1988 United Feature Syndicate, Inc.

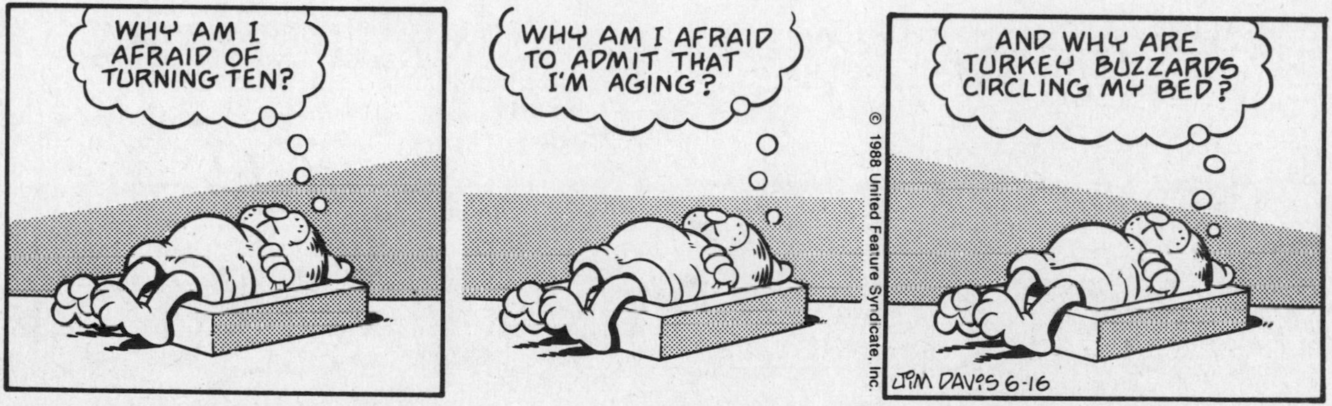
WHY AM I AFRAID OF TURNING TEN?
WHY AM I AFRAID TO ADMIT THAT I'M AGING?
AND WHY ARE TURKEY BUZZARDS CIRCLING MY BED?
JIM DAVIS 6-16
© 1988 United Feature Syndicate, Inc.

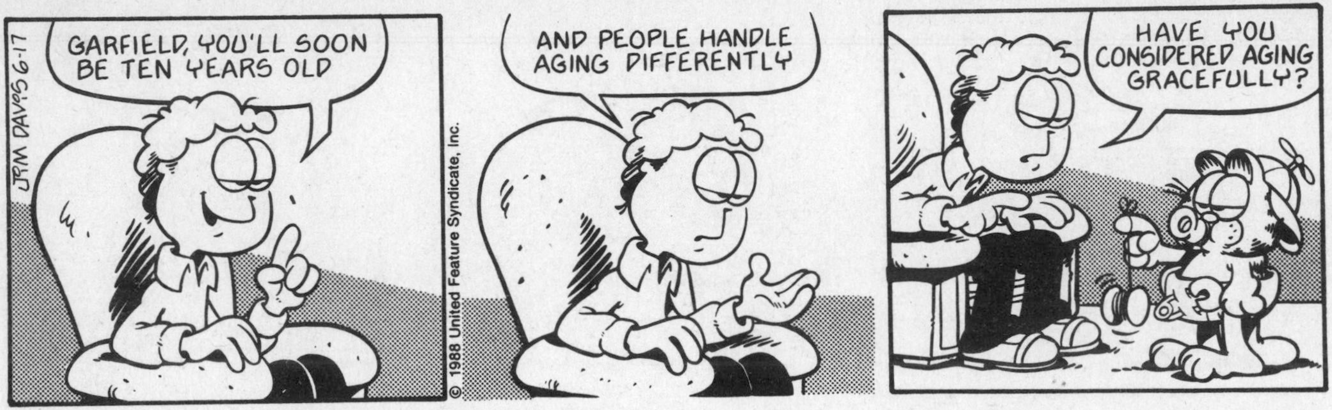
JPM DAV9S 6-17
GARFIELD, YOU'LL SOON BE TEN YEARS OLD
AND PEOPLE HANDLE AGING DIFFERENTLY
HAVE YOU CONSIDERED AGING GRACEFULLY?
© 1988 United Feature Syndicate, Inc.

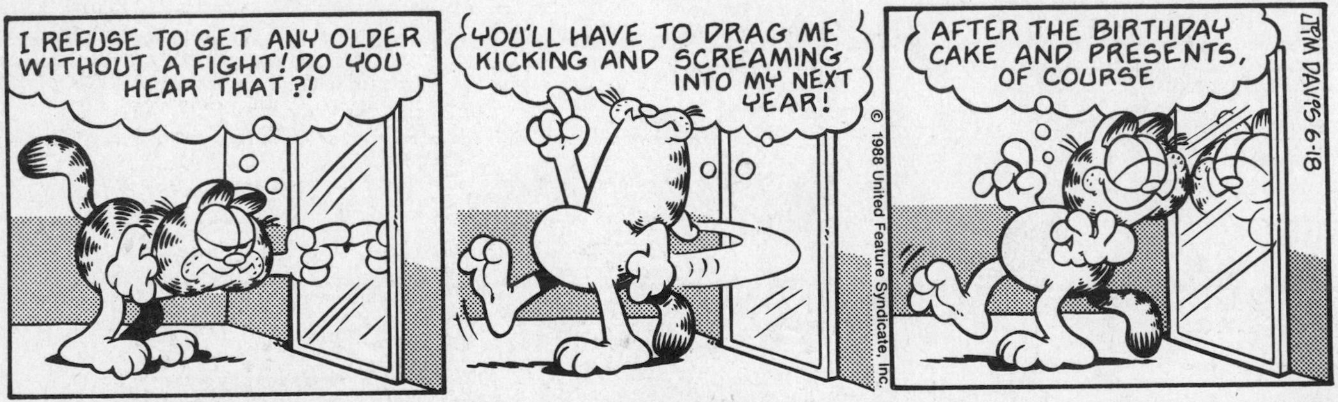
I REFUSE TO GET ANY OLDER WITHOUT A FIGHT! DO YOU HEAR THAT?!
YOU'LL HAVE TO DRAG ME KICKING AND SCREAMING INTO MY NEXT YEAR!
AFTER THE BIRTHDAY CAKE AND PRESENTS, OF COURSE
JPM DAV9S 6-18
© 1988 United Feature Syndicate, Inc.

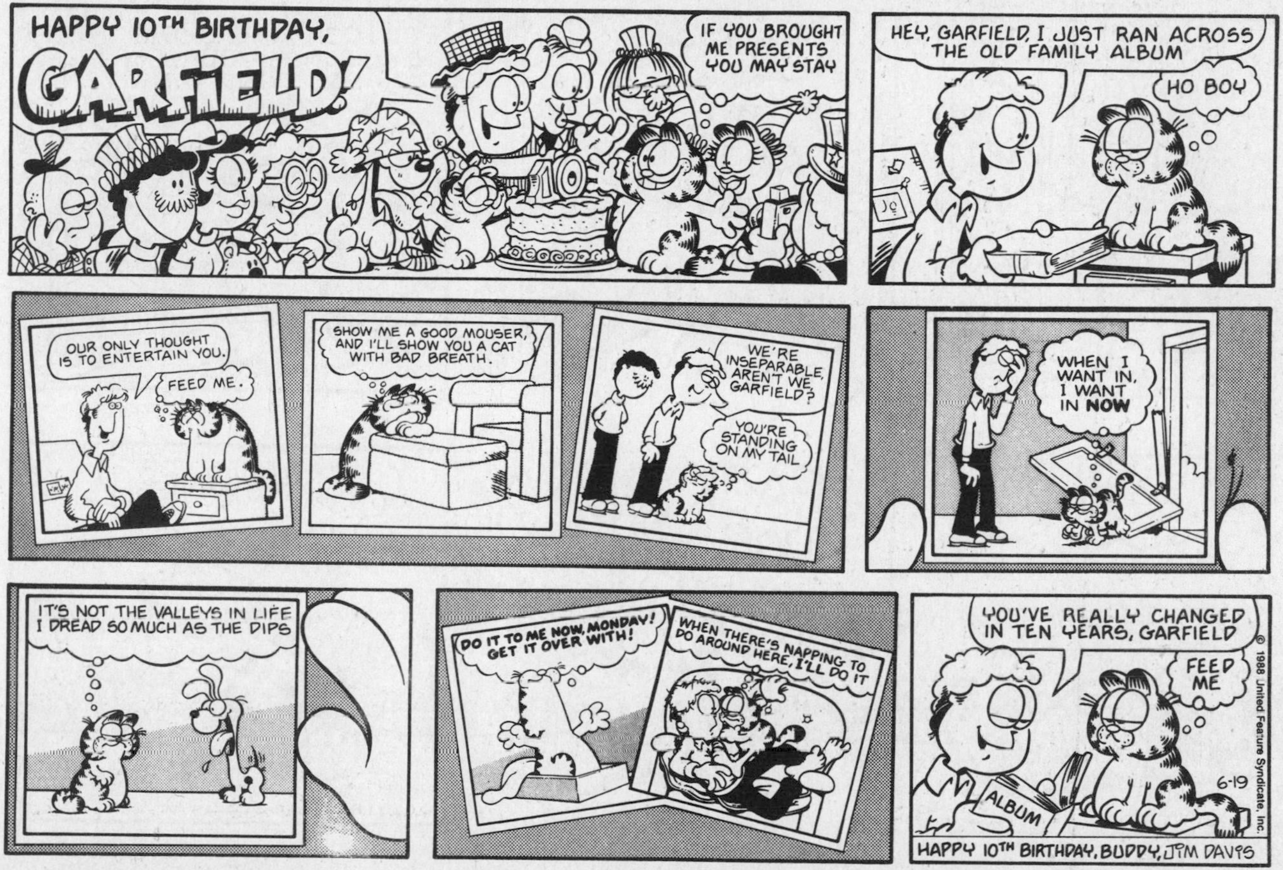
HAPPY 10TH BIRTHDAY,
GARFIELD!
IF YOU BROUGHT ME PRESENTS YOU MAY STAY
HEY, GARFIELD, I JUST RAN ACROSS THE OLD FAMILY ALBUM
HO BOY
OUR ONLY THOUGHT IS TO ENTERTAIN YOU.
FEED ME.
SHOW ME A GOOD MOUSER, AND I'LL SHOW YOU A CAT WITH BAD BREATH.
WE'RE INSEPARABLE, AREN'T WE, GARFIELD?
YOU'RE STANDING ON MY TAIL
WHEN I WANT IN, I WANT IN NOW
IT'S NOT THE VALLEYS IN LIFE I DREAD SO MUCH AS THE DIPS
DO IT TO ME NOW, MONDAY! GET IT OVER WITH!
WHEN THERE'S NAPPING TO DO AROUND HERE, I'LL DO IT
YOU'VE REALLY CHANGED IN TEN YEARS, GARFIELD
FEED ME
ALBUM
6-19
© 1988 United Feature Syndicate, Inc.
HAPPY 10TH BIRTHDAY, BUDDY, JIM DAVIS

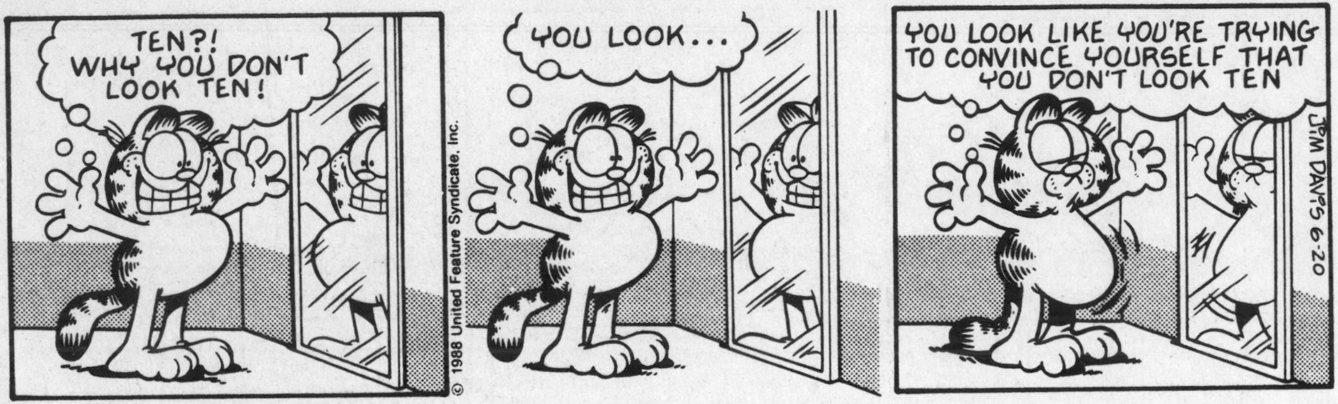
TEN?! WHY YOU DON'T LOOK TEN!
YOU LOOK...
YOU LOOK LIKE YOU'RE TRYING TO CONVINCE YOURSELF THAT YOU DON'T LOOK TEN
© 1988 United Feature Syndicate, Inc.
JIM DAVIS 6-20

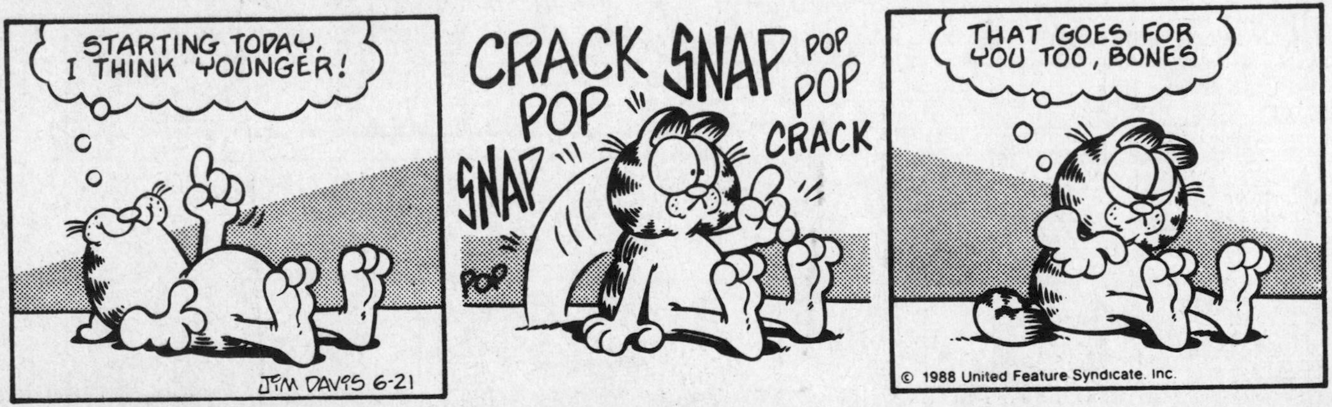
STARTING TODAY, I THINK YOUNGER!
JIM DAVIS 6-21
CRACK
POP
SNAP
SNAP
POP
POP
POP
CRACK
POP
THAT GOES FOR YOU TOO, BONES
© 1988 United Feature Syndicate, Inc.

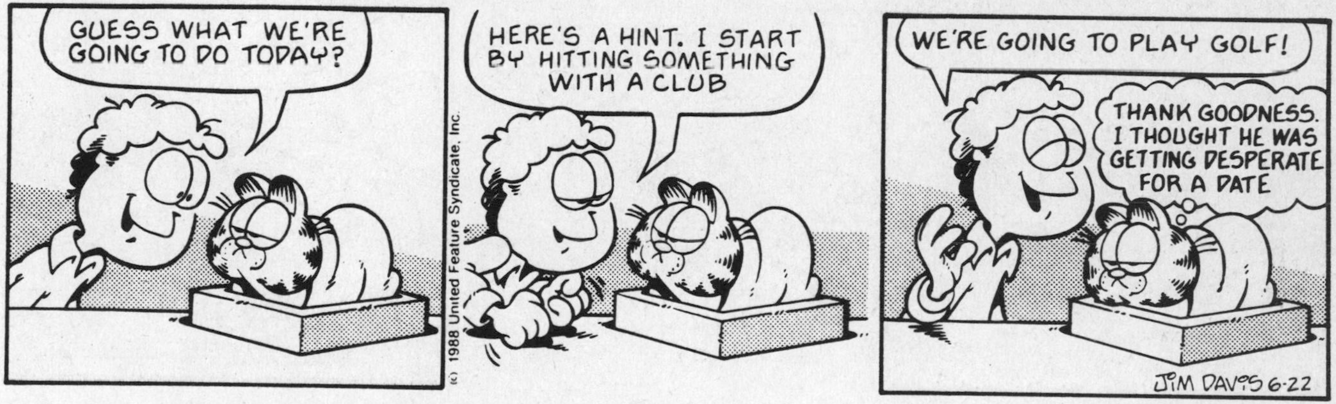
GUESS WHAT WE'RE GOING TO DO TODAY?
HERE'S A HINT. I START BY HITTING SOMETHING WITH A CLUB
WE'RE GOING TO PLAY GOLF!
THANK GOODNESS. I THOUGHT HE WAS GETTING DESPERATE FOR A DATE
(c) 1988 United Feature Syndicate, Inc.
JIM DAVIS 6-22

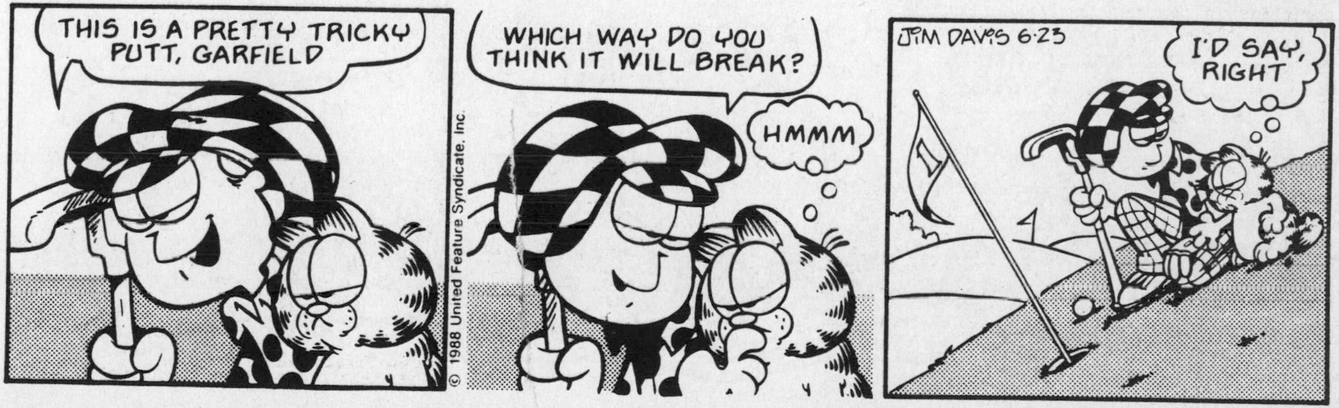
THIS IS A PRETTY TRICKY PUTT, GARFIELD
WHICH WAY DO YOU THINK IT WILL BREAK?
HMMM
I'D SAY, RIGHT
© 1988 United Feature Syndicate, Inc.
JIM DAVIS 6-23

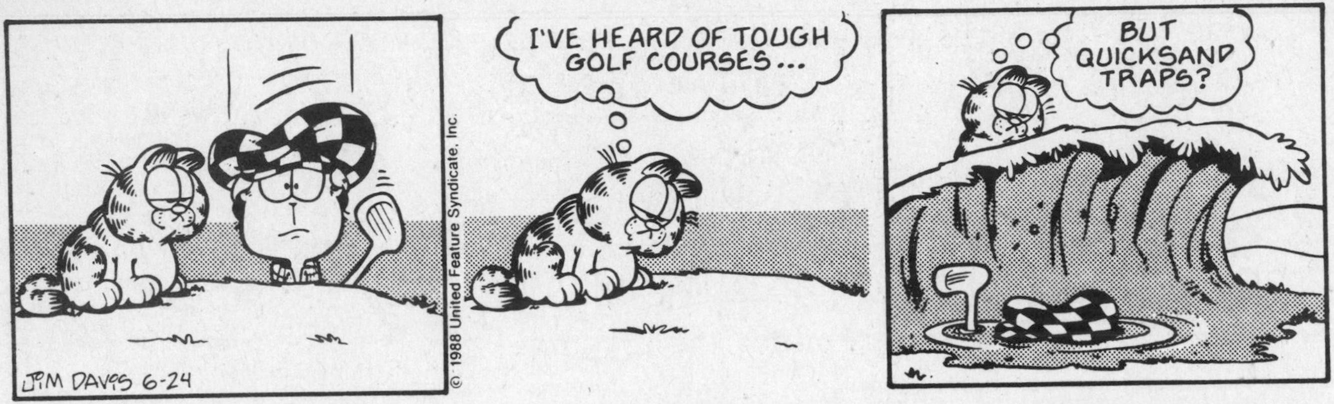
JIM DAVIS 6-24
© 1988 United Feature Syndicate, Inc.
I'VE HEARD OF TOUGH GOLF COURSES...
BUT QUICKSAND TRAPS?

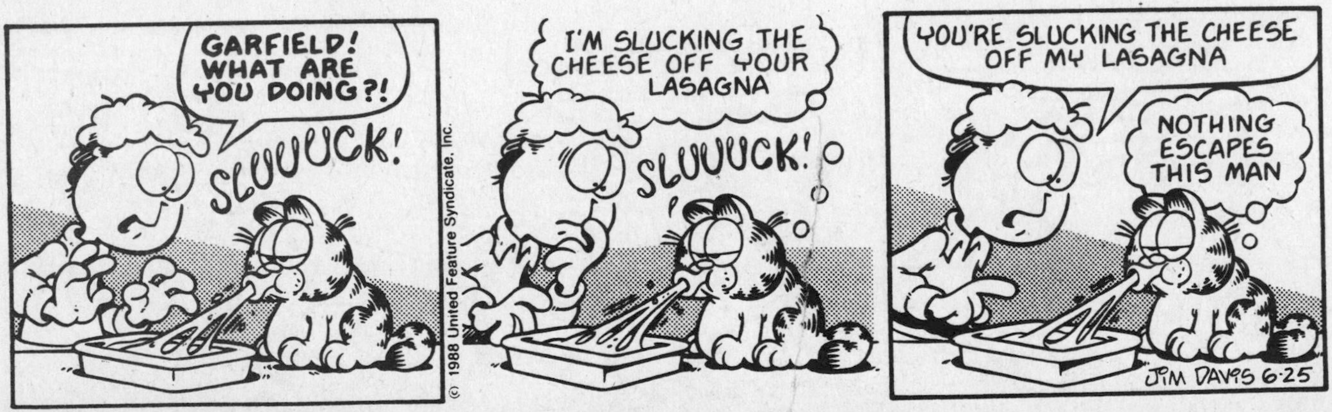
GARFIELD! WHAT ARE YOU DOING?!
SLUUUCK!
© 1988 United Feature Syndicate, Inc.
I'M SLUCKING THE CHEESE OFF YOUR LASAGNA
SLUUUCK!
YOU'RE SLUCKING THE CHEESE OFF MY LASAGNA
NOTHING ESCAPES THIS MAN
JIM DAVIS 6-25

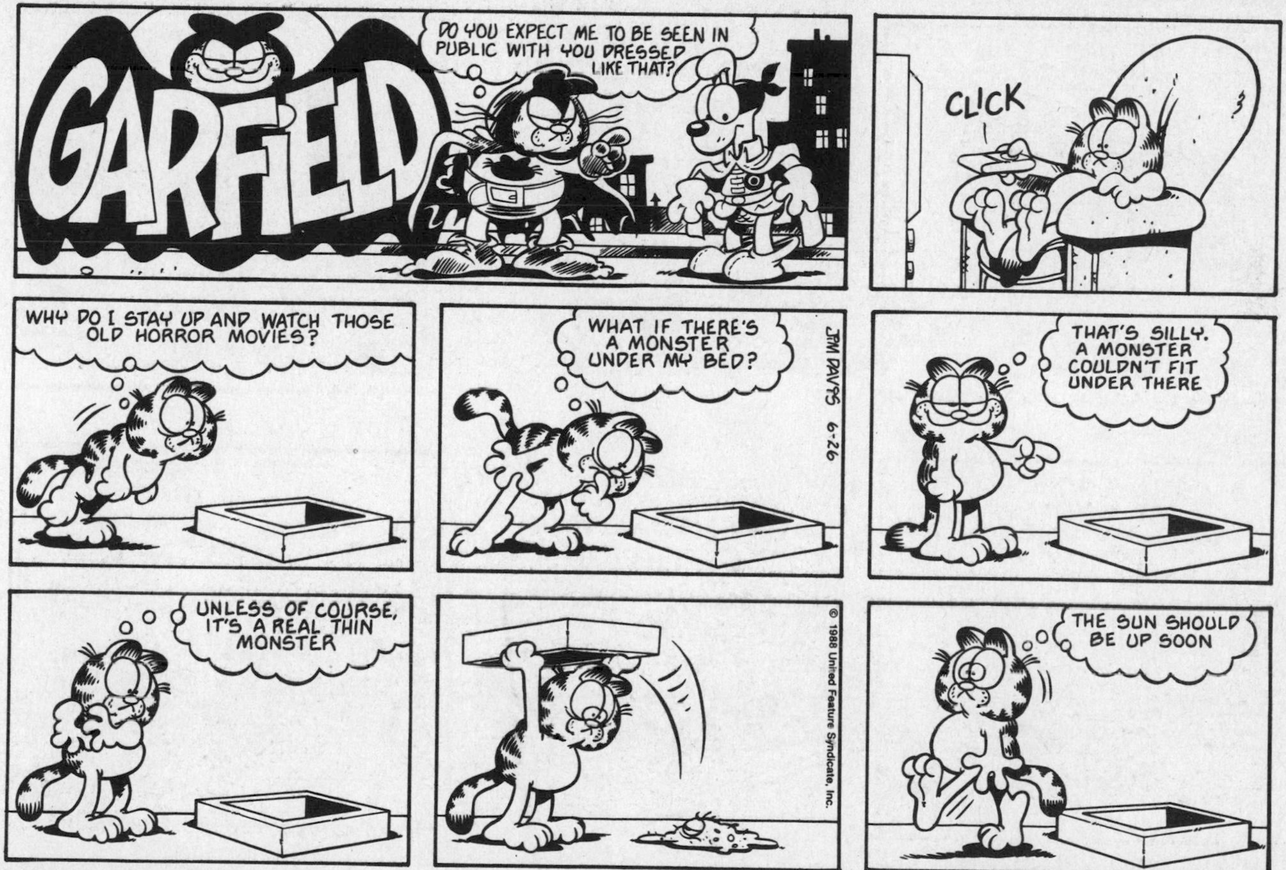
GARFIELD
DO YOU EXPECT ME TO BE SEEN IN PUBLIC WITH YOU DRESSED LIKE THAT?
CLICK
WHY DO I STAY UP AND WATCH THOSE OLD HORROR MOVIES?
WHAT IF THERE'S A MONSTER UNDER MY BED?
JIM DAVIS 6-26
THAT'S SILLY. A MONSTER COULDN'T FIT UNDER THERE
UNLESS OF COURSE, IT'S A REAL THIN MONSTER
© 1988 United Feature Syndicate, Inc.
THE SUN SHOULD BE UP SOON

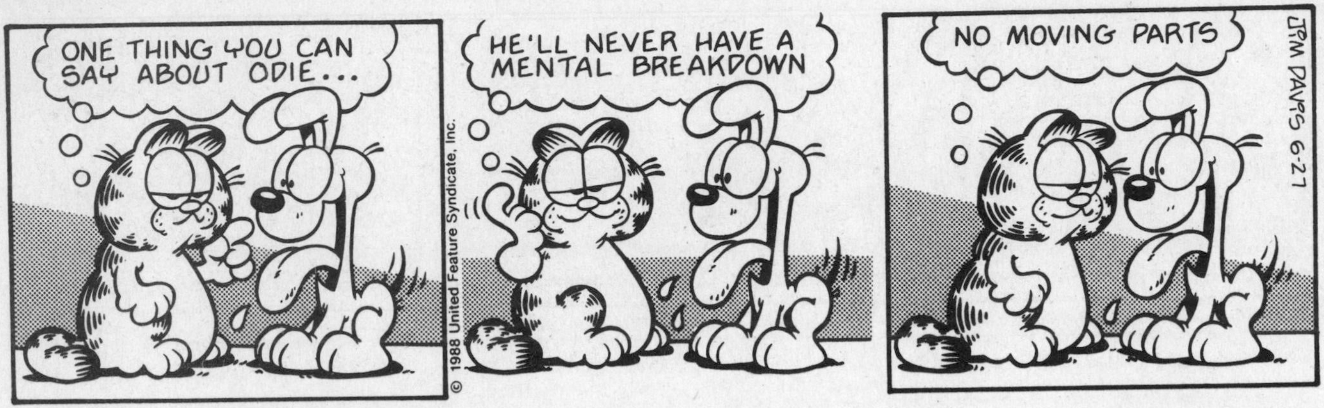
ONE THING YOU CAN SAY ABOUT ODIE...
HE'LL NEVER HAVE A MENTAL BREAKDOWN
NO MOVING PARTS
JPM DAVPS 6-27
© 1988 United Feature Syndicate, Inc.

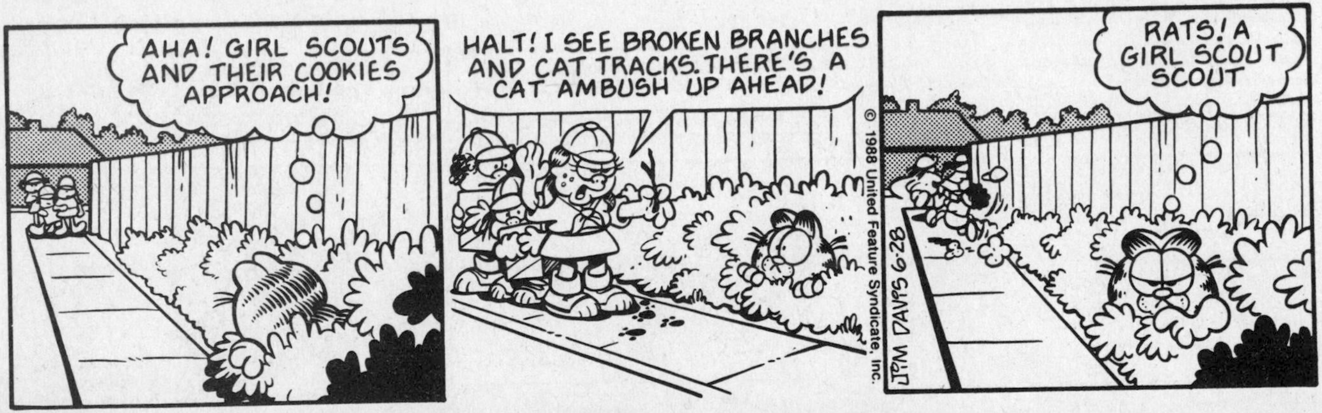
AHA! GIRL SCOUTS AND THEIR COOKIES APPROACH!
HALT! I SEE BROKEN BRANCHES AND CAT TRACKS. THERE'S A CAT AMBUSH UP AHEAD!
RATS! A GIRL SCOUT SCOUT
JPM DAVPS 6-28
© 1988 United Feature Syndicate, Inc.

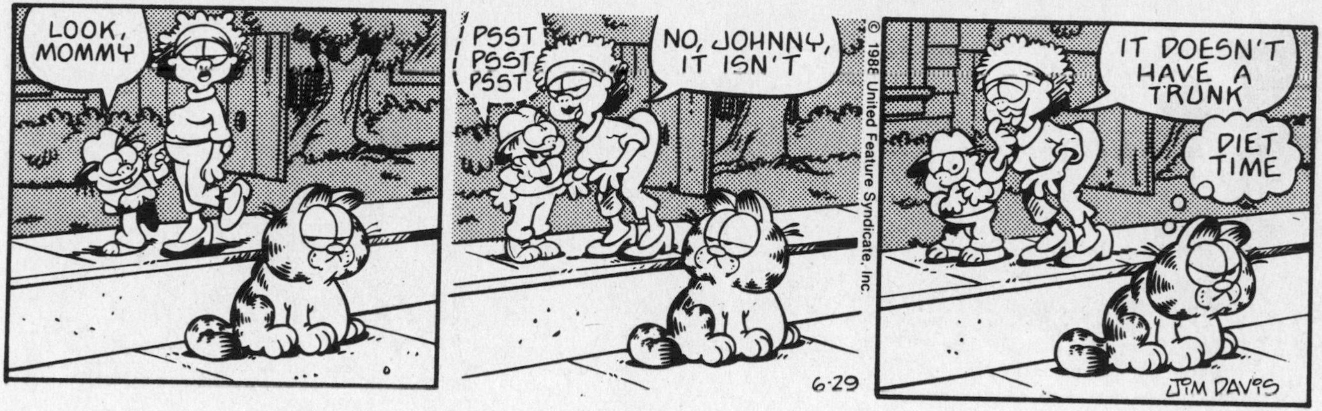
LOOK, MOMMY
PSST PSST PSST
NO, JOHNNY, IT ISN'T
© 1988 United Feature Syndicate, Inc.
6-29
IT DOESN'T HAVE A TRUNK
DIET TIME
JIM DAVIS

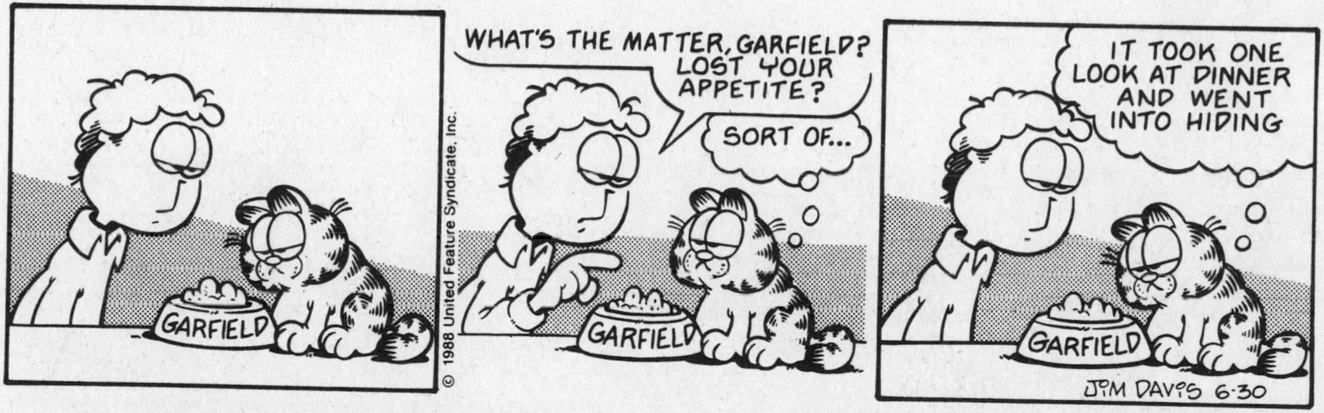
GARFIELD
© 1988 United Feature Syndicate, Inc.
WHAT'S THE MATTER, GARFIELD? LOST YOUR APPETITE?
SORT OF...
GARFIELD
IT TOOK ONE LOOK AT DINNER AND WENT INTO HIDING
GARFIELD
JIM DAVIS 6-30

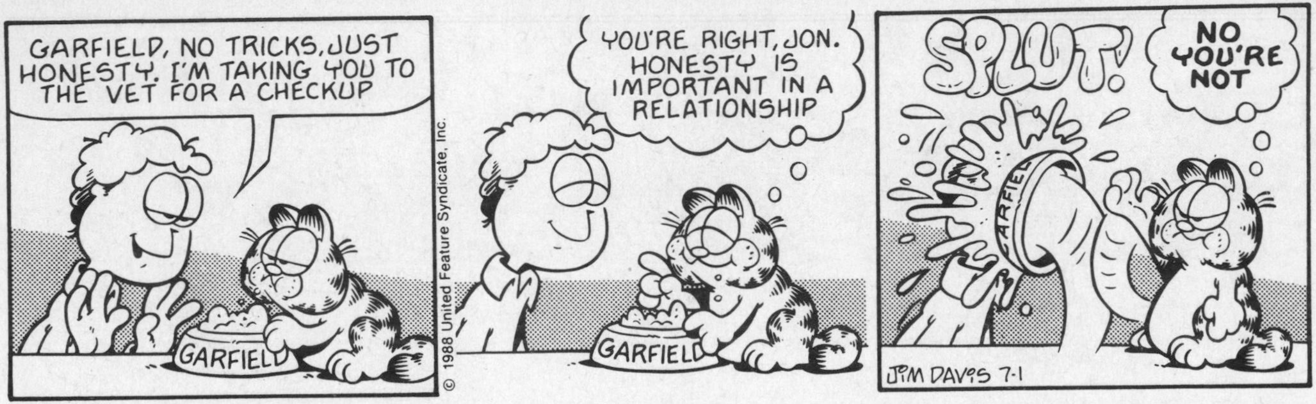
GARFIELD, NO TRICKS, JUST HONESTY. I'M TAKING YOU TO THE VET FOR A CHECKUP
GARFIELD
© 1988 United Feature Syndicate, Inc.
YOU'RE RIGHT, JON. HONESTY IS IMPORTANT IN A RELATIONSHIP
GARFIELD
SPLUT!
NO YOU'RE NOT
JIM DAVIS 7-1

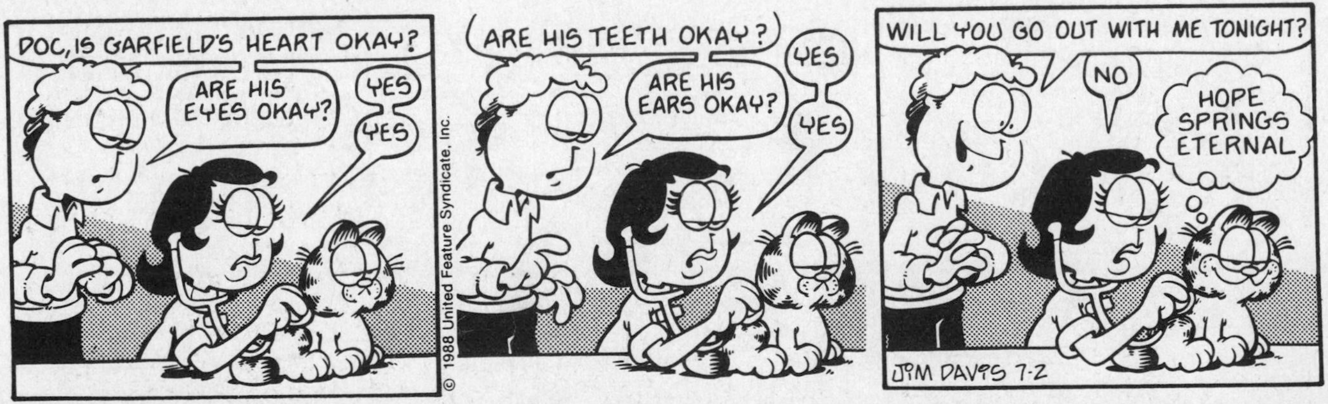
DOC, IS GARFIELD'S HEART OKAY?
ARE HIS EYES OKAY?
YES
YES
© 1988 United Feature Syndicate, Inc.
ARE HIS TEETH OKAY?
ARE HIS EARS OKAY?
YES
YES
WILL YOU GO OUT WITH ME TONIGHT?
NO
HOPE SPRINGS ETERNAL
JIM DAVIS 7-2

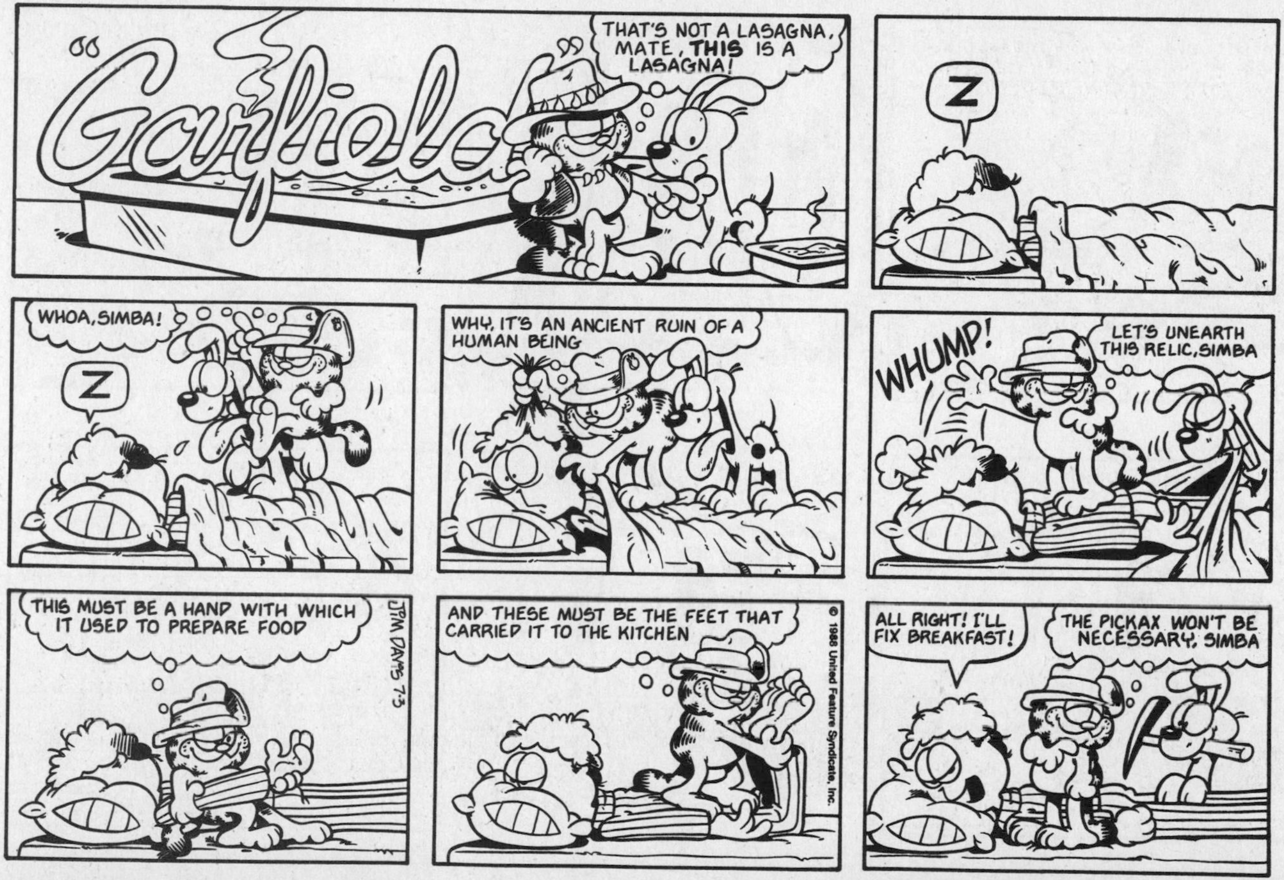

Garfield
THAT'S NOT A LASAGNA, MATE, THIS IS A LASAGNA!
Z
WHOA, SIMBA!
Z
WHY, IT'S AN ANCIENT RUIN OF A HUMAN BEING
WHUMP!
LET'S UNEARTH THIS RELIC, SIMBA
THIS MUST BE A HAND WITH WHICH IT USED TO PREPARE FOOD
JIM DAVIS 7-3
AND THESE MUST BE THE FEET THAT CARRIED IT TO THE KITCHEN
© 1988 United Feature Syndicate, Inc.
ALL RIGHT! I'LL FIX BREAKFAST!
THE PICKAX WON'T BE NECESSARY, SIMBA

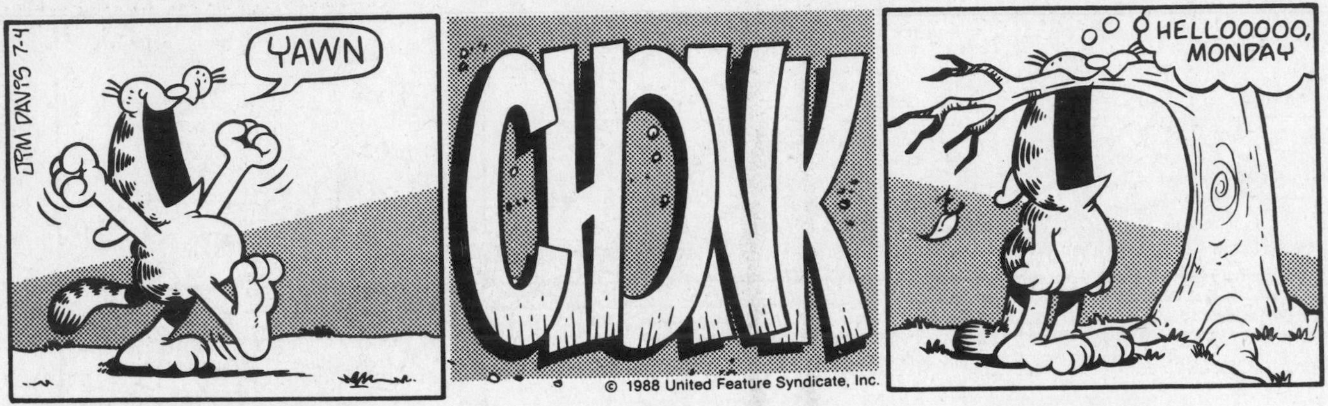
JIM DAVIS 7-4
YAWN
CHONK
© 1988 United Feature Syndicate, Inc.
HELLOOOOO, MONDAY

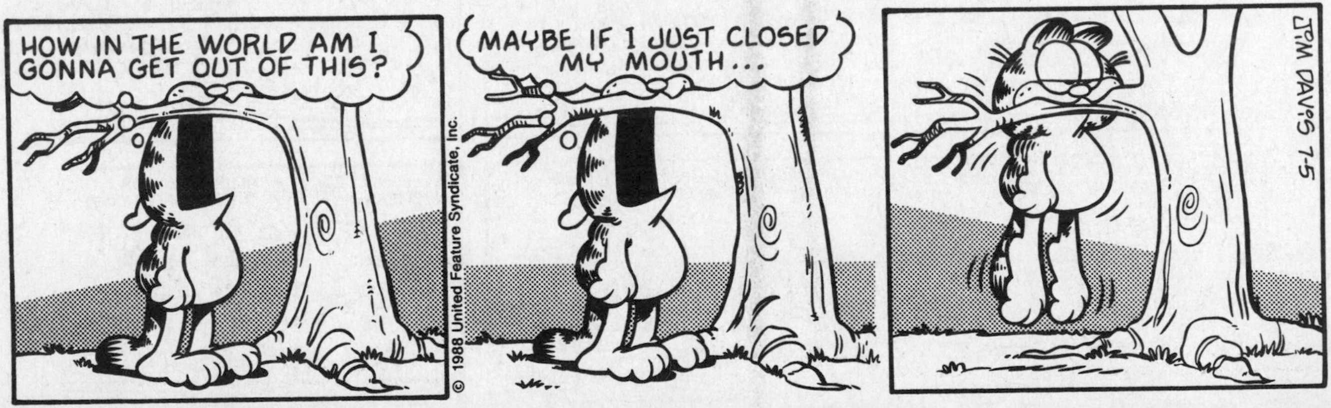
HOW IN THE WORLD AM I GONNA GET OUT OF THIS?
© 1988 United Feature Syndicate, Inc.
MAYBE IF I JUST CLOSED MY MOUTH...
JIM DAVIS 7-5

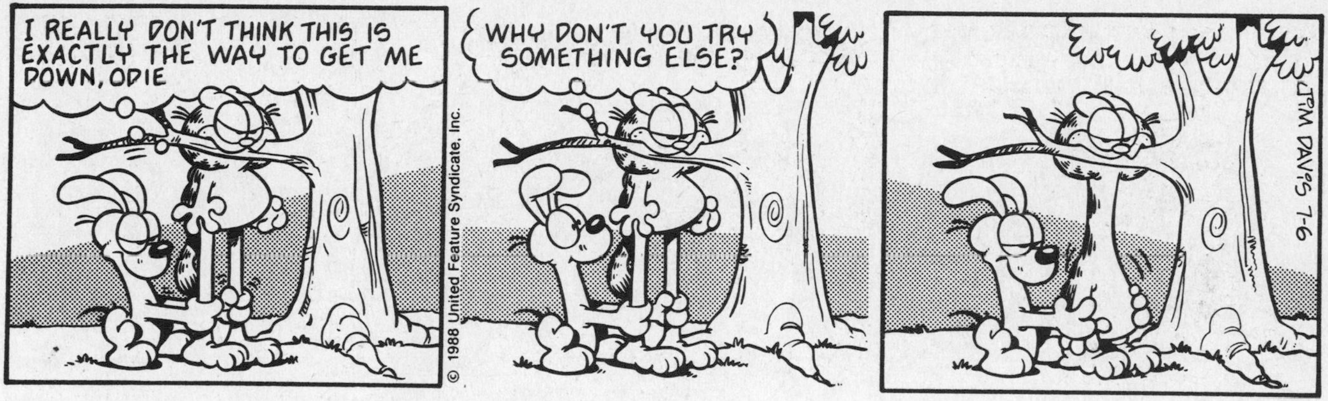
I REALLY DON'T THINK THIS IS EXACTLY THE WAY TO GET ME DOWN, ODIE
© 1988 United Feature Syndicate, Inc.
WHY DON'T YOU TRY SOMETHING ELSE?
JIM DAVIS 7-6

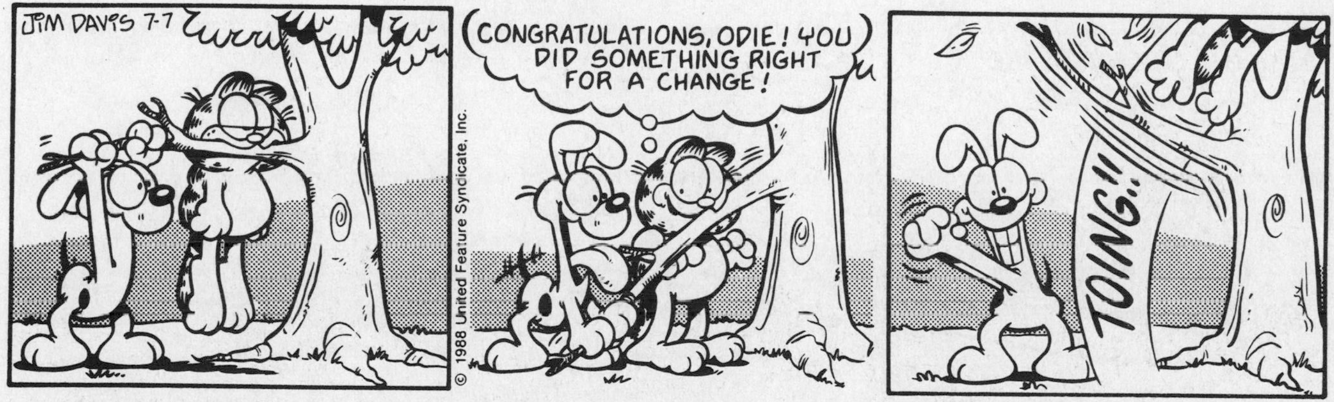
JIM DAVIS 7-7
© 1988 United Feature Syndicate, Inc.
CONGRATULATIONS, ODIE! YOU DID SOMETHING RIGHT FOR A CHANGE!
TOING!!

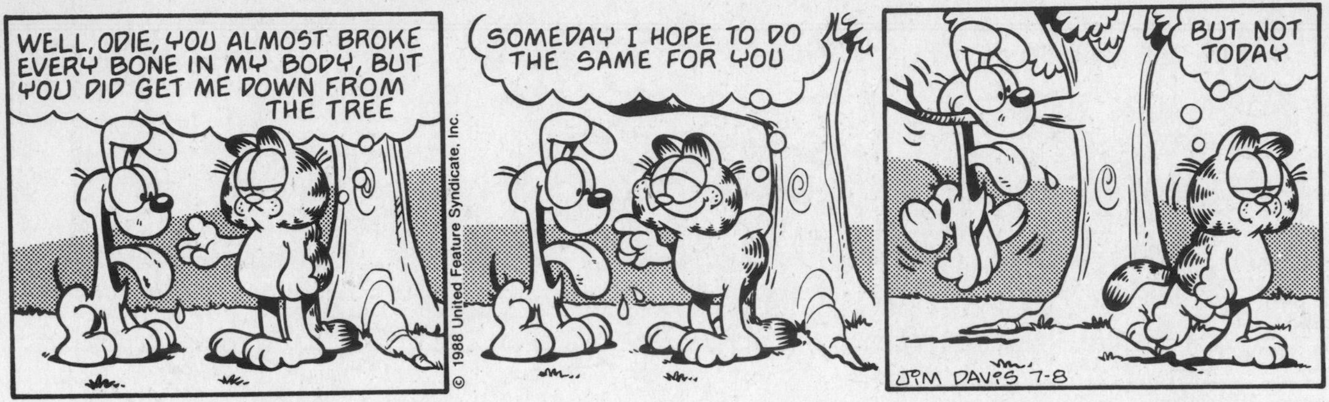
WELL, ODIE, YOU ALMOST BROKE EVERY BONE IN MY BODY, BUT YOU DID GET ME DOWN FROM THE TREE
SOMEDAY I HOPE TO DO THE SAME FOR YOU
BUT NOT TODAY
JIM DAVIS 7-8
© 1988 United Feature Syndicate, Inc.

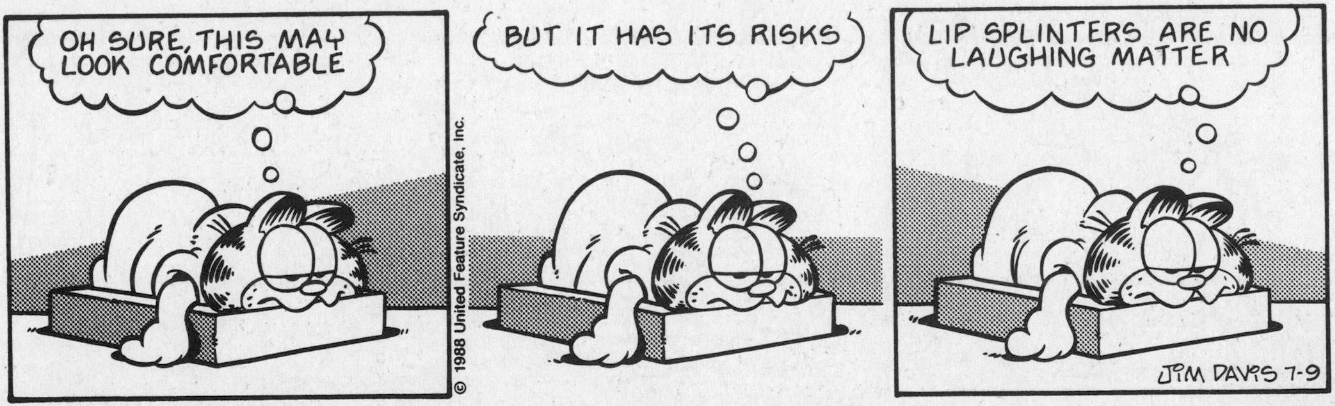
OH SURE, THIS MAY LOOK COMFORTABLE
BUT IT HAS ITS RISKS
LIP SPLINTERS ARE NO LAUGHING MATTER
JIM DAVIS 7-9
© 1988 United Feature Syndicate, Inc.

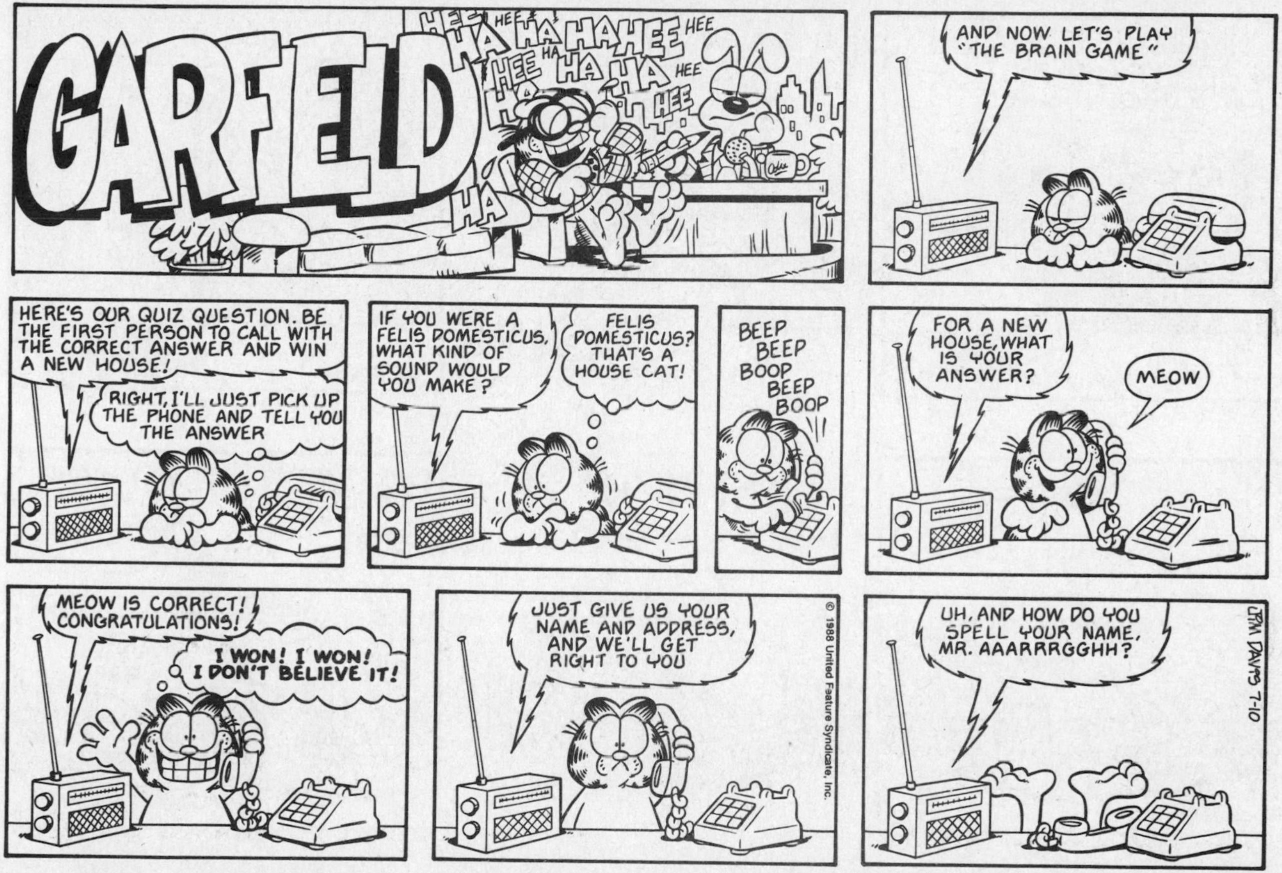
GARFIELD
HEE HEE HA HA HA HAHEE HEE HEE HA HEE HA HA HEE HA HEE HA
AND NOW LET'S PLAY "THE BRAIN GAME"
HERE'S OUR QUIZ QUESTION. BE THE FIRST PERSON TO CALL WITH THE CORRECT ANSWER AND WIN A NEW HOUSE!
RIGHT, I'LL JUST PICK UP THE PHONE AND TELL YOU THE ANSWER
IF YOU WERE A FELIS DOMESTICUS, WHAT KIND OF SOUND WOULD YOU MAKE?
FELIS DOMESTICUS? THAT'S A HOUSE CAT!
BEEP BEEP BOOP BEEP BOOP
FOR A NEW HOUSE, WHAT IS YOUR ANSWER?
MEOW
MEOW IS CORRECT! CONGRATULATIONS!
I WON! I WON! I DON'T BELIEVE IT!
JUST GIVE US YOUR NAME AND ADDRESS, AND WE'LL GET RIGHT TO YOU
© 1988 United Feature Syndicate, Inc.
UH, AND HOW DO YOU SPELL YOUR NAME, MR. AAARRRGGHH?
JPM DAVIS 7-10

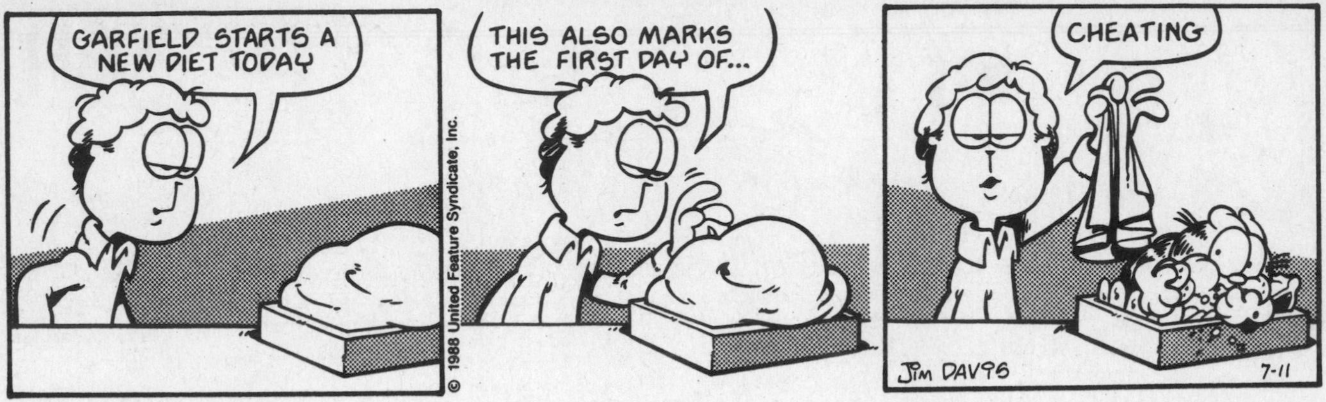
GARFIELD STARTS A NEW DIET TODAY
© 1988 United Feature Syndicate, Inc.
THIS ALSO MARKS THE FIRST DAY OF...
CHEATING
JIM DAVIS
7-11

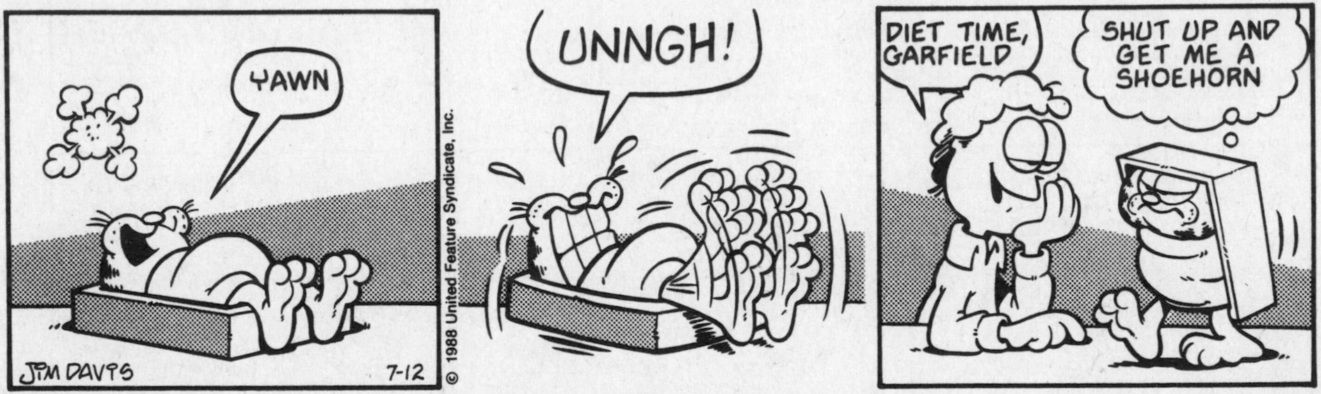
YAWN
JIM DAVIS
7-12
© 1988 United Feature Syndicate, Inc.
UNNGH!
DIET TIME, GARFIELD
SHUT UP AND GET ME A SHOEHORN

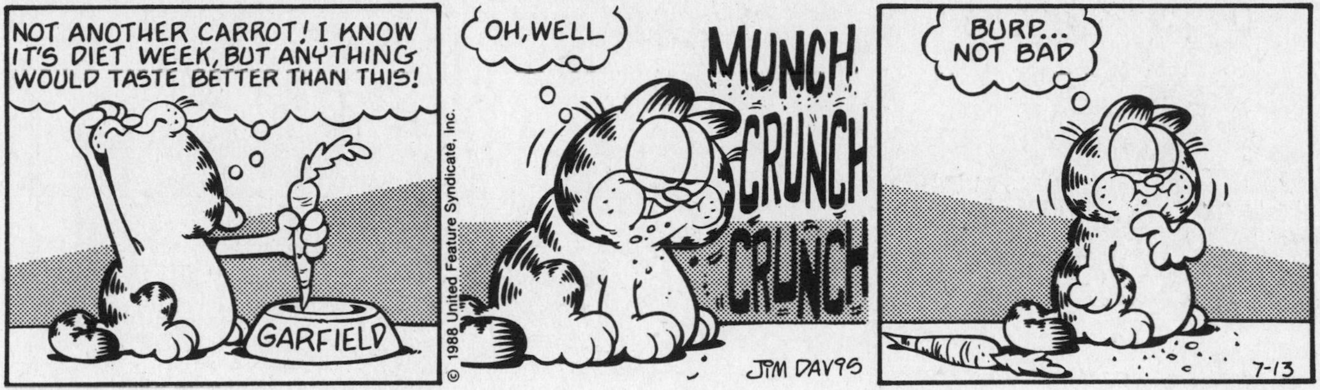
NOT ANOTHER CARROT! I KNOW IT'S DIET WEEK, BUT ANYTHING WOULD TASTE BETTER THAN THIS!
GARFIELD
© 1988 United Feature Syndicate, Inc.
OH, WELL
MUNCH
CRUNCH
CRUNCH
JIM DAVIS
BURP... NOT BAD
7-13

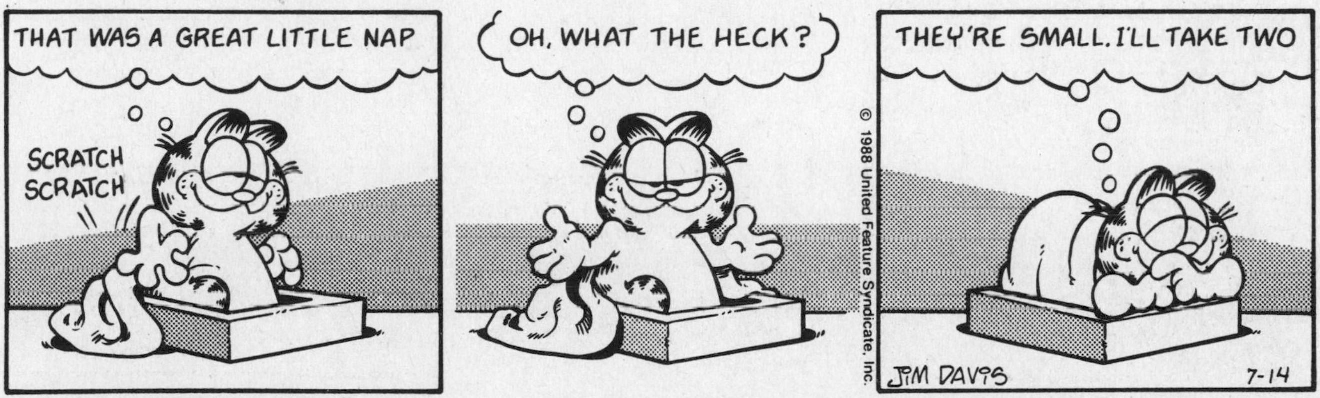
THAT WAS A GREAT LITTLE NAP
SCRATCH
SCRATCH
OH, WHAT THE HECK?
© 1988 United Feature Syndicate, Inc.
THEY'RE SMALL. I'LL TAKE TWO
JIM DAVIS
7-14

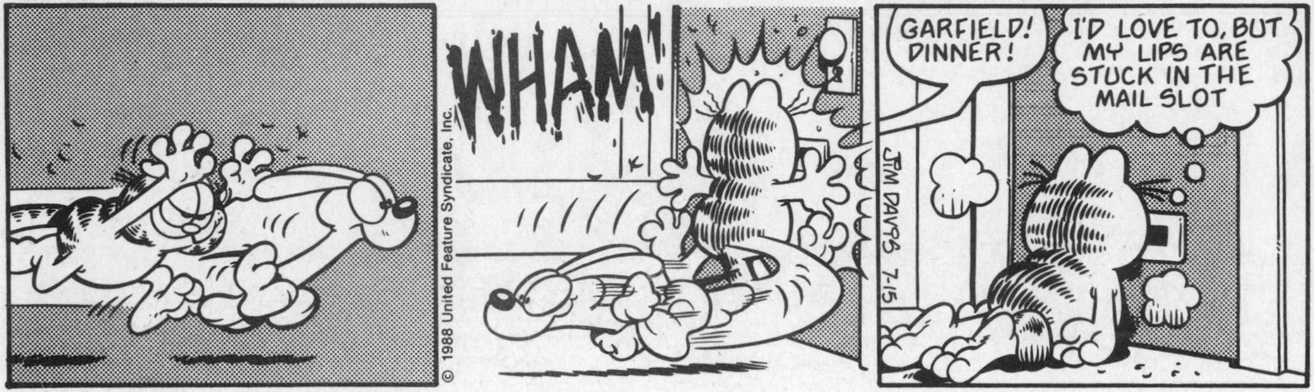
© 1988 United Feature Syndicate, Inc.
WHAM!
JIM DAVIS 7-15
GARFIELD! DINNER!
I'D LOVE TO, BUT MY LIPS ARE STUCK IN THE MAIL SLOT

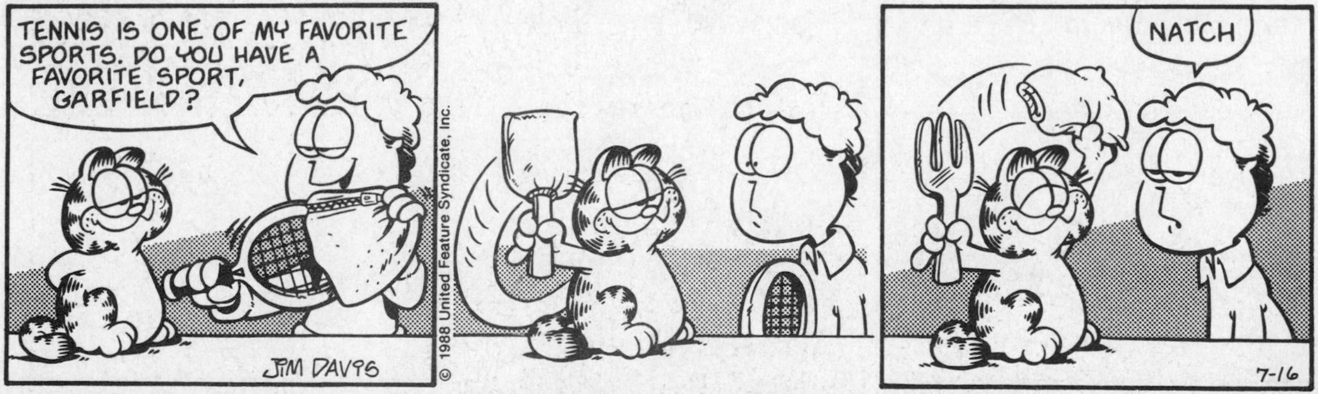
TENNIS IS ONE OF MY FAVORITE SPORTS. DO YOU HAVE A FAVORITE SPORT, GARFIELD?
JIM DAVIS
© 1988 United Feature Syndicate, Inc.
NATCH
7-16

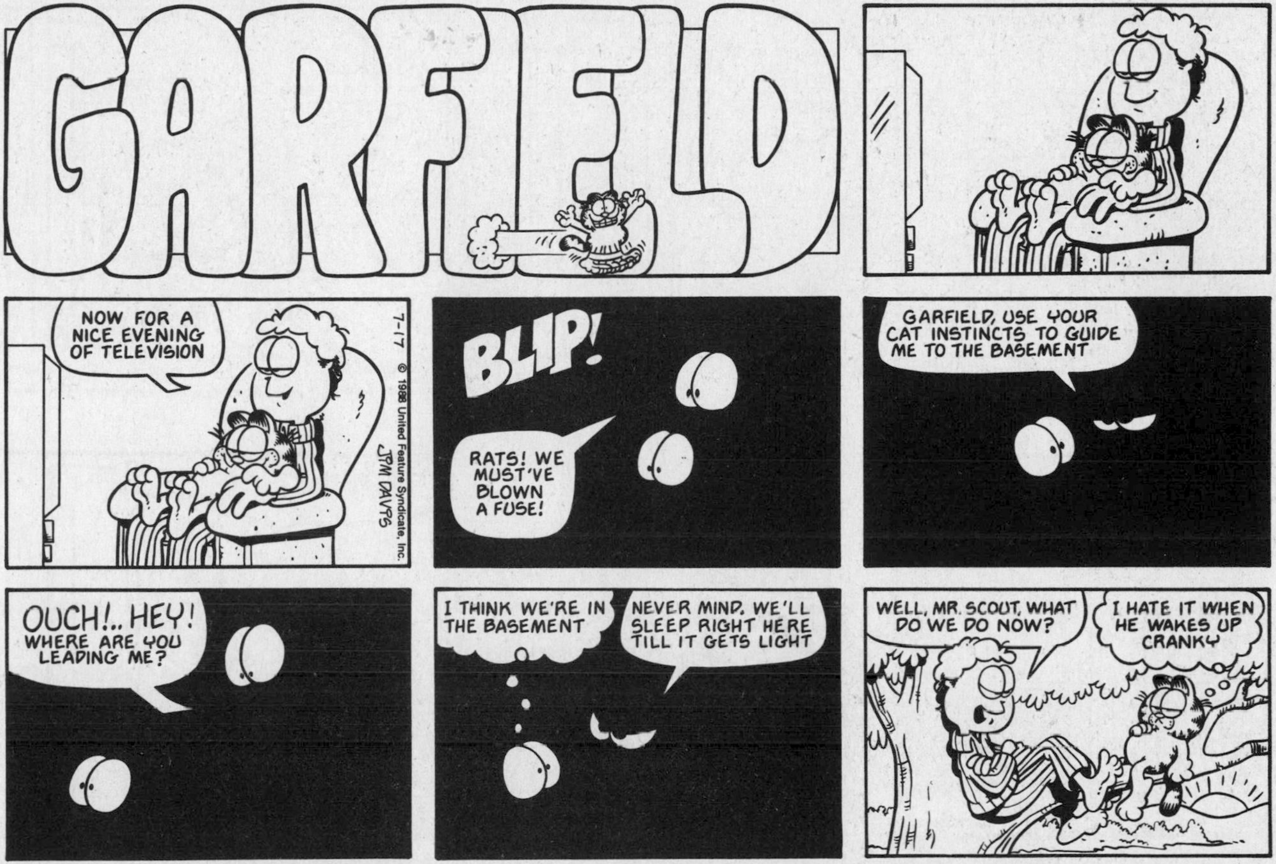
GARFIELD
NOW FOR A NICE EVENING OF TELEVISION
7-17
© 1988 United Feature Syndicate, Inc.
JIM DAVIS
BLIP!
RATS! WE MUST'VE BLOWN A FUSE!
GARFIELD, USE YOUR CAT INSTINCTS TO GUIDE ME TO THE BASEMENT
OUCH!.. HEY! WHERE ARE YOU LEADING ME?
I THINK WE'RE IN THE BASEMENT
NEVER MIND. WE'LL SLEEP RIGHT HERE TILL IT GETS LIGHT
WELL, MR. SCOUT, WHAT DO WE DO NOW?
I HATE IT WHEN HE WAKES UP CRANKY

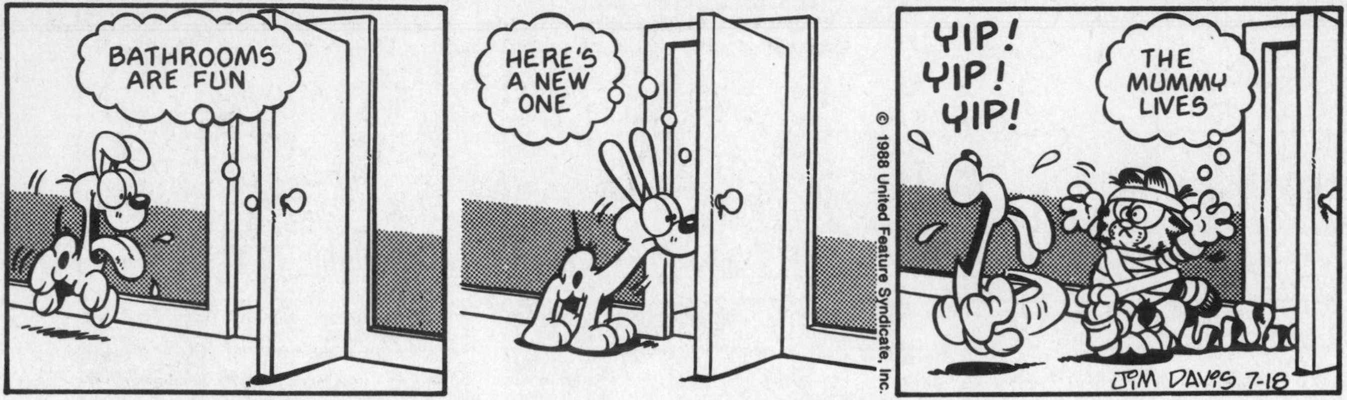
BATHROOMS ARE FUN
HERE'S A NEW ONE
YIP! YIP! YIP!
THE MUMMY LIVES
JIM DAVIS 7-18

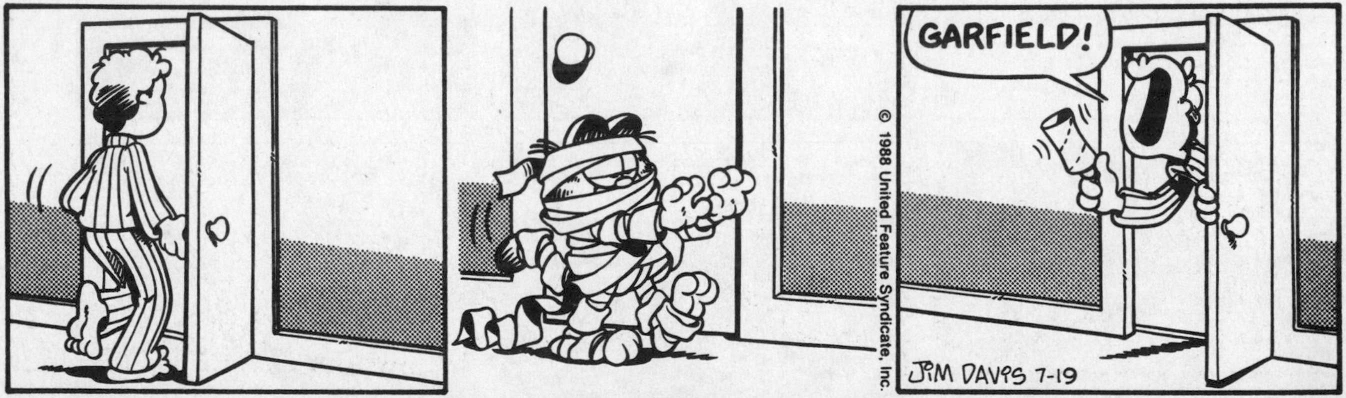
GARFIELD!
JIM DAVIS 7-19

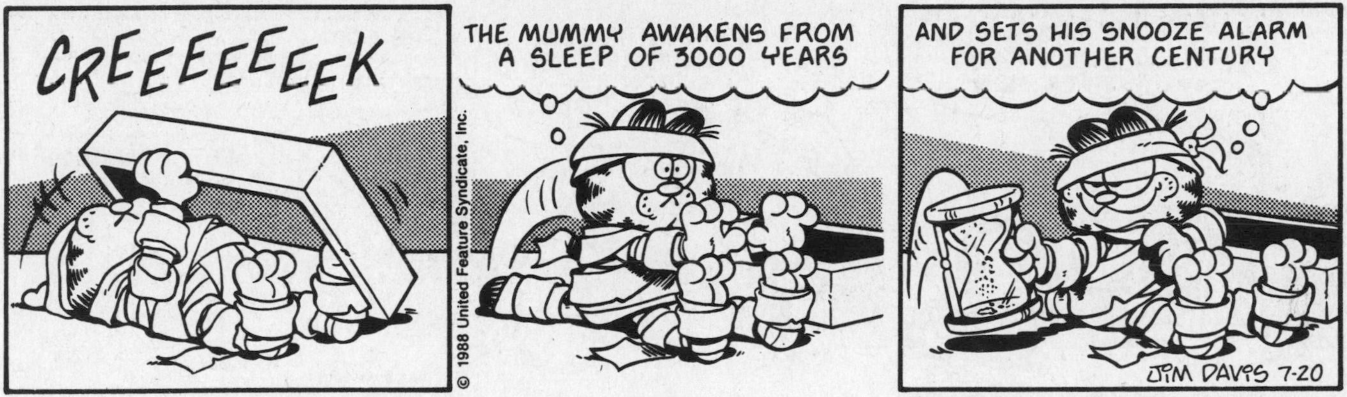
CREEEEEEEK
THE MUMMY AWAKENS FROM A SLEEP OF 3000 YEARS
AND SETS HIS SNOOZE ALARM FOR ANOTHER CENTURY
JIM DAVIS 7-20
© 1988 United Feature Syndicate, Inc.

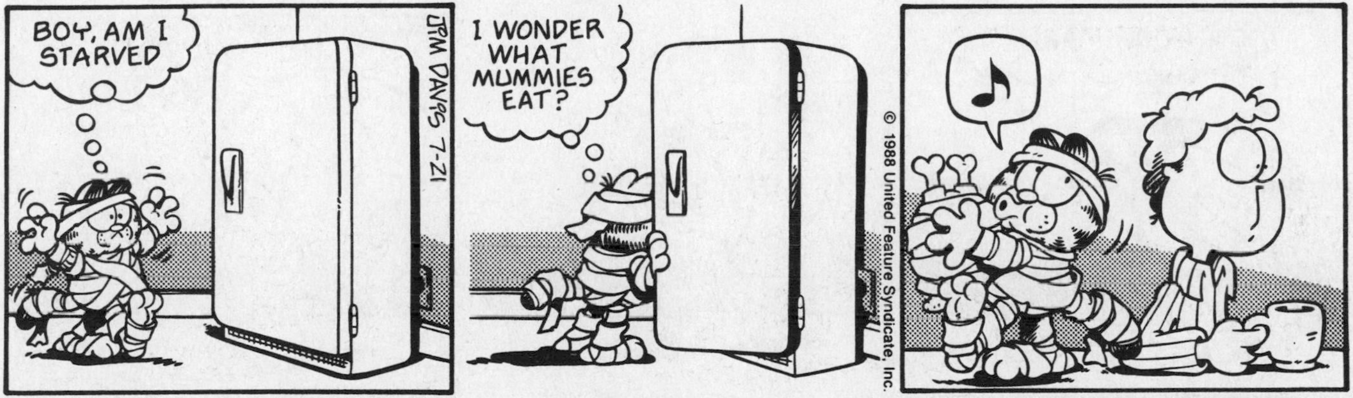
BOY, AM I STARVED
JIM DAVIS 7-21
I WONDER WHAT MUMMIES EAT?
© 1988 United Feature Syndicate, Inc.
♪

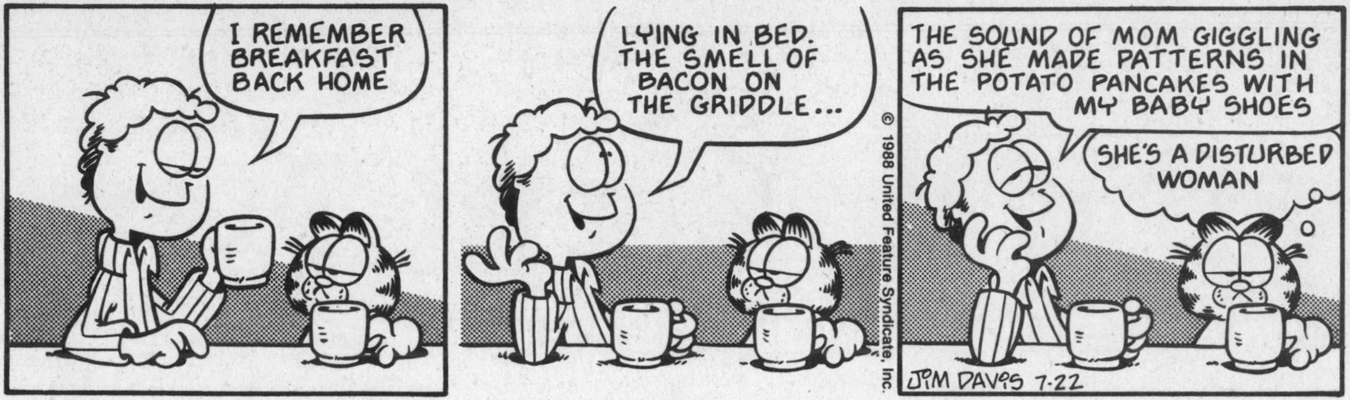
I REMEMBER BREAKFAST BACK HOME
LYING IN BED. THE SMELL OF BACON ON THE GRIDDLE...
© 1988 United Feature Syndicate, Inc.
THE SOUND OF MOM GIGGLING AS SHE MADE PATTERNS IN THE POTATO PANCAKES WITH MY BABY SHOES
SHE'S A DISTURBED WOMAN
JIM DAVIS 7-22

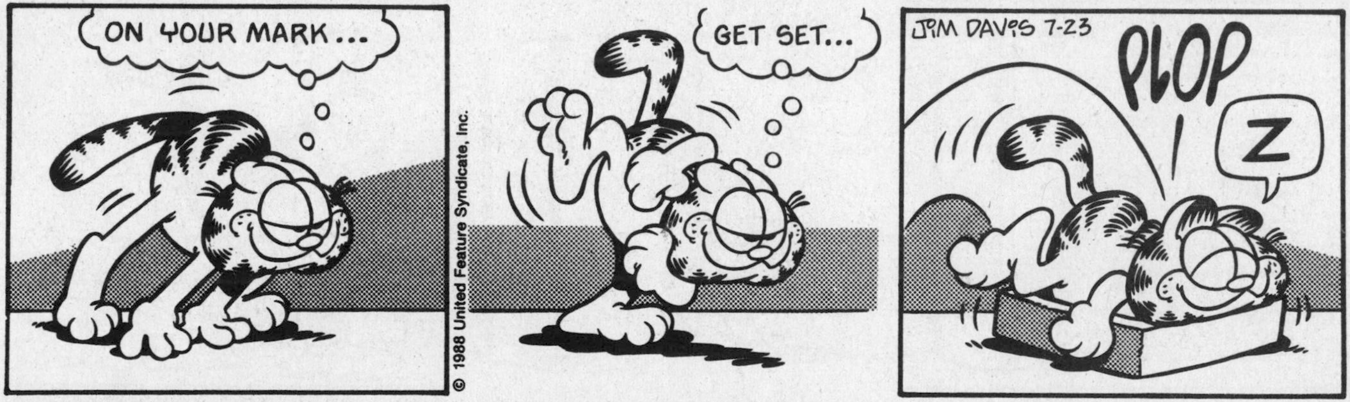
ON YOUR MARK...
© 1988 United Feature Syndicate, Inc.
GET SET...
JIM DAVIS 7-23
PLOP
Z

6 Best uses for an Odie

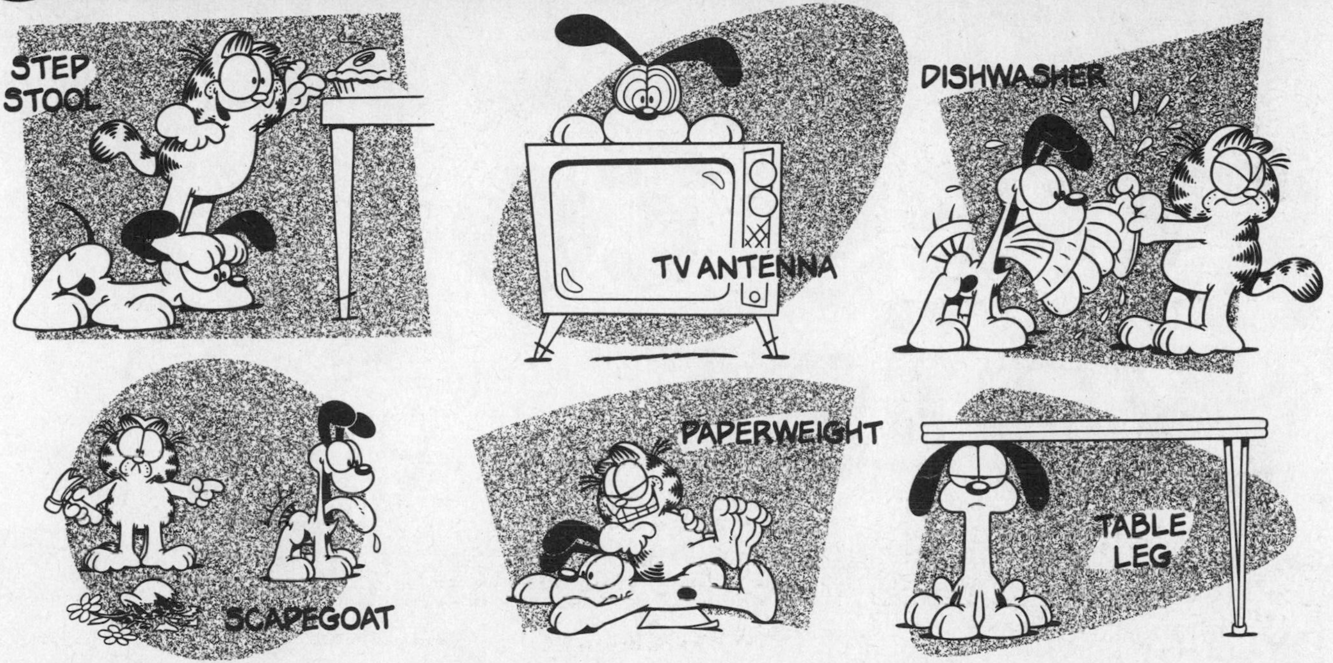
STEP STOOL
TV ANTENNA
DISHWASHER
SCAPEGOAT
PAPERWEIGHT
TABLE LEG

Garfield goes to waist

BY: JIM DAVIS

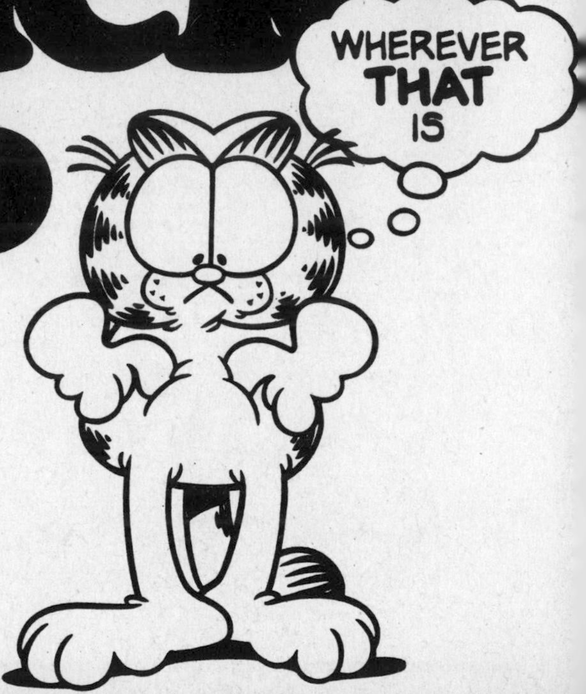
WHEREVER THAT IS

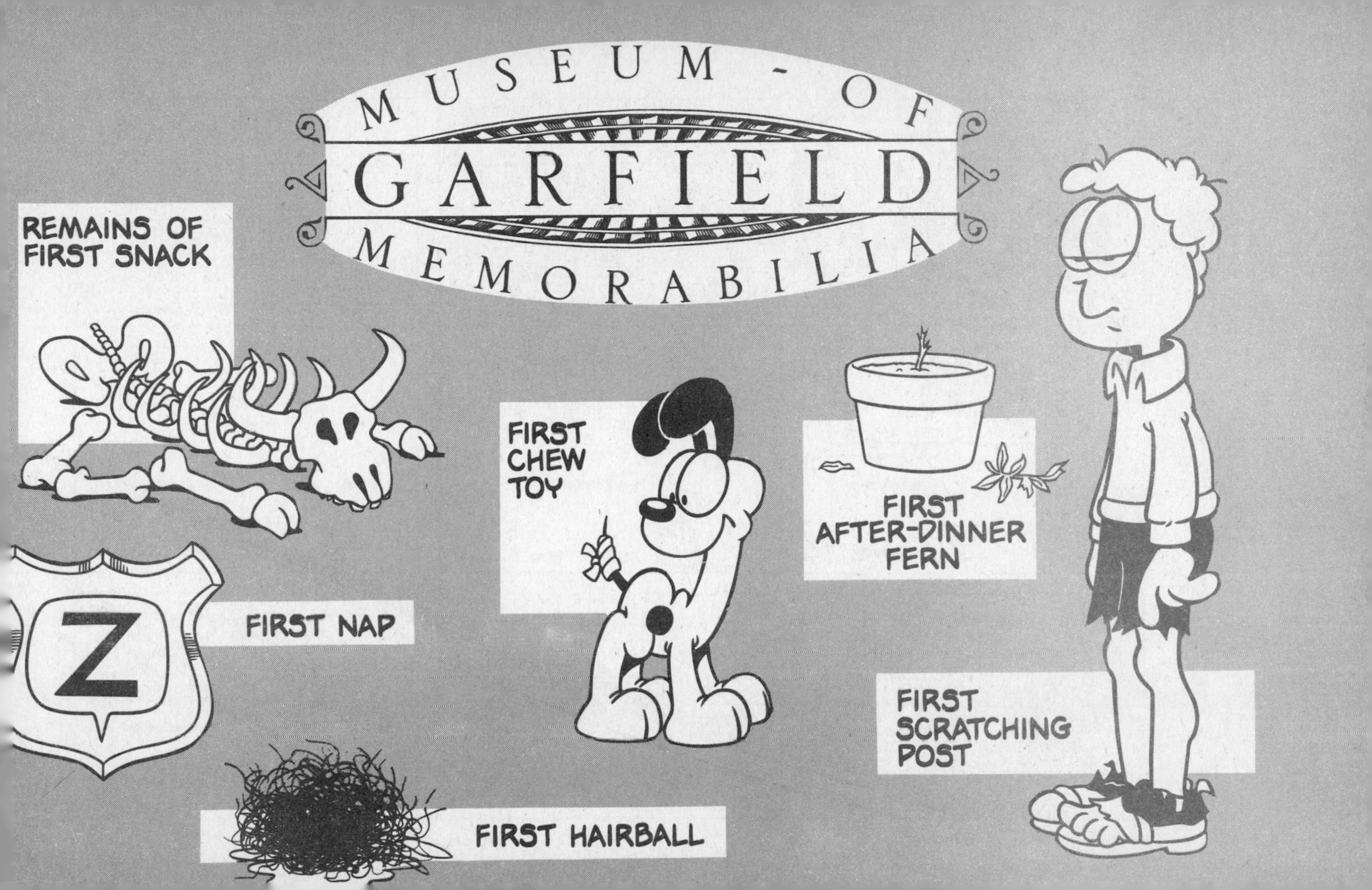
MUSEUM - OF
GARFIELD
MEMORABILIA
REMAINS OF FIRST SNACK
FIRST CHEW TOY
FIRST AFTER-DINNER FERN
Z
FIRST NAP
FIRST SCRATCHING POST
FIRST HAIRBALL

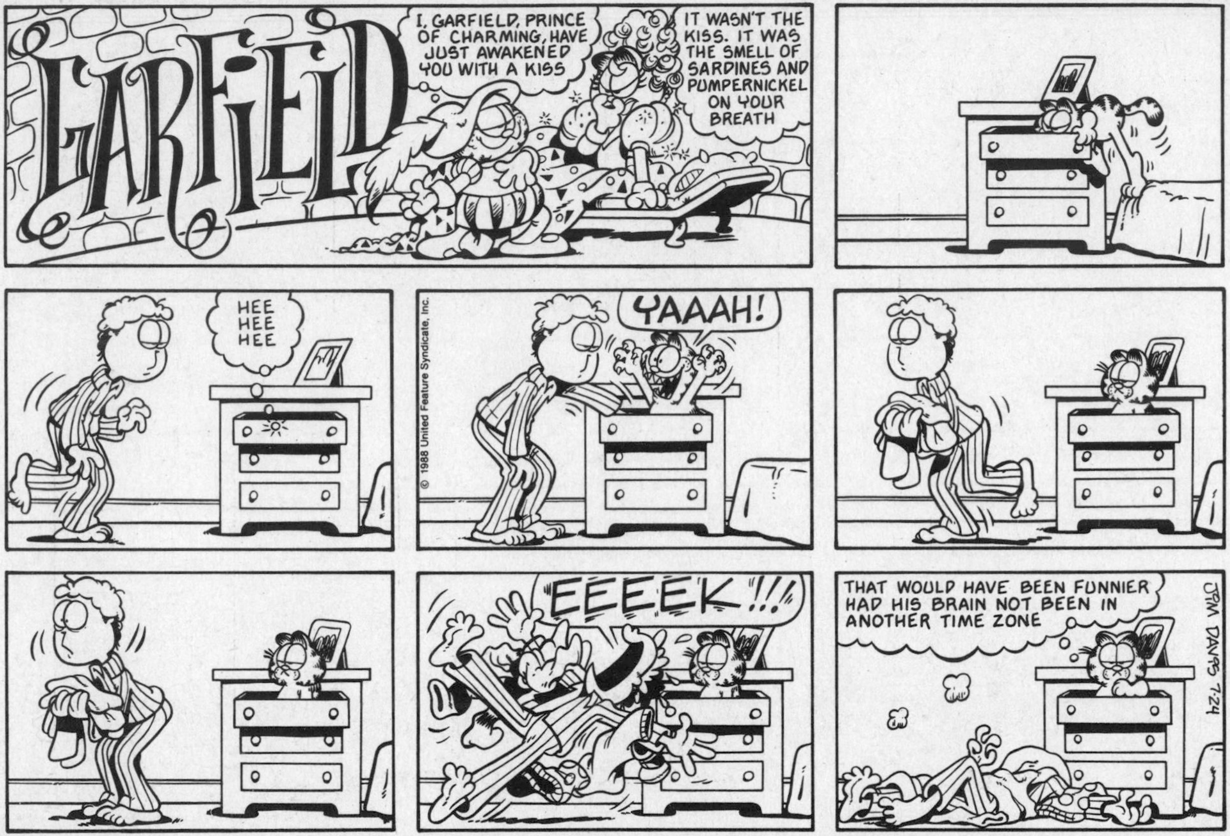
GARFIELD
I, GARFIELD, PRINCE OF CHARMING, HAVE JUST AWAKENED YOU WITH A KISS
IT WASN'T THE KISS. IT WAS THE SMELL OF SARDINES AND PUMPERNICKEL ON YOUR BREATH
HEE HEE HEE
© 1988 United Feature Syndicate, Inc.
YAAAH!
EEEEK!!!
THAT WOULD HAVE BEEN FUNNIER HAD HIS BRAIN NOT BEEN IN ANOTHER TIME ZONE
JPM DAVPS 7-24

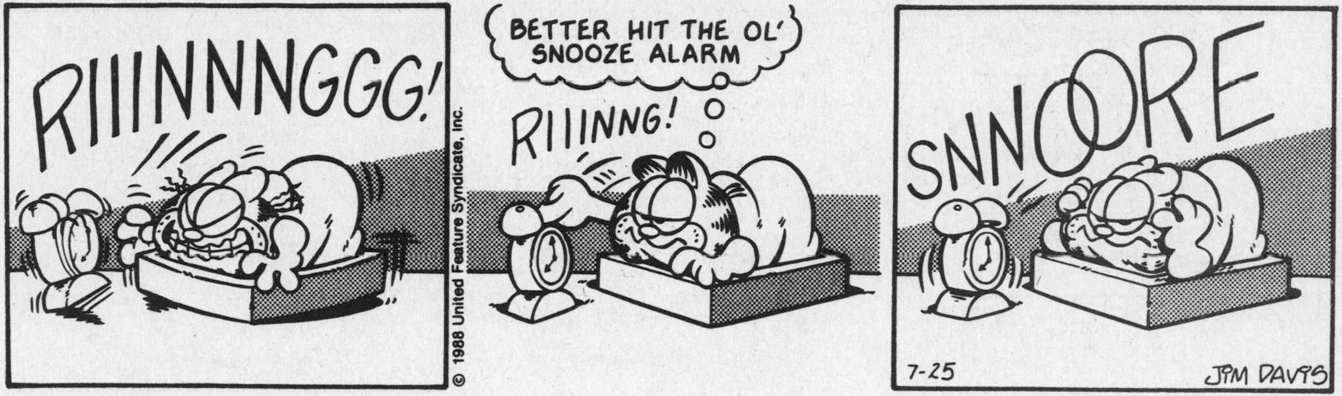
RIIINNNGGG!
BETTER HIT THE OL' SNOOZE ALARM
RIIINNG!
SNNOORE
© 1988 United Feature Syndicate, Inc.
7-25
JIM DAVIS

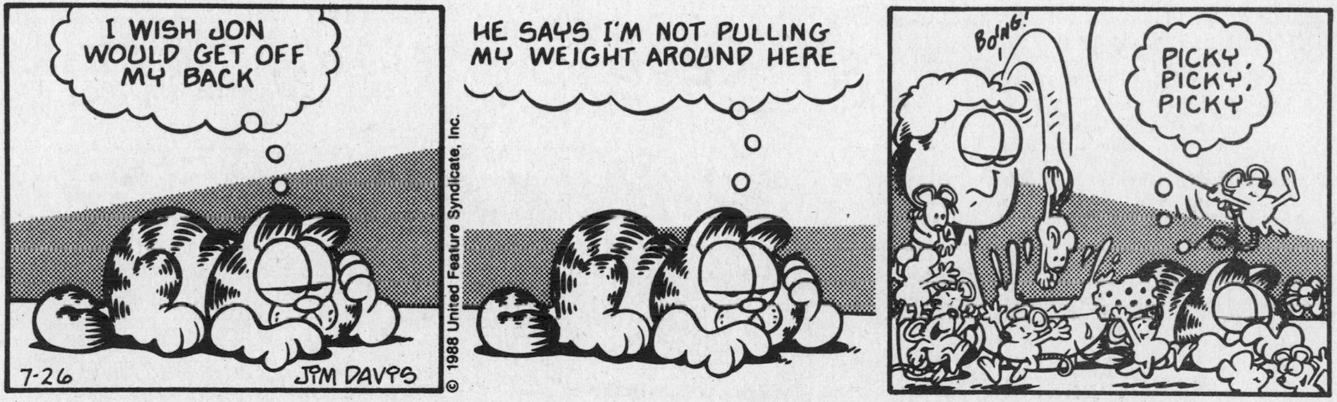
I WISH JON WOULD GET OFF MY BACK
HE SAYS I'M NOT PULLING MY WEIGHT AROUND HERE
BOING!
PICKY, PICKY, PICKY
© 1988 United Feature Syndicate, Inc.
7-26
JIM DAVIS

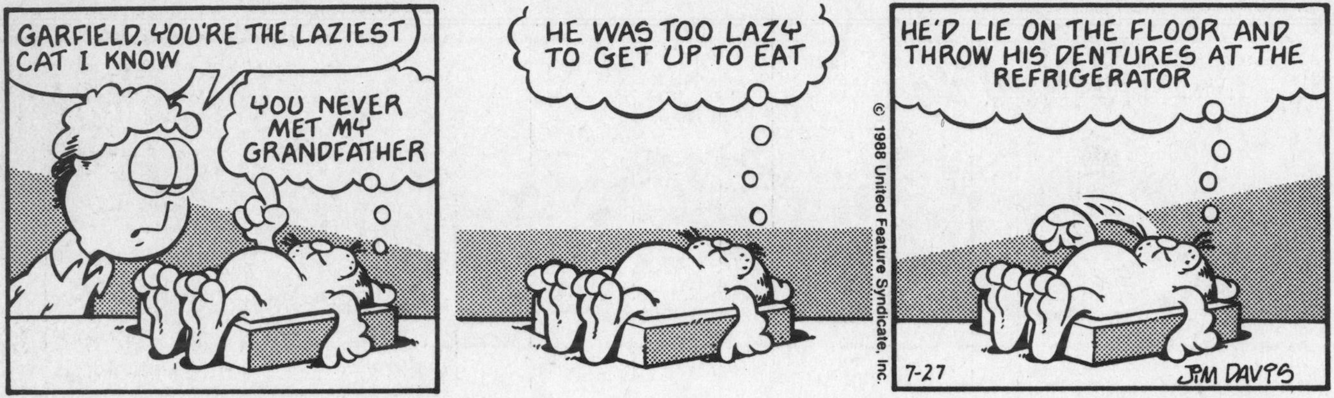
GARFIELD, YOU'RE THE LAZIEST CAT I KNOW
YOU NEVER MET MY GRANDFATHER
HE WAS TOO LAZY TO GET UP TO EAT
HE'D LIE ON THE FLOOR AND THROW HIS DENTURES AT THE REFRIGERATOR
© 1988 United Feature Syndicate, Inc.
7-27
JIM DAVIS

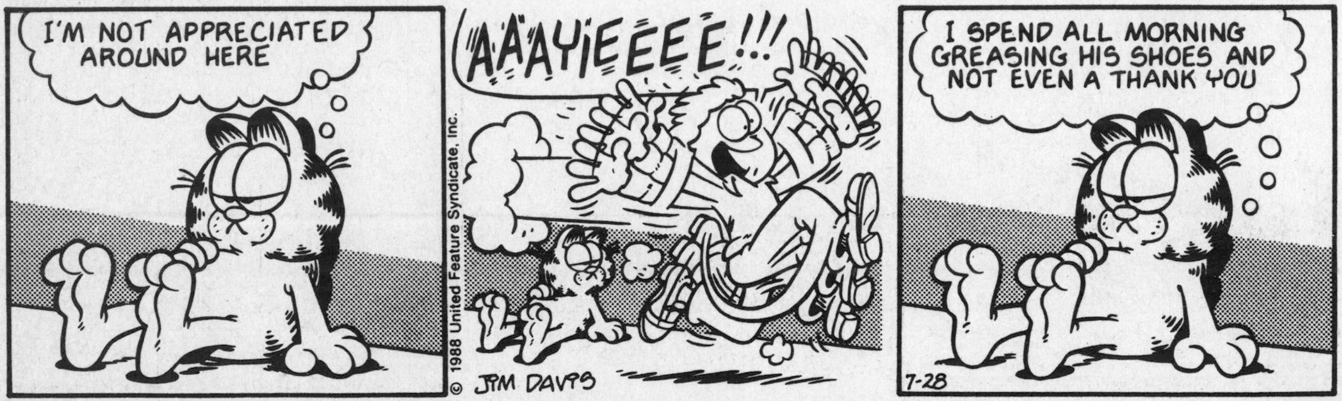
I'M NOT APPRECIATED AROUND HERE
AAAYIEEEEE!!!
© 1988 United Feature Syndicate, Inc.
JIM DAVIS
I SPEND ALL MORNING GREASING HIS SHOES AND NOT EVEN A THANK YOU
7-28

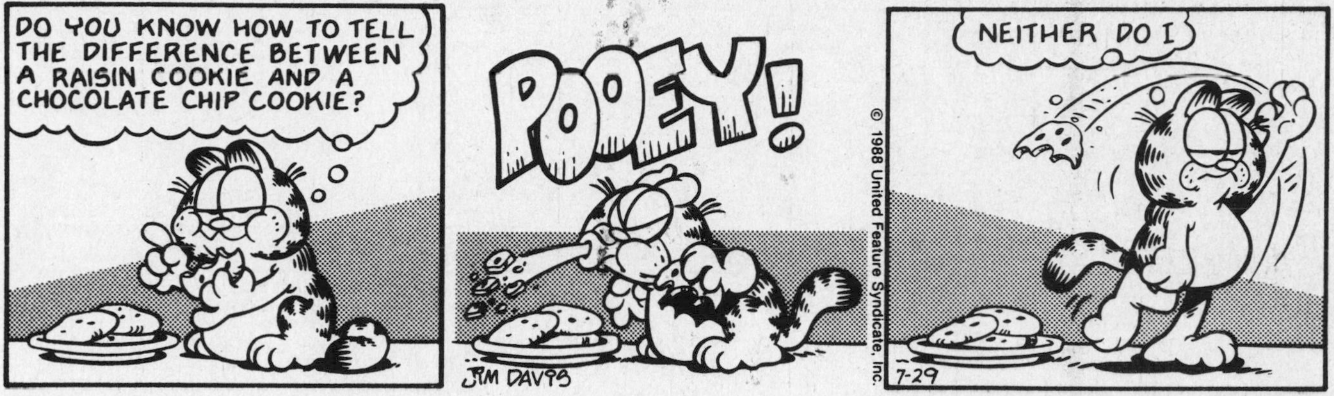
DO YOU KNOW HOW TO TELL THE DIFFERENCE BETWEEN A RAISIN COOKIE AND A CHOCOLATE CHIP COOKIE?
POOEY!
JIM DAVIS
© 1988 United Feature Syndicate, Inc.
NEITHER DO I
7-29

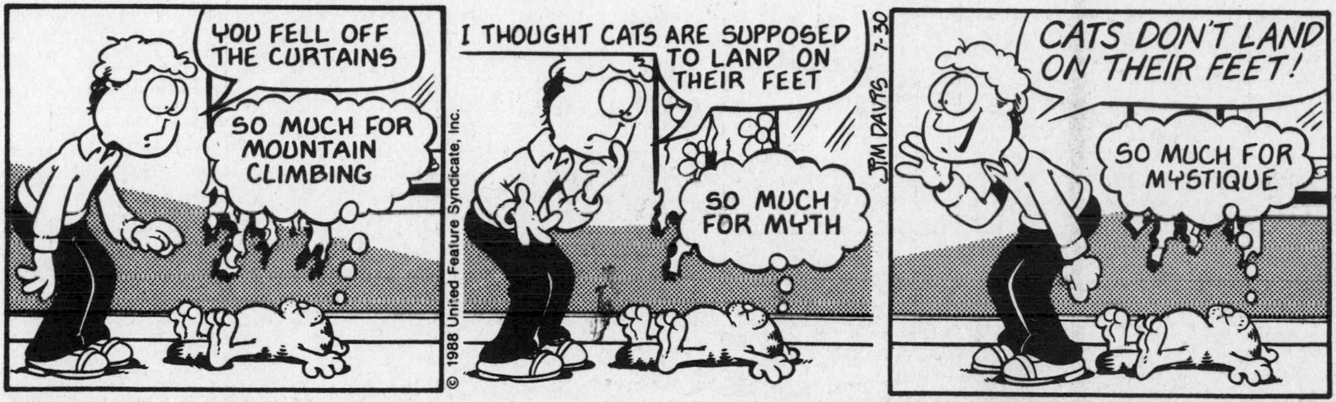
YOU FELL OFF THE CURTAINS
SO MUCH FOR MOUNTAIN CLIMBING
© 1988 United Feature Syndicate, Inc.
I THOUGHT CATS ARE SUPPOSED TO LAND ON THEIR FEET
SO MUCH FOR MYTH
JIM DAVIS 7-30
CATS DON'T LAND ON THEIR FEET!
SO MUCH FOR MYSTIQUE

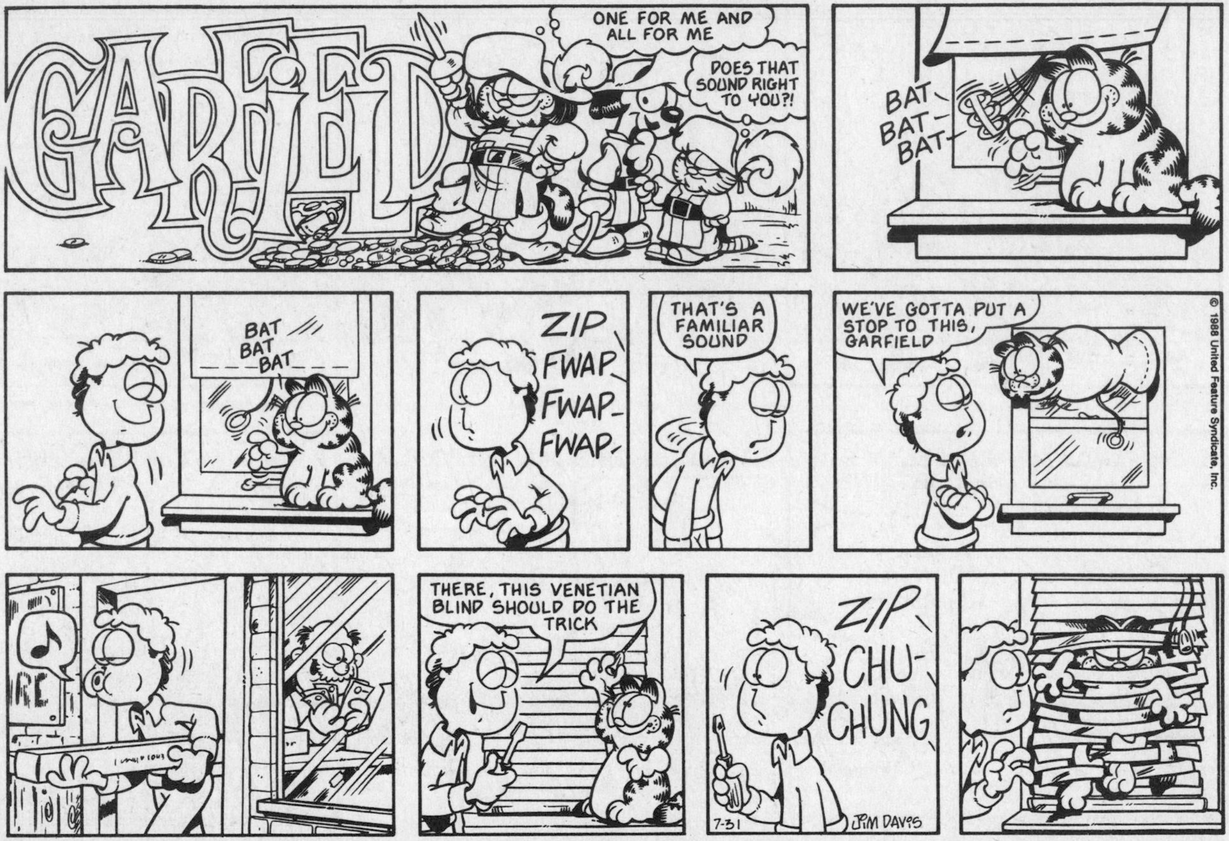
GARFIELD
ONE FOR ME AND ALL FOR ME
DOES THAT SOUND RIGHT TO YOU?!
BAT BAT BAT
BAT BAT BAT
ZIP FWAP FWAP FWAP
THAT'S A FAMILIAR SOUND
WE'VE GOTTA PUT A STOP TO THIS, GARFIELD
© 1988 United Feature Syndicate, Inc.
THERE, THIS VENETIAN BLIND SHOULD DO THE TRICK
ZIP CHU-CHUNG
7-31
JIM DAVIS

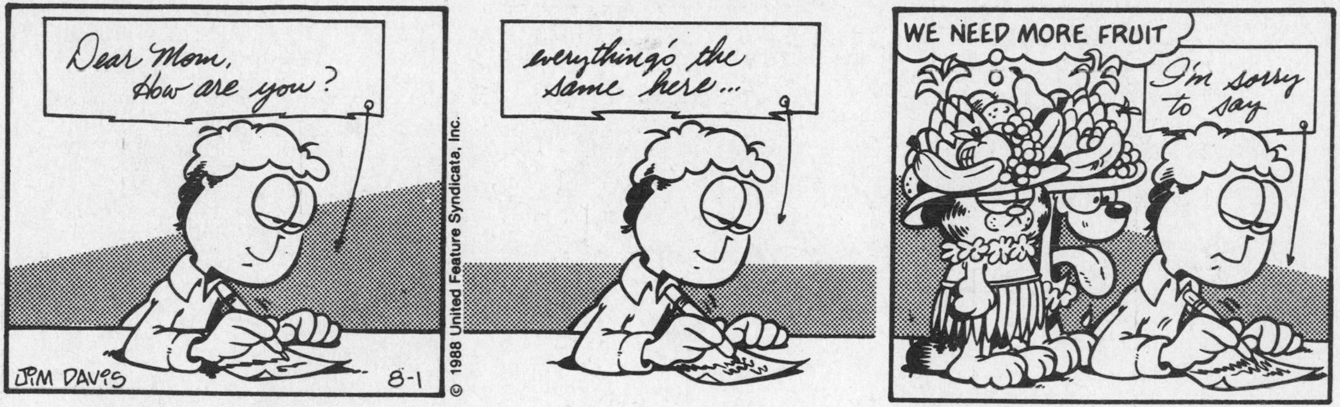
Dear Mom,
How are you?
everything's the same here...
WE NEED MORE FRUIT
I'm sorry to say
JIM DAVIS 8-1
© 1988 United Feature Syndicate, Inc.

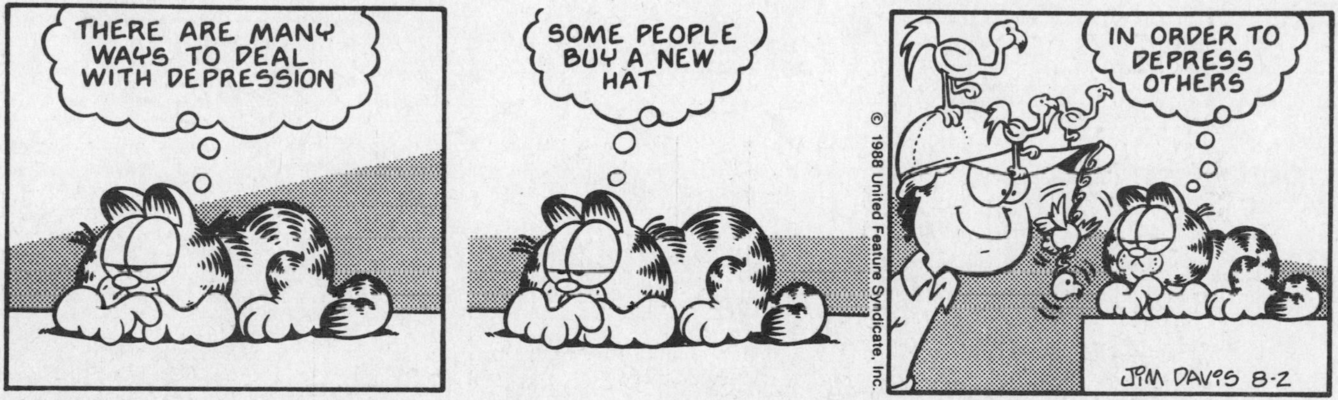
THERE ARE MANY WAYS TO DEAL WITH DEPRESSION
SOME PEOPLE BUY A NEW HAT
IN ORDER TO DEPRESS OTHERS
JIM DAVIS 8-2
© 1988 United Feature Syndicate, Inc.

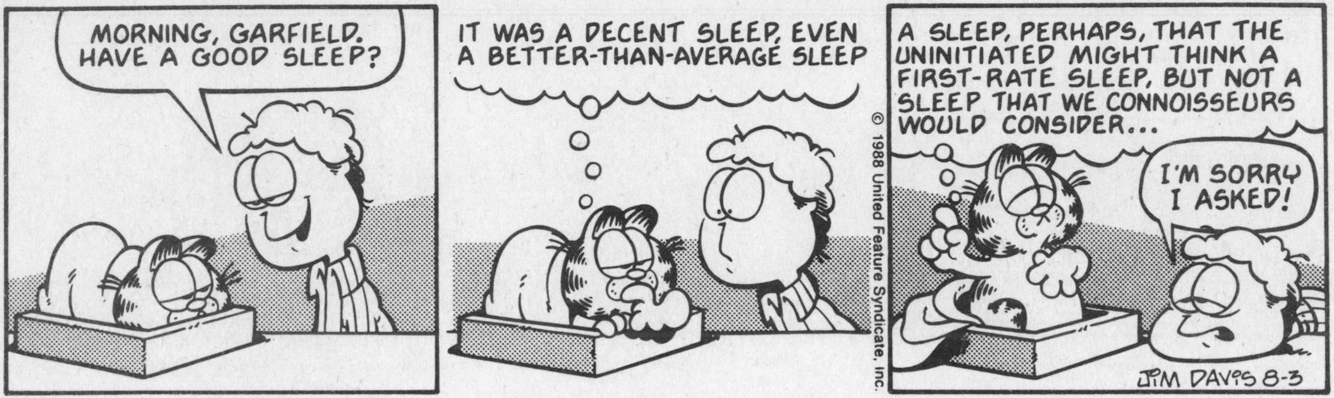
MORNING, GARFIELD. HAVE A GOOD SLEEP?
IT WAS A DECENT SLEEP, EVEN A BETTER-THAN-AVERAGE SLEEP
A SLEEP, PERHAPS, THAT THE UNINITIATED MIGHT THINK A FIRST-RATE SLEEP, BUT NOT A SLEEP THAT WE CONNOISSEURS WOULD CONSIDER...
I'M SORRY I ASKED!
JIM DAVIS 8-3
© 1988 United Feature Syndicate, Inc.

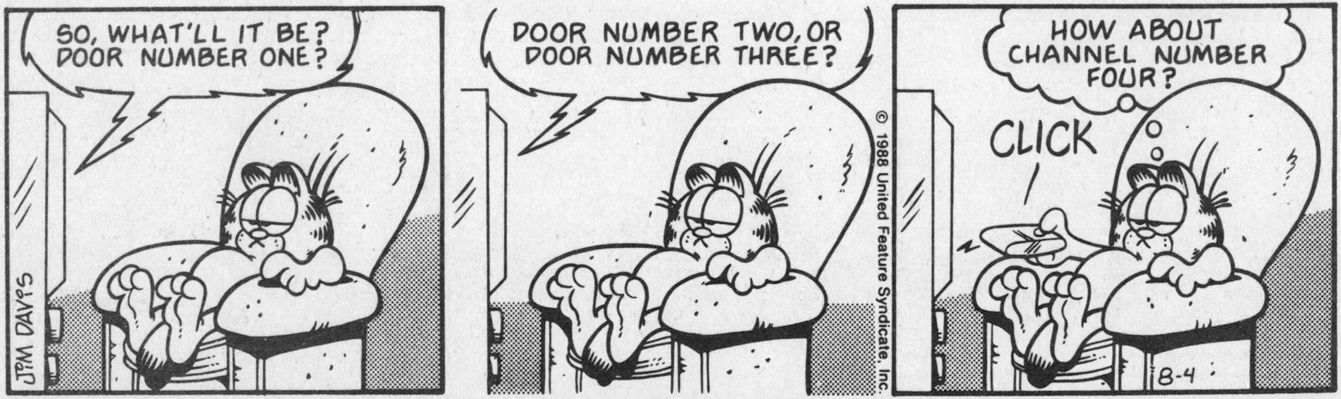
SO, WHAT'LL IT BE? DOOR NUMBER ONE?
JIM DAVIS
DOOR NUMBER TWO, OR DOOR NUMBER THREE?
HOW ABOUT CHANNEL NUMBER FOUR?
CLICK
8-4
© 1988 United Feature Syndicate, Inc.

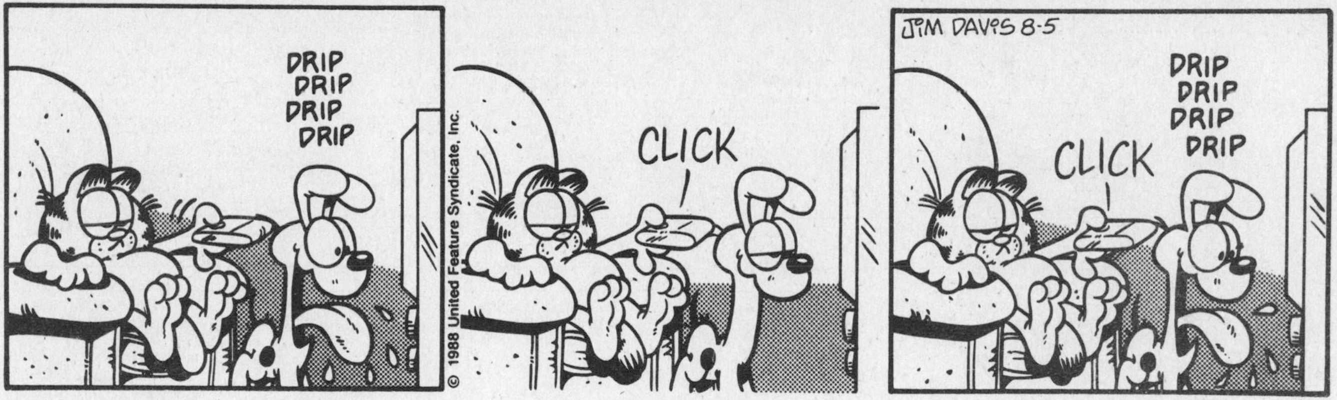
DRIP DRIP DRIP DRIP
© 1988 United Feature Syndicate, Inc.
CLICK
JIM DAVIS 8-5
CLICK
DRIP DRIP DRIP DRIP

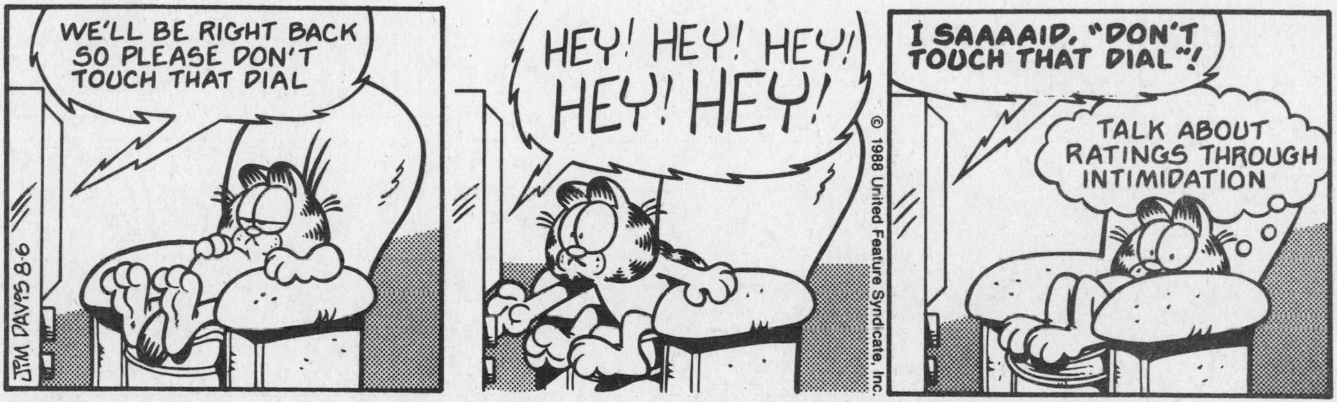
WE'LL BE RIGHT BACK SO PLEASE DON'T TOUCH THAT DIAL
JIM DAVIS 8-6
HEY! HEY! HEY! HEY! HEY!
© 1988 United Feature Syndicate, Inc.
I SAAAAID. "DON'T TOUCH THAT DIAL"!
TALK ABOUT RATINGS THROUGH INTIMIDATION

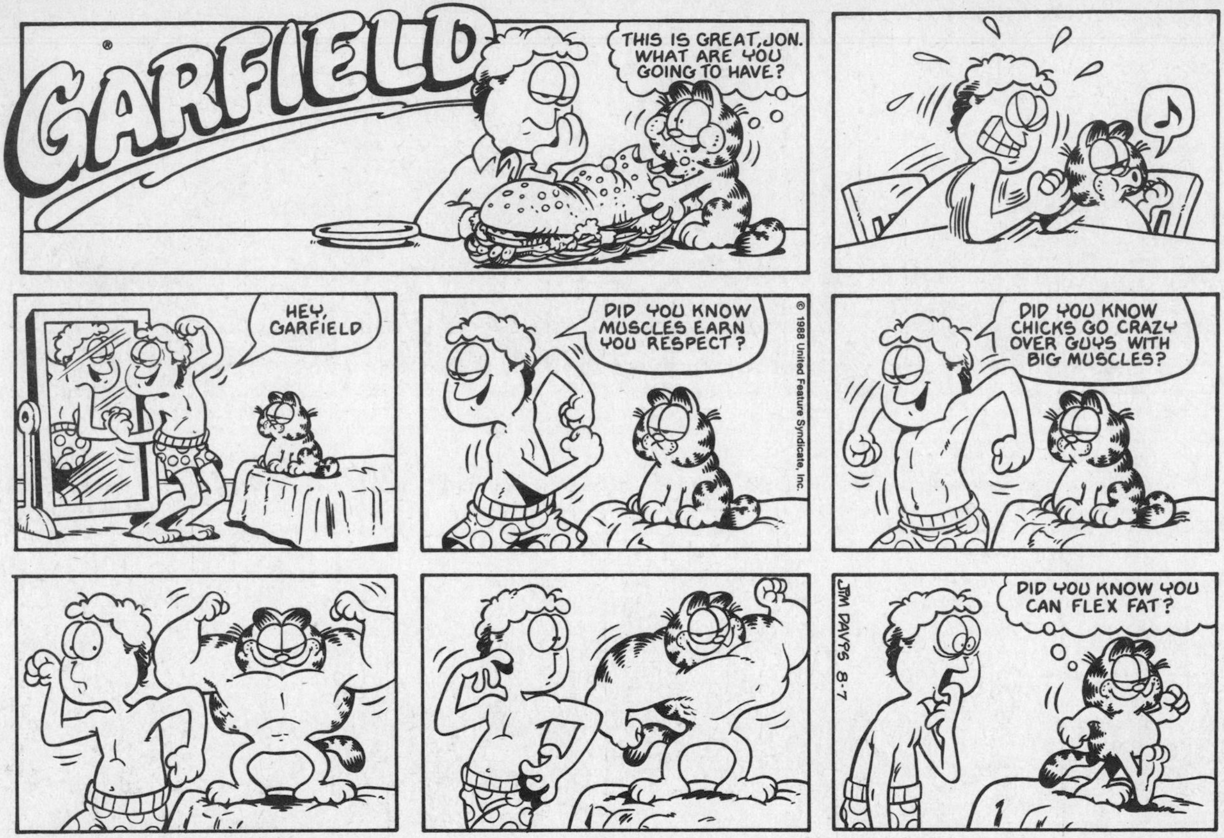
GARFIELD®
THIS IS GREAT, JON. WHAT ARE YOU GOING TO HAVE?
♪
HEY, GARFIELD
DID YOU KNOW MUSCLES EARN YOU RESPECT?
© 1988 United Feature Syndicate, Inc.
DID YOU KNOW CHICKS GO CRAZY OVER GUYS WITH BIG MUSCLES?
JIM DAVIS 8-7
DID YOU KNOW YOU CAN FLEX FAT?

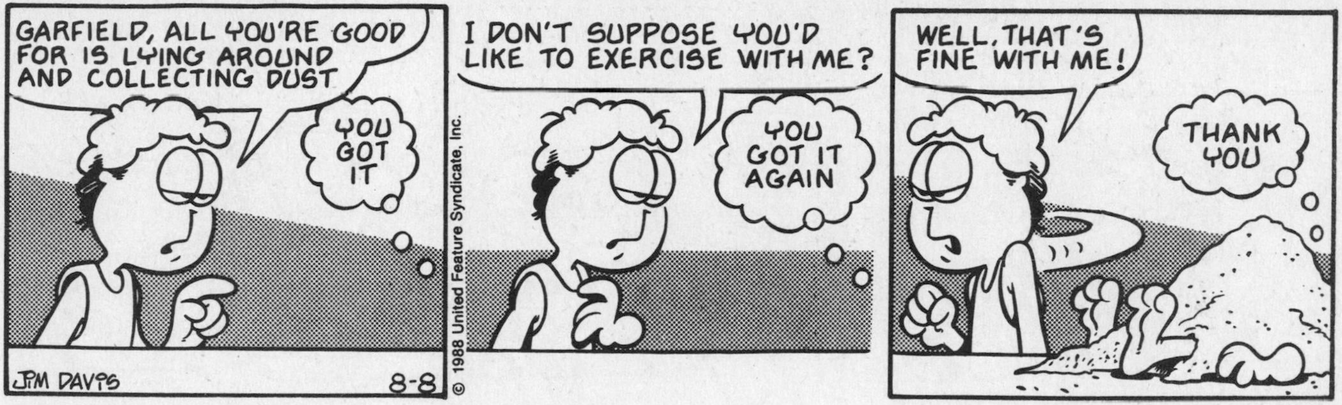
GARFIELD, ALL YOU'RE GOOD FOR IS LYING AROUND AND COLLECTING DUST
YOU GOT IT
JIM DAVIS
8-8
© 1988 United Feature Syndicate, Inc.
I DON'T SUPPOSE YOU'D LIKE TO EXERCISE WITH ME?
YOU GOT IT AGAIN
WELL, THAT'S FINE WITH ME!
THANK YOU

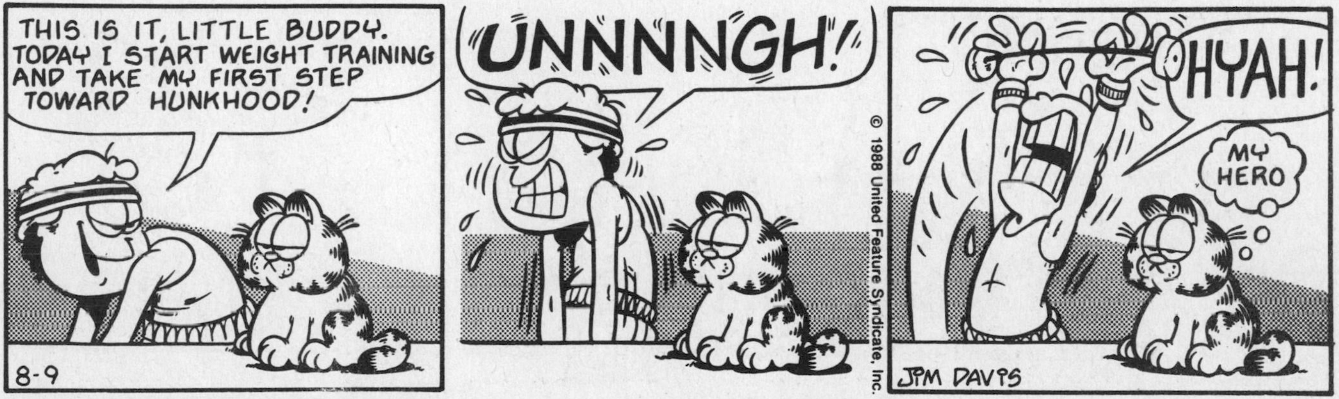
THIS IS IT, LITTLE BUDDY. TODAY I START WEIGHT TRAINING AND TAKE MY FIRST STEP TOWARD HUNKHOOD!
8-9
UNNNNGH!
© 1988 United Feature Syndicate, Inc.
HYAH!
MY HERO
JIM DAVIS

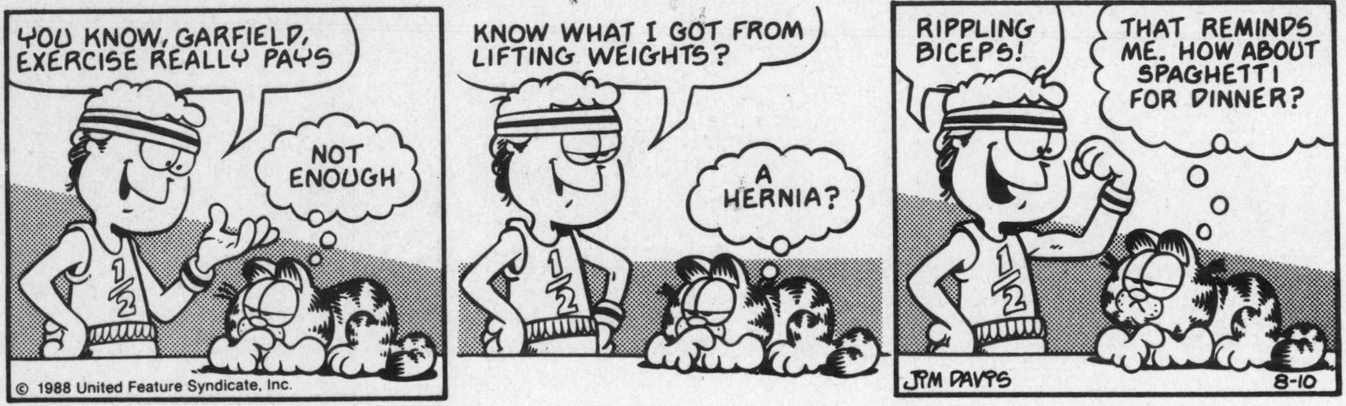
YOU KNOW, GARFIELD, EXERCISE REALLY PAYS
NOT ENOUGH
KNOW WHAT I GOT FROM LIFTING WEIGHTS?
A HERNIA?
RIPPLING BICEPS!
THAT REMINDS ME. HOW ABOUT SPAGHETTI FOR DINNER?
© 1988 United Feature Syndicate, Inc.
JIM DAVIS
8-10

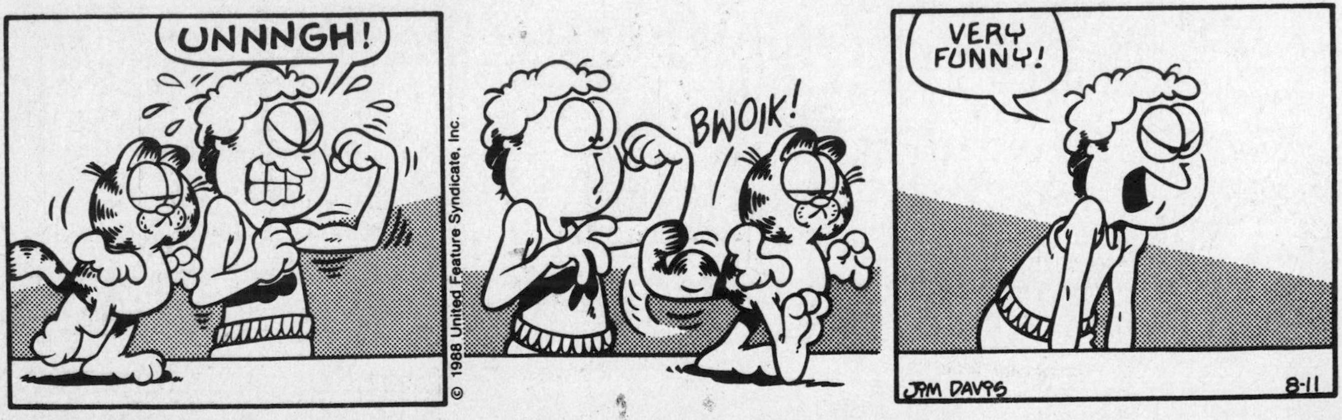
UNNNGH!
BWOIK!
VERY FUNNY!
© 1988 United Feature Syndicate, Inc.
JIM DAVIS
8-11

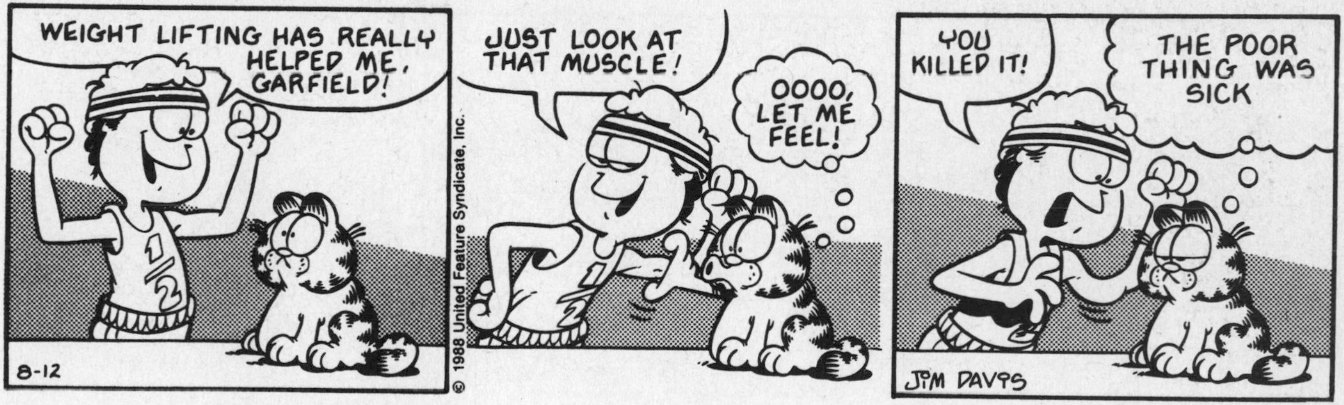

WEIGHT LIFTING HAS REALLY HELPED ME, GARFIELD!
JUST LOOK AT THAT MUSCLE!
OOOO, LET ME FEEL!
YOU KILLED IT!
THE POOR THING WAS SICK
8-12
© 1988 United Feature Syndicate, Inc.
JIM DAVIS

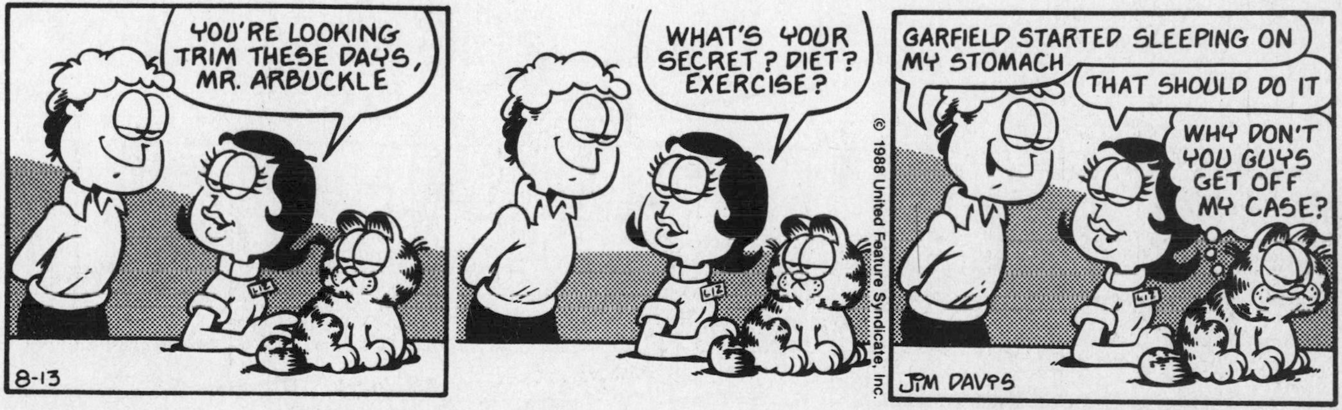

YOU'RE LOOKING TRIM THESE DAYS, MR. ARBUCKLE
WHAT'S YOUR SECRET? DIET? EXERCISE?
GARFIELD STARTED SLEEPING ON MY STOMACH
THAT SHOULD DO IT
WHY DON'T YOU GUYS GET OFF MY CASE?
8-13
© 1988 United Feature Syndicate, Inc.
JIM DAVIS

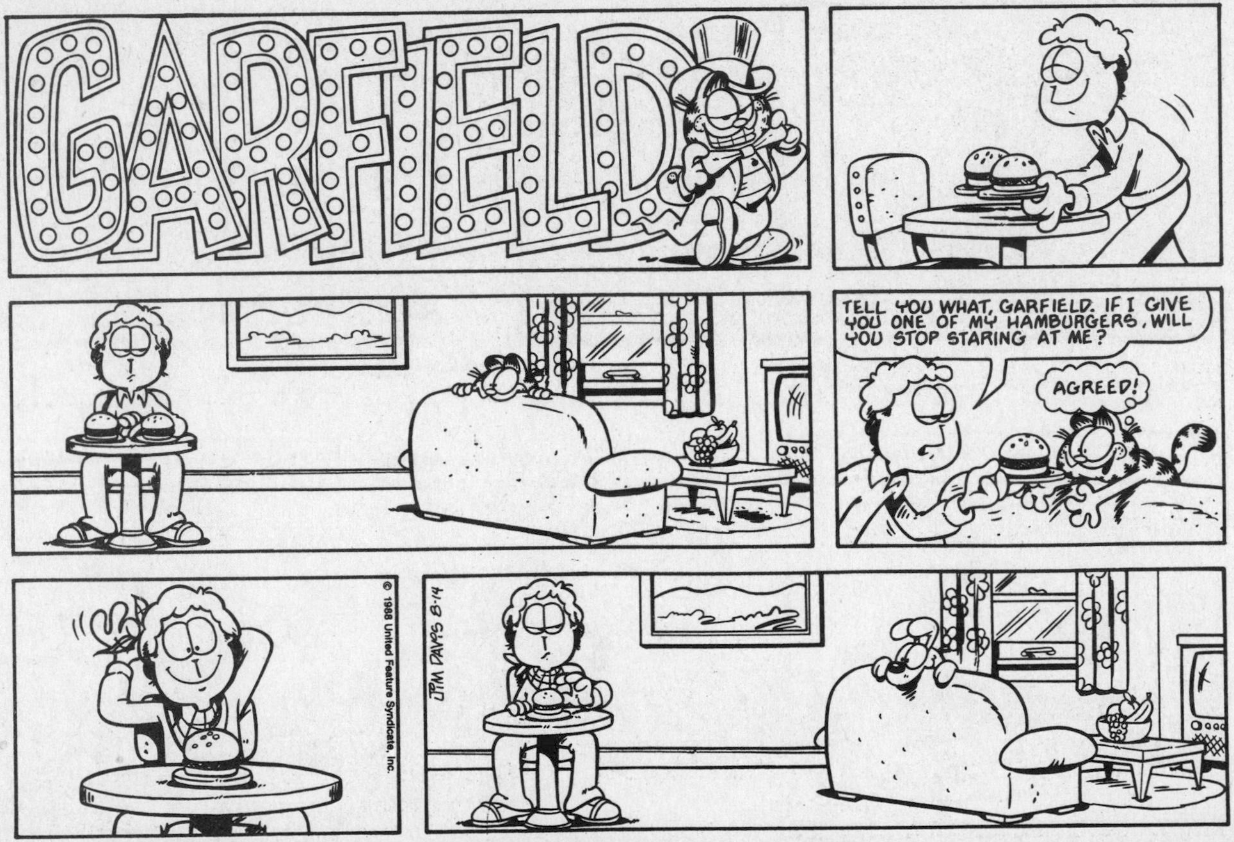
GARFIELD
TELL YOU WHAT, GARFIELD. IF I GIVE YOU ONE OF MY HAMBURGERS, WILL YOU STOP STARING AT ME?
AGREED!
JPM DAVPS 8-14
© 1988 United Feature Syndicate, Inc.

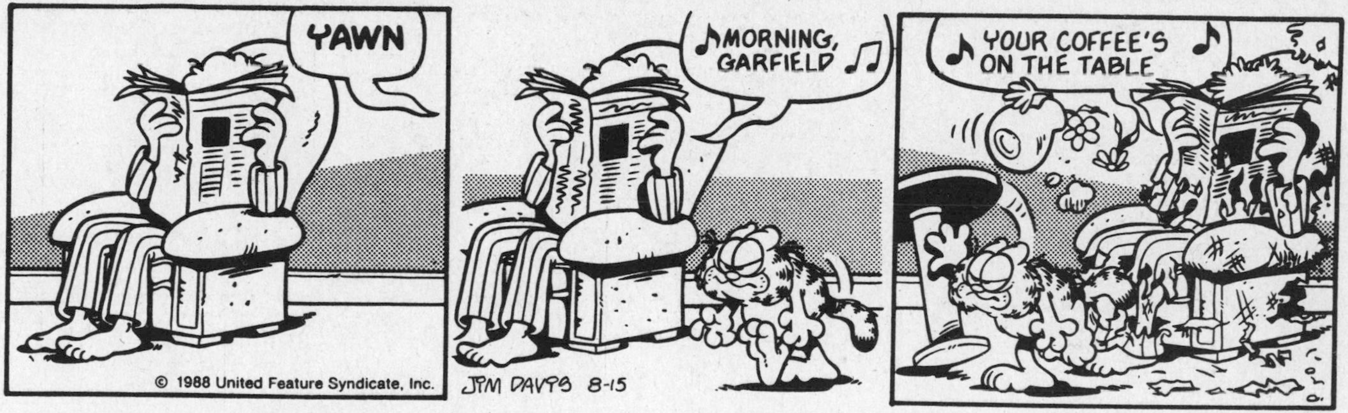
YAWN
MORNING, GARFIELD
YOUR COFFEE'S ON THE TABLE
© 1988 United Feature Syndicate, Inc.
JIM DAVIS 8-15

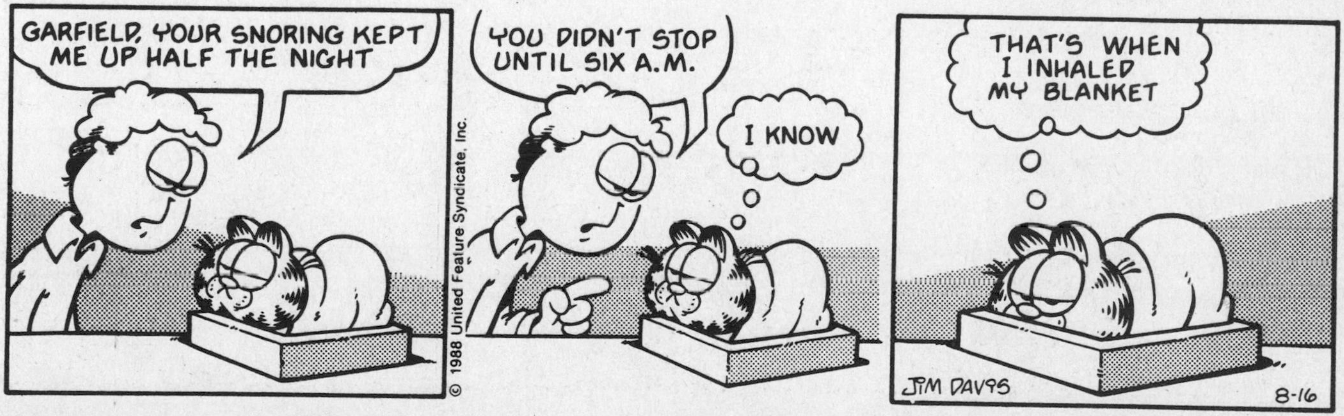
GARFIELD, YOUR SNORING KEPT ME UP HALF THE NIGHT
YOU DIDN'T STOP UNTIL SIX A.M.
I KNOW
THAT'S WHEN I INHALED MY BLANKET
© 1988 United Feature Syndicate, Inc.
JIM DAVIS
8-16

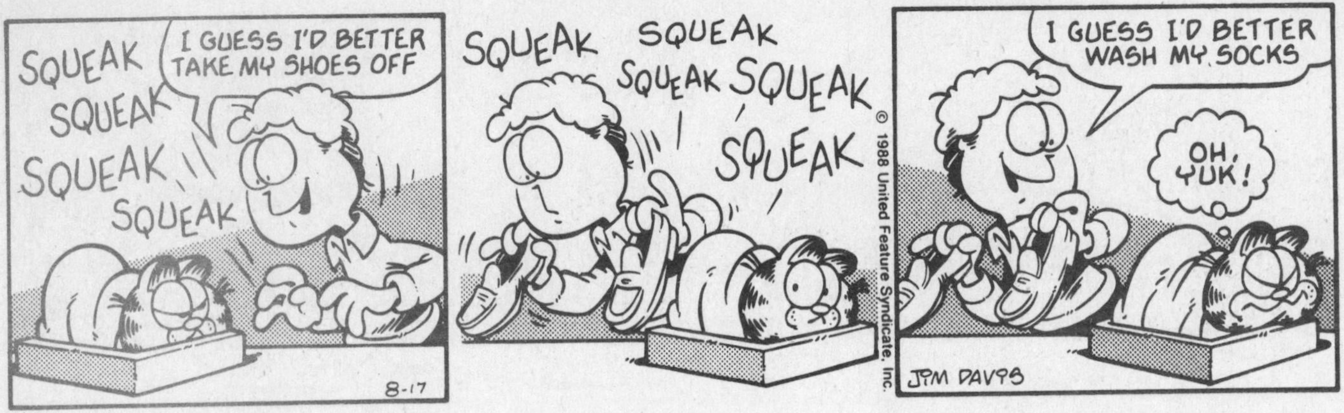
SQUEAK
SQUEAK
SQUEAK
SQUEAK
I GUESS I'D BETTER TAKE MY SHOES OFF
8-17
SQUEAK
SQUEAK
SQUEAK
SQUEAK
SQUEAK
© 1988 United Feature Syndicate, Inc.
I GUESS I'D BETTER WASH MY SOCKS
OH, YUK!
JIM DAVIS

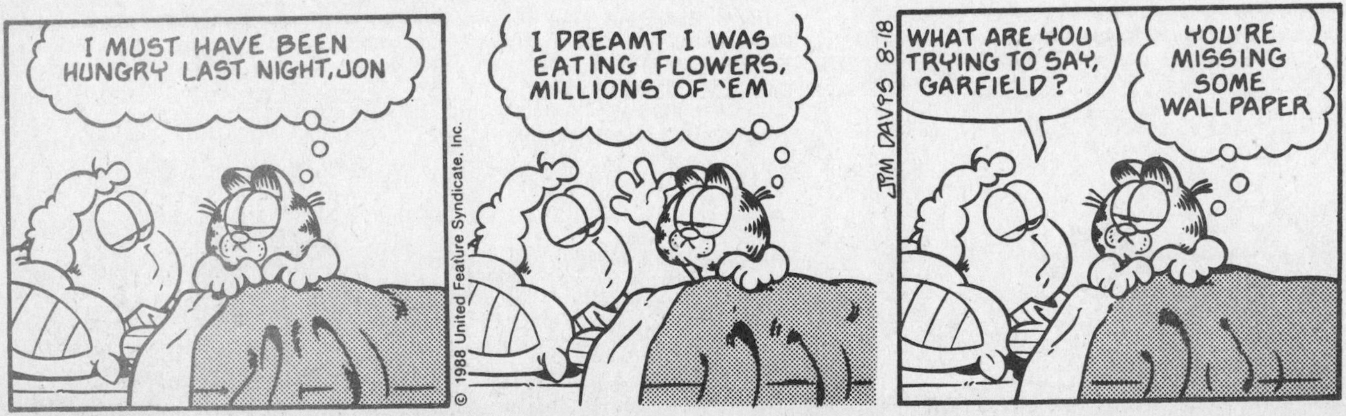
I MUST HAVE BEEN HUNGRY LAST NIGHT, JON
© 1988 United Feature Syndicate, Inc.
I DREAMT I WAS EATING FLOWERS, MILLIONS OF 'EM
JIM DAVIS 8-18
WHAT ARE YOU TRYING TO SAY, GARFIELD?
YOU'RE MISSING SOME WALLPAPER

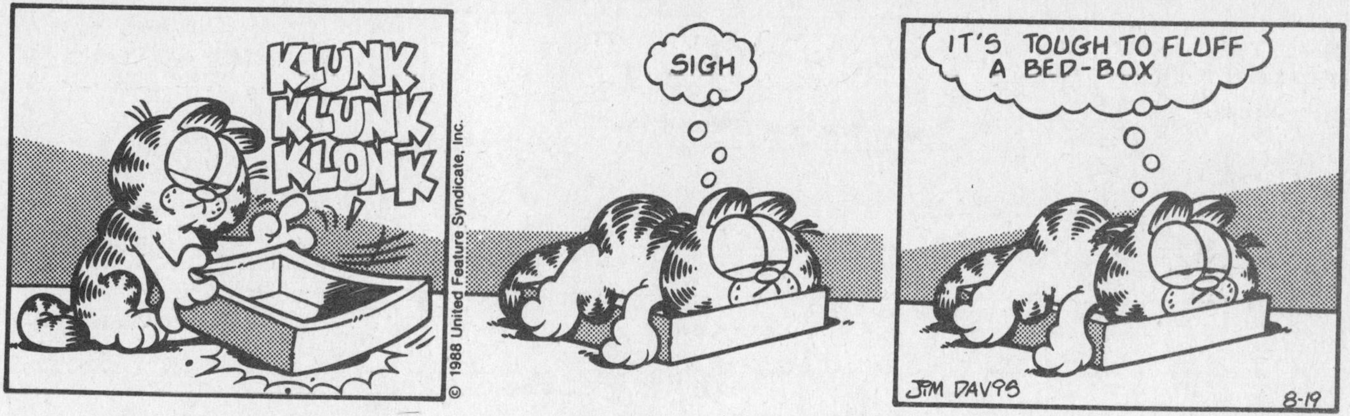
KLUNK
KLUNK
KLONK
© 1988 United Feature Syndicate, Inc.
SIGH
IT'S TOUGH TO FLUFF A BED-BOX
JIM DAVIS
8-19

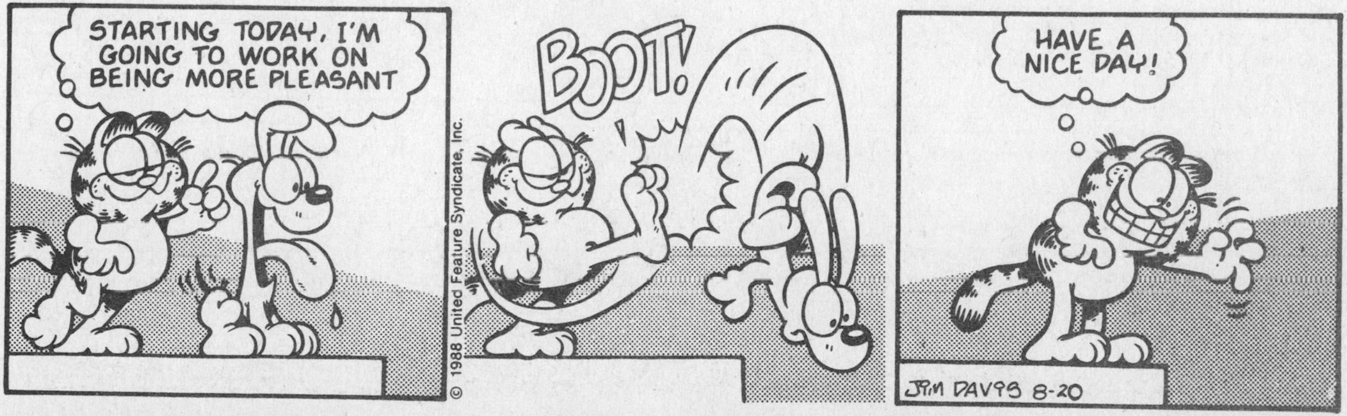
STARTING TODAY, I'M GOING TO WORK ON BEING MORE PLEASANT
© 1988 United Feature Syndicate, Inc.
BOOT!
HAVE A NICE DAY!
JIM DAVIS 8-20

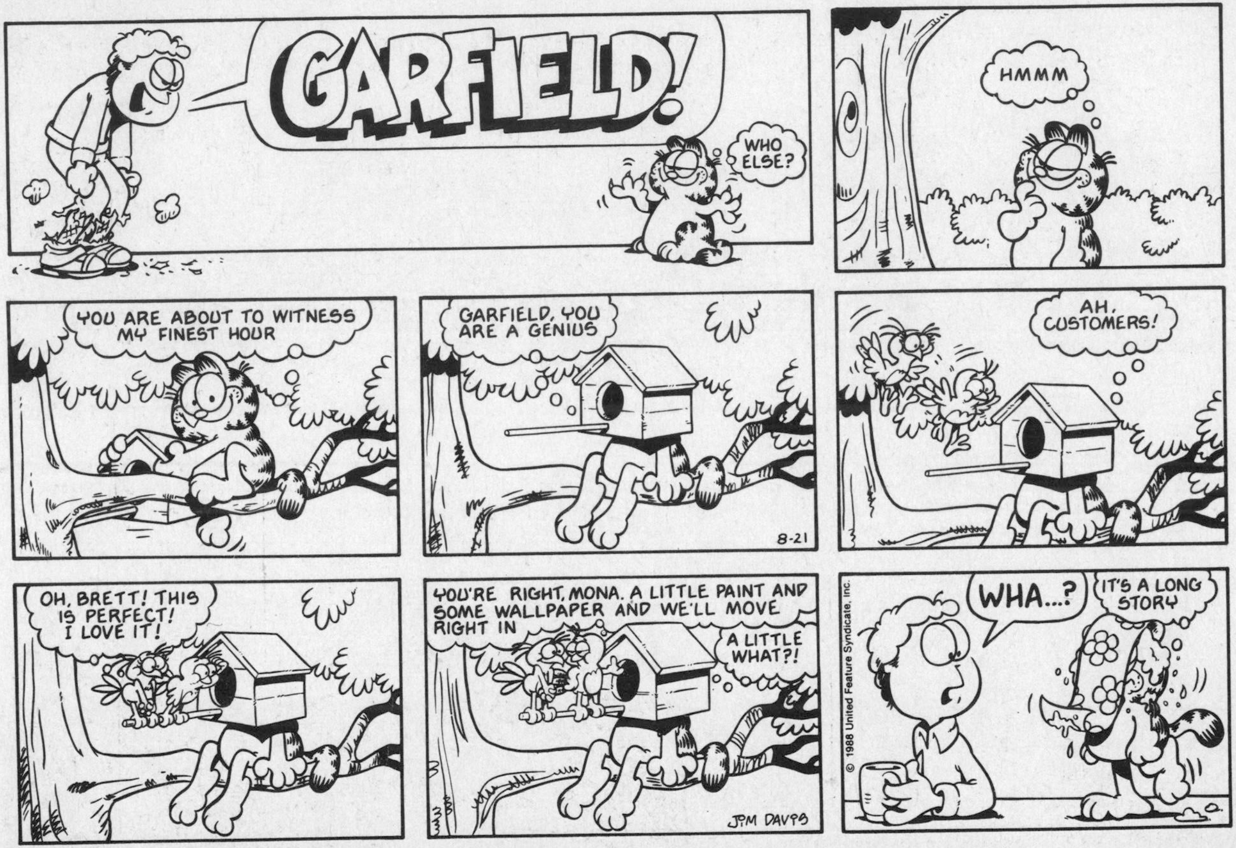
GARFIELD!
WHO ELSE?
HMMM
YOU ARE ABOUT TO WITNESS MY FINEST HOUR
GARFIELD, YOU ARE A GENIUS
8-21
AH, CUSTOMERS!
OH, BRETT! THIS IS PERFECT! I LOVE IT!
YOU'RE RIGHT, MONA. A LITTLE PAINT AND SOME WALLPAPER AND WE'LL MOVE RIGHT IN
A LITTLE WHAT?!
JIM DAVIS
© 1988 United Feature Syndicate, Inc.
WHA...?
IT'S A LONG STORY

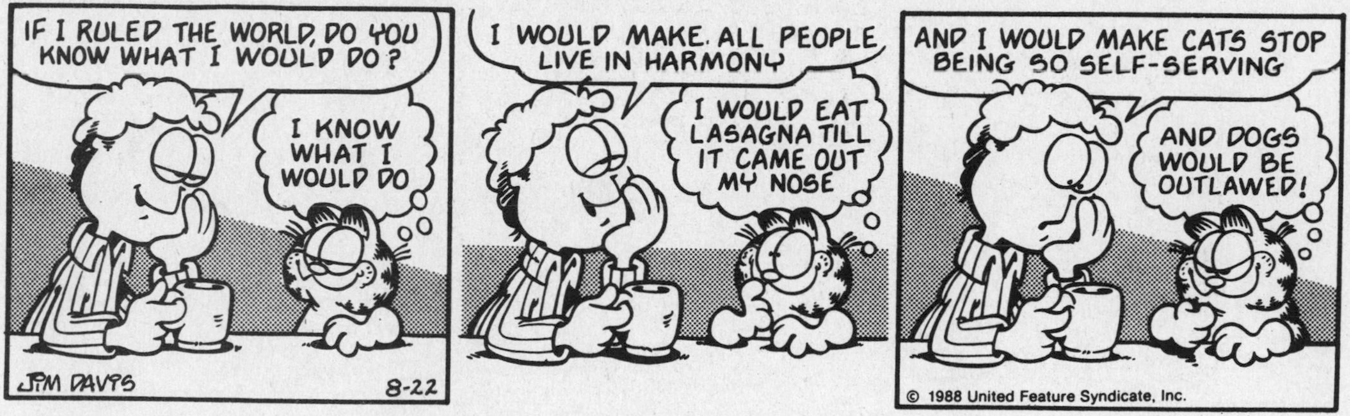
IF I RULED THE WORLD, DO YOU KNOW WHAT I WOULD DO?
I KNOW WHAT I WOULD DO
JIM DAVIS
8-22
I WOULD MAKE ALL PEOPLE LIVE IN HARMONY
I WOULD EAT LASAGNA TILL IT CAME OUT MY NOSE
AND I WOULD MAKE CATS STOP BEING SO SELF-SERVING
AND DOGS WOULD BE OUTLAWED!
© 1988 United Feature Syndicate, Inc.

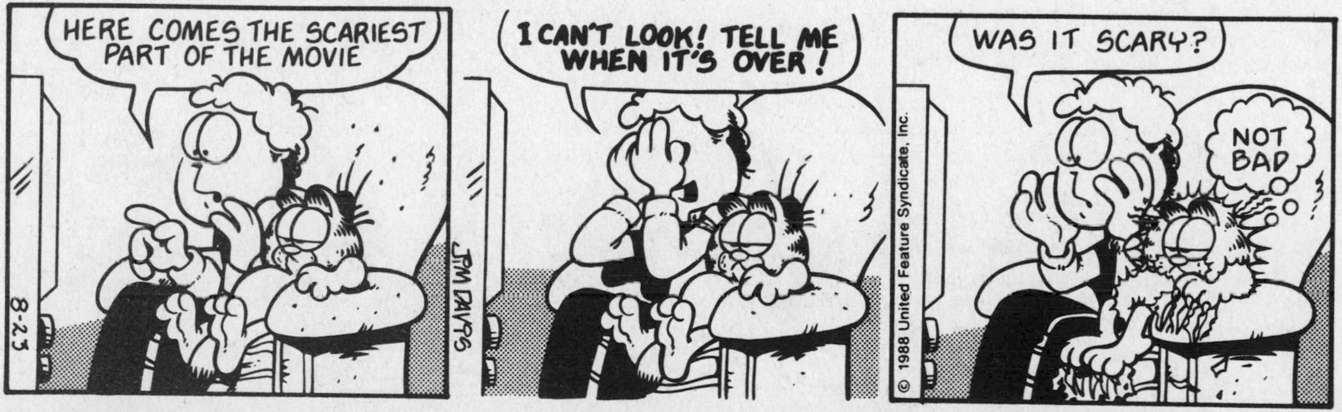
HERE COMES THE SCARIEST PART OF THE MOVIE
8-23
JIM DAVIS
I CAN'T LOOK! TELL ME WHEN IT'S OVER!
WAS IT SCARY?
NOT BAD
© 1988 United Feature Syndicate, Inc.

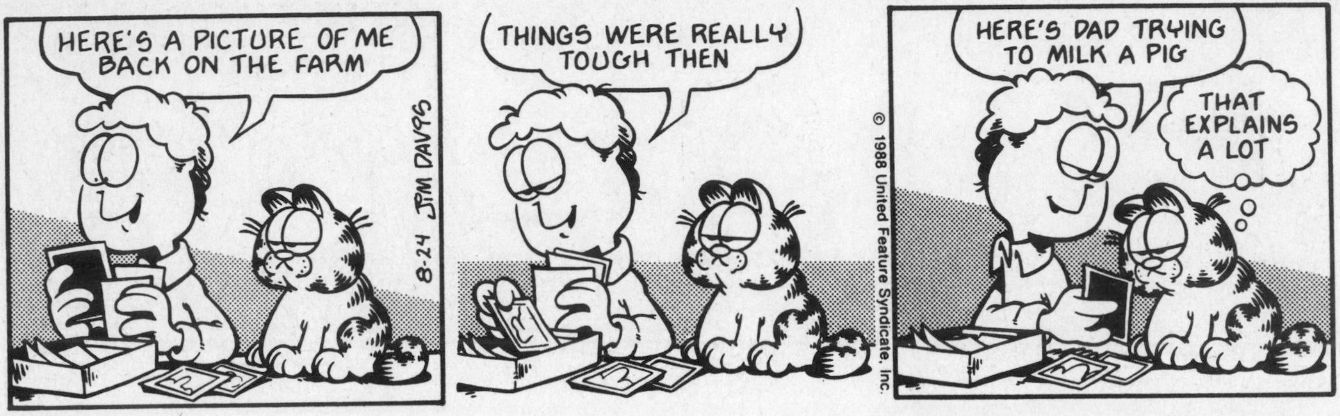
HERE'S A PICTURE OF ME BACK ON THE FARM
JIM DAVIS 8-24
THINGS WERE REALLY TOUGH THEN
© 1988 United Feature Syndicate, Inc.
HERE'S DAD TRYING TO MILK A PIG
THAT EXPLAINS A LOT

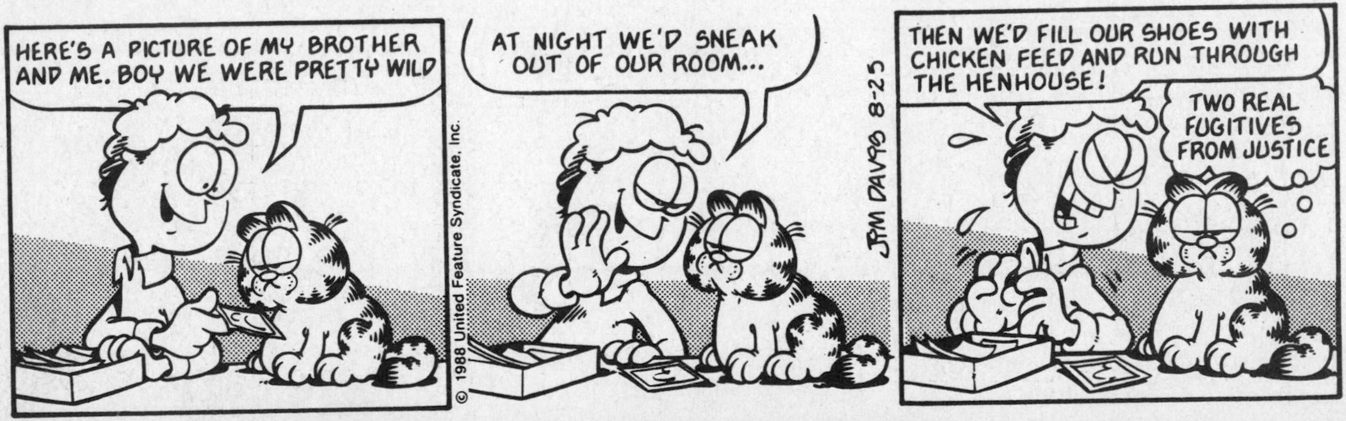
HERE'S A PICTURE OF MY BROTHER AND ME. BOY WE WERE PRETTY WILD
© 1988 United Feature Syndicate, Inc.
AT NIGHT WE'D SNEAK OUT OF OUR ROOM...
JIM DAVIS 8-25
THEN WE'D FILL OUR SHOES WITH CHICKEN FEED AND RUN THROUGH THE HENHOUSE!
TWO REAL FUGITIVES FROM JUSTICE

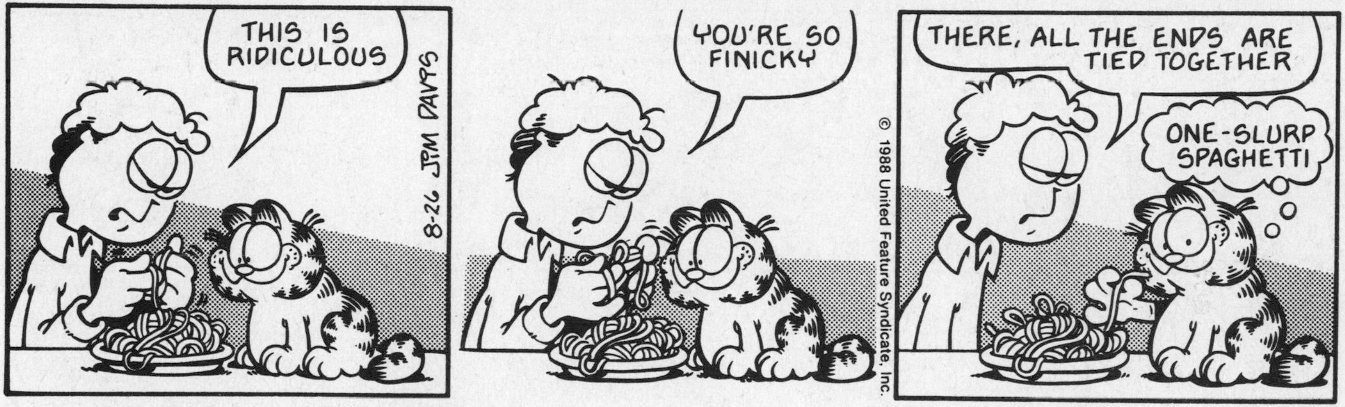
THIS IS RIDICULOUS
JIM DAVIS 8-26
YOU'RE SO FINICKY
© 1988 United Feature Syndicate, Inc.
THERE, ALL THE ENDS ARE TIED TOGETHER
ONE-SLURP SPAGHETTI

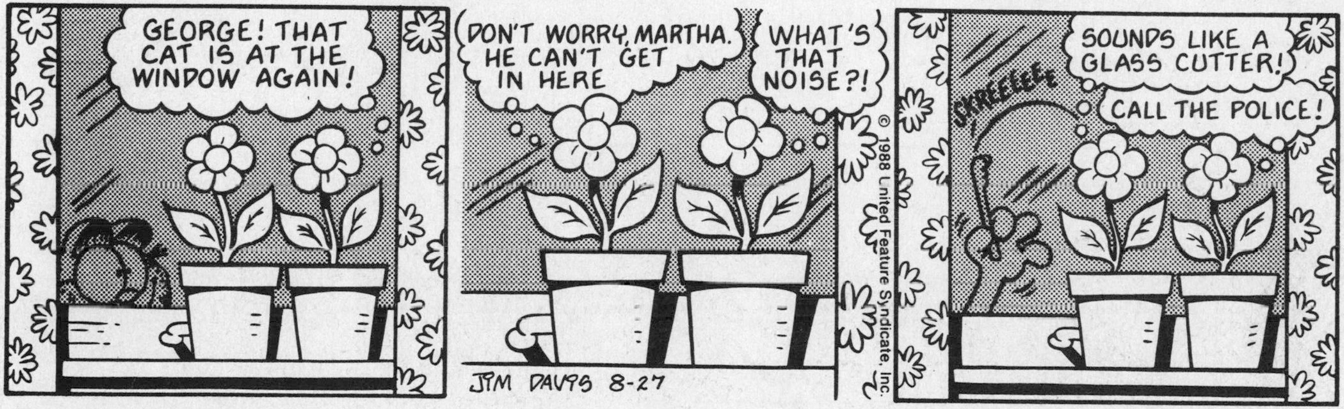
GEORGE! THAT CAT IS AT THE WINDOW AGAIN!
DON'T WORRY, MARTHA. HE CAN'T GET IN HERE
WHAT'S THAT NOISE?!
JIM DAVIS 8-27
© 1988 United Feature Syndicate, Inc.
SKREEEEEE
SOUNDS LIKE A GLASS CUTTER!
CALL THE POLICE!

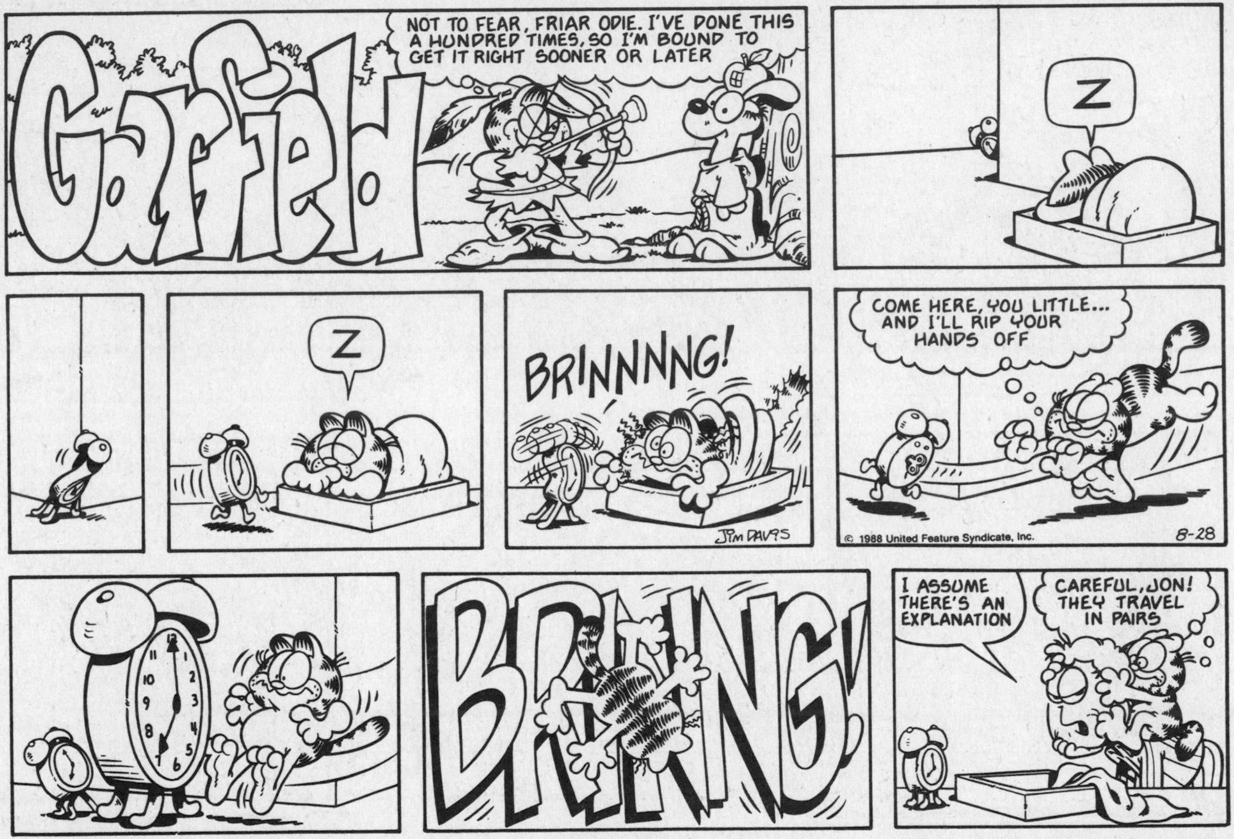

Garfield
NOT TO FEAR, FRIAR ODIE. I'VE DONE THIS A HUNDRED TIMES, SO I'M BOUND TO GET IT RIGHT SOONER OR LATER
Z
Z
BRINNNNG!
JIM DAVIS
COME HERE, YOU LITTLE... AND I'LL RIP YOUR HANDS OFF
© 1988 United Feature Syndicate, Inc.
8-28
BRRING!
I ASSUME THERE'S AN EXPLANATION
CAREFUL, JON! THEY TRAVEL IN PAIRS

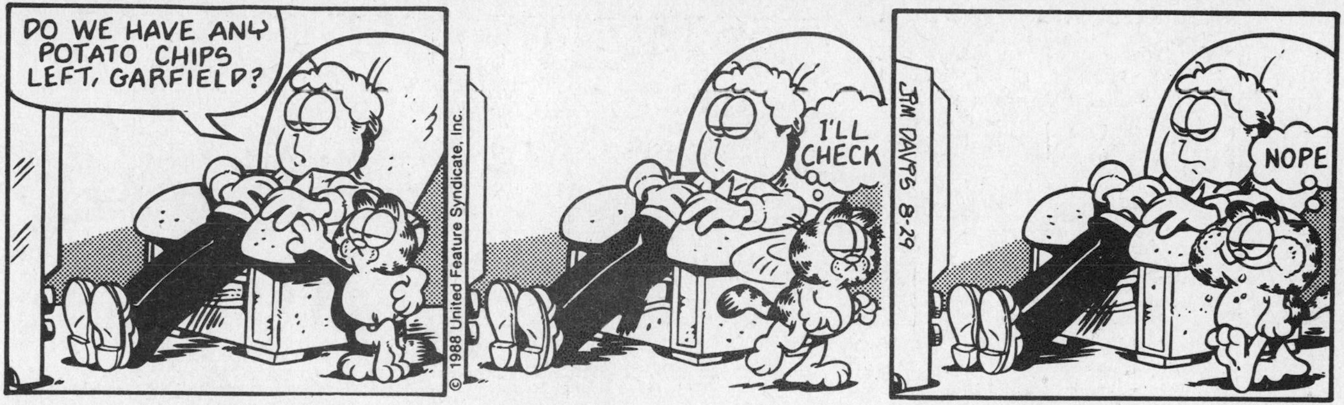
DO WE HAVE ANY POTATO CHIPS LEFT, GARFIELD?
© 1988 United Feature Syndicate, Inc.
I'LL CHECK
JIM DAVIS 8-29
NOPE

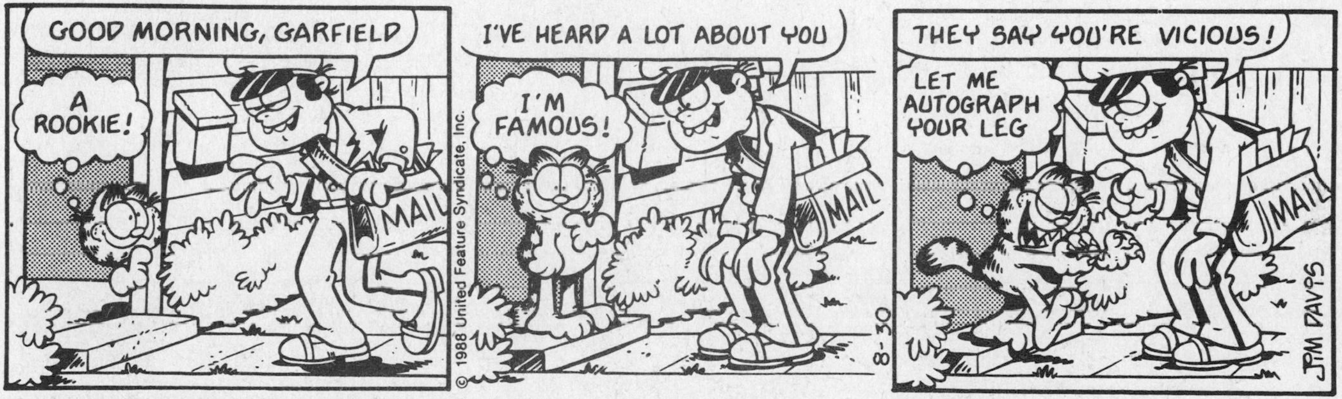
GOOD MORNING, GARFIELD
A ROOKIE!
© 1988 United Feature Syndicate, Inc.
I'VE HEARD A LOT ABOUT YOU
I'M FAMOUS!
8-30
THEY SAY YOU'RE VICIOUS!
LET ME AUTOGRAPH YOUR LEG
JIM DAVIS

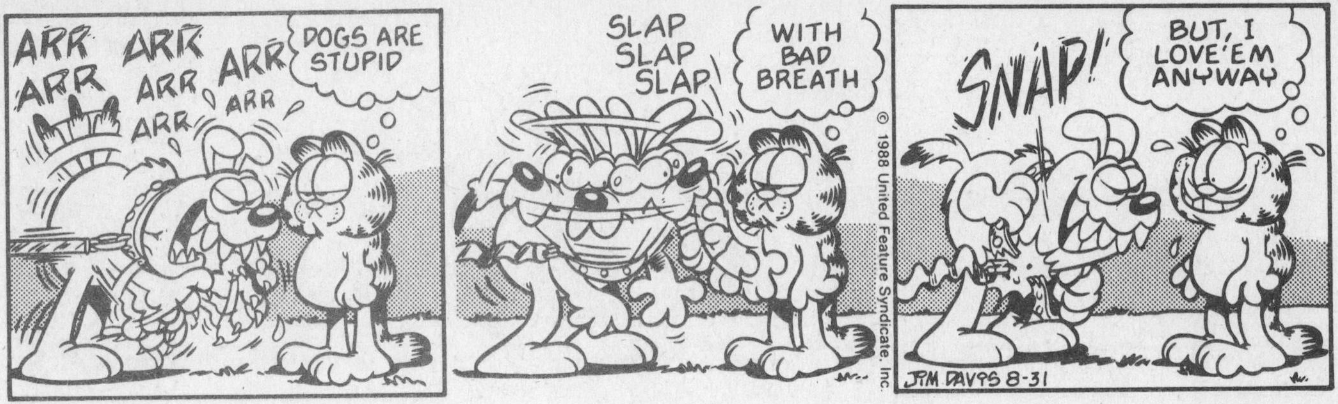
ARR ARR ARR ARR ARR ARR ARR ARR
DOGS ARE STUPID
SLAP SLAP SLAP
WITH BAD BREATH
© 1988 United Feature Syndicate, Inc.
SNAP!
BUT, I LOVE'EM ANYWAY
JIM DAVIS 8-31

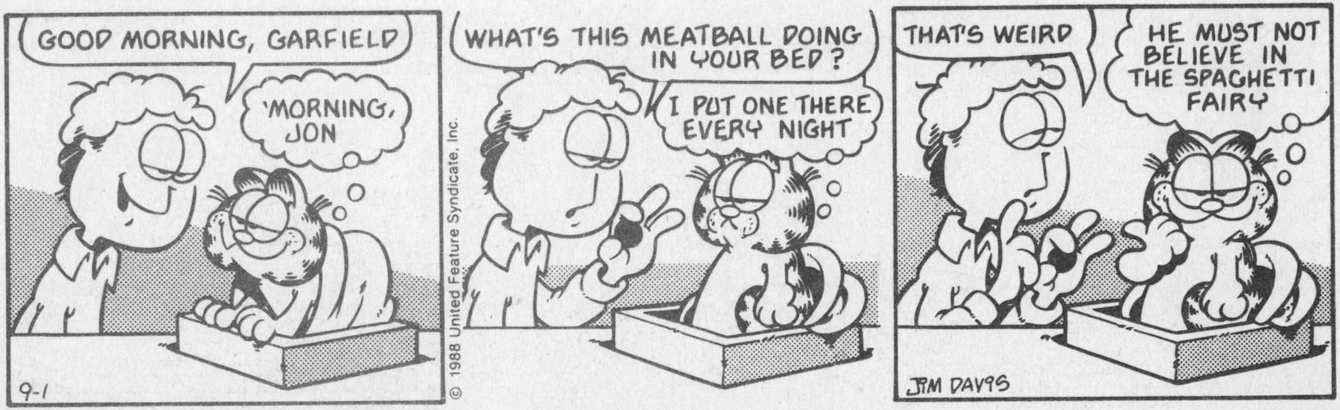
GOOD MORNING, GARFIELD
'MORNING, JON
9-1
© 1988 United Feature Syndicate, Inc.
WHAT'S THIS MEATBALL DOING IN YOUR BED?
I PUT ONE THERE EVERY NIGHT
THAT'S WEIRD
HE MUST NOT BELIEVE IN THE SPAGHETTI FAIRY
JIM DAVIS

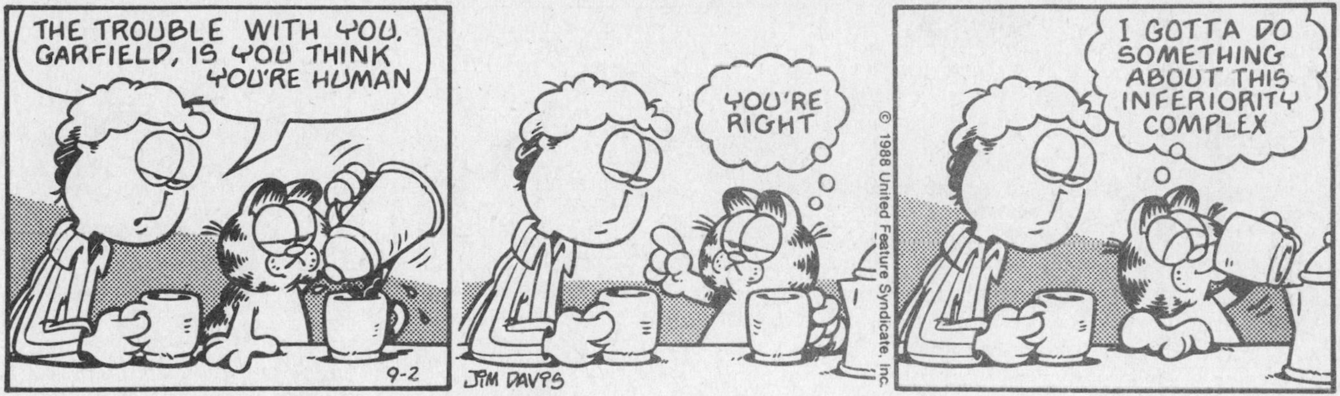
THE TROUBLE WITH YOU, GARFIELD, IS YOU THINK YOU'RE HUMAN
9-2
JIM DAVIS
YOU'RE RIGHT
© 1988 United Feature Syndicate, Inc.
I GOTTA DO SOMETHING ABOUT THIS INFERIORITY COMPLEX

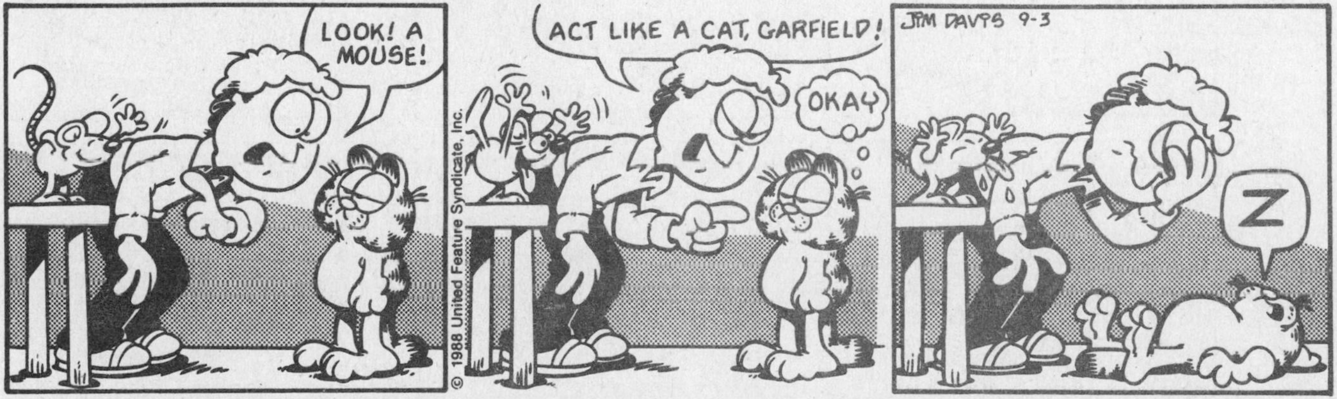
LOOK! A MOUSE!
© 1988 United Feature Syndicate, Inc.
ACT LIKE A CAT, GARFIELD!
OKAY
JIM DAVIS 9-3
Z

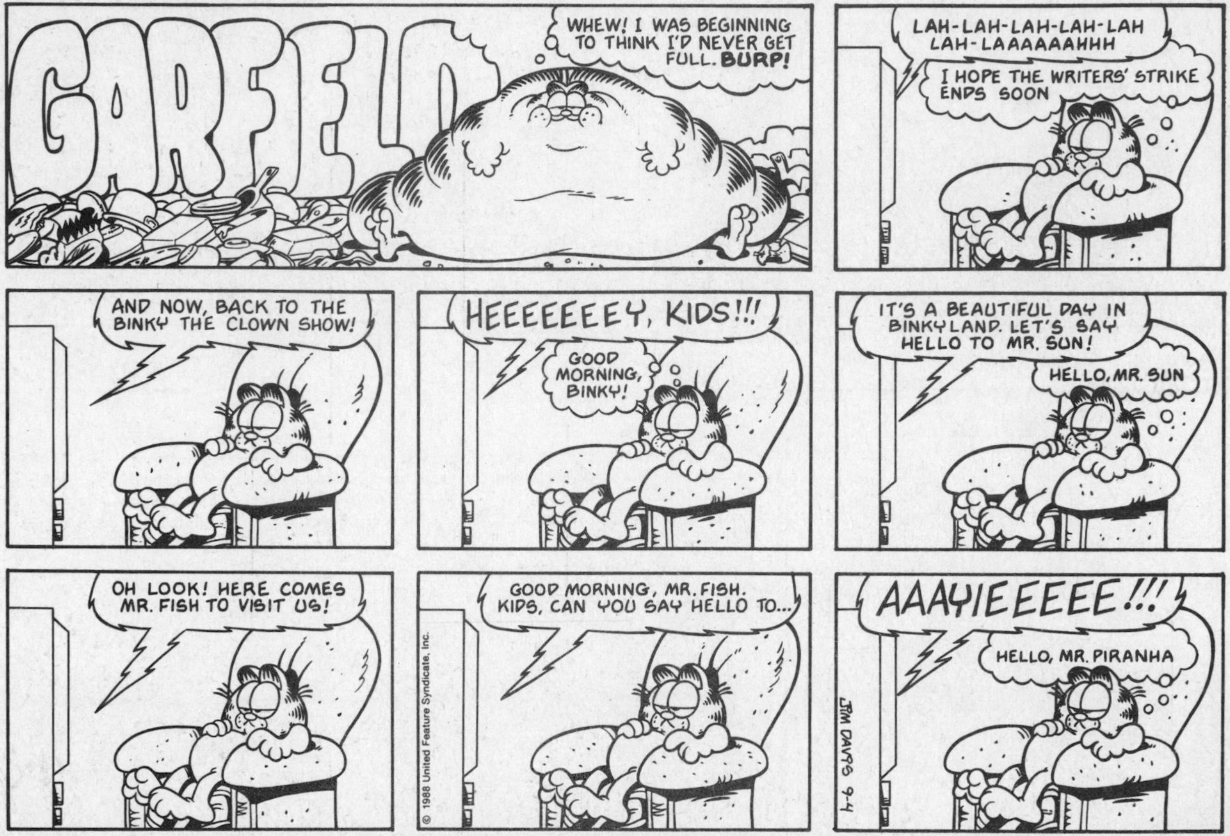
GARFIELD
WHEW! I WAS BEGINNING TO THINK I'D NEVER GET FULL. BURP!
LAH-LAH-LAH-LAH-LAH LAH-LAAAAAAHHH
I HOPE THE WRITERS' STRIKE ENDS SOON
AND NOW, BACK TO THE BINKY THE CLOWN SHOW!
HEEEEEEEY, KIDS!!!
GOOD MORNING, BINKY!
IT'S A BEAUTIFUL DAY IN BINKYLAND. LET'S SAY HELLO TO MR. SUN!
HELLO, MR. SUN
OH LOOK! HERE COMES MR. FISH TO VISIT US!
GOOD MORNING, MR. FISH. KIDS, CAN YOU SAY HELLO TO...
AAAYIEEEEE!!!
HELLO, MR. PIRANHA
© 1988 United Feature Syndicate, Inc.
JIM DAVIS 9-4

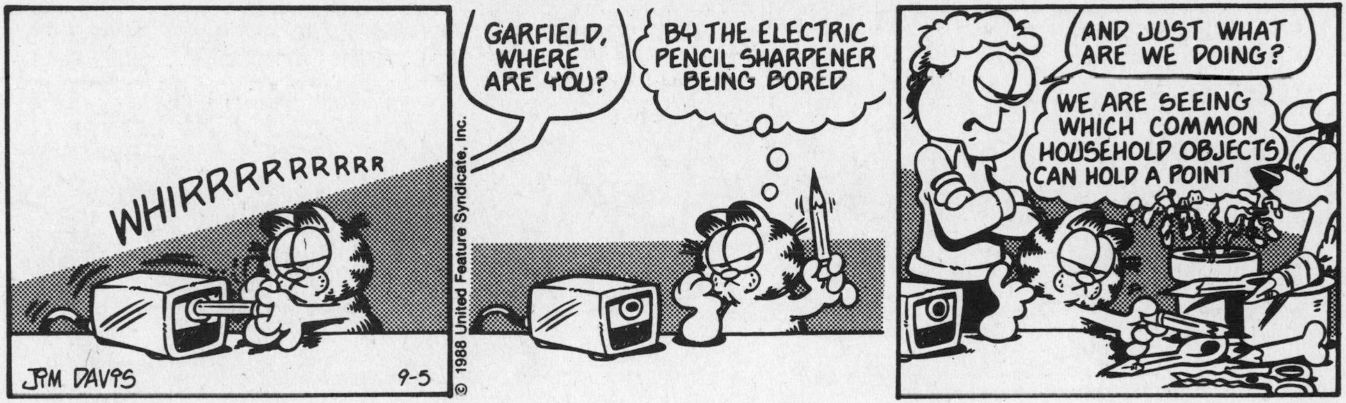
WHIRRRRRRRRRR
JIM DAVIS
9-5
© 1988 United Feature Syndicate, Inc.
GARFIELD, WHERE ARE YOU?
BY THE ELECTRIC PENCIL SHARPENER BEING BORED
AND JUST WHAT ARE WE DOING?
WE ARE SEEING WHICH COMMON HOUSEHOLD OBJECTS CAN HOLD A POINT

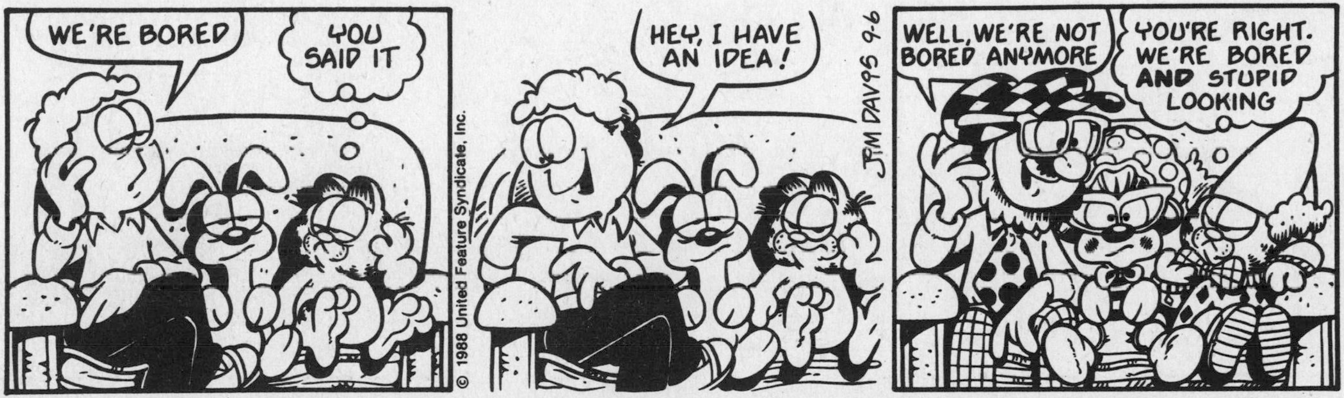
WE'RE BORED
YOU SAID IT
© 1988 United Feature Syndicate, Inc.
HEY, I HAVE AN IDEA!
JIM DAVIS 9-6
WELL, WE'RE NOT BORED ANYMORE
YOU'RE RIGHT. WE'RE BORED AND STUPID LOOKING

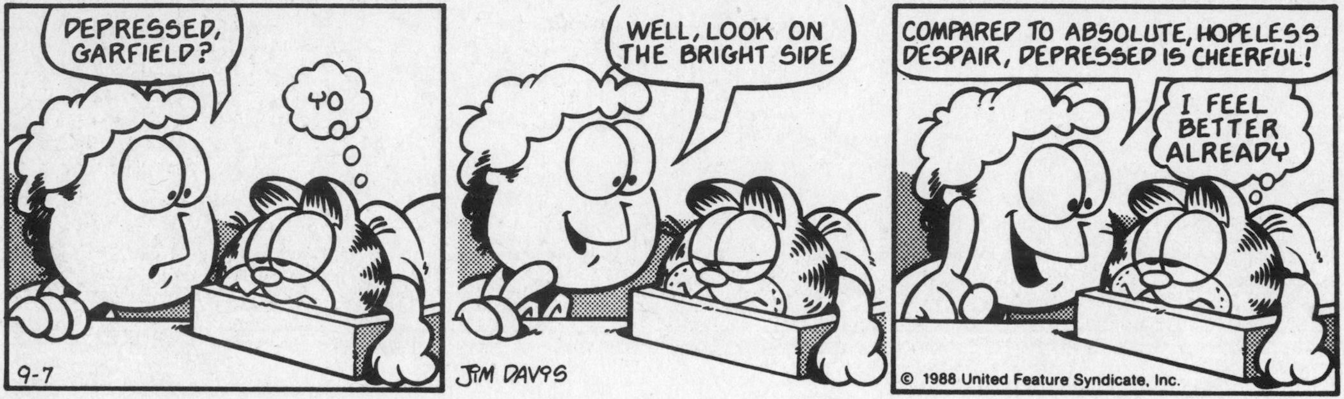
DEPRESSED, GARFIELD?
YO
9-7
WELL, LOOK ON THE BRIGHT SIDE
JIM DAVIS
COMPARED TO ABSOLUTE, HOPELESS DESPAIR, DEPRESSED IS CHEERFUL!
I FEEL BETTER ALREADY
© 1988 United Feature Syndicate, Inc.

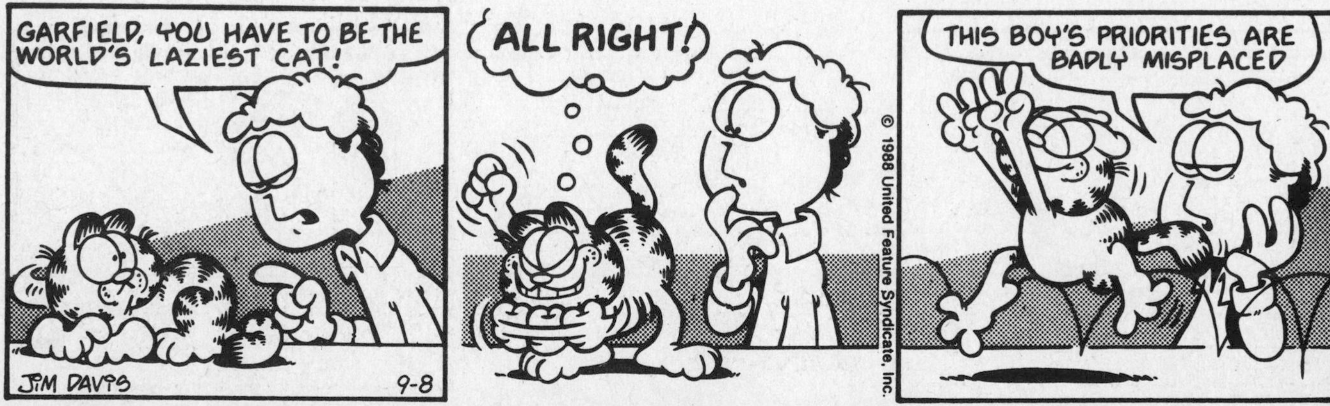
GARFIELD, YOU HAVE TO BE THE WORLD'S LAZIEST CAT!
JIM DAVIS
9-8
ALL RIGHT!
© 1988 United Feature Syndicate, Inc.
THIS BOY'S PRIORITIES ARE BADLY MISPLACED

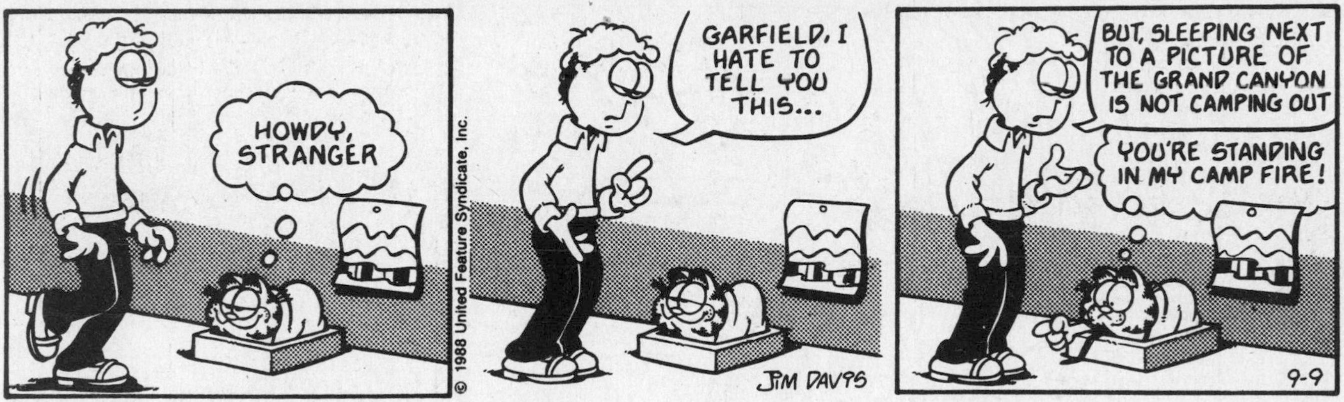
HOWDY, STRANGER
GARFIELD, I HATE TO TELL YOU THIS...
BUT, SLEEPING NEXT TO A PICTURE OF THE GRAND CANYON IS NOT CAMPING OUT
YOU'RE STANDING IN MY CAMP FIRE!
© 1988 United Feature Syndicate, Inc.
JIM DAVIS
9-9

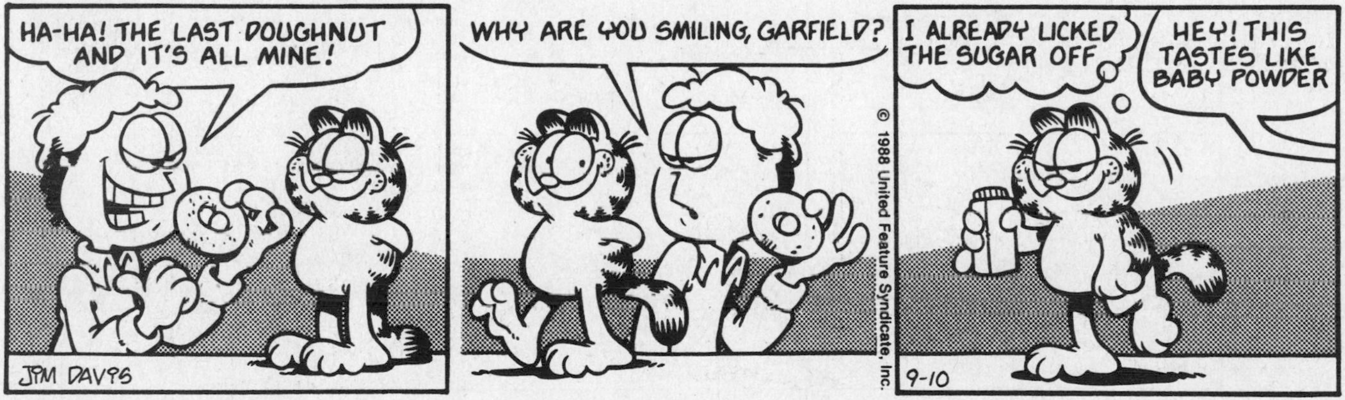
HA-HA! THE LAST DOUGHNUT AND IT'S ALL MINE!
WHY ARE YOU SMILING, GARFIELD?
I ALREADY LICKED THE SUGAR OFF
HEY! THIS TASTES LIKE BABY POWDER
© 1988 United Feature Syndicate, Inc.
JIM DAVIS
9-10

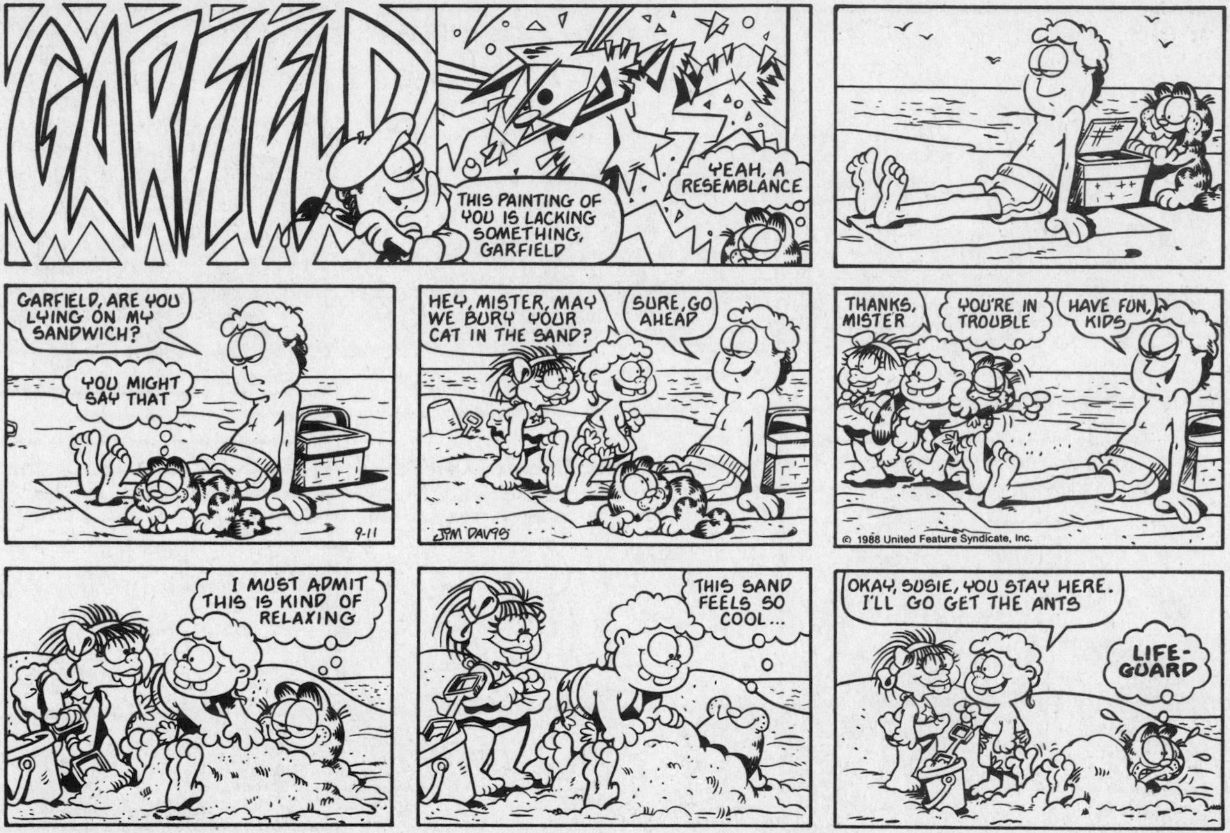
GARFIELD
THIS PAINTING OF YOU IS LACKING SOMETHING, GARFIELD
YEAH, A RESEMBLANCE
GARFIELD, ARE YOU LYING ON MY SANDWICH?
YOU MIGHT SAY THAT
9-11
HEY, MISTER, MAY WE BURY YOUR CAT IN THE SAND?
SURE, GO AHEAD
JIM DAVIS
THANKS, MISTER
YOU'RE IN TROUBLE
HAVE FUN, KIDS
© 1988 United Feature Syndicate, Inc.
I MUST ADMIT THIS IS KIND OF RELAXING
THIS SAND FEELS SO COOL...
OKAY, SUSIE, YOU STAY HERE. I'LL GO GET THE ANTS
LIFE-GUARD

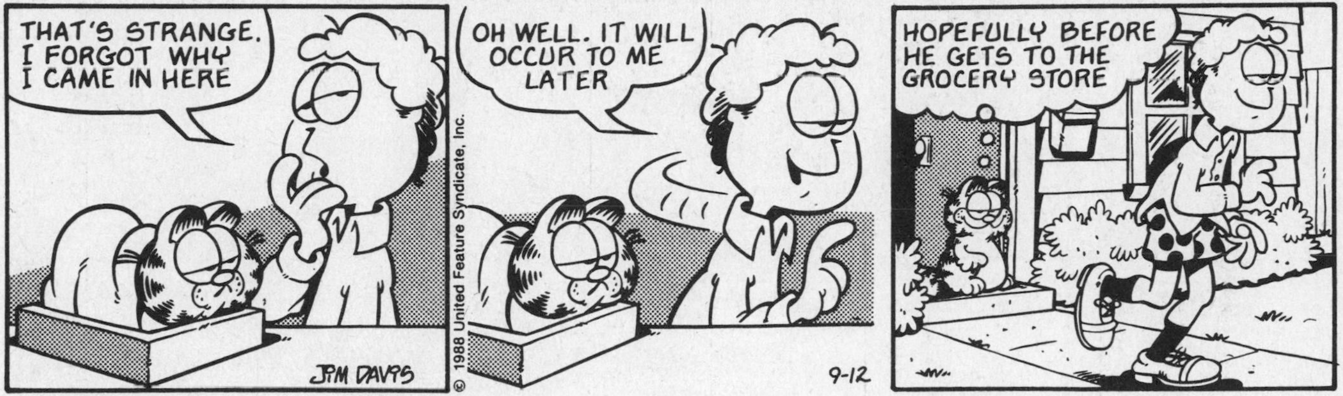
THAT'S STRANGE. I FORGOT WHY I CAME IN HERE
JIM DAVIS
© 1988 United Feature Syndicate, Inc.
OH WELL. IT WILL OCCUR TO ME LATER
9-12
HOPEFULLY BEFORE HE GETS TO THE GROCERY STORE

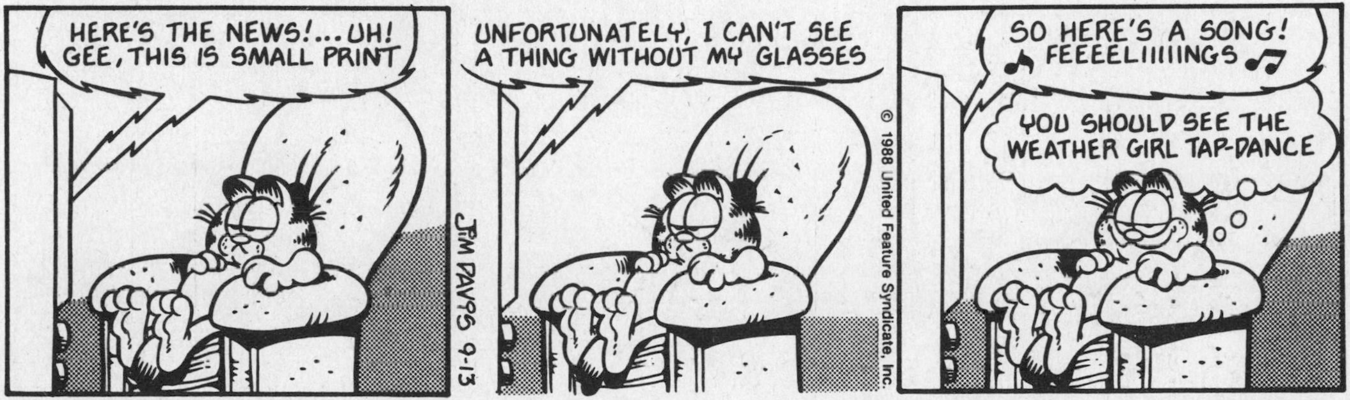
HERE'S THE NEWS!...UH! GEE, THIS IS SMALL PRINT
JIM DAVIS 9-13
UNFORTUNATELY, I CAN'T SEE A THING WITHOUT MY GLASSES
© 1988 United Feature Syndicate, Inc.
SO HERE'S A SONG! FEEEELIIIIINGS
YOU SHOULD SEE THE WEATHER GIRL TAP-DANCE

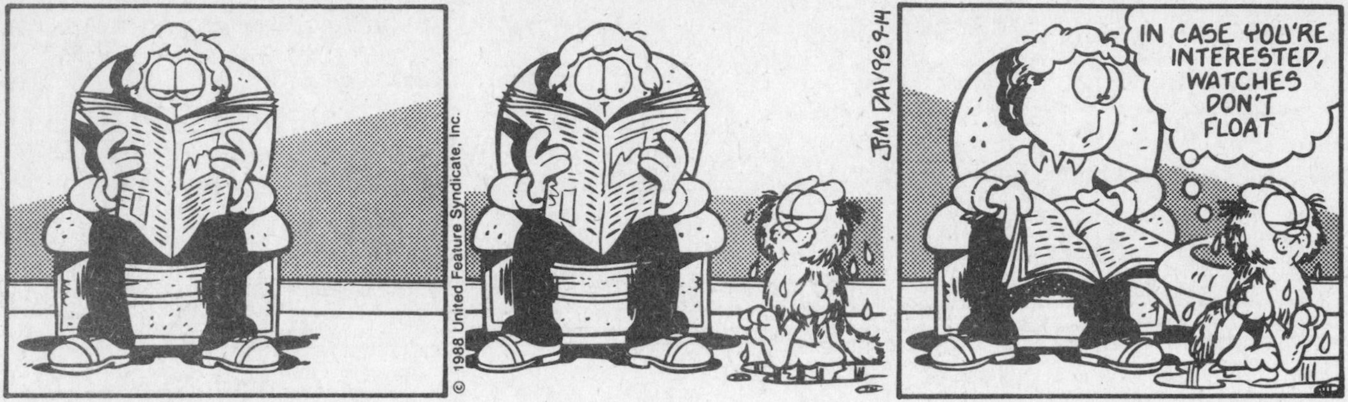
© 1988 United Feature Syndicate, Inc.
JIM DAVIS 9-14
IN CASE YOU'RE INTERESTED, WATCHES DON'T FLOAT

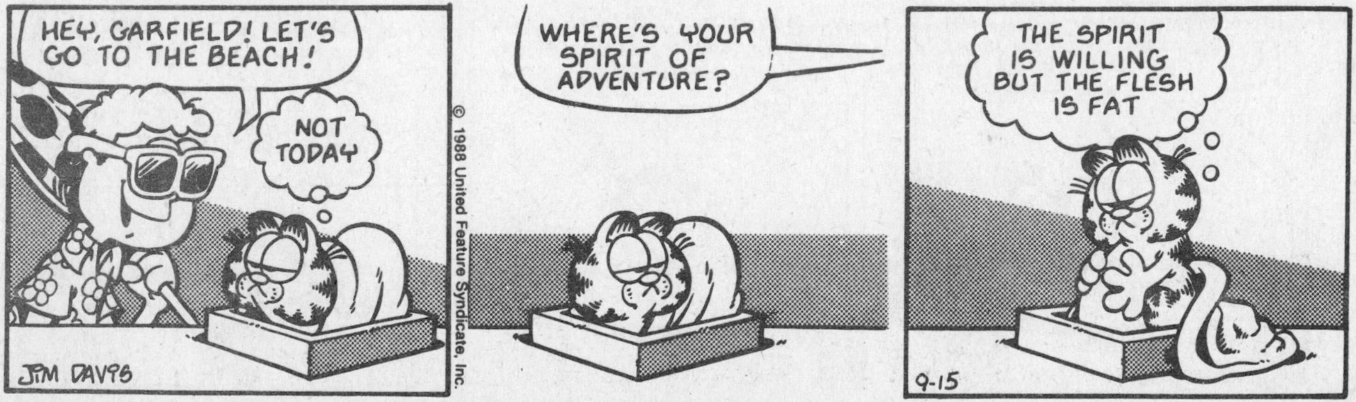
HEY, GARFIELD! LET'S GO TO THE BEACH!
NOT TODAY
JIM DAVIS
© 1988 United Feature Syndicate, Inc.
WHERE'S YOUR SPIRIT OF ADVENTURE?
THE SPIRIT IS WILLING BUT THE FLESH IS FAT
9-15

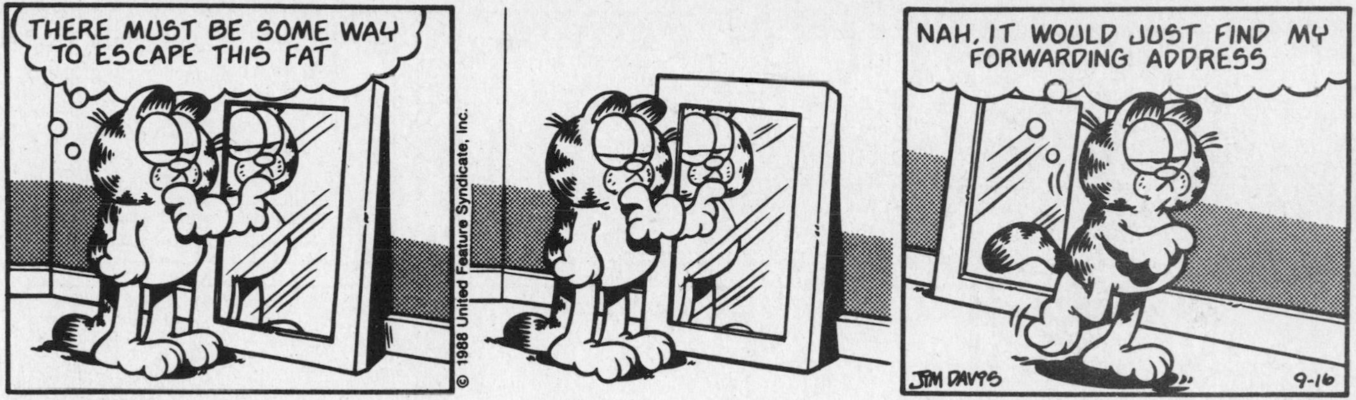
THERE MUST BE SOME WAY TO ESCAPE THIS FAT
© 1988 United Feature Syndicate, Inc.
NAH, IT WOULD JUST FIND MY FORWARDING ADDRESS
JIM DAVIS
9-16

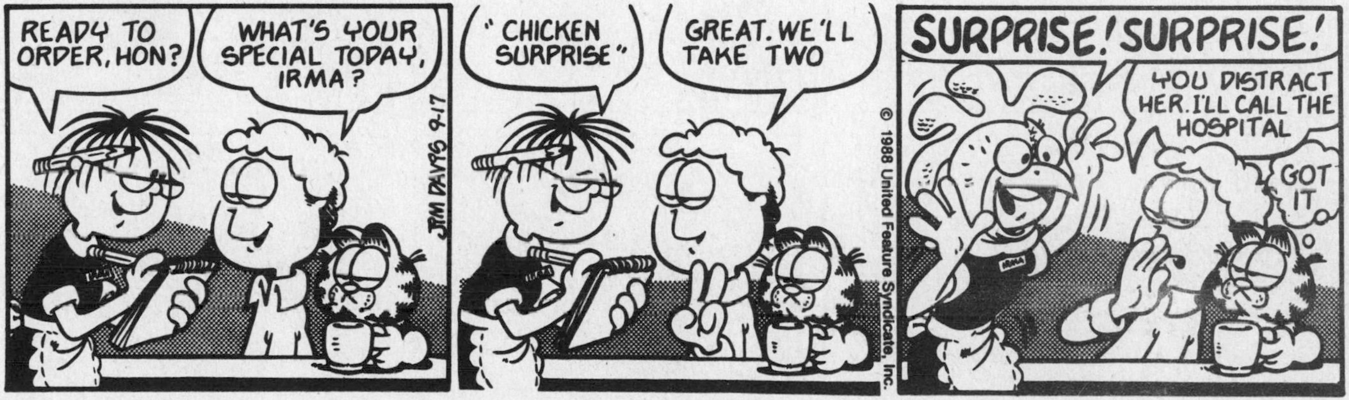
READY TO ORDER, HON?
WHAT'S YOUR SPECIAL TODAY, IRMA?
JIM DAVIS 9-17
"CHICKEN SURPRISE"
GREAT. WE'LL TAKE TWO
© 1988 United Feature Syndicate, Inc.
SURPRISE! SURPRISE!
YOU DISTRACT HER. I'LL CALL THE HOSPITAL
GOT IT

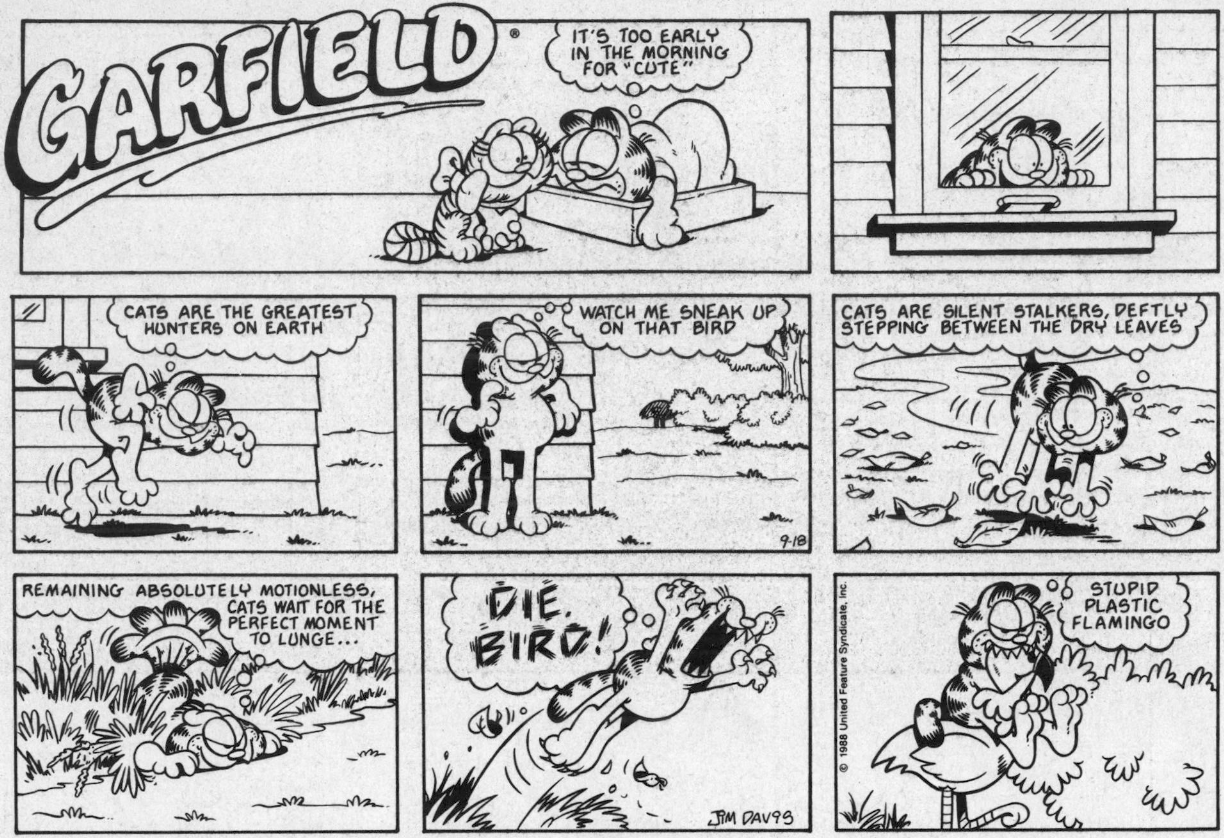
GARFIELD®
IT'S TOO EARLY IN THE MORNING FOR "CUTE"
CATS ARE THE GREATEST HUNTERS ON EARTH
WATCH ME SNEAK UP ON THAT BIRD
9-18
CATS ARE SILENT STALKERS, DEFTLY STEPPING BETWEEN THE DRY LEAVES
REMAINING ABSOLUTELY MOTIONLESS, CATS WAIT FOR THE PERFECT MOMENT TO LUNGE...
DIE, BIRD!
JIM DAVIS
© 1988 United Feature Syndicate, Inc.
STUPID PLASTIC FLAMINGO

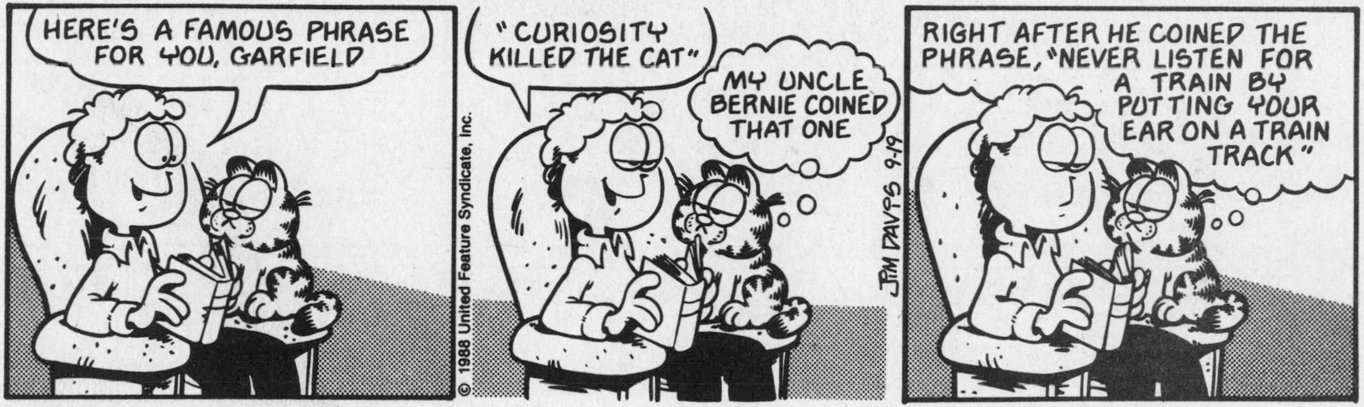
HERE'S A FAMOUS PHRASE FOR YOU, GARFIELD
"CURIOSITY KILLED THE CAT"
MY UNCLE BERNIE COINED THAT ONE
RIGHT AFTER HE COINED THE PHRASE, "NEVER LISTEN FOR A TRAIN BY PUTTING YOUR EAR ON A TRAIN TRACK"
JIM DAVIS 9-19
© 1988 United Feature Syndicate, Inc.

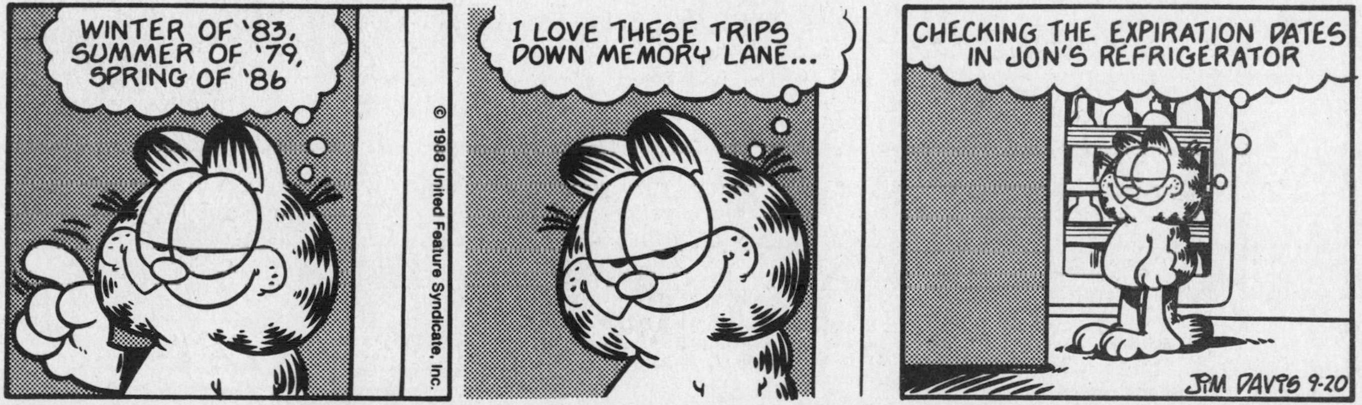
WINTER OF '83, SUMMER OF '79, SPRING OF '86
I LOVE THESE TRIPS DOWN MEMORY LANE...
CHECKING THE EXPIRATION DATES IN JON'S REFRIGERATOR
JIM DAVIS 9-20
© 1988 United Feature Syndicate, Inc.

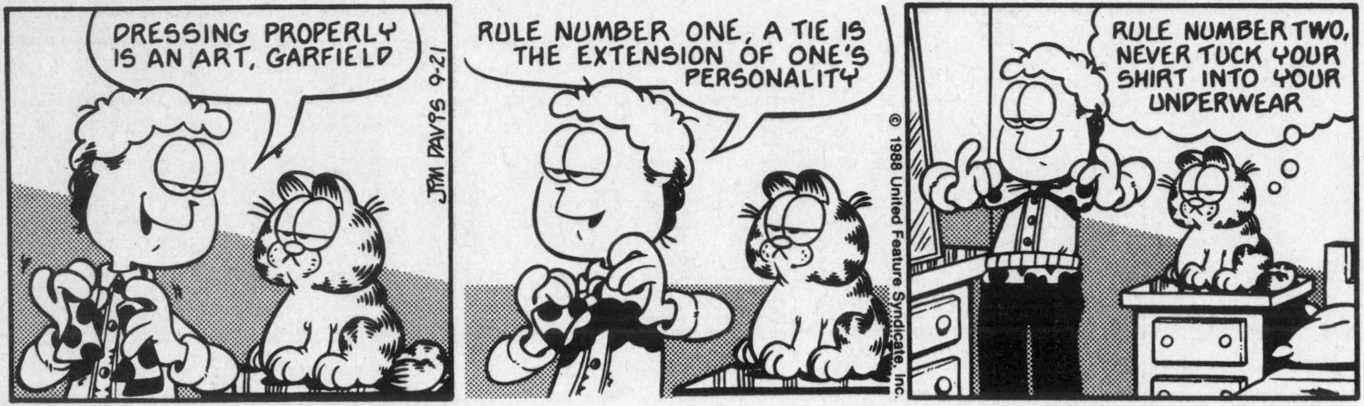
DRESSING PROPERLY IS AN ART, GARFIELD
JIM DAVIS 9-21
RULE NUMBER ONE, A TIE IS THE EXTENSION OF ONE'S PERSONALITY
© 1988 United Feature Syndicate, Inc.
RULE NUMBER TWO, NEVER TUCK YOUR SHIRT INTO YOUR UNDERWEAR

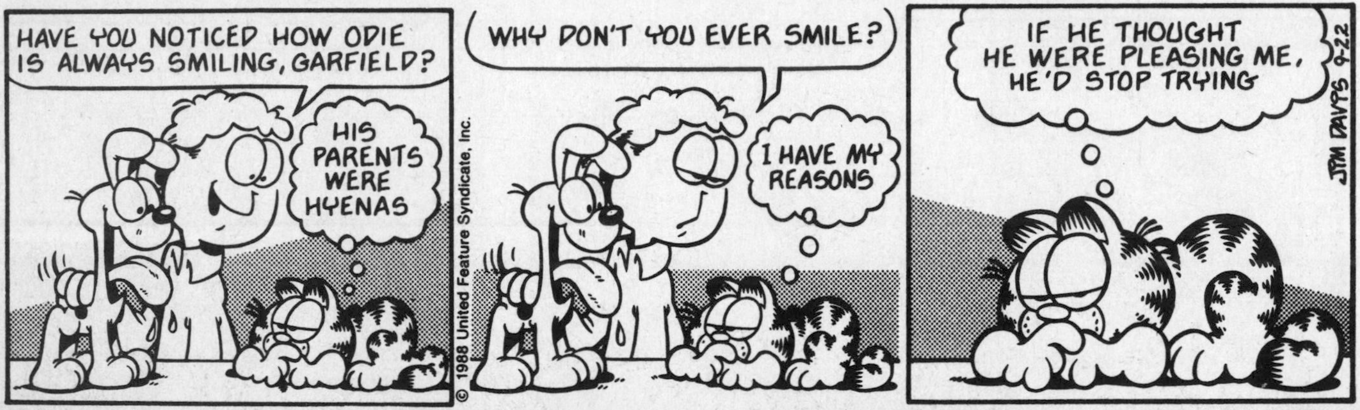
HAVE YOU NOTICED HOW ODIE IS ALWAYS SMILING, GARFIELD?
HIS PARENTS WERE HYENAS
© 1988 United Feature Syndicate, Inc.
WHY DON'T YOU EVER SMILE?
I HAVE MY REASONS
IF HE THOUGHT HE WERE PLEASING ME, HE'D STOP TRYING
JIM DAVIS 9-22

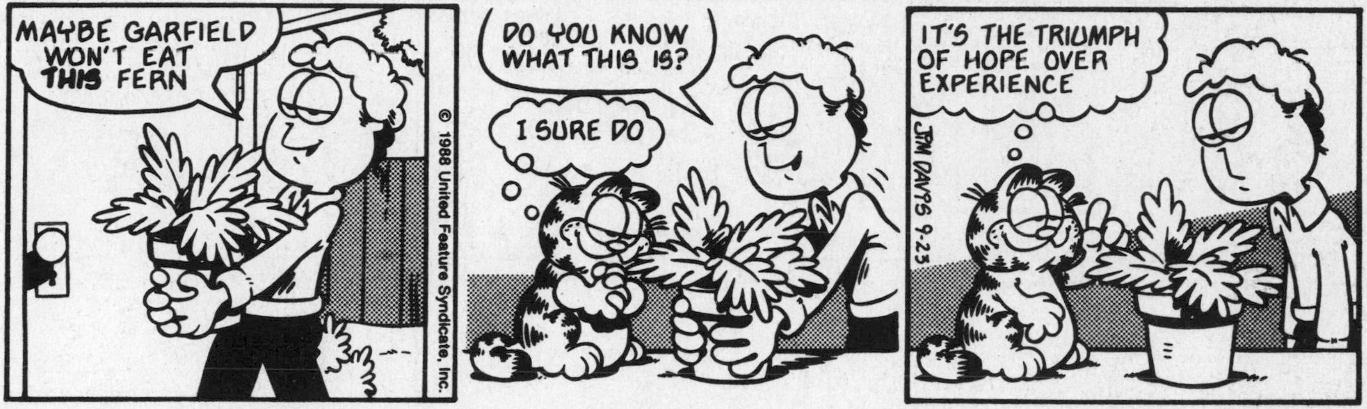
MAYBE GARFIELD WON'T EAT THIS FERN
© 1988 United Feature Syndicate, Inc.
DO YOU KNOW WHAT THIS IS?
I SURE DO
JIM DAVIS 9-23
IT'S THE TRIUMPH OF HOPE OVER EXPERIENCE

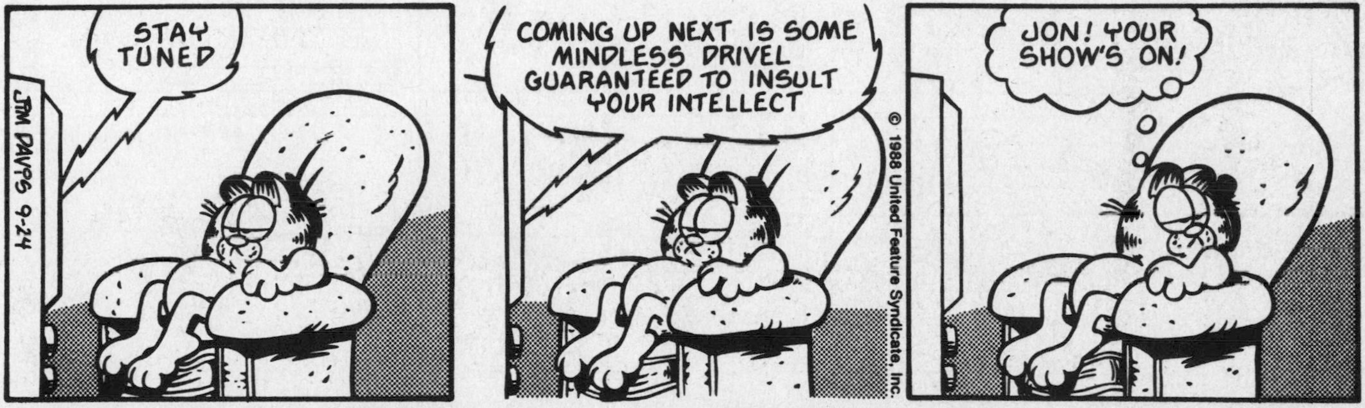
JIM DAVIS 9-24
STAY TUNED
COMING UP NEXT IS SOME MINDLESS DRIVEL GUARANTEED TO INSULT YOUR INTELLECT
© 1988 United Feature Syndicate, Inc.
JON! YOUR SHOW'S ON!

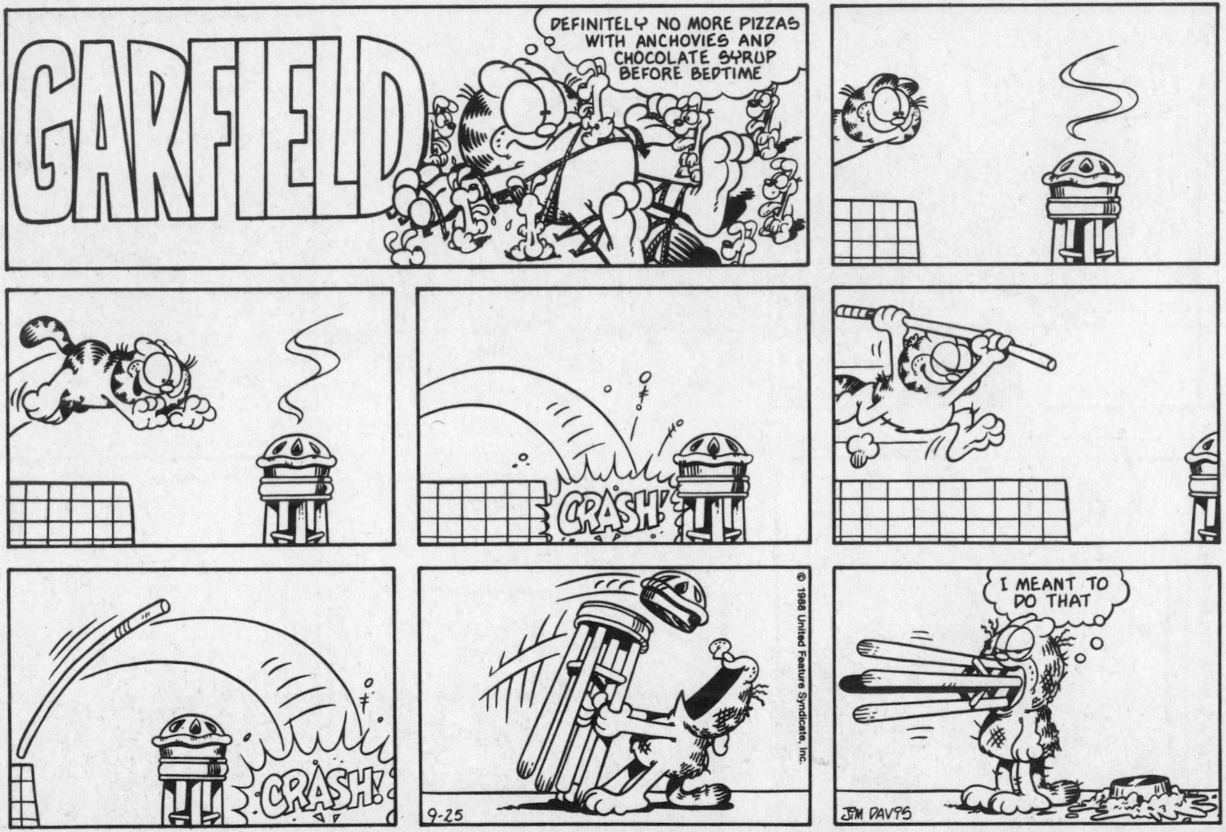
GARFIELD
DEFINITELY NO MORE PIZZAS WITH ANCHOVIES AND CHOCOLATE SYRUP BEFORE BEDTIME
CRASH!
CRASH!
9-25
© 1988 United Feature Syndicate, Inc.
I MEANT TO DO THAT
JIM DAVIS

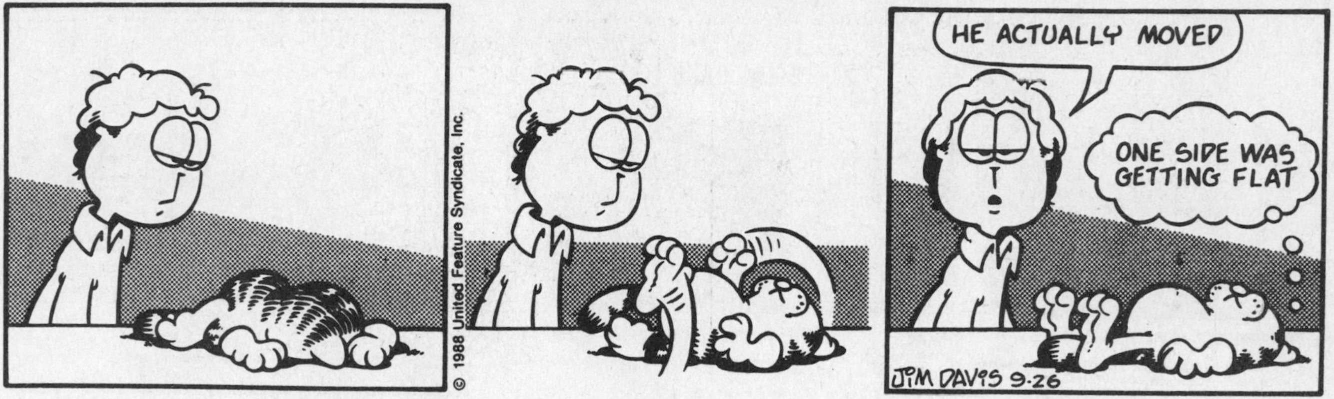
© 1988 United Feature Syndicate, Inc.
HE ACTUALLY MOVED
ONE SIDE WAS GETTING FLAT
JIM DAVIS 9-26

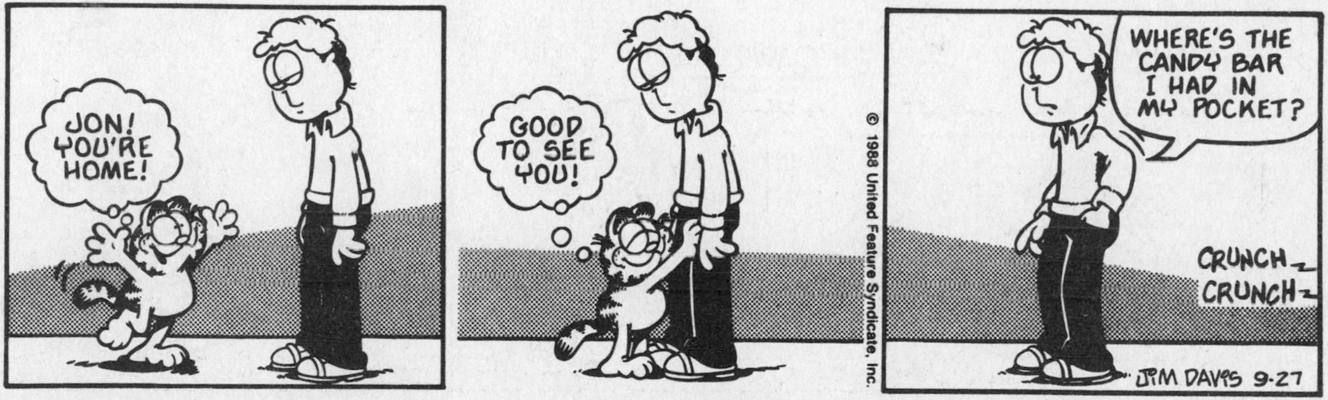
JON! YOU'RE HOME!
GOOD TO SEE YOU!
© 1988 United Feature Syndicate, Inc.
WHERE'S THE CANDY BAR I HAD IN MY POCKET?
CRUNCH
CRUNCH
JIM DAVIS 9-27

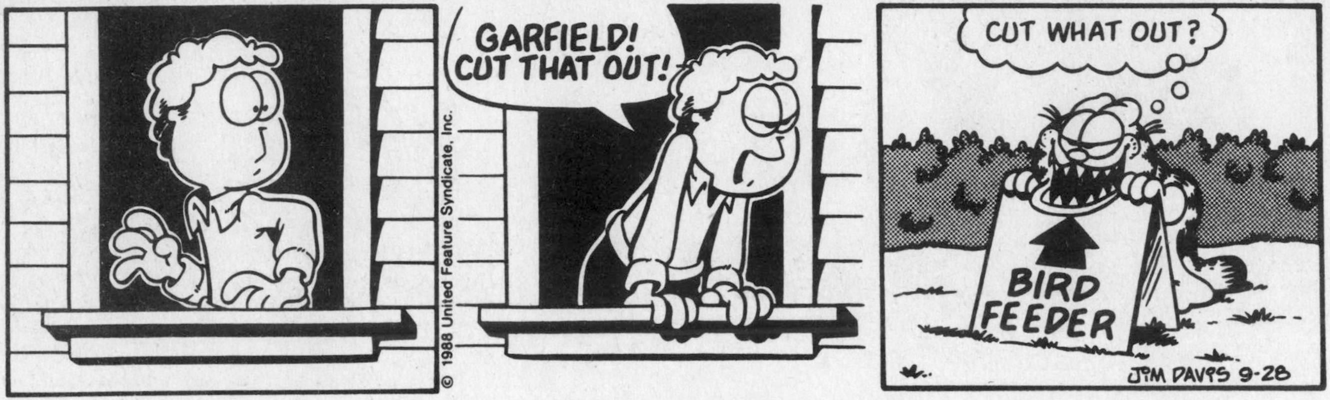
GARFIELD! CUT THAT OUT!
CUT WHAT OUT?
BIRD FEEDER
© 1988 United Feature Syndicate, Inc.
JIM DAVIS 9-28

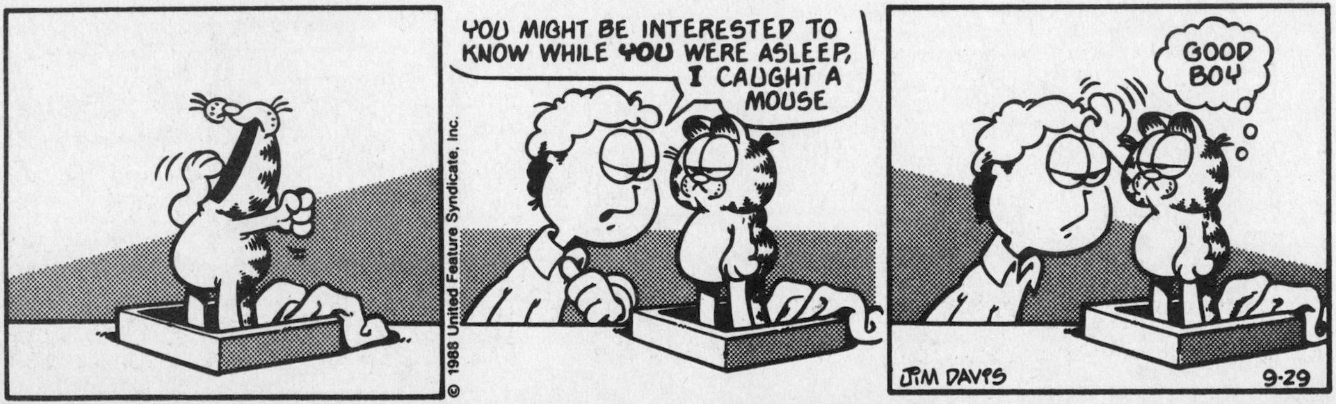
YOU MIGHT BE INTERESTED TO KNOW WHILE YOU WERE ASLEEP, I CAUGHT A MOUSE
GOOD BOY
© 1988 United Feature Syndicate, Inc.
JIM DAVIS
9-29

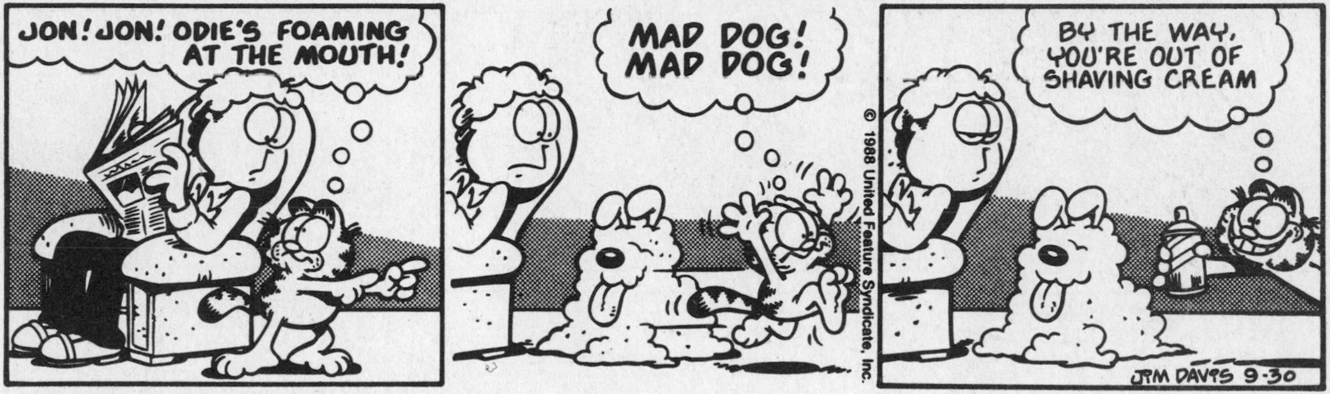
JON! JON! ODIE'S FOAMING AT THE MOUTH!
MAD DOG! MAD DOG!
© 1988 United Feature Syndicate, Inc.
BY THE WAY, YOU'RE OUT OF SHAVING CREAM
JIM DAVIS 9-30

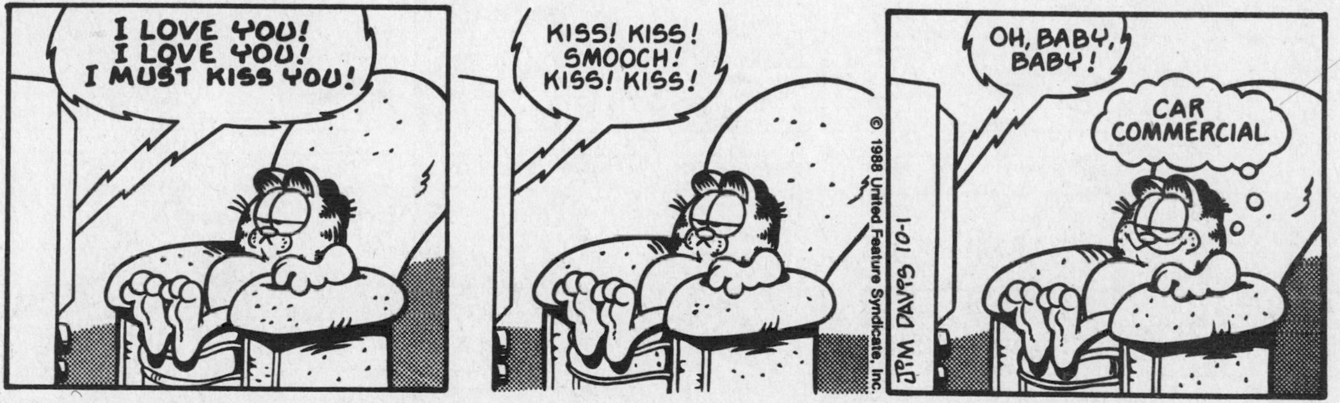
I LOVE YOU! I LOVE YOU! I MUST KISS YOU!
KISS! KISS! SMOOCH! KISS! KISS!
© 1988 United Feature Syndicate, Inc.
JIM DAVIS 10-1
OH, BABY, BABY!
CAR COMMERCIAL

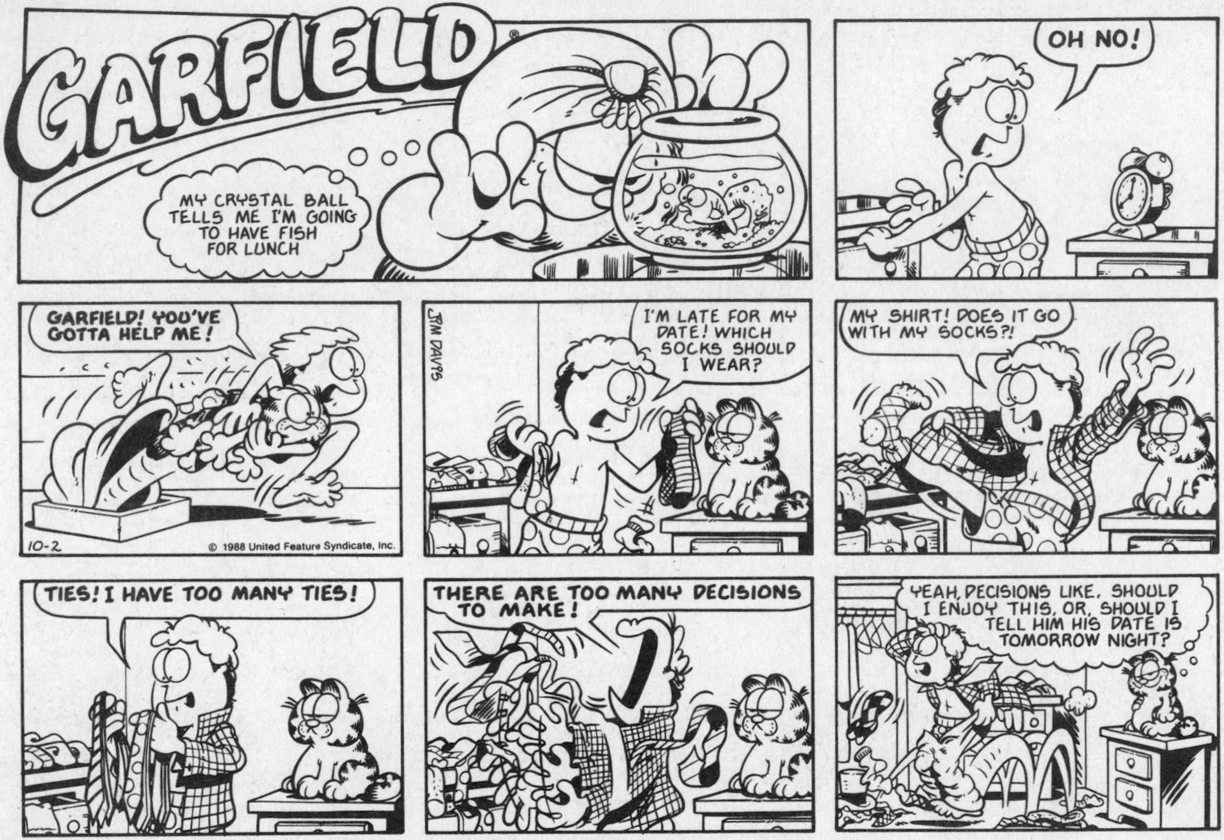
GARFIELD®
MY CRYSTAL BALL TELLS ME I'M GOING TO HAVE FISH FOR LUNCH
OH NO!
GARFIELD! YOU'VE GOTTA HELP ME!
10-2
© 1988 United Feature Syndicate, Inc.
JIM DAVIS
I'M LATE FOR MY DATE! WHICH SOCKS SHOULD I WEAR?
MY SHIRT! DOES IT GO WITH MY SOCKS?!
TIES! I HAVE TOO MANY TIES!
THERE ARE TOO MANY DECISIONS TO MAKE!
YEAH, DECISIONS LIKE, SHOULD I ENJOY THIS, OR, SHOULD I TELL HIM HIS DATE IS TOMORROW NIGHT?

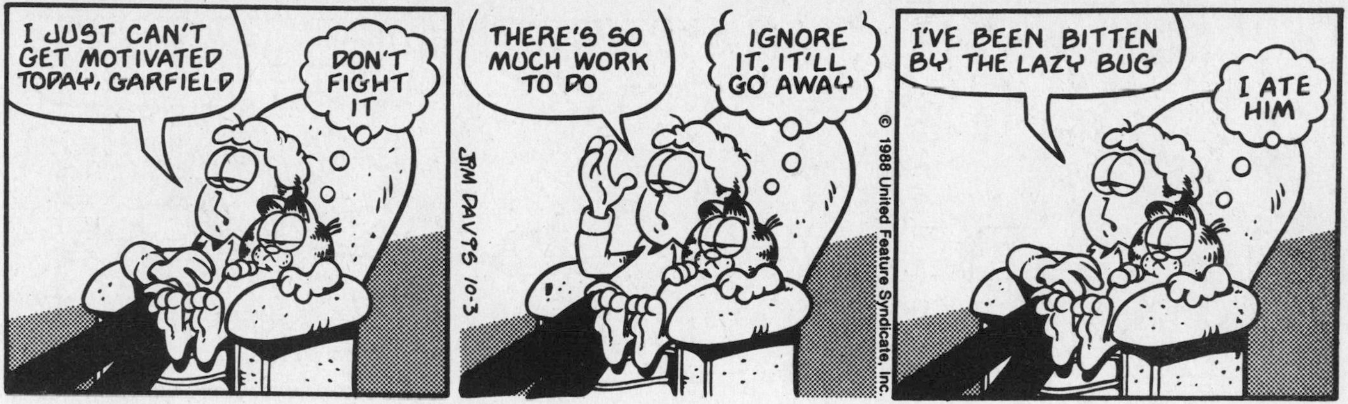
I JUST CAN'T GET MOTIVATED TODAY, GARFIELD
DON'T FIGHT IT
THERE'S SO MUCH WORK TO DO
IGNORE IT. IT'LL GO AWAY
I'VE BEEN BITTEN BY THE LAZY BUG
I ATE HIM
JIM DAVIS 10-3
© 1988 United Feature Syndicate, Inc.

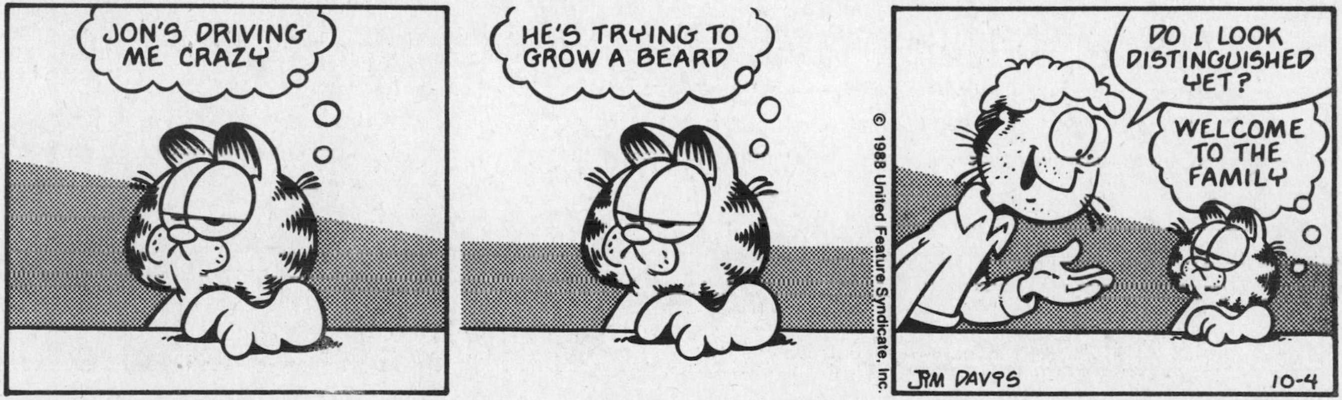
JON'S DRIVING ME CRAZY
HE'S TRYING TO GROW A BEARD
DO I LOOK DISTINGUISHED YET?
WELCOME TO THE FAMILY
JIM DAVIS 10-4
© 1988 United Feature Syndicate, Inc.

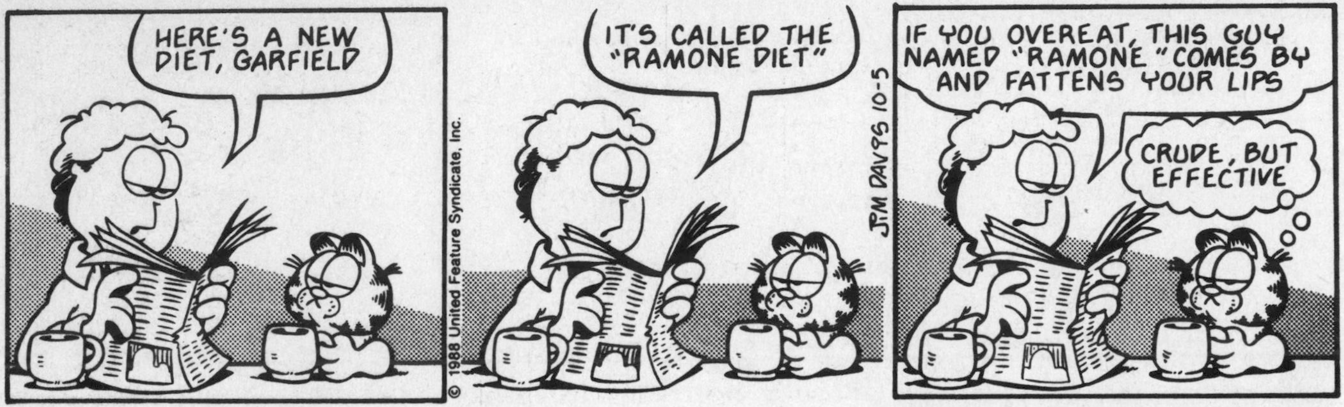
HERE'S A NEW DIET, GARFIELD
IT'S CALLED THE "RAMONE DIET"
IF YOU OVEREAT, THIS GUY NAMED "RAMONE" COMES BY AND FATTENS YOUR LIPS
CRUDE, BUT EFFECTIVE
JIM DAVIS 10-5
© 1988 United Feature Syndicate, Inc.

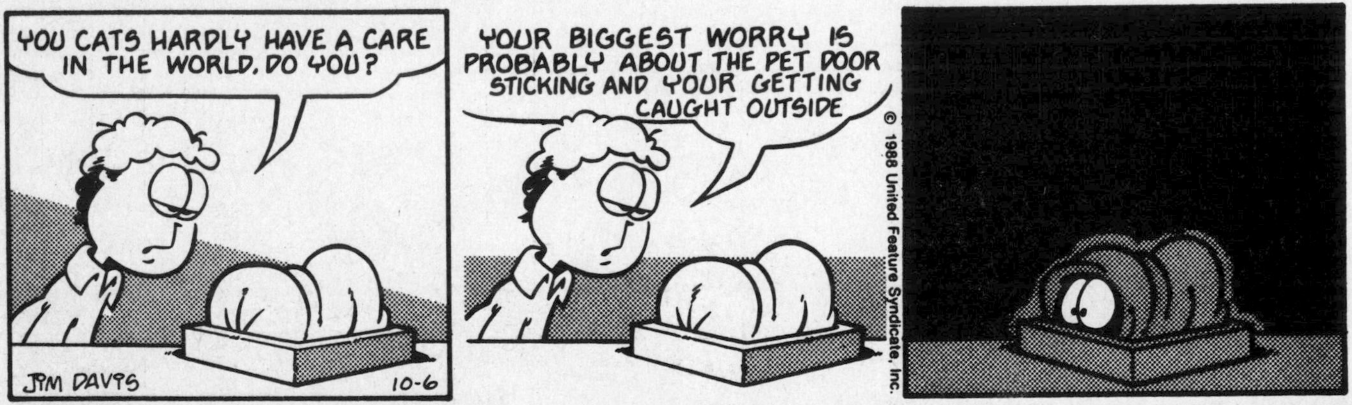
YOU CATS HARDLY HAVE A CARE IN THE WORLD. DO YOU?
YOUR BIGGEST WORRY IS PROBABLY ABOUT THE PET DOOR STICKING AND YOUR GETTING CAUGHT OUTSIDE
JIM DAVIS
10-6
© 1988 United Feature Syndicate, Inc.

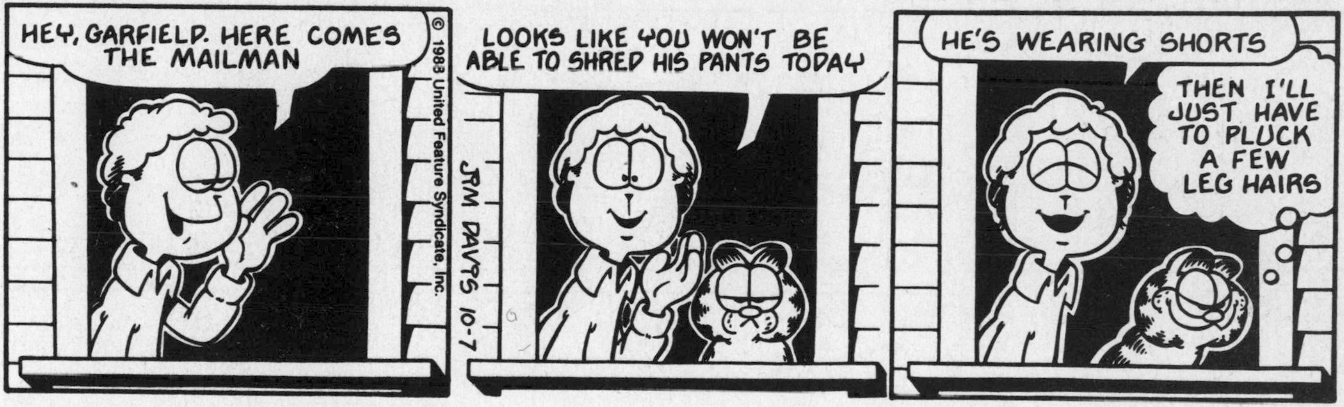
HEY, GARFIELD. HERE COMES THE MAILMAN
© 1983 United Feature Syndicate, Inc.
JIM DAVIS 10-7
LOOKS LIKE YOU WON'T BE ABLE TO SHRED HIS PANTS TODAY
HE'S WEARING SHORTS
THEN I'LL JUST HAVE TO PLUCK A FEW LEG HAIRS

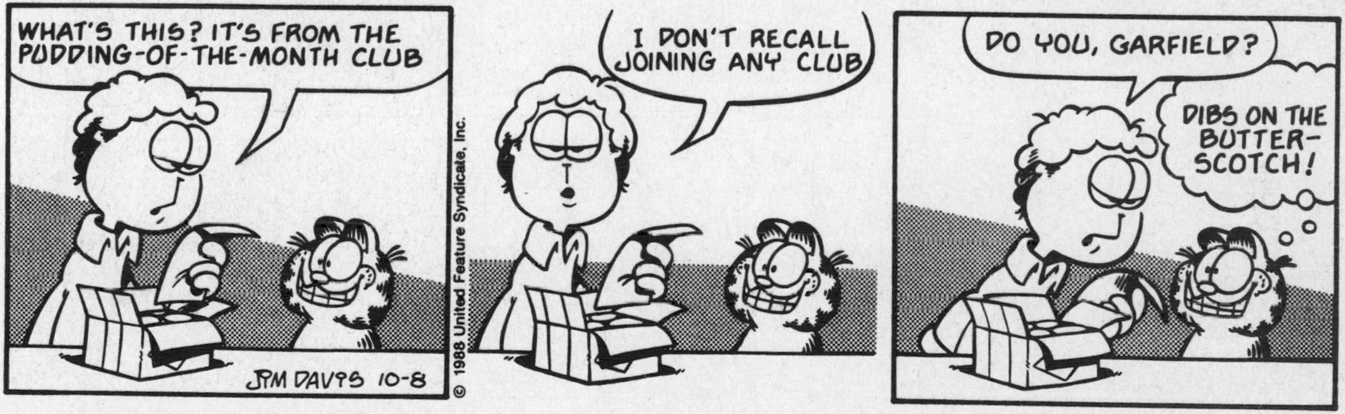
WHAT'S THIS? IT'S FROM THE PUDDING-OF-THE-MONTH CLUB
JIM DAVIS 10-8
© 1988 United Feature Syndicate, Inc.
I DON'T RECALL JOINING ANY CLUB
DO YOU, GARFIELD?
DIBS ON THE BUTTER-SCOTCH!

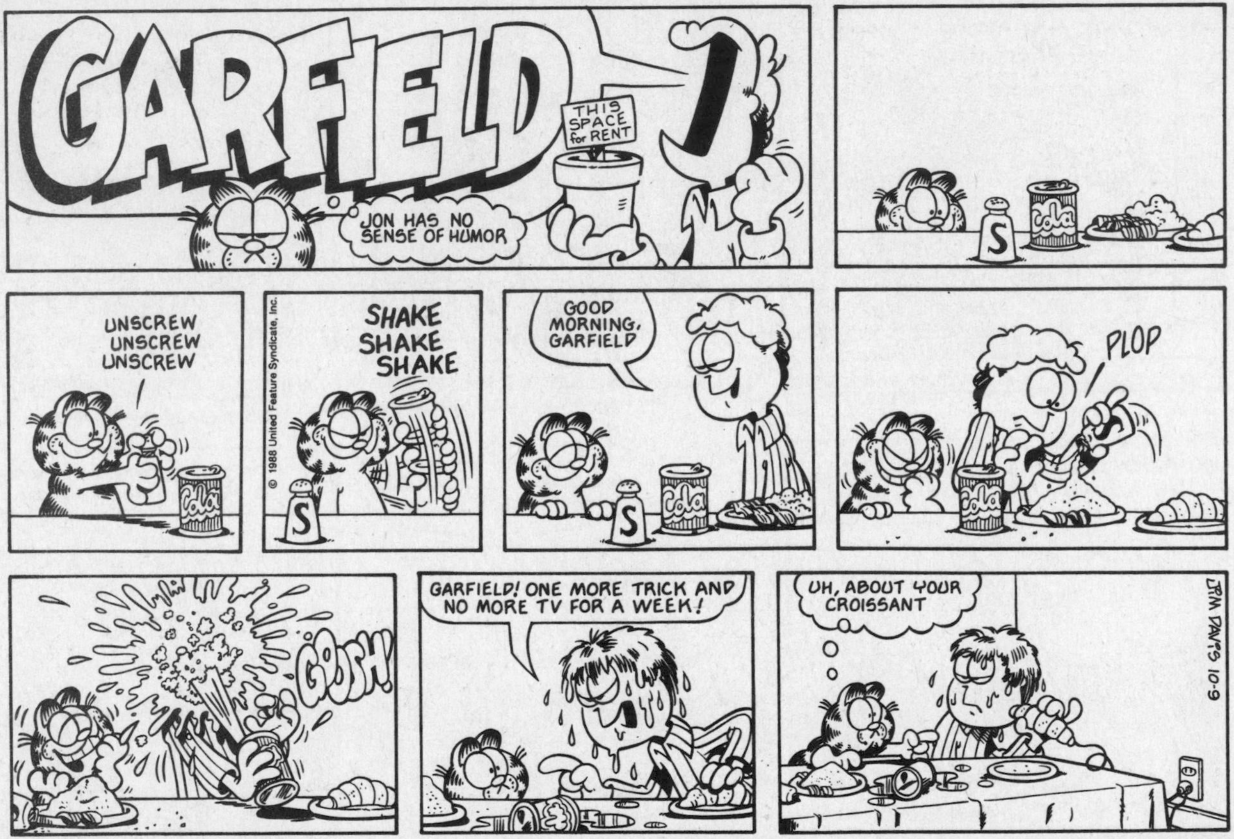
GARFIELD
THIS SPACE for RENT
JON HAS NO SENSE OF HUMOR
UNSCREW UNSCREW UNSCREW
© 1988 United Feature Syndicate, Inc.
SHAKE SHAKE SHAKE
GOOD MORNING, GARFIELD
PLOP
GOOSH!
GARFIELD! ONE MORE TRICK AND NO MORE TV FOR A WEEK!
UH, ABOUT YOUR CROISSANT
JIM DAVIS 10-9

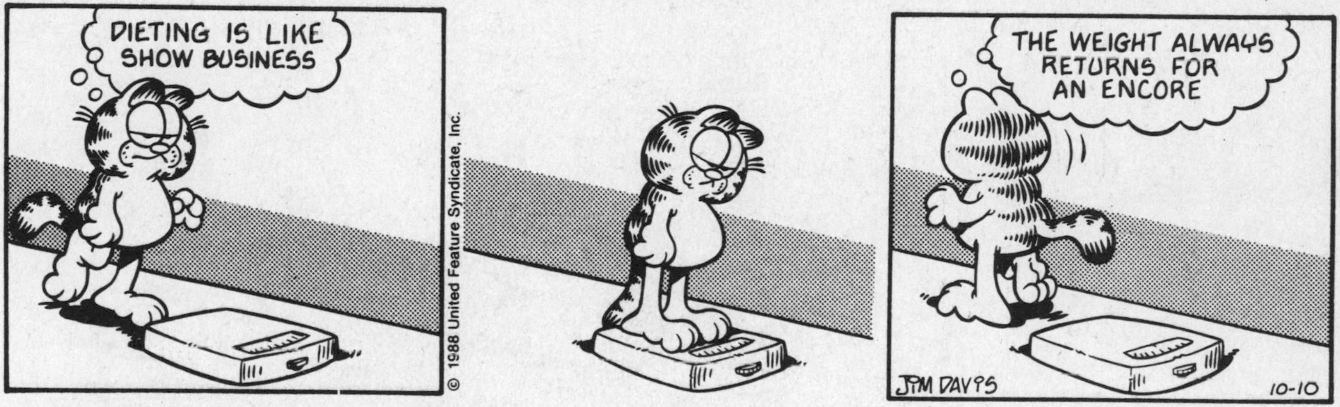
DIETING IS LIKE SHOW BUSINESS
THE WEIGHT ALWAYS RETURNS FOR AN ENCORE
JIM DAVIS
10-10

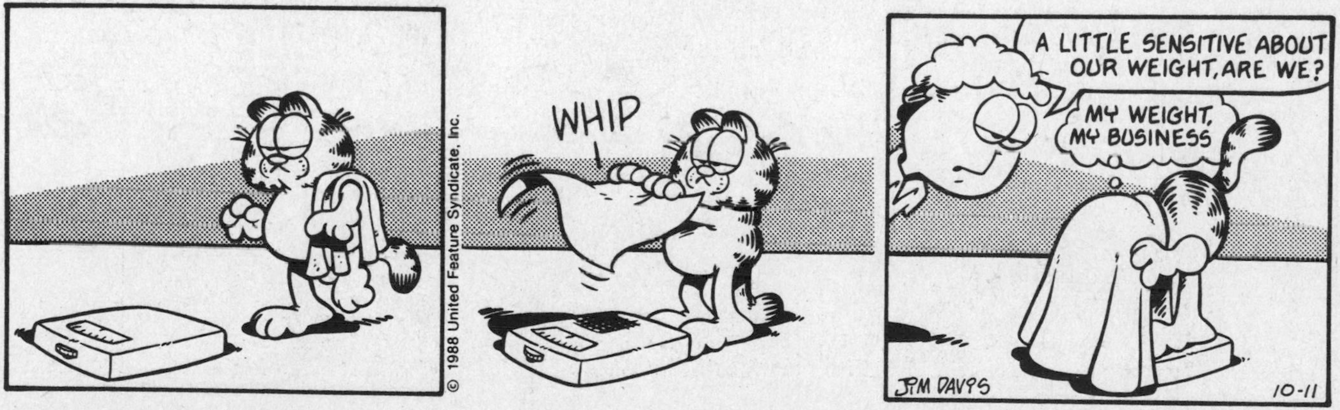
WHIP
A LITTLE SENSITIVE ABOUT OUR WEIGHT, ARE WE?
MY WEIGHT, MY BUSINESS
JIM DAVIS
10-11

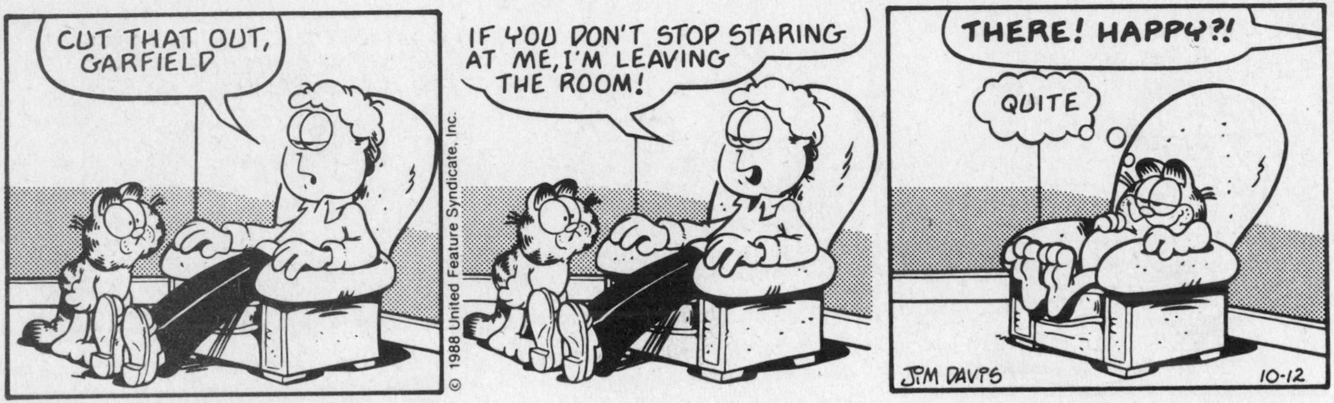
CUT THAT OUT, GARFIELD
© 1988 United Feature Syndicate, Inc.
IF YOU DON'T STOP STARING AT ME, I'M LEAVING THE ROOM!
THERE! HAPPY?!
QUITE
JIM DAVIS
10-12

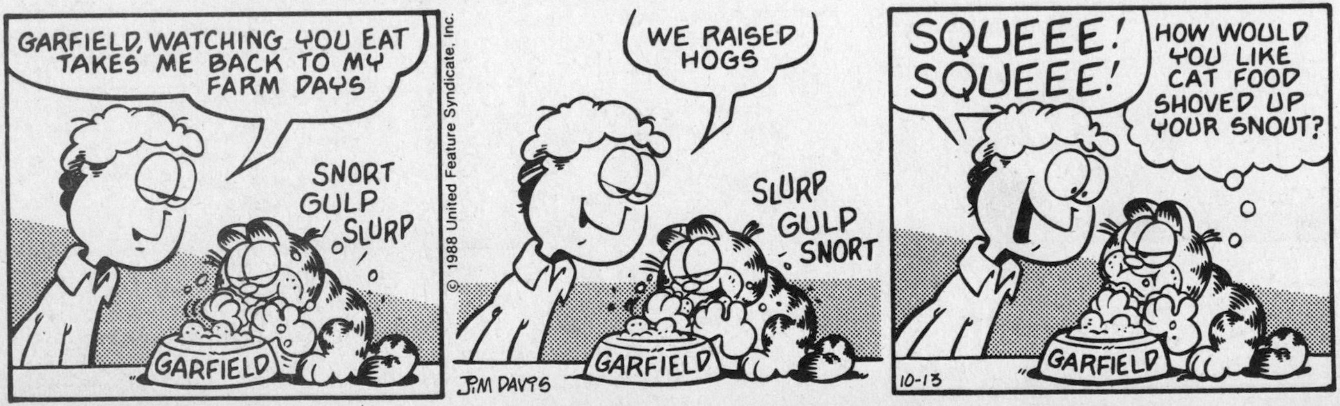
GARFIELD, WATCHING YOU EAT TAKES ME BACK TO MY FARM DAYS
SNORT
GULP
SLURP
GARFIELD
© 1988 United Feature Syndicate, Inc.
WE RAISED HOGS
SLURP
GULP
SNORT
GARFIELD
JIM DAVIS
SQUEEE! SQUEEE!
HOW WOULD YOU LIKE CAT FOOD SHOVED UP YOUR SNOUT?
GARFIELD
10-13

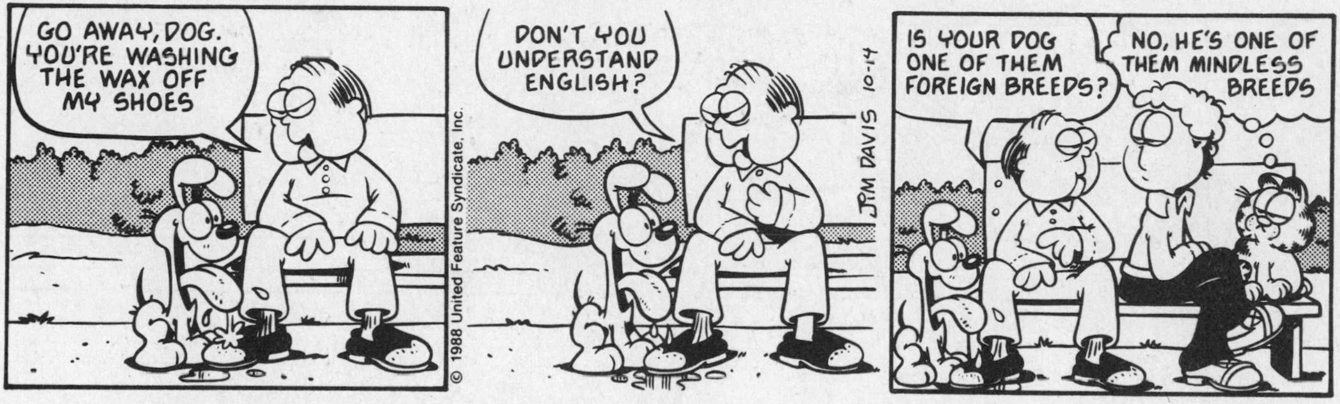
GO AWAY, DOG. YOU'RE WASHING THE WAX OFF MY SHOES
© 1988 United Feature Syndicate, Inc.
DON'T YOU UNDERSTAND ENGLISH?
JIM DAVIS 10-14
IS YOUR DOG ONE OF THEM FOREIGN BREEDS?
NO, HE'S ONE OF THEM MINDLESS BREEDS

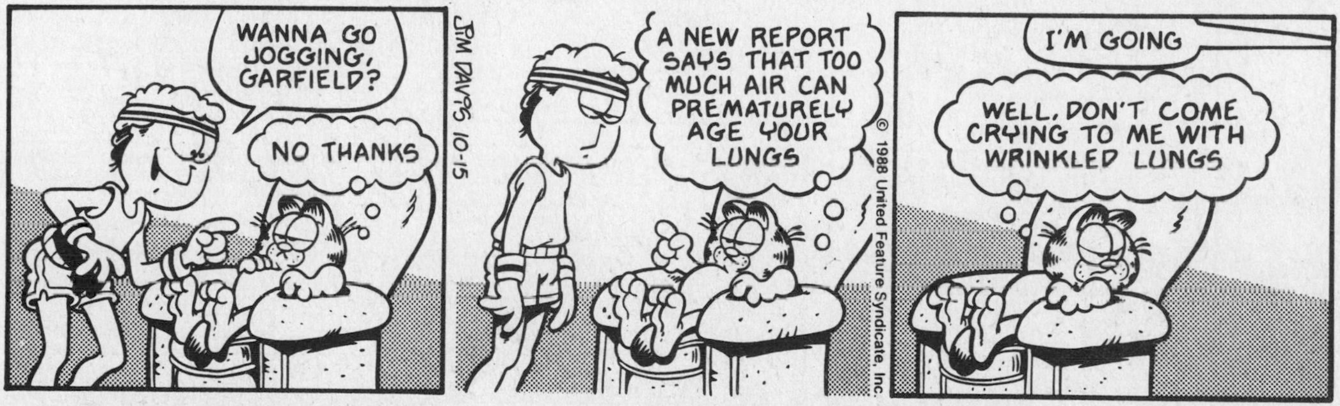
WANNA GO JOGGING, GARFIELD?
NO THANKS
JIM DAVIS 10-15
A NEW REPORT SAYS THAT TOO MUCH AIR CAN PREMATURELY AGE YOUR LUNGS
© 1988 United Feature Syndicate, Inc.
I'M GOING
WELL, DON'T COME CRYING TO ME WITH WRINKLED LUNGS

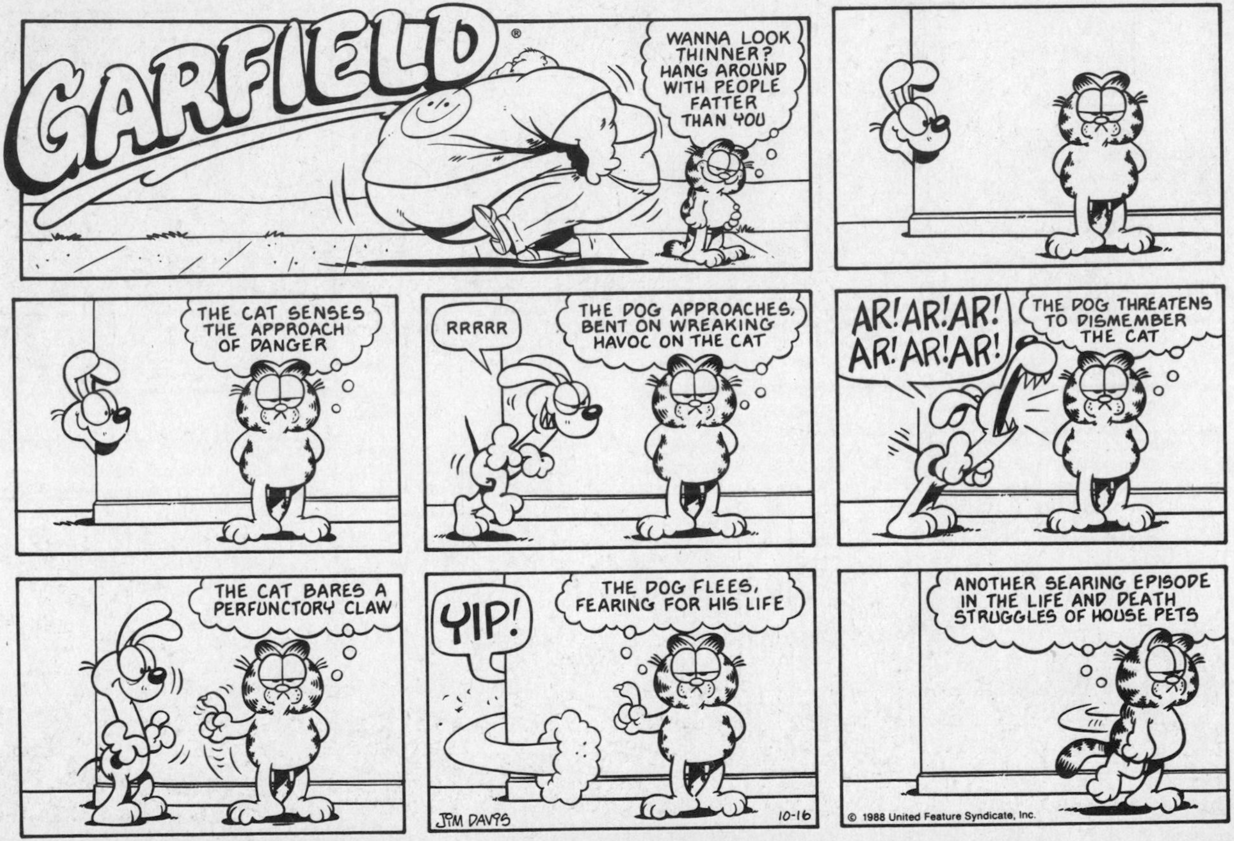
GARFIELD®
WANNA LOOK THINNER? HANG AROUND WITH PEOPLE FATTER THAN YOU
THE CAT SENSES THE APPROACH OF DANGER
RRRRR
THE DOG APPROACHES, BENT ON WREAKING HAVOC ON THE CAT
AR! AR! AR! AR! AR! AR!
THE DOG THREATENS TO DISMEMBER THE CAT
THE CAT BARES A PERFUNCTORY CLAW
YIP!
THE DOG FLEES, FEARING FOR HIS LIFE
JIM DAVIS
10-16
ANOTHER SEARING EPISODE IN THE LIFE AND DEATH STRUGGLES OF HOUSE PETS
© 1988 United Feature Syndicate, Inc.

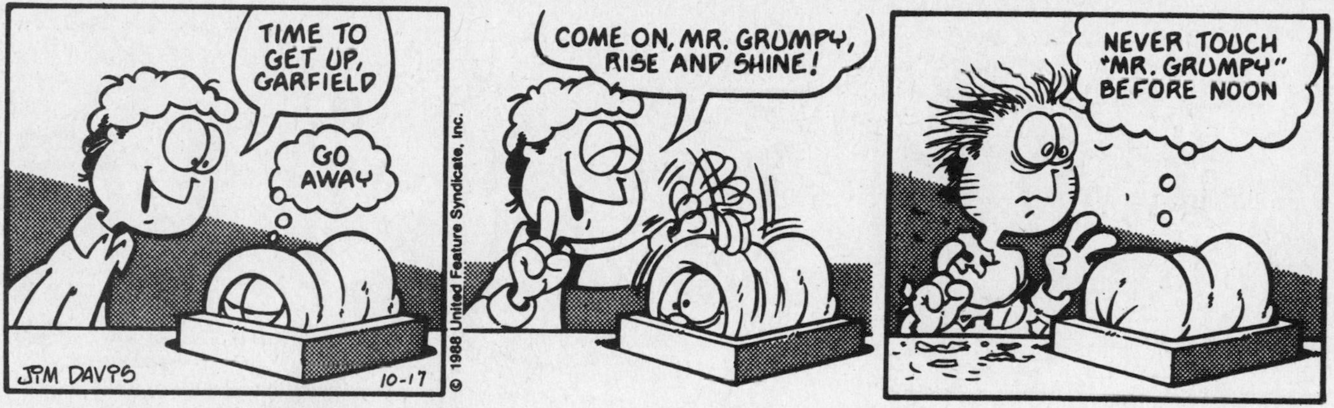
TIME TO GET UP, GARFIELD
GO AWAY
JIM DAVIS
10-17
© 1988 United Feature Syndicate, Inc.
COME ON, MR. GRUMPY, RISE AND SHINE!
NEVER TOUCH "MR. GRUMPY" BEFORE NOON

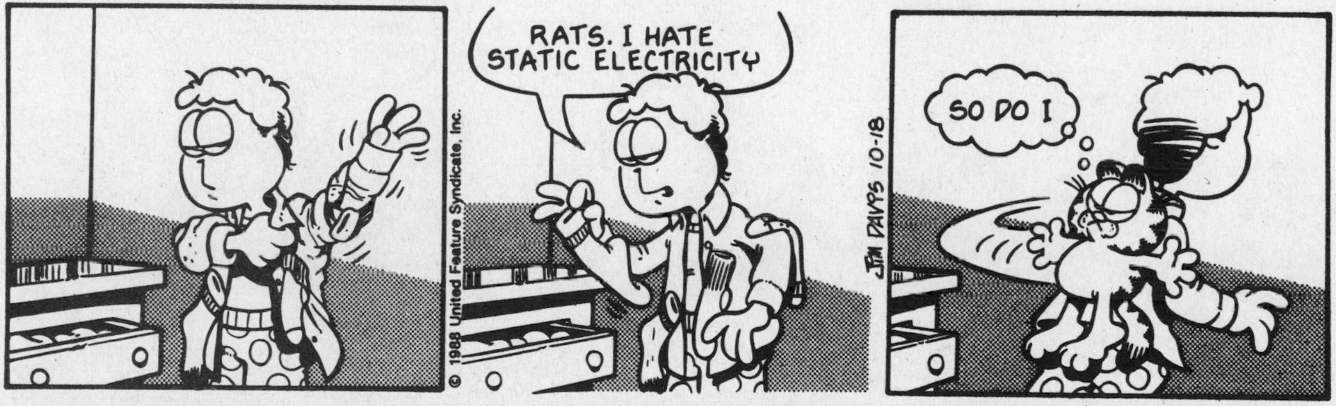
© 1988 United Feature Syndicate, Inc.
RATS. I HATE STATIC ELECTRICITY
JIM DAVIS 10-18
SO DO I

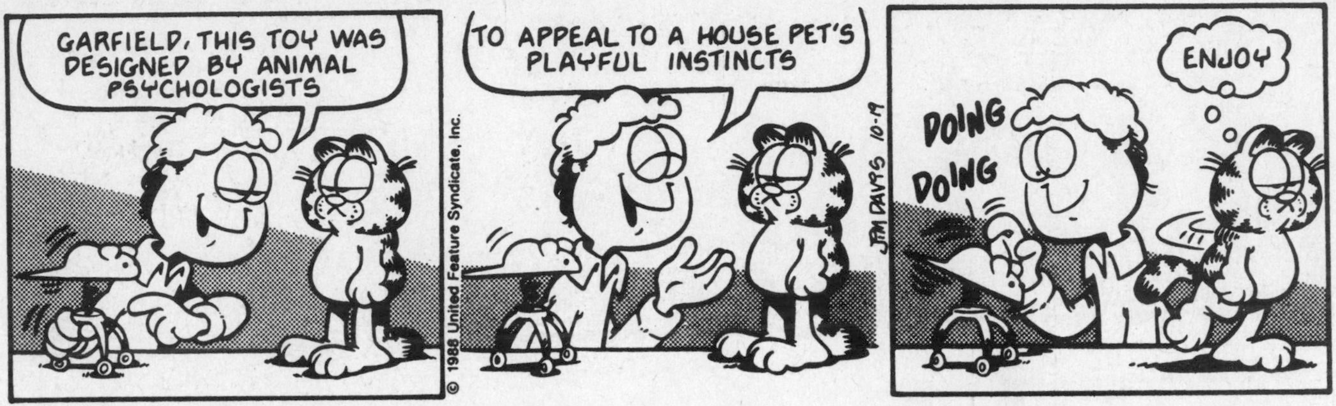

GARFIELD, THIS TOY WAS DESIGNED BY ANIMAL PSYCHOLOGISTS
TO APPEAL TO A HOUSE PET'S PLAYFUL INSTINCTS
© 1988 United Feature Syndicate, Inc.
JIM DAVIS 10-19
DOING
DOING
ENJOY

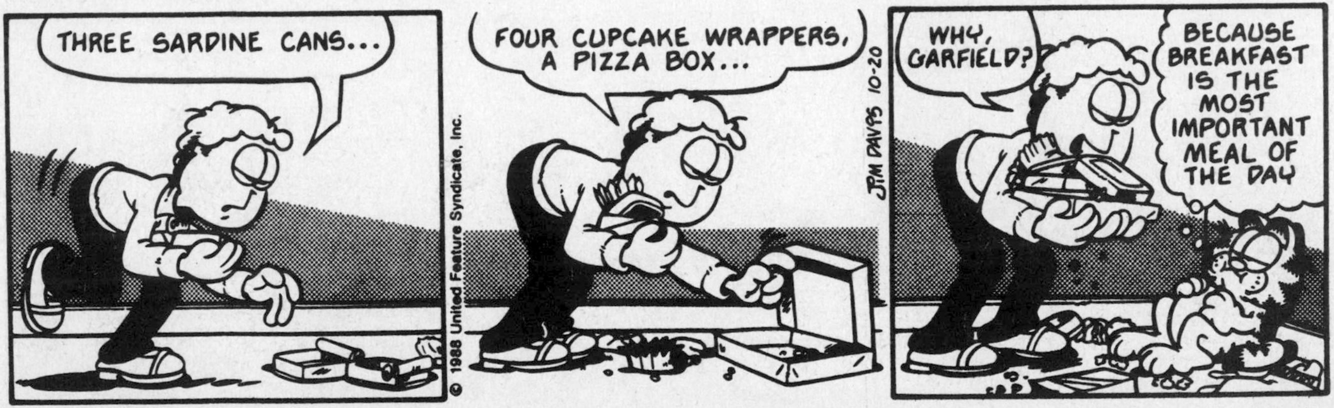

THREE SARDINE CANS...
FOUR CUPCAKE WRAPPERS, A PIZZA BOX...
© 1988 United Feature Syndicate, Inc.
JIM DAVIS 10-20
WHY, GARFIELD?
BECAUSE BREAKFAST IS THE MOST IMPORTANT MEAL OF THE DAY

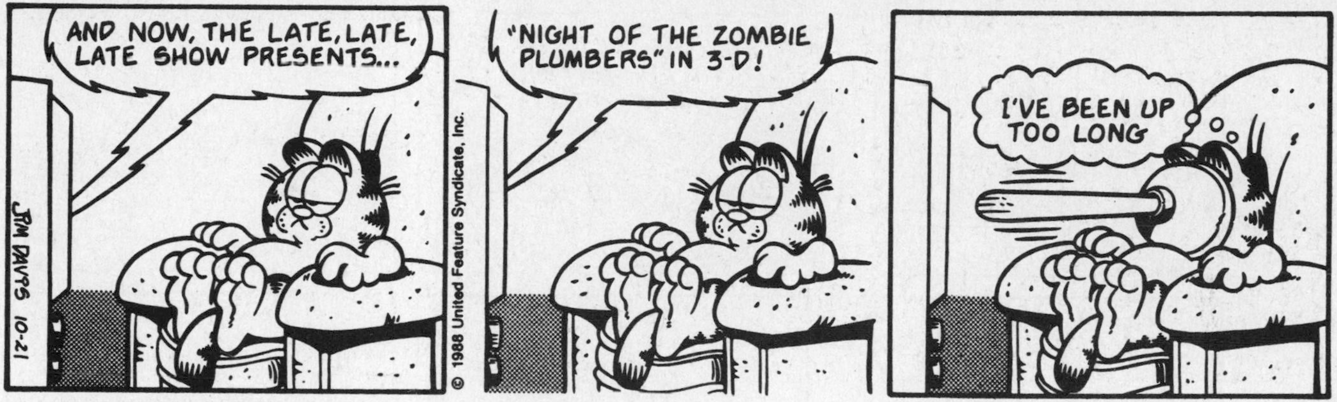
AND NOW, THE LATE, LATE, LATE SHOW PRESENTS...
"NIGHT OF THE ZOMBIE PLUMBERS" IN 3-D!
I'VE BEEN UP TOO LONG
JIM DAVIS 10-21
© 1988 United Feature Syndicate, Inc.

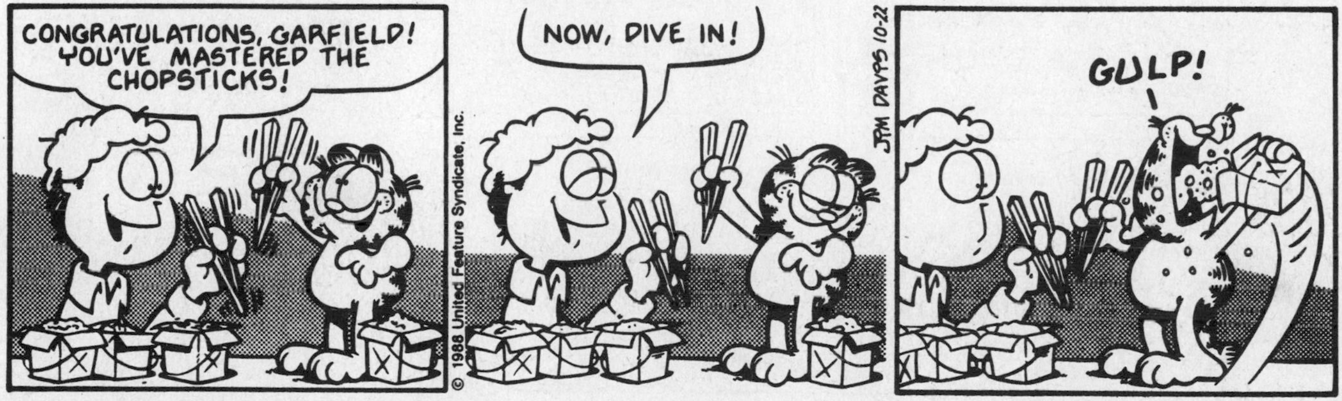
CONGRATULATIONS, GARFIELD! YOU'VE MASTERED THE CHOPSTICKS!
NOW, DIVE IN!
GULP!
JIM DAVIS 10-22
© 1988 United Feature Syndicate, Inc.

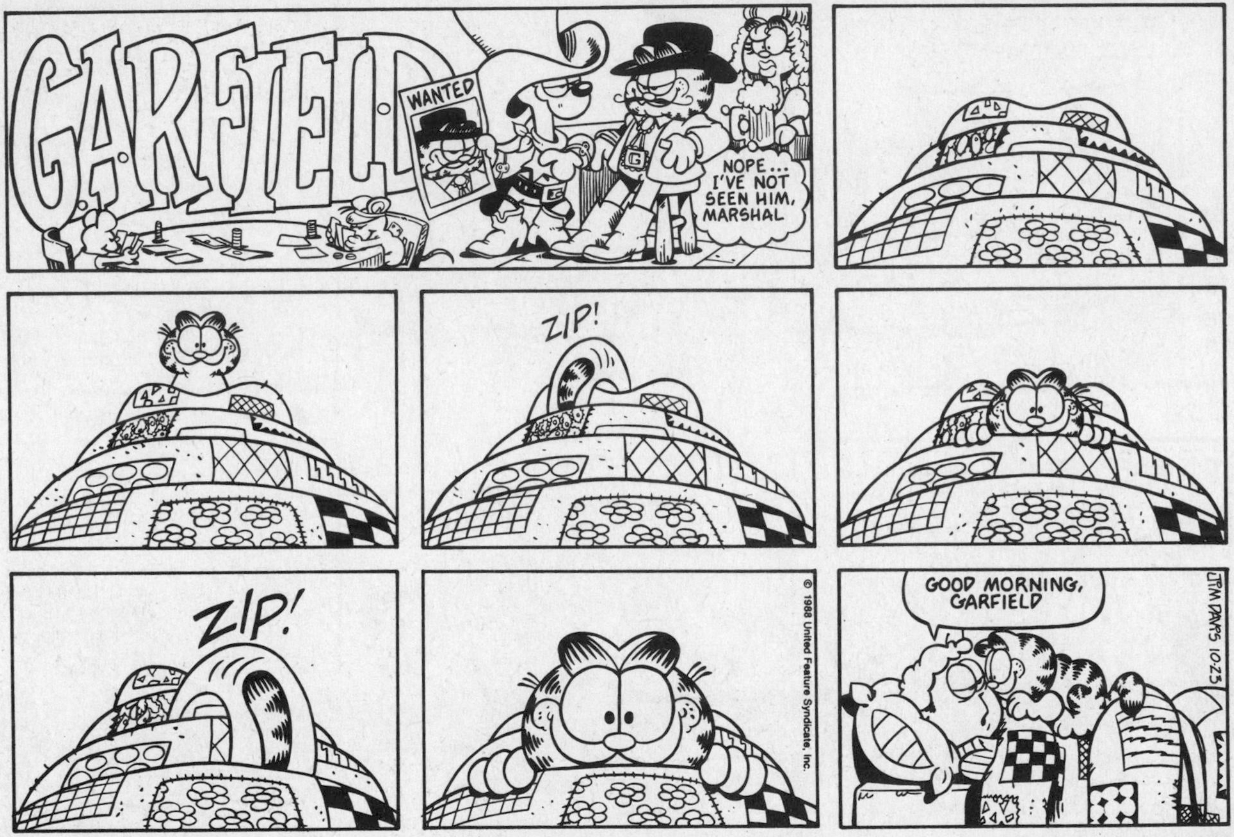
GARFIELD
WANTED
NOPE... I'VE NOT SEEN HIM, MARSHAL
ZIP!
ZIP!
© 1988 United Feature Syndicate, Inc.
JPM DAVIS 10-23
GOOD MORNING, GARFIELD

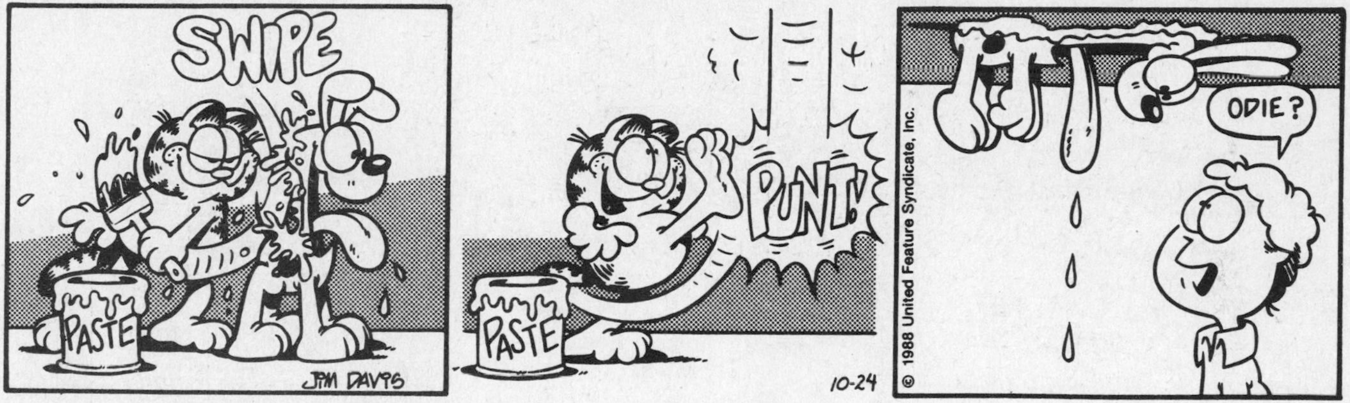

SWIPE
PUNT!
ODIE?
JIM DAVIS
10-24
© 1988 United Feature Syndicate, Inc.

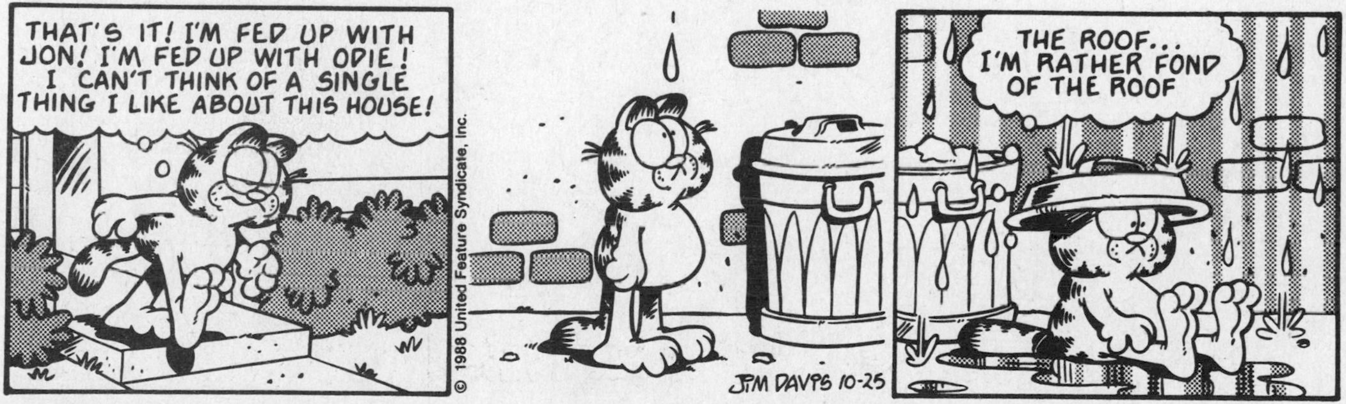

THAT'S IT! I'M FED UP WITH JON! I'M FED UP WITH ODIE! I CAN'T THINK OF A SINGLE THING I LIKE ABOUT THIS HOUSE!
© 1988 United Feature Syndicate, Inc.
JIM DAVIS 10-25
THE ROOF... I'M RATHER FOND OF THE ROOF

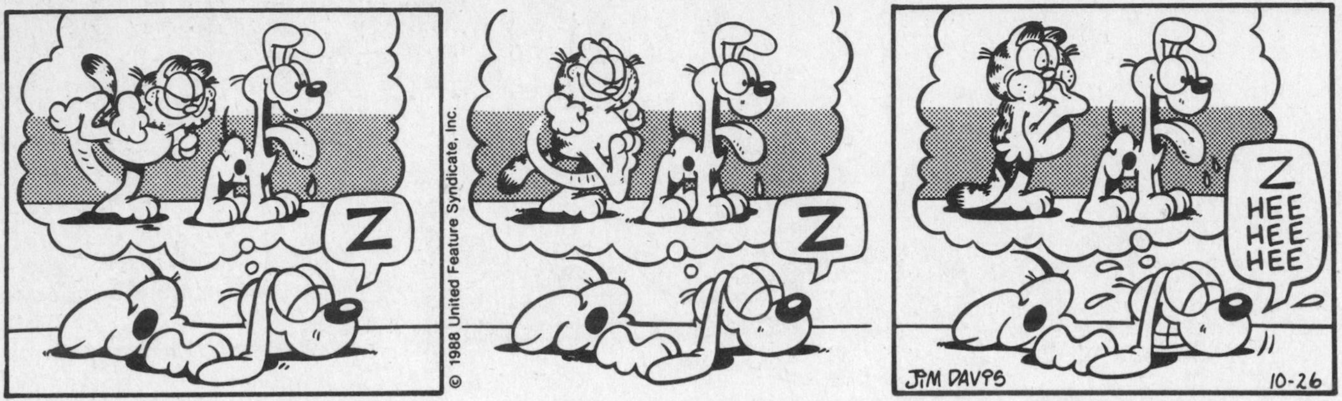
Z
Z
Z
HEE
HEE
HEE
JIM DAVIS
10-26
© 1988 United Feature Syndicate, Inc.

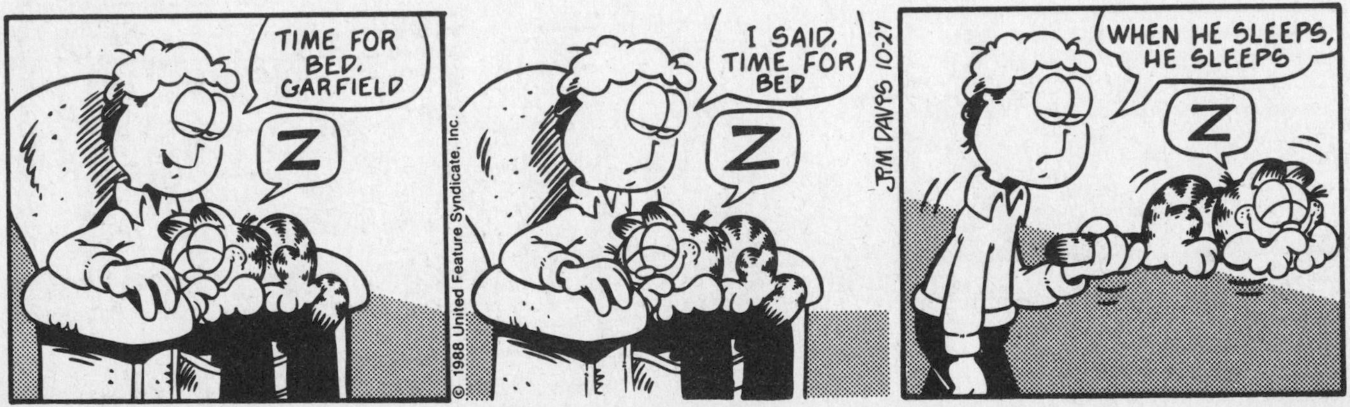
TIME FOR BED, GARFIELD
Z
I SAID, TIME FOR BED
Z
WHEN HE SLEEPS, HE SLEEPS
Z
JIM DAVIS 10-27
© 1988 United Feature Syndicate, Inc.

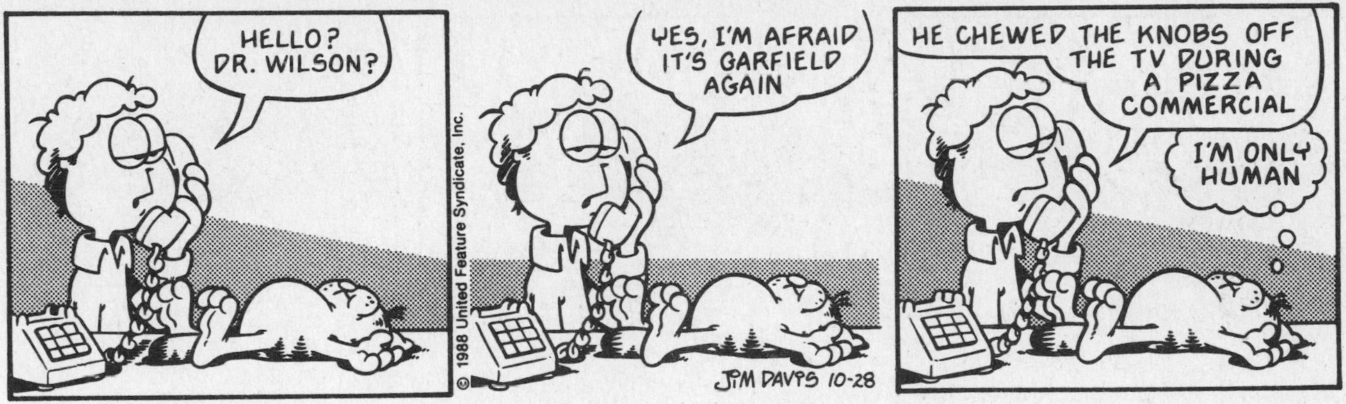
HELLO? DR. WILSON?
© 1988 United Feature Syndicate, Inc.
YES, I'M AFRAID IT'S GARFIELD AGAIN
JIM DAVIS 10-28
HE CHEWED THE KNOBS OFF THE TV DURING A PIZZA COMMERCIAL
I'M ONLY HUMAN

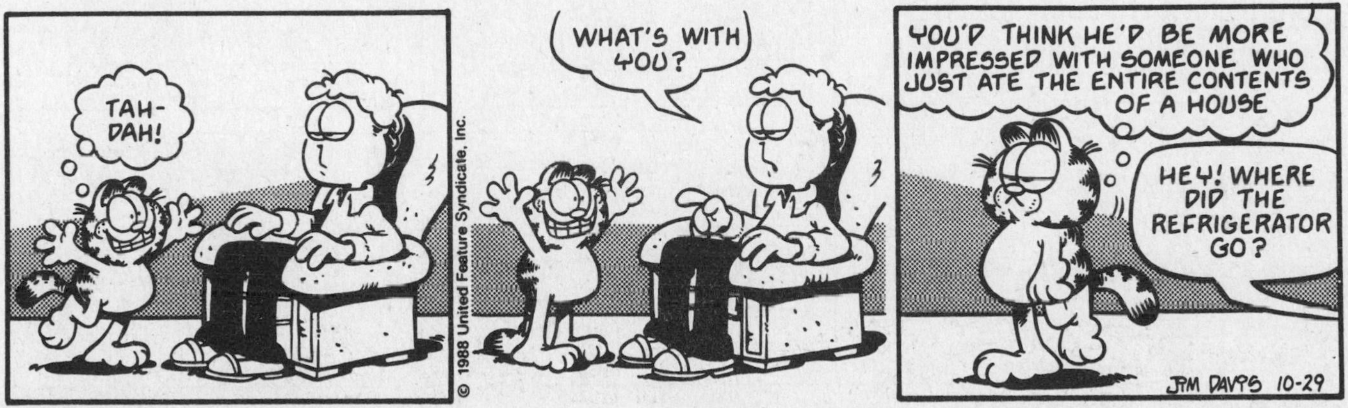
TAH-DAH!
© 1988 United Feature Syndicate, Inc.
WHAT'S WITH YOU?
YOU'D THINK HE'D BE MORE IMPRESSED WITH SOMEONE WHO JUST ATE THE ENTIRE CONTENTS OF A HOUSE
HEY! WHERE DID THE REFRIGERATOR GO?
JIM DAVIS 10-29

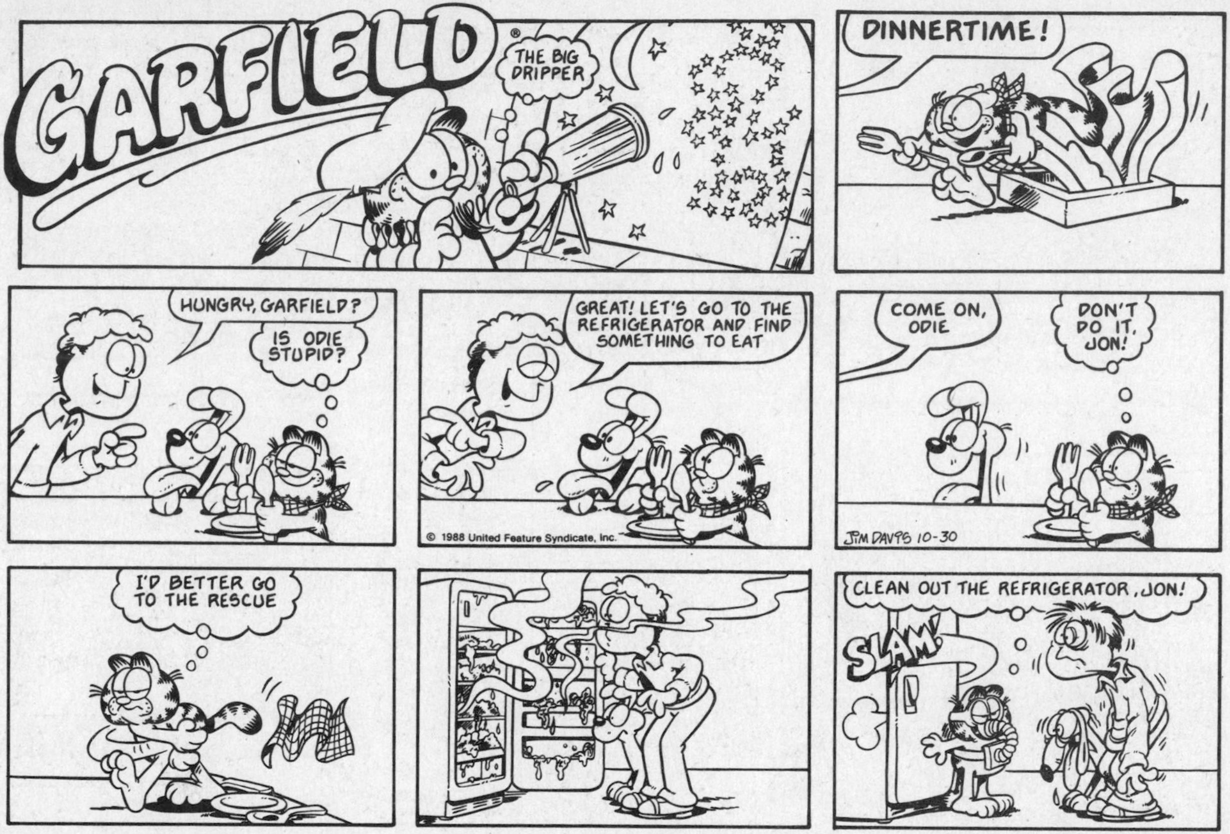
GARFIELD®
THE BIG DRIPPER
DINNERTIME!
HUNGRY, GARFIELD?
IS ODIE STUPID?
GREAT! LET'S GO TO THE REFRIGERATOR AND FIND SOMETHING TO EAT
© 1988 United Feature Syndicate, Inc.
COME ON, ODIE
DON'T DO IT, JON!
JIM DAVIS 10-30
I'D BETTER GO TO THE RESCUE
CLEAN OUT THE REFRIGERATOR, JON!
SLAM!

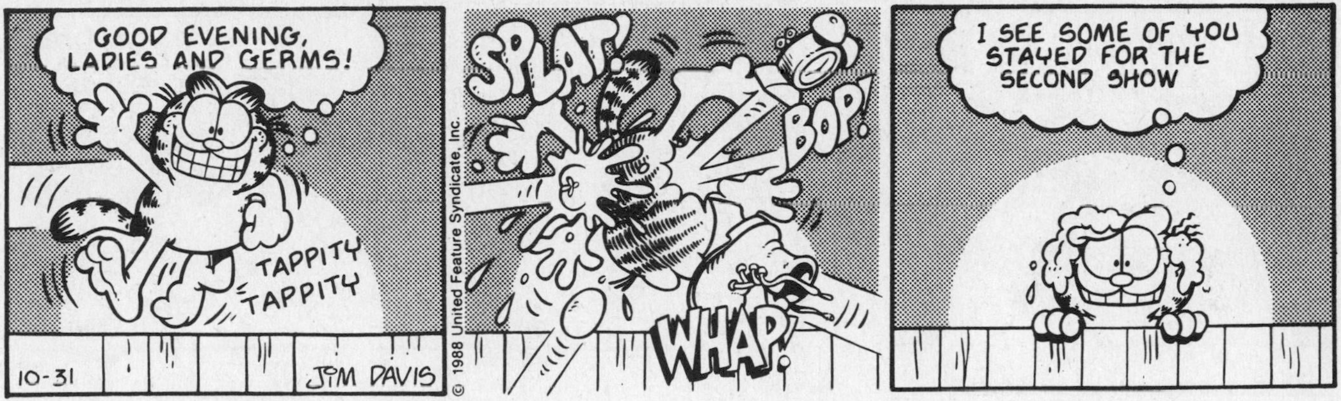
GOOD EVENING, LADIES AND GERMS!
TAPPITY TAPPITY
10-31
JIM DAVIS
© 1988 United Feature Syndicate, Inc.
SPLAT!
BOP!
WHAP!
I SEE SOME OF YOU STAYED FOR THE SECOND SHOW

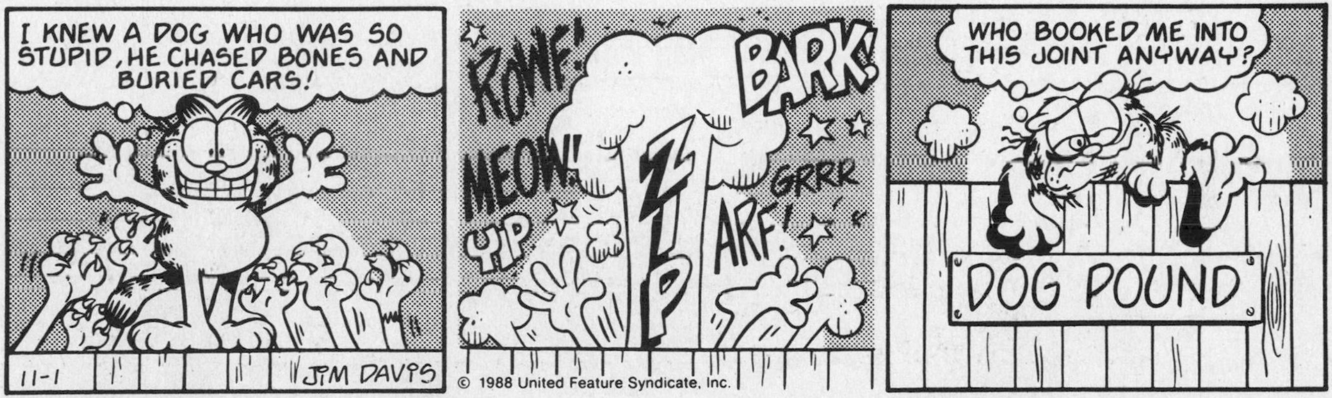
I KNEW A DOG WHO WAS SO STUPID, HE CHASED BONES AND BURIED CARS!
11-1
JIM DAVIS
ROWF!
BARK!
MEOW!
YIP
GRRR
ARF!
© 1988 United Feature Syndicate, Inc.
WHO BOOKED ME INTO THIS JOINT ANYWAY?
DOG POUND

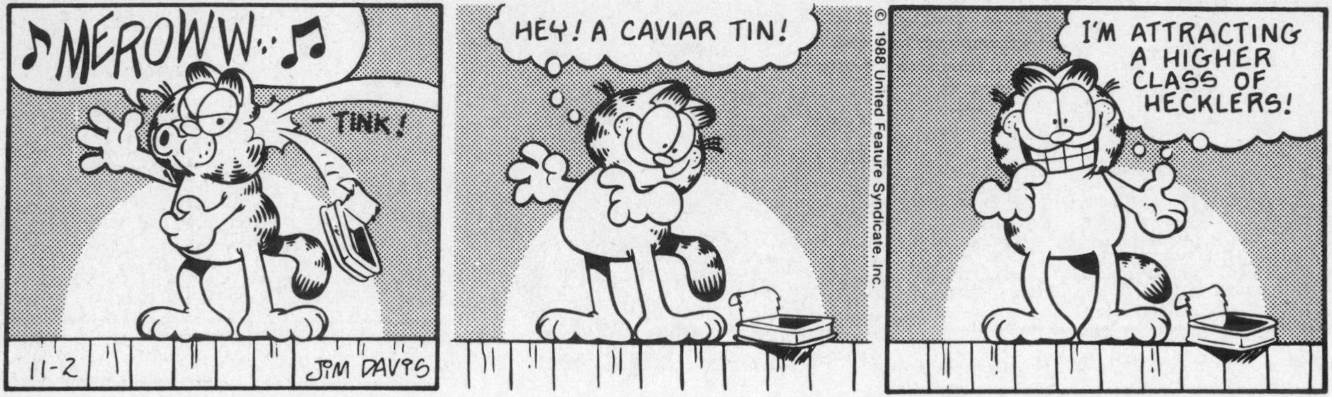
MEROWW
-TINK!
11-2
JIM DAVIS
HEY! A CAVIAR TIN!
© 1988 United Feature Syndicate, Inc.
I'M ATTRACTING A HIGHER CLASS OF HECKLERS!

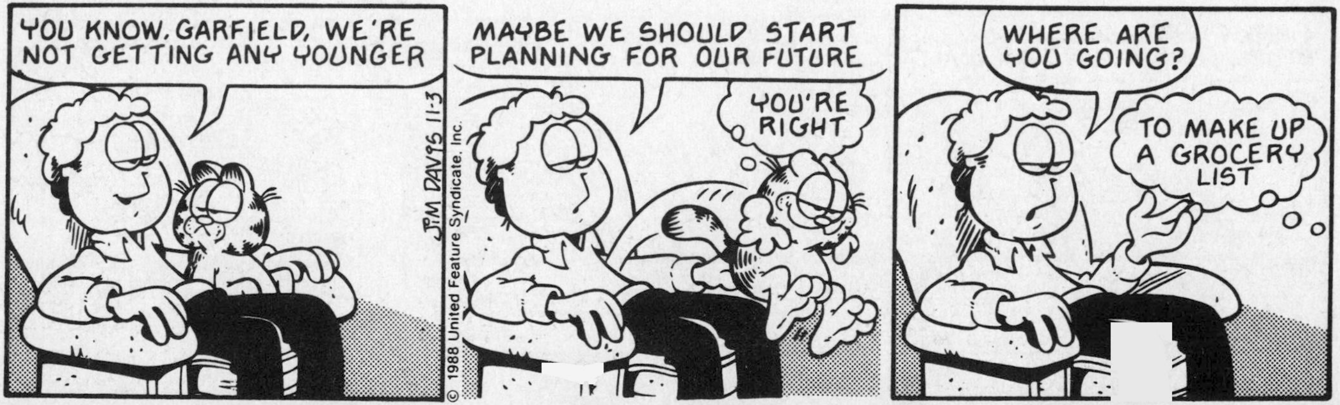
YOU KNOW, GARFIELD, WE'RE NOT GETTING ANY YOUNGER
JIM DAVIS 11-3
© 1988 United Feature Syndicate, Inc.
MAYBE WE SHOULD START PLANNING FOR OUR FUTURE
YOU'RE RIGHT
WHERE ARE YOU GOING?
TO MAKE UP A GROCERY LIST

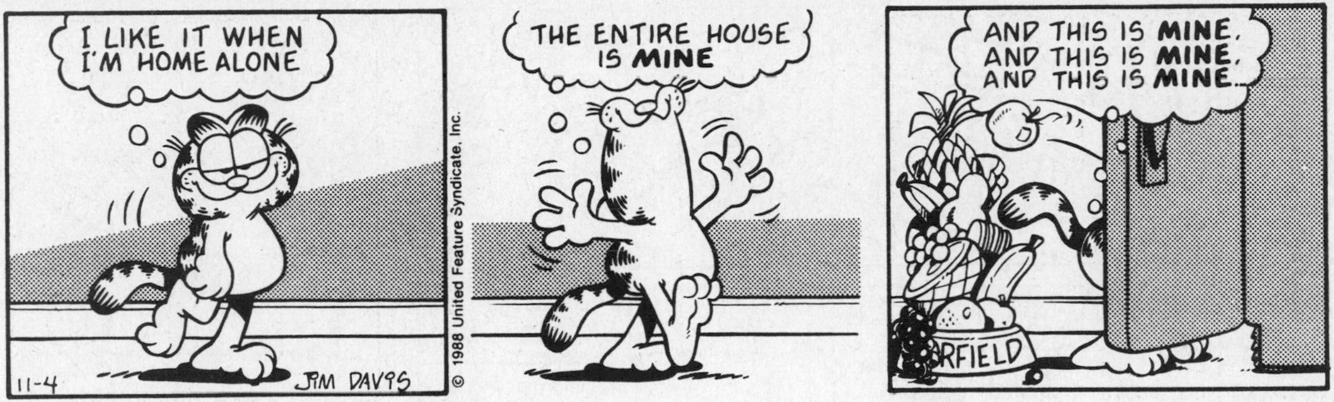

I LIKE IT WHEN I'M HOME ALONE
11-4
JIM DAVIS
© 1988 United Feature Syndicate, Inc.
THE ENTIRE HOUSE IS MINE
AND THIS IS MINE, AND THIS IS MINE, AND THIS IS MINE...
GARFIELD

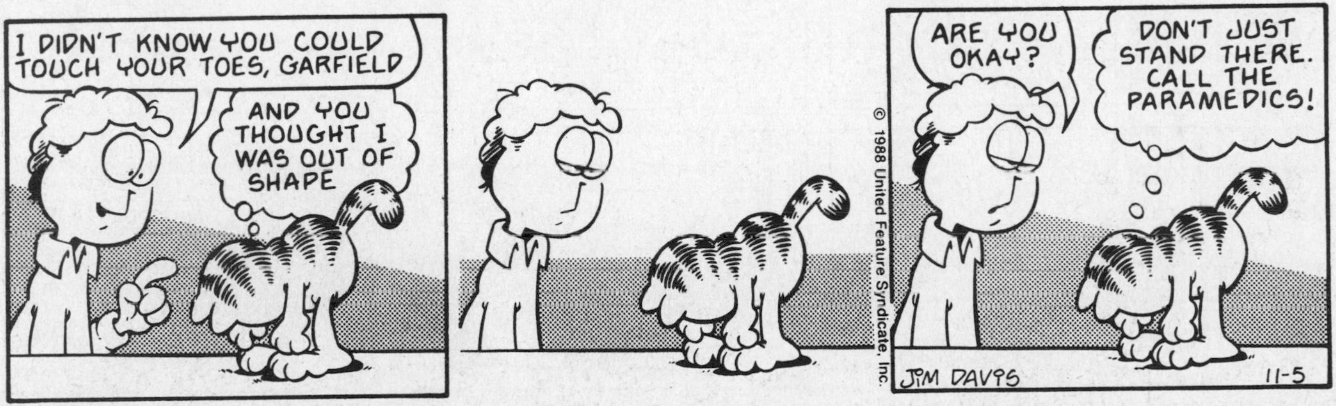

I DIDN'T KNOW YOU COULD TOUCH YOUR TOES, GARFIELD
AND YOU THOUGHT I WAS OUT OF SHAPE
© 1988 United Feature Syndicate, Inc.
ARE YOU OKAY?
DON'T JUST STAND THERE. CALL THE PARAMEDICS!
JIM DAVIS
11-5

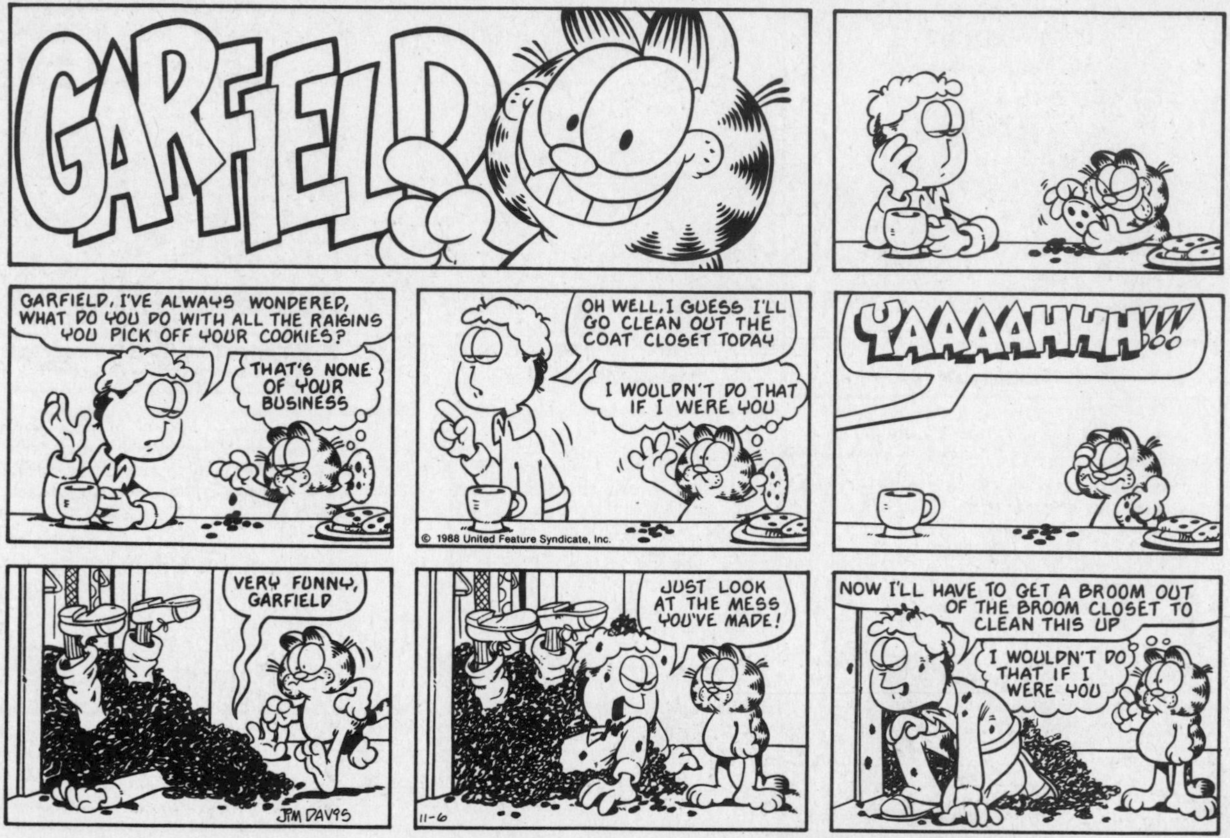
GARFIELD
GARFIELD, I'VE ALWAYS WONDERED, WHAT DO YOU DO WITH ALL THE RAISINS YOU PICK OFF YOUR COOKIES?
THAT'S NONE OF YOUR BUSINESS
OH WELL, I GUESS I'LL GO CLEAN OUT THE COAT CLOSET TODAY
I WOULDN'T DO THAT IF I WERE YOU
© 1988 United Feature Syndicate, Inc.
YAAAAHHH!!!
VERY FUNNY, GARFIELD
JIM DAVIS
JUST LOOK AT THE MESS YOU'VE MADE!
11-6
NOW I'LL HAVE TO GET A BROOM OUT OF THE BROOM CLOSET TO CLEAN THIS UP
I WOULDN'T DO THAT IF I WERE YOU

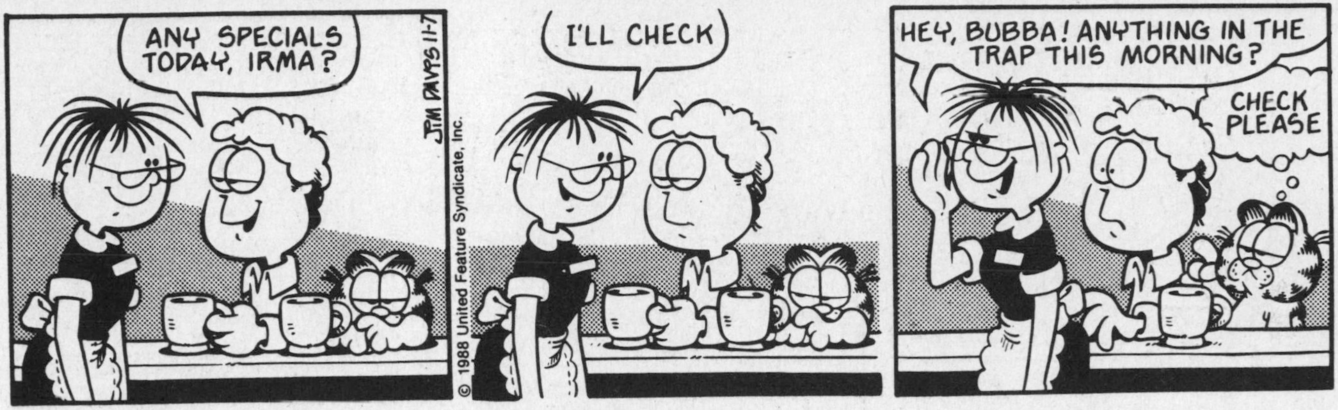
ANY SPECIALS TODAY, IRMA?
JIM DAVIS 11-7
© 1988 United Feature Syndicate, Inc.
I'LL CHECK
HEY, BUBBA! ANYTHING IN THE TRAP THIS MORNING?
CHECK PLEASE

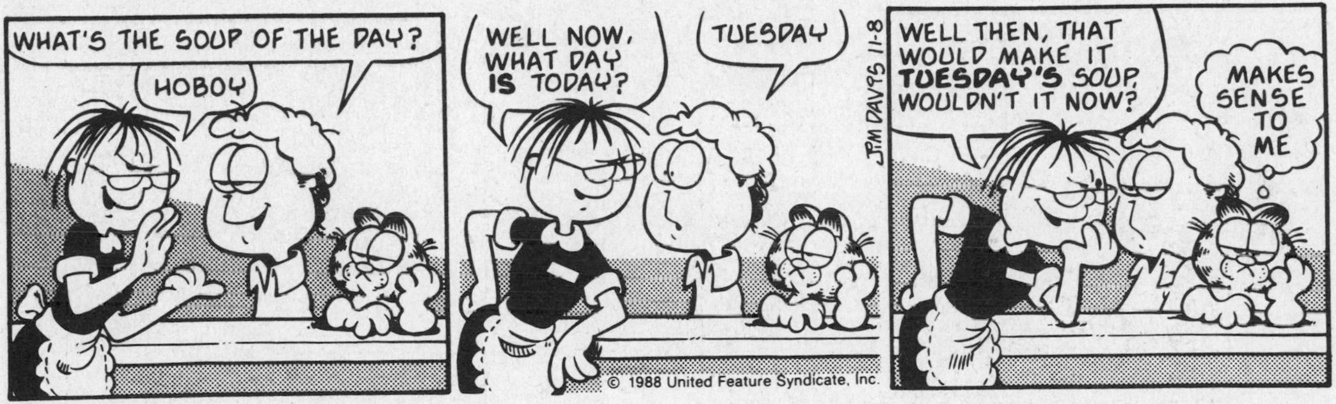
WHAT'S THE SOUP OF THE DAY?
HOBOY
WELL NOW, WHAT DAY **IS** TODAY?
TUESDAY
© 1988 United Feature Syndicate, Inc.
JIM DAVIS 11-8
WELL THEN, THAT WOULD MAKE IT **TUESDAY'S** SOUP, WOULDN'T IT NOW?
MAKES SENSE TO ME

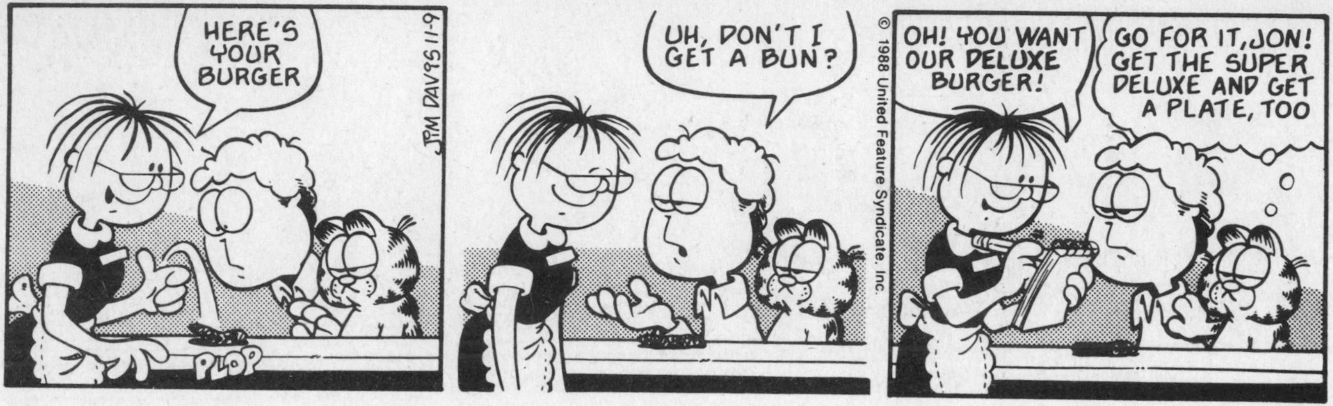
HERE'S YOUR BURGER
JIM DAVIS 11-9
PLOP
UH, DON'T I GET A BUN?
© 1988 United Feature Syndicate, Inc.
OH! YOU WANT OUR DELUXE BURGER!
GO FOR IT, JON! GET THE SUPER DELUXE AND GET A PLATE, TOO

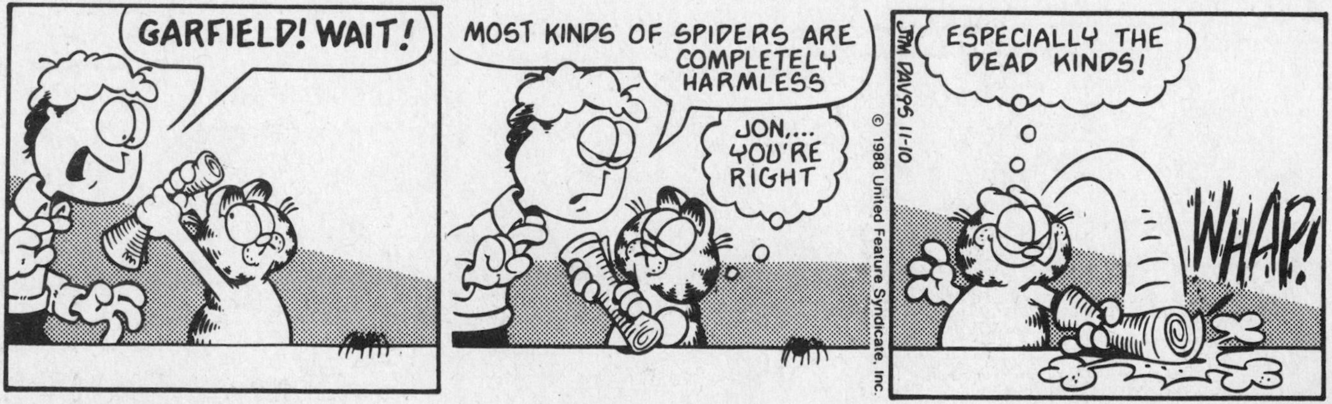
GARFIELD! WAIT!
MOST KINDS OF SPIDERS ARE COMPLETELY HARMLESS
JON,... YOU'RE RIGHT
© 1988 United Feature Syndicate, Inc.
JIM DAVIS 11-10
ESPECIALLY THE DEAD KINDS!
WHAP!

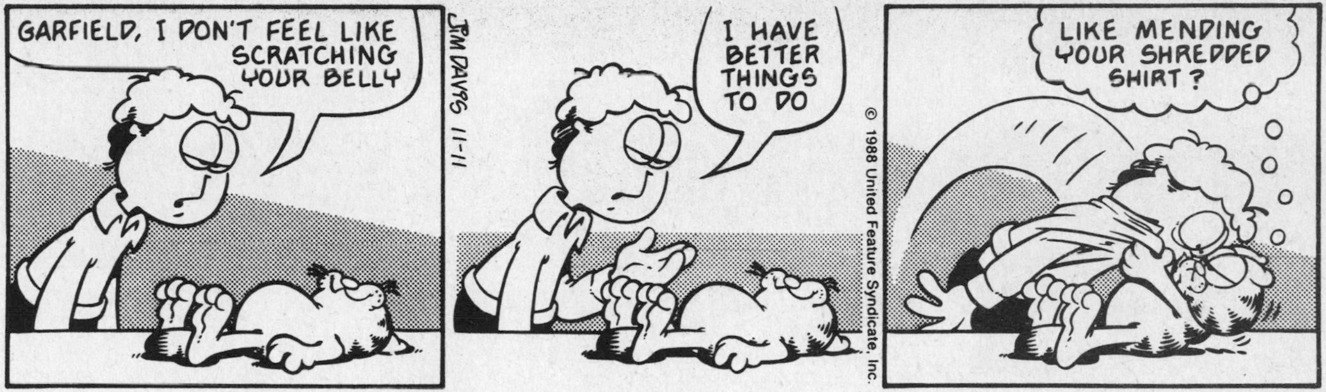
GARFIELD, I DON'T FEEL LIKE SCRATCHING YOUR BELLY
JIM DAVIS 11-11
I HAVE BETTER THINGS TO DO
© 1988 United Feature Syndicate, Inc.
LIKE MENDING YOUR SHREDDED SHIRT?

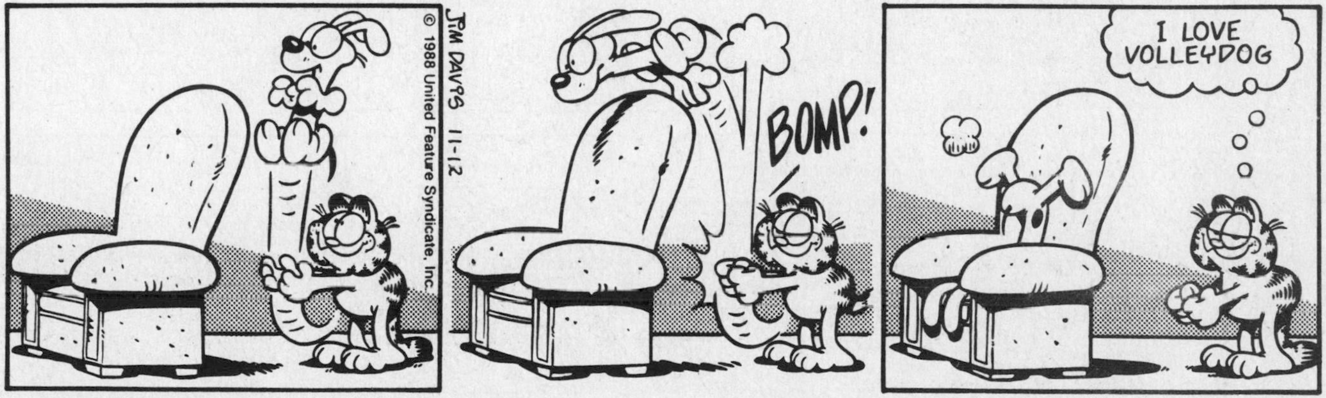
© 1988 United Feature Syndicate, Inc.
JIM DAVIS 11-12
BOMP!
I LOVE VOLLEYDOG

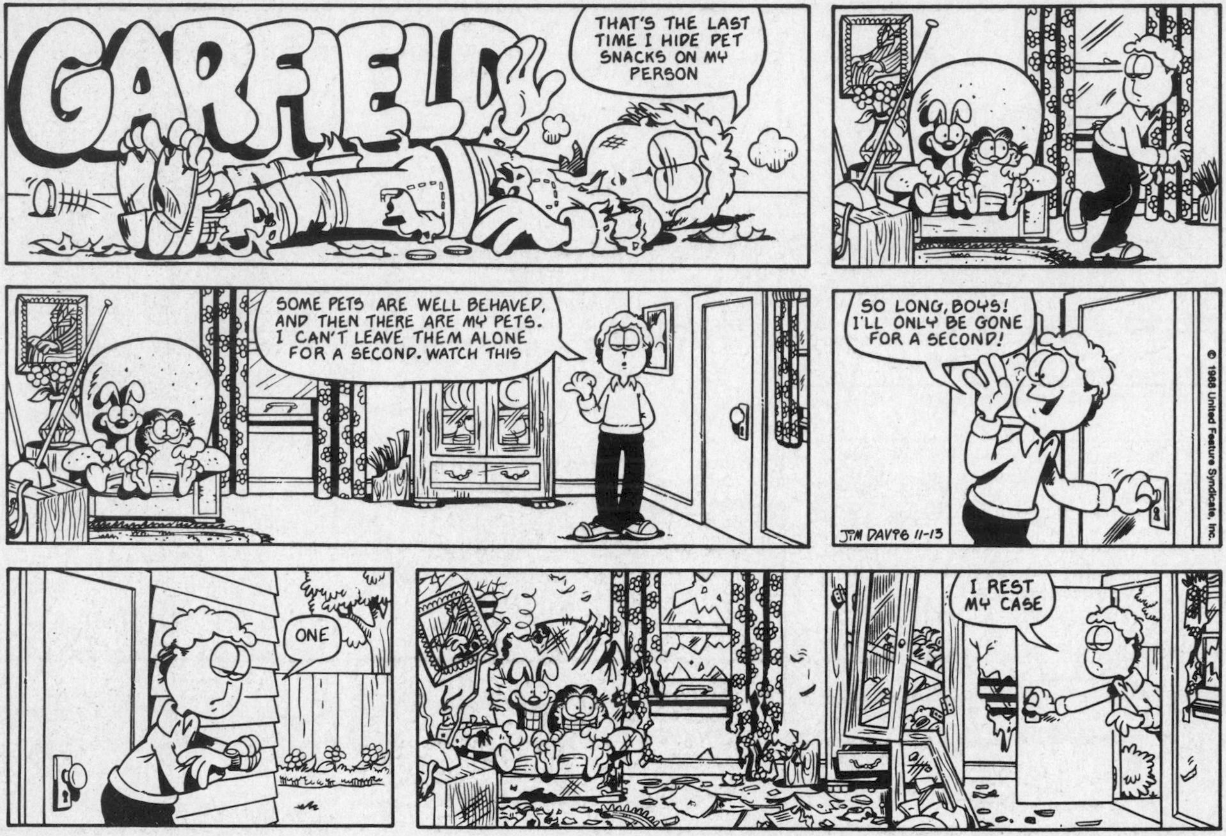
GARFIELD
THAT'S THE LAST TIME I HIDE PET SNACKS ON MY PERSON
SOME PETS ARE WELL BEHAVED, AND THEN THERE ARE MY PETS. I CAN'T LEAVE THEM ALONE FOR A SECOND. WATCH THIS
SO LONG, BOYS! I'LL ONLY BE GONE FOR A SECOND!
JIM DAVIS 11-13
© 1988 United Feature Syndicate, Inc.
ONE
I REST MY CASE

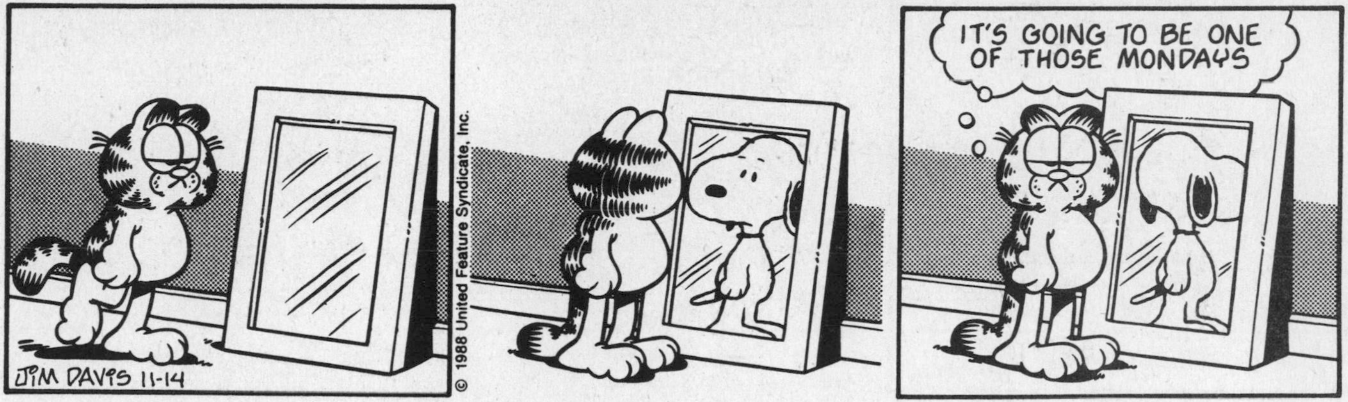
JIM DAVIS 11-14
© 1988 United Feature Syndicate, Inc.
IT'S GOING TO BE ONE OF THOSE MONDAYS

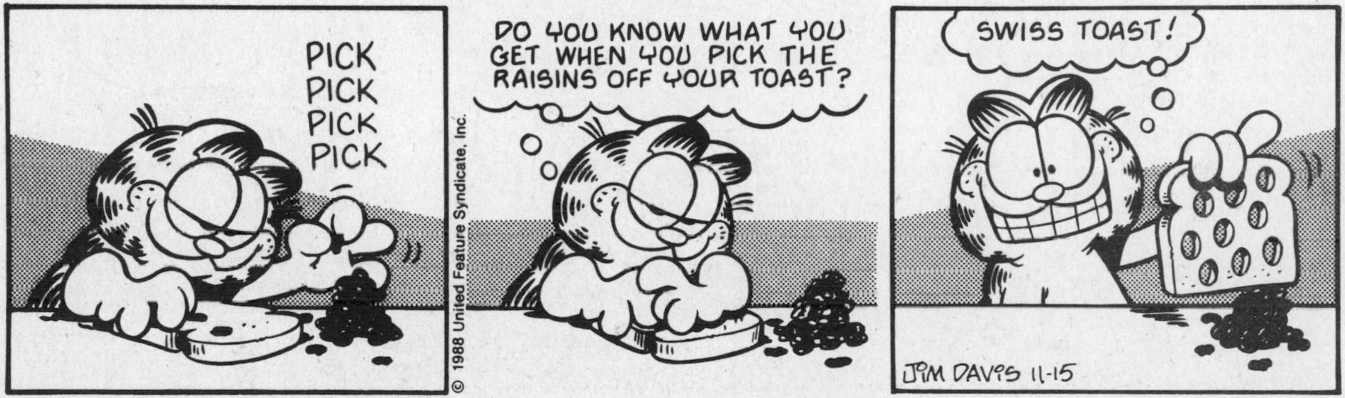
PICK
PICK
PICK
PICK
© 1988 United Feature Syndicate, Inc.
DO YOU KNOW WHAT YOU GET WHEN YOU PICK THE RAISINS OFF YOUR TOAST?
SWISS TOAST!
JIM DAVIS 11-15

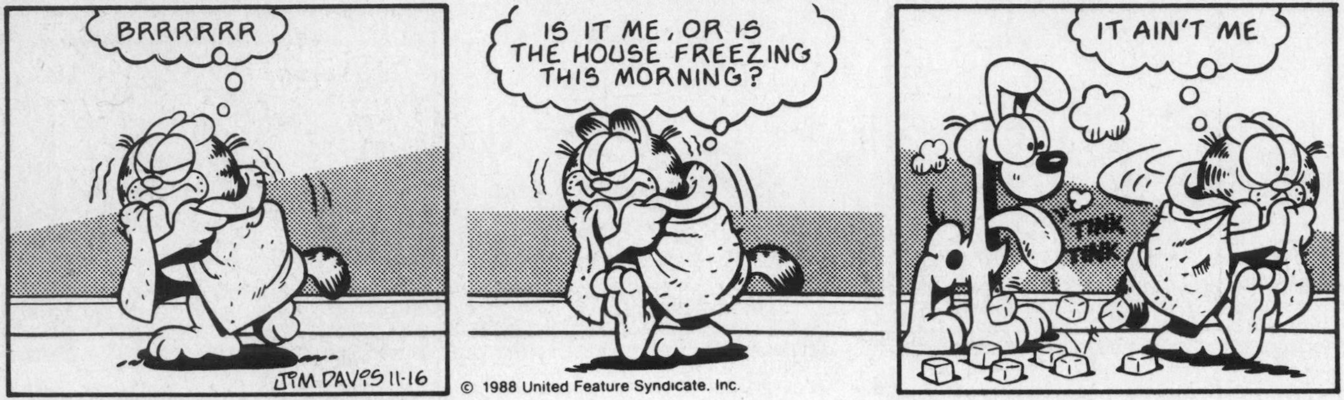
BRRRRRR
IS IT ME, OR IS THE HOUSE FREEZING THIS MORNING?
IT AIN'T ME
TINK
TINK
JIM DAVIS 11-16
© 1988 United Feature Syndicate, Inc.

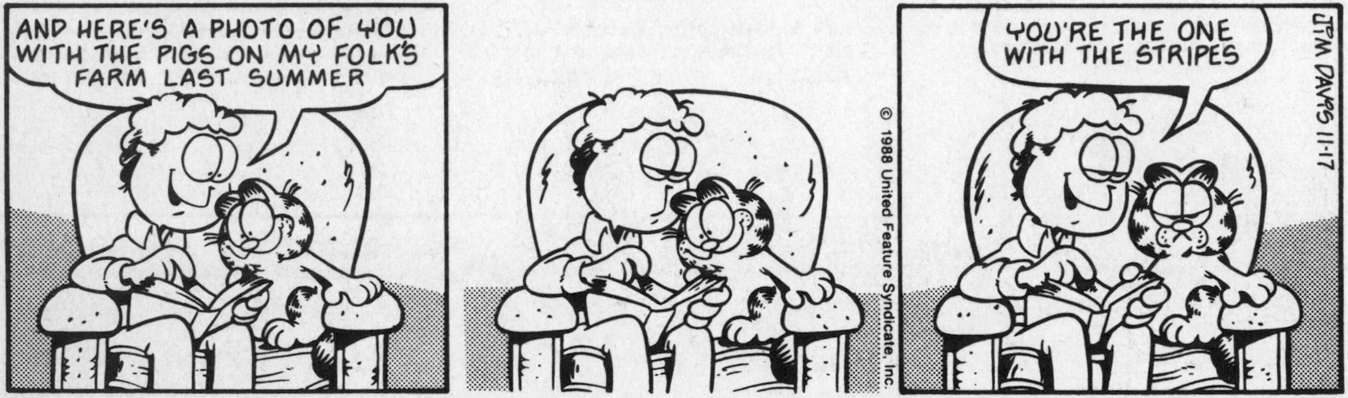
AND HERE'S A PHOTO OF YOU WITH THE PIGS ON MY FOLK'S FARM LAST SUMMER
YOU'RE THE ONE WITH THE STRIPES
JIM DAVIS 11-17
© 1988 United Feature Syndicate, Inc.

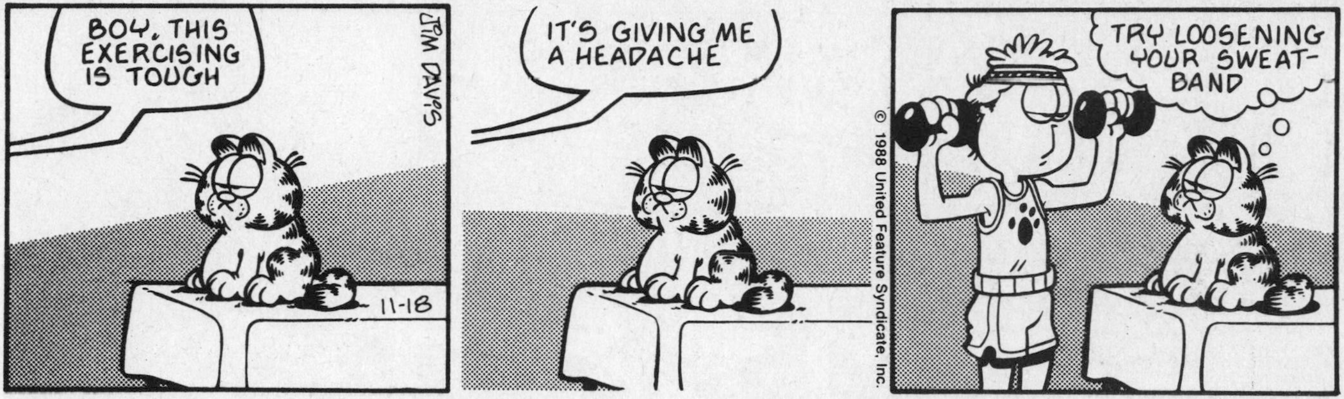
BOY, THIS EXERCISING IS TOUGH
JIM DAVIS
11-18
IT'S GIVING ME A HEADACHE
© 1988 United Feature Syndicate, Inc.
TRY LOOSENING YOUR SWEAT-BAND

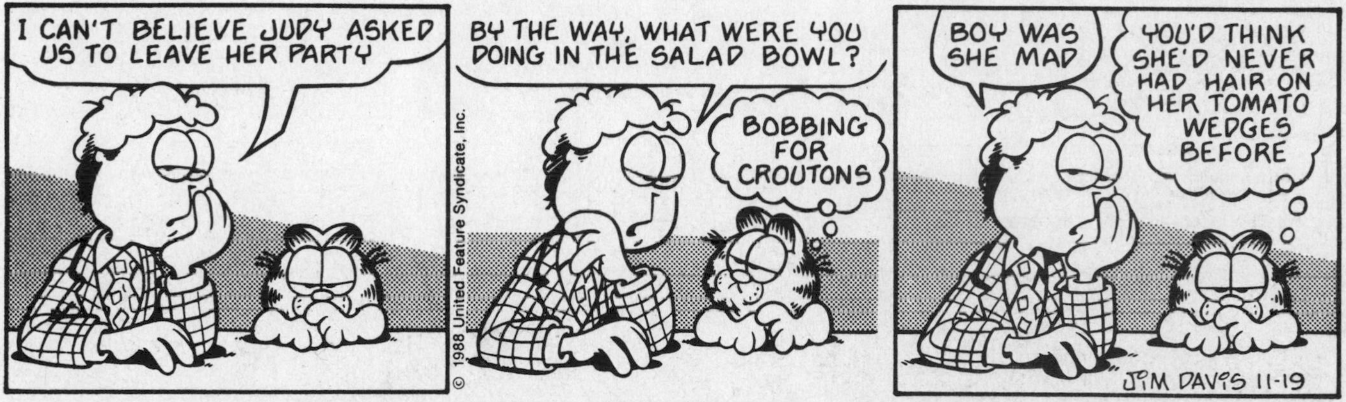
I CAN'T BELIEVE JUDY ASKED US TO LEAVE HER PARTY
© 1988 United Feature Syndicate, Inc.
BY THE WAY, WHAT WERE YOU DOING IN THE SALAD BOWL?
BOBBING FOR CROUTONS
BOY WAS SHE MAD
YOU'D THINK SHE'D NEVER HAD HAIR ON HER TOMATO WEDGES BEFORE
JIM DAVIS 11-19

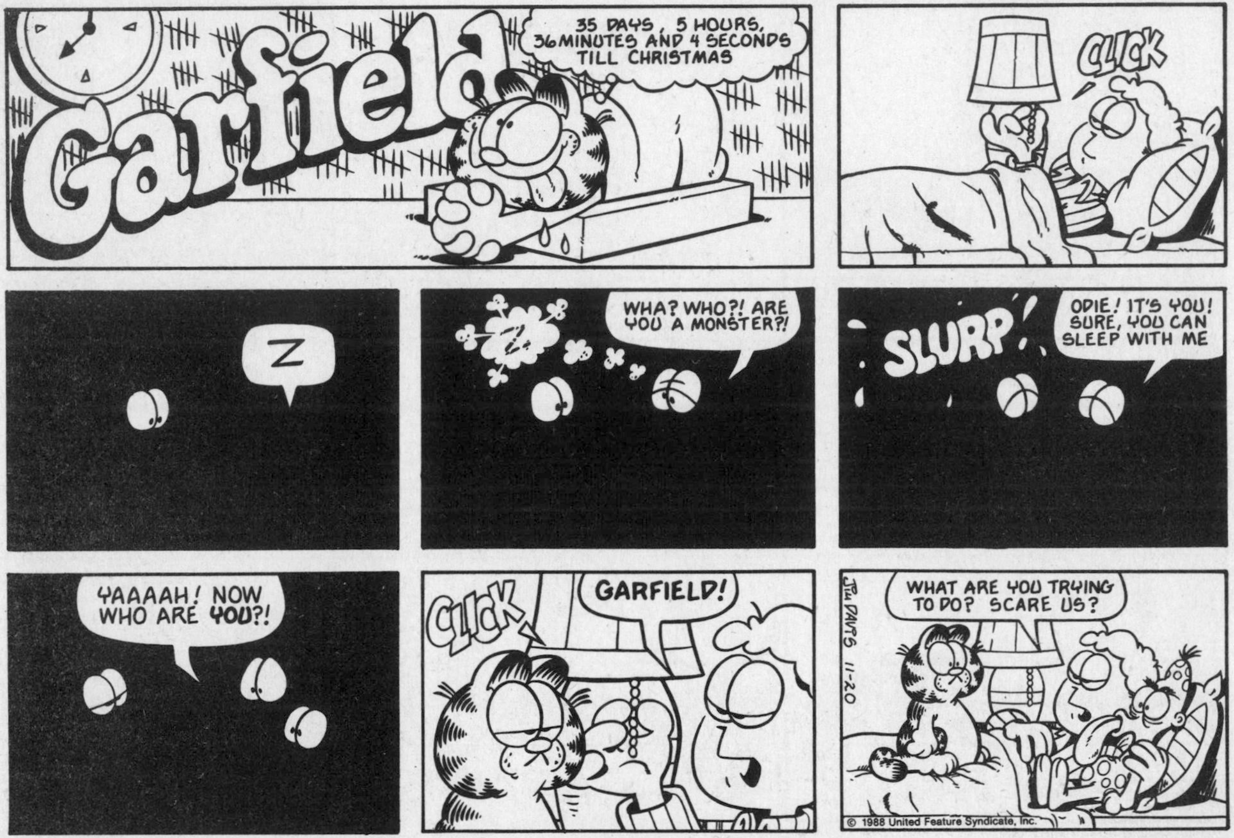
Garfield
35 DAYS, 5 HOURS, 36 MINUTES AND 4 SECONDS TILL CHRISTMAS
CLICK
Z
WHA? WHO?! ARE YOU A MONSTER?!
SLURP!
ODIE! IT'S YOU! SURE, YOU CAN SLEEP WITH ME
YAAAAH! NOW WHO ARE YOU?!
CLICK
GARFIELD!
JIM DAVIS 11-20
WHAT ARE YOU TRYING TO DO? SCARE US?
© 1988 United Feature Syndicate, Inc.

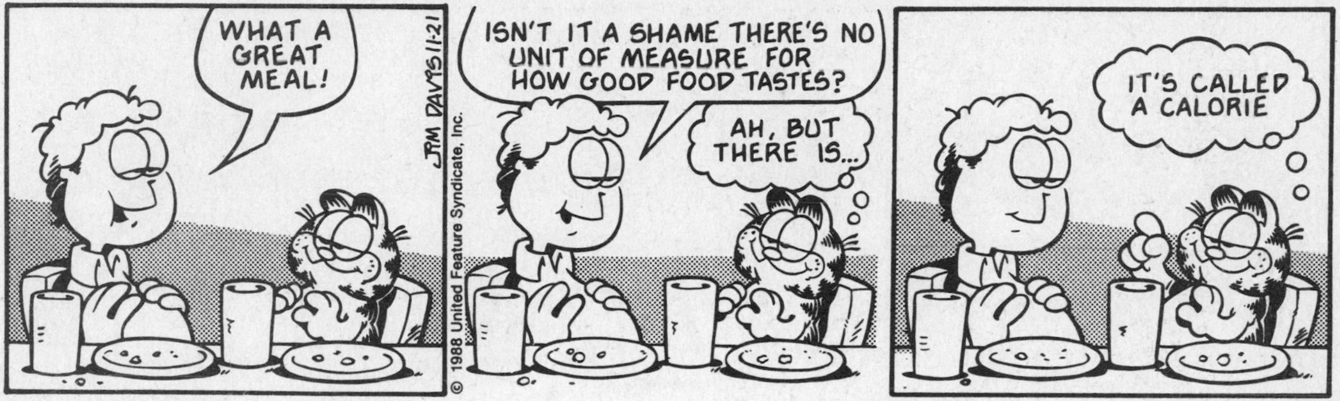
WHAT A GREAT MEAL!
JIM DAVIS 11-21
© 1988 United Feature Syndicate, Inc.
ISN'T IT A SHAME THERE'S NO UNIT OF MEASURE FOR HOW GOOD FOOD TASTES?
AH, BUT THERE IS...
IT'S CALLED A CALORIE

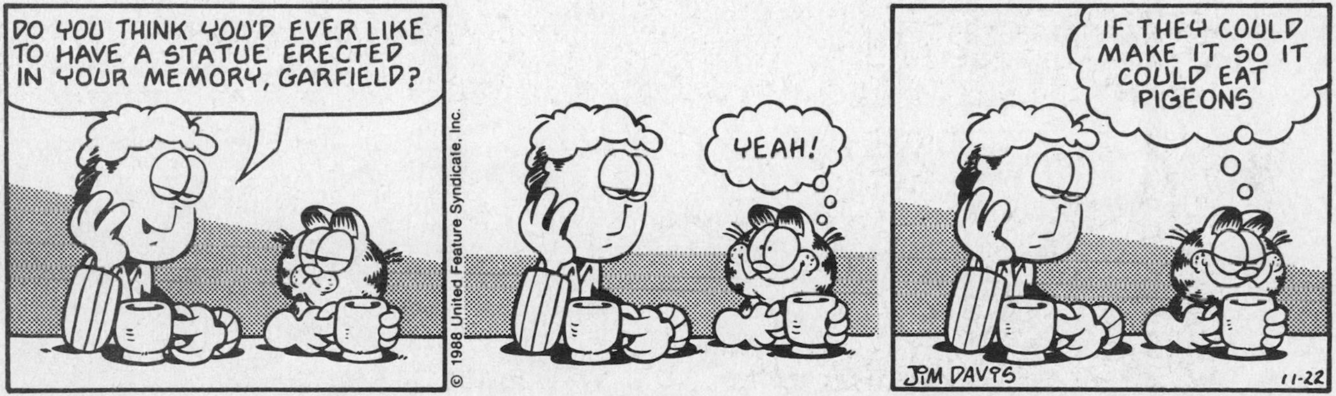
DO YOU THINK YOU'D EVER LIKE TO HAVE A STATUE ERECTED IN YOUR MEMORY, GARFIELD?
© 1988 United Feature Syndicate, Inc.
YEAH!
IF THEY COULD MAKE IT SO IT COULD EAT PIGEONS
JIM DAVIS
11-22

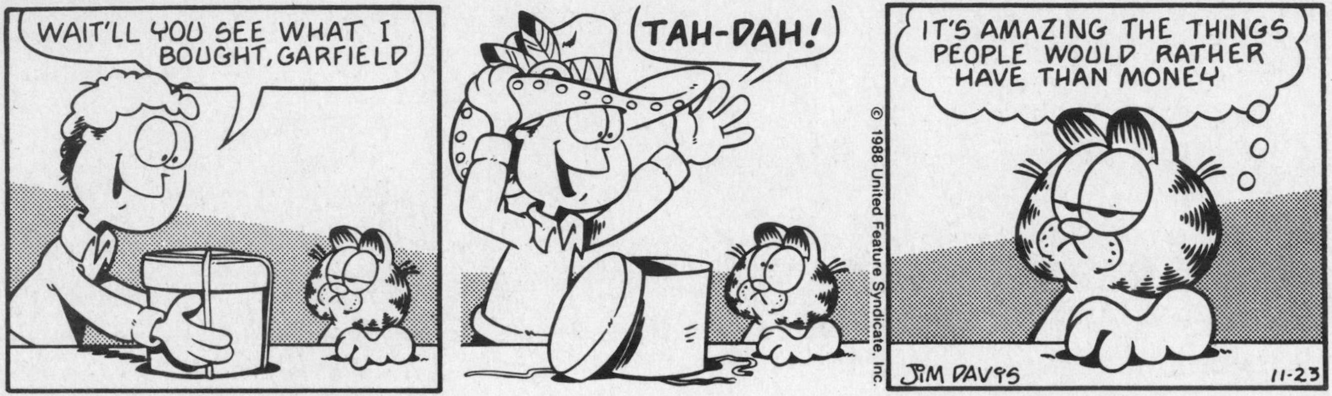
WAIT'LL YOU SEE WHAT I BOUGHT, GARFIELD
TAH-DAH!
IT'S AMAZING THE THINGS PEOPLE WOULD RATHER HAVE THAN MONEY
JIM DAVIS
11-23
© 1988 United Feature Syndicate, Inc.

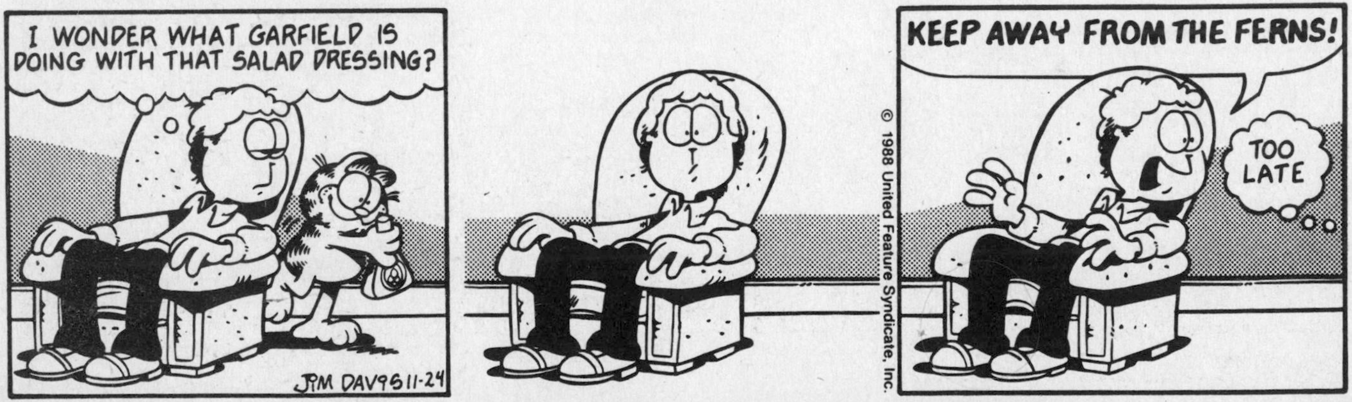
I WONDER WHAT GARFIELD IS DOING WITH THAT SALAD DRESSING?
JIM DAVIS 11-24
KEEP AWAY FROM THE FERNS!
TOO LATE
© 1988 United Feature Syndicate, Inc.

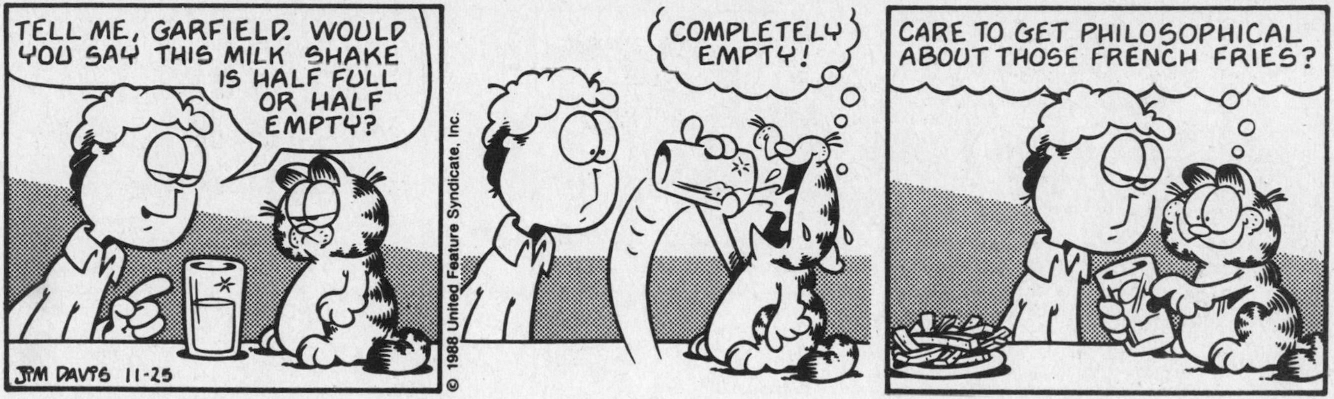
TELL ME, GARFIELD. WOULD YOU SAY THIS MILK SHAKE IS HALF FULL OR HALF EMPTY?
JIM DAVIS 11-25
© 1988 United Feature Syndicate, Inc.
COMPLETELY EMPTY!
CARE TO GET PHILOSOPHICAL ABOUT THOSE FRENCH FRIES?

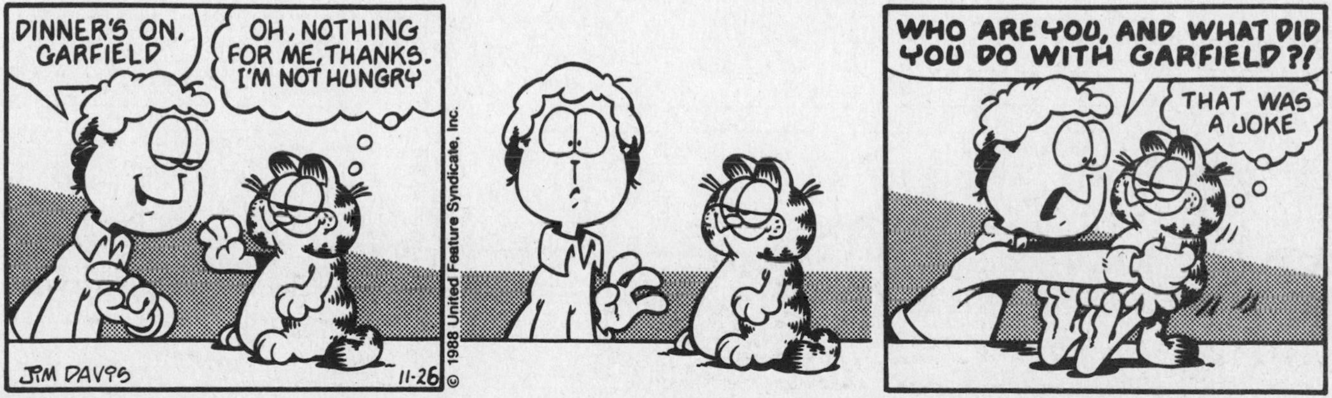
DINNER'S ON, GARFIELD
OH, NOTHING FOR ME, THANKS. I'M NOT HUNGRY
JIM DAVIS
11-26
© 1988 United Feature Syndicate, Inc.
WHO ARE YOU, AND WHAT DID YOU DO WITH GARFIELD?!
THAT WAS A JOKE

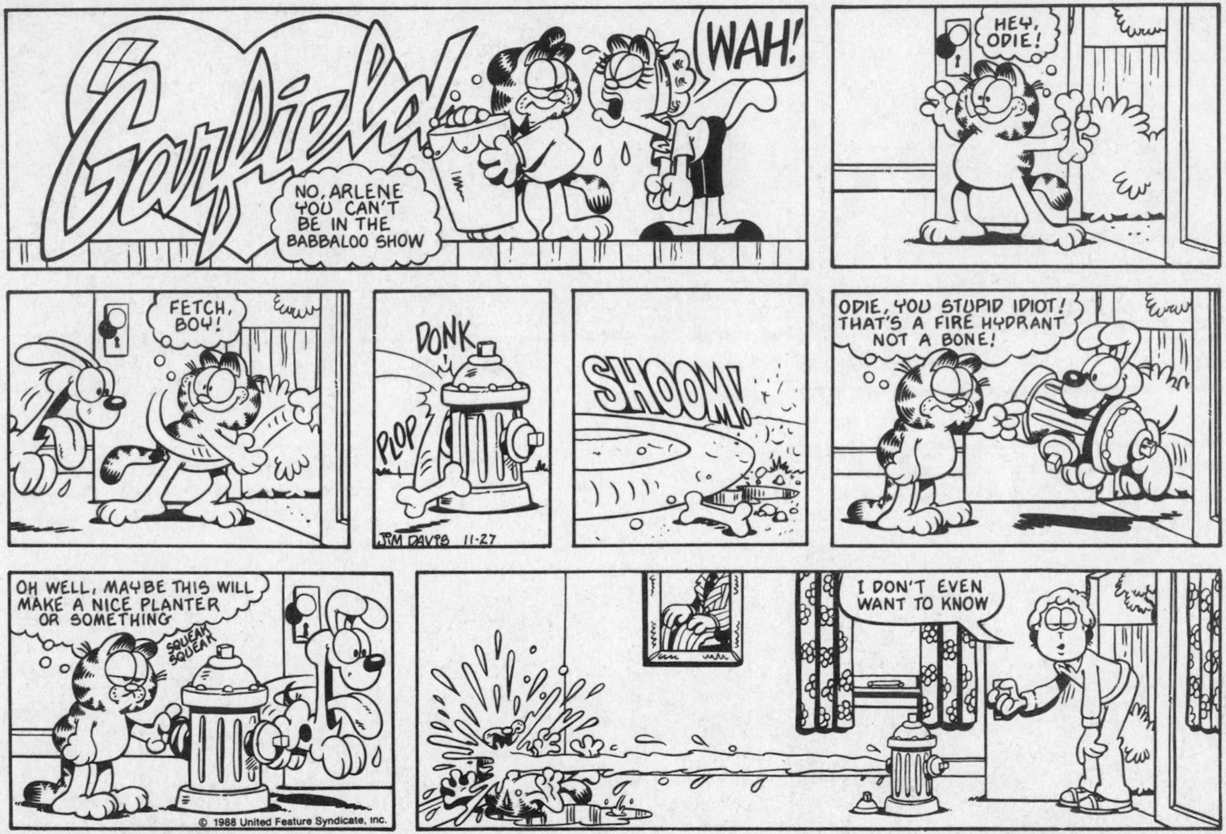

Garfield
NO, ARLENE YOU CAN'T BE IN THE BABBALOO SHOW
WAH!
HEY, ODIE!
FETCH, BOY!
DONK
PLOP
JIM DAVIS 11-27
SHOOM!
ODIE, YOU STUPID IDIOT! THAT'S A FIRE HYDRANT NOT A BONE!
OH WELL, MAYBE THIS WILL MAKE A NICE PLANTER OR SOMETHING
SQUEAK SQUEAK
© 1988 United Feature Syndicate, Inc.
I DON'T EVEN WANT TO KNOW

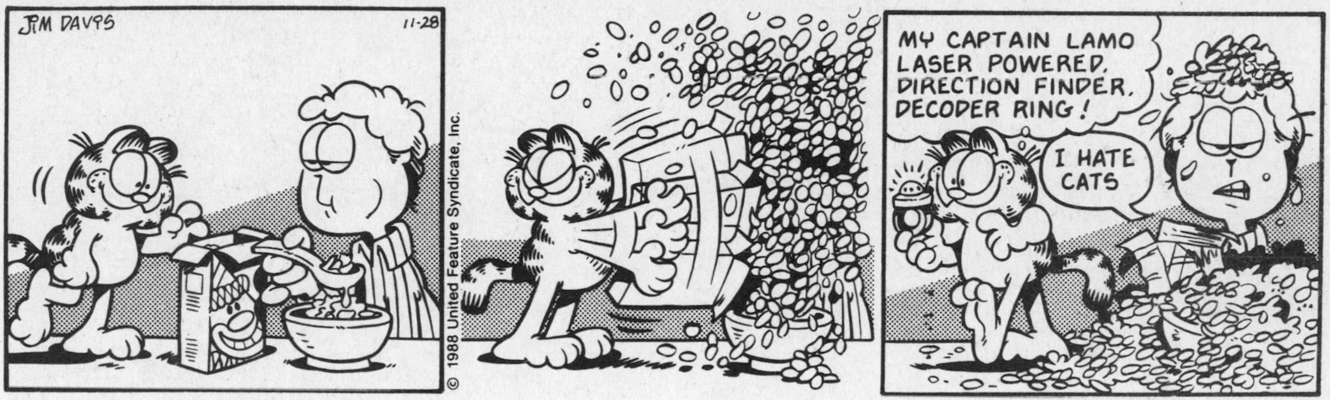
JIM DAVIS
11-28
© 1988 United Feature Syndicate, Inc.
MY CAPTAIN LAMO LASER POWERED, DIRECTION FINDER, DECODER RING!
I HATE CATS

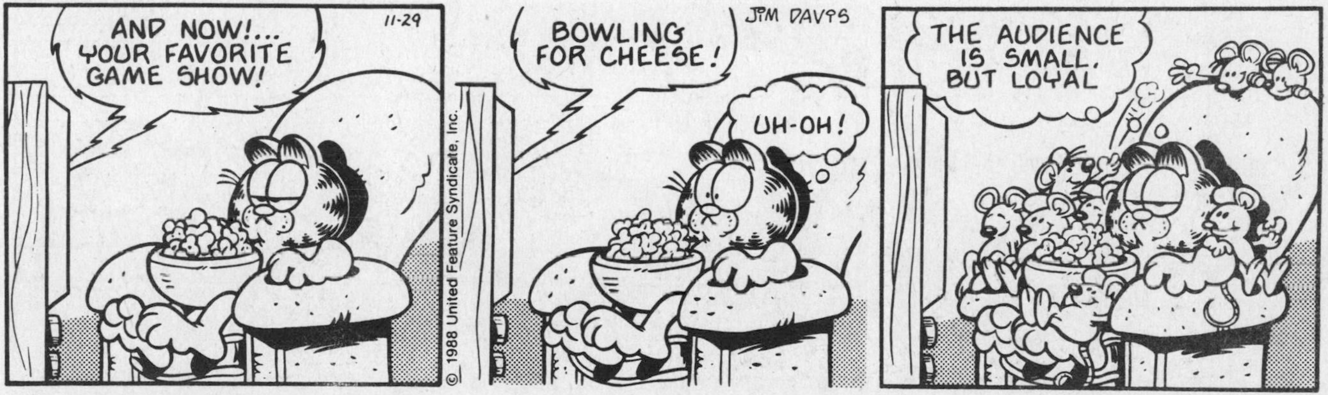
AND NOW!... YOUR FAVORITE GAME SHOW!
11-29
© 1988 United Feature Syndicate, Inc.
BOWLING FOR CHEESE!
JIM DAVIS
UH-OH!
THE AUDIENCE IS SMALL, BUT LOYAL

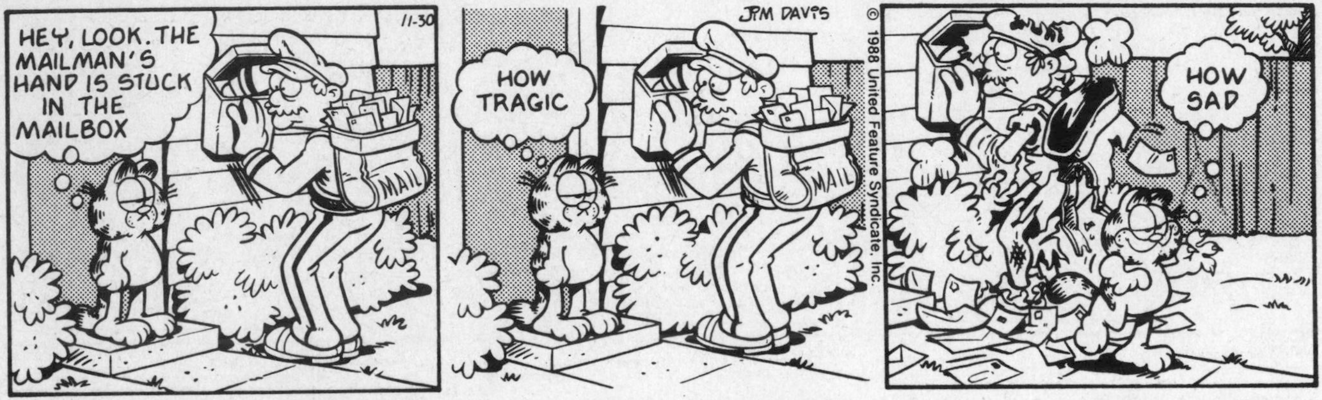
11-30
HEY, LOOK. THE MAILMAN'S HAND IS STUCK IN THE MAILBOX
HOW TRAGIC
JIM DAVIS
© 1988 United Feature Syndicate, Inc.
HOW SAD

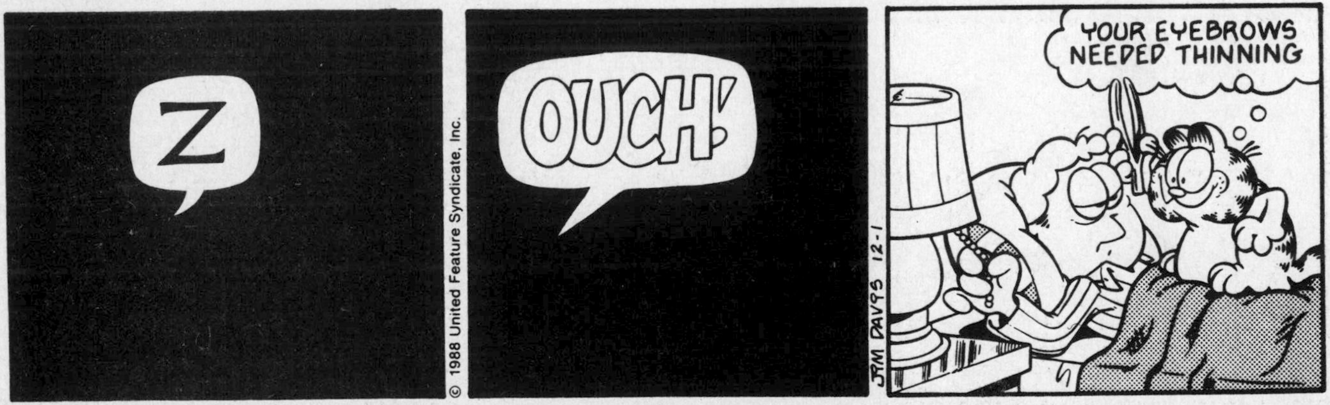
Z
© 1988 United Feature Syndicate, Inc.
OUCH!
JIM DAVIS 12-1
YOUR EYEBROWS NEEDED THINNING

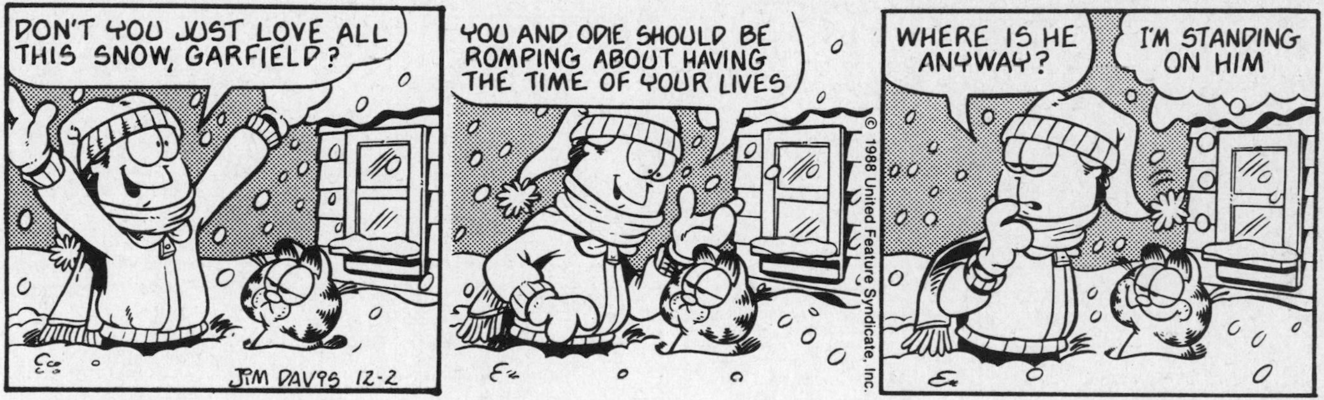
DON'T YOU JUST LOVE ALL THIS SNOW, GARFIELD?
JIM DAVIS 12-2
YOU AND ODIE SHOULD BE ROMPING ABOUT HAVING THE TIME OF YOUR LIVES
© 1988 United Feature Syndicate, Inc.
WHERE IS HE ANYWAY?
I'M STANDING ON HIM

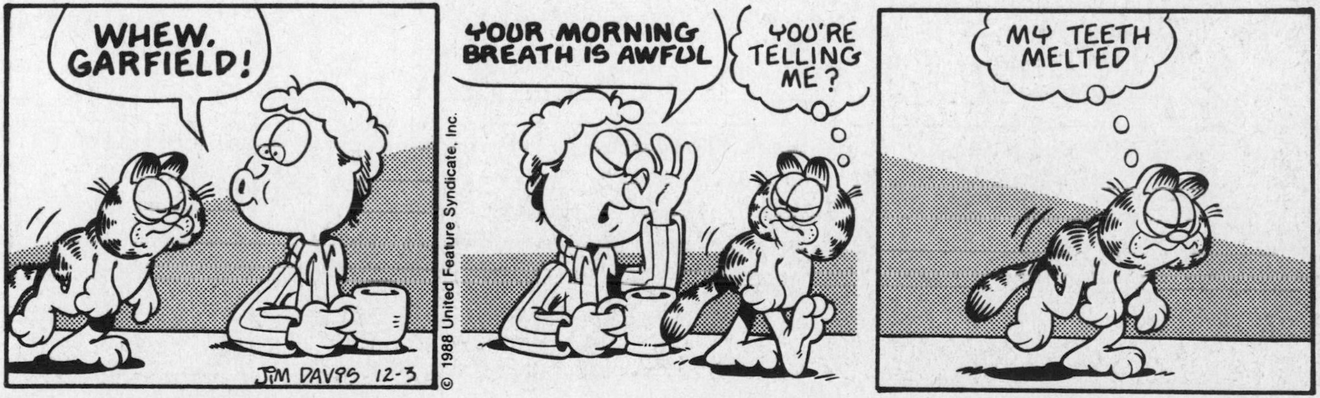
WHEW. GARFIELD!
JIM DAVIS 12-3
© 1988 United Feature Syndicate, Inc.
YOUR MORNING BREATH IS AWFUL
YOU'RE TELLING ME?
MY TEETH MELTED

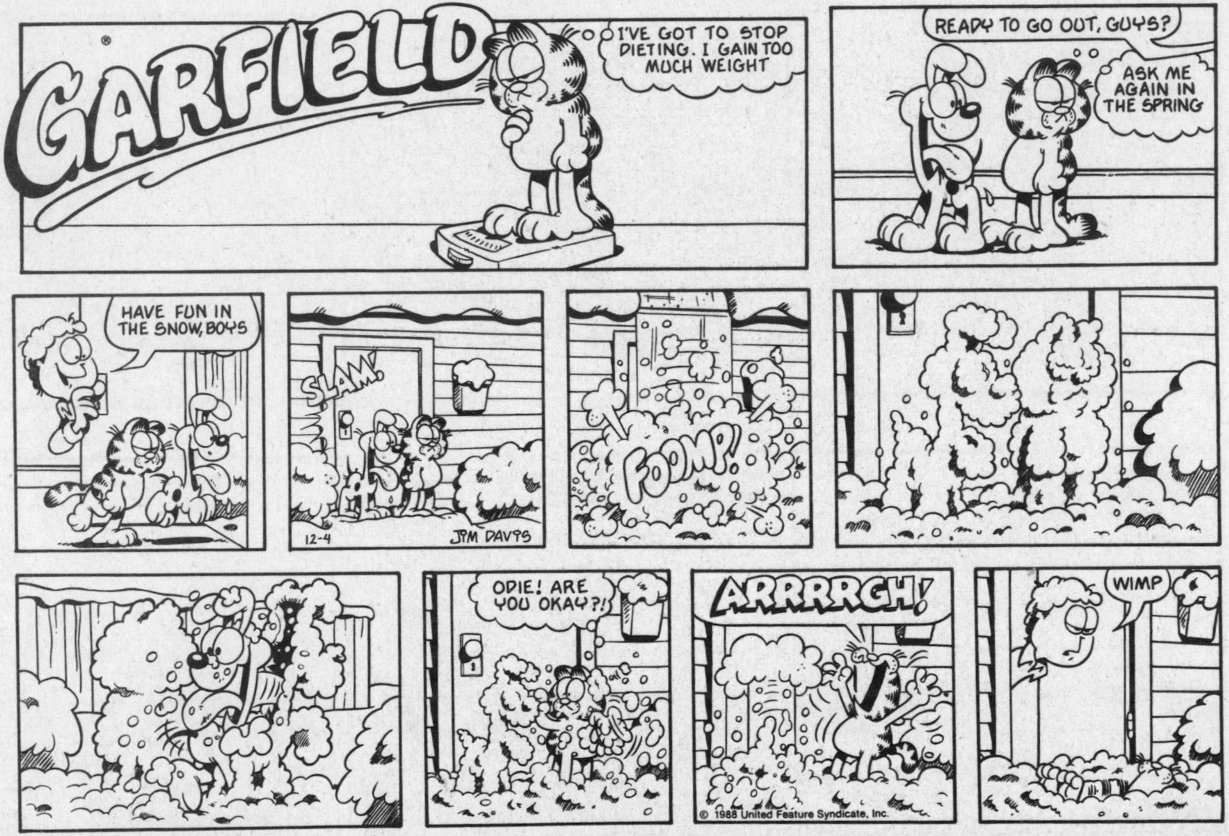
GARFIELD
I'VE GOT TO STOP DIETING. I GAIN TOO MUCH WEIGHT
READY TO GO OUT, GUYS?
ASK ME AGAIN IN THE SPRING
HAVE FUN IN THE SNOW, BOYS
SLAM!
12-4
JIM DAVIS
FOOMP!
ODIE! ARE YOU OKAY?!
ARRRRGH!
© 1988 United Feature Syndicate, Inc.
WIMP

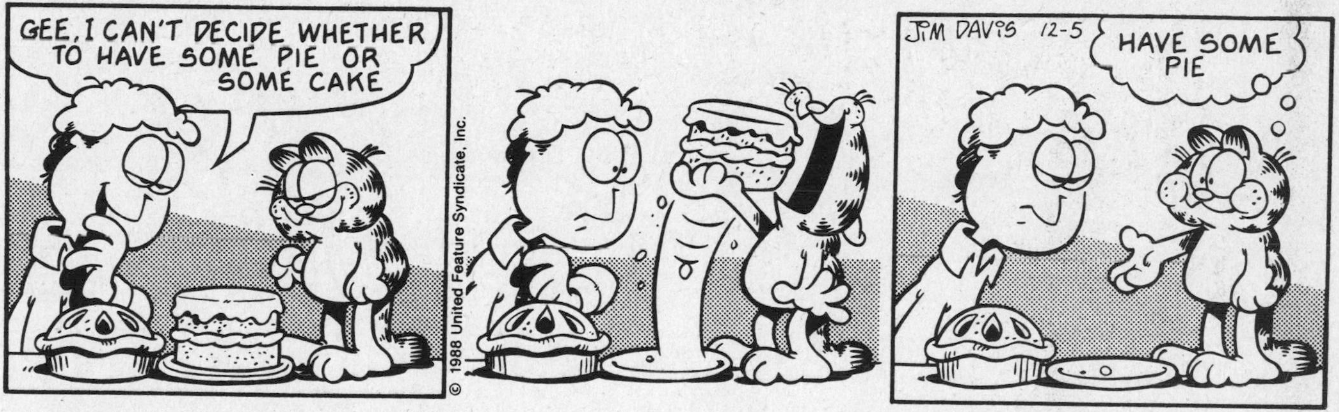
GEE, I CAN'T DECIDE WHETHER TO HAVE SOME PIE OR SOME CAKE
© 1988 United Feature Syndicate, Inc.
JIM DAVIS 12-5
HAVE SOME PIE

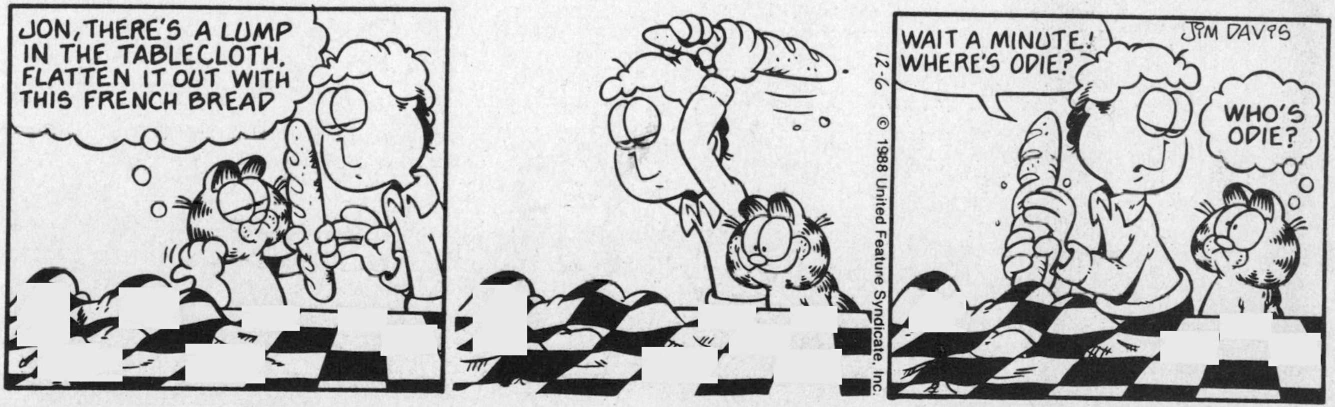
JON, THERE'S A LUMP IN THE TABLECLOTH. FLATTEN IT OUT WITH THIS FRENCH BREAD
12-6 © 1988 United Feature Syndicate, Inc.
WAIT A MINUTE! WHERE'S ODIE?
JIM DAVIS
WHO'S ODIE?

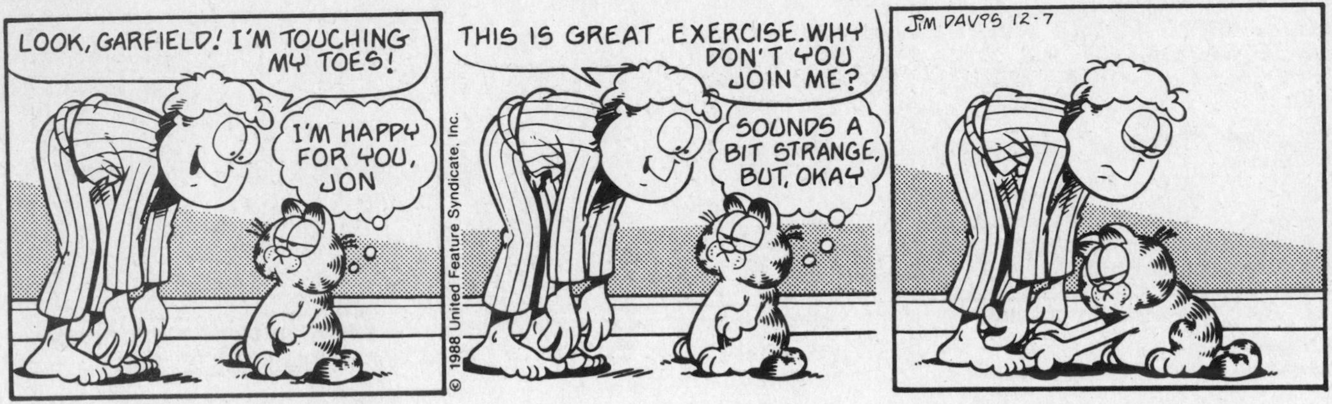
LOOK, GARFIELD! I'M TOUCHING MY TOES!
I'M HAPPY FOR YOU, JON
© 1988 United Feature Syndicate, Inc.
THIS IS GREAT EXERCISE. WHY DON'T YOU JOIN ME?
SOUNDS A BIT STRANGE, BUT, OKAY
JIM DAVIS 12-7
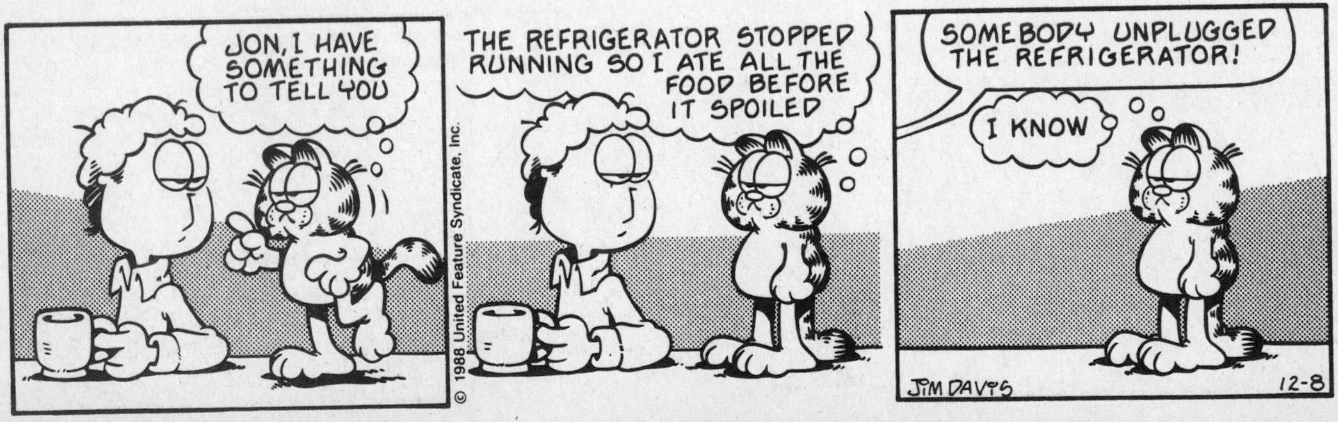
JON, I HAVE SOMETHING TO TELL YOU
© 1988 United Feature Syndicate, Inc.
THE REFRIGERATOR STOPPED RUNNING SO I ATE ALL THE FOOD BEFORE IT SPOILED
SOMEBODY UNPLUGGED THE REFRIGERATOR!
I KNOW
JIM DAVIS
12-8

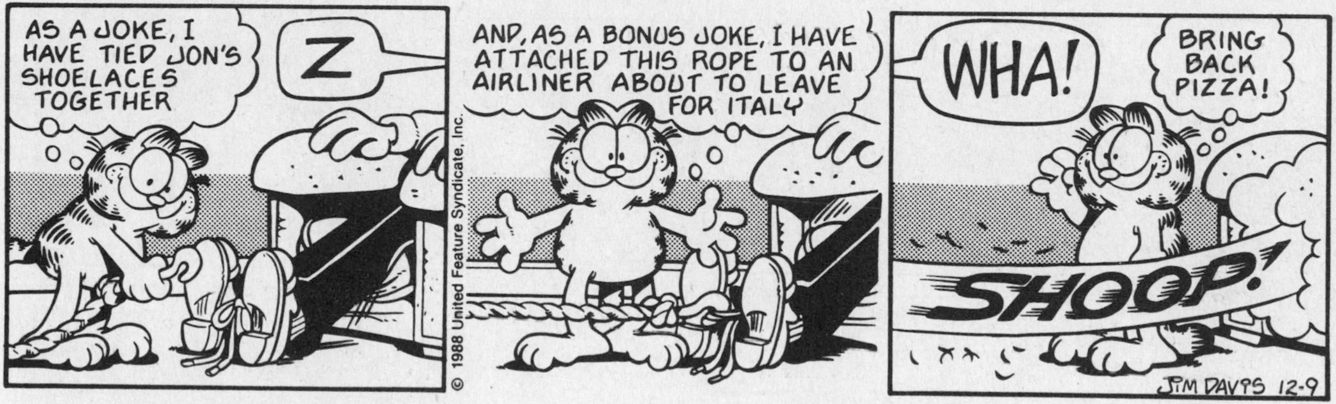
AS A JOKE, I HAVE TIED JON'S SHOELACES TOGETHER
Z
AND, AS A BONUS JOKE, I HAVE ATTACHED THIS ROPE TO AN AIRLINER ABOUT TO LEAVE FOR ITALY
WHA!
BRING BACK PIZZA!
SHOOP!
© 1988 United Feature Syndicate, Inc.
JIM DAVIS 12-9

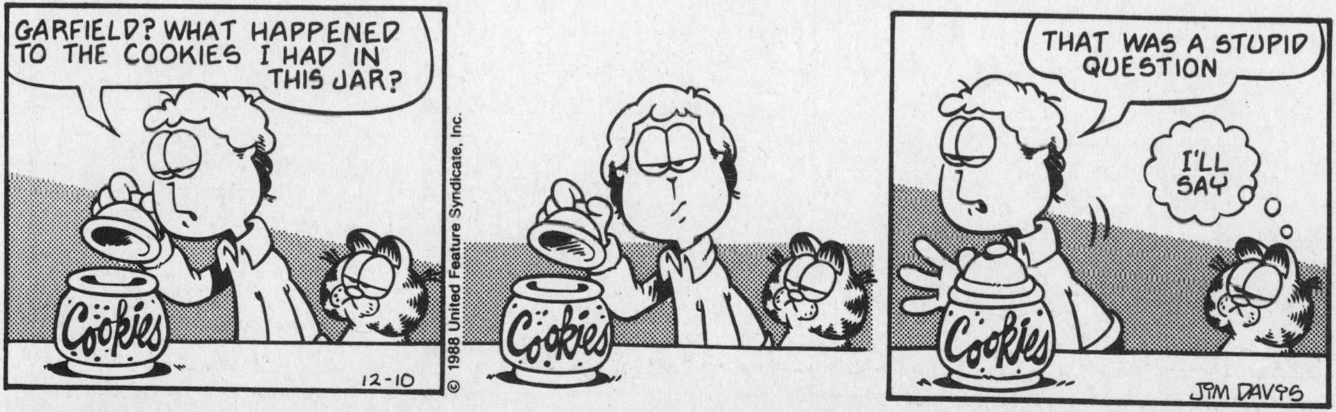
GARFIELD? WHAT HAPPENED TO THE COOKIES I HAD IN THIS JAR?
Cookies
THAT WAS A STUPID QUESTION
I'LL SAY
© 1988 United Feature Syndicate, Inc.
12-10
JIM DAVIS

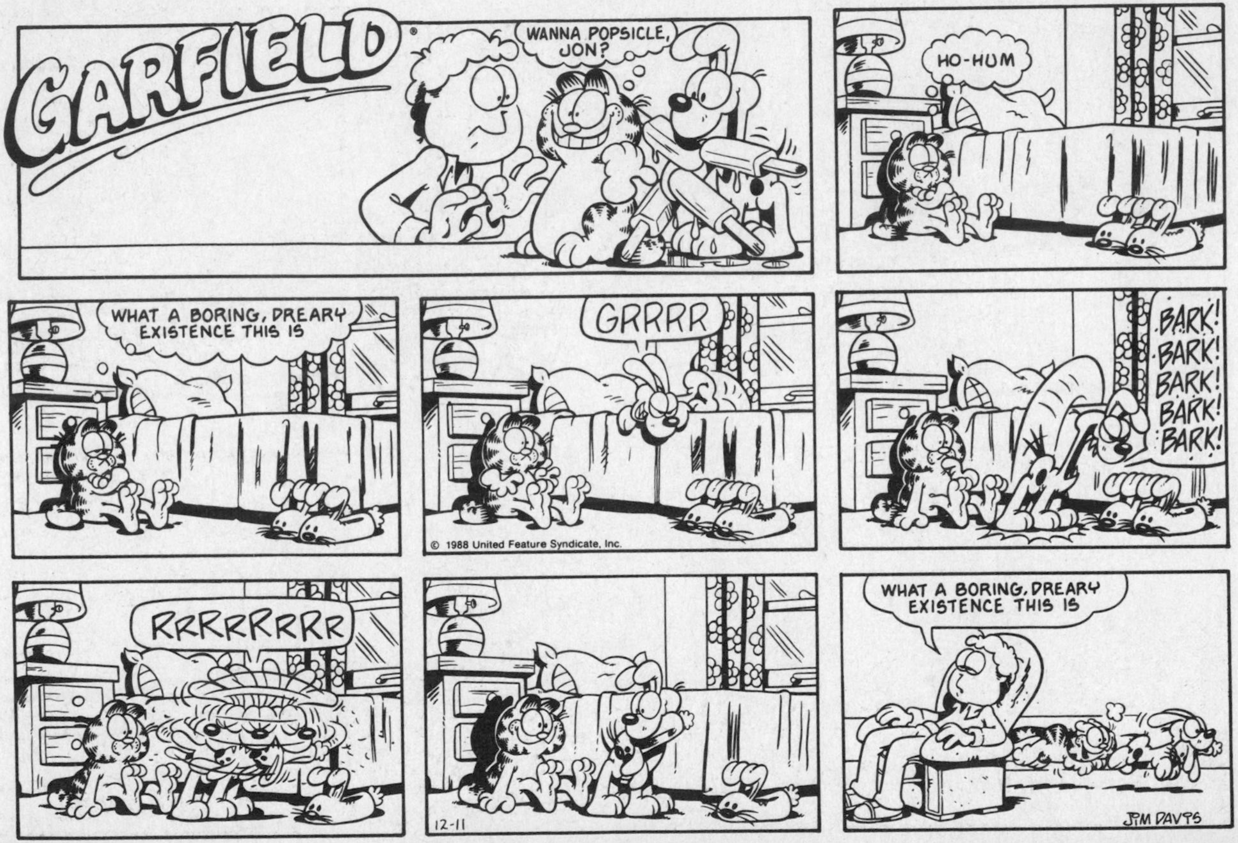
GARFIELD®
WANNA POPSICLE, JON?
HO-HUM
WHAT A BORING, DREARY EXISTENCE THIS IS
GRRRR
© 1988 United Feature Syndicate, Inc.
BARK! BARK! BARK! BARK! BARK!
RRRRRRRR
12-11
WHAT A BORING, DREARY EXISTENCE THIS IS
JIM DAVIS

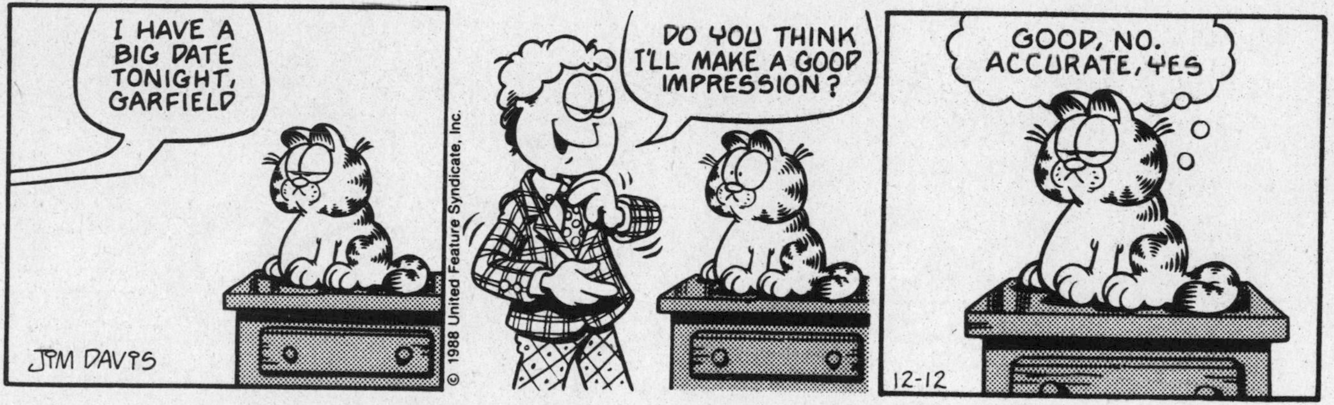
I HAVE A BIG DATE TONIGHT, GARFIELD
DO YOU THINK I'LL MAKE A GOOD IMPRESSION?
GOOD, NO. ACCURATE, YES
JIM DAVIS
© 1988 United Feature Syndicate, Inc.
12-12

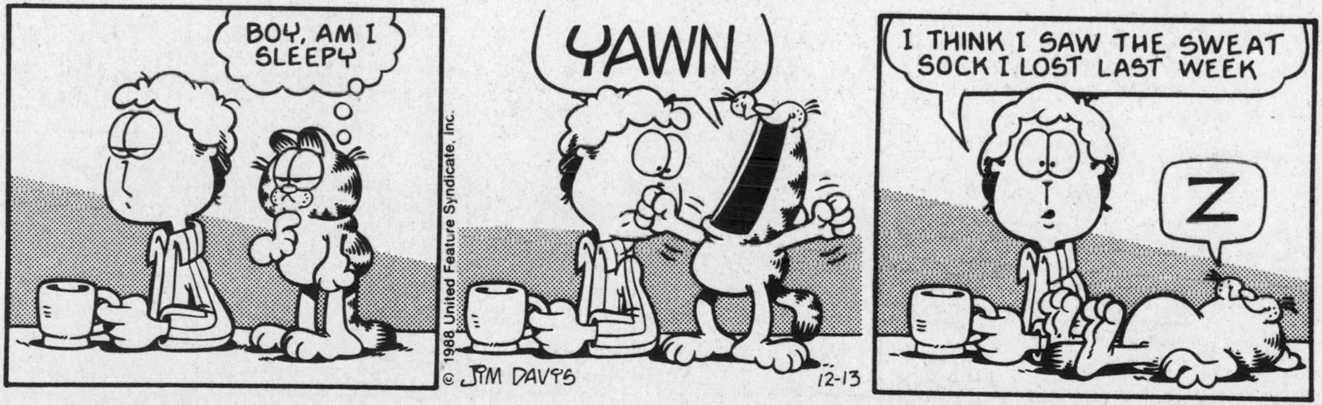
BOY, AM I SLEEPY
YAWN
I THINK I SAW THE SWEAT SOCK I LOST LAST WEEK
Z
© 1988 United Feature Syndicate, Inc.
JIM DAVIS
12-13

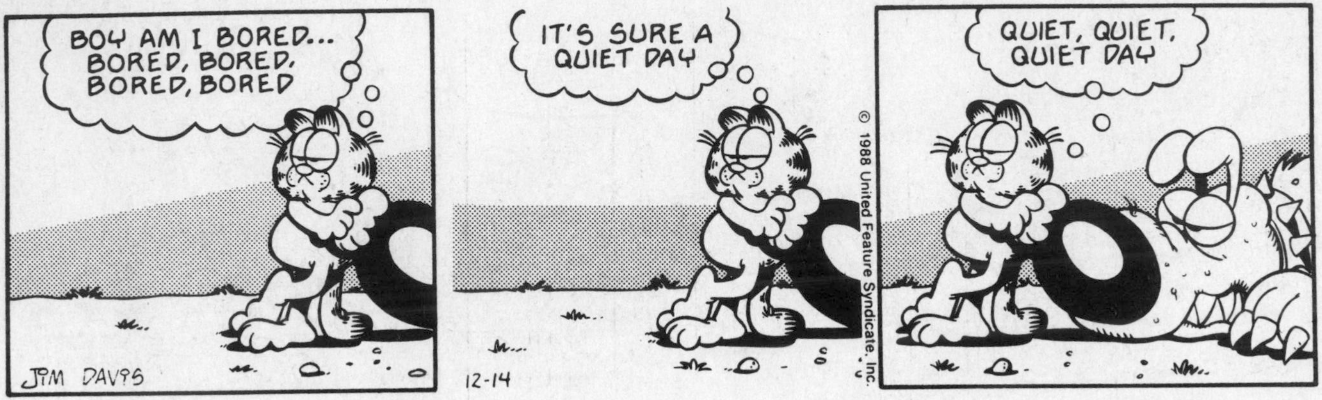
BOY AM I BORED... BORED, BORED, BORED, BORED
JIM DAVIS
IT'S SURE A QUIET DAY
12-14
© 1988 United Feature Syndicate, Inc.
QUIET, QUIET, QUIET DAY

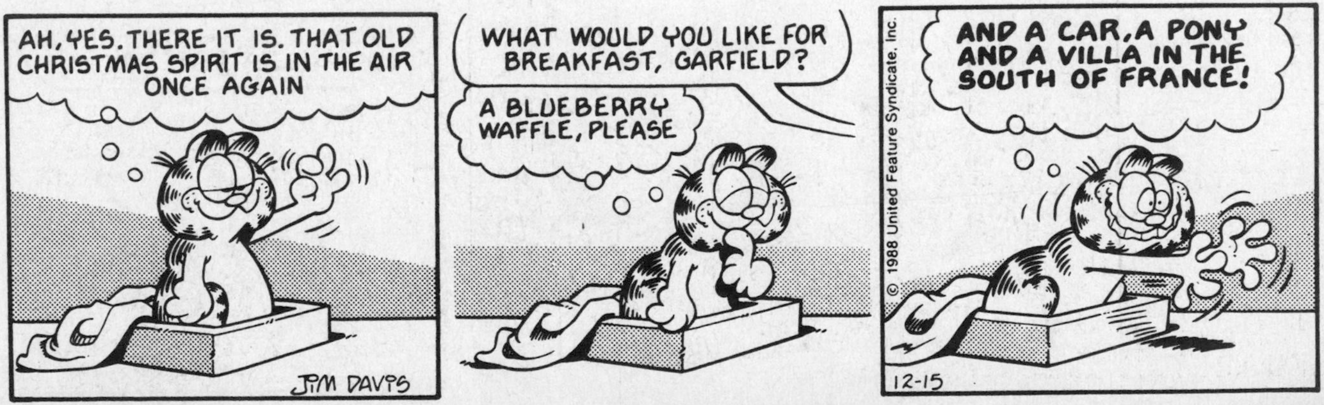
AH, YES. THERE IT IS. THAT OLD CHRISTMAS SPIRIT IS IN THE AIR ONCE AGAIN
JIM DAVIS
WHAT WOULD YOU LIKE FOR BREAKFAST, GARFIELD?
A BLUEBERRY WAFFLE, PLEASE
© 1988 United Feature Syndicate, Inc.
AND A CAR, A PONY AND A VILLA IN THE SOUTH OF FRANCE!
12-15

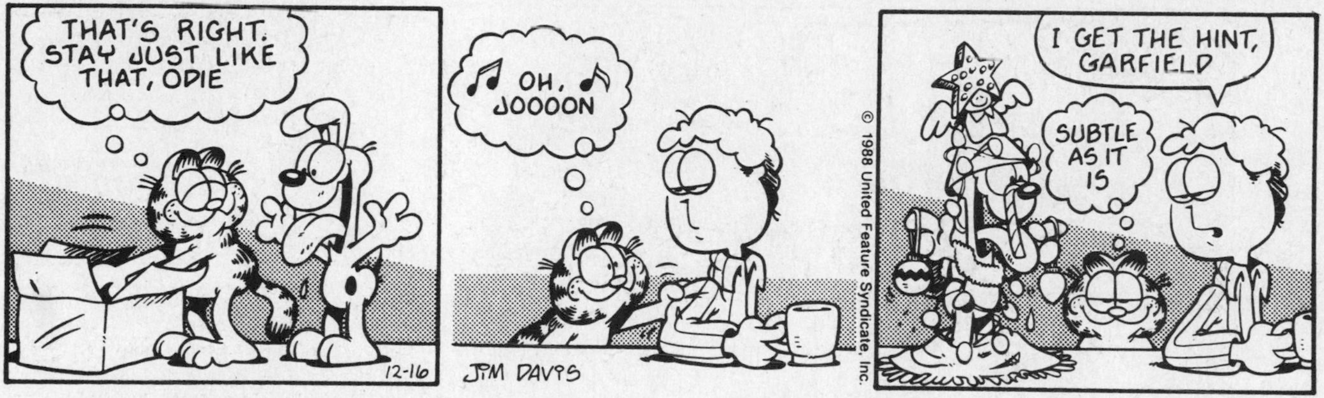
THAT'S RIGHT. STAY JUST LIKE THAT, ODIE
12-16
♪ OH, ♪ JOOOON
JIM DAVIS
© 1988 United Feature Syndicate, Inc.
I GET THE HINT, GARFIELD
SUBTLE AS IT IS

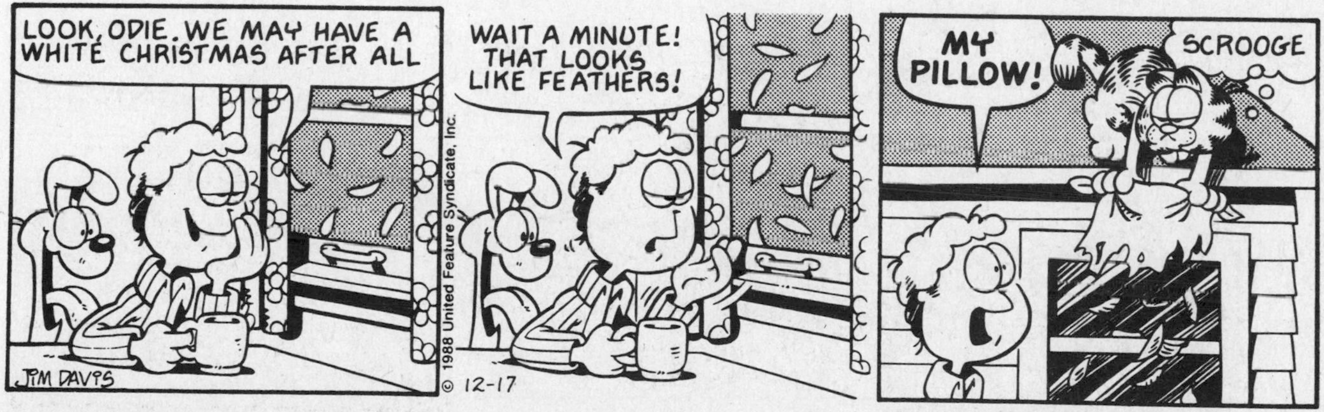
LOOK, ODIE. WE MAY HAVE A WHITE CHRISTMAS AFTER ALL
JIM DAVIS
© 1988 United Feature Syndicate, Inc.
12-17
WAIT A MINUTE! THAT LOOKS LIKE FEATHERS!
MY PILLOW!
SCROOGE

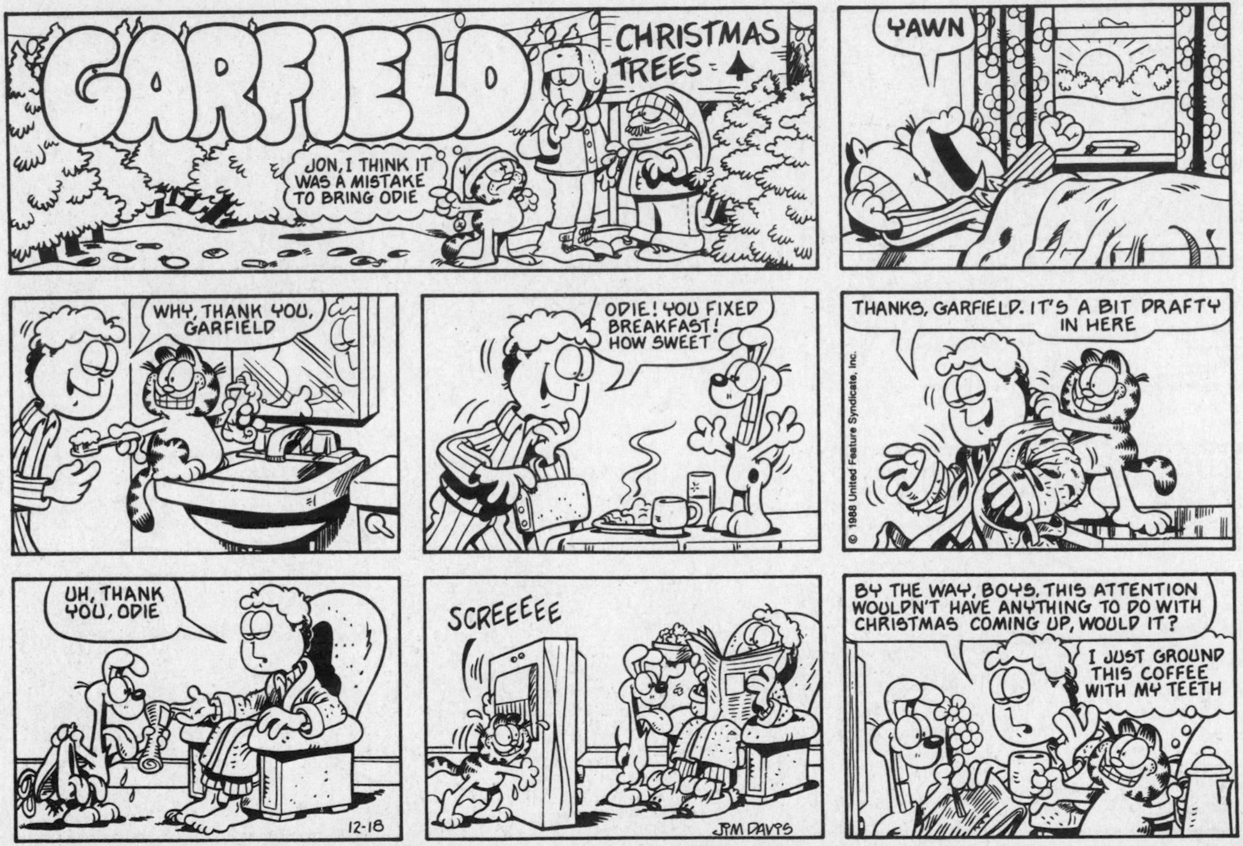
GARFIELD
CHRISTMAS TREES
JON, I THINK IT WAS A MISTAKE TO BRING ODIE
YAWN
WHY, THANK YOU, GARFIELD
ODIE! YOU FIXED BREAKFAST! HOW SWEET
THANKS, GARFIELD. IT'S A BIT DRAFTY IN HERE
© 1988 United Feature Syndicate, Inc.
UH, THANK YOU, ODIE
12-18
SCREEEEE
JIM DAVIS
BY THE WAY, BOYS, THIS ATTENTION WOULDN'T HAVE ANYTHING TO DO WITH CHRISTMAS COMING UP, WOULD IT?
I JUST GROUND THIS COFFEE WITH MY TEETH

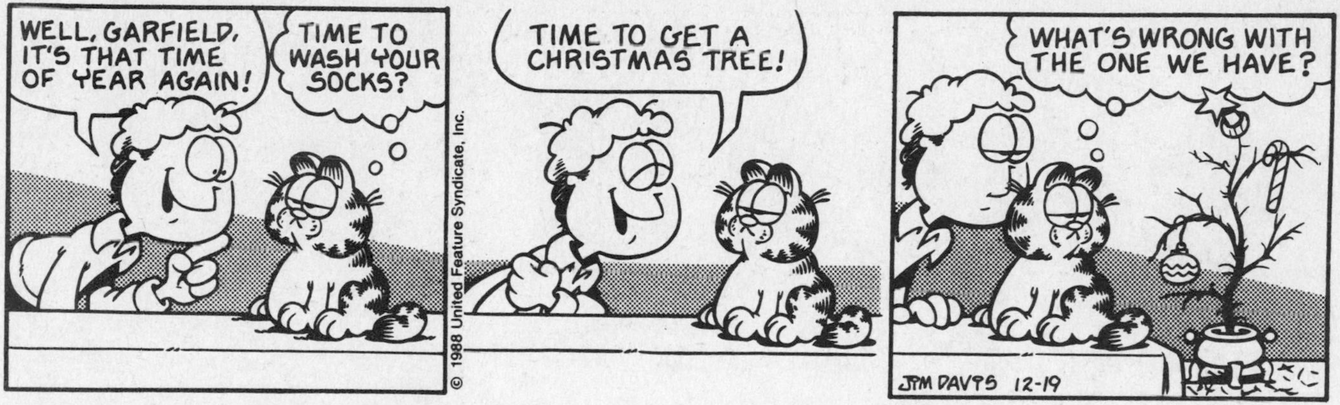
WELL, GARFIELD, IT'S THAT TIME OF YEAR AGAIN!
TIME TO WASH YOUR SOCKS?
© 1988 United Feature Syndicate, Inc.
TIME TO GET A CHRISTMAS TREE!
WHAT'S WRONG WITH THE ONE WE HAVE?
JIM DAVIS 12-19

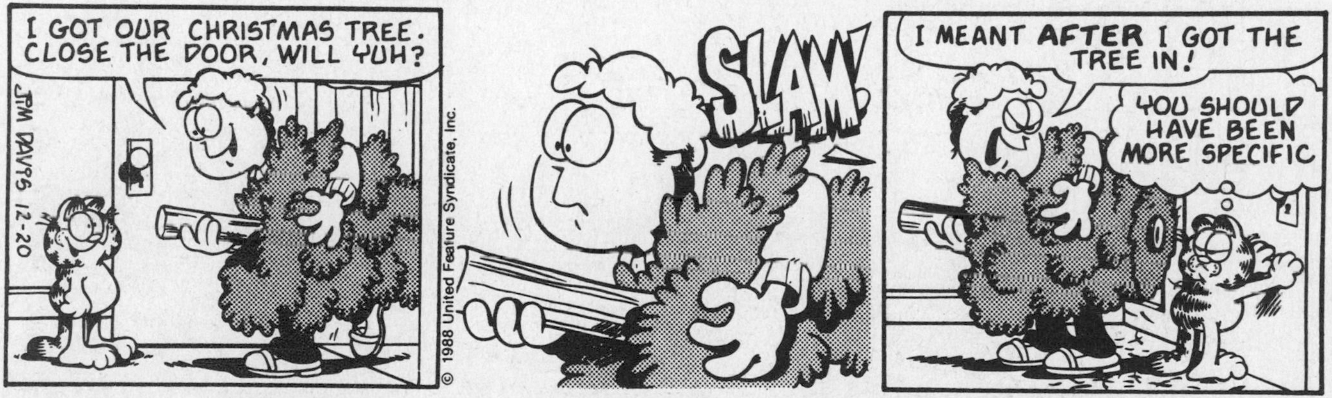
I GOT OUR CHRISTMAS TREE. CLOSE THE DOOR, WILL YUH?
JIM DAVIS 12-20
© 1988 United Feature Syndicate, Inc.
SLAM!
I MEANT **AFTER** I GOT THE TREE IN!
YOU SHOULD HAVE BEEN MORE SPECIFIC

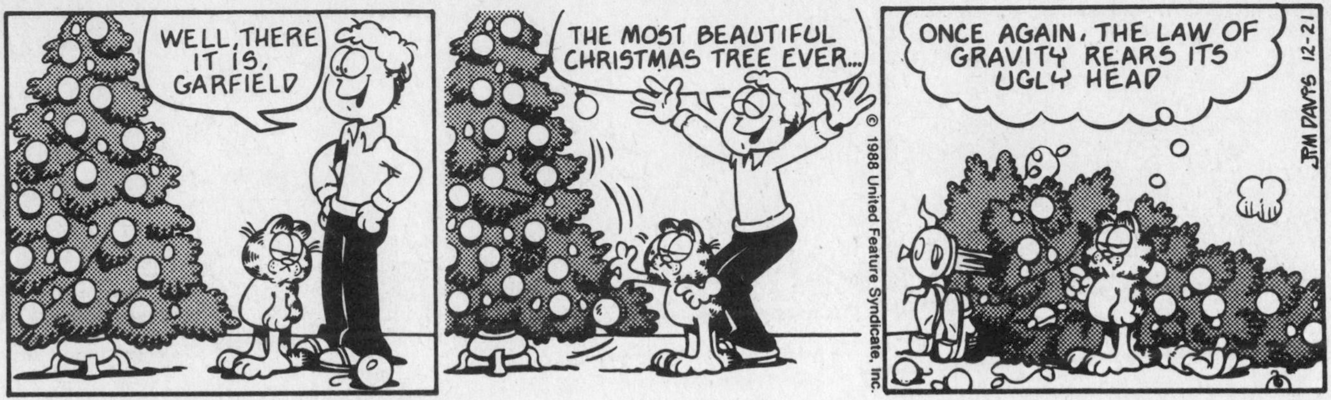
WELL, THERE IT IS, GARFIELD
THE MOST BEAUTIFUL CHRISTMAS TREE EVER...
ONCE AGAIN, THE LAW OF GRAVITY REARS ITS UGLY HEAD
JPM DAVIS 12-21
© 1988 United Feature Syndicate, Inc.

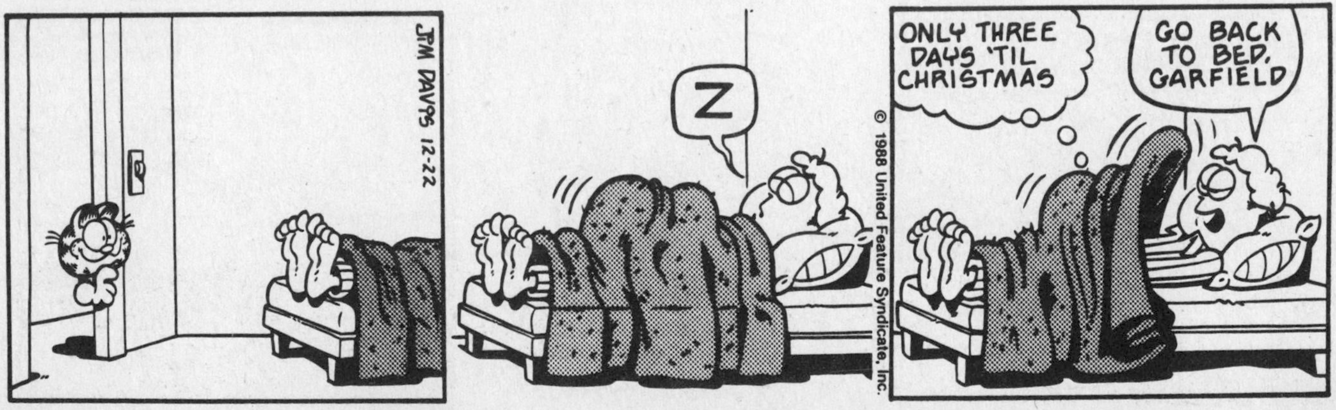
JPM DAVIS 12-22
Z
ONLY THREE DAYS 'TIL CHRISTMAS
GO BACK TO BED, GARFIELD
© 1988 United Feature Syndicate, Inc.

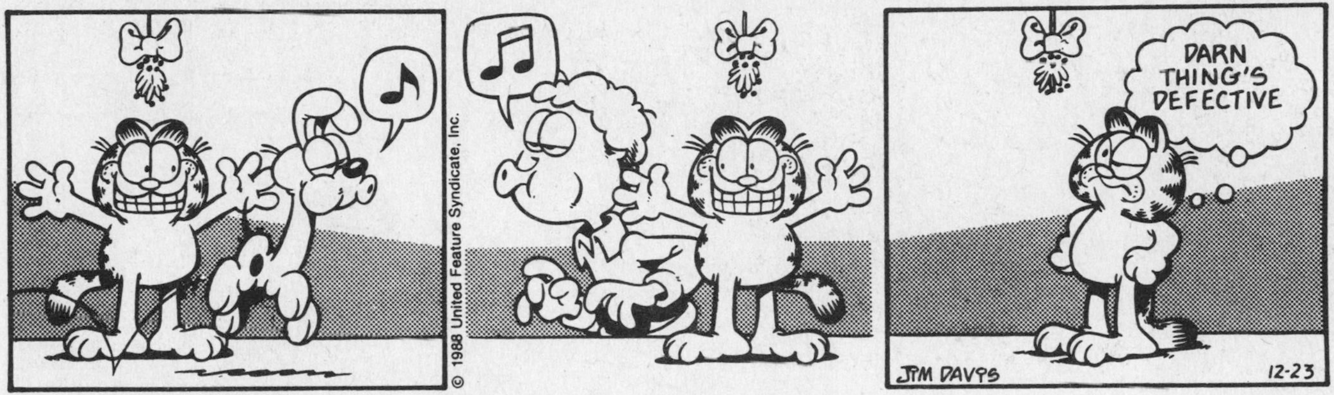
DARN THING'S DEFECTIVE
© 1988 United Feature Syndicate, Inc.
JIM DAVIS 12-23

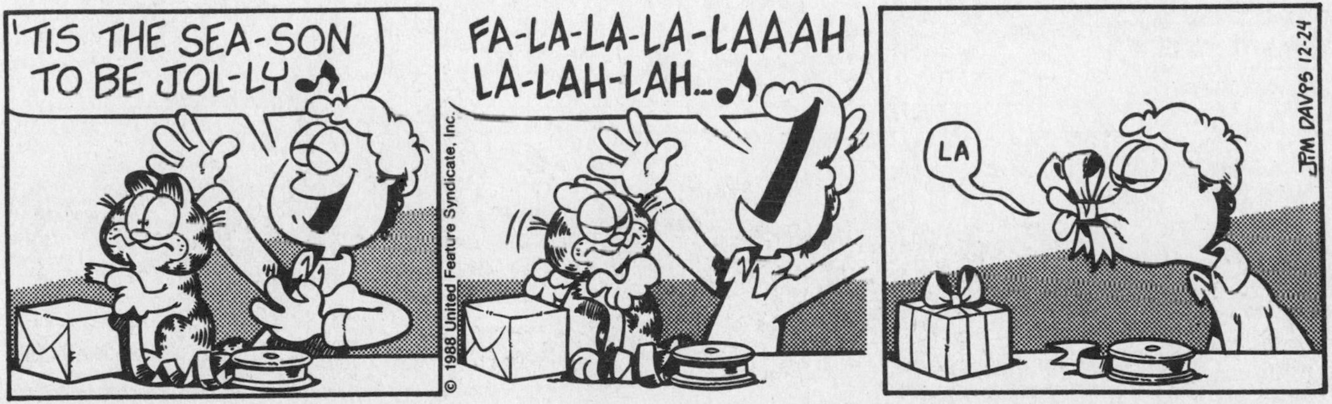
'TIS THE SEA-SON TO BE JOL-LY
FA-LA-LA-LA-LAAAH LA-LAH-LAH...
LA
© 1988 United Feature Syndicate, Inc.
JIM DAVIS 12-24

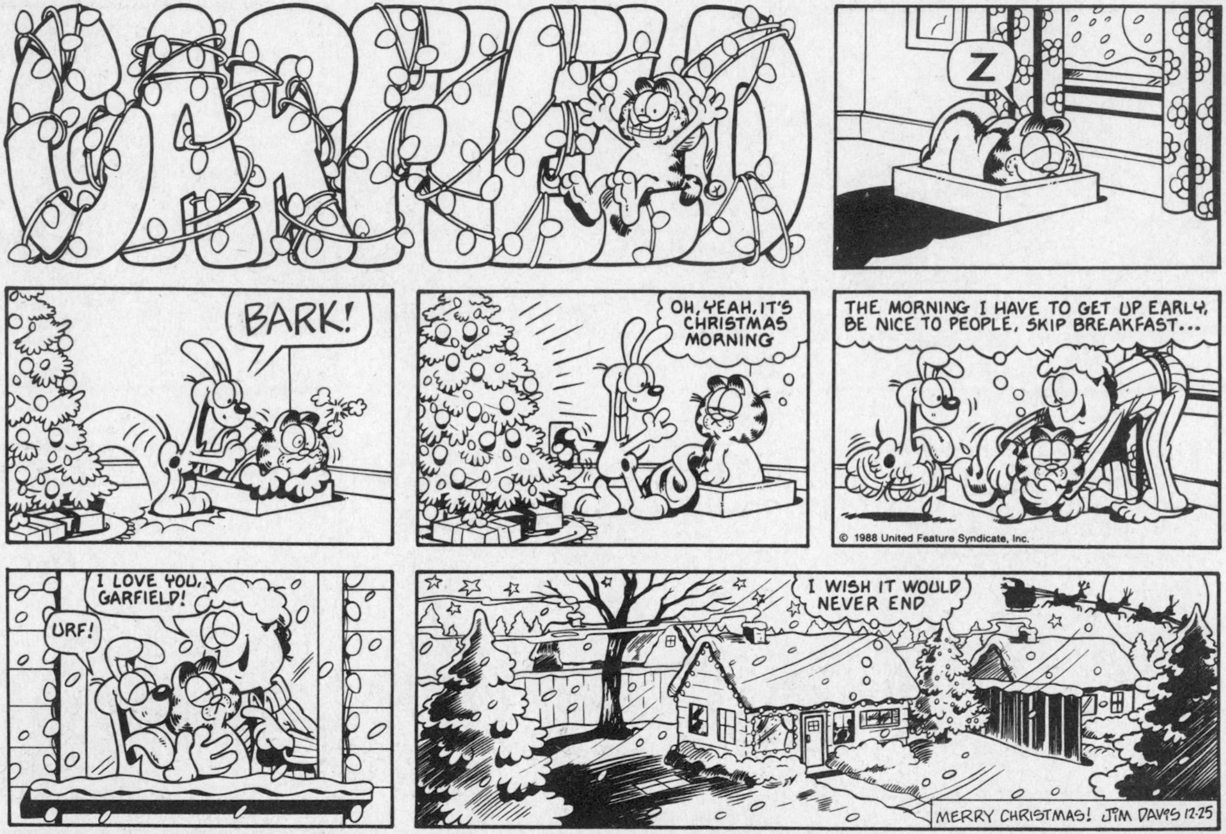

Z
BARK!
OH, YEAH, IT'S CHRISTMAS MORNING
THE MORNING I HAVE TO GET UP EARLY, BE NICE TO PEOPLE, SKIP BREAKFAST...
© 1988 United Feature Syndicate, Inc.
I LOVE YOU, GARFIELD!
URF!
I WISH IT WOULD NEVER END
MERRY CHRISTMAS! JIM DAVIS 12-25

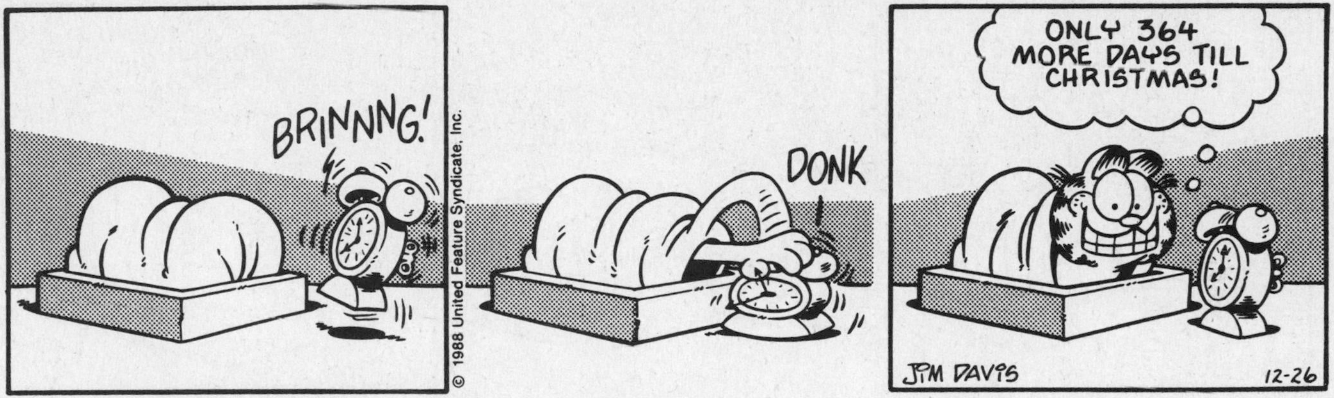
BRINNNG!
DONK
ONLY 364 MORE DAYS TILL CHRISTMAS!
JIM DAVIS
12-26

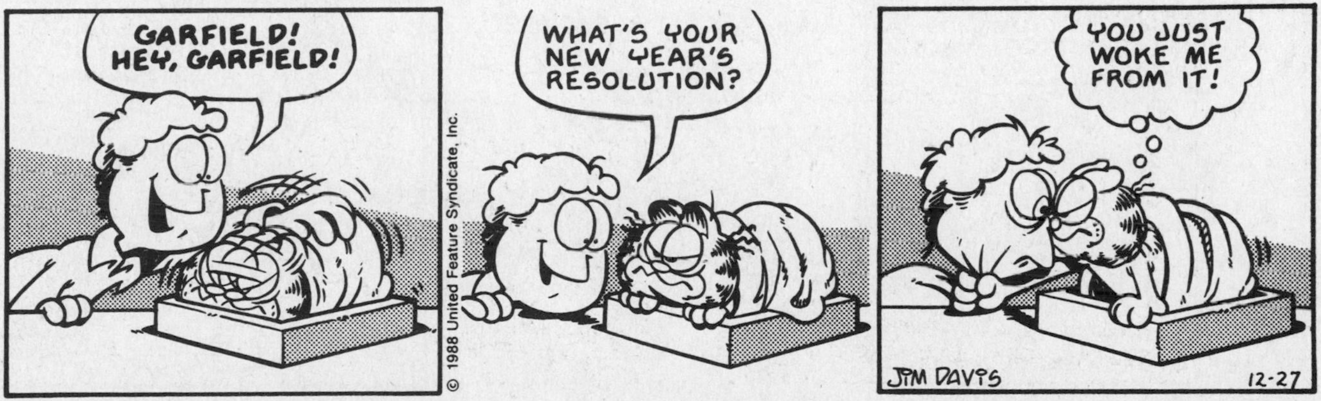
GARFIELD! HEY, GARFIELD!
WHAT'S YOUR NEW YEAR'S RESOLUTION?
YOU JUST WOKE ME FROM IT!
JIM DAVIS
12-27

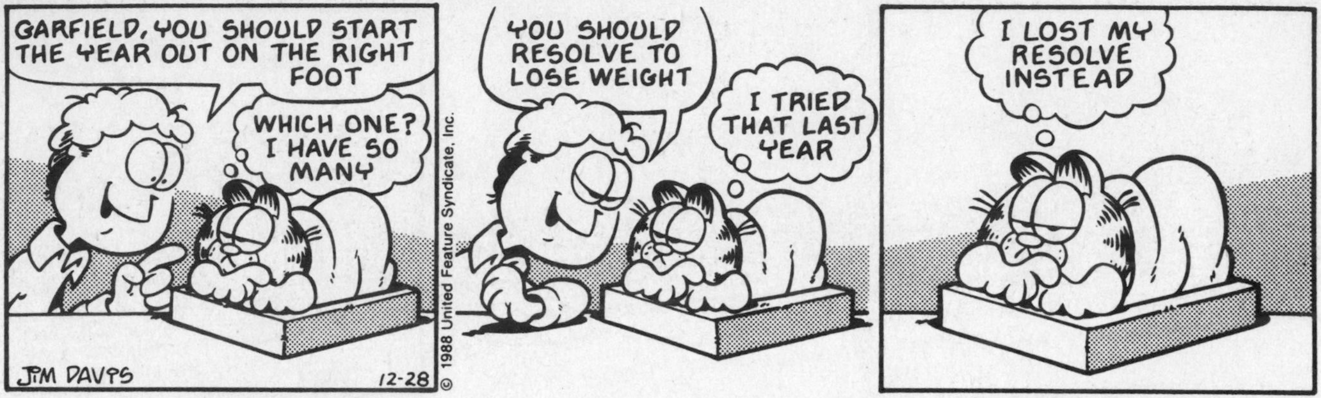
GARFIELD, YOU SHOULD START THE YEAR OUT ON THE RIGHT FOOT
WHICH ONE? I HAVE SO MANY
JIM DAVIS
12-28
© 1988 United Feature Syndicate, Inc.
YOU SHOULD RESOLVE TO LOSE WEIGHT
I TRIED THAT LAST YEAR
I LOST MY RESOLVE INSTEAD

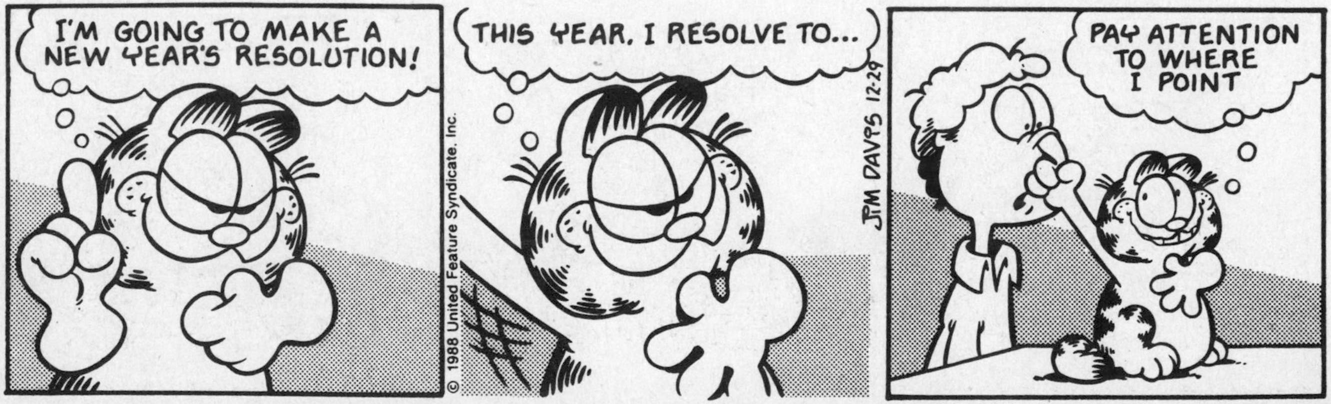
I'M GOING TO MAKE A NEW YEAR'S RESOLUTION!
© 1988 United Feature Syndicate, Inc.
THIS YEAR, I RESOLVE TO...
JIM DAVIS 12-29
PAY ATTENTION TO WHERE I POINT

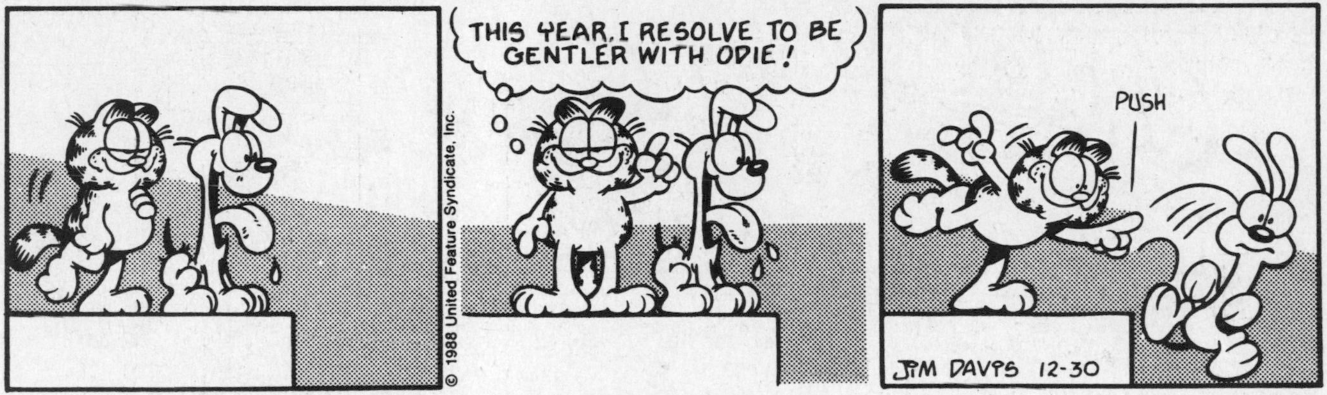
THIS YEAR, I RESOLVE TO BE GENTLER WITH ODIE!
PUSH
JIM DAVIS 12-30
© 1988 United Feature Syndicate, Inc.

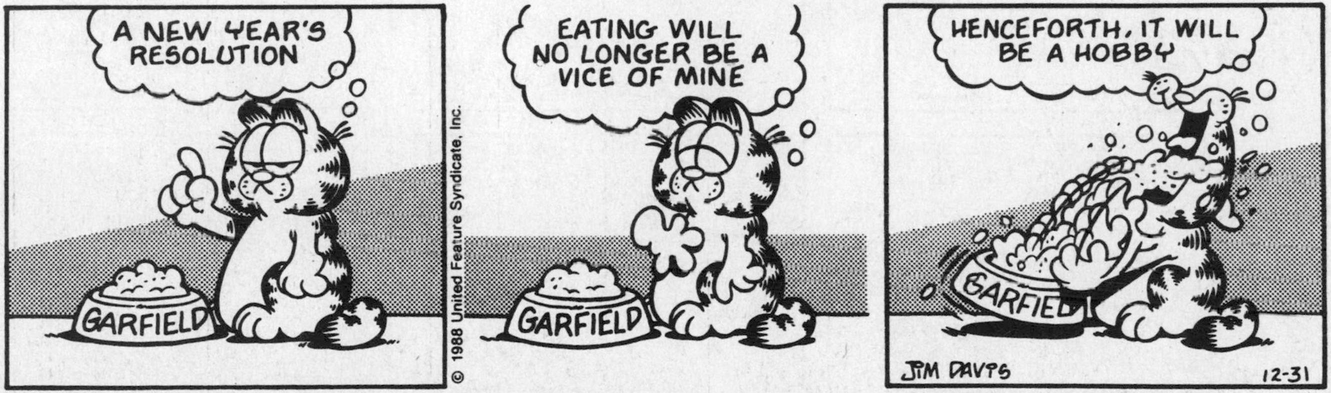
A NEW YEAR'S RESOLUTION
GARFIELD
EATING WILL NO LONGER BE A VICE OF MINE
GARFIELD
HENCEFORTH, IT WILL BE A HOBBY
GARFIELD
JIM DAVIS 12-31
© 1988 United Feature Syndicate, Inc.

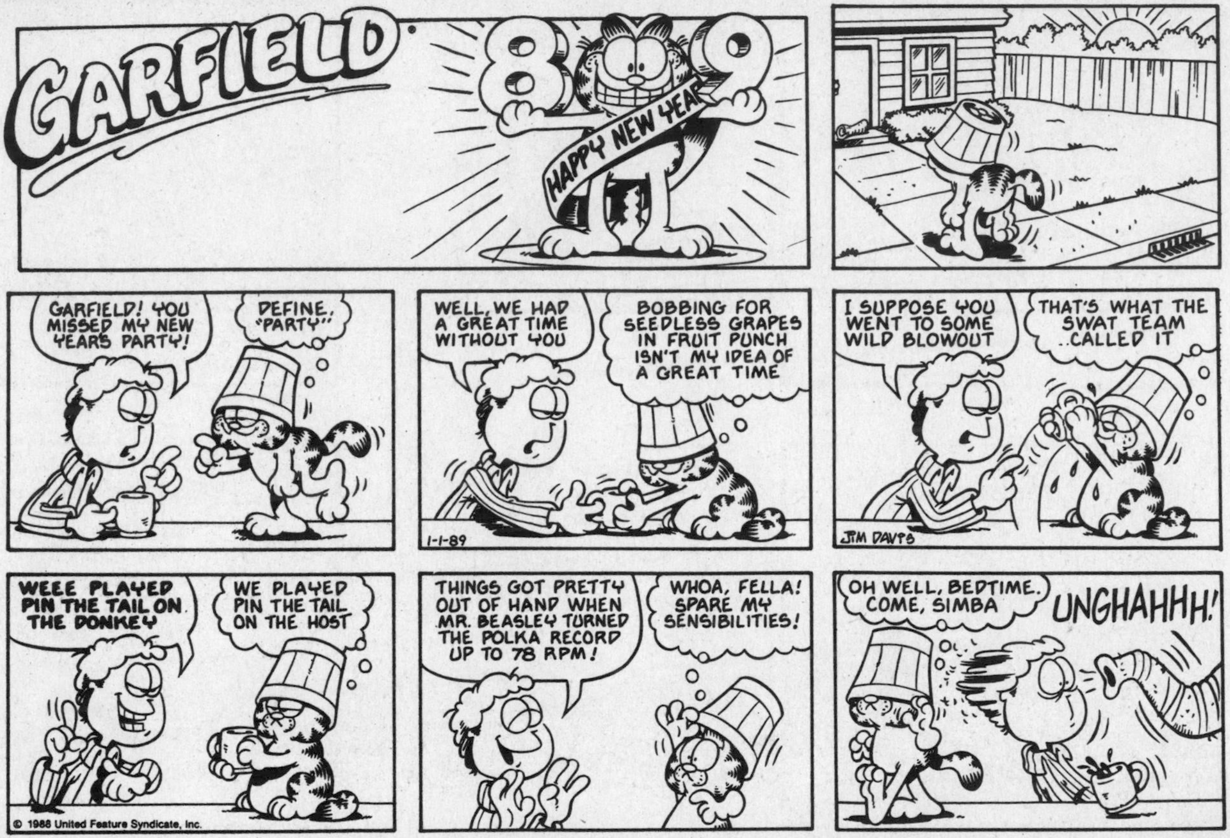
GARFIELD
8 9
HAPPY NEW YEAR
GARFIELD! YOU MISSED MY NEW YEAR'S PARTY!
DEFINE, "PARTY"
WELL, WE HAD A GREAT TIME WITHOUT YOU
BOBBING FOR SEEDLESS GRAPES IN FRUIT PUNCH ISN'T MY IDEA OF A GREAT TIME
1-1-89
I SUPPOSE YOU WENT TO SOME WILD BLOWOUT
THAT'S WHAT THE SWAT TEAM ..CALLED IT
JIM DAVIS
WEEE PLAYED PIN THE TAIL ON THE DONKEY
WE PLAYED PIN THE TAIL ON THE HOST
© 1988 United Feature Syndicate, Inc.
THINGS GOT PRETTY OUT OF HAND WHEN MR. BEASLEY TURNED THE POLKA RECORD UP TO 78 RPM!
WHOA, FELLA! SPARE MY SENSIBILITIES!
OH WELL, BEDTIME. COME, SIMBA
UNGHAHHH!

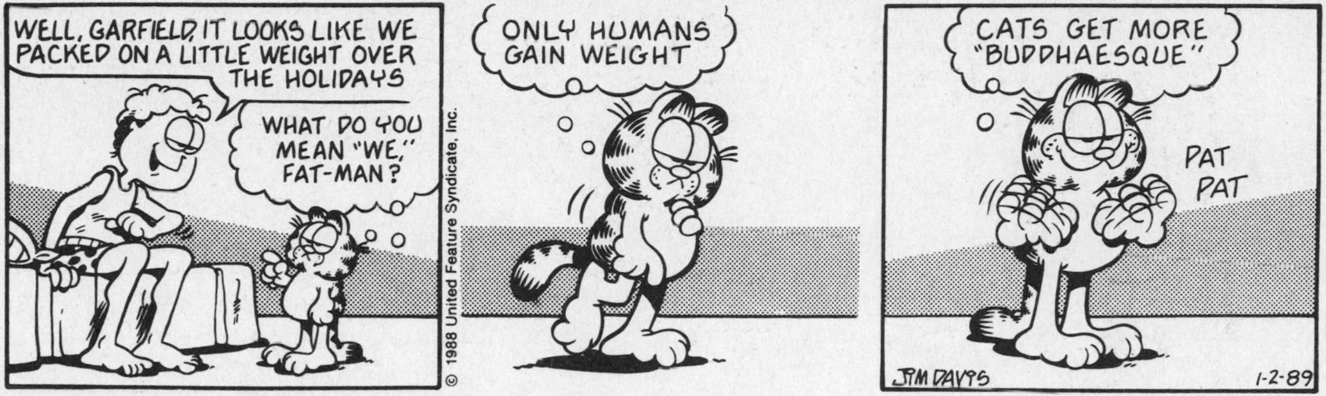
WELL, GARFIELD, IT LOOKS LIKE WE PACKED ON A LITTLE WEIGHT OVER THE HOLIDAYS
WHAT DO YOU MEAN "WE," FAT-MAN?
ONLY HUMANS GAIN WEIGHT
CATS GET MORE "BUDDHAESQUE"
PAT PAT
JIM DAVIS
1-2-89
© 1988 United Feature Syndicate, Inc.

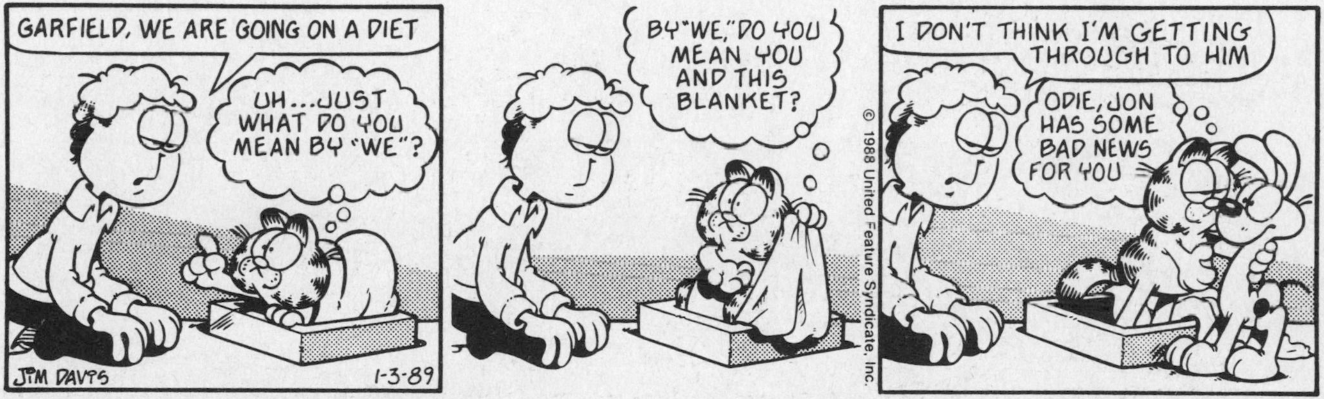
GARFIELD, WE ARE GOING ON A DIET
UH...JUST WHAT DO YOU MEAN BY "WE"?
BY "WE," DO YOU MEAN YOU AND THIS BLANKET?
I DON'T THINK I'M GETTING THROUGH TO HIM
ODIE, JON HAS SOME BAD NEWS FOR YOU
JIM DAVIS
1-3-89
© 1988 United Feature Syndicate, Inc.

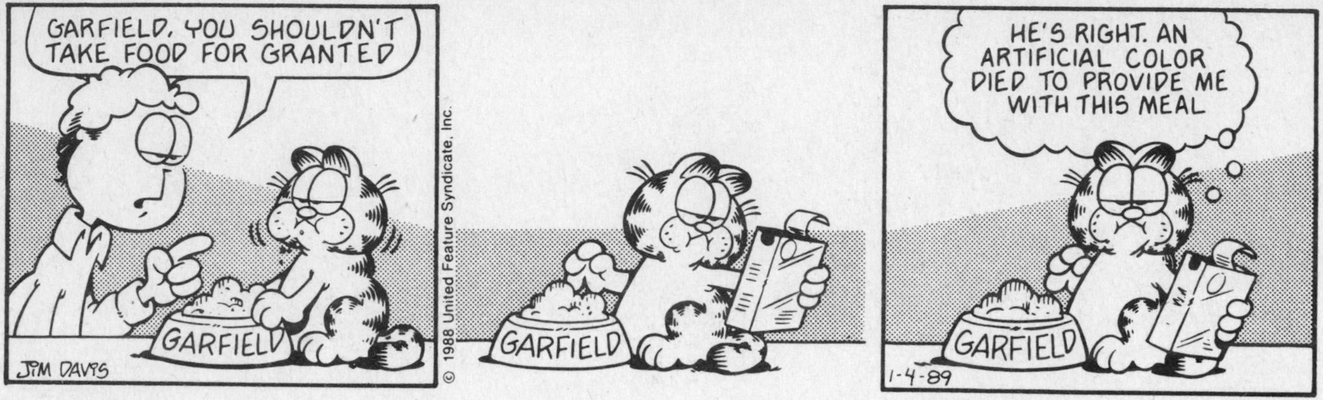
GARFIELD, YOU SHOULDN'T TAKE FOOD FOR GRANTED
GARFIELD
JIM DAVIS
© 1988 United Feature Syndicate, Inc.
GARFIELD
HE'S RIGHT. AN ARTIFICIAL COLOR DIED TO PROVIDE ME WITH THIS MEAL
GARFIELD
1-4-89

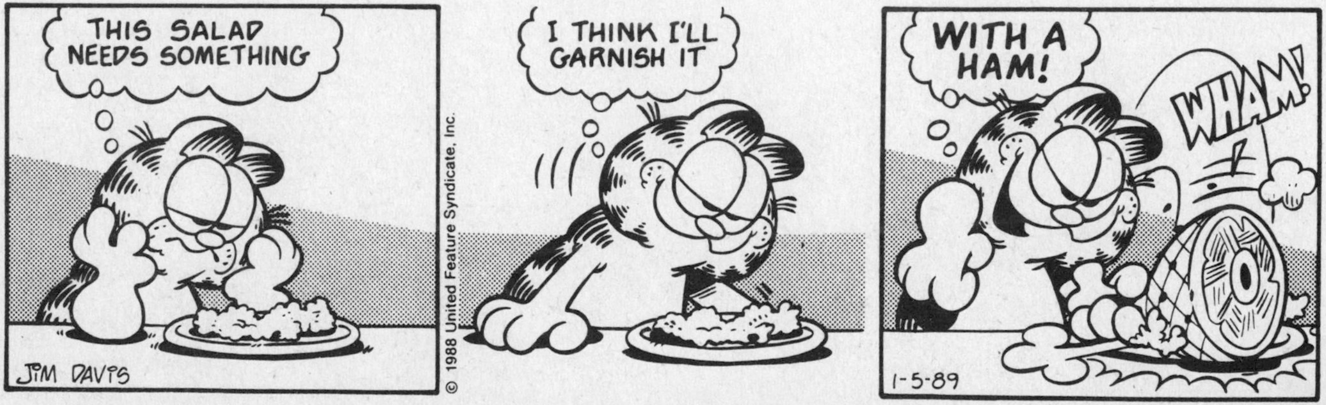
THIS SALAD NEEDS SOMETHING
JIM DAVIS
© 1988 United Feature Syndicate, Inc.
I THINK I'LL GARNISH IT
WITH A HAM!
WHAM!
1-5-89

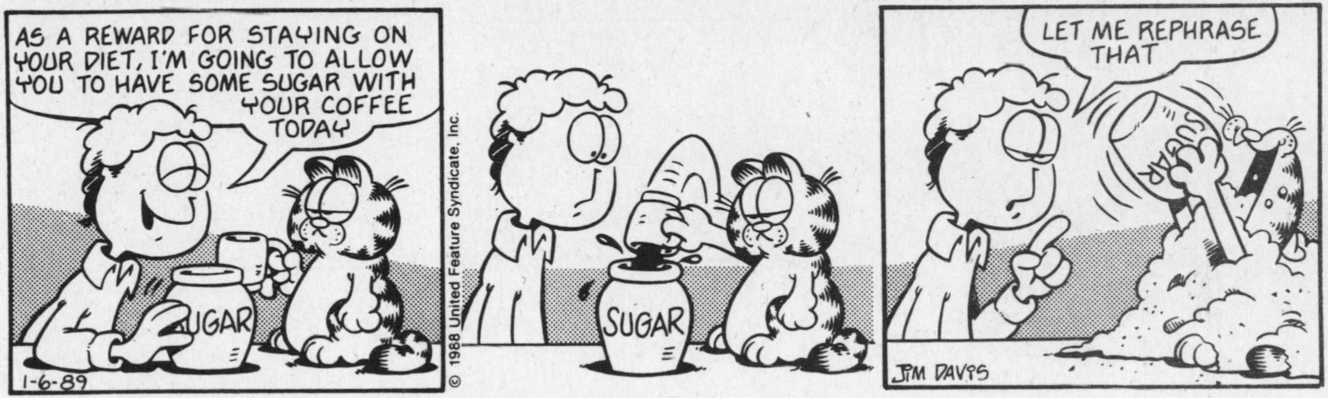
AS A REWARD FOR STAYING ON YOUR DIET, I'M GOING TO ALLOW YOU TO HAVE SOME SUGAR WITH YOUR COFFEE TODAY
SUGAR
1-6-89
© 1988 United Feature Syndicate, Inc.
SUGAR
LET ME REPHRASE THAT
SUGAR
JIM DAVIS

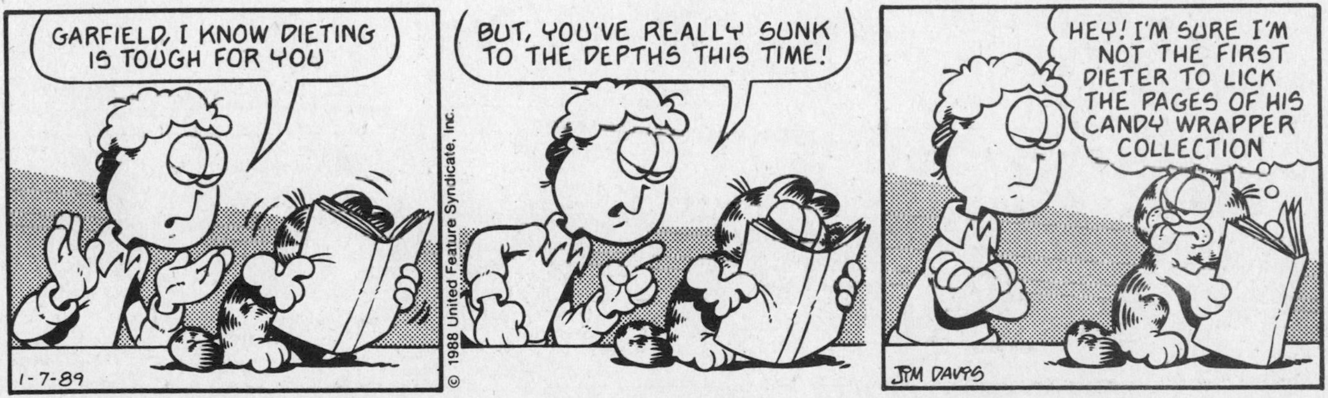
GARFIELD, I KNOW DIETING IS TOUGH FOR YOU
1-7-89
© 1988 United Feature Syndicate, Inc.
BUT, YOU'VE REALLY SUNK TO THE DEPTHS THIS TIME!
HEY! I'M SURE I'M NOT THE FIRST DIETER TO LICK THE PAGES OF HIS CANDY WRAPPER COLLECTION
JIM DAVIS

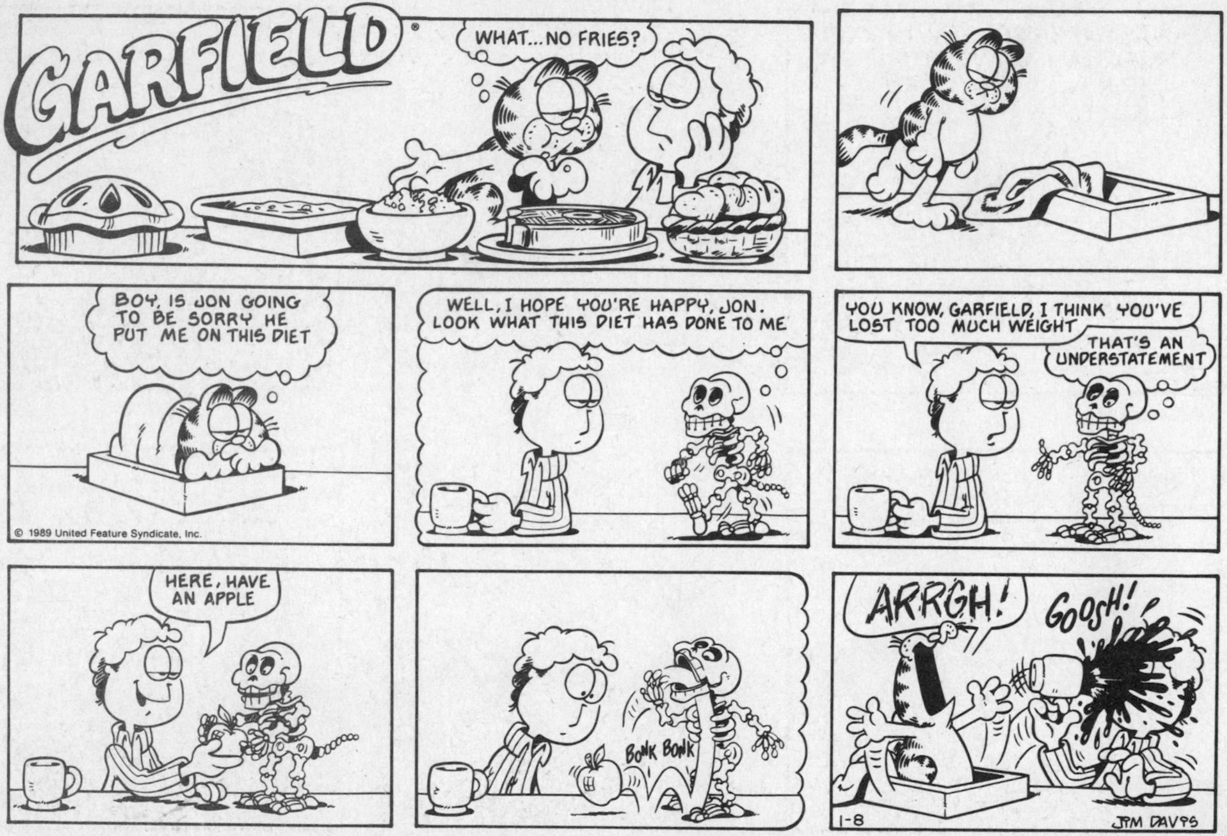

GARFIELD
WHAT... NO FRIES?
BOY, IS JON GOING TO BE SORRY HE PUT ME ON THIS DIET
WELL, I HOPE YOU'RE HAPPY, JON. LOOK WHAT THIS DIET HAS DONE TO ME
YOU KNOW, GARFIELD, I THINK YOU'VE LOST TOO MUCH WEIGHT
THAT'S AN UNDERSTATEMENT
HERE, HAVE AN APPLE
BONK BONK
ARRGH!
GOOSH!
1-8
JIM DAVIS
© 1989 United Feature Syndicate, Inc.

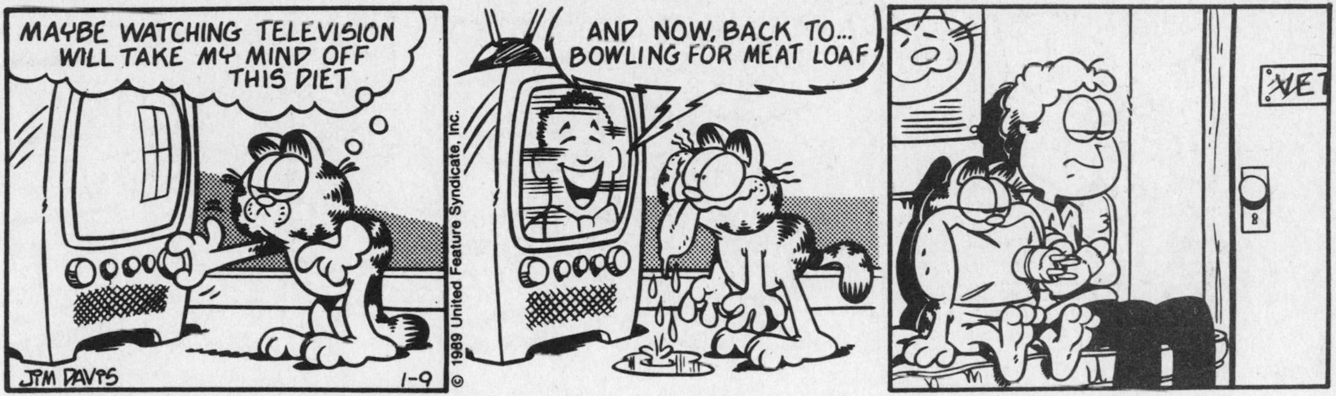
MAYBE WATCHING TELEVISION WILL TAKE MY MIND OFF THIS DIET
AND NOW, BACK TO... BOWLING FOR MEAT LOAF
VET
JIM DAVIS 1-9
© 1989 United Feature Syndicate, Inc.

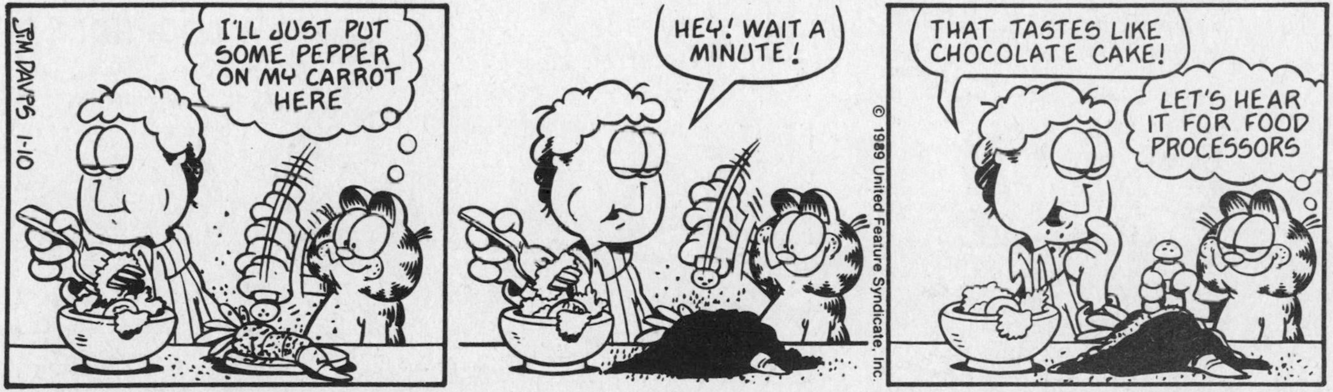
JIM DAVIS 1-10
I'LL JUST PUT SOME PEPPER ON MY CARROT HERE
HEY! WAIT A MINUTE!
THAT TASTES LIKE CHOCOLATE CAKE!
LET'S HEAR IT FOR FOOD PROCESSORS
© 1989 United Feature Syndicate, Inc.

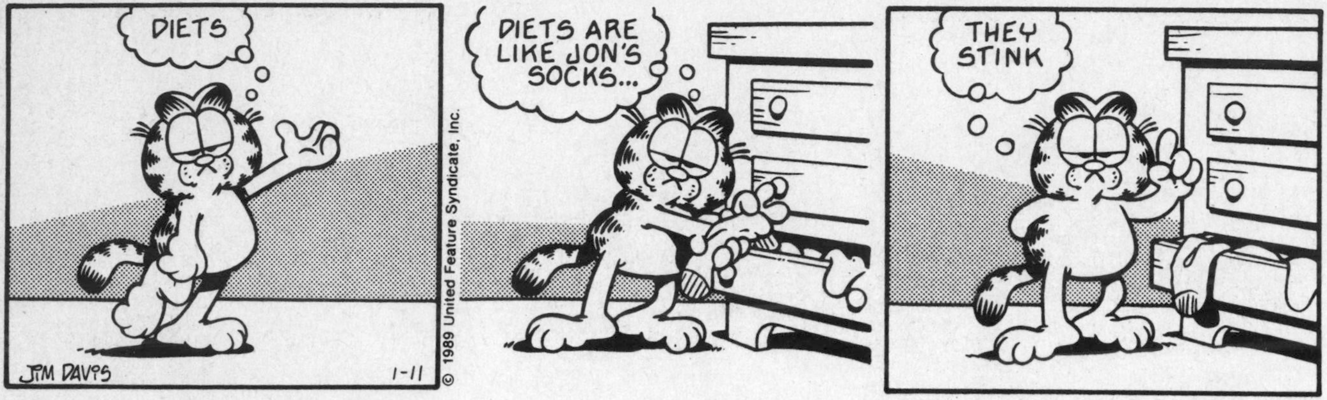
DIETS
DIETS ARE LIKE JON'S SOCKS...
THEY STINK
JIM DAVIS
1-11
© 1989 United Feature Syndicate, Inc.

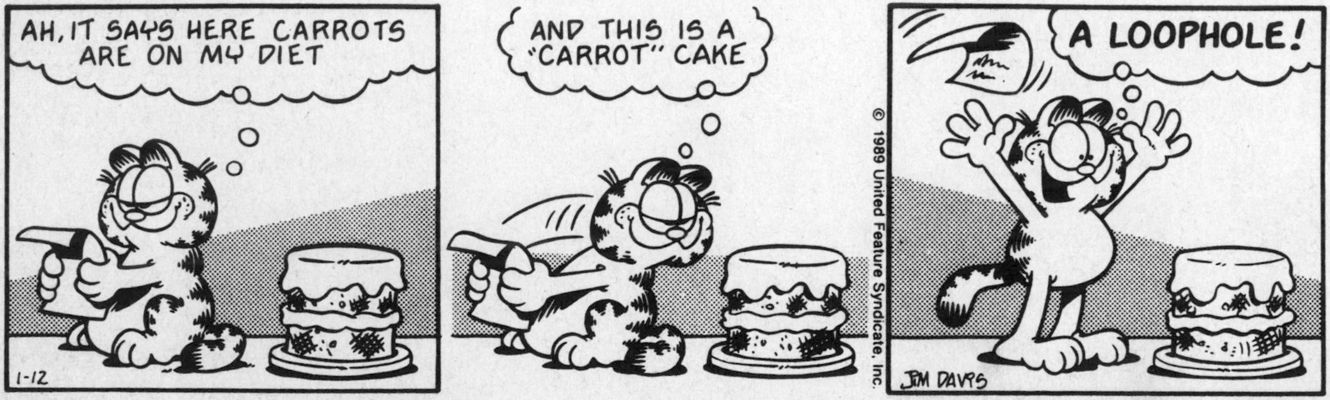
AH, IT SAYS HERE CARROTS ARE ON MY DIET
AND THIS IS A "CARROT" CAKE
A LOOPHOLE!
1-12
JIM DAVIS
© 1989 United Feature Syndicate, Inc.

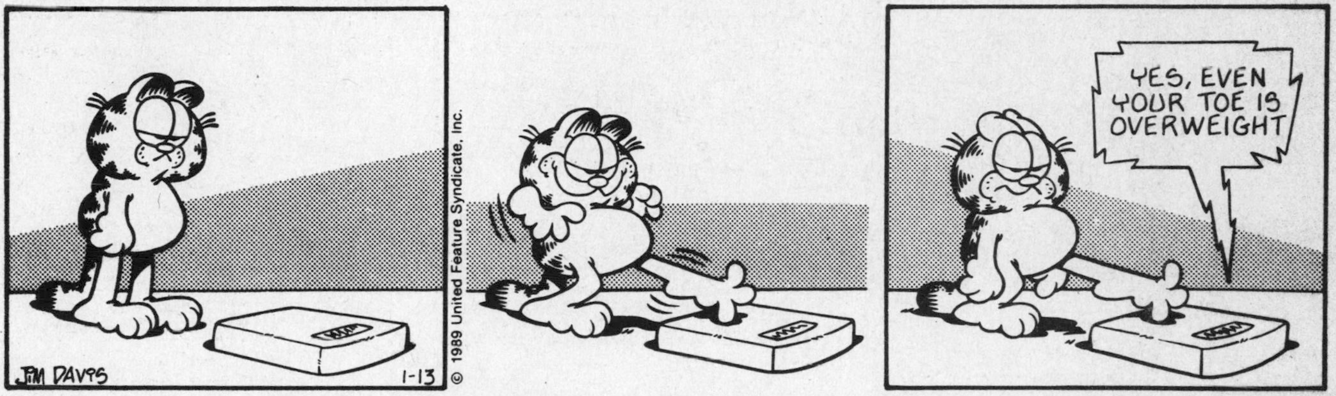
JIM DAVIS
1-13
© 1989 United Feature Syndicate, Inc.
YES, EVEN YOUR TOE IS OVERWEIGHT

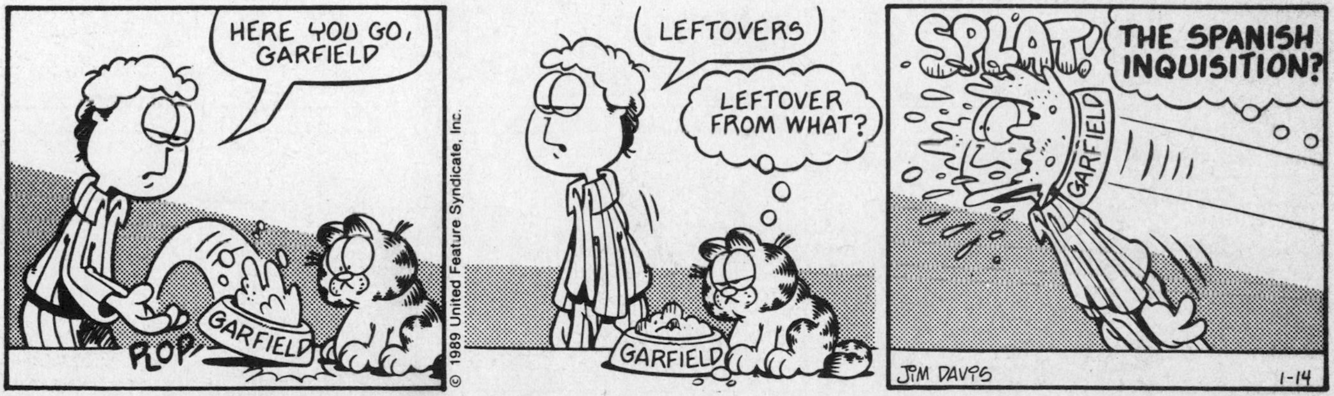
HERE YOU GO, GARFIELD
PLOP
GARFIELD
© 1989 United Feature Syndicate, Inc.
LEFTOVERS
LEFTOVER FROM WHAT?
GARFIELD
SPLAT!
THE SPANISH INQUISITION?
GARFIELD
JIM DAVIS
1-14

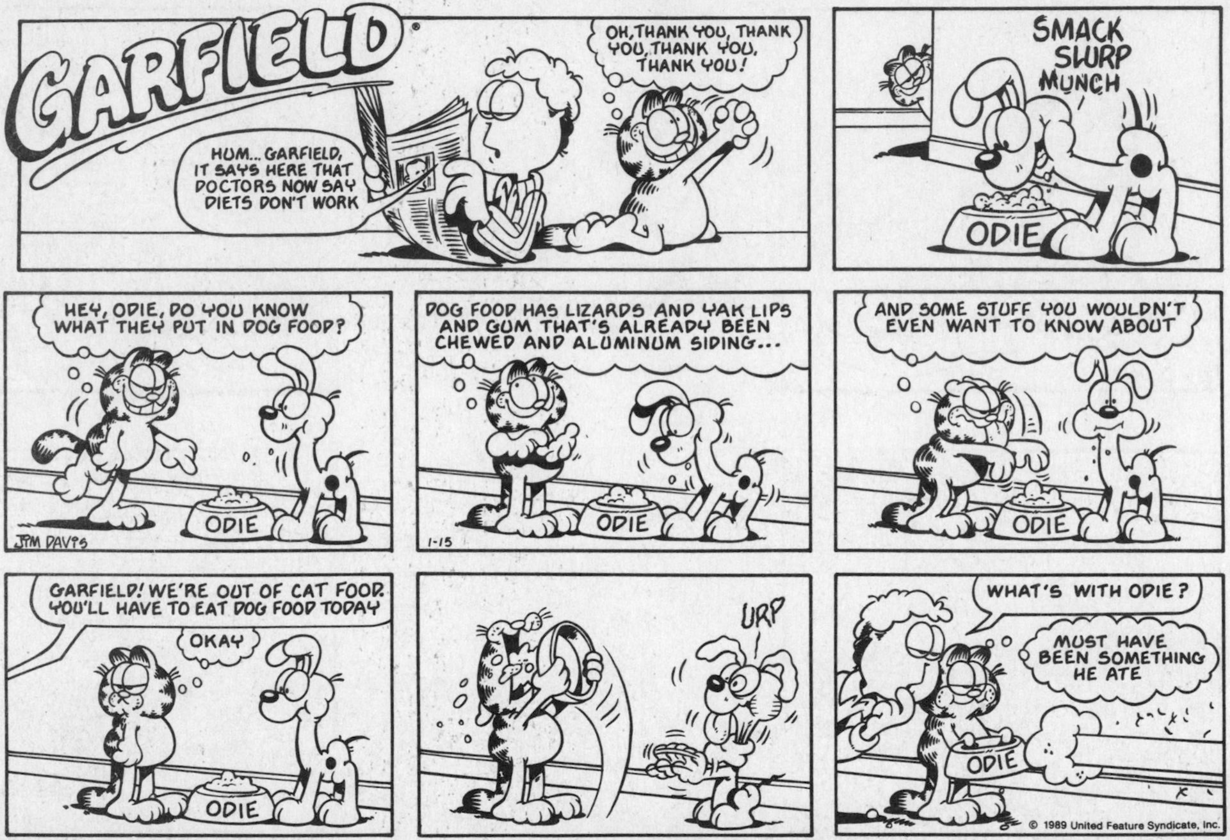
GARFIELD®
HUM... GARFIELD, IT SAYS HERE THAT DOCTORS NOW SAY DIETS DON'T WORK
OH, THANK YOU, THANK YOU, THANK YOU, THANK YOU!
SMACK
SLURP
MUNCH
HEY, ODIE, DO YOU KNOW WHAT THEY PUT IN DOG FOOD?
ODIE
JIM DAVIS
DOG FOOD HAS LIZARDS AND YAK LIPS AND GUM THAT'S ALREADY BEEN CHEWED AND ALUMINUM SIDING...
ODIE
1-15
AND SOME STUFF YOU WOULDN'T EVEN WANT TO KNOW ABOUT
ODIE
GARFIELD! WE'RE OUT OF CAT FOOD. YOU'LL HAVE TO EAT DOG FOOD TODAY
OKAY
ODIE
URP
WHAT'S WITH ODIE?
MUST HAVE BEEN SOMETHING HE ATE
ODIE
© 1989 United Feature Syndicate, Inc.

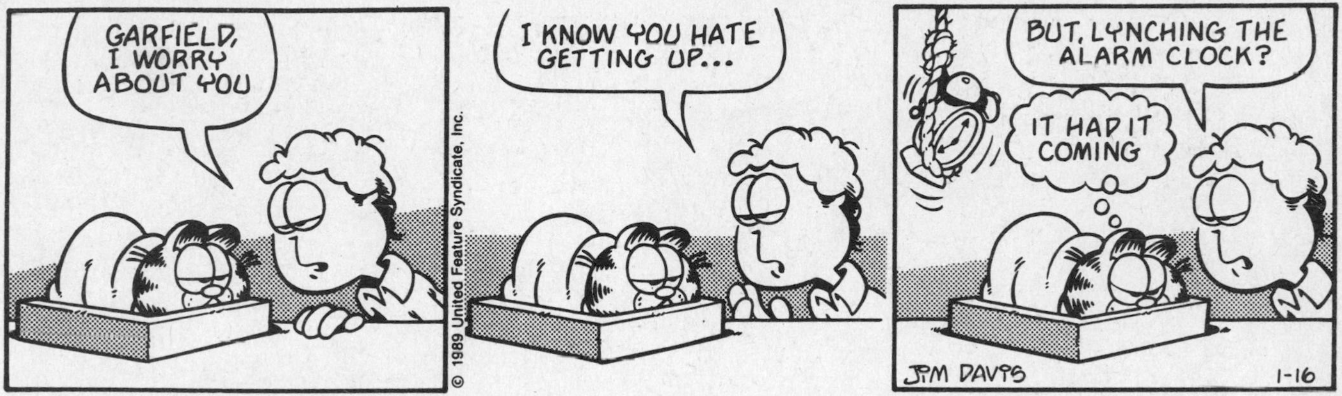
GARFIELD, I WORRY ABOUT YOU
I KNOW YOU HATE GETTING UP...
BUT, LYNCHING THE ALARM CLOCK?
IT HAD IT COMING
JIM DAVIS
1-16
© 1989 United Feature Syndicate, Inc.

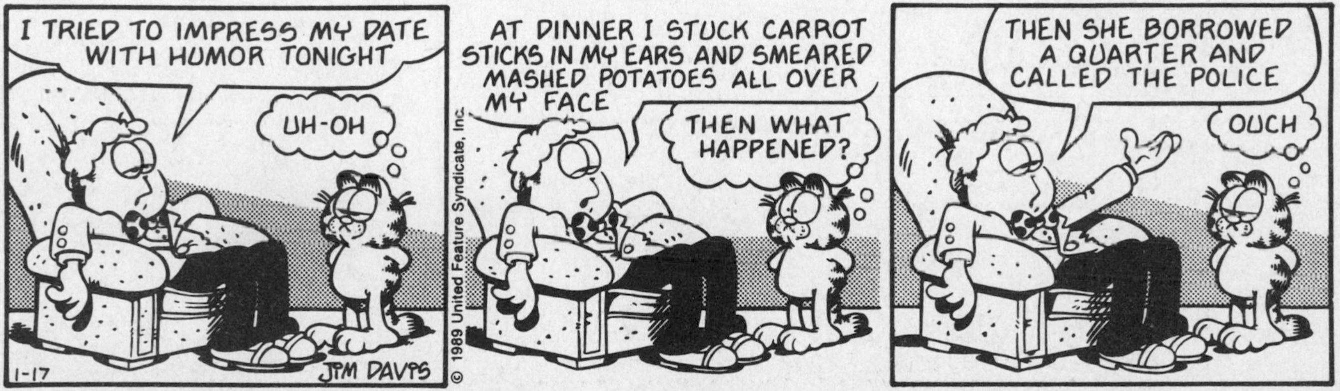
I TRIED TO IMPRESS MY DATE WITH HUMOR TONIGHT
UH-OH
AT DINNER I STUCK CARROT STICKS IN MY EARS AND SMEARED MASHED POTATOES ALL OVER MY FACE
THEN WHAT HAPPENED?
THEN SHE BORROWED A QUARTER AND CALLED THE POLICE
OUCH
1-17
JIM DAVIS
© 1989 United Feature Syndicate, Inc.

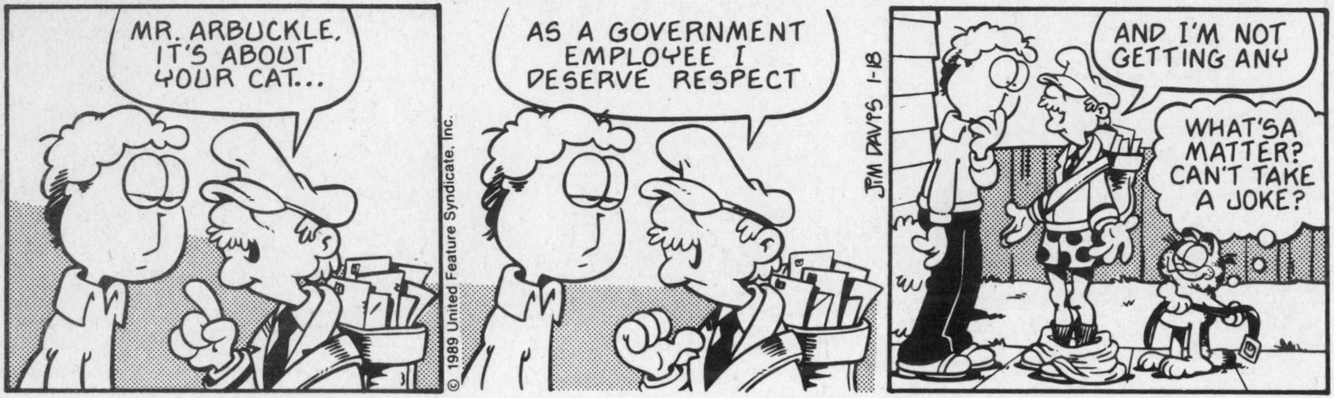
MR. ARBUCKLE, IT'S ABOUT YOUR CAT...
© 1989 United Feature Syndicate, Inc.
AS A GOVERNMENT EMPLOYEE I DESERVE RESPECT
JIM DAVIS 1-18
AND I'M NOT GETTING ANY
WHAT'SA MATTER? CAN'T TAKE A JOKE?

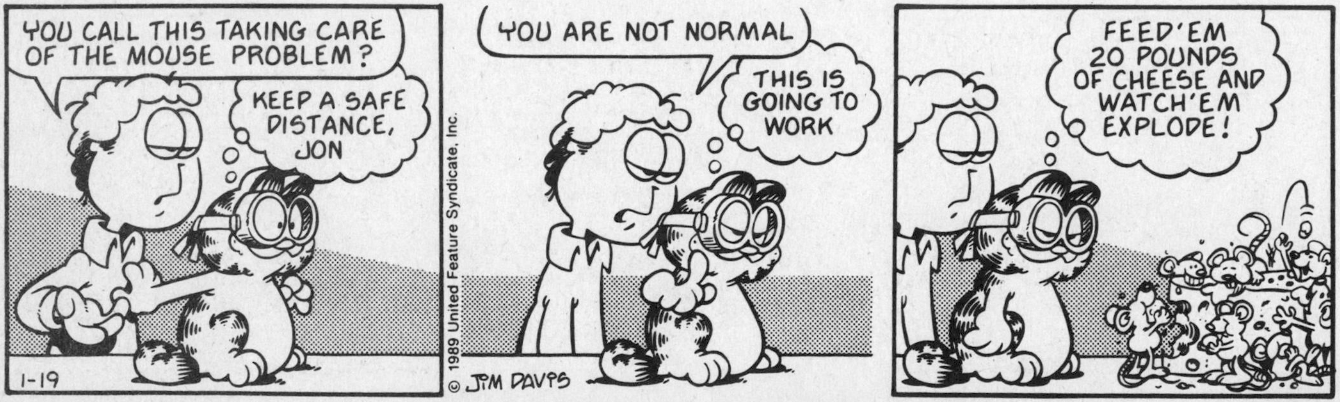
YOU CALL THIS TAKING CARE OF THE MOUSE PROBLEM?
KEEP A SAFE DISTANCE, JON
1-19
© 1989 United Feature Syndicate, Inc.
YOU ARE NOT NORMAL
THIS IS GOING TO WORK
© JIM DAVIS
FEED'EM 20 POUNDS OF CHEESE AND WATCH'EM EXPLODE!

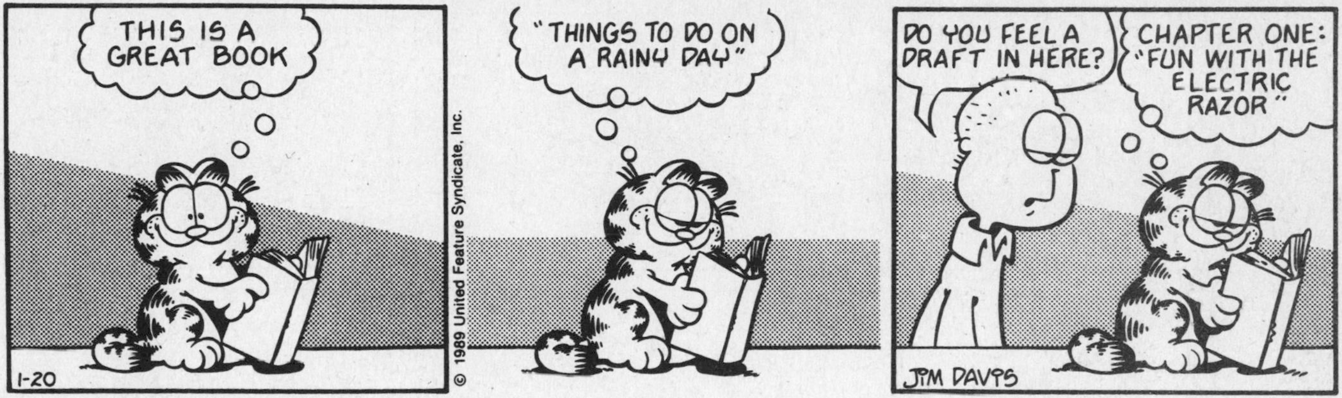
THIS IS A GREAT BOOK
1-20
"THINGS TO DO ON A RAINY DAY"
DO YOU FEEL A DRAFT IN HERE?
CHAPTER ONE: "FUN WITH THE ELECTRIC RAZOR"
JIM DAVIS

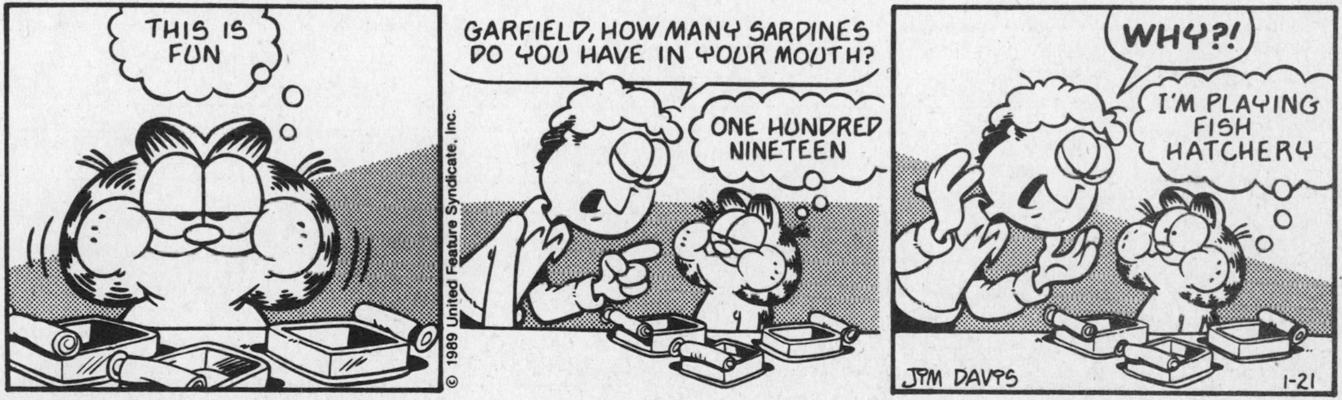
THIS IS FUN
GARFIELD, HOW MANY SARDINES DO YOU HAVE IN YOUR MOUTH?
ONE HUNDRED NINETEEN
WHY?!
I'M PLAYING FISH HATCHERY
JIM DAVIS
1-21

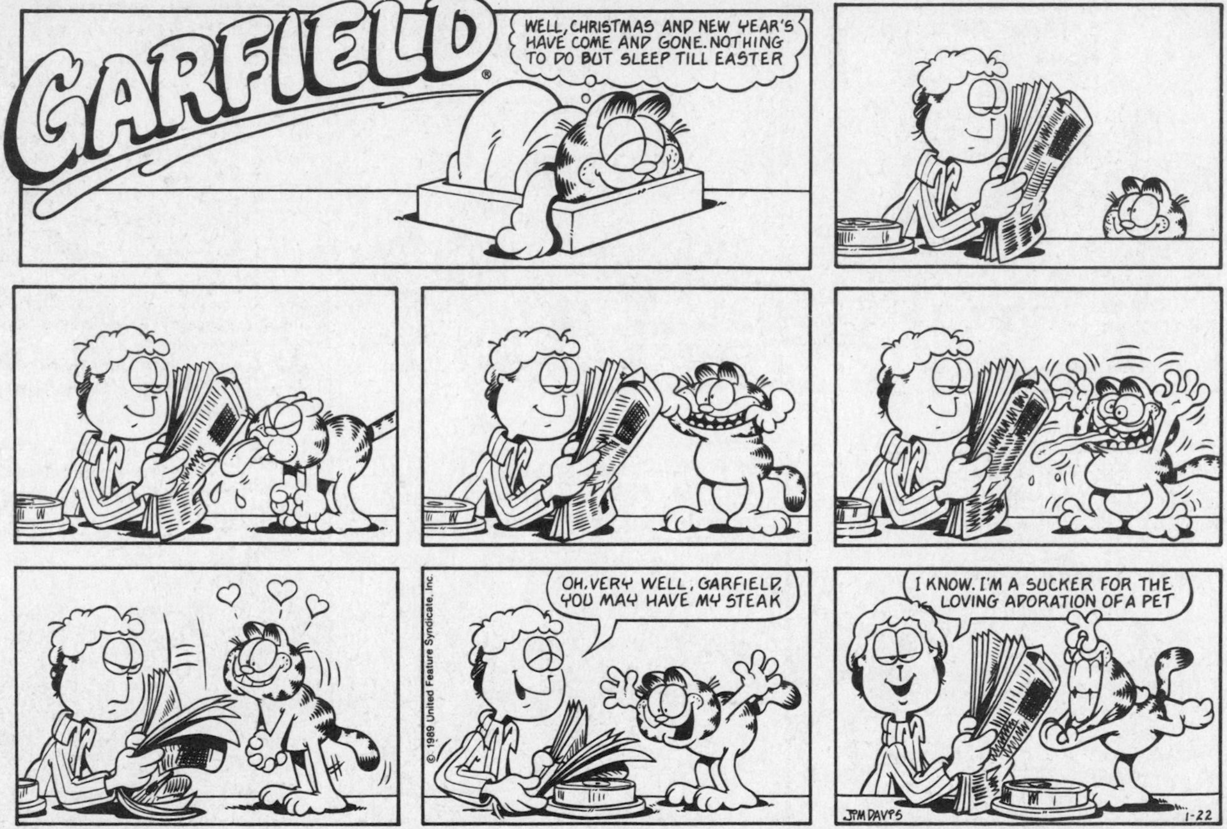
GARFIELD®
WELL, CHRISTMAS AND NEW YEAR'S HAVE COME AND GONE. NOTHING TO DO BUT SLEEP TILL EASTER
© 1989 United Feature Syndicate, Inc.
OH, VERY WELL, GARFIELD. YOU MAY HAVE MY STEAK
I KNOW. I'M A SUCKER FOR THE LOVING ADORATION OF A PET
JPM DAVIS
1-22

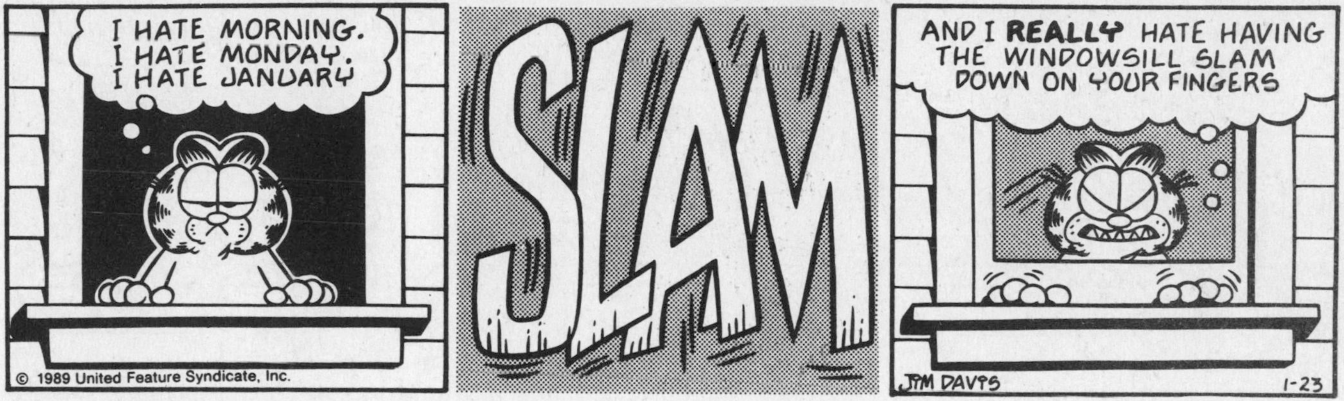

I HATE MORNING.
I HATE MONDAY.
I HATE JANUARY
© 1989 United Feature Syndicate, Inc.
SLAM
AND I **REALLY** HATE HAVING THE WINDOWSILL SLAM DOWN ON YOUR FINGERS
JIM DAVIS
1-23

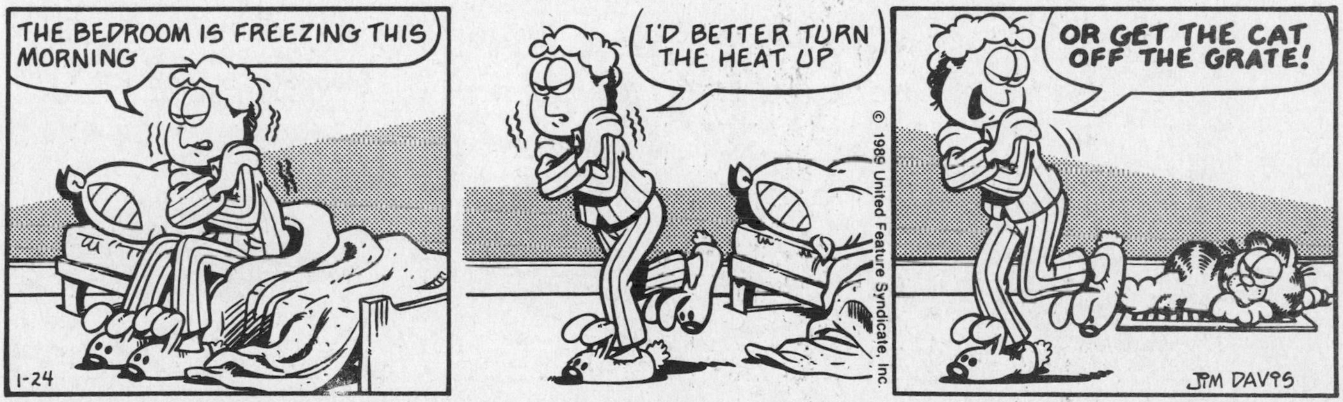

THE BEDROOM IS FREEZING THIS MORNING
1-24
I'D BETTER TURN THE HEAT UP
© 1989 United Feature Syndicate, Inc.
OR GET THE CAT OFF THE GRATE!
JIM DAVIS

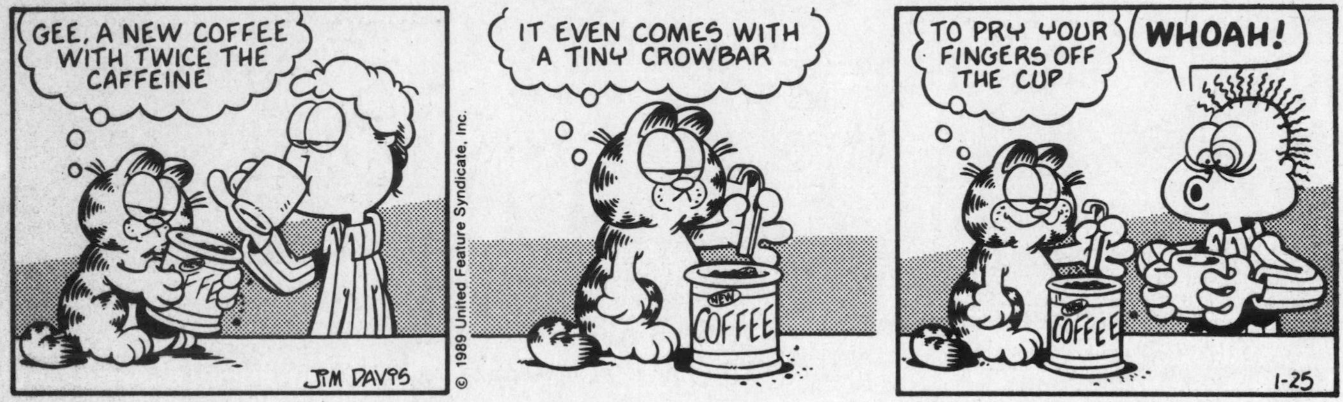
GEE, A NEW COFFEE WITH TWICE THE CAFFEINE
JIM DAVIS
© 1989 United Feature Syndicate, Inc.
IT EVEN COMES WITH A TINY CROWBAR
NEW
COFFEE
TO PRY YOUR FINGERS OFF THE CUP
WHOAH!
COFFEE
1-25

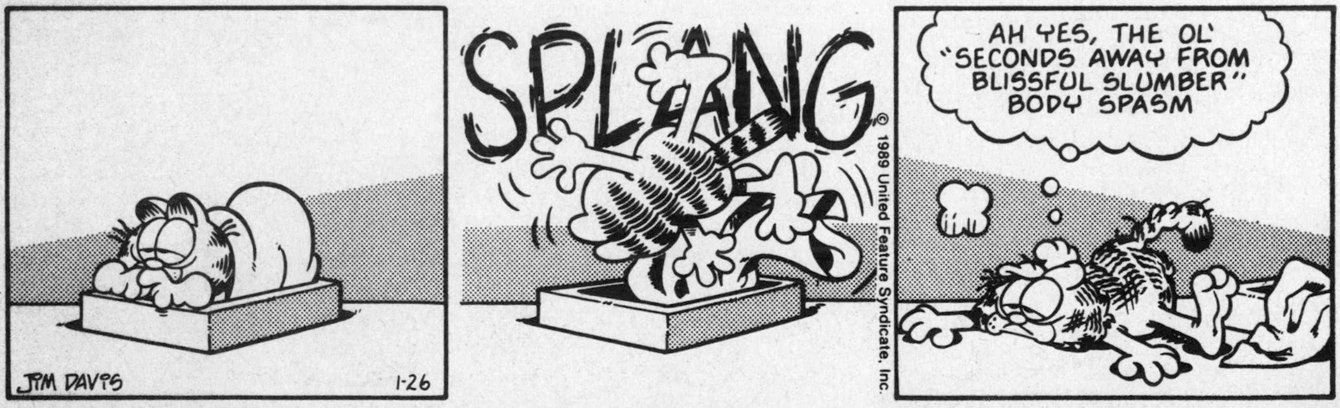
JIM DAVIS
1-26
SPLANG
© 1989 United Feature Syndicate, Inc.
AH YES, THE OL' "SECONDS AWAY FROM BLISSFUL SLUMBER" BODY SPASM

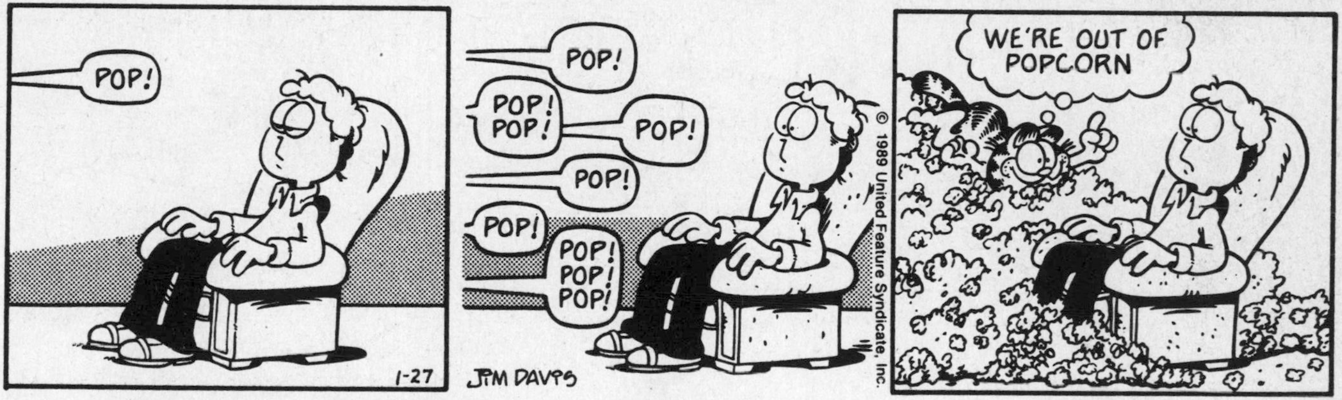
POP!
POP!
POP! POP!
POP!
POP!
POP!
POP! POP! POP!
WE'RE OUT OF POPCORN
1-27
JIM DAVIS
© 1989 United Feature Syndicate, Inc.

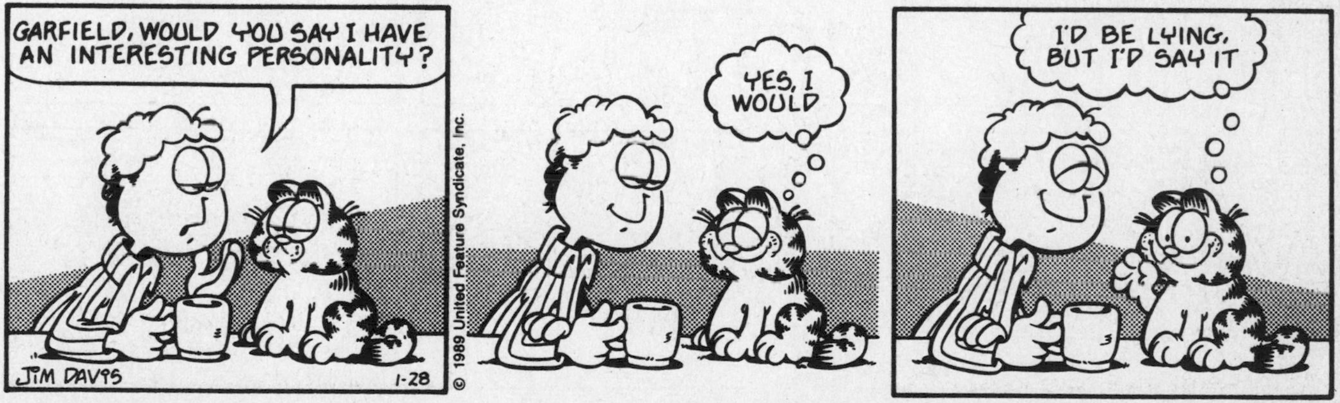
GARFIELD, WOULD YOU SAY I HAVE AN INTERESTING PERSONALITY?
YES, I WOULD
I'D BE LYING, BUT I'D SAY IT
JIM DAVIS
1-28
© 1989 United Feature Syndicate, Inc.

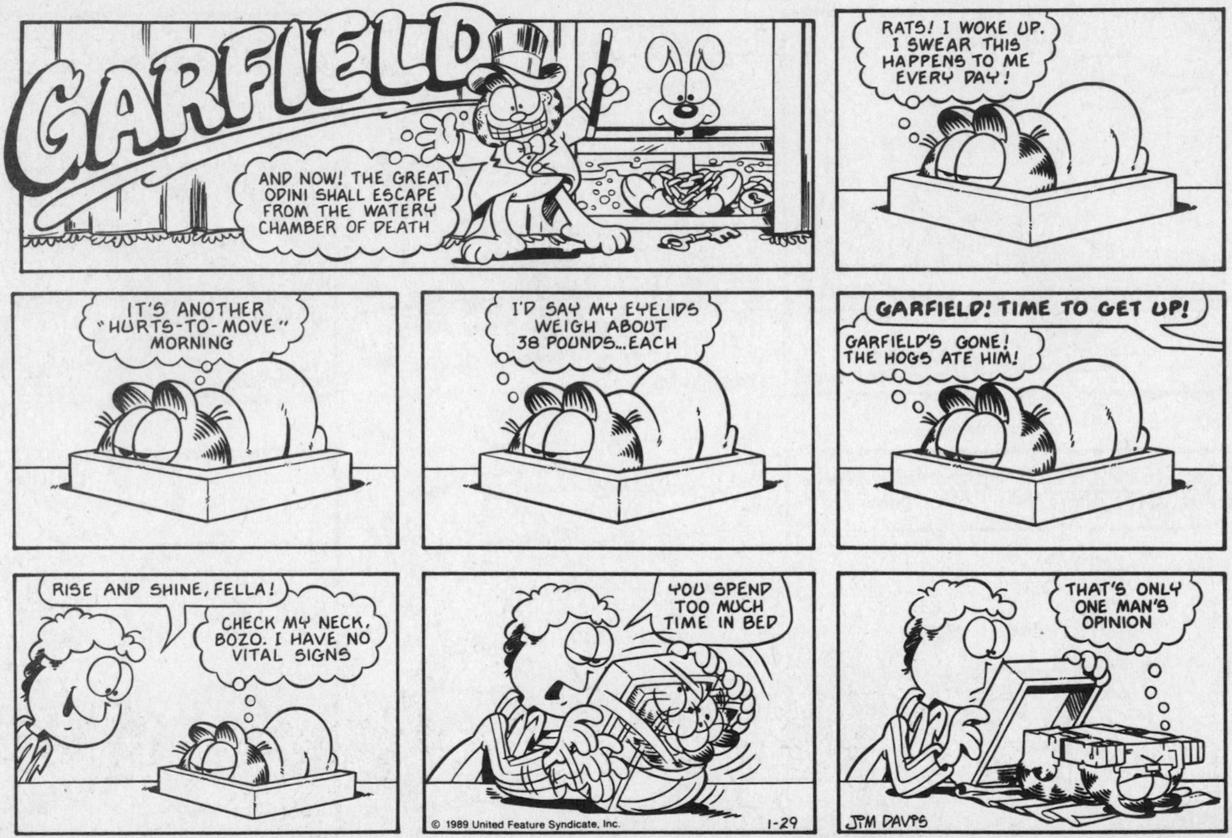
GARFIELD
AND NOW! THE GREAT ODINI SHALL ESCAPE FROM THE WATERY CHAMBER OF DEATH
RATS! I WOKE UP. I SWEAR THIS HAPPENS TO ME EVERY DAY!
IT'S ANOTHER "HURTS-TO-MOVE" MORNING
I'D SAY MY EYELIDS WEIGH ABOUT 38 POUNDS...EACH
GARFIELD! TIME TO GET UP!
GARFIELD'S GONE! THE HOGS ATE HIM!
RISE AND SHINE, FELLA!
CHECK MY NECK, BOZO. I HAVE NO VITAL SIGNS
YOU SPEND TOO MUCH TIME IN BED
THAT'S ONLY ONE MAN'S OPINION
© 1989 United Feature Syndicate, Inc.
1-29
JIM DAVIS

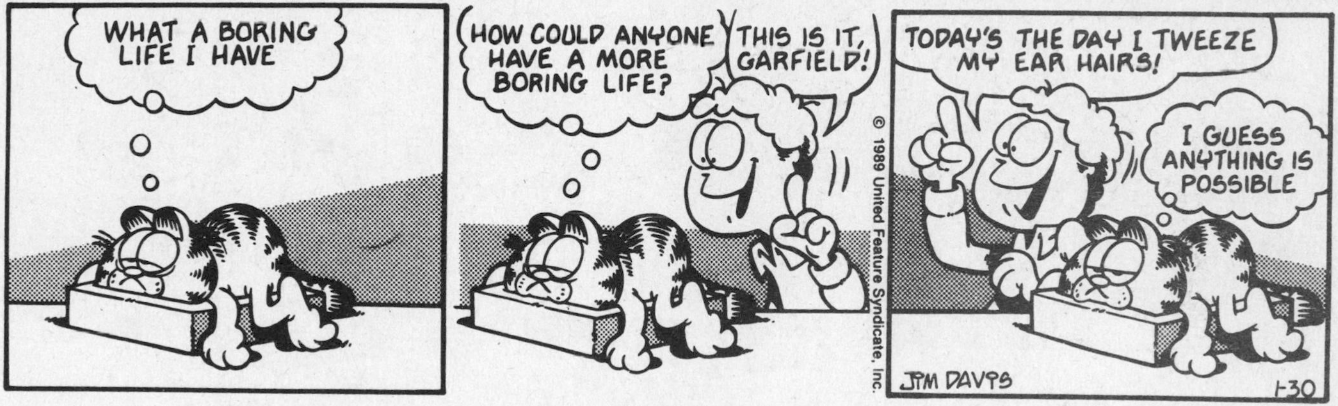
WHAT A BORING LIFE I HAVE
HOW COULD ANYONE HAVE A MORE BORING LIFE?
THIS IS IT, GARFIELD!
TODAY'S THE DAY I TWEEZE MY EAR HAIRS!
I GUESS ANYTHING IS POSSIBLE
© 1989 United Feature Syndicate, Inc.
JIM DAVIS
1-30

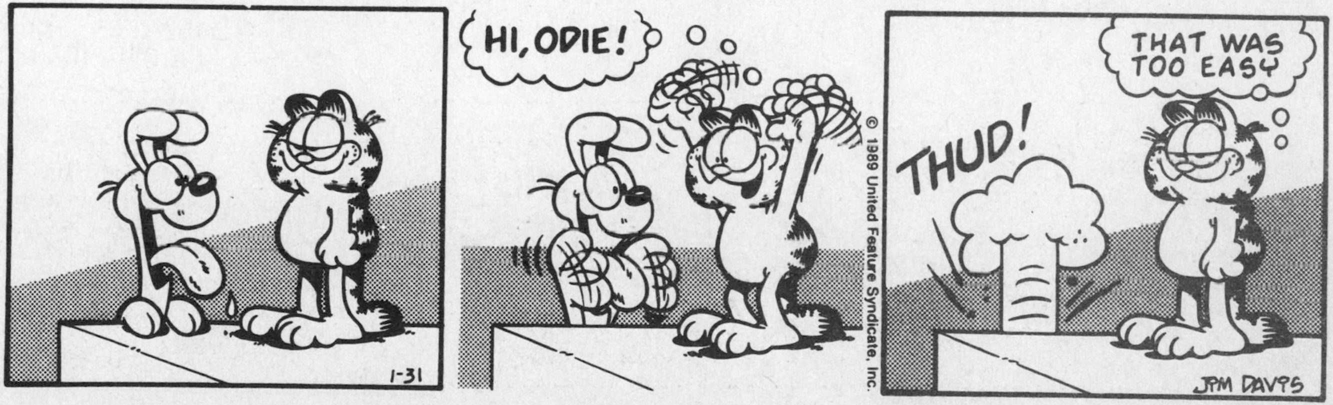
1-31
HI, ODIE!
© 1989 United Feature Syndicate, Inc.
THUD!
THAT WAS TOO EASY
JIM DAVIS

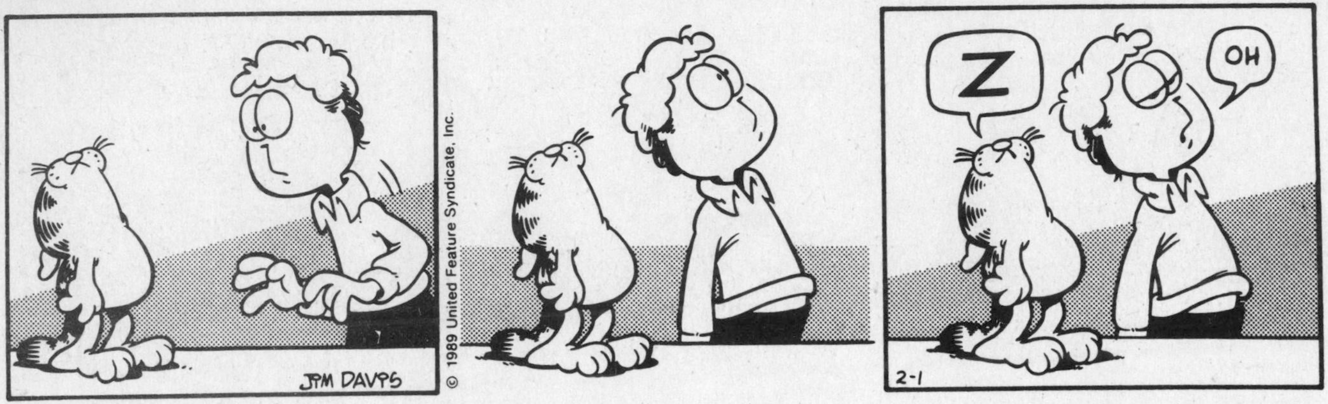
JIM DAVIS
© 1989 United Feature Syndicate, Inc.
Z
OH
2-1

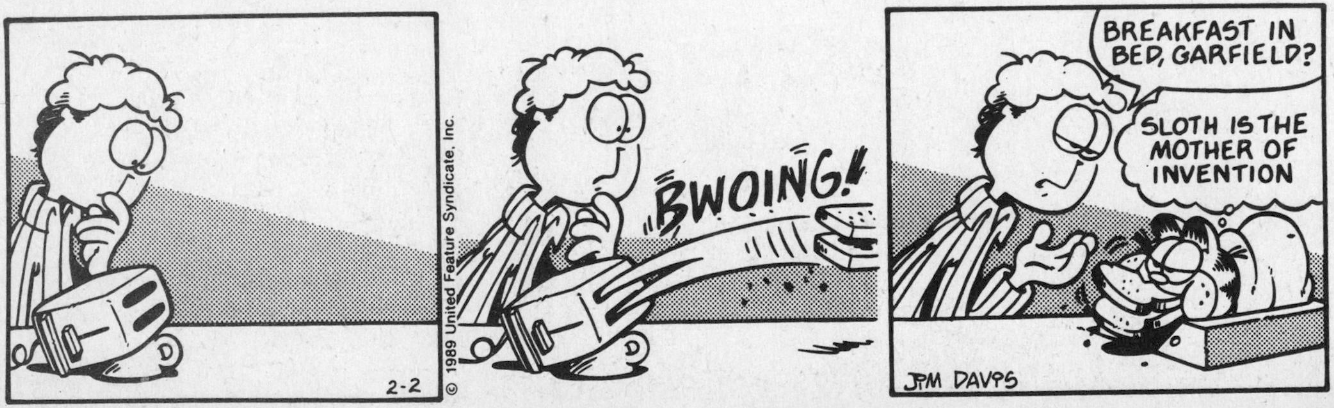
2-2
© 1989 United Feature Syndicate, Inc.
BWOING!
BREAKFAST IN BED, GARFIELD?
SLOTH IS THE MOTHER OF INVENTION
JIM DAVIS

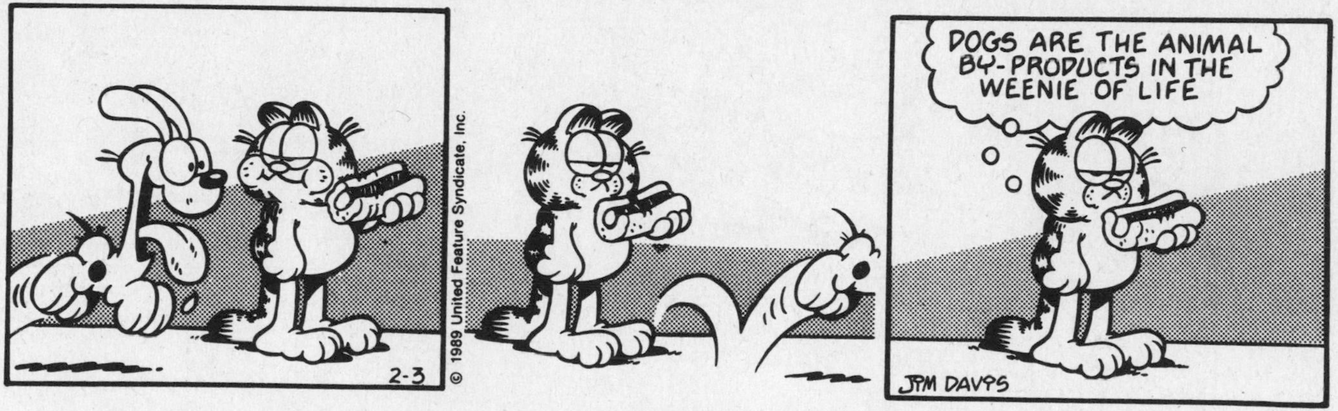
2-3
© 1989 United Feature Syndicate, Inc.
DOGS ARE THE ANIMAL BY-PRODUCTS IN THE WEENIE OF LIFE
JIM DAVIS

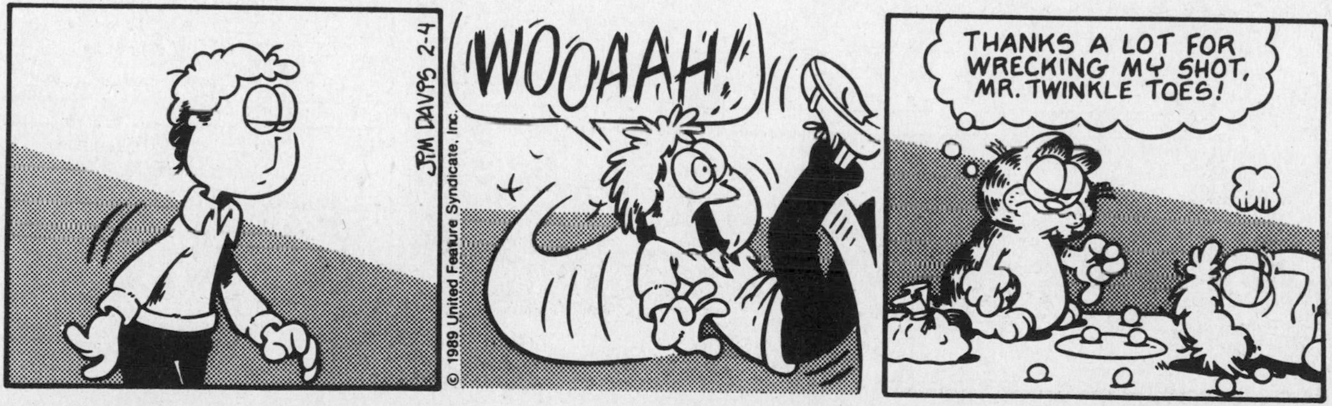
JIM DAVIS 2-4
© 1989 United Feature Syndicate, Inc.
WOOAAH!
THANKS A LOT FOR WRECKING MY SHOT, MR. TWINKLE TOES!

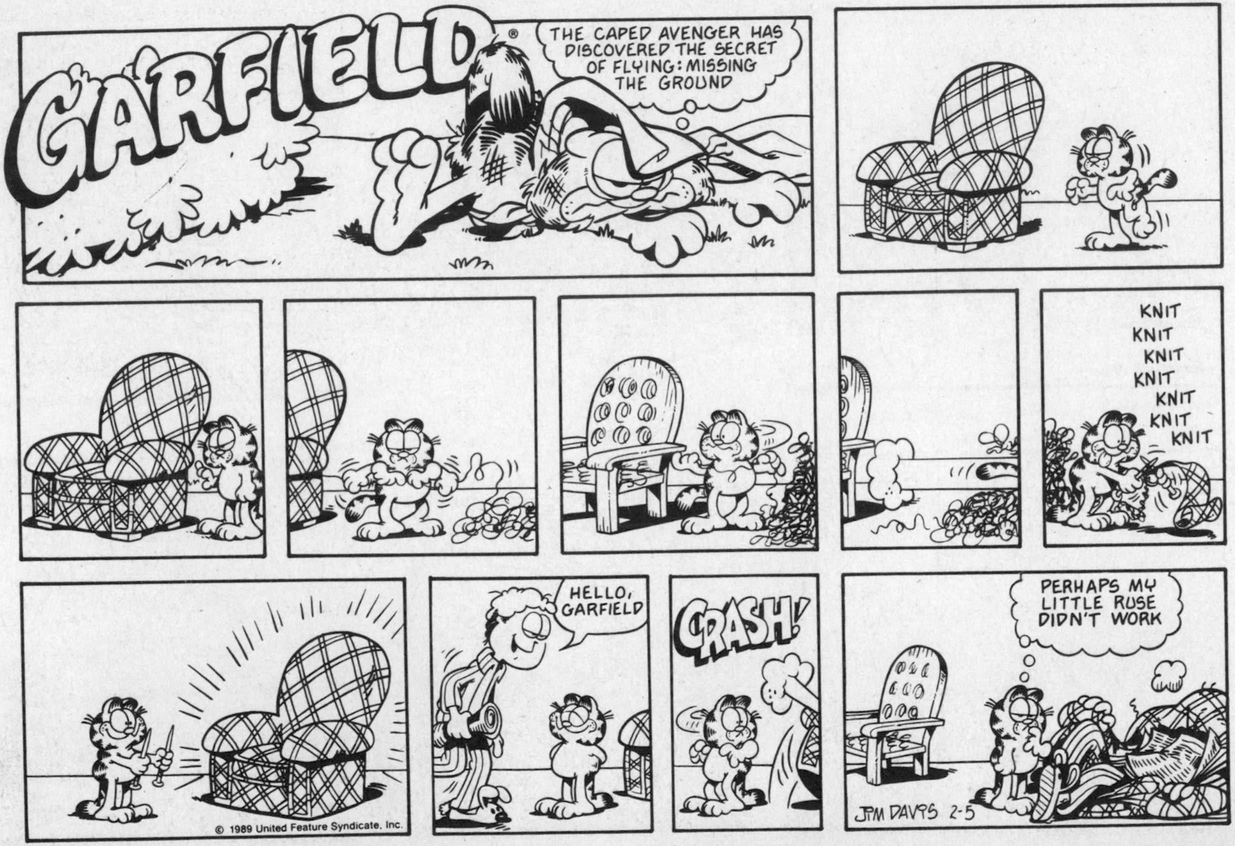
GARFIELD®
THE CAPED AVENGER HAS DISCOVERED THE SECRET OF FLYING: MISSING THE GROUND
KNIT
KNIT
KNIT
KNIT
KNIT
KNIT
KNIT
HELLO, GARFIELD
CRASH!
PERHAPS MY LITTLE RUSE DIDN'T WORK
© 1989 United Feature Syndicate, Inc.
JIM DAVIS 2-5

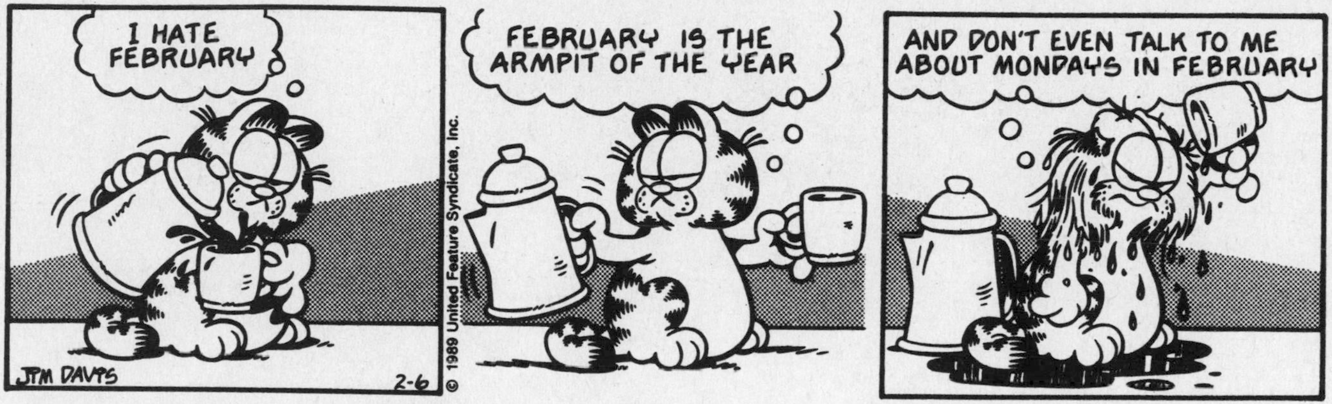
I HATE FEBRUARY
FEBRUARY IS THE ARMPIT OF THE YEAR
AND DON'T EVEN TALK TO ME ABOUT MONDAYS IN FEBRUARY
JIM DAVIS
2-6
© 1989 United Feature Syndicate, Inc.

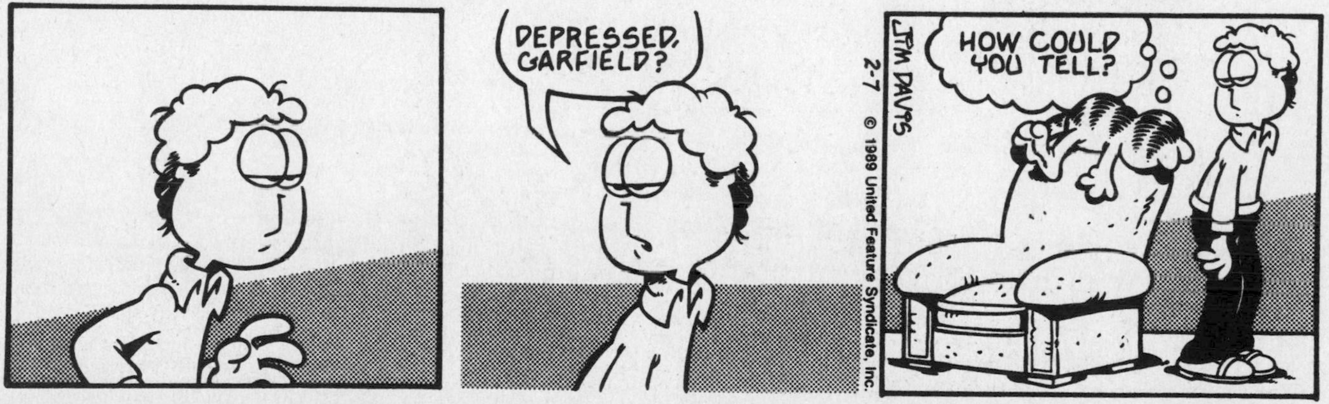
DEPRESSED, GARFIELD?
HOW COULD YOU TELL?
JIM DAVIS
2-7
© 1989 United Feature Syndicate, Inc.

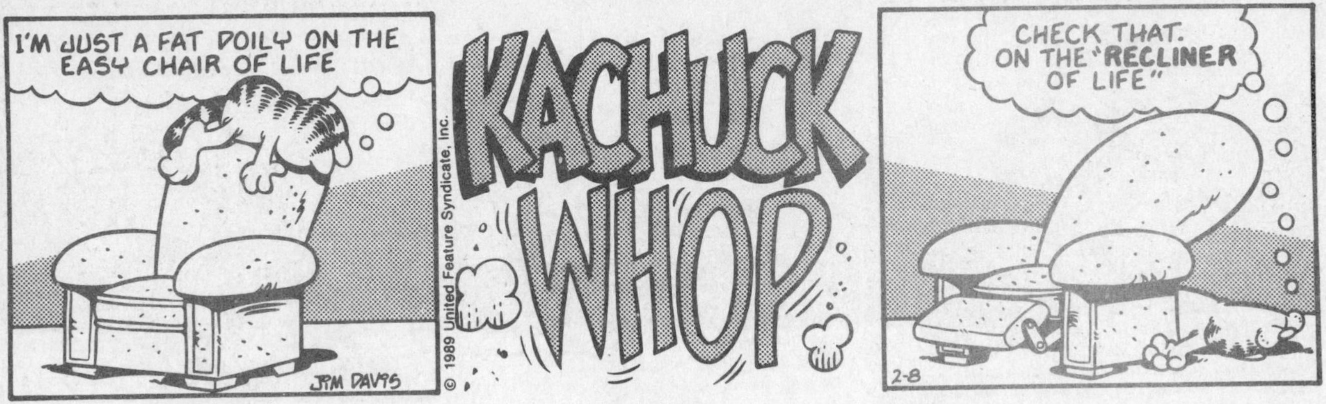
I'M JUST A FAT DOILY ON THE EASY CHAIR OF LIFE
KACHUCK
WHOP
CHECK THAT. ON THE "RECLINER OF LIFE"
JIM DAVIS
2-8
© 1989 United Feature Syndicate, Inc.

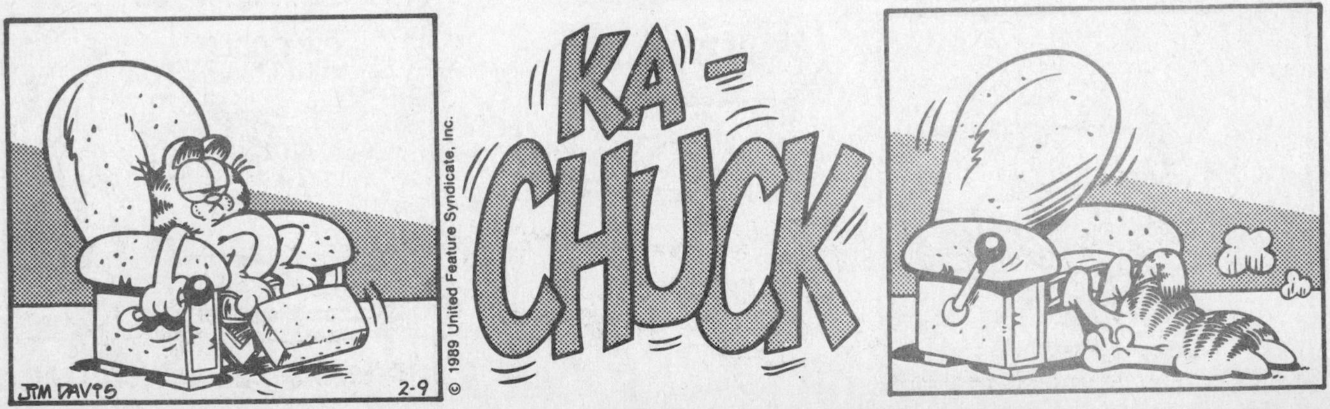
KA-
CHUCK
JIM DAVIS
2-9
© 1989 United Feature Syndicate, Inc.

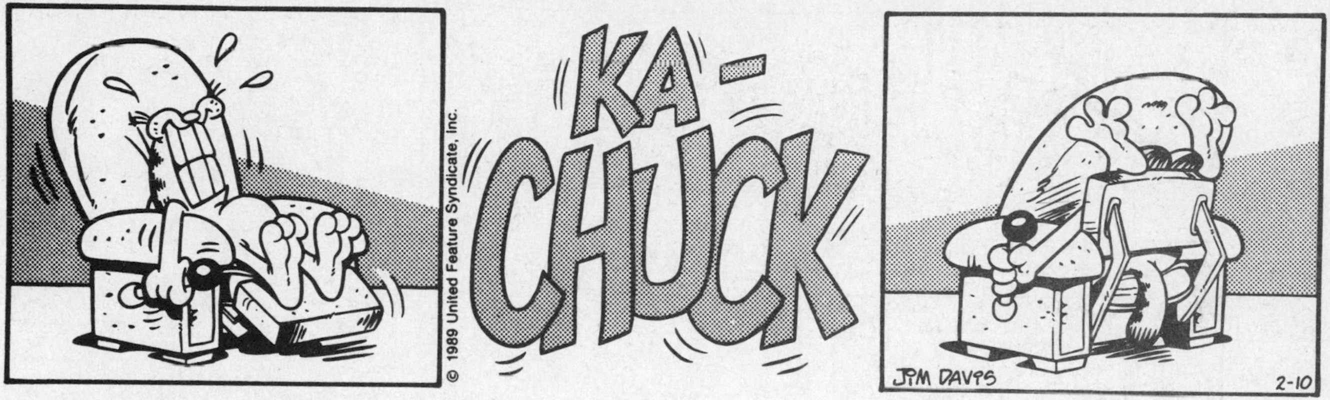
KA-CHUCK
© 1989 United Feature Syndicate, Inc.
JIM DAVIS
2-10

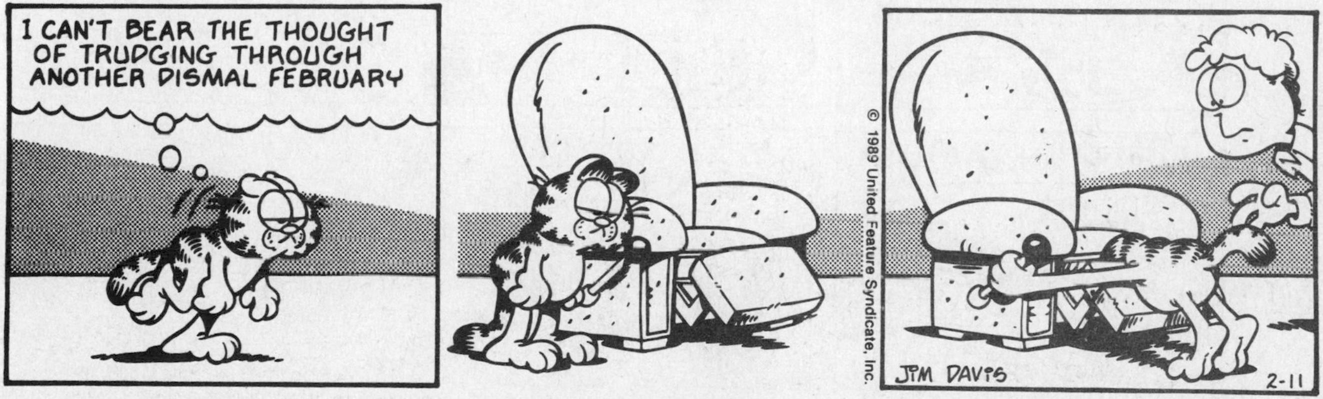
I CAN'T BEAR THE THOUGHT OF TRUDGING THROUGH ANOTHER DISMAL FEBRUARY
© 1989 United Feature Syndicate, Inc.
JIM DAVIS
2-11

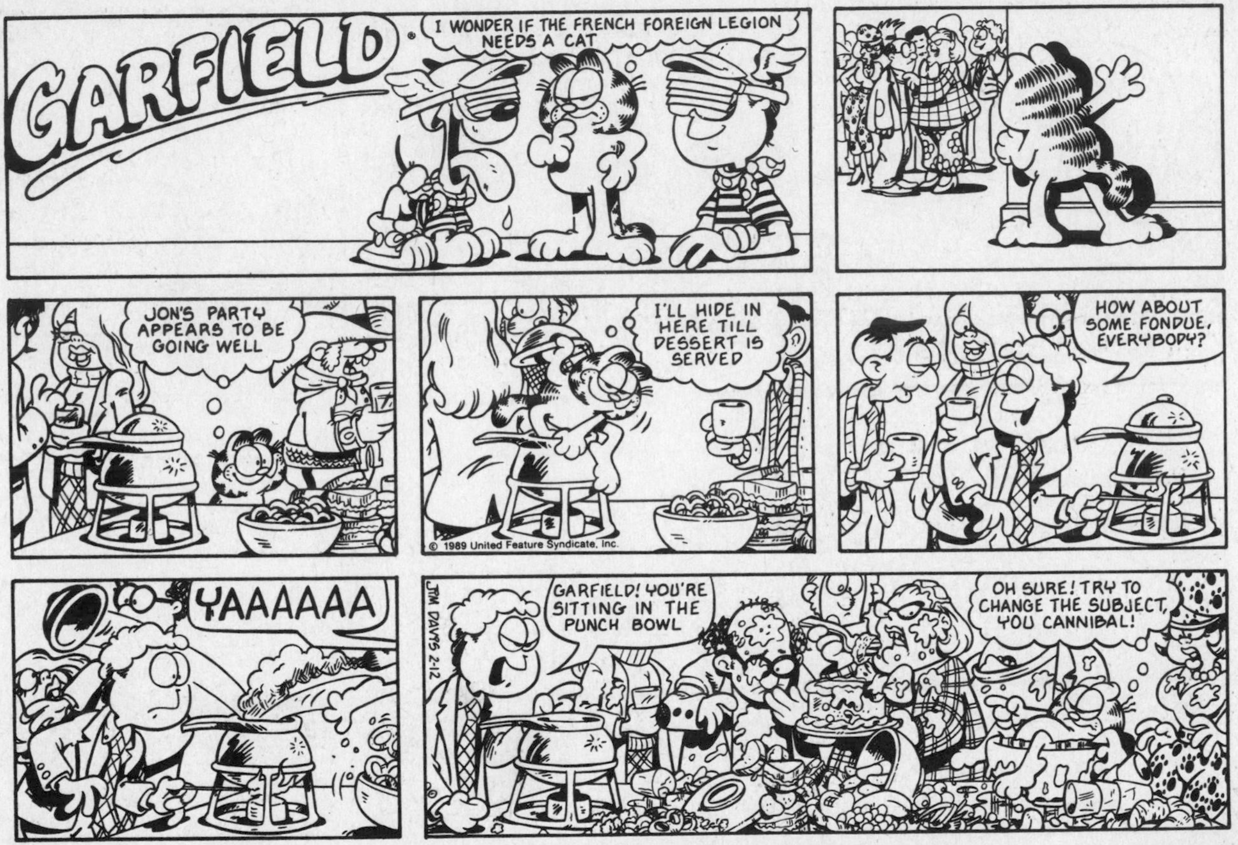
GARFIELD®
I WONDER IF THE FRENCH FOREIGN LEGION NEEDS A CAT
JON'S PARTY APPEARS TO BE GOING WELL
I'LL HIDE IN HERE TILL DESSERT IS SERVED
© 1989 United Feature Syndicate, Inc.
HOW ABOUT SOME FONDUE, EVERYBODY?
YAAAAAA
JIM DAVIS 2-12
GARFIELD! YOU'RE SITTING IN THE PUNCH BOWL
OH SURE! TRY TO CHANGE THE SUBJECT, YOU CANNIBAL!

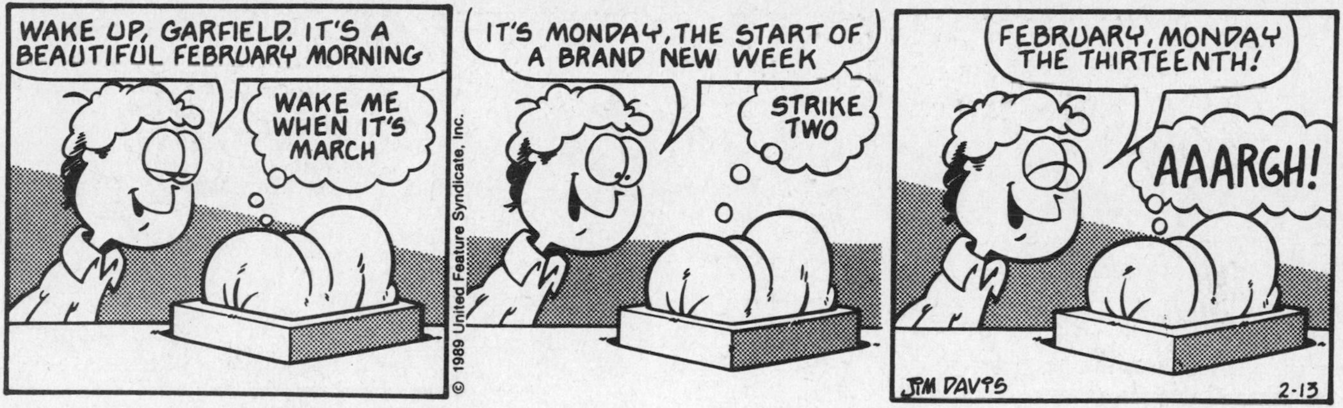
WAKE UP, GARFIELD. IT'S A BEAUTIFUL FEBRUARY MORNING
WAKE ME WHEN IT'S MARCH
© 1989 United Feature Syndicate, Inc.
IT'S MONDAY, THE START OF A BRAND NEW WEEK
STRIKE TWO
FEBRUARY, MONDAY THE THIRTEENTH!
AAARGH!
JIM DAVIS
2-13

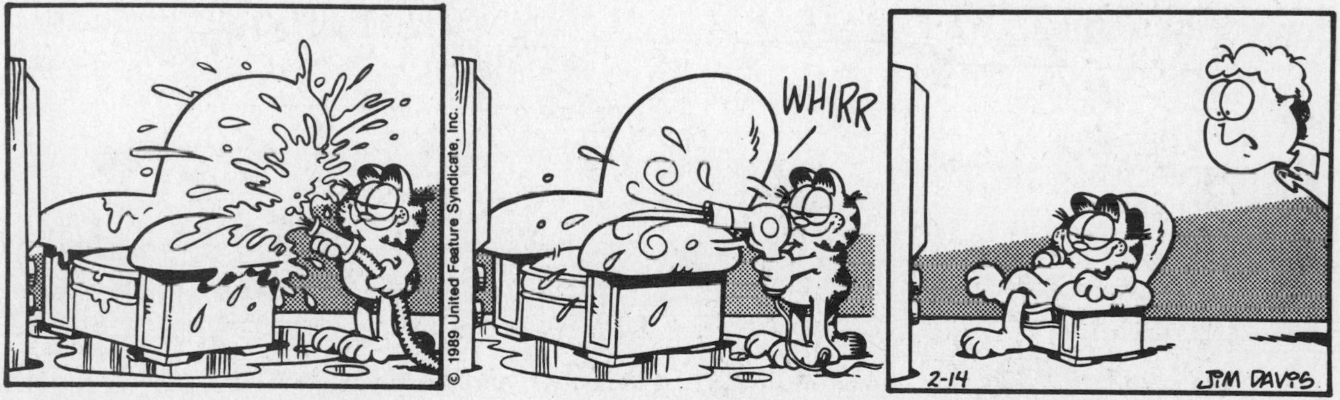
© 1989 United Feature Syndicate, Inc.
WHIRR
2-14
JIM DAVIS

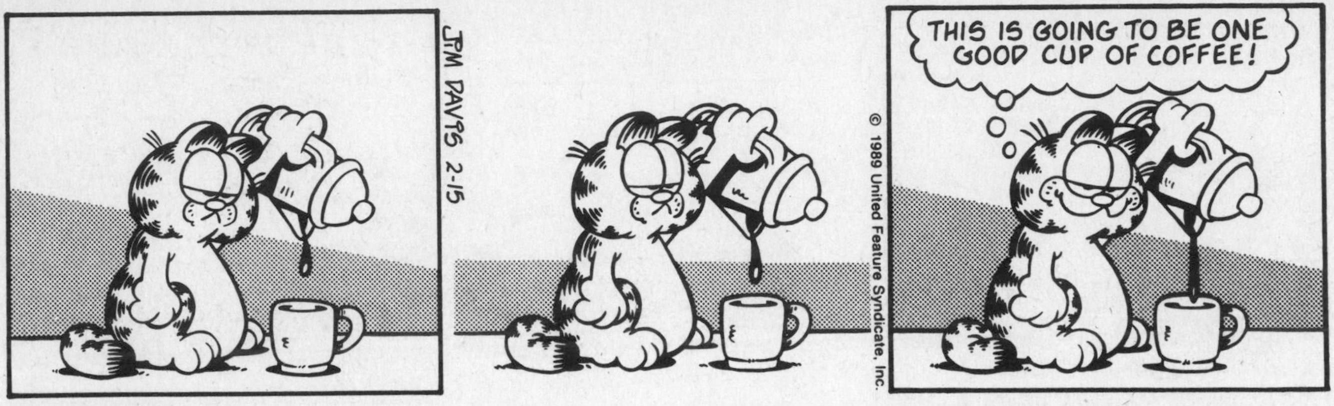
JIM DAVIS 2-15
© 1989 United Feature Syndicate, Inc.
THIS IS GOING TO BE ONE GOOD CUP OF COFFEE!

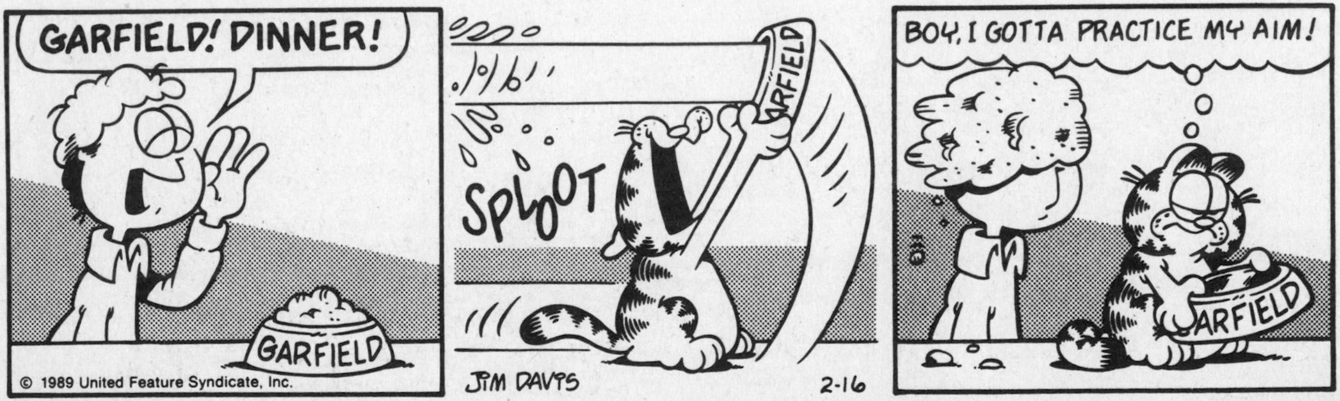
GARFIELD! DINNER!
GARFIELD
© 1989 United Feature Syndicate, Inc.
SPLOOT
GARFIELD
JIM DAVIS
2-16
BOY, I GOTTA PRACTICE MY AIM!
GARFIELD

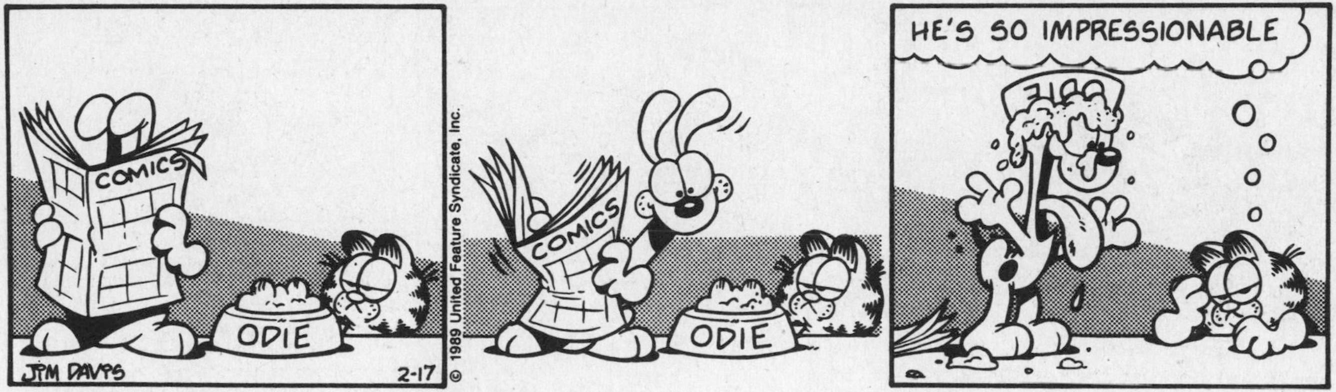
COMICS
ODIE
JIM DAVIS
2-17
© 1989 United Feature Syndicate, Inc.
COMICS
ODIE
HE'S SO IMPRESSIONABLE
ODIE

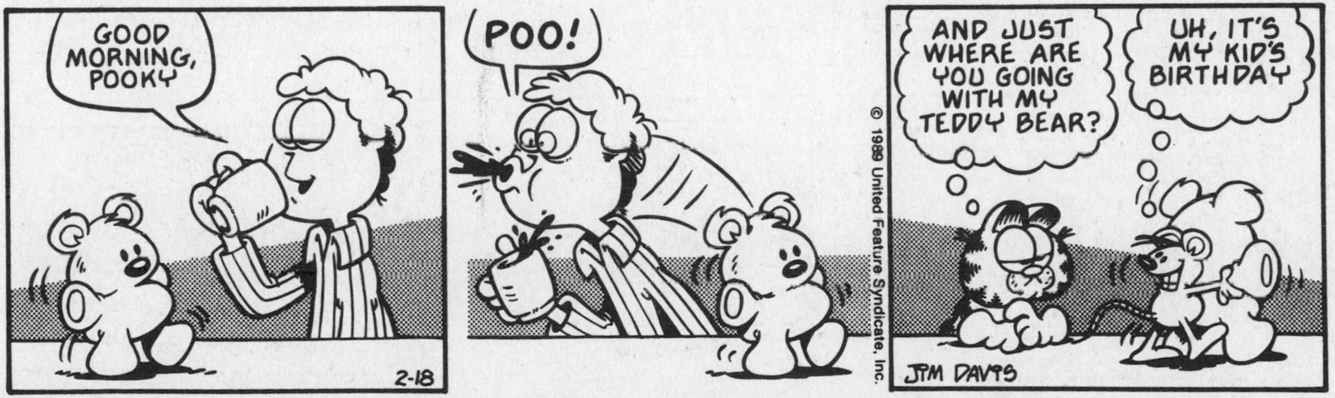
GOOD MORNING, POOKY
2-18
POO!
© 1989 United Feature Syndicate, Inc.
AND JUST WHERE ARE YOU GOING WITH MY TEDDY BEAR?
UH, IT'S MY KID'S BIRTHDAY
JIM DAVIS

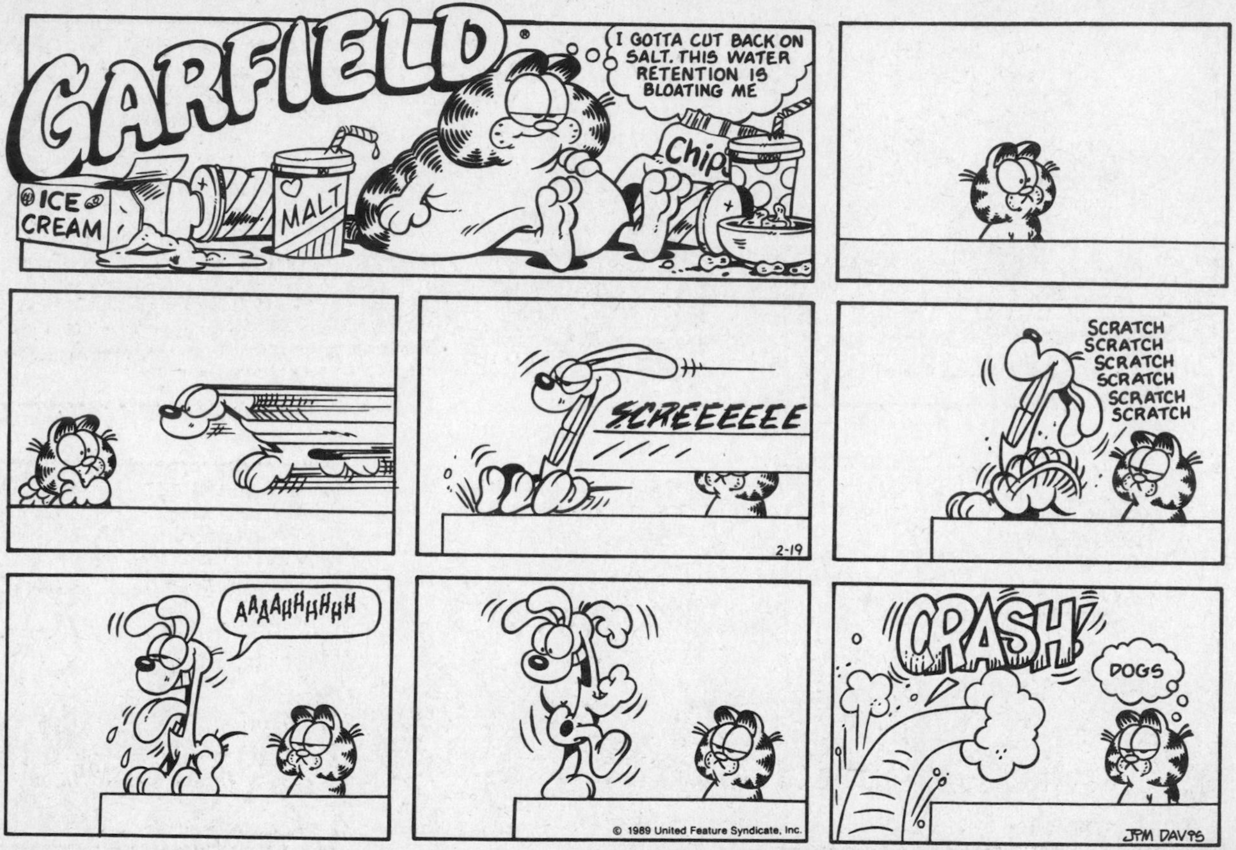
GARFIELD®
I GOTTA CUT BACK ON SALT. THIS WATER RETENTION IS BLOATING ME
ICE CREAM
MALT
Chip
2-19
SCREEEEEE
SCRATCH SCRATCH SCRATCH SCRATCH SCRATCH SCRATCH
AAAAHHHHHH
© 1989 United Feature Syndicate, Inc.
CRASH
DOGS
JPM DAVPS

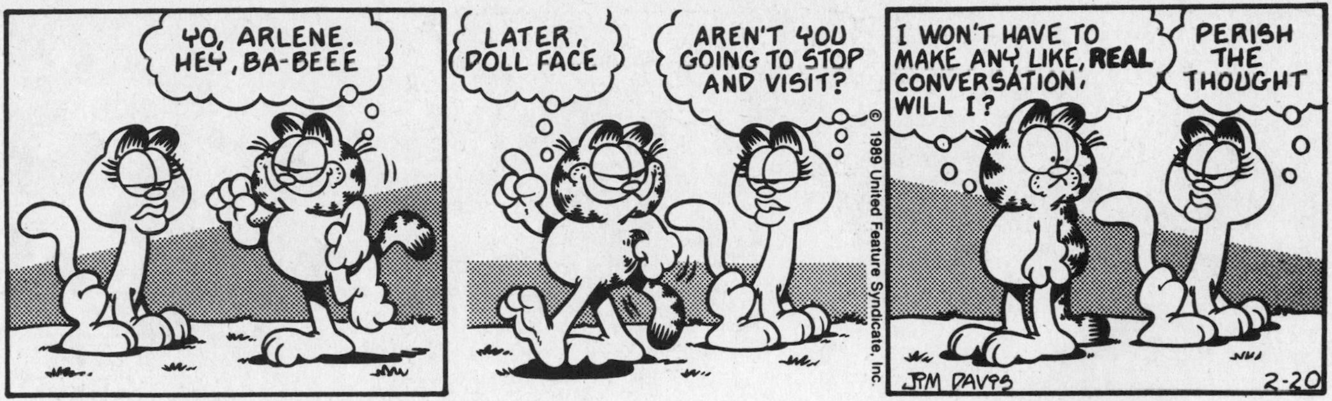
YO, ARLENE. HEY, BA-BEEE
LATER, DOLL FACE
AREN'T YOU GOING TO STOP AND VISIT?
I WON'T HAVE TO MAKE ANY LIKE, REAL CONVERSATION, WILL I?
PERISH THE THOUGHT
© 1989 United Feature Syndicate, Inc.
JIM DAVIS
2-20

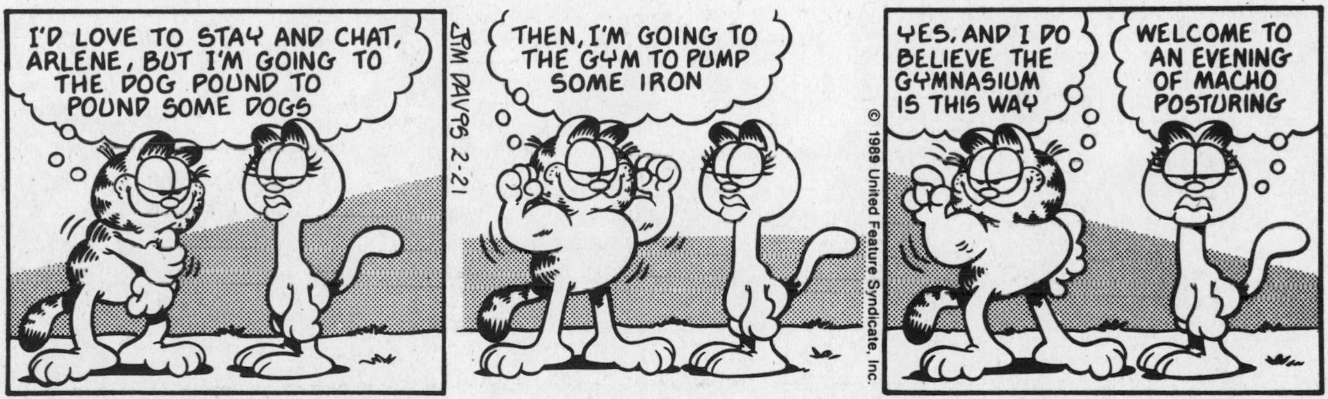
I'D LOVE TO STAY AND CHAT, ARLENE, BUT I'M GOING TO THE DOG POUND TO POUND SOME DOGS
JIM DAVIS 2-21
THEN, I'M GOING TO THE GYM TO PUMP SOME IRON
YES. AND I DO BELIEVE THE GYMNASIUM IS THIS WAY
WELCOME TO AN EVENING OF MACHO POSTURING
© 1989 United Feature Syndicate, Inc.

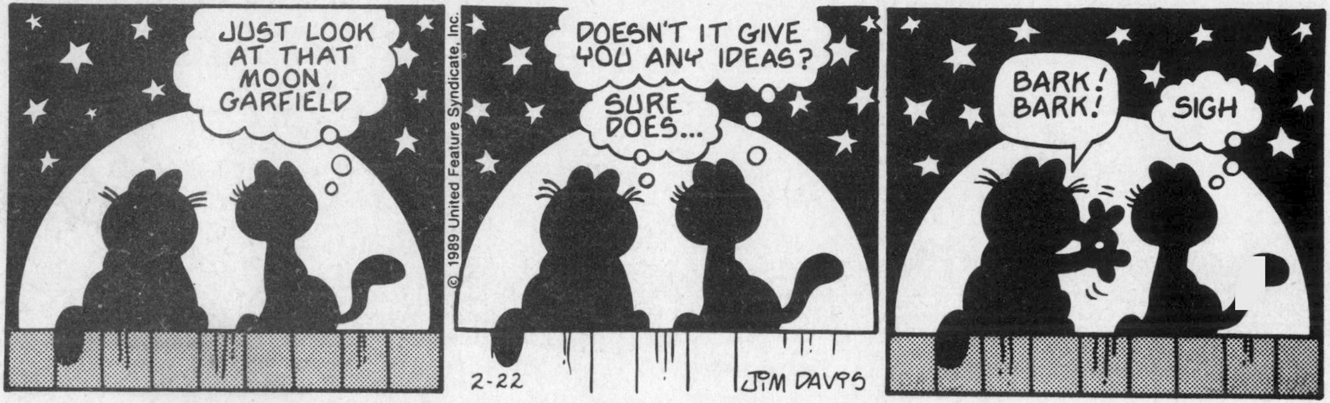
JUST LOOK AT THAT MOON, GARFIELD
© 1989 United Feature Syndicate, Inc.
DOESN'T IT GIVE YOU ANY IDEAS?
SURE DOES...
2-22
JIM DAVIS
BARK! BARK!
SIGH

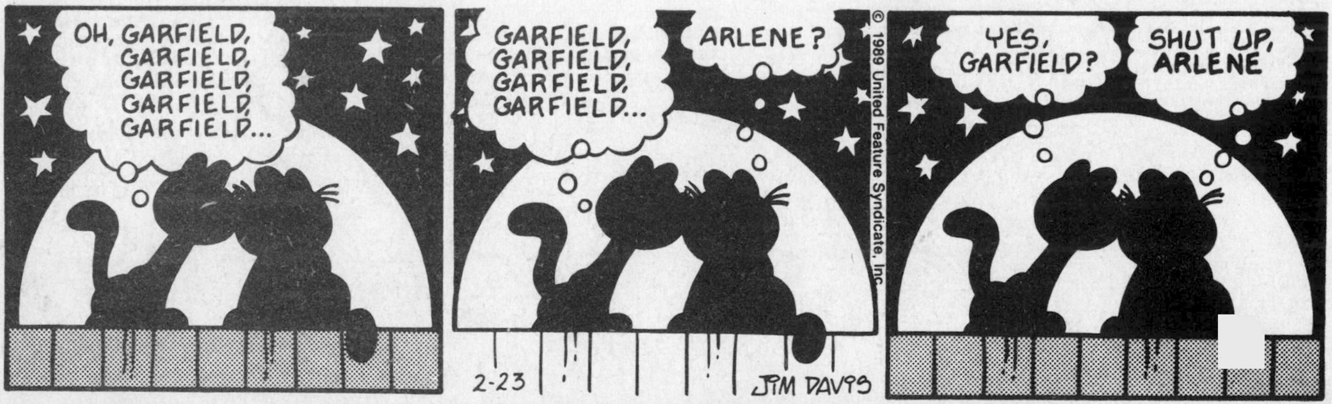
OH, GARFIELD, GARFIELD, GARFIELD, GARFIELD, GARFIELD...
GARFIELD, GARFIELD, GARFIELD, GARFIELD...
ARLENE?
2-23
JIM DAVIS
© 1989 United Feature Syndicate, Inc.
YES, GARFIELD?
SHUT UP, ARLENE

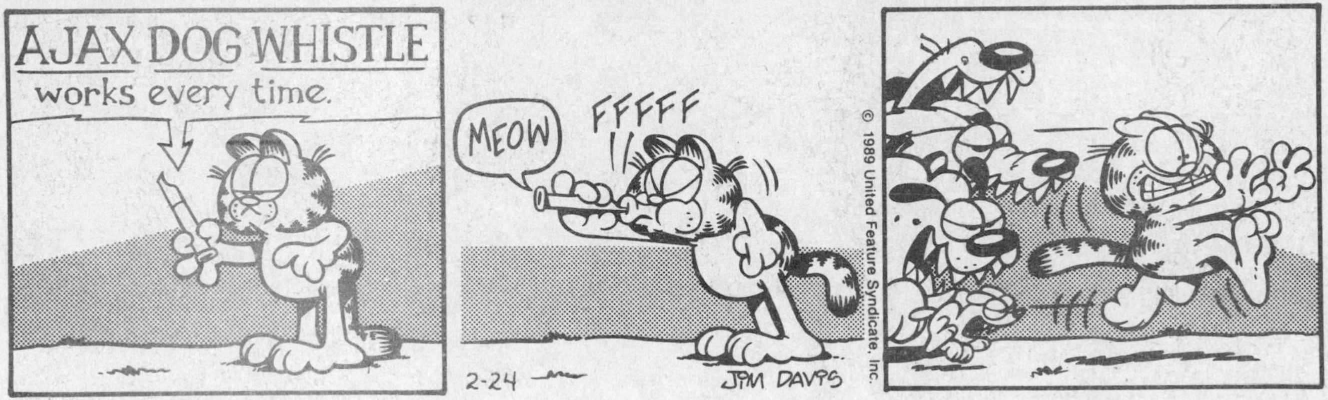
AJAX DOG WHISTLE
works every time.
MEOW
FFFFF
2-24
JIM DAVIS
© 1989 United Feature Syndicate, Inc.

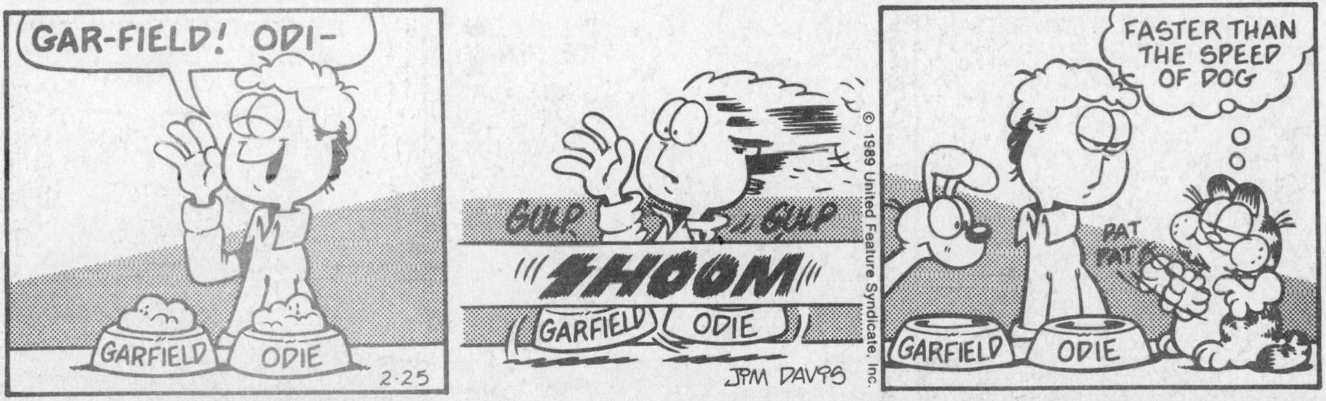
GAR-FIELD! ODI-
GARFIELD
ODIE
2-25
GULP
GULP
SHOOM
GARFIELD
ODIE
JIM DAVIS
© 1989 United Feature Syndicate, Inc.
FASTER THAN THE SPEED OF DOG
PAT PAT
GARFIELD
ODIE

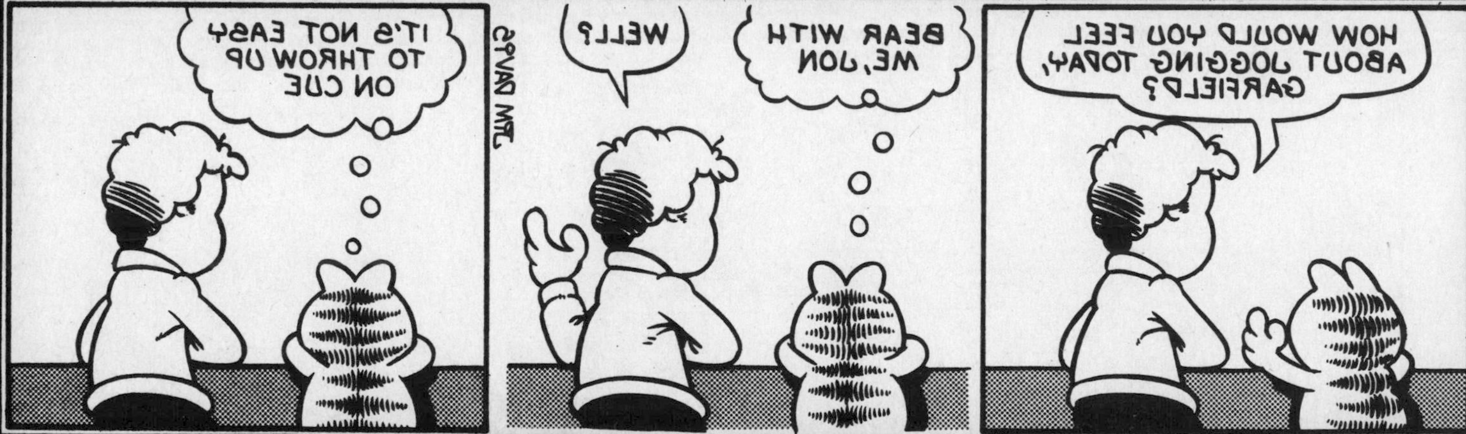

HOW WOULD YOU FEEL ABOUT JOGGING TODAY, GARFIELD?
BEAR WITH ME, JON
WELL?
JPM DAVIS
IT'S NOT EASY TO THROW UP ON CUE